THE BOOK

OF THE

PROPHET DANIEL.

THEOLOGICALLY AND HOMILETICALLY EXPOUNDED

BY

DR. OTTO ZÖCKLER,

PROFESSOR OF THEOLOGY IN THE UNIVERSITY OF GREIFSWALD, PRUSSIA.

TRANSLATED, ENLARGED, AND EDITED

BY

JAMES STRONG, S.T.D.,

PROFESSOR OF EXEGETICAL THEOLOGY IN DREW THEOLOGICAL SEMINARY, MADISON, N. J.

Wipf & Stock

PUBLISHERS

Eugene, Oregon

Wipf and Stock Publishers
199 W 8th Ave, Suite 3
Eugene, OR 97401

The Book of the Prophet Daniel
an Exegetical and Doctrinal Commentary
By Zöckler, Otto
ISBN 13: 978-1-55635-408-3
ISBN 10: 1-55635-408-8
Publication date 4/6/2007
Previously published by Charles Scribner, 1876

AUTHOR'S PREFACE.

In the following exposition of the Book of Daniel, the undersigned has occupied an exegetical and critical position, the peculiarity of which will probably not be overlooked, on a careful comparison with the views and methods of other recent expositors. While he has held fast to the authenticity of the book as a whole, although it was difficult for him to change his former opinion respecting the composition of the book, that it originated during the Maccabæan age, and to conform it to the results of the thorough investigations of M. v. Niebuhr, Pusey, Zündel, Kranichfeld, Volck, Füller, and others, which demonstrated its composition during the captivity, he is still obliged to retain his former doubts with respect to the greater portion of Chap. xi. (particularly vs. 5–39). The reasons which determine him to this conclusion, are certainly of an internal character only. They result in the conviction that a particularizing prophecy, embracing the history of centuries, as it is found in that section, forms so marked a contrast to everything in the line of specializing prediction that occurs elsewhere in the prophetic literature of the Old Testament, that only the theory of an interpolating revision of its prophetic contents, imposed on it during the period of the Seleucid persecutions, or soon afterward, seems to afford a really satisfactory explanation of its particulars. Granted, that in the face of the unanimous testimony of all the external witnesses to the integrity of the prophet's text, the subjective nature of a criticism, such as is involved in this conclusion, may be censured; granted, that it may be termed inconsequent, that the intimate unity of the well-planned, well-adapted, and well-arranged work is thus broken through at but a single point; yet the *analogia visionis propheticæ*, which furnishes the motive for our decision, appears to us to be no less a certain, objectively admissible, and most weighty criterion in critical questions like the present, than is the *analogia fidei* in the domain of Scriptural dogmatics. Nor was the solution of the many difficulties that were encountered, as it resulted from the assumption of an *ex eventu* interpolation at a single point, permitted to restrain us from submitting the progressive results of our investigation to the careful inspection of Biblical scholars belonging to wider circles, so far as the plan and design of the theological and homiletical Bible-work permitted such a course. [The American reviser has taken the liberty of combating the author's view as to the interpolation of the passage in question.]

In the treatment of a prophetic book like the one before us, it is evident that the homiletic element must occupy a very subordinate place. Nor could it be a principal aim for an exegete to obtain dogmatic results and modes of presenting them, from such a prophet as Daniel. For this reason we have preferred to follow the example of one of our esteemed co-laborers (Dr. Bähr, in his exposition of the Books of Kings), and accordingly we have given the title of "*Ethico*-fundamental principles *related to the history of salvation*" to the section ordinarily devoted to that object, and in the same connection we have noticed the apologetic questions that presented themselves, and also have indicated what was suitable for practical and homiletical treatment, in addition to the features designated by that heading.

We have devoted an especially careful attention, as in the case of our former exposition of the Song of Solomon, to the *history and literature of the exposition* of this prophet, both as a whole and with reference to its principal parts severally. Especially has the history of the exposition of the difficult and important vision of the 70 weeks of years, (chap. ix., 24–27,) been sketched by us as thoroughly as was possible, more thoroughly, we believe, than in any of the recent and latest commentaries on Daniel.

Of the most recent exegetical and critical literature on this prophet, it was unfortunately impossible to notice two works that appeared while this book was in press: the commentary of Keil (in Keil and Delitzsch's *Bible-work* on the O. T.), and the monograph by P. Caspari, *Zur Einführung in das Buch Daniel* (Leipsic, Dörffling und Franke).

May our attempt to add a further new and independent contribution to the exegetical literature on the most mysterious and difficult of all the prophets, which has recently been enriched by somewhat numerous, and in some respects not unimportant treatises, find that tolerant reception, at least on the part of Bible students who share our views in substance, which it may appropriately claim, in view of the unusual difficulty attending the execution of its object.

DR. ZÖCKLER.

Greifswald, April, 1869.

THE PROPHET DANIEL.

INTRODUCTION.

§ 1. The Book of Daniel, Considered as a Prototype of the Canonical Apocalypse.

The peculiarities of the book of Daniel, which explain, on the one hand, its position in the Jewish canon among the historical Hagiographa, and, on the other, its being classed in the Septuagint, Vulgate, and Luther, with the writings of the greater prophets, Isaiah, Jeremiah, and Ezekiel, are both internal and external. They arise chiefly from the circumstance that the writer lived and wrought *in Babylonia*, not as a member of the community of exiled Jews, but as a naturalized Babylonian at the court of Nebuchadnezzar and his successors—not, like Ezekiel, discharging priestly functions among his people, but performing duty as an officer of the state and chief of the Magi. He was thus possessed of honors and emoluments akin to those of Joseph, his patriarchal prototype, at the court of the Egyptian Pharaoh; but his removal, at a later date, from his prominent position, and his death, not long after the overthrow of the Chaldæan dynasty by the Persians, prevented his exerting a decisive influence on the welfare of his people.

The book of Daniel's prophecies owes its origin to a period of the deepest national misery of the people of God—a time of the profoundest degradation and confusion, which finds its only parallel in the condition of Israel, when, wholly separated from its native soil, it languished in Egypt, the ignominious "house of bondage" and oppressive "iron furnace" (Deut. v. 6; iv. 20; 1 Kings viii. 51; Jer. xi. 4); but this earlier period has its counterpart here, not only retrospectively as regards the severity of the judgment and humiliation, but also prospectively as respects the abundance of gracious visitation, and the wonderful displays of the Divine power, love, and faithfulness. Both the humiliation and the glory present in the humiliation are revealed in these prophecies. The *first* or historical division of the book records chiefly the miracles by which the grace of God was magnified in those who remained faithful during years of apostasy, suffering, and banishment. The comfortless condition and utter degeneracy of the nation are seen principally in the *second* part, the visions and prophetical pictures of which describe the present and immediate future as a period of severe oppression, universal apostasy, and unquestioned supremacy of the world-powers arrayed against God, at the close of which period the Messianic æra of salvation is finally introduced. According to this division the whole consists of two books—one of *narratives* (chap. i.–vi.), and the other of *visions* (chap. vii.–xii.)—which are about equal in length. This circumstance forms a marked peculiarity of Daniel, as compared with the other prophetical books of the Old Testament, which sometimes interweave the historical element with the prophetical (*e.g.*, Amos, Isa., Jer., etc.), and at others, either reduce the former to narrow limits (*e.g.*, Joel, Micah, Zechariah, etc.), or bring it into such prominence as to exclude the office of the seer (Jonah). This balance between narrative and prophecy, which exists only in Daniel, has its explanation in the origin of the book in a strange land and in a time of exile—circumstances which forbade an arrangement in direct and perfect harmony with the form of prophetical literature in general. These circumstances also serve to account for peculiarities in the *language* of the book; for its composition, to the extent of about one-half in Hebrew, and the remainder (chap. ii. 4 b.–chap. vii.) in the Aramæan or Chaldee idiom, which gradually, and as a consequence of the Babylonian captivity and of the Persian supremacy, became the language of the Palestinian Jews, is due solely to its origin, not only in a time of exile, but among the scenes of the exile, and at the court of the barbarous conquerors. The historical book of Ezra, which appeared immediately at the close of the exile, is the only one of the Old-Testament Scriptures which shares this peculiarity of language, while the prophetical books (*e.g.*, Jeremiah, which originated at the time of the exile and when its author was in constant intercourse with the Babylonians), merely contain isolated Aramæan words or paragraphs (see especially Jer. x. 11).

The peculiar literary traits and theological contents of this book, especially in its second or prophetical part, likewise find their explanation in its origin among the scenes of the captivity. The prophecies of Daniel, conveyed generally in the form of dreams and visions, and nowhere enforced by inspired addresses or exhortations, and concerning themselves chiefly, if not exclusively, with the fate of the all-controlling world-power, on the one hand, and, on the other, with the final triumph of the Messianic kingdom of God, are thus distinguished from the earlier prophetical writings by peculiarities which mark the book as the pattern for the so-called *apocalyptic* prophecies. In ordinary prophecies the people of God had usually occupied the foreground of vision, while the world-powers by which they were threatened, were only noticed incidentally, and made the objects of "burdens" or threatening prophecies, as isolated representatives of the spirit that opposes God. Daniel, on the contrary, takes his position in the heart of that world-power, which had overthrown and subjugated all the nations of the East, and among them the chosen race. From this point of vision he foretells the rise of a new world-kingdom, which shall destroy the present empire, to be followed, in turn, by another and still greater power, and so on to the end, when an eternal kingdom of truth and righteousness shall be established on their ruins, by the direct interference of the God of heaven. The result of all earthly development, and the succession of judgments visited on the enemies of God's people, closing with the Messianic or general judgment, form the subject of this prophecy; and the grandeur of its field of vision, compassing all history and embracing the world, together with the visional clothing of its teaching and the profound symbolism of its eschatological descriptions, constitute the features which stamp it as an apocalypse, in distinction from all earlier prophecy. Within the Old Testament, this form of prophetical writing is approached by the closing chapters of Ezekiel (xl.–xlviii.), but it is directly represented only in the former half of Zechariah (chap. i.–viii.), where the model found in Daniel was probably copied. In the New Testament it is found, if we except certain brief sections in the Gospels and Pauline epistles (the eschatological discourse in Matt. xxiv., xxv., and parallel passages, and 2 Thess. ii.), only in the Revelation of St. John, which is a direct copy and continuation of the prophecies of Daniel.

These peculiarities, as numerous as they are apparent and significant, explain why the book of Daniel was separated [in the Hebrew Bible] from the other prophets and placed among the Hagiographa, when the Old-Testament canon was formed. Its internal features, consisting in an embrace of all history with an eschatological aim, joined to a visional and symbolical dress, which stamp it as the model of all Biblical (and extra-Biblical or apocryphal) apocalypse, would not of themselves have compelled such a separation; since many of the later prophetical writings display clear transitions in matter and form to the field of apocalypse, and permit the distinction between this ripest fruit of Scriptural prophetical development and prophecy in the narrower sense, to appear as the result of the gradual growth. The decisive reason for the disposition made of this book, must be found in its peculiar division into historical and prophetical parts, and in its composition in Hebrew and Aramaic. This appears with irrefragable certainty from its assignment to *a place immediately before Ezra*, the only other book in the canon which frames in Chaldee a section of considerable extent between the Hebrew portions of its text.

An additional circumstance, which may have contributed to placing the present book among the Hagiographa, was the [presumed] *revision* of its prophetical portion, apparently by a pious seer of Maccabæan times, who sought to establish as exact a relation as was possible between the prophecy and its historical fulfillment, as observed by him. This later revision, which affected especially the contents of chapters x.-xii., will be considered below, in connection with the question of genuineness and integrity.

NOTE 1.—With reference to the *circumstances of the times*—so deplorable in their condition and yet so full of displays of Divine grace and wonderful providences—to which the book of Daniel owes its origin, Hävernick, in the introduction to his commentary (page 16 et seq.), is especially thorough and instructive. He justly disputes the opinion of Winer, de Wette, Lec (*Jüdische Geschichte*, p. 183), and others, according to which the situation of the captive Jews was not one of especial hardship. "The shame there inflicted on Israel was not exactly insignificant, when it could inspire pious and faithful men with a holy revenge, and lead them to invoke the Divine indignation on their tormentors! Remember the 137th Psalm and the audacious desecration of the Temple vessels by Belshazzar, as Dan. v. records, which lead to the conclusion that such conduct was of frequent occurrence. Even martyrs to the truth, cheerful and undismayed while testifying that Jehovah alone is God and none beside Him, are revealed in the history of Daniel and his friends (Dan. iii. and vi.); to which event the observation and experience of the wise preacher perhaps refer, when he remarks that 'there is a just man that perisheth in his righteousness' (Ecc. vii. 15).* When we consider the internal state of the nation in this period, we find further abundant reason for complaint, because of Israel's sin and misery. Ezekiel addressed the people with earnest censure, because they listened to his words, but refused to obey them, when he condemned their ways (Eze. xxxiii. 30, sq.), in which they dishonored God among the heathen, and continued to murder, work abomination, and violate chastity, until men asked, 'Are these the people of the Lord, that are gone forth out of His land?' (xxxiii. 26; xxxvi. 20, 21; cf. chap. xxxiv.). Where, indeed, could greater opportunity be found for indulgence in heathen customs by the Israelites, who were at all times excessively addicted to idolatry, than in Babylon, which was notorious as the home of luxury and idolatry? Hence, we must deplore the profound sense of sin, and of being forsaken by God, which is so clearly revealed, not only in the destruction of the temple, and the expulsion of Israel from the holy land, but also in the lack of prophecy (cf. Sam. ii. 9; Psa. lxxiv. 9); and which finds its most striking expression in the prayer of Daniel, uttered before the Lord in the name of the people, toward the end of the captivity.† A different class, who preferred the condition of the exile to the hairy garment of the prophet and the rigorous service of Jehovah, would doubtless enjoy their situation. If there were no other proof of this, it would appear from the fact that many preferred to remain in Babylon at the close of the exile. But the fate of these apostate souls, who, by the Divine decree, were at this exact juncture separated and cast out as dregs from the healthy and pious portion of the nation, was none the less deplorable on that account." . . . Further, page 20: "But the wretched and outcast nation was, and still continued to be, the *people of His covenant*, and, therefore, despite their low estate, the elect and favorite nation of the Lord. They were not merely to continue until the days of their great destiny were fulfilled, but, for Jehovah's sake, they were to be glorified among the heathen. As, therefore, He had always afforded them miraculous aid in seasons of great tribulation, so extraordinary signs and events, that transcended the ordinary course of nature, now occurred and secured the good of Israel while they alarmed the Gentiles; but at the same time these pointed forward, without exception, to the future realization of the great plan of salvation, whose end is the redemption of sinful man . . . Prophecies and wonders were the gracious means with which Jehovah overwhelmed Israel and compelled it to abide by Him, but through which, also, the determined apostates who would not turn to God, were finally cut out, so that a purified people, which agreed in confessing Israel's God at least in outward form, could return to the land of its fathers," etc.—This view of the time of Daniel and its significance, which is held by orthodox exegetes, with few exceptions (see particularly Auberlen, *Der Prophet Daniel*, etc., 2d ed., p. 26 et seq.) is rejected

* [These arguments of Hävernick, however, are not in point to show the general oppression of the Jews in the latter portion of the Babylonian exile. The treatment of the three Hebrew children, and at times of Daniel himself, are only occasional and exceptional instances of Oriental despotism, when aroused by opposition to an arbitrary and universal edict, as the immunity and even honors following evince. The book of Esther contains an apt commentary on these capricious vicissitudes. The reference to the passage in Eccles. is particularly inapposite, as that book belongs to the Solomonic age.]

† [On the contrary it appears that the chastisement of Israel by the captivity, became, as it was intended to be, an effectual cure of outward idolatry. The very sight of the abominations practised by their heathen captors, seems, as in the case of similar close contact with polytheism in Egypt, to have thoroughly disgusted and warned them from all such tendencies. The prayer of Daniel, alluded to by the author, is only a general confession of the *past* sins of the nation, for which the exile, now drawing near its close, is recognized as the just penalty. The passages in Ezekiel have a much earlier date.]

by rationalists, inasmuch, as has already been remarked, they do not admit that Israel's condition during the captivity was especially deplorable and fallen, nor acknowledge the historical character of the narratives respecting the wonderful displays of Divine power and grace, which are recorded in this book. And yet another collection of prophecies, whose origin in the time of the exile and at Babylon is considered by rationalistic critics to be an incontrovertible fact, substantiates the view in question concerning the conditions of the time which underlie our book, in all its bearings, and in many respects, even in its smallest details. The second part of the prophet Isaiah—whether with the modern critics, we consider it as the "Pseudo-Isaiah" or "the exilian Isaiah," or admit its genuineness and therewith its thoroughly prophetic character—describes the condition of the exiled nation in Babylon, as well as the striking contrast between their religious and national ruin and wickedness, and the miracles by which the grace of God was magnified in them, in precisely the same colors as does the book of Daniel, and therefore serves to establish the authenticity of the contents of this book in an impressive manner. Isaiah's lamentations because of the turning of many to idolatry (chap. xlvi. 6, etc.; lvii. 5, etc.; lx. 3, etc.); because of unrighteousness, wanton revelry, and violence (chap. lvi. 11; lviii. 2, etc.; lix. 3, etc); because of the discouragement and lack of faith among even the best of the exiles (chap. lx. 27; xlix. 24; li. 12, etc.; xlv. 9, etc.) and on account of the rebellious disposition and insolent stubbornness of the masses (xlviii. 4, 8, 10; lxiii. 17; lxiv. 7, etc.)—all these merely recapitulate in detail what is briefly comprehended in Daniel's priestly confession and penitential prayer in the affecting language of bitter lamentation.* Furthermore, the manner in which the deutero-Isaiah refers to the marvellous power and majesty of Jehovah, as revealed in wonderful signs of every sort (chap. xliv. 6; xlv. 11), in multitudes of prophecies and promises that have been realized (chap. xli. 21 et seq.; xliii. 9 et seq.; xliv. 7 et seq.; xlv. 19, 21; xlvi. 10; xlix. 3 et seq.), and in the humiliation and destruction of heathen idols and their worshippers, touches closely upon the corresponding descriptions in both parts of Daniel, the historical as well as the prophetical and symbolical (see especially chap. ii. 47; iii. 28; iv. 31 et seq.; vi. 27 et seq.; vii. 13 et seq.; ix. 24 et seq.). The relations of God's people to their heathen oppressors and their gods, on the one hand, and to their covenant God, Jehovah, and His displays of grace and promises of deliverance, on the other, are described by both prophets with substantially the same result; and there remains only this difference, that the mode of statement employed by Isaiah, accords with the older usage of spoken and written prophetical language, while Daniel illustrates the fate of kingdoms in the present and future from a decidedly apocalyptic point of view. The following note treats specifically of this important difference between our prophet and his earlier predecessors.

NOTE 2.—The relation of Daniel, as the original representative of Scriptural apocalypse, to the earlier prophets, is considered in an especially instructive manner by Auberlen (*Der Prophet Daniel*, etc., p. 2 sq.): "The prophets generally occupy an intro-Israelitish standpoint, from whence they view the future of God's kingdom. The congregation of His people constantly occupies the foreground with them, and the world-powers enter their range of vision only as they interfere in the present or immediate future of God's people. . . . The contrary holds with Daniel. Himself separated from the holy land and nation, and living and discharging duty as a high official at the Babylonian and Persian courts, he presents the development of the world-power at the outset as the chief object of his prophecies, and the kingdom of God is relegated significantly to the background. If the other prophets glance occasionally from their post in Zion to the south, the north, or the east, as one or another world-kingdom is presented to their vision, Daniel, from the heart of the world-power, overlooks its entire development, and not until his glance has penetrated through all its changing forms does he rest in Zion, recognizing her affliction and punishment, but also her triumph and exaltation. The prophecies of Daniel no longer relate merely to single and contemporaneous world-kingdoms of greater or less importance; but rather the period of universal monarchies has begun, which rise in succession to universal conquest, and in whose deportment the worldly principle that opposes the reign of God is revealed in steadily-increasing power and hostility. Intimately connected with this is the further peculiarity of Daniel, that his prophecies contain a much greater wealth of historical and political detail than those of all other prophets. While prophecy generally, viewing the near and the distant in perspective, is accustomed to regard the entire future from an eschatological point of view as the coming of the kingdom of God, Daniel, on the contrary, sees spread before him substantially the future history of the world which must transpire before the advent of the kingdom. Hence results the special form of prophecy which is peculiar to him alone. If this were in any case a history of the future, it would be with so him." The idea, that the notice in detail of the several

* [The passages of Isaiah here cited depict in part the idolatry of the heathen, with which the chosen nation are contrasted, and in part the degeneracy of the prophet's countrymen in his own day, for which the captivity was to be a punishment. Few, if any of them, necessarily imply anything more than that discouragement, which a long delay of the promised deliverance would naturally engender.]

features of progress in the future development of the world-power and its relations to God's people, is a final chief peculiarity of Daniel's prophecies, is based principally on the contents of chap. xi., which Auberlen regards as written throughout by Daniel and soon after the captivity. We believe ourselves warranted in holding a different view respecting this chapter, which is the chief support for the assumption of a continued series of the most special predictions, and therefore prefer to accept a revision in the time of Antiochus Epiphanes, by a pious apocalyptic investigator. Hence we charge the thorough description of the kingdoms of the Seleucidæ down to that tyrant, to the account of the modifying agency of this interpolator. We are not led to this view, either by a preconceived opinion that the Spirit of prophecy is incapable of producing such special predictions, or by a one-sided reference to the analogy of the remaining prophetical books of the Old Testament, which contain no such detailed descriptions of the future; but the decisive circumstance which arouses our suspicion concerning the assumption that Dan. xi. is throughout and in all its details a proper prediction, and which even directly forbids it, is the fact that the Revelation of St. John, besides our book the only independent and more comprehensive production of the canonical apocalypse, *everywhere presents only ideal pictures of the future.* We admit that the prophet, borne by the Spirit of prophecy, would, at the point in question, receive many surprisingly exact disclosures respecting the future history of the God-opposed world-power and its hostility towards the people of God, because we regard Daniel, the "vir desideriorum" (chap. x. 11), as pre-eminent in zeal and successful effort, among the Old-Testament prophets who, according to 1 Pet. i. 11, searched "what, or what manner of time the Spirit of Christ which was in them did signify." But precisely because he was only a *searcher* of the future and could be no more than this, we are compelled to reject everything that transforms his prophecy from a Divinely inspired *picture* of the future into a detailed and painfully exact *history* of the future, and we therefore charge this portion to the account of the reviser. Daniel is and remains for us a "prophetic light for the times devoid of revelation, during which Israel was given into the hands of the heathen," a "light that was designed to illumine the night of five hundred years from the Captivity to Christ and the destruction of Jerusalem by the Romans, for the understanding ones in Israel" (Auberlen, p. 80); but we cannot assume that the clear prophetic light which emanated from him was intended to penetrate to the smallest corners and most gloomy recesses of the history of God's people which was, for him, yet future.* But if we can assent to Auberlen's description of the canonical apocalypses as prophetical disclosures, intended to "serve the congregation of God's people as lights during the times of the Gentiles (Luke xxi. 24) in which there is no revelation," only on the condition that we conceive their light in an ideal sense, and as corresponding to the fundamental law in the Divine revelation of gradual and mediate disclosure, we are none the less compelled on the other hand to reject decidedly a special feature, admitted by Lücke, Hilgenfeld, and others, into their conception of the idea of apocalypse, a conception which otherwise conforms approximately to that of Auberlen. We refer to the idea of *pseudonymity*, concerning which Lücke (*Einleitung in die Offenbarung Johannis und die sogenannte apokalyptische Literatur*, 2d ed., p. 47 sq.) asserts that it is necessarily connected with the other two distinguishing features of apocalyptic prophecy, its eschatological, and its comprehensive character that covers all history, since only later writers who cunningly related the prophecies to the past and invented additions to the older prophets, were capable of such all-embracing vision. The one-sidedness and rashness of this assertion likewise appear from the mode of origin and the literary peculiarities of the Revelation by St. John, this most important and significant of apocalypses, against which no more unjust criticism can be offered than that of a pseudonymic origin; and not less from the notorious authenticity of the former half of the book of Zechariah (chap. i.–viii.), the remaining apocalyptic composition that has been admitted to the Old-Testament canon, and which may be regarded as the earliest imitation of Daniel. We can yield our assent to the charge of forgery as regards this form of writing, in so far only as it applies to the apocryphal apocalypses, and are therefore in accord with Hilgenfeld (*Die jüdische Apokalyptik in ihrer geschichtlichen Entwicklung*, 1857, p. 5 sq.)—whose view diverges somewhat from that of Lücke—no further than as he excepts the Johannean apocalypse from the canon of Lücke, which stamps pseudonymity as the invariable mark of apocalyptic literature; but to this exception we add the two apocalypses of the canonical Old Testament. † For the more special consideration of the relations of

* [To those far removed from all influence of the prevalent rationalism of German criticism, the insidious tincture of which, notwithstanding the author's disclaimer, is evident in his conclusion on this point, the ascription of any portion of the book of Daniel to a later nameless writer on such purely subjective grounds, must appear altogether gratuitous. The business of the interpreter is, not to prescribe what God was likely to cause a prophet to predict, but to accept and expound accordingly what historical and substantial testimony has delivered to us as the actual words of prophecy. There is no more evidence of a pseudo-Daniel than of a pseudo-Isaiah.]

† [The inconsistency of the author's position here is palpable, if we correctly apprehend his somewhat involved statement of it. The Revelation of St. John, if not the apostle's, is of course under a fictitious name, and the 11th chapter of Daniel, if not that prophet's, is equally pseudonymical, whoever may be conceived as the interpolator. The distinction in this respect between a whole work and a part only is too nice to escape the odium of a "pious fraud."]

Daniel to the apocryphal and pseudepigraphical apocalypses, which were mainly framed on its model, see below, § 11.*

NOTE 3.—With respect to the Chaldaic idiom in Dan. ii.–vii., which we represented above as a principal reason for leading the framers of the canon to assign to Daniel a place among the Hagiographa, and in the immediate neighborhood of Ezra, we remark in general, (1.) that this dialect, which gradually became the current language of the Palestinian Jews, was the eastern-Aramæan or Babylonian, a purely Shemitic idiom, which, as the *popular* tongue of the Babylonians, must be carefully distinguished from the לְשׁוֹן כַּשְׂדִּים, mentioned in Dan. i. 4, the latter being the *court* language of Nebuchadnezzar and the Chaldæan dynasty, and comprehending numerous Aryan or Turanian elements. This follows from Dan. ii. 4; Isa. xxxvi. 11; and Ezra iv. 7, where documents and speeches in this dialect are designated as such by the term אֲרָמִית (Luther [and English version]: "Syriac," rather *Aramaic*), while the "tongue of the Chaldeans" (לְ׳ כַּשְׂדִּים) mentioned in Dan. i. 4 is not again referred to, and is clearly distinguished from the ordinary Aramæan language as a peculiar dialect, current among the warrior and priestly caste then dominant in Babylon (possibly identical with those perpetuated in the Assyrio-Babylonish cuneiform inscriptions) by the manner in which it is there introduced; for Daniel and his companions would hardly have been obliged to undergo a regular course of instruction in the common Aramæan or Babylonian language, as it should be called, instead of Chaldee, which is less exact. Compare below, on chapter i. 4. (2.) The Aramæan of chapters ii.–vii. includes numerous Hebraisms, as the Hebrew of the remaining chapters Chaldaizes many expressions; a circumstance that can hardly be explained, except on the supposition of an intermingling of both dialects in the popular language, which may have begun at the time of the frequent Assyrian invasions, at first among the ten tribes, and later gradually extended also to Judah, and to which the strongly Aramaizing Hebrew of the prophet Ezekiel, most intimately related to the Hebrew of Daniel, bears testimony. (3.) The co-existence of the Hebrew and Aramæan, as dialects spoken and understood by the people, is substantiated further by the circumstance that our author could venture to express most of his narratives and predictions in the latter tongue; a feature that is repeated only in the book of Ezra, which was written a century later, while Isaiah (nearly two hundred years before Daniel) admits no Aramaic expressions into his text in a passage which would have afforded a suitable opportunity (chap. xxxvi. 11; cf. 2 Kings xviii. 26), and even Jeremiah contents himself with employing a brief Aramaic sentence (Jer. x. 11; compare the use of single words in Aram. in earlier books, *e.g.*, Gen. xxxi. 47; 2 Kings v. 12). (4.) The Aramaic idiom of Daniel corresponds closely to that of the book of Ezra and of Jer. x. 11, both in its grammatical and its lexical features. Its wealth of older words (*e.g.*, שְׁפַרְפָּרָה instead of the later שְׁפַר, עֲלוֹהִי for the later עַל־אֲפֵּר, תַּחְתּוֹהִי for the later מִלְּרָא, שִׂים טְעֵם for the later פְּקִיד, כָּל־קֳבֵל־דִּי, for the later אֲרֵי עַל כֵּן, יְוָלִי for קִלְקַלְתָּה, etc.) and its general grammatical peculiarities (where the forms, לְהוֹן, לְכוֹן, instead of the apparently more ancient לְהֹם, לְכֹם, which are found in Ezra, form the only exceptions) create the impression of a much higher antiquity than is represented by the otherwise closely related Chaldee of the Targums, which were composed about the beginning of the Christian æra. (5.) Of the seven notorious Parseeisms, or words derived from the Persian, which are found in the Aramaic portion of our book, only אַזְדָּא occurs in the Targums, while it has two others (פִּתְגָם and פַּרְתְּמִים) in common with the Chaldaizing Hebrew of the book of Esther and the Chaldee of Ezra, and a fourth (גִּזְבַר) occurs at least in the Chald. Ezra. There is thus in this respect also a more remarkable lingual relationship between Daniel and Ezra, than between them and the Chaldee Targums, and the position assigned to our book between Esther and Ezra on the forming of the canon, is fully justified by this consideration. We shall endeavor to show, in connection with the question of genuineness, that the weight of these lingual peculiarities, which point so decisively to the composition of this book during the period immediately preceding and following the captivity, is in no wise diminished by the occurrence in its Chaldee text of several phrases evidently derived from the Greek. We were only concerned in this connection, to show that the lingual peculiarities of the book formed a principal motive for its collocation with the Hagiographa, instead of its being placed in the series of prophetical books. Compare Hengstenberg, *Die Authentie des Daniel*, etc., p. 297 sq.; Hävernick, *Einleitung ins A. T.*, II. 2, 482 et seq.; Zündel, *Kritische Untersuchungen über die Abfassungszeit*

* [Auberlen (*Daniel and Revelation*, Clarke's ed., p. 77 sq.) notices several other "materialistic differences between the Apocalypse of the Old and of the New Testament," growing more or less directly out of the different position occupied by the people of God at their respective times. Those who have insisted that the Antichrist of the one is necessarily the Antichrist of the other, have therefore interpreted the symbols as having precisely the same significance, have unduly overlooked these differences in the standpoint and design of the two prophets.]

des Buches Daniel, p. 239 et seq. Concerning its place after Esther and before Ezra, compare in addition, Delitzsch, Art. "Daniel," in Herzog's *Real-Encycl.*, III. 272: "The book of Daniel stands between Esther and Ezra, because Esther, for a sufficient reason, is the last of the five Megilloth (festival volumes), and because *the principal contents of Daniel belong to the time before Ezra and Nehemiah.*" Accordingly, this book was regarded as belonging among the historical Hagiographa (in view of its really historical character throughout the first half), and it was placed at the head of these books, because of its lingual relationship with Ezra, and also because of its pre-eminently holy and inspired character. This arrangement is not chronological, indeed, for in this respect the Chronicles should precede, and Daniel, Ezra, Nehemiah, and Esther follow in their order. But considerations of a different nature prevailed, on the whole, in the collocation of these final constituents of the Old-Testament canon. The following section will illustrate one of the leading considerations which enable us definitely to understand the position of this book, in connection with its remarks on the call of Daniel to the prophetic office.

§ 2. The Personal Relations of the Prophet.

The name *Daniel* (דָּנִיֵּאל, chap. i. 6; also defective, דָּנִאֵל in Ezek. xiv. 14, 20; xxviii. 3), which signifies "judge of God, judge who pronounces judgment in the name of God," * belongs to two persons besides our prophet in Old-Testament history, of whom one was a son of David (1 Chron. iii. 1), and the other a Levite of the house of Ithamar. The latter flourished but little later than our prophet, according to Ezra viii. 2; Neh. x. 7, and has, on that account, been identified with him by the Septuagint in the apocryphal additions to the book of Daniel, as well as by several recent critics. The difference in time is, however, too considerable to admit of this opinion; and the fact that among the contemporaries of the priest Daniel were found a Mishael (Neh. viii. 4), Hananiah, and Azariah (Neh. x. 3, 24), must be regarded as a mere accident, from which, in view of the notorious frequency of these names, the conclusion cannot be drawn, that the Daniel of our book, together with his three pious associates, are the creatures of a fictitious collocation and pre-dating of those persons, who lived almost a century later (compare the arguments against Bleek in note 1).

According to chapter i. 3, Daniel seems to have been of royal descent, and therefore born at Jerusalem. The passage in chapter ix. 24, however, will hardly serve in proof of this (Harenberg and other expositors), since Jerusalem might have been termed the "holy city" by Daniel, even if he belonged to any other city or tribe of the holy land. † He was, at any rate, of high birth, and, together with three other noble Jewish youths, was in early life transported to Babylon in the first deportation under Jehoiakim, in order to become a page at the Chaldæan court.‡ Here their Hebrew names were changed for others of Chaldæan origin, and Hananiah received the name of Shadrach, Mishael that of Meshach, and Azariah that of Abednego, while Daniel was known as *Belteshazzar* (בֵּלְטְשַׁאצַּר). This name, if explained solely according to the Shemitic analogy, seems to be synonymous with "Beli princeps," or "princeps, cui Belus favet" (בֵּלְשַׁאצַּר), and therefore likewise indicates the princely rank of Daniel. That he bore in addition the probably Persian name of *Sheshbazzar*, by which Zerubbabel was known at the court of Cyrus (Ezra i. 8), rests on an unsupported Rabbinical tradition, which is found in Rashi and several later writers, and which seems to have grown out of a false etymological interpretation of שֵׁשְׁבַּצַּר as = "who was in six-fold tribulation."

The instruction in the wisdom of the Chaldee magians and in the manners of the court, which Daniel received in Babylon under the supervision of the chief eunuch, Ashpenaz, did

---

* So Gesenius and Dietrich, in the *Handwörterbuch*, explain, in connection with many older expositors, while Fürst interprets the name by "judge *through* God," and a majority render it "God is my judge" (*e.g.*, Hävernick, with reference to Gen. xxx. 6), or also, "God is judge" (*e.g.*, Reinke, *Die messianischen Weissagungen*, etc., iv. 1, 167).

† The Jewish tradition found in Pseudo-Epiphanius, *De vit. prophet.*, c. 10, which locates the birth-place of Daniel ἐν Βεθεβόρῳ τῇ ἀνωτέρᾳ πλησίον Ἱερουσαλήμ, or, by another reading (preferred by Reland, *Palaest.*, p. 694), ἐν Βεθέρων τῇ ἀνωτέρᾳ, is of no historical value, and perhaps originated in the desire to place the birth of the prophet, who, on the authority of Ezra, viii. 2, was held to be a Levite, in a Levitical city (see Josh. xxi. 22).

‡ ["The history of that period, in Kings and Chronicles, seems to warrant the supposition that the Jewish lads in question were *hostages*, who were drawn from the upper classes of society at Jerusalem, in order to secure the quiet and submission of the Jewish king and his nobles in their tributary condition."—*Stuart.*]

not prevent him from observing the injunctions of the Mosaic law in regard to food and drink, with conscientious care, and from astonishing the officials who had him in charge by the almost miraculous effects produced in his appearance through this ascetic course, in which his three friends participated (chap. i. 8–10). But marked as were these effects of his piety, his fame was increased still further by the extraordinary proofs of his prudence, wisdom, and learning, which he manifested at an early period, especially in the interpretation of dreams, visions, etc. This extended his reputation beyond the bounds of Babylon before he had attained maturity, and must even have made his name proverbial among his countrymen at least, as designating a marvel of wisdom. * Only thus can we explain the fact that Ezekiel, his contemporary, although considerably older in years, refers to Daniel in several passages of his prophecies (which were brought to a close in B. C. 572, that is, about the middle of the captivity), as a model of pious wisdom, and in two instances classes him with Noah and Job, the great wise men of antiquity (Ezek. xiv. 14, 28; xxviii. 3; compare note 2).

That Daniel was not merely trained under the oversight of the chief eunuch, or chief palace official ("prince of the eunuchs") of Nebuchadnezzar, but also himself became a eunuch in the proper sense, and was trained in that capacity, is an ancient Jewish tradition, which appears to rest on a combination of Dan. i. 3 et seq. with the prophecy of Isaiah to Hezekiah (Isa. xxxix. 7, where סריסים was held to designate actual eunuchs). It is, however, without any historical support, either in the book of Daniel itself, or in other Old-Testament records; and Ezek. xiv. 20 seems even to directly contradict this tradition, since it ascribes sons and daughters to him, as it does also to Noah and Job. But it could not be otherwise than welcome to the ascetically disposed Jews of later times, as well as to many church fathers and Roman Catholic expositors, to discover in Daniel a eunuch, even though an involuntary one, and an example of perpetual virginity. Hence the Targums report this tradition (on Esther iv. 5, in connection with the mention of Hatach, the Persian eunuch who was appointed to serve Esther), as do others of the more ancient rabbins (Pseudo-Epiphanius, *Vitæ Prophet.*, c. 10, ἦν ἀνὴρ σώφρων ὥστε δοκεῖν τοὺς Ἰουδαίους εἶναι σπάδοντα). Of later rabbins, *e.g.*, Rashi ad Dan. i. 21 (but not Ibn-Ezra, ad Dan. i. 3); of church fathers, Origen (*Hom.* iv. *in Ezech.*), Jerome (*Adv. Jovin.* i. 1; *Comm. in Jes.* xxxix. 7; in Dan. i. 3), John Damascenus (*De fide orthod.* iv. 25); of later Roman Catholics, Cornelius à Lapide, Huetius, and others, hold to this tradition. [It is also strongly confirmed by the well-known usages of Oriental courts, in which eunuchs are admitted to privileges allowed to none others, especially in personal offices near the king. Haman, indeed, was not of this class in the book of Ezra, but Nehemiah was doubtless such in the Persian court. In the light of this circumstance, the dietetic regimen imposed upon Daniel and his three companions had a sanitary reason, and their voluntary temperance may actually have had a good effect during their period of convalescence after the operation. The reference to Daniel in Ezekiel does not so explicitly allude to children as to invalidate this conclusion, being merely an implication of kindred.]

After three years of training and instruction, in which early period the apocryphal narrative in the interpolated Daniel of the Septuagint places the celebrated decision in favor of Susannah, who was unjustly condemned to death, as an instance of the extraordinary wisdom of the youthful prophet, Daniel and his three companions entered on their duties at the court of Nebuchadnezzar. † Through the miraculous aid of the enlightening grace of God, he was

* ["The reader will recall some points of close analogy between Daniel and Joseph. Both were captives; each rose in a foreign kingdom to the same rank of prime minister, by the same qualities of personal character—sterling integrity, unselfish devotion to their work, great business capacity, and unfaltering faith in God. Each became, under God, a patron and protector to his suffering people. To each was given of God extraordinary prophetic powers, which served to raise him to general notice and confidence, and manifestly in the case of Daniel, served to exalt the God of the Hebrew race highly in the convictions of the monarchs under whom he served. Each was able to distance and confound all the pretenders to supernatural knowledge, of whom there were many both in Egypt and Babylon."—*Cowles.*]

† ["This custom of taking young men of the finest parts from a captive or subject race to fill responsible positions about the king has prevailed in many despotic governments, and is essentially the usage of the Turkish empire to this day. It finds its motives (1.) In the fact that such monarchs need men about them of the very first abilities; (2.) In the difficulty they would experience in getting young men of such ability among their own people, who might not, by virtue of their social position or connections, become dangerous to the throne."—*Cowles.*]

enabled to interpret a remarkable dream of the king, in consequence of which he was promoted to the royal favor, as was Joseph at the court of Pharaoh, until he became the most influential official in the province of Babylonia, and chief of the caste of magians (chap. ii. 48 et seq.). He appears to have occupied this important position until the close of Nebuchadnezzar's reign, although the narrative of the persecution of Daniel's friends and fellow-worshippers, contained in chap. iii., and that of his interpretation of Nebuchadnezzar's second dream and of the madness of that king, which is found in chap. iv., warrant the opinion that his glory was not without an occasional but transitory eclipse in the course of that protracted period.

Under Belshazzar, the son and (possibly not immediate, but rather third or fourth) successor of Nebuchadnezzar, Daniel regained the royal favor and influential position of which he had been temporarily deprived. After having been entirely forgotten, he succeeded in interpreting an extraordinary appearance which had alarmed the king, but the prophetic meaning of which, relating to his approaching overthrow by the Persian world-power, none of the magians were able to reveal. The great honors with which Belshazzar rewarded him immediately before his fall (enrobing in purple, placing a chain of gold about his neck, and proclaiming him the third ruler in the kingdom) remained to him under the first Medo-Persian ruler, Darius the Mede (Cyaxeres). This monarch appointed him one of the three princes who were placed over all the one hundred and twenty governors of his kingdom; and he even thought to place him over his whole realm (as minister of state or grand-vizier) chap. vi. 1–4. For this reason, the other princes and governors, moved with envy, sought to destroy Daniel by bringing his steadfast adherence to the faith of his fathers into conflict with the established religion of Persia, or rather with an extraordinary decree of the king, which provided that during the space of one month the honor of Divine worship should be rendered only to him, the ruler of the kingdom. As Daniel persisted in the regular discharge of his religious duties, and, according to the custom of pious Jews, offered prayer at an open window, and with his face turned toward Jerusalem, three times in each day, he became subject to the fearful penalty imposed by the king, of being devoured by lions. The wondrous care of God, however, preserved him unharmed through the night which he spent in their den, and, in consequence, he rose still higher in the favor of the king, while his accusers were thrown into the den, and perished by the death they had designed for him. When Cyrus assumed the sole government over the Medo-Persian world-kingdom, after the two years' reign of Darius the Mede, the dignities and honors of Daniel were continued to him. He therefore survived the expiration of the Babylonian Captivity and the beginning of Israel's return to the holy land (see chap. i. 21), which ensued on the accession of that king, "the anointed of the Lord" (Isa. xlv. 1); and although the book of his prophecies records nothing of his agency in restoring his people to their land, his indirect influence was probably not unimportant. The closing series of his prophecies (chap. x.–xii.), which disclose the future history of Israel down to the erection of Messiah's kingdom on the ruins of the world-powers, testify that in spirit he cherished a warm sympathy for the physical and moral welfare of his people.

He died probably soon after receiving and recording these final revelations, which he himself places in the third year of the reign of Cyrus; but when, and under what circumstances, his death occurred is unknown. The attempts to state his circumstances at the close of life, together with the time and manner of his death, which are found in Jewish and Arabic authors, and also in church fathers, are based on empty traditions which are wholly without support. We class among these the statement of Josephus (*Antiq. Jud.* x. 11, 7) that Daniel immortalized himself as early as the reign of Darius the Mede by building a splendid royal castle of marble at Ecbatana, which was still standing and in the charge of a Jewish priest in the time of Josephus; * also the Jewish-oriental legend, perhaps derived from Dan. i. 21, and Ezra viii. 2, concerning his return to Palestine among the first exiles under Zerubbabel (D'Herbelot, *Bibl. Orient.*, p. 283); further, the statement of Pseudo-Epiphanius, that he died

* Cf. Jerome, *Comment. in Dan.* viii. 2, where the erection of this palace is erroneously transferred to Susa.

at Babylon and was buried in the royal tomb; the statement, perhaps, of later origin, but more widely circulated than the one last mentioned, which is held by Abdul-faraj and Benj. of Tudela, that he died in Shushan—a tradition upon which rests the still practised adoration of the reputed tomb of the prophet in that city, in which Jews and Christians are said to participate, as well as Moslems (see *Ausland*, 1853, p. 960); and finally the Romish tradition, which is to the effect that Daniel died as a martyr, and which commemorates him on the 21st of July (cf. Stadler and Heim, *Vollst. Heiligen-Lexikon*, vol. i., p. 722 ss.).

The above historical notices concerning Daniel show, that by reason of his relations to the Babylonian, and later to the Medo-Persian dynasties, as well as on account of his growth to maturity and continued dwelling and labors in a foreign land, he occupies an entirely exceptional position among the Old-Testament prophets—a position that makes it seem really doubtful whether the prophetic office was his proper and chief vocation. In any case, he appears as much a Chaldæan wise man as an Israelitish prophet, and thus intervenes between the Old-Testament prophetism and the position of the Divinely enlightened seers among the nations that bordered on Israel, who were supernaturally chosen to be the bearers of Messianic prophecies, as in the case of Balaam in the time of Moses, and the Eastern magi on the threshold of New-Testament times. For this reason chiefly, it would seem, he was regarded by the framers of the canon as not belonging to the class of prophets in the narrower sense, but as more directly included among the writers of the Hagiographa (compare note 3).

NOTE 1.—Bleek, in *Einleitung ins A. Test.*, 2d ed., p. 610, remarks with reference to the persons mentioned in Ezra viii. 2, and Neh. viii. 4; x. 3, 7, 24, under the names of Daniel, Mishael, Hananiah, and Azariah: "This coincidence of names with those of the heroic believers represented in our book may be accidental, but nevertheless is remarkable, since it exists with reference to the entire four, and the names Daniel and Mishael occur but rarely elsewhere. The time, indeed, in which the four contemporaries of Ezra and Nehemiah flourished is later than that of Daniel and his friends, as about 160 years elapsed between the third year of Jehoiakim and the reading of the book of the law by Ezra; but still, it is not unreasonable to suppose that the composer of this book (who, according to Bleek, lived and wrote in the time of the Maccabees, about B. C. 167) borrowed the names of his faithful heroes from those four men. We cannot tell whether a more intimate acquaintance with their history and experience in Babylon led him to select their names." (Similarly De Wette, *Einleitung ins A. T.*, p. 360 et seq.) To us the supposition of Bleek seems about as vague a combination as the familiar attempts of Strauss to find in the names of Gospel history, Jacob, Joseph, Mary, and Elizabeth, mythical reproductions of the corresponding names in the primitive Scripture history, or to find the origin of the historical Lazarus in the Gospel of St. John, in the purely imaginary person of this name in the parabolical narrative found in Luke xvi. 19 et seq. (*Leben Jesu*, etc., 1864, p. 477 et seq.). The impossibility of identifying the four contemporaries of Ezra with our prophet and his friends appears from (1) the fact that, according to Dan. i. 21, which passage could not possibly have been known to the mythical writer, Daniel lived only to the beginning of the reign of Cyrus; (2) that the names Azariah, Daniel, and Hananiah, which are enumerated in Neh. x. 2–28, among the great number of names of leaders, priests, and Levites, who engaged to observe the law, became so unimportant and are so widely separated that only the most reckless arbitrariness or chance could associate them precisely as intimate companions, who filled a distinguished position at the royal court of Babylon as wise men and confessors; (3) that the name Mishael (Neh. viii. 4), in the list of those who stood on the left hand of Ezra while he read the law, occupies a no less isolated position; (4) that the identity of Daniel, of the sons of Ithamar, who is mentioned in Ezra viii. 2, with the priest or Levite of the same name, who is noticed in Neh. x. 7, is, at any rate, extremely doubtful, since their surroundings are wholly dissimilar; (5) that what is recorded in chaps. i. and iii., particularly the report concerning the Babylonian names conferred on them (chap. i. 7) bears too thoroughly the stamp of historical reminiscence to admit of the hypothesis of a later invention, for the purpose of exalting those obscure names, which were almost forgotten among the number of names in the book of Nehemiah.

NOTE 2.—The three-fold reference of Ezekiel to Daniel has been regarded by many modern critics as irreconcilable with the historical existence of a magian and prophet of this name, since in two instances (chap. xiv. 14, 20) Ezekiel places Daniel between Noah and Job, and since he clearly seems to treat him as a personage belonging to the earliest antiquity in those passages as well as in chap. xxviii. 3. On this account, they have either questioned the genuineness of these passages in Ezekiel (*e.g.*, Bernstein, in Tzschirner's *Analekten*, i. 3, p. 10), or given up the historical character of the exilian Daniel, and considered him a purely poetic invention like Job, or a wise man belonging to the patriarchal or primitive period of Israelitish history. The latter hypothesis especially has been received with favor, and has been variously developed by Bleek, Hitzig, Ewald, and Bunsen. According to Bleek (in Schleierm. u. Lücke's *Theologischer Zeitschrift*, III. 1822, p. 283 et seq., and in *Einl. ins A. T.*, p. 608 et seq.), we are not led by the manner in which he is mentioned to think of a person who shared in the Babylonian captivity with Ezekiel, but much rather, to conceive of a long-familiar personage of primitive times, who was historically connected with events in the experience of Israel, or, which is more probable, since we know no more concerning him, who was like Job, a mere product of the poetic fancy. From the manner in which Ezekiel refers to him, it is barely conceivable that he should have been, as the Daniel of our book is represented, a Jewish exile and contemporary with Ezekiel." De Wette (*Einl. ins A. T.*, p. 361) and Von Lengerke (*Das Buch Daniel ausgel.*, p. xciii. et seq.) likewise limit the choice to either a "man belonging to the gray antiquity" or to a purely imaginary personage. Hitzig, on the other hand, regards the Daniel of Ezek. xiv. as not, indeed, created by the writer, like Job, but still as the "child of tradition" like Noah and Melchizedek, and finds an intimate correspondence, amounting almost to identity, of our Daniel with the mysterious royal and priestly personage of the latter, who is assumed to be a junior contemporary of Noah—a relation which exists especially in respect of his name (דניאל, "divine judge," nearly synonymous with מלכיצדק, "king of righteousness." *Kurzgef. exeget. Handbuch zu Daniel*, p. viii.). Ewald, again (*Die Propheten des Alten Bundes*, vol. II., Appendix, p. 562 et seq), considers the Daniel mentioned by Ezekiel as having been descended from one of the ten tribes, and as having lived and prophesied at the heathen court of Nineveh, a hundred years before the Babylonian Captivity. To this participator in the Assyrian captivity were attributed prophetic oracles respecting the world-kingdoms, by an unknown Jewish author of the times of Alexander the Great or the earliest Seleucidæ, which were modified by a later writer, in the time of Antiochus Epiphanes, from whom they received their present form. Bunsen (*Gott in der Geschichte*, I. 514 et seq.) agrees in the main with the first part of this hypothesis. The historical Daniel lived at the royal court in Nineveh soon after the deportation of the Israelites by Shalmaneser; the fantastic representations of animals on the palaces of Nimrud and Khorsabad, which have become known to us through the researches of Botta and Layard, served as models for his visional descriptions of the world-kingdoms under the form of various imaginary animals, in chapters vii. and viii.; and the originator of the present book transformed the prophet of Nineveh by mistake into a Babylonian. Compare below, § 4, note 1. Two earlier opponents of the genuineness of this book, Bertholdt and Kirmss, endorse the opinion of Ewald and Bunsen, that Daniel was a real person of historical times; but instead of assigning this wise man, whom Ezekiel celebrates, to an earlier age, they make him the contemporary of that prophet, living at the court of Babylon. The author of this book, who belonged to a much later period, and derived his entire knowledge of Daniel from Ezekiel, merely clothed him in a mythical dress, etc. (Bertholdt, *Daniel*, etc., I. p. 7; *Einleit. ins A. T.*, p. 1506; Kirmss, *Commentatio historico-critica exhibens descriptionem et censuram recentiorum de Daniel libro opinionum*, Jen. 1828, p. 59 et seq.); in like manner also Winer in the *Realwörterb.*, Art. "Daniel" (I., p. 247).

The more recent defenders of the genuineness of Daniel's prophecies are in immediate correspondence with the arguments raised by these latter critics in support of the possibility of Daniel's contemporary existence with Ezekiel, *despite* the peculiar manner in which he is mentioned in Ezek. xiv. and xxviii. Hengstenberg especially (*Die Authentie des Daniel*, p. 70 et seq.) shows in a most discerning way that the chronological difficulty is of no importance, *since Daniel must have been thirty years old* when Ezekiel xiv. was composed, and since the rewards and honors conferred on him by Nebuchadnezzar *must have been received at least ten years before that period*; and further, that the book of Daniel itself (in such passages as chap. i. 17, 20; ii. 47; iv. 5; v. 11) testifies to the extraordinary and early-developed wisdom, by which this pious youth was distinguished, and with reference to which Ezekiel was already enabled to point the contemporary king of Tyre to him as a model of exalted wisdom and Divine illumination (chap. xxviii. 3). The position assigned to Daniel between Noah and Job in chapter xiv. 14 and 20, proves nothing whatever concerning his patriarchal age; rather, Job is placed at the end of the series because he was a less suitable example for the immediate purpose of Ezekiel, than Noah and Daniel, the preachers of righteousness in the midst of a godless world. In general agreement with this view of Hengstenberg are, Hävernick (*Komm. zu Ezechiel*, p. 206 et seq.; *Neue Untersuchungen über Daniel*, p. 23 et seq.; *Einl. ins A. T.*, ii. 2, 455), Kliefoth (*Das Buch Ezechiels übersetzt und erklärt*, p. 177 et seq.; and *Das Buch Daniels*, p. 31 et seq.), Delitzsch (in Herzog's *Real-Encykl.*, s. v. *Daniel*), and Zündel (*Krit. Untersuchungen*, etc., p. 258 et seq.). These later apologists, however, justly declare Hengstenberg's explanation of the circumstance that Daniel is placed between Noah and Job to be inadequate, and therefore endeavor to find a more appropriate explanation of this fact, which at the first blush seems so strange. Hävernick and Kliefoth assume a climax: "Noah saved himself and his family; Daniel was still able to provide for his friends, chap.

ii. 17, 18; Job, despite his uprightness, could not even save his children." Delitzsch explains the arrangement of names by assuming that Ezekiel "mentions first a righteous man belonging to the ancient world, next, a righteous man belonging to the present world, and lastly, a righteous man who belongs to the ideal world;" for Job is "presented to the eyes of Israel as a righteous man only in the book of Job, which, although not without a historical basis, is not historical, but rather poetical and didactic." Finally, Zündel seeks to explain this arrangement of names by the observation, that Daniel occupied a "thoroughly analogous central and universal position among his contemporaries," so to speak, as a mediator between God and His people, by virtue of which, as formerly did Noah and Job, he presented his uprightness and piety before God, in a reconciling and atoning way, when His anger was aroused because of the sins of His people. None of these attempts at explanation are entirely satisfactory to us; but that of Delitzsch seems to be the most adequate and plausible, because the most simple and unconstrained. But may not euphonic considerations have contributed to the arrangement of the three names נֹחַ, דָּנִיאֵל and אִיּוֹב, in like manner as such considerations appear to have prevailed in other enumerations of proper names? *e. g.*, of the three sons of Noah (Gen. vi. 9; ix. 18, etc.), among which Ham, although the youngest of the three, is always placed before Japheth; of the three daughters of Job (Job xlii. 14), etc. As examples of the neglect of chronological order in the enumeration of names, compare, in addition, Eccles., chap. xlix., where Josiah, Jeremiah, Ezekiel, Zerubbabel, Joshua, and Nehemiah (vs. 16–20) are placed before Enoch, Joseph, Seth, Shem, and Adam; also Heb. xi. 32 (Gideon, Barak, Samson, Jephthah, David, Samuel); Jude v. 9 et seq. (Moses, Cain, Balaam, Korah, Enoch); Matt. xvi. 14 (John the Baptist, Elijah, Jeremiah). The last of these examples is especially instructive, since it shows that living persons might be classed with persons of similar character belonging to the earliest antiquity without any regard to chronological sequence. [The fact that Daniel is thus associated by Ezekiel, a nearly contemporary writer, with an undoubtedly historical personage, Noah, has always been held to be a strong proof of his actual existence. The same holds true of Job, as mentioned in the same connection. Compare James v. 11. Indeed, the introduction of a purely *mythical* name in such a matter-of-fact connection would be irrelevant and nugatory.]

NOTE 3.—On the peculiarity of the prophetic character of Daniel, as constituting a principal reason for referring this book among the Hagiographa, see Delitzsch, p. 272: "The book of Daniel was placed among the Hagiographa, because he was *not a prophet by virtue of his office and calling*, although, like David and Solomon, he possessed the gift of prophecy." Origen remarks correctly: "Non si quis prophetat, ideo propheta est. Ac profecto si quis propheta est, is quidem prophetat, sed vero qui prophetat, non continuo etiam est propheta." The genuineness of the book is therefore not compromised by its position among the Hagiographa.* Compare also Auberlen, *Daniel*, p. 30 et seq.: "We may also refer to his instruction in the wisdom of the Chaldæan Magi; for the Holy Scriptures show that the mysterious knowledge and arts of the heathen were not an empty boast, *e. g.*, in the case of the Egyptian sorcerers who opposed Moses. The wise men who were led by the star to seek after the new-born king of the Jews, were such Chaldee Magians, which clearly shows that they were not deprived of all truth, and *in connection with which we may even inquire whether a tradition may not have been transmitted among them which had emanated from Daniel, their chief*, who had received such remarkable disclosures concerning this king of the Jews, reaching even to the *time* of his appearing? The circumstance, that in his youth he was instructed during three years in this wisdom of the Chaldæans, doubtless had the effect on the prophet himself, to develop the prophetic tendency which was natural to him, and to make him at home in these mysterious regions (chap. i. 4, 5, 17). It must have afforded him an education similar to that which Moses derived from his training at the Egyptian court, or that drawn by the modern theologian from the study of philosophy. He learned, however, nothing of importance from the Chaldæans, but rather soon excelled them all ten-fold in wisdom." Further, compare the same, page 34 et seq., where, conforming to the Rabbins, the isolated position of Daniel, the apocalyptist, among the other Old-Testament prophets, is explained and interpreted to mean that while he did not possess the רוּחַ נְבוּאָה or proper prophetic Spirit, he nevertheless partook of the רוּחַ הַקֹּדֶשׁ or "Holy Spirit," which was shared also by the remaining writers of the Hagiographa, for which reason his proper place was among this class, and not among the prophets. Compare also the definitions which are quoted in that connection from Witsius (Daniel was endowed with the gift of prophecy indeed, but not with the prophetic office); from Bengel (Daniel was "the politician, chronologer, and historian among the prophets"); and from M. Baumgarten (Daniel was "the official seer of Jehovah in the world-kingdom").—See infra, § 6, note 1.

* Kliefoth (*Das Buch Daniels*, p. 48) assents to this, and observes, that in addition to the fact that, "according to his office Daniel was not a prophet, but an officer of the state," "his book contained prophecies concerning the world-power," and further, that, "in view of its historical matter, his book is a historical document for the period during which Israel languished under the world-power of Babylon and Media."

§ 3 Contents and Form of Daniel's Prophecies.

The *first* or *historical* division (chap. i.–vi.) of the two which compose our book according to § 1, p. 1, has already, so far as its principal features are concerned, been analyzed in the preceding paragraph, which narrates the leading events of the prophet's life in exact chronological order. The *second* or *prophetical* division (chap. vii.–xii.) contains the prophetic elements of the book, but not so exclusively as not to interweave occasional historical and biographical notices with its predictions (see especially the mention of Daniel's illness, chap. viii. 27; of his fasting, mourning, and prayer, chap. ix. 1 et seq.; x. 2 et seq.; of his visions on the banks of the Tigris, chap. x. 4 et seq.; xii. 5). Nor are prophecies entirely wanting in the historical division; for besides the interpretation of the dream relating to the lycanthropy of Nebuchadnezzar (in chap. iv. 16–24), which is equivalent to an actual prophecy or special prophetical prediction, and also besides the interpretation of the mysterious writing on the wall of Belshazzar's banquet-hall, which likewise testifies to Daniel's prophetic endowments (chap. v. 17–28), the leading features of the narrative in chapter ii., relating to the interpretation of Nebuchadnezzar's first dream by Daniel, form a prophecy of the specifically apocalyptic kind in their reference to the history of kingdoms and of the world. The great image composed of gold, silver, brass, iron, and clay, the so-called *image of the monarchies*, together with the stone that destroys it, which were seen by Nebuchadnezzar in his dream, and afterward by the prophet, in a night vision, were interpreted by Daniel by virtue of Divine inspiration, to signify a succession of world-kingdoms that should precede the kingdom of Messiah or of God, commencing with the reign of Nebuchadnezzar himself. The golden head of the image represented the existing kingdom of Nebuchadnezzar with its exalted power and greatness. Upon it should follow a second and inferior kingdom, and a third, that should bear rule over all the earth with the power and hardness of brass; afterwards a fourth, strong as iron, which should crush and destroy all things; and finally a divided kingdom, partly of iron and partly of clay, *i. e.*, partly strong and partly brittle, which, though seeking to combine its several parts, should yet fail to develop into a united whole. In the time of this divided kingdom, God Himself would establish a kingdom on the earth, which, like the destroying stone, should overturn and crush all the world-kingdoms in order to flourish on their ruins forever (chap. ii. 37–45).*

* [Keil (*Commentary on Daniel,* Clarke's tr., p. 84) ingeniously traces the logical position of the chapters in this *historical portion* as follows. He regards chaps. ii.–iii. as comprising, after the introductory chap. i., the *first part* of the book, containing "the development of the world-power," and remarks that "this part contains in six chapters as many reports regarding the successive forms and the natural character of the world-powers. It begins (chap. ii.) and ends (chap. vii.) with a revelation from God regarding its historical unfolding in four great world-kingdoms following each other, and their final overthrow by the kingdom of God, which shall continue for ever. Between these chapters (ii. and vii.) there are inserted four events belonging to the times of the first and second world-kingdoms, which partly reveal the attempts of the rulers of the world to compel the worshippers of the true God to pray to their idols and their gods, together with the failure of this attempt (chaps. iii. and vi.), and partly the humiliations of the rulers of the world, who were boastful of their power, under the judgments of God (chaps. iv. and v.), and bring under our consideration the relation of the rulers of this world to the Almighty God of heaven and earth and to the true fearers of His name. The narratives of these four events follow each other in chronological order, because they are in actual relation bound together, and therefore also the occurrences (chaps. v. and vi.) which belong to the time subsequent to the vision in chap. vii. are placed before this vision, so that the two revelations regarding the development of the world-power form the frame within which is contained the historical section which describes the character of that world-power." The *second part* of the entire book, as distributed by Keil (chaps. viii.–xii.), is designated by him as "the development of the kingdom of God"—thus contrasted with the world power of the former section. This latter part Keil analyzes as follows: "This part contains three revelations which Daniel received during the reigns of Belshazzar, Darius the Mede, and Cyrus the Persian, regarding the development of the kingdom of God. After describing in the first part the development of the world-power and its relation to the people and kingdom of God from the days of Nebuchadnezzar, its founder, down to the time of its final destruction by the perfected kingdom of God, in this second part it is revealed to the prophet how the kingdom of God entered against the power and enmity of the rulers of the world, and amid severe oppressions, is carried forward to final victory, and is perfected. The first vision, chap. viii., represents what will happen to the people of God during the developments of the second and third world-kingdoms; the second revelation, chap. ix., gives to the prophet, in answer to his penitential prayer for the restoration of the ruined holy city and the desolated sanctuary, disclosures regarding the whole development of the kingdom of God, from the close of the Babylonian exile to the final accomplishment of God's plan of salvation. In the last vision, in the third year of Cyrus, chap. x.–xii., he received yet further and more special revelations regarding the severe persecutions which await the people of God for their purification, in the nearer future under Antiochus Epiphanes, and in the time of the end under the last foe, the Antichrist" (p. 283).]

This prophecy, which is interwoven with the first or historical part, is closely related to the *first* prediction of the prophetical part (chap. vii.), and indeed is identical with it in purport. This latter prophecy is also a dream-vision with a succeeding Divinely-disclosed interpretation, but revealed originally and solely to Daniel. The succession of the four world-kingdoms which began with that of Nebuchadnezzar, is in this instance represented by four beasts which rise in succession from the sea: a lion with eagle's wings and the heart of a man, a bear with three ribs in its ravenous jaws, a leopard with four wings and four heads, and a fourth terrible monster with iron teeth and ten horns, three of which were plucked up by the roots, and replaced by "another little horn" with human eyes and a mouth that spoke presumptuous blasphemies (chap. vii. 2–8). The fourth of these kingdoms is now described somewhat differently, and more particularly, as a fearful reign of tyranny, which devoured the earth and destroyed and ruined all things, and from which should proceed in succession ten kings, who are symbolized by the ten horns. Three of these kings are to be superseded by the final monarch, who is represented by the "little horn," and whose madness and blasphemous presumption exceed that of all who have preceded him, so that he speaks blasphemy against the Highest, makes war upon the saints of God, and aims to set aside the law and the holy seasons. The sufferings of the people of God at the hands of this tyrant are limited to three and a half years, at the end of which Divine judgments shall be visited on him through one like the Son of man, who comes with the clouds of heaven, and to whom is committed an everlasting dominion over all nations.

The *second* prophecy of the second part (chap. viii.) also stands connected in its subject and purport with the image of the monarchies, whose middle and lower parts it develops and illustrates more fully. Under the figure of a contest between a ram and a he-goat, it describes the overthrow of the third by the fourth world-kingdom, together with succeeding events down to the Messianic judgment. A ram with two horns, of which the taller appeared last, pushes fiercely towards the four quarters of the earth, until a he-goat with a notable horn, coming from the west, smites him to the ground, and breaks his two horns. Next, the great horn of the victorious goat is broken, and replaced by four other notable ones, toward the four winds of heaven. Out of one of these comes forth a little horn, which increases mightily toward the south, the east, and Judæa, grows even to the host of heaven and its prince, desecrates the sanctuary, and interrupts the offering of the daily sacrifice during a period of 2,300 evenings and mornings (*i.e.* 1,150 days, or three and a half years), vers. 3–14. The angel Gabriel interprets this vision to the prophet, and applies it to the Medo-Persian empire, which should be overthrown by the fourth world-power, founded by the king of Græcia (Alexander the Great), and also to the four more important kingdoms of the Diadochi, which should arise out of the Greek world-monarchy, on the early death of its founder. One of these latter kingdoms (that of the Seleucidæ) should become especially hurtful to the people of God and His sanctuary, through the craft and audacity of one of its rulers, until finally the breaking of this offender "without hand," *i. e.*, by the interference of a superior power should come to pass. [For a comparative table of all these prophecies see § 10, Note 3; and for a refutation of the "year-day" hypothesis on which the application of the fourth kingdom exclusively to Papal Rome rests, see § 10, Note 4.]

A *third* vision (chap. ix.) is vouchsafed to the prophet in connection with his meditating on the meaning of the seventy years, which Jeremiah had predicted should elapse before the rebuilding of Jerusalem. While addressing Jehovah in fervent penitential prayer, in connection with his meditations, and beseeching Him to forgive the sins of His people, and to turn away His fury from Jerusalem (vers. 3–19), the angel Gabriel discloses to him the meaning of Jeremiah's prophecy. The seventy years are to be understood as seventy weeks of years. Four hundred and ninety years were determined, in order to atone fully for the sins of the people, and to reanoint the Most Holy of His temple. The first seven of the seventy weeks of years were to include the period between the utterance of Jeremiah's prophecy and the "anointed prince" (Cyrus); in the course of the sixty-two weeks of years that should follow, the city (Jerusalem) was to be rebuilt, but in troublous times. The last, or seventieth, week of years should begin with the "cutting off of an anointed one," after which the people and their sanctuary were to be devastated by the armies of a tyrant, and the customary offering of the sacred sacrifices and oblations to be interrupted during the half of a week (evidently during the latter half of this final week of years), until, in the end, ruin should overtake the destroyer * (vers. 21–27).

The *final* vision (chaps. x.–xii.) contains the most thorough and detailed description of the developments of the future. After three weeks of fasting and mourning, an angel, whose clothing and appearance were wonderful (chap. x. 5–11), appeared to the prophet on the banks of the Tigris, and gave him an account of the contests which he was compelled to enter into with the "princes," or angelical protectors of Persia and Græcia, and in which he was aided only by Michael, the angel of God's people (chap. x. 12–xi. 1). To this account he added a representation, full of life and minute detail, of the immediate future, and extending to the time of the tyrannical oppressor of God's people, who has already been frequently described. In this connection he dwells especially upon the conflicts of the kings of a southern kingdom (Egypt) and a northern kingdom (Syria), which were to constitute the principal states that should arise from the ruins of the fourth (Greek or Macedonian) world-power (chap. xi. 2–20), and more than all, on the insolent, audacious, and blasphemous deportment of the last king of the northern realm, who should ultimately come to a terrible end, after inflicting the most horrible abominations on the holy nation, their sacred city, and its sanctuary (chap. xi. 21–45). After unparallelled tribulation and affliction, deliverance and salvation should come to Daniel's nation, in connection with the resurrection of the dead, which should lead to the exaltation of the righteous, but consign the ungodly to everlasting punishment (chap. xii. 1–3). † After the angel has directed the prophet to seal the prophecy to the time of the end (ver. 4), he supplements it by a final revelation in regard to the *duration* of the period of severe affliction before the introduction of Messiah's kingdom, which is fixed at 1,290, or, conditionally, at 1,335 days (vs. 7–12). The whole closes with the counsel of the angel to the prophet, to wait patiently until the end of all things, and until his resurrection to eternal life.

The arrangement of the four prophecies of the second part is strictly chronological, so that the order of their succession is parallel with that of the actual events in Daniel's life, as recorded in the first part. The first vision appeared to him "in the first year of Belshazzar" the king, in the form of a dream, which he at once recorded in writing (chap. vii. 1); the second, in the third year of the same reign, "in the palace of Shushan, in the province of Elam, by the river of Ulai,"—where the prophet in his exaltation at least believed himself to be (chap. viii. 1, 2); the third, in the first year of the reign of Darius the Mede, hence soon after the overthrow of Belshazzar (chap. ix. 1, 2; cf. v. 30; vi. 1); and the fourth, "in the third year of Cyrus, king of Persia," on the 24th day of the first month, while the prophet was on the banks of the Tigris, after completing his fast of three weeks (chap. x. 1–4; cf. xii. 5, 6). The first vision is included in the Aramaic portion of the book; the three others, like chap. i. and the opening verses of chap. ii. (vers. 1–4a), are recorded in Hebrew.

In a formal point of view, the marked difference between the prophecies of the second part and those of the first is to be noticed, namely, that in the latter instance the interpretation of the wonderful and prophetic appearance of the vision in Nebuchadnezzar's dream (chap. ii.), and of the mysterious writing, Mene, Mene, Tekel, etc., at the banquet of Belshazzar (chap. v.), was imparted to the prophet immediately through the Divine Spirit, and without the agency of angels; while in each of the four prophecies of the second part angels are employed, either to reveal the purport of the visions seen by Daniel while awake or dreaming (as in the case of the first two, chap. vii. and viii.), or to convey direct disclosures relating to the future, without any previous symbolical vision (as with the final prophecies, chap. ix. and x.–xii.). The prophet, however, is the only narrator, even when he recapitulates (as is the case especially in chap. x. 20–xii. 4) the extended remarks of the angel, his celestial teachers and interpreters. The epistolary form of narration which occurs once in the first part, chap. iii. 31–iv.

* In support of this statement of the contents of chap. ix. 22–27, and especially of the verse last mentioned, compare the exegetical remarks on that passage. [For counter arguments, see the additions thereto.]

† [See, however, the exegetical remarks on this last particular.]

34 (but which is not rigidly adhered to in that connection, since Nebuchadnezzar, the writer of the letter under our notice, is referred to in the third person, in chap. iv. 25–30), is not found in the second part.

NOTE.—In opposition to the division of the contents of this book into historical and prophetico-visional parts, which we have adopted, Auberlen (p. 38), and in connection with him Keil (*Einl. ins A. T.*, 2d ed., p. 389 et seq.), and also Kranichfeld (*Das Buch Daniel*, p. 2 et seq.), contends that chap. vii. should be included in the first part. The reasons adduced by the last mentioned exegete, as "material" in contrast with ours as merely "formal," are, first, the prophetico-visional elements which enter also into the first part, and particularly into chap. ii., and secondly, the identity of language in chap. vii. with chapters ii.–v., which forbids a wider separation between chapters vi. and vii. as contrary to the intention of the author. But the visional constituents of the first part are extremely meagre when compared with the far greater proportion of the narrative elements in this division; and the chronological difference between chapters vi. and vii. is decidedly more important than the affinities of language between chap. vii. and the five chapters that precede it. The dream-vision recorded in chapter vii. dates back to the reign of Belshazzar, the last (or one of the last) of the Babylonian kings, while the historical contents of the preceding chapter belong to the Medo-Persian period; hence the time of chapter vii. and also of chap. viii. corresponds to that of chapter v., while chapter vi. is contemporary with chapter ix. Since the general arrangement, both of the pre-eminently historical chapters of the first part, and of the chiefly visional contents of the second, is strictly chronological, the distribution of the entire book into the categories of history and prophecy seems to have been the leading idea by which its editor (whom we regard as identical with its author) was governed, while the identity of language in chapter vii. and the preceding chapters sinks into a merely accidental feature. The following section may serve to show the most probable explanation of this feature. For the present, we are only concerned to show that the arrangement adopted by us, even if it were based more on a formal than a material principle, conforms fully to the idea and design of the writer, and is therefore with justice retained by a majority of modern expositors—even by Zündel (p. 39 et seq.), Reusch (*Einl. ins A. T.*, 3d ed., p. 109), and others.

§ 4. UNITY OF THE BOOK OF DANIEL.

The integrity of this book may be conclusively shown, despite the occasional attempts essayed by recent critics to represent it as a compilation of several historical and prophetic fragments of various origin; for, as has been shown in § 3, the contents of the two principal divisions form a harmonious and closely-connected whole, which must have emanated from a single author. This author is frequently designated as one and the same person—as Daniel—particularly in chap. vii. 1; xiii. 1; ix. 2; x. 1; xii. 4; and he is mentioned either in the third person (chap. vii. 1; x. 1) or in the first (chap. vii. 2 et seq.; x. 2 et seq.). The same interchange of the first and third persons is found elsewhere in writings of the Old Testament that have emanated from a single author, *e.g.*, Isa. vii.; xxxvi.–xxxix., etc. The fact that Daniel is mentioned exclusively in the third person throughout the first six chapters is sufficiently explained by the historical and descriptive character of this first main division, which merely reports occasional expressions by Daniel, of greater or less extent (*e.g.*, chap. ii. 15, 20, 23, 30; iv. 16 et seq.; v. 17 et seq.; vi. 22 et seq.), but generally represents *other* persons as speaking and acting. The absence from this part of the formula, "I, Daniel, saw," or "I, Daniel, said," could only hold as an argument against the unity of the book, in case other discrepancies and contradictions of importance existed between the contents of the two parts. Such contradictions, however, do not occur. It is not impossible to reconcile chapter i. 21 with chapter x. 1, or chapter vi. 1 with chapters ix. 1 and xi. 1, etc., as the exposition of those passages will show in detail. The historical part is rather connected with the prophetical in manifold relations, and their chronological parallelisms especially bear the marks of design on the part of the composer. The series of remarkable events in his life, which are first recorded, is designed as a historical introduction, or scaffolding, for the prophetic visions which follow. But within the historical part itself, chapter i. is intimately connected, as an introduction, with the five chapters that follow. Daniel's prophetic power and skill in interpreting dreams, are remarked in chap. i. 17, 20, evidently with reference to the tests to which they were to be exposed, chap. ii. 4, 5. The mention of the three friends in chap. i. 6 et seq.

paves the way for the narrative respecting their official stations and confessorship (chap. ii. 49; iii. 1 et seq.). The statement that Nebuchadnezzar removed the sacred vessels of the temple from Jerusalem is a preparation for the history of their desecration by Belshazzar (chap. ii. 5 et seq.).

Nor does the diversity of language, as between the Chaldee of chapters ii.–vii. and the Hebrew of the remaining chapters, involve a multiplicity of authors; for, aside from the fact that a transition from the Hebrew to the Chaldee, exactly similar to that in Dan. ii. 4, occurs in Ezra iv. 7, the idea of a variety of authors becomes impossible in view of the intimate relation of the Hebrew chapter i. to the succeeding Aramaic sections, which has just been noticed. The last (chap. vii.) of the Aramaic portions, again, is so closely connected in its leading features with the Hebrew sections that follow—and especially with chapter viii. which is introduced by the indication of time, in a manner entirely analogous to chap. vii. 1—that the discrepancy of language in this case also appears evidently as a feature of secondary importance. The contrast between the use of the Hebrew in the introductory and the five closing chapters, and of the Chaldee in chapters ii.–vii. can appear as other than accidental, only as the latter sections seem to have been reduced to writing at an earlier period than the former. They were probably recorded during the Chaldæan supremacy or immediately afterward, whereas the Hebrew sections that enclose them were probably added at a considerably later date, and in the time of the Persian rule. This hypothesis (first assumed by Kranichfeld) of a gradual completion of the book, or of the framing of the Chaldæan sections, which originated during the exile proper, between the Hebrew portions, chaps. i. 1–ii. 4 and viii.–xii., that date in the Persian period, is favored by the note in chap. i. 21, which implies the later composition of the introduction, but more especially by the circumstance that the Chaldee fragments, without exception, convey the impression that they were recorded in the style of chronicles, immediately after the events transpired to which they relate. They also seem to indicate that the author employed this language for such journalistic minutes, as being more familiar, in view of his culture (compare § 2), while he adopted the Hebrew at a later period, perhaps because he had in the meantime acquired a sufficient readiness in its use, or because the different circumstances of the times subsequent to the captivity might lead him to regard the sacred language of the law and the earlier prophets as more appropriate for his purpose of instructing and edifying his theocratic compatriots. We therefore assert the integrity of this book with reference to all its leading divisions, and as being the work of a single author; but in the closing section of the second part, in the especially detailed prophecies of chapters x.–xii., we detect the hand of a later interpolating reviser of the time of Antiochus Epiphanes, for reasons which have been generally indicated (§ 1, note 2), but the more detailed elaboration of which must be reserved for the exposition (see especially on chap. xi. vs. 5 and 40, etc.). Such interpolations are apparent more particularly in chapter xi. 5–39 (*e.g.*, vs. 5, 6, 8, 14, 17, 18, 25, 27, 30–39).

NOTE 1.—J. D. Michaelis, Bertholdt, and Eichhorn (at least in the earlier editions of his *Einleitung*), among those who reject the integrity of this book, find a considerable number of independent compositions contained in it, which are said to have been written at different times and by various authors. Of such compositions Michaelis enumerates eight, Eichhorn ten (in vol. III. of his *Hebräische Propheten*, p. 428 et seq., at least five), and Bertholdt nine. The latter refers the first (chap. i.) of these "Danielana," as he calls them, to the time of Artaxerxes Longimanus; the second (chap. ii.) to that of Ptolemy Philadelphus; the third (chap. iii. 1–30) to a somewhat later date; the fourth (iii. 31–iv. 34) to the age of the first Asmonæans; the fifth, sixth, and seventh (chaps. v.–viii.) to the same period, under Antiochus Epiphanes; the eighth (chap. ix.) by a priest at Jerusalem, to a date but little later; and the ninth (chap. x.–xii.) to a still later time. The composers of the later sections are said generally to have known the earlier writers, and to have continued their work, in which effort they even imitated their predecessors in the use of single words and phrases. But despite their care numerous contradictions crept into the separate parts, so that, for instance, chap. i. 21 is opposed to x. 1; chap. i. 1, 5 to ii. 1; chap. ii. 48, 49 to v. 11–14, etc. (Bertholdt, *Daniel* i. 83 et seq.). The impropriety of such a mutilation of Scripture was soon understood, and was pointed out, with convincing arguments, especially by Bleek (in Schleiermacher's *Theol. Zeitschrift*, 1822, No. 3, p. 241 et seq.; compare his *Einleitung ins A. T.*, p. 585 et seq.),

Hävernick (*Einl.* II. 2, p. 443 et seq.), and De Wette (*Einleitung in das A. T.*, § 256). Hence Eichhorn, in the third and fourth editions of his *Einleitung*, contented himself with the assumption of merely two authors, of whom the one composed chap. ii. 4–vi. 29, and the other, chap. vii–xii., together with the Hebrew introduction, chap. i. 1–ii. 3, in each case long after the captivity. The two-fold authorship is also asserted by Sack (*Christl. Apologetik*, 1829), Herbst (*Histor.-krit. Einl.*, published by Welte, 1840 and later, ii. 2, § 34), F. Speil (*Zur Echtheit des B. Daniel*, in the *Tüb. Theol. Quartal-Schrift*, 1863, p. 194), Reusch (*Einl.*, p. 110), and several others, inasmuch as they regard the visional part of the book, beginning with chap. vii., as genuine, but claim that the narrative of Daniel's life and of the circumstances of his time, contained in chap. i.–vi., was added by a later hand, and based upon a revision of certain genuine memoranda, which were left by the prophet at his death. Hence, we are to distinguish between genuine originals, written by the prophet himself, and a later compilation which belongs to the Maccabæan period or to the age immediately preceding, and in which the author possessed the skill to imitate the prophet's mode of thought and expression, thus producing the impression of a united apocalyptic whole. Such an origin of the book cannot be branded as wholly impossible; but the impression of closely connected, systematic, and designed unity which it makes, in respect to both its form and matter, appears to favor the view stated above, by which the first and second editor constitute a single personage, identical with the prophet Daniel, and by which the whole appears as the work of one mind, despite its gradual production in the period immediately before and after the close of the exile (compare the following note).

Three additional hypotheses concerning the origin of the book deserve attention, which likewise proceed on the assumption of a two-fold authorship, or of a distinction between a genuine original and a later interpolating revision, but which differ greatly among themselves. According to the editor [Lange] of this *Bible-work* (*Einl. in das A. T.*, in the remarks preliminary to the exposition of Genesis, vol. I., p. 38 [of the Am. ed.]), the book, which otherwise originated entirely with the captive prophet Daniel, received two extensive additions in its final sections, at the hands of an apocalyptist of the Maccabæan period, who was led to make these interpolations in view of the severe trials of the time. These additions comprise chap. x. 1–xi. 44, and xii. 5–13; hence the predictions which relate specially to Antiochus Epiphanes and his time, and which bear pre-eminently the stamp of *vaticinia ex eventu*. The professed interpolation of 2 Pet. i. 20–iii. 3 from the epistle of Jude, which the editor has endeavored to establish, in vol. I. of his *Geschichte des apostolischen Zeitalters* (p. 152 et seq.), more thoroughly than this asserted addition to Daniel, is adduced as an analogous instance; but it does not seem to be sufficiently demonstrated, despite the manifold advantages it would afford to the apologist. We are obliged to prefer the view of a mere interpolating revision of chapters x.–xii. by a pious apocalyptist of the Asmonæan period, and to hold to the probable insertion of several brief passages, which cannot in our day be clearly distinguished, instead of accepting the introduction of the lengthy section, chap. x. 1–xi. 44, together with that in chap. xii. 5–13. A later inventor of the entire prophetic imagery of chapters x. and xi. would display an incredible talent in his imitations of the prophet's literary style. Moreover, the writer of Ecclesiasticus (about B. C. 180) seems to have recognized passages like chap. x. 13, 20, as original with Daniel, and to have imitated them as such; also the Septuagint. See below § 6, note 2, and compare the exegesis of the chapters in question.* The view of Ewald (*Die Propheten des A. Bds.*, 1st ed., II. 562 et seq.) is peculiar. According to him, the prophet Daniel lived at the heathen court of Nineveh as early as the Assyrian captivity, about B. C. 700. A Jewish contemporary of Alexander the Great invented prophecies relating to the world-kingdoms, and attributed them to this wise man of the Assyrian period, while another Jew, living in the time of the Maccabees, added further embellishments to the book as he found it. Somewhat more definite and thoughtful is Bunsen (*Gott in der Geschichte*, I. 514 et seq.). The Daniel of Assyrian times, who lived at Nineveh under Pul and Sargon, about the middle of the 8th century B. C., left behind him figurative prophecies concerning the destruction of Asshur (the winged lion) by the Babylonian empire (a devouring bear; cf. chap. vii. 2 et seq.); these ancient oracles, together with legendary records concerning the personal fortunes of Daniel, and particularly his deliverance from the den of lions, were transmitted, either verbally or in writing, until a writer of the Maccabæan period gave them their present form, in connection with which work, however, he committed the grave historical error of transferring the prophet to the period of the Babylonian captivity, and of substituting the Babylonian monarchy for the Assyrian, and the Medo-Persian for the original Babylonian (cf. above, § 2, note 2). Neither Ewald nor Bunsen are able to furnish any positive proof in support of these strained, artificial, and fantastic views. The assertion that the later Jewish writers constantly substituted Babylon for Asshur is entirely arbitrary and incapable of proof; and the removal of Daniel to "the great river which is Hiddekel" can no more be considered a mere echo of the history of Daniel in Nineveh, than the imaginary winged creatures with human visages

* [We shall there endeavor to show that all these suppositions of any interpolation whatever are gratuitous and unsupported.]

can be regarded as dark allusions to the colossal statues on the palaces of Nimrud. In our exposition of the related passages we will aim to show that both these features may be adequately explained on the assumption of a Babylonian career in the case of the prophet. Bunsen, however, appears to have subsequently given up his arbitrary view, in favor of the general pseudo-Daniel tendency-hypothesis (see the prefaces in vol. I. of his *Bibelwerk*, p. liv.); while the view of Ewald appears unchanged in the recent 2d edition of his *Propheten des Alten Bundes* (vol. III. p. 312 et seq.).

NOTE 2.—In support of the opinion laid down in this section, that the book was composed at different times by Daniel himself, compare Kranichfeld, *Das Buch Daniel* (*Einl.*, p. 4): "For the rest, the Chaldee fragments in their present state, without an incorporated introduction and conclusion, cannot in themselves have formed a separate work. Their formal and abrupt character produces rather the impression of an occasional composition in the manner of a diary, which was undertaken at different times, and perhaps in connection with corresponding events of the exile in the Chaldæan period, while the conception of the Hebrew introduction may have fallen, agreeably to the remark in chap. i. 21, in the time of the Persian supremacy. Presuming the genuineness of the book, the overthrow of both the Chaldæan and the Persian dynasties in Babylon would therefore have occurred between the composition of the several Chaldee fragments and that of the Hebrew section, chap. i. 1–ii. 4; and a very different condition of affairs, having an especial significance for Israel, would meanwhile have been introduced. This would also be sufficient to account for the choice of the Hebrew dress of chapters viii.–xii., and, in general, to establish their subsequent composition, which is now more than ever a question of interest." Compare the same writer, p. 53 et seq.: "The composition of the Chaldee fragments accordingly belonged to a time in which the heathen oppressors as such, and the measures of the heathen tyranny, were everywhere prominent; and it is natural that a theocratical writer of this period should fix his gaze on these features, and clothe his narrative in a form likely to be effective among the Chaldæan population, and serviceable to oppose their hostile and insolent measures, as well as that he should attempt this in the Chaldæan language, which was current among the oppressors. * With the close of the exile a new range of vision opened before the theocrat. The oppressive tyranny which was before his leading thought, is no longer prominent in that character; the hitherto passive people of the theocracy is now roused to a more active concern for its national interests. Appropriate as was the Chaldee tongue before the dawning of the new period, the language of his people and of the fathers, which the writer employs, in common with the prophets after the exile, to convey his supplemental and additional matter, is no less appropriate after that period has begun. With his attention fixed upon his people, the prophet now gave its final and united form to his book, during the first year of the sole reign of Cyrus, as has been noticed above. The Chaldee portions, which were composed during the captivity, and whose form was due to that circumstance, received their place in the book in connection with this final revision; and there was no reason why the existing Chaldee material should be rendered into Hebrew for the benefit of his compatriots, who were familiar with the language of Babylon, especially as the Chaldee dress itself contributed not a little to the vivid representation of the circumstances described."

We accept, in all its essential features, this hypothesis respecting the composition of our book as being highly probable and attractive; † but instead of finding in a designed reference to the Chaldæan oppressors the motive which induced the prophet to compose in Aramaic the portions (chap. ii.–vii.) belonging to the exile, we would adopt the more simple and natural view, that during that period he was accustomed to employ the Chaldee tongue, with which he was chiefly familiar; and that, in his written productions especially, he availed himself of its use, to the exclusion of all others. This does not involve the admission that he may not already at that time have acquired, by means of *reading and study*, that marked familiarity with the sacred language and literature of his people, which chap. i. 17, 20 (cf. with i. 4) seem to imply. In this connection we would also venture the supposition with respect to the "occasional journalizing notes" of events belonging to the Chaldæan (and Median) period, as found in chap. ii.–vii., that Daniel employed with design the chronicling style of the older

* [On the contrary, such a state of oppression, if it existed at the time (of which there is no evidence), would have rendered the foreign tongue odious, and therefore been the strongest possible reason for avoiding it. Such was certainly the effect at a later date, when Antiochus sought to introduce the Greek language and customs. In the Roman period, too, we know that the comparatively mild rule of the conquerors made the Jews only cling the more tenaciously to "the sacred tongue," at least for all their religious works.]

† [We beg leave, however, to dissent almost entirely from Kranichfeld's views on this head. A far more natural and sufficient reason for the insertion of the Chaldee portions of the book is found in the fact, stated or implied in their respective contents, that they were extracts, taken verbatim and as such *from the Babylonian state records*. The supposition that the whole book was originally written in Chaldee, and these parts alone left untranslated, is destitute of a particle of confirmation, either in the narrative, the style of the composition, or the usage of the contemporary Jewish writers. Especially the insinuation that Daniel was so ignorant of his mother tongue, that he was obliged to *learn* it in mature life by a slow and imperfect process, as the author a few sentences further on presumes, is contrary to all the probabilities in the case.]

prophets, which regarded all the facts to be related from a strictly theocratical point of view, and by which their supernatural features were rather intensified and idealized, than simplified and reduced to sober events of common occurrence. Compare § 9, Note 1.

§ 5. Authenticity of the Book.

a. *Review of the Attacks on, and Defence of, its Genuineness.*

The most ancient assailant of the genuineness of Daniel's prophecies of whom we have a certain knowledge, was the Neo-platonic Porphyry (died A. D. 304). In his fifteen books "against the Christians," which are known to us only through Jerome so far as they contain attacks on this book, he contends for its composition in Maccabæan times, and for the forged character of its prophecies as mere *vaticinia ex eventu.** It is uncertain whether Jewish rabbins who opposed Christianity were his predecessors and instructors in this assertion, or not. A passage in the Talmud, which attributes the "recording" of several books of the Old Testament, and among them *Daniel*, to the members of the Great Synagogue beginning with Ezra,† affords no support to the opinion that the authenticity of the book was denied in pre-Christian times in Jewish circles, since that "recording" is doubtless not to be understood in the sense of an original composition, but rather as a renewed recording on the authority of an exact tradition; or rather, of a new inspiration. The entire statement is, therefore, merely an empty legend of the sort which is represented by the Jewish tales concerning the marvellous reproduction of the Pentateuch by Ezra, the origin of the Septuagint, etc. The statement of Isidore of Seville (died A. D. 636) that "Ezekiel and Daniel are said to have been written by certain wise men"‡ points back to the same muddy Jewish-rabbinical source. The "wise men" in this case can scarcely be other than the men of the Great Synagogue, and their "writing" of the books of Ezekiel and Daniel cannot designate a forgery in any sense, but must be explained as in the Talmudic tradition referred to. In short, the older period exhibits no definite instance of the rejection of the authenticity of this prophetic book beyond the solitary one of Porphyry; and only the immediate opponents of this writer, as Methodius, Eusebius of Cæsarea, Apollinaris of Laodicea, or church fathers of the age next following, were engaged in the defense of the genuineness of the book, while refuting his objections.

In the 17th century the opponents of its genuineness became somewhat more numerous, but their objections were at first without any scientific value. Spinoza (*Tractat. theol.-polit.*, x. 130 et seq.) held, that only chap. viii.–xii. were genuine; chap. i.–vii. might originally have formed component parts of the annals of the Chaldæan reigns, which, together with the final five chapters, were probably collected and published by a later hand. Hobbes (*Leviathan*, c. 33) doubted whether Daniel himself or a subsequent writer had recorded his prophecies. Sir Isaac Newton (*Observations upon the prophecies of Daniel and the Apocalypse of St. John*, I. p. 10), whose view was followed, in the main, by Beausobre (*Remarques sur le N. Test.*, I. p. 70), thought that "the last six chapters contained prophecies composed at various times by Daniel himself, while the six former ones were a collection of historical essays by other authors." By this, however, he did not intend to attack the credibility or the inspired character of the book; on the contrary, he declared solemnly that "whoever rejects the prophecies of Daniel, does as much as if he undermined the Christian religion, which, so to speak, is founded on Daniel's prophecies of Christ." If he regarded the first six chapters as not the work of Daniel, it was not because he objected to the wonders recorded in them, as Zündel thinks (*Kritische Untersuchungen*, etc., p. 2), but because he believed that their mode of presentation indicated one or several authors other than Daniel. It was different, however, with Collins, the deisti

* Jerome, *Comm. in Dan. Prophet.*: "*Contra prophetam Danielem scripsit Porphyrius, nolens eum ab ipso, cuius inscriptus est nomine, esse compositum, sed a quodam, qui temporibus Antiochi Epiphanis fuerit in Judæa; et non tam Danielem ventura dixisse, quam illum narasse præterita. Denique quicquid usque ad Antiochum dixerit, veram historiam continere, si quid autem ultra opinatus est, quia futura nescierit, esse mentitum.*"

† *Baba Bathra*, f. 15: "*Viri Synagogæ magnæ scripserunt K. N. D. G., quibus literis significantur libri Ezechielis, duodecim prophetarum minorum, Danielis et Estheræ.*"

‡ Isidore, *Origg.*, vi. 2: "*Ezechiel et Daniel a viris quibusdam sapientibus scripti esse perhibentur.*" Cf. Hengstenberg, *Die Authentie des Daniel*, etc., p. 3, where the opinion of Bertholdt (*Einl. ins. A. T.*, iv. 1508), that a doubt of the genuineness of Daniel is here implied, is rejected, and certainly with justice.

cal contemporary of Newton, and with the somewhat older Jewish atheist Uriel Acosta (about A. D. 1630), who denied the credibility of the book together with its genuineness, but with a bungling criticism that is wholly involved in the prejudices of naturalistic dogmatism.*

Among the representatives of German rationalism, Semler contented himself with a very general denial of the inspiration of the book of Daniel, for the reason that he "could discover no such benefit in it as God always designs to secure to man when he employs very peculiar means for that end" (*Freie Untersuchung des Kanon*, III. 505). Michaelis and Eichhorn, while contesting the integrity of the book (see above § 4, note 1), endeavored to establish the genuineness of at least the last chapters. Eichhorn did not venture to assert the Maccabæan origin of the whole book (in the 3d and 4th ed. of his *Einleitung*), and consequently its forged character, until Corrodi had declared it to be wholly the work of an impostor of the times of Antiochus Epiphanes, † in his *Freimüthigen Versuchen über verschiedene in Theologie und bibl. Kritik einschlagende Gegenstände*. Bertholdt now followed with his super-ingenious mutilating hypothesis, which was wholly based on the assumption of forgery (cf. supra), and later, Griesinger, Gesenius, De Wette, Kirmss, Redepenning, Von Lengerke, Knobel, Hitzig, Stähelin, Hilgenfeld, and others. ‡ The greatest scientific ability and judgment in contesting the authenticity of this book, but, at the same time, in breaking the force of the assaults on its integrity, made by Bertholdt and Eichhorn, was displayed by Bleek. § The more recent deniers of the genuineness of the book, with but few exceptions, agree with him in giving up its historical character to a greater or less extent, and in assigning it to the Maccabæan period, and regarding its prophecies as *vaticinia ex eventu*—hence, in holding essentially the same critical position which was occupied by Porphyry. The grounds on which their assertions are based are partly internal and partly external in their nature. They are drawn in part from the place of the book in the canon and its relation to the later Jewish apocryphal literature, and in part from its peculiarities of language, the asserted mythical character of its historical part, the chronological difficulties which it is said to present, and the apocalyptical character of its prophecies. In the following section we shall engage in a more detailed examination of these arguments, and in that connection find opportunity to become acquainted with the substantial and enduring services of the more recent defenders of the genuineness of the book. Among them belong, of Protestants, Lüderwald, Stäudlin, Beckhaus, Hengstenberg, Hävernick, Keil, Auberlen, Delitzsch, Zündel, Volck, Kranichfeld, Pusey, Fuller, and others; of Roman Catholics, Jahn, Hug, Herbst, Scholz, Speil, Reusch, and others. ‖

* Cf. Wolf, *Bibl. Hebraica*, II., p. 161; Bertholdt, as cited above; and especially as affecting Newton's position on the question of Daniel, the instructive article "Is. Newton" by B . . . . . . t, in Michaud's *Biographie universelle*, tom. XXX., p. 397 ss.

† Cf. also *Beleuchtung der Geschichte des Kanon*, I. 75 et seq.; and *Kritische Geschichte des Chiliasmus*, I. 247 et seq., by the same author.

‡ Griesinger, *Neue Geschichte der Aufsätze im Buch Daniel*, 1812; Gesenius, *Allgem. Literaturzeitung*, 1816, Nos. 57 and 80; De Wette, *Einleitung ins. A. T.*, § 255 et seq.; Kirmss, *Commentatio historico-critica, exhibens descriptionem et censuram recentium de Danielis libro opinionum*, Jena, 1850; Redepenning, *Theol. Studien und Kritiken*, 1833, p. 831 et seq.; 1835, p. 163 et seq.; Von Lengerke, *Das Buch Daniel*, 1835; Knobel, *Prophetismus der Hebräer*, II. 389 et seq.; Hitzig, *Kurzgef. exeget. Handbuch zu Daniel*, 1850; Stähelin, *Spezielle Einleitung in die kanon. BB. des A. Test.*, 1862; Hilgenfeld, *Die jüdische Apokalyptik*, 1857. Compare also Dillmann, *Ueber die Bildung der Sammlung heiliger Schriften A. Tests.*, in the *Jahrbücher für deutsche Theologie*, 1858, p. 458 et seq.; Kahnis, *Luther. Dogmatik*, I. p. 369 et seq.; Th. Nöldeke, *Die alttestamentl. Literatur in einer Reihe von Aufsätzen dargestellt* (Leipsic, 1868), p. 216 et seq.; R. Baxmann, *Ueber das B. Daniel*, *Studien und Kritiken*, 1863, p. 452 et seq. (against Zündel); and Davidson, *Introd. to the Old Test.*, vol. III., p. 200 ss.

§ *Ueber Verfasser und Zweck des B. Daniel*, in the *Theol. Zeitschrift* of Schleiermacher, De Wette, and Lücke, 1822, III. 171 et seq. Further, *Die Messianischen Weissagungen im Buche Daniel* (Review of Auberlen's work) in the *Jahrbücher für deutsche Theologie*, 1860, I.; and *Einl. ins A. T.*, § 254 et seq.

‖ Lüderwald. *Die sechs ersten Kapitel Daniels nach historischen Gründen geprüft*, Helmstädt, 1787 (against Eichhorn, 1st ed.); Stäudlin, *Prüfung einiger Meinungen über den Ursprung des B. Daniel, in den Neuen Beiträgen zur Erläuterung der Propheten*, Göttingen, 1791 (specially against Corrodi); Beckhaus, *Die Integrität der prophetischen Schriften*, p. 279 et seq.; Hengstenberg, *Beitr. zur Einl.* I.; *Die Authentie des Daniel und die Integrität des Sacharja*, Berlin, 1831; Hävernick, *Kommentar über d. Buch Daniel*, 1832; *Neue krit. Untersuchung über d. Buch Daniel*, 1838; *Einleitung ins A. T.*, II. 2, p. 444 et seq.; Keil, *Einl.* § 135 et seq.; Auberlen, *Der Prophet Daniel und die Offenbarung Johannis*, Basle, 1854; 2d ed., 1857; F. Delitzsch, in Herzog's Real-Encycklop., Art. *Daniel* (III. 271 et seq.); W. Volck, *Vindiciæ Danielicæ*, Dorpat, 1866; David Zündel, *Kritische Untersuchung über die Abfassungszeit des Buches Daniel*, Basle, 1861; Kranichfeld, *Der Prophet Daniel*, Berlin, 1868, p. 6 et seq.; E. B. Pusey, *Daniel the prophet*, Oxford, 1864; J. M. Fuller, *An essay*

§ 6. Authenticity of the Book (Continued).

b. *Examination of the* EXTERNAL *reasons against the genuineness of Daniel.*

Among the external grounds on which opponents are accustomed to contest the origin of the book with Daniel, its position among the Hagiographa, in the third and last part of the Hebrew canon, generally forms their chief reliance. That this fact, so suspicious at first sight, is by no means inexplicable, but rather has its adequate explanation in the peculiar prophetic character of Daniel and his writings, as well as in the composition of the book, partly in Hebrew and partly in Chaldee, has already been shown (§ 1, particularly notes 2 and 3, and also § 2, note 3). We confine ourselves in this place to the suggestion that possibly the times of severe trial and of conflict with anti-Christian powers, which the prophet of the exile foretold to his people, might seem to the scribes of the centuries succeeding the captivity to present too great a contrast to the subjects of the other prophets, who dwelt chiefly on the prospects of deliverance that should come to the people of God; and that, consequently, they hesitated to acknowledge the full canonical value of this book,—in like manner as they questioned the canonical authority of Ecclesiastes during an extended period, through the influence of their optimistic hopes for the future (compare note 1). The book, however, is classed with the other three greater prophets in the Septuagint; but the conclusion that it originally occupied this position in the Hebrew Bible as well (so Herbst, Speil, and others contend) does not necessarily follow. Rather, the framers of the Hebrew canon seem to have attached greater importance to the literary and lingual peculiarities of the book than to anything else, and, for this reason, to have regarded its separation from the prophetical literature in the narrower sense, as necessary, however much they might recognize in it the genuine work of a prophet living under the exile.*

That the book was in fact so recognized appears highly probable, in view of the manifold references to its declarations in the later prophetic writings and in several of the Old-Testament apocrypha. Among the prophets after the captivity, whose reference to Daniel is utterly denied by Bleek, Zechariah at least seems to betray an acquaintance with the prophecies of Daniel, his apocalyptic model and predecessor, particularly in the vision of the four horns (chap. ii. 1), and in that of the four chariots (chap. vi. 1), which are referred by several expositors to the four world-kingdoms of Daniel; further, in chap. xi. 8, where the three shepherds, who should be cut off in one month by the Lord, are possibly a symbolizing of the first three world-kingdoms of Daniel, and of their overthrow in rapid succession (compare

---

on the authenticity of the book of Daniel, Cambridge, 1864. J. Jahn, *Einl. ins A. Test.*, II. 624 et seq.; L. Hug, *Zeitschrift für das Erzbisthum Freiburg*, VI. 150; Herbst. *Einl. mit Zusatz* by Welte, II. 2, p. 80 et seq.; Scholz, *Einl.* III. 482 et seq.; Speil, *De libri Danielis authentia*, Oppolii. 1860, and *Zur Echtheit des B. Daniel*, in the *Tüb. Theol. Quartalschrift*, 1863, p. 191 et seq.; Reusch, *Einl.*, 3d ed., p. 111 et seq.

* [We may remark here, once for all, that a simpler reason for the position of Daniel among the Hagiographa rather than among the Prophets, seems to be the fact that the author was not a prophet in the strictly technical sense of the term; *i.e.*, like John the Baptist (John x. 41), he wrought no *miracles*, and his *predictions* were not directly inspired, but only given mediately through angels or dreams, like those of Joseph (Gen. xli. 15, 16). Keil thus expresses it: "The place occupied by this book in the Hebrew canon perfectly corresponds with the place of Daniel in the theocracy. Daniel did not labor, as the rest of the prophets did whose writings form the class of the *Nebiyîn*, as a prophet among his people in the congregation of Israel, but he was a minister of state under the Chaldæan and Medo-Persian world-rulers. Although, like David and Solomon, he possessed the gift of prophecy, and therefore was called προφήτης (Sept. Josephus, N. T.), yet he was not a נָבִיא, *i.e.*, a prophet in his official position and standing. Therefore his book, in its contents and form, is different from the writings of the *Nebiyîn*. His prophecies are not prophetical discourses addressed to Israel or the nations, but visions, in which the development of the world-kingdoms and their relation to the kingdom of God are unveiled, and the historical part of his book describes events of the time when Israel went into captivity among the heathen. For these reasons his book is not placed in the class of the *Nebiyîn*, which reaches from Joshua to Malachi,—for these, according to the view of him who arranged the canon, are wholly the writings of such as held the prophetic office, *i.e.*, the office requiring them openly, by word of mouth and by writing, to announce the word of God,—but in the class of the *Kethubin*, which comprehends sacred writings of different kinds, whose common character consists in this, that their authors did not fill the prophetic office, as, *e.g.*, Jonah in the theocracy; which is confirmed by the fact that the Lamentations of Jeremiah are comprehended in this class, since Jeremiah uttered these Lamentations over the destruction of Jerusalem and Judah not as a prophet but as a member of that nation which was chastened by the Lord" (*Commentary on Dan.*, Introd., p. 29, 30, Edinb. ed.).]

note 2). Among the Apocrypha—aside from uncertain analogies, such as exist between Wisd. v. 17 and Dan. vii. 18, 27; Wisd. xiv. 16 and Dan. iii.—at least 1 Macc. i. 57 ("Abomination of desolation," cf. Dan. ix. 27) and ii. 59 et seq. (the deliverance of Hananiah, Mishael, and Azariah from the fiery furnace, and of Daniel from the lion's den; cf. Dan. iii. 16 et seq.; vi. 21 et seq.), and still more the book of Baruch, may be regarded as unquestionable witnesses for the canonical dignity of our book in pre-Maccabæan times. The analogies to the prayer of Daniel (Dan. ix.), which the latter book presents in chap. ii. (especially vs. 6, 11, 15, 19), and its references to Nebuchadnezzar and to "Belshazzar his son," in chap. i. 11, 12, are the more important and unquestionable as proof, because the Hebrew original, which we are compelled to receive, indicates with tolerable certainty the origin of this book in pre-Maccabæan times, and probably as early as the fourth century B. C. Under these circumstances, the fact that Ecclesiasticus, whose Hebrew original likewise indicates its composition before the period of the Maccabees, contains no definite allusions to Daniel, and especially that his name is not mentioned in its enumeration (chap. xlix.) of Israel's great religious heroes, which includes Jeremiah, Ezekiel, and the twelve minor prophets, is of no considerable importance. This feature may be regarded as purely accidental, and the rather, as the immediate context (chap. xlix. 13 et seq.) mentions Zerubbabel, Joshua, and Nehemiah among the great men of the time immediately after the exile, but omits the name of Ezra; as many of the prominent champions of Israel are not included in the remarkable list beginning with chap. xlv., *e.g.*, Joseph, Gideon, Samson, Jehoshaphat, etc.; and finally, as the silence of Ecclus. in regard to Daniel "is more than balanced by his mention in Ezek. xiv. and xxviii." (Reusch, p. 112; cf. supra, § 2, note 2). Moreover, the words ἑκάστῳ ἔθνει κατέστησεν ἡγούμενον in Ecclus. xvii. 17 probably contain an allusion to the angelology of Daniel, and are to be explained in accordance with Dan. x. 13, 20; xii. 1 (Hävernick, *Einl.* II. 2, p. 451). Concerning the *Sybilline Oracles* as an especially important source of proofs for the authenticity of Daniel, see note 3.

The passage in the *Jewish Antiquities* of Josephus, Book XI. chap. 8, which relates that, among others, the prophecies of Daniel were shown by the Jewish priests to Alexander the Great, on the occasion of his visit to Jerusalem, and that he was greatly pleased by the oracle respecting the overthrow of the Persian dynasty, which so clearly referred to him, might constitute an important testimony for the genuineness of this book, or for its origin during the exile; but many embellishments and internal improbabilities seem to lower the value of this tradition to a degree that forbids the definite conclusion that the statement concerning the book of Daniel is to be included in the genuine historical kernel of this incident, the essential truth of which, however, is indicated by various considerations (*e.g.* the noteworthy and certainly historical statement that, at the request of the high-priest, Alexander granted immunity from taxation to the Jews during every seventh or fallow year). So much the more decisive is the testimony of the New Testament in support of the inspired character of the book and of the prophetic dignity of its author, which occurs in the familiar reference of Our Lord to Daniel ix. 27, in his great eschatological discourse (Matt. xxiv. 15: ὅταν οὖν ἴδητε τὸ βδέλυγμα τῆς ἐρημώσεως τὸ ῥηθὲν διὰ Δανιὴλ τοῦ προφήτου ἑστὸς ἐν τόπῳ ἁγίῳ—ὁ ἀναγινώσκων νοείτω, etc.), and which is paralleled by other unmistakable allusions to Daniel's expressions in the discourses of Our Lord. Among these we reckon the constantly repeated designation of himself as "the Son of Man," the adoption of which phrase from Dan. vii. 13 is open to no serious objection, while its identity with Daniel's בַּר־אֱנָשׁ is unmistakably revealed, especially in prophetic descriptions, such as Matt. xix. 28; xxiv. 30; xxvi. 64. The prophecy concerning the resurrection of the good and the evil, in John v. 28, 29, likewise, is clearly based on chap. xii. 2, 3, of this book. Among the numerous allusions to our prophet which are found in the writings of the Apostles, we instance merely 2 Thess. ii. 3 et seq.; 1 Pet. i. 10–12 (cf. Dan. iii. and vi.), and the Apocalypse, which latter book is based throughout on the prophecies of Daniel, and therefore vouches, with its entire contents, for the Divinely inspired and canonical character of this book.

NOTE 1.—Kranichfeld, p. 8 et seq., explains in a striking manner to what extent the peculiar theological, or rather eschatological, character of Daniel's prophecies may have been influential in retarding their admission into the canon during the pre-Maccabæan period: "The prophecies of Daniel, in contrast with the oracles of earlier prophets, foretell a period of severe tribulation in the future, which the sufferings of the exile have not warded off; and they predict this far more constantly, positively, and directly than does the book of Zechariah, or any prophecy of the period succeeding the captivity, the aim of the latter being chiefly to comfort and encourage the returned exiles in their discouraging circumstances. There was thus a sufficient reason, in the character of the book itself, to warrant its being received with caution by the age succeeding the exile, and even to justify the temporary ignoring of its claims; for, on the one hand, it contradicted the sentiment of that age, which indulged in exalted hopes of deliverance based on the older prophecies, and, on the other, it had emanated from one who was not even a prophet by a specific call. A similar treatment appears to have been accorded to the book of Ecclesiastes during an extended period, which likewise resulted from its contents, although differing extremely from those of Daniel. In the Asmonæan period, however, the impression produced by the religious and political events which illustrated its prophecies, secured the book a ready reception into the canon, although it was excluded from the second part of the sacred writings, which had probably been closed for centuries, and was limited by traditional usage. This simple explanation, which removes every difficulty in relation to the place of the book in the canon, is not contradicted by the remark of Josephus (*Contra Apion*, I. 8) concerning the closing of the canon in the time of Artaxerxes, which is, in the main, correct. That statement, as Keil correctly observes (*Einl.* § 154), refers to the time of the *composition* of the sacred writings, in harmony with the fact that neither Ecclesiasticus nor 1 Maccabees (which were composed only two centuries before Christ) found a place in the canon; but it does not preclude the subsequent conclusion of the *collecting* and receiving into the third section of the canon of older sacred writings." Similar views are advanced, so far as the last question is concerned, by Hengstenberg, *Beitr.* I. 23 et seq., and Zündel, *Krit. Untersuchungen*, p. 196 et seq., 214 et seq. Also compare below, § 10.

NOTE 2.—Among older expositors, Jerome, Abarbanel, Kimchi, and Drusius, refer Zechariah's visions of the four horns (ii. 1), etc., and of the four chariots (vi. 1 et seq.), to the world-kingdoms of Daniel, as do Baumgarten (*Nachtgesichte des Sacharja*), Zündel (*Kritische Untersuchungen*, 249), Pusey (*Daniel*, p. 357), Füller, Kliefoth, and W. Volck (*Vindiciæ Danielicæ*, p. 3 et seq.), among moderns; while Köhler (*Nachexilische Propheten*, ii. 1) and a majority of later expositors deny the fact of such a relation. Köhler, however, (*ibid.*, II. p. 138) agrees with Von Hofmann, Ebrard, Kliefoth, Zündel, and Volck (*l. c.*, p. 26) in referring the "three shepherds," Zech. xi. 8, to the first three world-kingdoms, and assumes, in addition, a relation of the prophecy against Javan, Zech. ix. 13, to Dan. viii. 8 et seq. But the correspondence of these latter passages, if it is to be accepted at all, is of minor importance, because the chapters Zech. ix.–xi. possibly originated with a prophet Zechariah, who flourished before the exile, and therefore may be older than the Daniel of the captivity. Compare, however, the arguments adduced to the contrary by Hengstenberg, *Beitr.* I. 366 et seq.; also by the editor of this Bible-work, in vol. I. of the Old Test., p. 44 [Am. ed.].

NOTE 3.—In relation to the references in Ecclesiasticus to Daniel, see Zündel, p. 188; and the same, p. 191 et seq., concerning the much clearer and more important references in the book of Baruch, where the opinion of Dillmann, as stated in his essay on the formation of the Old-Test. canon (*Jahrbb. f. deutsche Theol.*, 1858, p. 480), is quoted: "The book of Baruch, by no means a contemptible after-piece of prophetical literature, may have been in circulation in its Hebrew form as early as the fourth century B. C.;" and where, at the same time, it is shown most clearly that the pseudo-Baruch was undeniably acquainted with the book of Daniel, and imitated many of its features, particularly the prophet's prayer, Dan. ix. Hengstenberg, p. 288 et seq., Hävernick, *Einl.* II. 2, 459 et seq., and Pusey, in his Commentary, p. 370, show that the echoes of this book found in 1 Maccabees (which are so clear and unmistakable, that scholars like Bleek, De Wette, and Grimm [on 1 Macc. i. 57] have acknowledged this occurrence) are entitled, despite the composition of the book toward the close of the second century B. C., to rank as indirect testimonies for the origin of Daniel prior to the Asmonæan period. Concerning Ecclus. and its omission of Daniel from the ὑμνὸς πατέρων, chapters xliv.–l., see Hävernick, p. 451 et seq.; Herbst, *Einl.* II. 2, 88; Keil, *Einl.*, p. 452; Hengstenberg, p. 21 sq.; Kranichfeld, p. 10, etc. Some of these writers, however (*e.g.*, Hävernick, Keil, Hengstenberg, together with Bretschneider and others), go too far when they reject the passage, chap. xlix. 12, as not genuine, and thus exclude all mention of the twelve minor prophets as well; for there is no sufficient reason to suspect that verse on critical grounds (cf. Bleek, *Einl.*, p. 589). It has been pointed out, especially by Hävernick (*Einl.* l. c., p. 457 et seq.) and Zündel (p. 173 et seq.; cf. p. 140 et seq.), that the Alexandrian version of the Old Testament in general, and of Daniel in particular (cf. infra, § 11), which probably originated in the second century B. C., reveals many traces of the existence of our prophetical book prior to the Maccabæan age; that, for instance, its rendering of Deut. xxxii. 8, ὅτε διεμέριζεν ὁ ὕψιστος ἔθνη, ἔστησεν ὅρια ἐθνῶν κατὰ ἀριθμὸν ἀγγέλων θεοῦ, seems to rest on Dan. x. 13, 20, like the passage, Ecclus. xvii. 17, which is cited above; and that citations from its version of Daniel occur in the first book of Maccabees (i. 57), as well as in the Sibylline oracles (iii. 396, 613, etc.); facts that argue with great force the origin of this Greek version in the Asmonæan period, and therefore, at the very time to which the negative criticism assigns the original Daniel itself. The testimonies drawn from the Apocrypha are, with rare exceptions, surpassed in importance and evidential force by the agreement of the Sibyllines with Daniel, since the unanimous consent of competent scholars, such as Bleek, Lücke, Friedlieb, and others, ascribes the composition of the portion of the *Oracula Sibyllina* in question (lib. III., v. 35–746) to an Alexandrian Jew, and dates it in the first half of the second century, or, more probably, about 160 B. C. The correspondence of many of these verses to passages in our prophetical book, or rather in its Alexandrian version, cannot be questioned; and the supposition ventured by Bleek, that both (pseudo-Daniel and the pseudo-Sibyllines) sprang from a common source of a more ancient time, is merely an arbitrary evasion to hide his embarrassment. Compare *Sibyll.*, lib. III., v. 396 ss.: Ῥίζαν ἰαν γε διδούς, ἣν καὶ κόψει βροτολοίγος. Ἐκ δέκα δὴ κεράτων· παρὰ δὴ φυτὸν ἄλλο φυτεύσει . . . . καὶ τότε δὴ παραφυόμενον κέρας ἄρξει, with the Sept. at Dan. vii. 7, 8, 11, 20;—also *Sibyll.*, III. 613: πάντα δὲ συγκόψει καὶ πάντα κακῶν ἀναπλήσει, with Sept., Dan. vii. 23, 24.

NOTE 4.—Hengstenberg (p. 258 et seq., 277 et seq.) is especially thorough and profound in his examination of the testimony of Christ and the apostles, and of Josephus in *Ant.*, XI. 8, 5. He may attempt too much in seeking to establish the historical character of all the details connected with the perhaps somewhat legendary narrative respecting the incident by which Alexander became acquainted with Daniel's prophecies; but his statements convey the decided impression that the narrative in question is not a pure invention without any foundation in fact. He quotes, on page 288, the significant judgment of H. Leo respecting the credibility of this account (as expressed in his *Vorlesungen über die Geschichte des jüdischen Volks*, p. 200, which, as is well known, breathe anything rather than a believing spirit): "The entire narrative contains nothing that is really improbable. An armed resistance on the part of the high-priest would have been madness; he may therefore have gone out to meet Alexander in peace. It is also well known that Alexander sought to impress the Asiatic world with the belief that he was in league with the gods of the nations whom he had conquered. It has been considered improbable that Alexander should not have hastened from Gaza directly to Egypt; but to go from Gaza to Egypt by way of Jerusalem involved at most an additional journey of a few days, and Judæa was not a point to be disregarded in an expedition to Egypt. It would be unwise to leave this mountain region in the rear, in the possession of an enemy." See also Zündel, p. 238 et seq., where the hypercritical objection of Hitzig, "The book was not produced, and if it had existed at the time, it would certainly have been shown" (*Heidelberger Jahrb.*, 1832, II., p. 235), is justly regarded as an indirect testimony for the trustworthiness of the account by Josephus.

§ 7. AUTHENTICITY OF THE BOOK (Continued).

c. *Examination of the* INTERNAL *reasons against its genuineness, and more particularly of those derived from peculiarities of language and style.*

It has already been repeatedly shown that the lingual structure of this book—the transition into Chaldee, chap. ii. 4, the essential identity of this idiom with the Chaldee of Ezra, the Hebraisms and Parseeisms contained in it, and finally, the marked Chaldaizing tendency of the Hebrew portions, similar to the style of Ezekiel—that all this corresponds fully with the assumption of an author who flourished at the Chaldæan court of Babylon, and who was of Jewish birth, but educated in the customs and wisdom of the Chaldæans (see § 1, note 3, and § 4, note 2). It is only necessary, in this connection, to refer to the Greek expressions, which have been regarded as proving the later origin of the work in an especially decisive way. Bertholdt was still able to enumerate ten such expressions, but the more recent opponents of the genuineness of the book find the number reduced to three or four, as the result of a careful word-criticism. All of these are names of musical instruments, such as might easily have been introduced at Babylon by commercial intercourse, even prior to the exile. They comprise the terms פְּסַנְתֵּרִין=ψαλτήριον, סוּמְפֹּנְיָה=συμφωνία, קִיתְרוֹס=κίθαρις, and סַבְּכָא=σαμβύκη, all of which occur in the history of Daniel's friends and the fiery furnace (chap. iii. 5, 7, 10, 15). But even among these the third is possibly of Oriental origin, and the last almost certainly so. The σαμβύκη or ζαμβύκη (also ἰαμβύκη) of the Greek was, according to Athenæus (*Deipnosoph.* iv. 182; xiv. 634), a Syrian invention, and the Shemitic סַבְּכָא (related to סבך, "to interweave") seems therefore to be the primitive form, from which the Græcized σαμβύκη is derived. קִיתְרוֹס may possibly be the Persian *Si-tareh*, "six-stringed," and may stand related to *κίθαρις*, which is to be derived from the same source, as a sister rather than as a mother. Pareau, Hengstenberg, Hävernick, Haneberg, and others, have even attempted to trace the two remaining terms to a Shemitic source, and have accordingly derived סומפניה from סוּף, "a reed, and פסנתרין from פַּס, "a hand," and נָתַר, "to leap" (therefore, "strings that are played by hand"). But excessive difficulties stand in the way of such an etymology, particularly the Greek sound in the endings of the two words (פסנתרין seems to be singular rather than plural), and the circumstance that *συμφωνία*, if not *ψαλτήριον*, occurs in the classics as the name of an instrument, as may be seen in the passage Polyb. *Fragm.*, 31, t. 4, and as may be concluded from the Italian designation of the bagpipe, *zambogna* or *sampogna*, which is probably derived from that source. On the other hand, the assumption that the instruments of the Greeks were in use among the Chaldæans early in the sixth century B. C., or even in the seventh and eighth, involves no difficulty whatever. It would seem strange, rather, if no traces of commercial intercourse with the Greeks at about the middle of the sixth century B. C. were found in Babylon, the primitive "city of merchants" (Ezek. xvii. 4, 12; cf. Josh. vii. 21), since the Assyrian kings Esar-haddon, Sargon, and Sennacherib were involved in either friendly or hostile relations with the Greeks of Asia Minor, as early as the eighth century B. C. Further, "Javan" is mentioned in the cuneiform inscriptions of Sargon among the nations who were tributary to Assyria; according to Strabo, xiii. 3, 2, a Greek, the brother of the poet Alcæus, served in the armies of Nebuchadnezzar as a mercenary, or, more probably, as the leader of a band of Greek mercenaries; the Ionian philosopher, Anaximander, displays considerable knowledge of the Orient in his map of the world, which was prepared in the same period; and finally, commercial relations of considerable importance were maintained between the lands of the Euphrates and the Greek colonies of Asia Minor, certainly in the eighth century B. C., and possibly, through Phœnician channels, as early as the days of Homer (see notes 1 and 2).

It appears, therefore, that no unanswerable objection against the origin of this book during the period of the captivity can be established on the ground of its peculiarities of language; nor do the *remaining literary peculiarities*, such as the method in which the prophet refers to himself and his personal relations, afford the slightest reason to doubt its composition by Daniel. "The honorable references to Daniel (chap. i. 17, 19; v. 11 et seq.; vi. 4; ix. 23; x. 11) are analogous to many expressions employed by the Apostle Paul concerning himself, *e.g.*, 1 Cor. xv. 10; 2 Cor. xi. 5 et seq.; xii. 2 et seq.; and they are necessary, either to complete the historical representation, as in the case of the predicate 'greatly beloved,' applied to him by the angel in chap. ix. 23; x. 11, or in the honorable mention of his name to Belshazzar by the queen, chap. v. 11, 12; or they belong to passages which aim to honor God, who had endowed his servant with miraculous wisdom (i. 17 et seq.; vi. 4). Consequently, they contain no trace of Pelagian self-laudation which could militate against the opinion that the book which bears his name was composed by himself" (Keil, *Einl.*, p. 452 sq.).—Nor does the religiously moral deportment of the prophet, as it is described by himself in this book, afford a proof in any other direction against its composition in the period of the exile. His custom of observing three seasons of daily prayer, as mentioned in chap. vi. 11, his frequent fasts (chap. ix. 3; x. 3, 12), and the strict abstinence from profane food of himself and his youthful friends (chap. i. 8 et seq.), do not necessarily indicate a period subsequent to the exile, and even as late as that of the Asmonæans, as is abundantly shown by passages like Psa. lv. 18; Ezra viii. 21 et seq.; ix. 3 et seq.; Neh. i. 4; ix. 1; Zech. vii. 3; viii. 19; Hos. ix. 3, 4; Ezek. xxii. 26; xliv. 23; xxxiii. 25, etc. His *dogmatic position* no more requires an explanation based on the condition or experiences of God's people after the exile, than such ascetic habits, or the exalted value, which, according to chap. ii. 18; ix. 3; x. 2 et seq., he attaches to prayer and intercession, oblige us to regard him as involved in the narrow-minded legal and work-righteous conceptions of the later Judaism. His description of the Messiah and his kingdom—in contrast with the apocryphal literature of the period after the captivity, from which Messianic ideas and hopes are almost entirely wanting—is intimately related to the predictions of the older prophets, and especially of Isaiah (cf. Isa. ix. 4 et seq. with Dan. vii. 13 sq.). The relation between the expected founding of Messiah's kingdom and the general resurrection of the dead, which he indicates in chap. xii. 2 et seq., corresponds to the older prophetic descriptions in Isa. xxiv.; lxvi. 22–24; Ezek. xxxvii., but finds no analogy in the later apocryphal literature, unless we except 2 Macc. vii. 9 et seq., which passage, however, is probably based on Dan. xii. as its model. Nor does the angelology of the book present any specific feature which points to a period later than the exile; much less does it indicate that its teachings result from the influence of the religious thought of Persia on Judaism. Rather, they are closely related, on the one hand, to the angelology of Ezekiel and Zechariah (cf., *e.g.*, Ezek. ix. 10; also i. 26, and Zech. i.–vi.), and, on the other, they are rooted in the much older views and experiences of the time before the exile; *e.g.*, the idea of protecting spirits of single states is founded in Isa. xxiv. 21; that concerning princes of the angels (chap. x. 13, 20; xii. 1), doubtless in the familiar account in the book of Joshua respecting the "captain of the Lord's host" (Josh. 14). Therefore, in this direction also, the literary character of the book reveals nothing that indicates an anti-Daniel or a pseudo-Daniel (cf. note 3).

NOTE 1.—Delitzsch observes, p. 274, on the relationship of the Hebrew of Daniel to that of Ezekiel, that "the Hebrew of this book is closely related especially to that of Ezekiel, whose book may be, and doubtless is, included among the ספרים in chap. ix. 2; and it is a surprising accident that it conforms somewhat to Habakkuk also, whom tradition associates with Daniel." The following expressions are adduced in support of the former correspondence, by Hävernick (*N. krit. Unterss.*, p. 97 et seq.) and Keil (*Einl.*, p. 446): the vocative בֶּן אָדָם, chap. viii. 17; זֹהַר, brightness, xii. 3, cf. Ezek. viii. 2; חַיֵּב, to render liable to penalty, i. 10, and חוֹב, debt, Ezek. xviii. 7; כְּתָב for סֵפֶר, x. 21, cf. Ezek. xiii. 9; לָבוּשׁ בַּדִּים, x. 5, cf. Ezek. ix. 2, 3; פַּתְבַּג, royal food, i. 5, and בַּג, food, Ezek. xxv. 27; קָלָל, polished, x. 6, cf. Ezek. i. 7, etc. With reference to the relation of the Aramaic of Daniel to that of Ezra, and to the Chaldee of the Targums of a later age, consult Hävernick and Keil, as above, and cf. supra, § 1, note 3. It is the peculiar merit of Pusey to have established, in his profoundly learned commentary, the high antiquity of the Chaldaism of Daniel, in comparison with that of the Targums and the rabbins, by his examination of numerous individual forms, and especially of the many asserted Hebraisms of this book.

NOTE 2.—On the question whether the musical instruments of the Greeks may have been known to the Babylonians, and even to the Assyrians, consult Delitzsch, p. 274; Auberlen, p. 12 et seq.; Kranichfeld, p. 48 et seq., and the passage cited by the two former from Joh. Brandis, *Ueber den histor. Gewinn aus der Entzifferung der assyrischen Inschriften*, 1856, p. 1 et seq., where the observation is made, in relation to the commercial intercourse of the ancient Greeks, that "the extended commerce of the Greek colonies would frequently lead their merchants to Assyrian countries, since they penetrated even to the inhospitable steppes on the Dnieper and the Don. Their most important enterprises were probably connected with the Assyrian provinces of Asia Minor, and above all with the countries on the coasts of Pontus and along the Mediterranean Sea, doubtless including Lydia also, where the Assyrian supremacy seems to have been maintained during more than five hundred years, and almost to the close of the eighth century B. C. These nations must also have met in Cyprus, where the Greeks traded at an early period, and where the Assyrians had firmly established themselves. We are obliged to be content with a supposition that Greeks came as far as Assyria proper, in the capacity of merchants; but Greek soldiers certainly accompanied Esar-haddon, the first among the Assyrian rulers to form a corps of mercenaries (Abydenus in Euseb., *Chron. Armen.*, ed. Aucher I., p. 53), on his marches through Asia," etc. Compare also the interesting work by Brandis, *Das Münz-, Mass- und Gewichtswesen in Vorderasien bis auf Alexander d. Gr.*, 1867. Respecting the Greeks as the musicians κατ' ἐξοχήν in the world, see Auberlen, as above: "Attention may also be directed to the fact that the Greeks, as the patrons of art, occupied a position in the ancient world similar to that conceded to the Italians in the modern; and how many are the musical terms which we Germans have adopted from the Italians! Poetry and music flourished at first precisely among the Greeks of Asia Minor, and prior to the ninth century B. C., about the middle of which Homer lived there, according to the not improbable statement of Herodotus (II. 53). Greek artists were employed by the Lydians, among whom music was likewise cultivated, so that the Greeks adopted the Lydian key from them. But Lydia was not merely dependent on Assyria to a greater or less extent, down to the close of the eighth century, but afterward maintained intimate relations with Babylon," etc. Concerning the ψαλτήριον or *Pesanterin*, compare, in addition, the remark of Kranichfeld: "It may be observed, in relation to the objection that the ψαλτήριον is mentioned only by later writers among the Greeks, that the *argumentum ex silentio* raised, on that ground, against the earlier existence of that instrument, is sufficiently met by the probable representation of a ψαλτήριον on the monuments of Sennacherib, cf. Layard, *Nineveh and Babylon*, c. 20, p. 454. The persons who there welcome the Assyrian leaders with dances, songs, and plays, are preceded by five musicians, three of whom carry harps with many strings, a fourth has a double flute, and the fifth is furnished with an instrument which Layard compares to the *Santer* of Egypt = פסנתרין (Gesenius, *Thes.*, p. 1116). It consists of a number of strings which are stretched on a resonant frame, and corresponds to the description of the psalterium furnished by Augustine (on Psa. xxxii.)."

NOTE 3.—With reference to the feasibility of reconciling the religious-ethical representations of this book with the hypothesis of its origin during the captivity, see Hengstenberg, p. 137 et seq.; Hävernick, *Neue krit. Unterss.*, p. 32 et seq.; and Oehler in Tholuck's *Literarischer Anzeiger*, 1843, Nos. 49 and 50, and particularly p. 388 et seq. The dependence of Daniel's angelology on that of Zoroaster has been frequently asserted, since it was first stated by Gesenius, Bertholdt, Winer, and others; but Martin Haug, of Bombay, decidedly advocates the opinion, in his *Essays on the Sacred Languagė, Writings, and Religion of the Parsees* (Bombay, 1862), that the religious development of Judaism was independent of that of Parseeism, without, on that account, attempting to deny to them a common source, as an explanation of their manifold analogies (compare *Ausland*, 1862, p. 937; 1865, p. 1079 et seq.). The simple circumstance that a scholar so thoroughly acquainted with the Zend religion and literature, should hold to this opinion, may serve as a warning to receive with caution such views of their relations as are above referred to. The opinion of Max Müller, as expressed in his philosophical meditations on religion (*Chips from a German Workshop*, London, 1867), agrees fully with that of Haug; while E. Rénan (*De l'Origine du Language*, p. 230; *Vie de Jésus*, p. 15 s.) and Fr. Spiegel (*Genesis und Avesta*, in *Ausland*, 1868, No. 12 et seq.) assert a direct adoption from the religious writings of the ancient Persians of many theological and angelological conceptions by the later Judaism after the time of the Achæmenidæ. Hilgenfeld also (*Das Judenthum im persischen Zeitalter* in the *Zeitschrift für wissenschaftl. Theologie*, 1866, No. 4, p. 398 et seq.) and Alex. Kohut, *Ueber die jüdische Angelologie und Dämonologie in ihrer Abhängigkeit vom Parsismus* (taken from the *Zeitschrift der deutsch-morgenl. Gesellsch.*, Vol. IV., No. 3) Leipsic, 1866, advocate the same view. But the sober investigations of men of the most diverse tendencies agree in reaching substantially the same result, namely, proving that at most a few names of angels remain to a profounder and more unprejudiced criticism, as elements of the Jewish angelology which are really derived from Parseeism, and that even these names are not chiefly of Aryan, but of Shemitic and even genuinely Hebrew origin—as is especially true of those found in Daniel (Michael and Gabriel). Compare Reuss (*Histoire de la théologie Chrétienne au Siècle apostolique*, I., 92 et seq.), Dillmann (*Jahrbb. für deutsche Theologie*, 1858, p. 419 et seq.), Hävernick (*Vorll. über die Theologie des A. Ts.*, 2d ed., published by H. Schultz, p. 92 et seq.; 118 et seq.); Hofmann (*Schriftbeweis*, I. 281, 291 et seq.); A. Köhler (*Nachexilische Propheten*, II. 23 et seq.); Haneberg (in Reusch, *Theol. Literaturbl.*, 1867, No. 3, p. 72). See the exegetical notes on chap. viii. 10, 15, and compare the instructive treatise of Erich Haupt, *Ueber die Berührungen des A. Ts. mit der Religion Zarathustra's* (Treptow on the Rhine, 1867), which argues positively against the adoption from Parseeism of any religious conceptions whatever in the canonical portions of the O. T.

§ 8. AUTHENTICITY OF THE BOOK (Continued).

d. *Examination of the internal evidences against its genuineness, based on* HISTORICAL DIFFICULTIES.

The charges raised against the book of Daniel, on the ground of asserted contradictions of the accounts of extra-biblical history respecting the Babylonian and Medo-Persian kingdoms, are either historico-social in their nature, or politico-historical. They relate either to the antiquities of those kingdoms, or to their chronological relations and changes of dynasties.

1. The former class of difficulties, namely those affecting the social progress and customs of the times, lie within the domain of the *history of civilization and morals.* They arise from the deportment of Nebuchadnezzar and Belshazzar toward the oneirocritical magicians on the one hand, and toward Daniel on the other (chaps. ii. and v.); further, from the colossal size and ugliness of the image which was to be worshipped, and from the cruelty of the punishment imposed on the friends of Daniel, because of their refusal to obey the decree which required such worship (chap. iii.); from the lycanthropy of Nebuchadnezzar, as not substantiated by extra-biblical historians (chap. iv.); from the alleged incredibility of the statement that king Darius issued a decree ordaining that divine honors should be paid exclusively to him; and from the assumed funnel-like shape of the lion's den into which Daniel was thrown (chap. vi.). All of these difficulties are merely such in appearance. An observer who understands the

spirit of the ancient as well as the modern Oriental despotism (of which the case of Theodore of Abyssinia, with his whims and fluctuating views, may serve as a late example), and especially who at the same time remembers the tendency of the Babylonian and Medo-Persian rulers to syncretistic arbitrariness and mingling of religions, will not deem it strange that Nebuchadnezzar should address to his magicians the unreasonable demand, not merely to interpret his dream, but even to recall its contents, which were forgotten by him, and that he should condemn them to death when they failed to satisfy his demands, while he rewarded Daniel, who accomplished the task, with the highest honors and emoluments. Such an observer will not be surprised to find the king, in chap. iii., directing a monstrous idolatrous demonstration against the God of Daniel and his friends, and consigning the latter to so glorious a martyrdom; nor to behold, in chap. v., the striking contrast between the blasphemous insults and excesses of Belshazzar at the first, and the favor afterward bestowed by him on Daniel; nor yet, in chap. vi., the similar change in the disposition of Darius as revealed in his conduct. That, by Divine retribution, the arbitrary and passionate temper of Nebuchadnezzar should develop into madness, and result in the infliction, during several years, of a mental disorder of the most terrible nature, is no more surprising than are any of the various cases of lycanthropy recorded in the annals of psychiatry, among which that of the Armenian king, Tiridates III., is the most familiar and historically important. Traces of this awful episode in the reign of Nebuchadnezzar, although not found in other historians of ancient times, may yet be shown with sufficient clearness in the Babylonian Berosus and in Abydenus (see note 1). With regard to the less important details which have excited criticism, as being legendary or at least suspicious, it may be observed that the description of the idol in the plain of Dura (chap. iii. 1 et seq.), which reached a height of sixty cubits, corresponds substantially with the descriptions transmitted through other channels of uncouth colossal images, such as the coarse and excessively fanciful art of ancient Oriental heathendom was accustomed to erect to the honor of its gods. The non-appearance of Daniel and the other magians before Belshazzar (chap. v. 7) is sufficiently explained by the Oriental custom of removing the priests from office with every change of rulers. The decree of Darius, limiting the ascription of divine honors during an entire month to himself (chap. vi. 8 et seq.) agrees fully with the statements of Herodotus, Xenophon, and Plutarch, respecting the deifying of kings among the ancient Medes and Persians. And finally, the designation of the lion's den by גּוֹב or גֻּבָּא (chap. vi. 8, 18) does not necessitate the view that it was "a funnel-shaped cavern or cistern," since the term in question is applied in the Syriac, not merely to dungeons, but also especially to the dens or cages of wild beasts (cf. the exegetical remarks on the several passages cited in this connection).

2. The following difficulties and alleged contradictions or anachronisms belong to the domain of *political history and chronology :*

(1.) According to the statement in chap. i. 1, that "In the third year of Jehoiakim came (בָּא) Nebuchadnezzar, king of Babylon, unto Jerusalem and besieged it," our book seems to place the first siege and capture of Jerusalem by Nebuchadnezzar *as early as the third year of Jehoiakim.* This contradicts Jer. xxv. 1, 9 (cf. xlvi. 2; xxxvi. 9), where the arrival of Nebuchadnezzar before Jerusalem appears to be placed in the fourth or even the fifth year of Jehoiakim's reign; and it also conflicts with Dan. ii. 1, where the *second* year of Nebuchadnezzar is given as the time in which Daniel interpreted the monarch's dream, and thus attained to great distinction, whereas the conquest of Judæa and the transportation of Daniel and his friends, together with other prisoners, to Babylon, and the instruction of the Hebrew youth (according to chap. i. 5, 18) during three years in the wisdom of the Chaldæans, all transpired several years before. The only adequate solution of this two-fold difficulty is found in the hypothesis, that Dan. i. 1 does not relate the *arrival* of Nebuchadnezzar before Jerusalem, but merely his *departure* for that place, or the beginning of his march (בּוֹא as in Jon. i. 3; cf. Gen. xiv. 5; xlv. 7; Dan. xi. 13, 17, 28); and also that the designation of Nebuchadnezzar as king, in chap. i. 1, 3, 5, is to be regarded as proleptical, his position at that time being that of a military leader and representative of his father Nabopolassar, while his accession to the throne was delayed about two years later. From this hypothesis results an interval of more than three years between the removal of Daniel to Babylon, and his elevation to the headship of the magian caste (see note 2).

(2.) According to chap. v., Belshazzar seems to be the successor, or, at least, one of the successors, of his father Nebuchadnezzar on the throne of Babylon, while ver. 30 represents him as the last ruler before the introduction of the Medo-Persian dynasty. The extra-biblical authorities, however, mention four kings of his family who succeeded Nebuchadnezzar (Evil-merodach, Neriglissar, Laborasoarchad, and Nabonidus), none of whom bears the name of Belshazzar. Of the two methods possible for the solution of this difficulty, the one identifies Belshazzar with Evil-merodach, and the other with Nabonidus. The former is the more probable one, because the relation of chap. vi. 1, to v. 30 by no means requires that the subjection of Babylon to the Medo-Persians should have *immediately* followed on the death of Belshazzar; and further, because Nebuchadnezzar is mentioned as the father of Belshazzar in chap. vii., while the profane sources call Evil-merodach a son of Nebuchadnezzar, but not Nabonidus, the last Chaldæan king (see note 3). Moreover, the two years of the reign of Evil-merodach, mentioned in Jer. lii. 31, may be easily reconciled with the statement in Dan. viii. 1, that a vision was seen by Daniel "in the third year of Belshazzar;" for it might be said that Belshazzar-Evil-merodach reigned two years even if he lived until about the middle of his "third year." *

(3.) It is said that chap. vi. 1 implies that the monarch who overthrew the Chaldæan dynasty, and established the Medo-Persian rule in Babylon, was not *Cyrus*, but "Darius the Mede." But since, according to chap. vi. 29 (cf. i. 21), the author had knowledge of Cyrus as the successor of this Darius, there can be no doubt that by the latter name he designates the Cyaxeres II. of Xenophon, who was the son of Astyages and uncle of Cyrus, and consequently the sovereign whose reign, according to Æschylus, Xenophon, Abydenus, and Josephus, intervened between the last Median king Astyages and the founding of the Persian Achæmenidean dynasty by Cyrus. It follows, that the narrative of Herodotus, which relates that Cyrus defeated his Median grandfather Astyages near Pasargardæ, and became his immediate successor, has its source in an inexact or incomplete tradition, from whence the father of history derived his facts in relation to the Persian as well as the Babylonian kingdom (see note 4).

NOTE 1.—With reference to the mention of diseases and the actual occurrence of lycanthropy, compare generally Bartholinus, *De morbis biblicis*, c. 13; Rich. Mead, *Medica sacra*, c. 7; J. D. Müller, *Diss. de Nebuchadnezaris* μεταμορφώσει ad Dan., c. iv., Lips., 1747; Freind, *Historia medic.*, p. 380 (where the important testimony of Oribasius, physician to the emperor Julian, is given, showing the occurrence of this disease in his time); Forestus, *Observationes*

* [A better solution of the difficulty is proposed by Rawlinson (*Herodotus*, i. 424, Am. ed.), as being suggested by the recently discovered inscriptions on the Babylonian monuments. "According to Berosus, Nabonadius was not in Babylon, but at Borsippa, at the time when Babylon was taken, having fled to that comparatively unimportant city when his army was defeated in the field (apud Joseph., *Contra Apion*, i. 21). He seems, however, to have left in Babylon a representative in the person of his son, whom a few years previously he had associated with him in the government. This prince, whose name is read as *Bil-shar-uzur*, and who may be identified as the Belshazzar of Daniel, appears to have taken the command in the city when Nabonadius threw himself for some unexplained reason into Borsippa, which was undoubtedly a strong fortress, and was also one of the chief seats of Chaldæan learning, but which assuredly could not compare, either for magnificence or for strength, with Babylon, and Belshazzar, who was probably a mere youth, left to enjoy the supreme power without check or control, neglected the duty of watching the enemy, and gave himself up to enjoyment." "Two difficulties stand in the way of this identification, which (if accepted) solve one of the most intricate problems of ancient history. The first is the relationship in which the Belshazzar of Scripture stands to Nebuchadnezzar, which is throughout represented as that of son (verses 2, 11, 13, 18, etc.); the second is the accession immediately of 'Darius the Mede.' With respect to the first of these, it may be remarked that although Nabonadius was not a descendant, or indeed any relative of Nebuchadnezzar, Belshazzar may have been, and very probably was. Nabu-nahit, on seizing the supreme power, would naturally seek to strengthen his position by marriage with a daughter of the great king, whose son, son-in-law, and grandson had successively held the throne. He may have taken to wife Neriglissar's widow, or he may have married some other daughter of Nebuchadnezzar. Belshazzar may thus have been grandson of Nebuchadnezzar *on the mother's side*. It is some confirmation of these probabilities or possibilities to find that the name of Nebuchadnezzar was used as a family name by Nabu-nahit. He must certainly have had a son to whom he gave that appellation, or it would not have been assumed by two pretenders in succession, who sought to personate the legitimate heir to the Babylonian throne." The second objection, respecting the immediate succession of "Darius the Mede," is elsewhere considered, and applies not particularly to this identification.]

medic., X. 15; Welcker, *Allgem. Zeitschrift für Psychiatrie*, vol. IX., No. 1; Trusen, *Sitten, Gebräuche, und Krankheiten der alten Hebräer*, 1853; Reil, *Rhapsodien über die Anwendung der psychischen Kurmethode auf Geisteszerrüttungen*, pp. 296, 336 et seq. The last work contains many interesting examples of insanity, in which the patients believed themselves transformed into dogs, wolves, bears, cats, etc., and were able to imitate the calls of those animals with surprising exactness. Important historical examples of this character are: Lycaon (Pausan., VIII. 2; Ovid, *Metam.*, I. 216); king Tiridates III. of Armenia, the persecutor of Gregory the illuminator about A. D. 300 (Moses of Chorene, *Hist. Armeniaca*, l. III., ed. Whiston, p. 256 et seq.; M. Samueljan, *Bekehrung Armeniens durch Gregor. Illuminator, nach national-historischen Quellen bearb.*, Vienna, 1844; S. C. Malan, *The Life and Times of S. Gregory the Illuminator, the Founder and Patron Saint of the Armenian Church, Translated from the Armenian*, London, 1868;—cf. the Basle *Missions-Magazin*, 1832, p. 530); Latronianus, a persecutor of Christians in the time of Diocletian, who was temporarily bestialized because of his cruelty (see the acts of the martyrs, s. vv., Epictetus and Astion, in the *Acta Sanct.*, Jul., T. II. p. 538); Simon of Tournay, an Aristotelian philosopher in Paris about A. D. 1200 (who is said to have received a roaring voice like a beast, in punishment of a blasphemy publicly uttered against Christ, Moses, and Mohammed; see Schröckh, *Kirchengesch.*, vol. XXVI., p. 380); Simon Brown, an English dissenting minister, 1733 (who, while in a melancholy state of mind, believed himself, during a considerable period, to be changed into a beast, although in other respects he was rational and in the possession of his faculties; see Stäudlin and Tzschirner, *Archiv*, etc., vol. III., p. 562 et seq.); a prince of Condé, who at times believed himself transformed into a dog (Schubert, *Symbolik des Traums*, 3d ed., p. 166); an English boy at Norwich, about A. D. 1603, whose disease assumed the form of lycanthropy (Reitz, *Historie der Wiedergeborenen*, II. 56 et seq.). Compare also the fabulous accounts of werewolves, *i.e.*, persons who rage with wolfish cruelty and rapacity against their fellow men, in Görres, *Die Christl. Mystik*, vol. IV. 2, p. 472 et seq.; also Waitz, *Anthropologie der Naturvölker*, vol. II., p. 180, concerning the belief of the African nations in the disease *marafilnas*, *i.e.*, lycanthropy. Among the profane testimonies to the lycanthropy of Nebuchadnezzar, that of the inscriptions on the Babylonian monuments (which, so far as they date back to that king, indicate the interruption of his great building enterprises during a considerable period; see Rawlinson, *Bampton Lectures*, V., p. 166 and p. 440, n. 29), is not sufficiently positive and clear. The statement of Berosus (in Josephus, *Contra Apion.* I. 20): Ναβουχοδονόσορος μὲν οὖν μετὰ τὸ ἄρξασθαι τοῦ προειρημένου τείχους, ἐμπεσὼν εἰς ἀῤῥωστίαν, μετηλλάξατο τὸν βίον, βεβασιλευκὼς ἔτη τεσσεράκοντα τρία, is likewise very indefinite, and leaves room for the opinion that it refers to a disease not at all unusual in its character, which immediately preceded the death of Nebuchadnezzar (although the mention of the ἀῤῥωστία which preceded his death can hardly be accidental and without significance with Berosus, whose narrative in other cases is always as concise as possible. Cf. Kranichfeld on the passage, p. 204 et seq.). The Chaldæan tradition concerning the wonderful close of Nebuchadnezzar's life, as reported by Abydenus (in Euseb., *Præpar. Evang.*, IX. 41; cf. *Chron. Armen.*, I., p. 59), contains, on the other hand, a positive although frequently clouded and distorted testimony to that fact. It states that Nebuchadnezzar, after concluding his wars of conquest, "ascended to the summit of his royal palace, where he was seized by one of the gods" (ὡς, ἀναβὰς ἐπὶ τὰ βασιλήϊα, κατασχηθείη θεῷ ὅτεῳ δή). "With a loud voice he said, 'I, Nebuchadnezzar, foretell your misfortune, which neither Bel, my ancestor, nor the queen Beltis, can prevail on the fates to avert! The *Persian mule* shall come, being in league with your own gods, and shall bring you into bondage; the Mede, the pride of the Assyrians, shall be his helper! Would that a whirlpool or a flood (χάρυβδίν τινα ἢ θάλασσαν) might sweep him previously away and utterly destroy him! Or that, at any rate, he might be driven by other ways through the desert, where there are neither cities nor human paths, but where only wild beasts and birds roam about—that he might wander in solitude among rocks and precipices! And would that I had met a better end before this knowledge was imparted to me!'. After this prophecy he immediately became invisible" (Ὁ μὲν θεσπίσας παραχρῆμα ἠφάνιστο). We have here, clearly, a specifically Chaldæan version of the same tradition, whose original form appears in Dan. iv. The prophecy respecting the impending overthrow of the Chaldæan kingdom appears to have been taken from the mouth of the Hebrew prophet, and ascribed to the great king himself, as being suddenly overwhelmed by the gods (as a מְשֻׁגָּע, cf. Jer. xxix. 26; 2 Kings ix. 11). The banishment of the king while controlled by a bestializing mania is represented as a mysterious disappearance; and the popular tradition seeks to escape the typical allusion to the humiliation and punishment of the proud Chaldæan kingdom, which is conveyed in that insanity—in that disgraceful, though temporary, degradation of its ruler, by invoking the fate which actually came upon Nebuchadnezzar, on the head of the Medo-Persian, the hated national foe. The popular wit of the ancient Orientals, which delighted to ridicule Cyrus as the Πέρσης ἡμίονος (cf. Herodotus I. 55, 91), may have been not altogether without influence in bringing about this peculiar perversion, or rather reversal, of the original prophecy, as is suggested by a comparison of Abydenus, as quoted above, with Dan. v. 21 (עֲרָדַיָּא, "a wild ass"). Compare

Hengstenb., p. 107 et seq.; Hävernick, *Neue krit. Unterss.*, p. 52 et seq.; Kranichfeld, pp. 203-209; Pusey, p. 294 et seq.

NOTE 2.—The most simple solution of the historical difficulty in chap. i. 1, and that which has the greatest exegetical support, has been indicated above. It may be found in Perizonius, *Origines Ægyptiacæ et Babylonicæ*, II., p. 430, and more recently in Hengstenberg, p. 54 et seq.; Delitzsch, p. 275; Keil, *Einl.*, § 133, p. 440; and substantially, in Kranichfeld, p. 16 et seq. (but cf. infra, No. 2). It regards the verb בּוֹא as not designating the arrival of Nebuchadnezzar before Jerusalem, but as merely indicating his departure from Babylon (for the feasibility of this interpretation cf. the proof-texts cited above, to which may be added Num. xxxii. 6; Isa. vii. 24; xxii. 15, and many others; see Gesenius and Dietrich under בּוֹא, No. 3). Further incidents in the campaign, whose beginning is thus indicated are: the victory of Nebuchadnezzar over Pharaoh-Necho near Carchemish, or Circesium, on the Euphrates (an event which, according to Jer. xlvi. 2, transpired in the course of *the fourth year of Jehoiakim*); the pursuit of the defeated Egyptians by the Chaldæans in a southerly direction (Jer. xlvi. 5 et seq.); the arrival of the victor before Jerusalem, and the taking of the city, which followed soon afterwards (2 Kings xxiv. 1 et seq.; 2 Chron. xxxvi. 6 et seq.), and probably near the close of the fourth year of Jehoiakim, with which was connected the first deportation of captive Jews, and of a portion of the vessels of the temple, to Babylon. In the following year, and some time after the departure of the Chaldæans, the fast was proclaimed, of which Jeremiah remarks (xxxvi. 9) that it was observed in the ninth month of the fifth year of Jehoiakim. It may therefore, in analogy with Zech. viii. 19, be regarded as an anniversary of mourning, commemorative of the fall of the city in the preceding year, instead of being considered a prophylactic, penitential fast, designed to secure deliverance from the impending danger of Nebuchadnezzar's arrival, and thus as similar to those described in Joel i. 14; 2 Chron. xx. 3, 4, etc. (as Hitzig, Schmeidler, and others, hold). This simple and natural combination of events is contradicted by no statement whatever, in relation to the history of Jehoiakim and his time, whether found in this or any other prophetical or historical book. The passages Dan i. 2 and 2 Chron. xxxvi. 6 (Heb. text) do not actually state that Jehoiakim was carried to Babylon by Nebuchadnezzar after his capture of Judæa; but if this were the case, their statements would by no means conflict with the account in 2 Kings xxiv. 1, according to which Jehoiakim became the tributary of Nebuchadnezzar during three years after his first subjugation, and afterwards revolted from him anew. Neither the brief sketch in Chronicles, nor the subject of Daniel, which is not specially concerned with the fortunes of that king, would require the mention of the return of Jehoiakim to his capital soon after his transportation (see on chap. i. 2); and in view of his undecided character, his revolt, after three years of vassalage, may be readily accepted, despite the fact that he had felt the proud Chaldæan's power but a few years before. Nor will it be surprising that 2 Kings xxiv. 11 et seq. relates another taking of Jerusalem and deportation of many Jews so soon after the first as the reign of king Jehoiachin or Jeconiah, if we regard this second deportation (6–7 years later than the first; cf. 2 Kings xxiii. 36, with xxiv. 8) as the punishment which Nebuchadnezzar was compelled to inflict on the Jews, because of Jehoiakim's revolt, but which was not executed until some time after it was decided on, and thus affected the son and successor, before he had attained his majority, instead of crushing the father (cf. 2 Chron. xxxvi. 8–10). Finally, the designation of Nebuchadnezzar as *king* while engaged in his campaign against Necho and the allied Jehoiakim (Dan. i. 1),—while the successful interpretation of the dream by Daniel, which transpired, according to chap. ii. 1, in the *second* year of that monarch's reign—must date at least three years later, involves no contradiction whatever, if we regard the title in the first instance as *proleptical*. There would be no impropriety in applying it to him as joint ruler with his father and leader of his armies, even during the life of Nabopolassar,—especially if we remember that Berosus (in Josephus, *contra Apion.*, I. 19) makes Nebuchadnezzar to achieve his great victories over the "satraps" of Egypt, Cœle-Syria, and Phœnicia, before the death of the aged Nabopolassar, and to hasten to Babylon to assume the sole government, only after receiving the tidings of his father's death (B. C. 605 or 604, and soon after the first capture of Jerusalem). Jer. xxv. 1, also, in harmony with Dan. i. 1, when correctly understood, represents the fourth year of Jehoiakim as the first of Nebuchadnezzar's reign, inasmuch as he regards the leader of the Chaldæans as the king of Babylon after his victory over Necho, whether he might be for the time the commander-in-chief and co-regent, and also the prospective successor to the throne, or not. But a comparison of Jer. lii. 31 with 2 Kings xxv. 27 shows clearly that this prophet was by no means unacquainted with the correct chronology of Nebuchadnezzar's reign (beginning with the death of Nabopolassar). This method of reconciling Dan. i. 1, with all the remaining data affecting the chronology, is so satisfactory in all respects, that we are led to reject every other combination as decidedly as we do the course of the negative criticism which finds the statements of this book in general to conflict with history, and which, therefore, despairs especially of being able to reconcile the passage chap. i. 1 with the statements in Jeremiah, Kings, and Chronicles (Bertholdt, Kirmss, Bleek, De Wette, Hitzig, etc.). Among the methods of arrangement which differ from ours we reckon:

(1.) The account of Josephus (*Ant.*, X. 6, 1), which, in view of 2 Kings xxiv. 1 et seq admits indeed that Nebuchadnezzar possessed all the territory west of the Euphrates after his victory over Necho, but fixes the conquest of Judæa fully three or four years later (in the 8th year of Jehoiakim); a perversion of history that resulted probably from a misunderstanding of Jer. xxii. 18, 19, and against which Keil and Thenius (on 2 Kings in many places), Hitzig, Graf, Hasse (*De prima Nebuchadnezaris adv. Hierosol. expeditione*, Bonnæ, 1856), and others have justly declared themselves.

(2.) The view of Kranichfeld, who does not date the capture of Jerusalem three or four years after Nebuchadnezzar's victory near Carchemish, but still one year later, or "not earlier than the ninth month of the fifth year of Jehoiakim," because that author believes himself compelled to regard the fast mentioned in Jer. xxxvi. 9, as having preceded the fall of the city; a hypothesis which is opposed by the fact that it fixes the transportation of Daniel and other Jewish youths to Babylon, and the beginning of their three years' course of instruction in the wisdom of the Chaldæans, before the capture of Jerusalem—thus involving an inherent improbability, and conflicting directly with Dan. i. 2 et seq. (cf. the exegetical remarks on that place).

(3.) The assumption of Kleinert (in the *Dorpater theolog. Beiträgen*, II. 128 et seq.); Hoffmann (*Die 70 Jahre des Jeremia und die 70 Jahrwochen Daniels*, Nuremberg, 1836, p. 16 et seq.; *Weissagung und Erfüllung*, I. 297 et seq.), Hävernick (*Neue krit. Unterss.*, p. 62 et seq.), Oehler (in Tholuck's *Literar. Anzeiger*, 1849, p. 395 et seq.), and Zündel (p. 20 et seq.), that Jerusalem was taken by Nebuchadnezzar a year before the battle of Carchemish. What Keil has remarked (*Einl.*, § 133, p. 440) will suffice to refute this view: "This combination is untenable, because it cannot be reconciled with Jer. xxv. In that passage the fourth year of Jehoiakim is mentioned, beyond the possibility of being mistaken, as marking an epoch for the theocracy and for all the nations of Western Asia, in which the Lord would bring Nebuchadnezzar and all the tribes of the north against Jerusalem, that the land of Judæa might become a wilderness and its inhabitants, together with all neighboring nations, be subjected to Babylon during seventy years (chap. xxv. 9–11). So emphatic a prophecy in the mouth of Jeremiah would be utterly incomprehensible, if Jerusalem had been taken by Nebuchadnezzar and Jehoiakim been made tributary a year previously, while in the *fourth* year of Jehoiakim, which the prophet so strongly emphasizes (xxv. 3 et seq.), nothing of moment had transpired, and even later in the reign of Jehoiakim nothing had occurred beyond his revolt from the Chaldæans some years afterward, by which he became involved in hostilities with bands of Chaldæans, Syrians, Moabites, and Ammonites (2 Kings xxiv. 2). But this view becomes wholly untenable from the consideration that, at a time when the Egyptian king, who had advanced towards Carchemish at the beginning of Jehoiakim's reign, was doubtless in possession of that fortress, Nebuchadnezzar could not possibly pass by this hostile force and proceed to Judæa, while exposing Babylonia to so powerful a foe. But had this been possible, and, incredible as it is, had it actually occurred, it is certain that Pharaoh-Necho would not have permitted him quietly to operate in the rear of his army and overcome Jehoiakim his vassal; nor would Nebuchadnezzar, after conquering Jerusalem, have returned to capture Carchemish and defeat his principal enemy, instead of proceeding to Egypt, and making an easy conquest of the country, which was deprived of its defenders. But aside from this, the method under consideration is irreconcilable with the extracts from Berosus furnished by Josephus (*Ant.* X. 11, 1; *contra Ap.*, I. 19)." Views exactly similar are expressed by Hitzig, p. 3, and Kranichfeld, p. 17 et seq.

NOTE 3.—Is the Belshazzar of chap. v. the same as Evil-merodach, the son and immediate successor of Nebuchadnezzar, or is he identical with Nabonidus, the last Babylonian king prior to the Persian invasion? The latter alternative, which is advocated by Jerome (*Comm. in Dan.*, V. 1) and more recently by Hengstenberg, Hävernick (in his Commentary), Auberlen, Keil, and in substance also by Pusey (with the distinction, however, that he considers Belshazzar as the son and co-regent of Nabonidus), is supported (1) by the fact that according to Herodotus, I. 191, and Xenophon, *Cyrop.*, VII. 5, 15 et seq., Babylon was taken by the Persians while a luxurious banquet was in progress, and (2) by the circumstance that Herodotus, I. 188, calls Labynetus (=Nabonidus) a son of Nebuchadnezzar, with which the introduction of the queen-mother in chap. v. 10 (possibly the Nitocris of Herodotus, or the Amuheer of Alexander Polyhistor), and the express mention of Nebuchadnezzar as the father of Belshazzar in chap. v. 11, would seem to correspond. But the following considerations militate against this view, and favor the alternative which identifies Belshazzar with Evil-merodach: (1) Both the Babylonian historians, Berosus (in Josephus, *Ant.*, X. 11, 1, and *contra Apion.*, I. 20) and Abydenus (in Euseb., *Præpar. Ev.*, IX. 41, and *Chron. Arm.*, p. 28, ed. Mai) agree, in contrast with Herodotus, in representing Nabonidus, the last Babylonian king, as a usurper and throne-robber of non-royal descent, who conspired with a number of others to deprive Laborasoarchad, the youthful grandson of Nebuchadnezzar, of his throne and life, and who afterward fell into the hands of the Persians, not at the taking of Babylon by Cyrus during a royal banquet, but some time after the capture of his capital. They relate that, having been defeated in the open field, he threw himself into the fortress of Borsippa, where he capitulated to Cyrus after the fall of Babylon, by whom he was exiled to Carmania (or, as Abydenus states, he was made governor of that province). That these traditions of Berosus and Abydenus by no means owe their origin to a boastful tendency, representing the Chaldæan national interests in a one-sided manner, but as certainly comprehend a part of the truth, as do the accounts of Herodotus and Xenophon, has been shown by Kranichfeld, as cited above, in the clearest and profoundest manner.* The identity of Daniel's Belshazzar with Evil-merodach is confirmed (2) by the repeated mention of Nebuchadnezzar as his father (אָב, chap. v. 11, 13, 18, 22), which could, in every case, be applied to a more distant relationship, *e. g.*, grandfather and grandson, only by a forced interpretation; † and further (3) by the circumstance that, according to Berosus (Josephus, as above), Evil-merodach also died a violent death, having been murdered by his brother-in-law Neriglissar (cf. Dan. v. 30). No arguments against this identification can be drawn (*a*) from the relation of Dan. v. 30 to vi. 1—since these passages are not necessarily connected (see exeget. remarks); nor (*b*) from Dan. viii. 1, where a "third year of Belshazzar is mentioned, while Berosus and the Ptolemaic canon limit the reign of Evil-merodach to two years—since these latter authorities may have slightly postdated the years of that reign, *i.e.*, may have included the first year, as being incomplete, in the reign of Nebuchadnezzar; and in fact the canon of Syncellus appears to assign three years to the reign of Evil-merodach; nor (*c*) from the prophetic descriptions in Isa. xxi. 5, and Jer. li. 39, which predict that Babylon should fall in its dissipation, but by no means assert that it should meet this fate while a banquet or carousal was in progress; nor finally (*d*) from Jer. lii. 31, and 2 Kings xxv. 27, where the immediate successor of Nebuchadnezzar is called Evil-merodach, as in profane authorities;—for the anomalous name in Dan. v. may be readily explained on the ground of the very general custom of Oriental sovereigns to bear several names (cf M. v. Niebuhr *Gesch. Assurs und Babels*, p. 20 et seq., where reference is made to Sargon=Shalmaneser,‡ Asshurdanipal=Kineladan, and many others), and nothing is more probable than that Evil-merodach bore, in addition to his proper name, a title containing the name of the god Bel, which title was similar to the appellative that Daniel himself, according to chap. i. 5, was compelled to assume. And it is probable that the prophet designedly avoided the real name of the king, when writing of Evil-merodach, on account of that homonymy (see on chap. v. 1 and 12). Beyond this, the fact that the name Belshazzar occurs as belonging to Chaldæan kings is substantially established by the notice deciphered on the cylinders of Mugheir by Oppert and Rawlinson, which refers to a "Belsarussur, son of Nabomit or Nabunituk" (see *Zeitschrift der deutsch morgenl. Gesellsch.*, viii. 598; *Athenæum*, 1854, p. 341); although the identity of this Belsarussur with the Belshazzar of Daniel, which is asserted by Rawlinson and Pusey (*Daniel the Prophet*, p. 402), appears to be highly improbable, since this son of Nabonidus cannot be shown to have been either of royal rank nor descended from Nebuchadnezzar. This method, which identifies Belshazzar with Evil-merodach, is supported by Marsham (*Canon chron.*, p. 596 et seq.), Hofmann (*Die 70 Jahre des Jeremia*, etc., p. 44 et seq.), Hävernick (*Neue krit. Unterss.*, p. 71 et seq.), Oehler (in Tholuck's *Anzeiger*, as above, p. 398), Hupfeld (*Exercitat. Herodot.*, spec. II., Rintel, 1843, p. 46), Schulze (*Cyrus der Grosse*, in the *Stud. u. Krit.*, 1853, No. 3), M. v. Niebuhr (*Geschichte Assurs und Babels*, Berlin, 1857), Röckerath (*Bibl. Chronologie*, Munster, 1865, p. 123), Zündel (*Krit. Unterss.*, p. 29 et seq.), Kranichfeld (p. 24 et seq.), Füller (*Der Prophet Daniel*, p. 12), A. Scheuchzer (*Assyrische Forschungen*, in Heidenheim's *Vierteljahrsschrift*, etc., Vol. IV., No. 1), Kliefoth (p. 146 et seq.), and others. §

---

* See especially p. 35 et seq.: "The remarkable incident of the mysterious writing (chap. v. 5 et seq.), which raised Daniel to be the third ruler over the kingdom, and which of itself would have aroused attention and excited remark, the interpretation which connected two events as contemporary, and the fact that some of the events foretold in the mysterious writing actually came to pass the same night—all these taken together might, in the course of time, give rise, even among the natives, to the legend that the remaining facts contained in the writing and its interpretation transpired in that night as well; and this might occur still more easily among foreigners, in view of the clouded form which the tradition would naturally assume among them, as, *e.g.*, in the case of the Persians. Whether the recollection of the writing and interpretation were preserved or not would probably not modify the legend. In this way the Persian and Median tradition might easily conceive of the natural son of Nebuchadnezzar, who was murdered in that night, as being also the last Chaldæan king, and could therefore designate him by the name Λαβύνητος, which is found to correspond with the name of the last king in Berosus —Ναβόννηδος. In addition to the name which Herodotus gives to the king in question in agreement with Berosus, such a confusion of two distinct facts by the tradition is confirmed by the circumstance that these authors, in contrast with Xenophon, speak of a battle which preceded the taking of Babylon, and further, that Herodotus does not allude to the presence of Nabonidus, nor to his death, on the occasion of the fall of the city—thus agreeing with Berosus, who relates that that king had retreated towards Borsippa. Thus the facts in relation to the fall of the Chaldæan dynasty, as they are preserved in Berosus, were thrown together and commingled with the statements of Daniel, concerning the wonderful writing (in which the end of the king and of his empire were co-ordinated); and this cloudy tradition is before us in the accounts of Herodotus and Xenophon, while the correct account, as it is given in Dan. v., forms the transition from the sketch in Berosus, to the form which it assumed in Herodotus and Xenophon."

† [Yet this usage of אָב for *forefather* is a very common one, as any Hebrew Lexicon will show.]

‡ [The cuneiform inscriptions show that Sargon was Shalmaneser's son and successor.]

§ [It is beset, however, with many insuperable difficulties, the chief of which are cited and but imperfectly met in the

Together with the hypothesis of Pusey, already referred to, we are compelled to reject that indicated by Hofmann (*Die 70 Jahre*, etc., p. 44) and adopted by Delitzsch (p. 278) and by Ebrard (*Die Offenb. Joh.*, p. 55), which identifies Belshazzar with Laborasoarchad, the nephew of Evil-merodach and son of Neriglissar (and by descent from him, or rather from his consort, the grandson of Nebuchadnezzar). This view becomes untenable, because it is opposed by the expression, "Nebuchadnezzar, thy father" (אֲבוּךְ), in chap. v. 11, by the brief reign of the child Laborasoarchad, extending, according to Berosus, only over nine months (cf. with this Dan. viii. 1), and finally, by the impossibility of substituting Nebo-Shadrach for Laborasoarchad, and Bel-Shadrach for that; for, according to Isa. xlvi. 1, Bel and Nebo are not the same, but different divinities.

NOTE 4.—The identity of *Darius the Mede* (chap. vi. 1) with the Cyaxares of Xenophon, the son of Astyages and father-in-law of Cyrus, as well as his co-regent for a time, may be still more positively established than that of Belshazzar (chap. v. 1) with Evil-merodach. Even the critical opponents of this book generally acknowledge the reign of such a Cyaxares, as intervening between the Median Astyages and the Persian Cyrus, and thereby recognize the truth of Xenophon's account, despite its being found in the *Cyropædia*—a work which so largely bears the character of a romance (Bertholdt, Gesenius, Von Lengerke, and even Hitzig; also Holtzmann, in the *Deutsch-morgenl. Zeitschr.*, VIII. 3, 547, etc.). The existence of this second Cyaxares, as the immediate predecessor of Cyrus, is attested, not merely by numerous statements in the *Cyropædia* (I. 4, 7; 5, 2, 5; III. 3, 20; VIII. 5, 19; 7, 1), but also by Æschylus in his Περσαι, v. 762–65: Μῆδος γὰρ ἦν ὁ πρῶτος ἡγεμὼν στρατοῦ (Astyages), Ἄλλος δ' ἐκείνου παῖς (Cyaxares) τόδ' ἔργον ἤνυσε . . . . . Τρίτος δ' ἀπ αὐτοῦ Κῦρος, εὐδαίμων ἀνήρ, etc., and by Abydenus, in Euseb., *Præp. Evang.*, IX. 14, where the prophecy of Nebuchadnezzar concerning the fall of Babylon as quoted above (Note 1), declares with reference to Cyrus, that "the Mede, the pride of the Assyrians, should be his helper" (οὗ δὴ συναίτιος ἔσται Μήδης, τὸ Ἀσσυρίων αὔχημα), and in addition, by Josephus (*Ant.*, X. 11, 4), who states that the Greeks gave "another name" to the son of Astyages—the Darius of Daniel—which was doubtless Κυαξάρης, as transmitted by Xenophon. Nor can the circumstance that Herodotus does not mention this Cyaxares, and makes Cyrus the immediate successor of his grandfather Astyages, reflect doubt on the existence of this intervening king, since the remark of Gesenius (*Thesaur.*, p. 350) holds good of Herodotus as a writer of the earlier Assyrio-Babylonian and Medo-Persian history: "*Solere Herodotum prætermissis mediocribus hominibus ex longa rerum serie nonnisi unum alterumve memorare reliquis eminentiorem, ut aliunde constat et ipsa Babyloniæ historia docet, ex qua unius Nitocris reginæ mentionem injicit, reliquos reges usque ad Labynetum, ne Nebuchadnezare quidem excepto, silentio transit.*" The only real difficulty connected with the identification of the Median king in chap. vi. and the Cyaxares of the *Cyropædia* consists in the name Darius (דָּרְיָוֶשׁ) given to the former. It is to be observed, however, in relation to this circumstance:

(1.) In general, the bearing of two names is no more remarkable among the Ancient Median and Persian kings, than among the Assyrio-Babylonian; for the two-fold language and literature which all these nations employed promoted the use of various names to designate one and the same person, as did also the custom of connecting honorable appellatives with the proper names of kings and other eminent persons; cf. note 3.

(2.) The names דָּרְיָוֶשׁ = old Persic *Dârjawus*, and Κυαξάρης = the Pers. or Med. *Uvakshatara*, appear to be related in one sense, inasmuch as the former seems to be synonymous with "holder, or governor" (ἑρξείης, *sceptrum tenens*), and the latter with "direct," or "actual ruler," and the one to be of Persian origin, the other of Median (Delitzsch, p. 278).

(3.) Both names, and especially the latter, appear to have been stereotyped royal honorary titles, and, accordingly, to have been conferred on various persons; for

(*a.*) Cyaxares I., the father of Astyages and ally of Nabopolassar and conqueror of Nineveh (639–604), bore this name.

(*b.*) Consequently it must have descended to Astyages himself; for, according to Dan. ix 1, the father of Darius the Mede was named Ahasuerus, the Hebrew form of which, אֲחַשְׁוֵרוֹשׁ, is analogous in sound with the Persian *Uvakshatara*, and also with the Greek Κυαξάρης. But further

(*c.*) Cyrus himself appears occasionally to have borne the name of Cyaxares or Uvakshatara as an honorary title; for, according to Holtzmann (*Deutsch-morgenl. Zeitschrift*, as above), an old Persian cuneiform inscription contains the names Cyrus (*Qurus*) and Uvakshatara in immediate consecution: "*Ego Cyrus Cyaxares*," which may be synonymous with "*Ego Cyrus imperator*" (cf. Niebuhr, *Gesch. Ass. und Bab.*, p. 214, note 4), but can scarcely be rendered by "*Ego Cyrus Cyaxeres, sc. filius*," as Holtzmann suggests. Finally,

(*d.*) The name Cyaxares corresponds also to Xerxes, as is indicated by the Pers. form *Kshjârcha* or *Kshjârsha*, an abbreviation or contraction of Uvakshatara; also by the Hebrew

foregoing discussion. The hypothesis has far less to recommend it than the identification of Belshazzar with Nabonadius's son—Balsaruzur of the inscriptions. See foot-note at the end of No. 2 above.]

אֲחַשְׁוֵרוֹשׁ; and since a Persian king is designated, in Ezra iv. 6, by the latter name, who can hardly be any other than Cambyses, in view of the chronology; and further, since the Ahasuerus of the book of Esther is the same as Artaxerxes I. Longimanus (instead of Xerxes, as most moderns since Scaliger hold), according to the opinion which prevails in the Septuagint, Josephus, and the ancients generally, and which has not been refuted,* we may regard the name Cyaxares-Xerxes as being in fact a standing title, which descended from the last Median kings to all the Achæmenians. Similarly, the early Median kings seem generally to have borne the name *Ajis-Dahaka* or *Ashdahak* (*i.e.*, *dragon*) since both Deioces, who founded Ecbatana about 700 (Herod. I. 102), and Cyaxares I., who, according to Berosus and Abydenus, was also called Astyages (*i.e.*, Ashdahak), and also Astyages, the father of Cyaxares II., were designated by this title. The descent of names to others also finds its parallel among the rulers of other ancient Oriental kingdoms, *e.g.*, of Armenia, Cappadocia, Pontus, and even among the Egyptians after Ptolemy (cf. Niebuhr, as above, pp. 32, 44, etc.). It might possibly be shown that the name Darius (*Darjawus*) belongs to this class of standing royal titles among the Persians, from the designation of the golden coins of that kingdom as *Darics*. This designation dates back, indeed, to Darius Hystaspis, according to Herodotus, IV. 166, but according to Suidas, Harpocration, and the scholiast on Aristophanes' *Ecclesiaz.*, it traces its origin "to an older king of that name"—who, however, is not necessarily the same as Daniel's Darius-Cyaxares (as also the reference in the *Chron. Armen.* of Eusebius, p. 58: "*Darius rex de regione depulit aliquantulum*," need not be applied to the Darius of this book). But in any case, it is clear from what has been stated, that the difference between the names Cyaxares and Darius does not compel us to assume a difference between the persons who are thus designated by Xenophon and Daniel, and that all other views become superfluous in proportion as the identity of the two becomes probable. Of such we mention that of M. v. Niebuhr (pp. 91, 223), which identifies Darius, Dan vi. 1 et seq., with the last Median king Astyages, who is said to have subjugated Babylon after the death of Belshazzar or Evil-merodach, and to have been deprived of his Median kingdom in the following year by Cyrus, so that Babylon again became independent; that of Kleinert (in the *Dorp. Beiträge*), which assumes that Darius the Mede was a natural son of Cyaxares I., and younger brother to Astyages, while Cyaxares II. was his nephew and shared in his government; and that of Schulze (*Cyrus der Grosse*, in the *Stud. u. krit.*, as above, p. 685), which is also favored by Zündel (p. 36 et seq.), by which Cyaxares II., who is held to be identical with Darius the Mede, was not the son, but a younger brother of Astyages, and therefore a son of Cyaxares I. (Ahasuerus, Dan. ix. 1), whom Xenophon erroneously transformed from a Cyaxarides into an Astyagides, by which error the great-uncle of Cyrus was converted into his uncle. The correct view is advocated by Josephus (supra), Jerome on Dan. vi. 1, and among moderns, Offerhaus (*Spicilegia histor.-chronolog.*, lib. III., Gron., 1739, p. 265 ss.), Jehring (*Bibliotheka Bremensis*, VIII. 580 ss.), Gesenius (*Thesaur.*, I. 349 et seq.), Winer (*Realw.*, I. 250), Hengstenberg (p. 48 et seq.), Hävernick (*Comm.*, p. 203 et seq.; *Neue krit. Unterss.*, p. 74 et seq.), Keil (p. 457), Delitzsch (p. 278), Kranichfeld (p. 39 et seq.), Auberlen (pp. 16, 212), Füller (p. 141), and Kliefoth (p. 160 et seq.).† In relation to the passage, chap. vi. 2 (the 120 satraps of Darius), which apparently conflicts with the view advocated above, see the exegetical remarks on that place, where also the effort of Ebrard (*Die Offenb. Johannes erklärt*, p. 55 et seq.), and several others, to identify Darius with the Nabonidus of Berosus will be sufficiently considered.

§ 9. AUTHENTICITY OF THE BOOK (Concluded).

e. *Examination of the* INTERNAL *reasons against its genuineness, which are based on its* MIRACLES *and* PROPHECIES.

The narration of miracles and prophecies by Daniel is no more irreconcilable with the view that the book originated with him than are the historico-chronological difficulties which are asserted to be insuperable; for

(1.) The miracles recorded in the first part, and particularly the preservation of the three men in the flames of the fiery furnace (chap. iii.), the appearance of the mysterious hand upon the wall (chap. v. 5), and the deliverance of Daniel from the den of lions (chap. vi.), present no features whatever which fundamentally distinguish them from other miracles of the Old-Testament stage of revelation, or which mark them as the invention of a later period. On

* [But this identification of the Ahasuerus of Esther with Artaxerxes Longimanus instead of Xerxes is beset with so many difficulties that it is now almost universally rejected.]

† [On the ground of the superior authority, however, of the other Greek historians over the single testimony of the romance of Xenophon, this identification of "Darius the Mede" with Cyaxares II., or even the existence of the latter, is still strongly contested by many writers on classical history, who do not seem to allow the passage in Daniel sufficient weight in the discussion.]

the contrary, the principal periods of Old-Testament development in its earlier stages, and especially the Mosaic period and that of Elijah and Elisha, that is to say, the primitive stages of the legal and prophetic periods, abound with incidents of a still more extraordinary character; *e.g.*, the passages through the Red Sea and the Jordan; the pillar of cloud and of fire; the writing of the law on tables by the hand of God (Ex. xxxi. 18; xxxii. 16); the consuming of Nadab and Abihu by fire from the Lord (Lev. x. 1); the feeding of Elijah at the brook Cherith by ravens (1 Kings xvii. 4); the destruction of Ahaziah's captain and his fifty in the presence of Elijah (2 Kings i. 10 et seq.); Elisha's raising of the dead and providing of food; the floating iron in the Jordan, etc. If the Divine economy of revelation required such miracles for the founding of the theocracy, for the attestation of its principal bearers and supporters, and for the inauguration of the prophetic institution, why should it not require them at this juncture, when the continuation of the theocracy was endangered by an oppressive heathendom, which was to be feared the more, because of its sensual, luxurious, and syncretistic character, and when a large portion of the people had yielded to these evil influences to an extent that threatened the utter absorption of the worship of Jehovah by the conglomerate religions of Babylonia and Medo-Persia? The critical epoch at the close of the captivity required—with an urgency almost equal to that which existed in the opening period of the Old Covenant—that Jehovah should display his power in the face of the proud world-kingdoms and their scornful rulers, who laid claim to Divine honors and even to deification, and that He should thus at once confirm the tottering faith of His followers by appearing as the same faithful and living God of the covenant, and crush the insolent daring and silly superstition of those tyrants, by demonstrating His right to rank as the King of all kings, and as the Lord of heaven and earth. Wonders of a similar character, although not so striking and extraordinary as those in Daniel, had been wrought by the principal representative of the prophetic office, as early as the age of Isaiah and Hezekiah, while Shalmaneser and Sennacherib were bringing like oppression and temptations to bear on the faithful ones among the people of God (*e.g.*, the retrogression of the shadow on the dial of Ahaz; the healing of Hezekiah, etc.). Toward the close of the exile such Divine self-attestations were repeated, but in increased measure; and the agent was again the leading prophet of the time, who thus became the analogue and successor of Isaiah. These facts will be the less surprising when we reflect that it was now important to make a profound impression, not only on the members of the theocracy, but likewise on their oppressors, the heathen rulers; an impression such as the miracles of Moses were designed to produce on Pharaoh, and such as actually was produced in the case of the Chaldæan and Medo-Persian antitypes of Pharaoh—unless, indeed, the statements relating to repeated acts of homage rendered to Daniel's God by Nebuchadnezzar and Darius (Dan. ii. 46 et seq.; iii. 28 et seq.; iv. 31 et seq.; vi. 29 et seq.), and also that concerning the public recognition of the supreme divinity of Israel's God by Cyrus in the edict of liberation (Ezra i. 1–4), which is supported by other historical authorities, are to be remanded to the realm of myths and fables—a conclusion which, in the latter instance, only the most radical hyper-criticism could reach. This comparison with the Mosaic period affords the only valid basis on which to form a proper estimate of the age of Daniel, with its peculiar national conditions and its miracles, since the sufferings and trials of that period, which assailed the faith of God's children and threatened the further existence of the theocratic community, were met, like those of the captivity, on *foreign soil*, in the house of bondage and the land of misery. The sufferings, together with the inducements to idolatry, of the time of the Judges, were experienced by Israel on its own domestic soil; the afflictions of the period subsequent to the exile, *e.g.*, in the times of Ezra and of the Maccabees, likewise befell God's people while dwelling in the land of their fathers, and for that very reason were less dangerous to their religious and national life, than were the sufferings during either of those seasons of tribulation and persecution, which were undergone in "a strange land" (Psa. cxxxvii. 4). It is, therefore, decidedly impertinent and unhistorical to allege, as do the opponents of the genuineness of this book, that it owes its origin solely to a supposed analogy between the periods of the captivity and of the Asmonæans, and to ascribe to this invented Daniel the design of exhibiting the humiliations experienced by Nebuchadnezzar and Darius

Medus, in consequence of the Divine miracles and of the gracious strength and unyielding firmness of the theocratic witnesses to the truth, as a warning to Antiochus Epiphanes, the imitator of the religious tyranny of those monarchs. A certain typical analogy between Nebuchadnezzar and Antiochus may readily be granted; but the fundamental difference, or rather contrast, between these two periods of persecution, that Israel suffered during the one while in captivity, and during the other while domiciled on its native soil, is none the less apparent. The inability of Israel to resist the oppressors with armed force, and also the necessity for God to interfere with his wonder-working power, resulted immediately from the conditions of the former instance; while in the latter case the nation could struggle for its country, its sanctuary, and its faith, and therefore required no other miracles than those of warlike enterprise and of devoted courage that even courted martyrdom, such as are described in the Maccabæan books (see note 1).

(2.) Nor can the *prophecies* contained in this book be made to serve as witnesses against its genuineness; for, despite their visional form throughout (which, however, they bear in common with the former half of Zechariah, with numerous portions of Ezekiel, and even with extended sections of older prophetic books, *e.g.*, Amos, Isaiah, etc.), they exhibit the general characteristic features of Old-Testament prophecy everywhere, since they relate to the conditions and requirements of the time, are steadily possessed with the idea of the triumph of God's kingdom in its conflict with the world-powers, and develop this conflict in harmony with its growing intensity down to the time of the final Messianic triumph and judgment, in descriptions that become more and more minute as they progress. The book describes this Messianic period during which the Deliverer is to appear, as immediately connected with the resurrection of the just and the unjust to their final judgment (chap. xii. 1–3); and it assigns that event to a time that follows closely on the death of a raging Antichrist, whose description seems to be largely met in many traits belonging to Antiochus Epiphanes (see chap. xi. 21–45). But it does not follow from this that its author was a contemporary of that king, who described the historical events from the captivity to his time in the style of prophecy; since this feature is merely another illustration of the general law of prophetic visional perspective. At the farthest, certain of the more detailed predictions of the section (chap. x. and xi.) relating to the development of the world-powers after the fall of the Persian kingdom, might, as has already been observed (§ 1, note 2, and § 9), be regarded as the later additions of an apocalyptist living in the time of Antiochus, who sought to give a more definite form to the prophecy of Daniel. Aside from these external and unessential singularities, there is included in the prophetic contents of the book nothing connected with the development of the world-kingdoms until the advent of the Messiah, that might not have been foreseen and predicted by a Divinely-enlightened seer in the closing period of the captivity. Although such a seer had witnessed the supplanting of but one great world-kingdom by another, and although the extended range of observation which he enjoyed might reveal in the more distant political horizon but a single additional power in the progress of development; still nothing is easier to conceive than that, by the enlightening influence of the Holy Spirit, a long succession of world-monarchies, previous to Messiah's kingdom, should open to his vision, and that he should symbolically represent this succession of powers by certain figures taken from the products of Babylonian and Medo-Persian culture and art, as in the visions of chap. vii.–x. Nor do the attempts to reach a more exact chronological exposition of the development represented by the succession of these kingdoms, which are found more especially in the last four chapters of the book, involve any feature that does not suggest a parallel, on the one hand in the earlier prophets (*e.g.*, Isa. vii. 8; xxiii. 15; Jer. xxv. 11 et seq.; xxix. 10), and on the other, in the mathematical studies of Babylonian astronomers, and the attempted application of these to (astrological) calculations of the future. The indefinite character which probably attached to these symbolico-chronological descriptions of the future in their original form, did *not* correspond to the historical succession of events as such, and may have been now and then removed by the hand of the later reviser in order to give place to features harmonizing more exactly with the facts. But, upon the whole, even these chapters contain far more prophecy of an ideally descriptive character than of detailed historical prediction, calculated to excite the suspicion of a composition subsequent to the event; and the book, therefore, bears the character of a work whose origin during the captivity, and whose inspired prophetic nature are decidedly more probable than its forged and simulated composition in the Maccabæan age. Especially is the mention by Peter of an anxious looking for the period in which the Messiah should appear (1 Pet. i. 10–12), as a characteristic of the inspired prophets of the Old Covenant, more directly applicable to this work than to any other prophetical book in the canon (see notes 2 and 3).

NOTE 1.—In relation to the miracles of the time of Daniel, as demanded by the oppressed condition of Israel (see § 1, note 1), and especially the remarks of Hävernick there quoted, compare further, Hävernick, *Neue krit. Unterss.*, p. 85: "Without such a revelation of Jehovah, the theocracy would have been involved in heathendom, or absorbed by it. Jehovah's signs and wonders showed, despite the presence of the powerful world-kingdoms, that He still was the King of kings, and through them the question of the continued existence of the theocracy was really decided." See *ibid.*, p. 87, for the fact that the Asmonæan period, on the contrary, was characterized by an *absence* of miracles: "In the Maccabæan period the forsaking of the nation by God was manifested precisely in a manner that excluded miracles. The dead form remained to the people in petrified traditions; but the freshness and life of the old theocratic and prophetic spirit was wanting. This consciousness (that the ancient prophetism with its miraculous power must first be revived) finds expression in the monuments of that time with sufficient clearness. The first book of Maccabees has not a single reference to miracles; the disheartened age cannot even expect them," etc. See, further, Kranichfeld, who observes, in correspondence with the parallelism above established between the miracles of Daniel and those of Moses and Elijah, "Precisely the periods of an especially hopeless condition of the theocracy are found to present suitable conditions for the intervention of the Scriptural miracle, designed, as it is, to strengthen the theocratic consciousness." The assertion of Hitzig, that a *susceptibility* of the human mind and disposition for the usual influence of especially wonderful events, *i.e.*, a faith in them, could not have been developed during the "night of the exile," is without either historical or psychological support. If there was ever a night of discouragement for Israel, it was in the circumstances of the Egyptian period, as described in Exod. vi. 9, 12; yet that period contained the germ of a far-reaching exaltation of faith and trust, such as is frequently found in intimate connection with resignation and a gloomy sense of both outward and spiritual oppression. The 137th Psalm, as an example of the actual current of theocratic thought, may serve to indicate, that during the "night of the exile" as well, complaints and tears might consist with an internal profound and glowing excitation which longs for the Divine Deliverer. It has already been remarked that the descriptions relating to the circumstances of the captivity, in the second part of Isaiah's prophecies, represent an apparently hopeless demoralization of the religious and national spirit as coexistent with the strengthening and elevation of the theocratic consciousness by means of miracles. The extent to which the prophetic office of Ezekiel—the prophet of the opening period of the captivity—corresponds, in view of the conditions of the time, and of his personal traits, with that of Daniel, the prophet of the closing period, and also the significant contrast between them, are remarked by Hävernick, as cited above: "While the duty of influencing the captives during the exile *through the word* is devolved mainly on Ezekiel, everything in the position of Daniel unfolds a different field of activity, viz.: to defend the rights of the people of God in their relations to the heathen. This peculiar duty constituted a *man of action* (like Moses, Elijah, etc.), who opposed the superior Divine wisdom to the confused wisdom of men, and brought the deeds of victorious kings into contrast with the more powerful energy of God. His relation to Ezekiel is therefore complementary, and thus becomes a truly glorious testimony to the grace of God," etc. Keil, pp. 459, 461, shows the injustice of the charge occasionally raised against the author (*e.g.*, by Von Lengerke, *Dan.*, p. LXII.), that he is guilty of a "useless expenditure" or "needless accumulation" of miracles. As the really miraculous is confined to the three wonders mentioned in chapters iii., v., and vi., there can be no reason for the assertion of such an accumulation of wonders or rage for miracles on the part of the author, especially when compared with the far greater number of the miracles of Moses or Elisha. But it has already been observed in § 4, note 2, as a characteristic peculiarity of Daniel's method of narration, that he does not avoid the recognition of the Divine power and grace, as displayed in miracles, but rather avails himself of every opportunity afforded by his experience to call attention to the hand of Providence, and to place the events of his time in the light of a childlike believing and theocractical pragmatism. It must be reserved for the detailed exposition of the historical part to illustrate more specifically this peculiarity, in which the books of Esther and of Chronicles likewise participate, and which we would characterize as the *theocratic chronicling* style of the captivity and the succeeding period (see the observations on chap. iii.).

NOTE 2.—In opposition to the assertion of Lücke, that the apocalyptic character of our book as a prophecy, necessarily involves its pseudonymy, see above, § 1, note 2. It is important, in view of the assertion by Bleek (*Einl.*, § 259), that "the especially definite character of the predictions extends precisely to the time of Antiochus Epiphanes, and no farther," to observe the many obscure, indefinite, and ambiguous features which are found in the prophecies in the second part of the book, and which indicate with sufficient clearness that the position of the writer was that of a seer who looks forward, and whose descriptions are therefore only ideal, instead of that of a prophetic historian who recalls the past. Compare Kranichfeld, p. 58: "The prophecies of the book of Daniel, in their descriptions, are never independent of the course of history as such, and nowhere bear the character of *absolute*, unconditioned, and *therefore* miraculous predictions. They do not contain a single paragraph (?) which, when viewed entirely apart from its fulfilment, might not be considered as merely the independent development of a theocratical thought, or complexity of thoughts, founded on historical facts. For this reason detailed descriptions of the course of future events are met with which do not fully correspond to the actual history; and this is as readily conceivable as it is natural. The critics have no difficulty about explaining away such differences, which become especially prominent on a comparison of the description of the *last* heathen kingdom and its final conformation in the times of the Seleucidæ and the Maccabees (chap. x. and xi.); and the product of such arbitrary interpretation is ranged with the remaining occasional correspondences of the prophecy with the course of history, which are *natural*, because they have their basis in religious and ethical truth. The resultant caricature of Scriptural prophecy, similar to that presented in the later so-called apocalypse of Judaism, the Jewish Sibyls, the book of Enoch, the 4th book of Esdras, thus, in the end, becomes a certain prize." The opinion here expressed is correct in all its essential features, and will bear modifying only in the single statement relating to the alleged unexceptionally ideal character of the descriptions of the future, contained in chapters x. and xi. We regard it as exceedingly probable that in this connection, but only here, occasional *vaticinia ex eventu* were interpolated by a later hand, and doubtless by a theocrat of the time of Antiochus Epiphanes; for the congruity between the prophecy and the facts by which it is fulfilled, is frequently more apparent than the fundamental law of Old-Testament prophecy appears to warrant (cf. § 1, note 2). None of the special predictions which are usually cited as being analogous to Dan. x., xi.—whether Isa. vii. 8 (possibly an interpolated passage), Isa. xiii. 1–14; xxi. 1–10; Jer. xxv. 11 et seq.; xxix. 10; or Ezek. xxiv. 25–27, etc.—do, in fact, compare with Dan. xi. in point of remarkable and often directly particularizing correspondence between prophecy and fulfillment; cf. Auberlen, p. 71 et seq.; Hengstenberg, p. 173 et seq.* The decidedly eschatological character of chap. xii. 1 et seq., may be insisted on, as a special argument against the assertion that the book was written from the point of view which prevailed in the Maccabæan age, and that, more particularly, its final chapters were composed "immediately after the death of Antiochus Epiphanes became known" (Bleek). That passage does not merely assign the beginning of the future Messianic period to the time immediately following the death of Antichrist (xi. 45), but also its close, and may therefore have originated with a prophet belonging to an earlier age, who saw the anti-christian tyrant as a vision of the distant future (cf. similar perspective descriptions of the future, following upon gloomy prophecies of evil, in Amos ix. 11 et seq.; Mic. vii. 12 et seq.; Isa. xi. 1 et seq., etc.), but can hardly have emanated from a designing forger of the troubled times of the Asmonæans. To employ this passage as a proof of the origin of the book under Epiphanes, or to postpone the composition of the closing chapters, x.–xii., until even after the death of that tyrant, is to manifest a gross misapprehension of the nature of Messianic prophecy—its complex and apotelesmatic character, its necessary co-ordinating of the near and distant future in perspective vision (cf. Delitzsch, p. 286). Compare infra, on chap. vii. 8; ix. 24 et seq.; and see the exegetical remarks in general, which may serve to explain in detail how difficult it is to adapt this book to the Maccabæan period, in the character of a pseudo-prophetical work.

NOTE 3.—With reference to the difficult, but, for the exegesis of this book, exceedingly important question, "Which world-kingdoms of the last pre-Christian time correspond to the four characteristic figures of Daniel's monarchies (chap. ii. 31 et seq.; vii. 2 et seq.)?" we offer the preliminary remark, that the interpretation by which the fourth kingdom represents the Roman supremacy—an interpretation which was accepted by Josephus and a majority of the church fathers, and which has become traditional and is in almost universal favor—does

* [We need hardly point out to the student how purely conjectural and subjective is this supposition of the interpolation of certain parts of these wonderful prophecies, nor how fatal to the genuineness of the book as a whole is such an admission. *Falsus in uno, falsus in omnibus.* Who is to draw the line of distinction between the authentic and the spurious parts? None is apparent in the text, and if interpreters are allowed to pick and choose for themselves what they conceive it *likely* that God would have revealed, and what they may be free to attribute to later hands, the whole ground is virtually conceded to Rationalism. The true explanation of the minuteness of the prophecies in chap. xi. of Daniel lies in their intimate connection with the *nearer* future of the chosen people, and the fact that Antiochus Epiphanes, being the first *foreign* persecutor of the Jewish religion as such, is set forth as the type of all coming Antichrists.]

not to us seem to meet the sense of the prophet.* Nor can we, with Ephraem Syrus, Hitzig, Ewald, Delitzsch, and others, find in this fourth kingdom the Macedonian or Grecian empire of Alexander the Great, *together with the kingdoms of the Diadochi*, which sprang from it; but instead, the divided nature of the fourth kingdom (chap. ii. 41) appears to us to symbolize *only* the empire of the Greek Diadochi after Alexander, while the kingdom of Alexander himself must be considered as the third. See above, § 3 [also § 10, Notes 3 and 4]; and compare the exegesis of chap. ii. 40 et seq. See ibid. in relation to the number *four* and its symbolical meaning as applied to the world-kingdoms. Meanwhile compare Kranichfeld, p. 57: "It is an unquestionable peculiarity of Daniel that he attempts to cover this period by four of such kingdoms; but the general application by the Hebrews of the number four to extensions of time or space is equally unquestioned (cf. the four winds, Dan. vii. 2; viii. 8; the four quarters of the heavens, four ages of the world, four principal metals, etc.). If we therefore consider the composer of the book to have been a person who estimated the political condition of his time and its consequences understandingly and naturally, and at the same time clung decidedly and immovably to his faith in the realization of the Messianic hopes which rested on previous prophecies, it will be evident that the Messianic period would present itself to his mind as connected with the fourth, *i.e.*, extreme development of heathen supremacy, which was so significant to the reflections of a scholar as such; and this conception would be as natural as that, for instance, of Isaiah and Jeremiah, in whom the predominance of religious and theocratic thought, together with the corresponding subordination of political interests as such, produced an association of the Messianic period with the fall of Babylon," etc. See the same author, p. 58, in relation to the peculiarly definite character of the *chronological* predictions of Daniel: "There is not a single prediction relating to a definite point of time, in the prophecies of Daniel, which is not the expression of an idea that would be perfectly intelligible to a theocratic contemporary of the writer. The *manner* in which he determines a point of time might, indeed, seem to be somewhat peculiar; but this consists merely in the astronomically arithmetical *measurement* of a current *conception of time*, which reminds us of Babylon, the cradle of astronomical as well as astrological definitions, and which, by its union with the thoroughly Babylonian feature presented in the use of animal symbols, and with the grotesquely descriptive style of the narrative in general, harmonizes with the Babylonian origin of the book."

§ 10. Design of the Book of Daniel.

According to the opponents of the genuineness of this book, who assign it to the Maccabæan period, its author aimed merely to exhort and comfort, and even invented the contents of the first or historical part for this purpose. Both the narratives relating to the heroic faith and steadfastness of Daniel and his friends, when exposed to the threatenings and persecu-

* [Dr. Pusey, the latest scholarly advocate of this reference of the fourth kingdom to Rome (pagan rather than papal), offers the following special considerations in its favor (p. 69 et seq.): 1. "Even an opponent (De Wette, in the *Hall. Encykl.* s. v. Daniel) has said, 'It is in favor of this interpretation [of the 4th empire as Roman] that the two feet of iron can be referred to the eastern and western emperors.'" But so is the 3d empire described by the *plural* "breasts (חֲדוֹהִי) and arms," where the Medo-Persian coalition affords but a faint parallel. 2. "The ten horns are explained to be kings or kingdoms which should issue *out of it.* 'And the ten horns out of (*i.e.*, going forth from) this kingdom are ten kings that shall arise.' Throughout these prophecies the king represents the kingdom, and the kingdom is concentrated in its king. The kings, then, or kingdoms, which should arise out of this kingdom must, from the force of the term as well as from the context, be kings or kingdoms which should arise at some later stage of its existence, not those first kings without which it could not be a kingdom at all." The force of this reasoning is somewhat difficult to perceive, and its whole validity is destroyed by the Masoretic accents of the text quoted, which should be translated thus: "The ten horns [are] the kingdom thence, [namely] ten kings [that] shall arise." 3. "These ten horns or kingdoms are also to be contemporaneous. They are all prior in time to the little horn which is to arise out of them. 'Another shall arise after them, and is diverse from the rest.' Yet the ten horns or kingdoms are to continue on together until the eleventh shall have risen up; for it is to rise up *among* them and destroy three of them." The inconclusiveness of this argument is palpable. Antiochus certainly was later than his predecessors, but of the same line, and he displaced three of them. The correspondence is as perfect as could be desired; far more so than on any other scheme. 4. "The period after the destruction of that power [the eleventh horn], and of the whole fourth kingdom which is to perish with him, is indicated by these words: 'And the rest of the beasts (the other kingdoms), their dominion was taken away, yet their lives were prolonged on' to the time appointed by God. The sentence seems most naturally to relate to a time after the destruction of the 4th empire; for it continues the description." This was exactly true of the Maccabæan deliverance, which for the first time effected the independence of the Jews from Antiochus, who was but the sequel and climax of the long subjugation ever since the captivity. If the theory in question has no better support than these arguments, it is weak indeed. Its main prop, as to *pagan* Rome, is the superficial resemblance in the extent and power of the latter—which is at once dissipated when the prophecy is viewed from the stand-point of the Jewish martyrs; and as to *papal* Rome, its great bulwark is the year-for-a-day interpretation, with the overthrow of which it utterly falls. The subject is argued at length by Dr. Cowles, *Commentary on Daniel*, p. 354 et seq.].

tions of the Babylonian tyrants, and the apocalyptic visions of the second part, were designed to admonish the compatriots and contemporaries of the writer to "emulate these men in their unconquerable faith, as shown in their public and disinterested confession of the God of their fathers, and to remind them that this only true God would, at the proper time, know how to humble and destroy those who, like Antiochus Epiphanes, should exalt themselves against Him in their reckless pride, and should seek to cause His people to renounce His service, as well as how to secure the final victory to his faithful and steadfast adherents" (Bleek, *Einleit.*, p. 602). The book, if really composed in the time of Antiochus Epiphanes, would certainly correspond to this design but imperfectly. The hortative and typical bearing of many of its marvelous narratives upon the sufferings, temptations, and religious duties of Israel in a later age, would not have been at all understood. Nebuchadnezzar, Belshazzar, and Darius would hardly have been recognized as types of that Seleucidian tyrant, since their relations to the theocracy were wholly different from his. The latter aimed at the complete extirpation and annihilation of the worship of Jehovah, and would never have consented to even a temporary recognition of the supreme power and majesty of the Covenant God of the Old Dispensation, such as was secured from each of those rulers; and the cordial relations which Daniel maintained throughout the exile towards the Chaldæan and Medo-Persian heathendom, as chief of the Magian caste, and as an influential political officer and confidential adviser of their heathen rulers, would certainly have exerted a forbidding influence on the narrow-minded, illiberal, and fanatically-inclined Jews of Maccabæan times, instead of encouraging them, quickening their faith, and inspiring them with the zeal of martyrs. With the exception of three men in the fiery furnace, not a single really suitable example would have been presented to the martyrs of this period for their encouragement and comfort, while, at the same time, the prophetic portions of the book would have been burdened with much that was superfluous, obscure, and incomprehensible, and therefore with much that contradicted its design (cf. the note 1 below).

On the other hand, everything reveals a definite plan, and is adapted to a practical end, which is easily apprehended when it is examined from the position of the nation during the exile and immediately afterward. The Chaldee fragments, chap. ii.–vii., which were recorded first, are seen in this light to be a collection of partly narrative and partly prophetic testimonies to Jehovah, as the only true God, in contrast with the vain gods of the Babylonians. These fragments were designed to strengthen the faith of the captives, and this design is indicated by the unvarying manner in which each section closes, viz.: by an ascription of praise to Jehovah, which generally falls from the lips of one of the heathen sovereigns himself (see chap. ii. 47; iii. 28 et seq.; iv. 34; v. 29; vi. 26 et seq.; vii. 27). The Hebrew text was composed somewhat later, and was designed directly and solely for Israel, which appears, not only from the absence of doxologies expressive of the triumph of the faith in Jehovah over the worship of idols, at the end of the several paragraphs, but also from the fact that, aside from the historical introduction to the book as a whole (chap. i. 1–ii. 4), it contains *only* prophecies, which are, moreover, exclusively of a *comforting* nature. They are designed "to comfort the Hebrew people in the trying political circumstances under which they are either newly engaged in arranging their affairs in Palestine, or are still languishing in the land of the exile. In view of the fact that to the human understanding the duration of this trying condition is unknown, they present the assurance that the continued and increasing tribulations, which must keep pace with the moral corruption of heathendom, *are designed by God for the purifying of the faithful* (cf. chap. xi. 35; xii. 10), *and cannot be imposed a single day beyond what He has determined*" (Kranichfeld, p. 60); and with a view to afford a still more effectual comfort and encouragement, they contain repeated references to the *Messianic period of salvation* (chap. ix. 25 et seq.; xii. 1 et seq.; cf. vii. 13 et seq.), that long predicted glorious conclusion at which the history of God's people must arrive after passing through many previous clouds and shadows, and *which contains in and of itself the assurance that Israel shall be saved out of every affliction, however great.*

From their connection with these comforting prophecies, the older records relating to the marvelous displays of Divine power and grace as witnessed by Daniel and his companions, receive an additional significance, as examples tending to encourage, comfort, and quicken the faith of Israel in succeeding ages, and serving, especially in the more sad and troublous seasons, as shining way-marks and guiding stars through the dark nights of a condition in which God had apparently forsaken them, although they were originally recorded for a different situation. This comforting tendency of the book, however, did not reveal itself fully, until, as has been shown elsewhere (§ 6, note 1), almost three hundred and fifty years after the captivity, the religious tyranny of the Seleucidæ brought the full measure of the sufferings predicted by Daniel to bear upon Israel. In consequence, this prophetical book, which up to that time had perhaps been partially misconceived, or at least misunderstood and undervalued, attained its rightful position in the public mind; for the sufferings of the time revealed not only the marked keenness of vision displayed by the Divinely-enlightened seer, but also the fullness of consoling power contained in his wonderful narratives and visions. The Maccabæan period served, therefore, to fully demonstrate the practical design of the book, and thereby to solve its prophetical riddles, to bring to view the depths of wisdom which underlie its meditations on the relations of the world-powers to the kingdom of God, and to secure permanently to its author the honorable rank of the fourth among the greater prophets.

NOTE 1.—Hävernick, *Einl.*, II. 488, shows in a striking manner, the untenable character of the assumption that the book is a fiction of the Maccabæan age, invented to serve a purpose, especially in view of the marked difference between the religious and political circumstances of that time and those prevailing in the captivity: "How marked is the distinction between the heathen kings of this book and Antiochus Epiphanes! Collisions with Judaism occur, indeed, but how different is the conduct of Nebuchadnezzar, Belshazzar, and Darius the Mede, in relation to the recognition of Judaism and its God! Where is the evidence in this case of a desire to extirpate Judaism, or to inaugurate a formal persecution of the Jews, such as entered into the designs of Antiochus. There can hardly be two things more dissimilar than are the deportment of a Belshazzar or Darius and that of the Seleucidian king." Compare page 487: "That Daniel, together with his companions, receives instruction in the language and wisdom of Chaldæa, that he even appears as the head of the Magian caste, and bears a heathen name, fills political positions at heathen courts, maintains relations of intimate friendship with heathen princes, and even manifests the warmest interest in them (cf. iv. 16)—all these are traits in thorough harmony with the history, and corresponding to the circumstances resulting from the captivity, but not according with the rigid exclusiveness of the Maccabæan period," etc. Cf. Herbst, *Einleit.*, II. 2, 98; Zündel, p. 60 et seq.; Pusey, p. 374 et seq.

[NOTE 2.—We introduce here, as an appropriate connection, some valuable remarks from Keil's *Commentary on Daniel* (Clark's ed., Introd., § ii., p. 5 et seq.), on *Daniel's place in the history of the kingdom of God*, so far as these relate to the chosen people of Israel. "The destruction of the kingdom of Judah and the deportation of the Jews into Babylonian captivity, not only put an end to the independence of the covenant people, but also to the continuance of that constitution of the kingdom of God which was founded at Sinai; and that not only temporarily but forever, for in its integrity it was never restored. . . . . The abolition of the Israelitish theocracy, through the destruction of the kingdom of Judah and the carrying away of the people into exile by the Chaldæans, in consequence of their continued unfaithfulness and the transgression of the laws of the covenant on the part of Israel, was foreseen in the gracious counsels of God; and the perpetual duration of the covenant of grace, as such, was not dissolved, but only the then existing condition of the kingdom of God was changed, in order to winnow that perverse people, who, notwithstanding all the chastisements that had hitherto fallen upon them, had not in earnest turned away from their idolatry, by that the severest of all the judgments that had been threatened them; to exterminate by the sword, by famine, by the plague, and by other calamities, the incorrigible mass of the people; and to prepare the better portion of them, the remnant who might repent, as a holy seed to whom God might fulfill His covenant promises. Accordingly the exile forms a great turning-point in the development of the kingdom of God which He had founded in Israel. With that event the form of the theocracy established at Sinai comes to an end, and then begins the period of the transition to a new form, which was to be established by Christ, and has actually been established by Him. . . . . The restoration of the Jewish state after the exile was not a re-establishment of the Old-Testament kingdom of God. When Cyrus granted liberty to the Jews to return to their own land, and commanded them to rebuild the temple of Jehovah in Jerusalem, only a very small band of captives returned; the greater part remained scattered among the heathen. Even those who went home from Babylon to Canaan were not set free from subjection to the heathen world-power, but remained, in the land which

History.	Chap. II.	Chap. II.	Chap. VII.
I. *Babylonian Empire.* This is depicted at its acme under Nebuchadnezzar, who attained the universal sovereignty of Western Asia and Egypt. Griffins or winged lions are a common emblem on the Assyrian sculptures. The empire subsequently degenerated, and, at the same time, became more civilized.	31 Thou, O king, sawest, and behold a great image. This great image, whose brightness *was* excellent, stood before thee; and the form thereof *was* terrible. 32 This image's head *was* of fine gold,	37 Thou, O king, *art* a king of kings: for the God of heaven hath given thee a kingdom, power, and strength, and glory. 38 And wheresoever the children of men dwell, the beasts of the field and the fowls of the heaven hath he given into thine hand, and hath made thee ruler over them all. Thou *art* this head of gold.	2 Daniel spake and said, I saw in my vision by night, and, behold, the four winds of the heaven strove upon the great sea. 3 And four great beasts came up from the sea, diverse one from another. 4 The first *was* like a lion, and had eagle's wings: I beheld till the wings thereof were plucked, and it was lifted up from the earth, and made stand upon the feet as a man, and a man's heart was given to it.
II. *Persian Empire.* The original element was Media, where bears abound. Persia was the higher horn and more elevated side. The three ribs are probably Lydia, Assyria, and Babylonia, which were successively absorbed by Cyrus. He was victorious in every direction except eastward. The kings following him were: 1. Cambyses; 2. Smerdis; 3. Darius Hystaspis; 4. Xerxes, who first exerted all his resources against Greece.	his breast and his arms of silver,	39 And after thee shall arise another kingdom inferior to thee,	5 And behold another beast, a second, like to a bear, and it raised up itself on one side, and *it had* three ribs in the mouth of it between the teeth of it: and they said thus unto it, Arise, devour much flesh.
III. *Macedonian Empire.* Copper denotes the mercenary Greeks. The leopard represents their slyness and pertinacity. The four wings are indicative of double velocity. Alexander marched with unexampled rapidity. He was the sole ruler of his dynasty. His dominions were divided, shortly after his premature death, between, 1. Ptolemy, in Egypt and the Mediterranean coast; 2. Seleucus, in Asia; 3. Lysimachus, in Thrace; 4. Cassander, in Greece.	his belly and his thighs of brass,	and another third kingdom of brass, which shall bear rule over all the earth.	6 After this I beheld, and lo another, like a leopard, which had upon the back of it four wings of a fowl; the beast had also four heads; and dominion was given to it.
IV. *Syrian Monarchy.* This was of a mongrel character, the native Oriental element corresponding to the clay, and the foreign Greek to the iron. These were combined in all sorts of affinities. The ten toes may symbolize the numerous satrapies which fell to the share of Seleucus. This dynasty is depicted as fierce, from contrast with the lenient governments preceding, and especially from its intolerance towards the Jewish religion.	33 His legs of iron, his feet part of iron and part of clay.	40 And the fourth kingdom shall be strong as iron: forasmuch as iron breaketh in pieces and subdueth all *things*: and as iron that breaketh all these, shall it break in pieces and bruise. 41 And whereas thou sawest the feet and toes, part of potters' clay, and part of iron, the kingdom shall be divided; but there shall be in it of the strength of the iron, forasmuch as thou sawest the iron mixed with miry clay. 42 And *as* the toes of the feet *were* part of iron and part of clay, *so* the kingdom shall be partly strong and partly broken. 43 And whereas thou sawest iron mixed with miry clay, they shall mingle themselves with the seed of men: but they shall not cleave one to another, even as iron is not mixed with clay.	7 After this I saw in the night visions, and behold a fourth beast, dreadful and terrible, and strong exceedingly; and it had great iron teeth: it devoured and brake in pieces, and stamped the residue with the feet of it: and it *was* diverse from all the beasts that *were* before it;
1. *Seleucus Nicator* was originally Ptolemy's general at Babylon, but soon managed to secure not only the entire East, but also the province of Syria (including Palestine). 2. *Antiochus Soter* was engrossed with subduing the Gauls. 3. *Antiochus Theos* made peace with Ptolemy Philadelphus by marrying Berenice, his daughter; but soon repudiated her in favor of Laodice, his former wife, who revenged herself by poisoning him and killing her rival with her infant.			and it had ten horns.
Berenice's brother, Ptolemy Euergetes, avenged her death by invading Syria, carrying away immense spoil.			
4. *Seleucus Callinicus* attempted to retaliate by attacking the Egyptian provinces [translate, ver. 9, "And he (the king of the north) shall come into the kingdom of the king of the south"], but was forced to retire with defeat. 5. *Seleucus Ceraunus*, his son, renewed the attempt, but was slain; and his brother, 6. *Antiochus the Great*, pushed the campaign to the border of Egypt.			
This roused Ptolemy Philopator, who assembled an army, with which he totally routed Antiochus at Gaza; but he then concluded a truce with him.			
Fourteen years afterwards, Antiochus returned with the spoils of his Eastern campaigns to renew his designs against			

Chap. VII.	Chap. VII.	Chap. VIII.	Chap. VIII.	Chap. XI.
17 These great beasts, which are four, *are* four kings, *which* shall arise out of the earth.				
		3 Then I lifted up mine eyes, and saw, and, behold, there stood before the river a ram which had *two* horns: and the *two* horns *were* high; but one *was* higher than the other, and the higher came up last. 4 I saw the ram pushing westward, and northward, and southward; so that no beasts might stand before him, neither *was there any* that could deliver out of his hand; but he did according to his will, and became great.	20 The ram which thou sawest having *two* horns *are* the kings of Media and Persia.	2 And now will I show thee the truth. Behold, there shall stand up yet three kings in Persia; and the fourth shall be far richer than *they* all:
		5 And as I was considering, behold, a he-goat came from the west on the face of the whole earth, and touched not the ground: and the goat *had* a notable horn between his eyes. 6 And he came to the ram that had *two* horns, which I had seen standing before the river, and ran unto him in the fury of his power. 7 And I saw him come close unto the ram, and he was moved with choler against him, and smote the ram, and brake his two horns: and there was no power in the ram to stand before him, but he cast him down to the ground, and stamped upon him: and there was none that could deliver the ram out of his hand.	21 And the rough goat *is* the king of Grecia: and the great horn that *is* between his eyes *is* the first king.	and by his strength through his riches he shall stir up all against the realm of Grecia. 3 And a mighty king shall stand up, that shall rule with great dominion, and do according to his will.
		8 Therefore the he-goat waxed very great: and when he was strong, the great horn was broken; and for it there came up four notable ones toward the four winds of heaven.	22 Now that being broken, whereas four stood up for it, four kingdoms shall stand up out of the nation, but not in his power.	4 And when he shall stand up, his kingdom shall be broken, and shall be divided toward the four winds of heaven; and not to his posterity, nor according to his dominion which he ruled: for his kingdom shall be plucked up, even for others besides those.
19 Then I would know the truth of the fourth beast, which was diverse from all the others, exceeding dreadful, whose teeth *were of* iron, and his nails *of* brass; *which* devoured, brake in pieces, and stamped the residue with his feet.	23 Thus he said, The fourth beast shall be the fourth kingdom upon earth, which shall be diverse from all kingdoms, and shall devour the whole earth, and shall tread it down, and break it in pieces.			
20 And of the ten horns that *were* in his head,	24 And the ten horns out of this kingdom *are* ten kings *that* shall arise:			5 And the king of the south shall be strong, and *one* of his princes; and he shall be strong above him, and have dominion; his dominion *shall be* a great dominion. 6 And in the end of years they shall join themselves together; for the king's daughter of the south shall come to the king of the north to make an agreement: but she shall not retain the power of the arm; neither shall he stand, nor his arm: but she shall be given up, and they that brought her, and he that begat her, and he that strengthened her in *these* times. 7 But out of a branch of her roots shall *one* stand up in his estate, which shall come with an army, and shall enter into the fortress of the king of the north, and shall deal against them, and shall prevail. 8 And shall also carry captives into Egypt their gods, with their princes, *and* with their precious vessels of silver and of gold; and he shall continue *more* years than the king of the north. 9 So the king of the south shall come into *his* kingdom, and shall return into his own land. 10 But his sons shall be stirred up, and shall assemble a multitude of great forces: and *one* shall certainly come, and overflow, and pass through: then shall he return, and be stirred up, *even* to his fortress. 11 And the king of the south shall be moved with choler, and shall come forth and fight with him, *even* with the king of the north: and he shall set forth a great multitude; but the multitude shall be given into his hand. 12 *And* when he hath taken away the multitude, his heart shall be lifted up; and he shall cast down *many* ten thousands: but he shall not be strengthened *by it*. 13 For the king of the north shall return, and shall set forth a multitude greater than the former, and shall certainly come after certain years with a great army and with much riches.

	CHAP. II.	CHAP. II.	CHAP. VII.	CHAP. VII.
the Egyptian provinces, and, with the assistance of a party of the Jews, he defeated the Egyptian general at the sources of the Jordan, besieged and captured the remainder of the Egyptian force in Zidon, and got full possession of Palestine. He now concluded a hollow alliance with Ptolemy Epiphanes, giving him his daughter Cleopatra, with the Palestinian provinces as a dowry, hoping that she would favor his purposes, an expectation in which he was ultimately disappointed. He then				
turned his arms against the Greek colonies of Asia Minor and the Ægæan till checked by the Romans under Scipio, who compelled him to sue for peace on the most humiliating terms. He was killed while attempting to plunder a temple in his own dominions. 7. *Seleucus Philopator* was engrossed with efforts to raise the enormous fine imposed by the Romans upon his father as the price of peace, and was at length assassinated by his minister, 8. *Heliodorus*, who held the throne a short time, although, 9. *Demetrius Soter*, son of the last king, was rightfully heir, and, 10. *Ptolemy Philometor* was entitled to the Palestinian provinces by virtue of his mother's dower right. 11. ANTIOCHUS EPIPHANES, brother of Seleucus, artfully and quietly secured the succession, expelling Heliodorus, and ignoring the claims of his nephews Demetrius and Ptolemy. (Daniel styles him "vile," in contrast with his surname "illustrious," and notes the Hellenizing corruptions of his reign in Judæa, as detailed below.) The guardians of the latter			8 I considered the horns, and, behold, there came up among them another little horn, before whom there were three of the first horns plucked up by the roots: and, behold, in this horn *were* eyes like the eyes of man, and a mouth speaking great things.	and *of* the other which came up, and before whom three fell; even *of* that horn that had eyes, and a mouth that spake very great things, whose look *was* more stout than his fellows.
prince resenting this, a struggle ensued, in which Antiochus twice defeated the Egyptians in a pitched battle on their own borders. He then pretended to make a truce with them, but only used it as a cover for entering Egypt with a small force, and seizing quietly upon the capital and other points. On his				
return from his second campaign into Egypt, he endeavored to carry out the scheme of introducing Greek customs among the Jews. In a third campaign he continued his successes, and in a fourth he was likely to capture Alexandria and reduce the whole Egyptian power, when he was peremptorily ordered to desist by the Romans. On is way home he vented his cha-				
grin at this interference upon the unhappy Jews, in whose quarrels he meddled, deposing the high-priest, abolishing th sacrificial offerings, interdicting the ritual, and bitterly persecuting all who refused to apostatize to paganism. The Temple remained closed to all but heathen victims for three years and a half (1290 days), and was shortly afterwards rededicated on Dec. 25, B.C. 165 (making 1335 days), six and a half years (2300 days) from the first act of profanation in the removal of the legitimate pontiff. Antiochus's disregard for even the native deities is evident from his renewal of his father's attempt to plunder the temple of the Syrian Venus. Yet he made the most violent efforts to introduce the worship of Jupiter Capitolinus.	34 Thou sawest till that a stone was cut out without hands, which smote the image upon his feet *that* *we* of iron and cl.., an brake them to pie.. 35 Then was the iron, the clay, the brass, the silver, and the gold, broken to pieces together, and became like the chaff of the summer threshing-floors; and the wind carried them away, that no place was found for them:	44 And in the days of these kings shall the God of heaven set up a kingdom which shall never be destroyed: and the kingdom shall not be left to other people, *but* it shall break in pieces and consume all these kingdoms, and it shall stand forever. 45 Forasmuch as thou sawest that the stone was cut out of the mountain without hands, and that it brake in pieces the iron, the brass, the clay, the silver, and the gold, the great God hath made known to the king what shall come to pass hereafter: and the dream *is* certain, and the interpretation f.	9 I beheld till the thrones were cast down, and the Ancient of days did sit, whose garment *was* white as snow, and the hair of his head like the pure wool: his throne *was like* the fiery flame, *and* his wheels *as* burning fire. 10 A fiery stream issued and came forth from before him: thousand thousands ministered unto him, and ten thousand times ten thousand stood before him: the judgment was set, and the books were opened. 13 I saw in the night visions, and, behold, *one* like the Son of man came with the clouds of heaven, and came to the Ancient of days, and they brought him near before him. 14 And there was given him dominion, and glory, and a kingdom, that all people, nations, and languages should serve him: his dominion *is* an everlasting dominion, which shall not pass away, and his kingdom *that* which shall not be destroyed.	11 I beheld then, because of the voice of the great words which the horn spake, I beheld *even* till the beast was slain, and his body destroyed, and given to the burning flame. 12 As concerning the rest of the beasts, they had their dominion taken away: yet their lives were prolonged for a season and time.
The remainder of his reign is obscure, owing to the nearly total loss of the ancient records concerning it. We have therefore but slight intimations of the final expedition against Egypt, etc., referred to by Daniel as being so successful. It is certain, however, that the last act of his reign was a campaign in the north-eastern provinces, and that he perished miserably (one account says as a raving maniac) as he was hastening to the support of his generals, who had been defeated by the Jewish patriots and zealots. The Maccabees had raised the standard of civil and religious liberty in Judæa, and, after a long and severe struggle, the Jews secured their independence. This they retained for a century, a period of great political and spiritual prosperity in general, which Daniel and the other prophets speak of in such glowing terms as being introductory to the Messianic times, the Gospel "kingdom of Heaven," never to end.	and the stone that smote the image became a great mountain, and filled the whole earth.			18 But the saints of the Most High shall take the kingdom, and possess the kingdom forever, even forever and ever.

Chap. VII.

and another shall rise after them; and he shall be diverse from the first, and he shall subdue three kings.

21 I beheld, and the same horn made war with the saints, and prevailed against them;

25 And he shall speak *great* words against the Most High, and shall wear out the saints of the Most High, and think to change times and laws: and they shall be given into his hand until a time and times and the dividing of time.

22 Until the Ancient of days came, and judgment was given to the saints of the Most High; and the time came that the saints possessed the kingdom.

26 But the judgment shall sit, and they shall take away his dominion, to consume and to destroy *it* unto the end.

27 And the kingdom and dominion, and the greatness of the kingdom under the whole heaven, shall be given to the people of the saints of the Most High, whose kingdom *is* an everlasting kingdom, and all dominions shall serve and obey him.

Chap. VIII.

9 And out of one of them came forth a little horn, which waxed exceeding great, toward the south, and toward the east, and toward the pleasant *land*.

11 And it waxed great, *even* to the host of heaven; and it cast down *some* of the host and of the stars to the ground, and stamped upon them.

11 Yea, he magnified *himself* even to the prince of the host, and by him the daily *sacrifice* was taken away, and the place of his sanctuary was cast down.

12 And a host was given *him* against the daily *sacrifice* by reason of transgression, and it cast down the truth to the ground; and it practised and prospered.

13 Then I heard one saint speaking, and another saint said unto that certain *saint* which spake, How long *shall be* the vision *concerning* the daily *sacrifice*, and the transgression of desolation, to give both the sanctuary and the host to be trodden under foot?

14 And he said unto me, Unto two thousand and three hundred days; then shall the sanctuary be cleansed.

Chap. VIII.

23 And in the latter time of their kingdom, when the transgressors are come to the full, a king of fierce countenance, and understanding dark sentences, shall stand up.

24 And his power shall be mighty, but not by his own power: and he shall destroy wonderfully, and shall prosper, and practise, and shall destroy the mighty and the holy people.

25 And through his policy also he shall cause craft to prosper in his hand; and he shall magnify *himself* in his heart, and by peace shall destroy many: he shall also stand up against the Prince of princes;

but he shall be broken without hand.

26 And the vision of the evening and the morning which was told *is* true: wherefore shut thou up the vision; for it *shall be* for many days.

Chap. XI.

14 And in those times there shall many stand up against the king of the south: also the robbers of thy people shall exalt themselves to establish the vision; but they shall fail.

15 So the king of the north shall come, and cast up a mound, and take the most fenced cities: and the arms of the south shall not withstand, neither his chosen people, neither *shall there be any* strength to withstand.

16 But he that cometh against him shall do according to his own will, and none shall stand before him: and he shall stand in the glorious land, which by his hand shall be consumed.

17 He shall also set his face to enter with the strength of his whole kingdom, and upright ones with him; thus shall he do: and he shall give him the daughter of women, corrupting her: but she shall not stand *on his side*, neither be for him.

18 After this shall he turn his face unto the isles, and shall take many: but a prince for his own behalf shall cause the reproach offered by him to cease; without his own reproach he shall cause *it* to turn upon him.

19 Then he shall turn his face toward the fort of his own land: but he shall stumble and fall, and not be found.

20 Then shall stand up in his estate a raiser of taxes *in* the glory of the kingdom: but within few days he shall be destroyed, neither in anger, nor in battle.

21 And in his estate shall stand up a vile person, to whom they shall not give the honor of the kingdom: but he shall come in peaceably, and obtain the kingdom by flatteries.

22 And with the arms of a flood shall they be overflown from before him, and shall be broken; yea, also the prince of the covenant.

23 And after the league *made* with him he shall work deceitfully: for he shall come up, and shall become strong with a small people.

24 He shall enter peaceably even upon the fattest places of the province; and he shall do *that* which his fathers have not done, nor his fathers' fathers; he shall scatter among them the prey, and spoil, and riches: *yea*, and he shall forecast his devices against the strong holds, even for a time.

25 And he shall stir up his power and his courage against the king of the south with a great army; and the king of the south shall be stirred up to battle with a very great and mighty army; but he shall not stand; for they shall forecast devices against him.

26 Yea, they that feed of the portion of his meat shall destroy him, and his army shall overflow: and many shall fall down slain.

27 And both these kings' hearts *shall be* to do mischief, and they shall speak lies at one table; but it shall not prosper: for yet the end *shall be* at the time appointed.

28 Then shall he return into his land with great riches; and his heart *shall be* against the holy covenant; and he shall do *exploits*, and return to his own land.

29 At the time appointed he shall return, and come toward the south; but it shall not be as the former, or as the latter.

30 For the ships of Chittim shall come against him: therefore he shall be grieved, and return, and have indignation against the holy covenant: so shall he do; he shall even return, and have intelligence with them that forsake the holy covenant.

31 And arms shall stand on his part, and they shall pollute the sanctuary of strength, and shall take away the daily *sacrifice*, and they shall place the abomination that maketh desolate.

32 And such as do wickedly against the covenant shall he corrupt by flatteries: but the people that do know their God shall be strong, and do *exploits*.

33 And they that understand among the people shall instruct many: yet they shall fall by the sword, and by flame, by captivity, and by spoil, *many* days.

34 Now when they shall fall, they shall be holpen with a little help: but many shall cleave to them with flatteries.

35 And *some* of them of understanding shall fall, to try them, and to purge, and to make *them* white, *even* to the time of the end: because *it is* yet for a time appointed.

36 And the king shall do according to his will; and he shall exalt himself, and magnify himself above every god, and shall speak marvellous things against the God of gods, and shall prosper till the indignation be accomplished: for that that is determined shall be done.

37 Neither shall he regard the god of his fathers, nor the desire of women, nor regard any god: for he shall magnify himself above all.

38 But in his estate shall he honor the God of forces: and a god whom his fathers knew not shall he honor with gold, and silver, and with precious stones, and pleasant things.

39 Thus shall he do in the most strong holds with a strange god, whom he shall acknowledge *and* increase with glory: and he shall cause them to rule over many, and shall divide the land for gain.

40 And at the time of the end shall the king of the south push at him: and the king of the north shall come against him like a whirlwind, with chariots, and with horsemen, and with many ships; and he shall enter into the countries, and shall overflow and pass over.

41 He shall enter also into the glorious land, and many *countries* shall be overthrown: but these shall escape out of his hand, *even* Edom, and Moab, and the chief of the children of Ammon.

42 He shall stretch forth his hand also upon the countries: and the land of Egypt shall not escape.

43 But he shall have power over the treasures of gold and of silver, and over all the precious things of Egypt: and the Libyans and the Ethiopians *shall be* at his steps.

44 But tidings out of the east and out of the north shall trouble him: therefore he shall go forth with great fury to destroy, and utterly to make away many.

45 And he shall plant the tabernacles of his palace between the seas in the glorious holy mountain; **yet he shall come to his end, and none shall help him.**

Chap. XII.

7 And I heard the man clothed in linen, which was upon the waters of the river, when he held up his right hand and his left hand unto heaven, and sware by him that liveth forever, that *it shall be* for a time, times, and a half; and when he shall have accomplished to scatter the power of the holy people, all these *things* shall be finished.

Chap. XII.

10 Many shall be purified, and made white, and tried; but the wicked shall do wickedly: and none of the wicked shall understand; but the wise shall understand.

11 And from the time *that* the daily *sacrifice* shall be taken away, and the abomination that maketh desolate set up, *there shall be* a thousand two hundred and ninety days.

12 Blessed *is* he that waiteth, and cometh to the thousand three hundred and five and thirty days.

the Lord had given to their fathers, servants to it. Though now again the ruined walls of Jerusalem and the cities of Judah were restored, and the temple also was rebuilt, and the offering up of sacrifice renewed, yet the glory of the Lord did not again enter into the new temple, which was also without the ark of the covenant and the mercy-seat, so as to hallow it as the place of His gracious presence among His people. The temple worship among the Jews after the captivity was without its soul, the real presence of the Lord in the sanctuary; the high priest could no longer go before God's throne of grace in the holy of holies to sprinkle the atoning blood of sacrifice toward the ark of the covenant, and to accomplish the reconciliation of the congregation with their God, and could no longer find out, by means of the Urim and Thumim, the will of the Lord. When Nehemiah had finished the restoration of the walls of Jerusalem, prophecy ceased, the revelations of the Old Covenant came to a final end, and the period of expectation (during which no prophecy was given) of the promised Deliverer, of the seed of David, began. . . . . . If the prophets before the captivity, therefore, connect the deliverance of Israel from Babylon, and their return to Canaan, immediately with the setting up of the kingdom of God in its glory, without giving any indication that between the end of the Babylonian exile and the appearance of the Messiah a long period would intervene, this uniting together of the two events is not to be explained only from the perspective and apotelesmatic character of the prophecy, but has its foundation in the very nature of the thing itself. The prophetic perspective, by virtue of which the inward eye of the seer beholds only the elevated summits of historical events as they unfold themselves, and not the valleys of the common incidents of history which lie between these heights, is indeed peculiar to prophecy in general, and accounts for the circumstance that the prophecies as a rule give no fixed dates, and apostelesmatically bind together the points of history which open the way to the end with the end itself. But this formal peculiarity of prophetic contemplation we must not extend to the prejudice of the actual truth of the prophecies. The fact of the uniting together of the future glory of the kingdom of God under the Messiah with the deliverance of Israel from exile, has perfect historical veracity. The banishment of the covenant people from the land of the Lord, and their subjection to the heathen, was not only the last of those judgments which God threatened against His degenerate people, but it also continues till the perverse rebels are exterminated, and the penitents are turned with sincere hearts to God the Lord and are saved through Christ. Consequently the exile was for Israel the last space for repentance which God in His faithfulness to His covenant granted to them. Whoever is not brought by this severe chastisement to repentance and reformation, but remains opposed to the gracious will of God, on him falls the judgment of death: and only they who turn themselves to the Lord, their God and Saviour, will be saved, gathered from among the heathen, brought in within the bonds of the covenant of grace through Christ, and become partakers of the promised riches of grace in His kingdom."]

[Note 3.—As a conspectus of Daniel's entire series of prophecies respecting the world-kingdoms, showing their complete harmony and mutual illustration, as well as their exact accordance with history, we insert (on pages 44–47) a table of all the passages, taken from M'Clintock and Strong's *Cyclopædia*, s. v. Daniel.]

[Note 4.—Dr. Cowles, in his *Commentary on Daniel* (N. Y. 1871), devotes an Excursus (pp. 459 sq.) to the consideration of that theory, generally called the "year-for-a-day" view, which results in applying the prophecy of the fourth kingdom of Rome, and especially the Papacy. His arguments are perfectly conclusive to candid minds. As the work is easily accessible we forbear to quote or abridge his remarks. See further the exegetical observations on the passages where the dates are given.]

§ 11. The Alexandrian Version of the Book of Daniel, and its Apocryphal Additions.

The Alexandrian translation of this book was, during a long time, supposed to be no more in existence, because the church, as far back as the time of Eusebius of Cæsarea and Pamphylius, had adopted the version of the Jewish proselyte Theodotian, which was considerably more exact and free from errors.* The genuine Septuagint text of Daniel was not published until 1772, when Simon de Magistris, a Romish priest of the oratory, published it from a Codex Chisianus. The editions by J. D. Michaelis (1773–4) and Segaar (1775) served to farther introduce and multiply this version. H. A. Hahn finally published a truly critical edition (1845), for which he had availed himself of a Syriac-Hexaplarian version published in 1788 by Cajetan Bugati, from a Codex Ambrosianus. This hexapla offers a Septuagint

* Cf. Jerome, *Comm. in Dan.* iv., 16; "*Septuaginta hæc omnia nescio qua ratione prætertierunt. Unde judicio magistrorum Ecclesiæ editio eorum in hoc volumine repudiata est et Theodotionis vulgo legitur, quæ et Hebræo et cæteris translatoribus congruit.*"

text corrected after Theodotian, as Origen had prepared it for his *Hexapla*, while the text edited after the Cod. Chisianus represents the genuine and unadulterated language of the Alexandrian version, as it had stood in Origen's *Tetrapla* beside the unchanged text of Theodotian (cf. Delitzsch, p. 286).

The Alexandrian version of this book probably originated before, or at any rate *about*, the middle of the second century before Christ, and therefore at the time in which the opposing criticism finds the Hebrew original to have been written (cf. § 6, note 3). The numerous departures from the original which this version presents, and which consist in the change of words and phrases (*e.g.* I. 3, 11, 16; II. 8, 11, 28; VII. 6, 8, etc.), in part of abbreviations and omissions (*e.g.* III. 31 et seq.; IV. 2–6; V. 17–25; 26–28), and finally, also in extensions of the text (*e.g.* IV. 34; VI. 20, 22–29), are by many critics traced to a Hebrew or Chaldee text diverse from the original, upon which this version is based (*e.g.* Michaelis, Bertholdt, Eichhorn). But they owe their existence, more probably, to the labors of the translator, since they are merely interpretations or paraphrases, designed to clear up the text, to indicate the connection, or to simplify or intensify the wonderful (cf. Hävernick, *Kommentar*, p. xlvii et seq.; De Wette, *Einl.*, § 258; Keil, § 137).

Nor do the longer interpolations inserted into the book of Daniel, in both the Alexandrian and Theodotian's versions, and generally bearing the name of *apocryphal additions to Daniel*, contain any feature that could compel the assumption of a Hebrew or Chaldee original on which they are based. Their lingual features testify rather to an original composition in the Greek (particularly the paronomasias or plays on Greek words, which were remarked by Porphyry,—such as σχῖνος, σχίσειμπρῖνος, πρίσει, which can scarcely be traced back to Hebrew paronomasias that were copied by the translator *), which is therefore accepted by Michaelis, De Wette, Bleek, Hävernick, etc., while other critics contend that these fragments were wholly, or in part, translated from a Hebrew or Aramaic original. (The latter include not merely Roman Catholics, as Dereser, Welte, Haneberg, Reusch, but also Protestants, among whom are Bertholdt, Eichhorn, Delitzsch [*De Habacuci prophetæ vita atque ætate*, 1844, p. 52 et seq.], Fritzsche [*Exeget. Handbuch zu den Apokryphen*, I. 111 et seq.], Zündel, etc.) This hypothesis of a Shemitic original may be justified, at most, with regard to two of these additions (the prayer of Azariah, and the song of the three children), but not with reference to the two that remain. These latter fragments (the history of "Susanna and Daniel," and that of "Bel and the dragon") bear a decidedly legendary character, being designed to glorify Daniel, and involving many improbabilities, and even impossibilities. They are therefore regarded, and with justice, as being of still later origin than the other component parts of the Greek Daniel. In the Alexandrian version they compose the closing sections of the book (chapters xiii. and xiv., by the modern arrangement of chapters), but are introduced with formulas (*e.g.* chap. xiv., or Bel and the dragon, with the puzzling superscription: ἐκ τῆς προφητείας Ἀμβακοὺμ υἱοῦ Ἰησοῦ ἐκ τῆς φυλῆς Λευί), the peculiarity of which is of itself sufficient to indicate their origin subsequently to the time of Daniel, whether an otherwise unknown prophet pseudo-Habakkuk be regarded as their author, or their origin be ascribed to one or several Jewish or Hellenistic writers. In Theodotian's translation these additions are organically incorporated with the Book of Daniel, Susanna being placed before Chap. i., as belonging to the history of the prophet's youth—the "prayer of Azariah" and the "song of the three children", being inserted between vs. 23 and 24 of chap. iii. (similar to their position in the Sept.), while only "Bel and the dragon" is consigned to the end of the book after chap. xii.

The question relating to the time and place in which these apocryphal fragments were composed cannot be solved, and we can only venture the supposition that the four emanated from different authors. This appears in the case of the "prayer of Azariah" and the "song of the three children" (chap. III. 24–45 and 51–90), from the circumstance, that in the former (v. 38) the temple is represented as destroyed, and its services as having ceased, while the other

* Jerome, *Comm. in Dan. Proph.*: "*Sed et hoc nosse debemus, inter cætera Porphyrium de Danielis libro nobis objicere, idcirco illum apparere confictum, nec haberi apud Hebræos, sed Græci sermonis esse commentum: quia in Susannæ fabula contineatur, dicente Daniele ad presbyteros,* ἀπὸ τοῦ σχίνου σχίσαι, καὶ ἀπὸ τοῦ πρίνου πρίσαι, *quam etymologiam magis Græco sermoni convenire quam Hebræo, cui et Eusebius et Apollinaris pari sententia responderunt: Susannæ Belisque, et Draconis fabulas non contineri in Hebraico, sed partem esse prophetiæ Habacuc filii Jesu,*" etc.

fragment presumes the existence of both these institutions (vs. 54, 84 et seq.). Of the two remaining additions, that relating to Susanna (possibly containing a grain of historical truth belonging to the age of the canonical book of Daniel) seems to have been composed at an early day, and without any reference to the canonical Daniel; while "Bel and the dragon," or the "Prophecy of Habakkuk, the son of Jesus, of the tribe of Levi," appears to have been written, with special reference to Dan. vii., by a Palestinian author of a much later time. All of these apocryphal appendages to the questions relating to Daniel furnish a very important testimony in attestation of the superior historical rank and genuine prophetical character of the canonical Daniel, inasmuch as their artificial stamp and legendary tone present a contrast to the far more sober and credible contents of that book, analogous to the familiar contrast between the apocryphal and the canonical Gospels, which serves so strongly to endorse the credibility of the latter. These remarks will also apply to the contrast between Daniel and the pseudonymous apocalypses of the last Jewish, or pre-Christian age, *e.g.* the "Sibylline Oracles," Enoch, and the "Fourth Book of Esdras," whose partial dependence on our book has already been considered (§ 6, especially note 3), and which are unquestionably the earlier or later products of an apocalyptic and simulated authorship, like that of the unknown originators of the additions to our book.

NOTE.—In relation to the apologetic importance of the apocryphal supplements to chap. iii. 13 and 14 in the Greek Daniel, compare Delitzsch, p. 186: "How favorable is the testimony for the historical and prophetical character of the canonical book, which results from its contrast with these apocryphal legends!"—and also Zündel, p. 187: "These apocryphal additions to Daniel therefore, did not all originate at the same time, or in the same place; but one appeared on Grecian (?) soil, another on Palestinian, and a third perhaps on Babylonian. They were translated before they were received by the Septuagint (without exception? —see above); and prior to their reception, they had been partially gathered, and ascribed to a spurious Habakkuk. . . . If Daniel, therefore, was not composed until B. C. 168, how could the translation in question, together with these additions, have existed as early as B. C. 130? Even though an unusually rapid formation of legends be assumed, from the oldest, relating to Susanna, to the latest αἴνεσις τῶν τριῶν παίδων, how is it possible to conceive the contrast between the original work and the oldest forgery, as developed within the limits of a single generation? And from the earliest forgery again, down to the latest, would not a considerable contrast have arisen here, *e.g.* between the προσευχή and the αἴνεσις? . . . And beyond this, their being translated and collected! All these considerations compel us to assume *a period, covering many generations, between the origin of the book of Daniel and its Alexandrian version.*"—See *ibid.*, p. 134 et seq., and especially p. 137, on the relation of the *Jewish apocalypses* of the pre-Christian period to Daniel: "A pre-Christian, or, upon the whole, a progressive development, cannot be asserted in connection with these apocalypses; for, with the exception of the Sibyllines, none of them was sufficiently important to give rise to imitations. They did not spring from each other, but are co-ordinate, and the only connection among themselves consists in their imitating the earlier prophets, and in their tendency to describe the facts of history in an apocalyptic manner. But on the other hand, *nearly all of them contain imitations of Daniel.* The "Book of Enoch" treats of the interpretation of the number seventy in his seventy regents; Esdras's eagle with wings and feathers is evidently the fourth [? first] beast of Daniel; and the person who incessantly inquires why the covenant people is afflicted, is merely a copy of Daniel while mourning because of the delay in the fulfilment of prophecy (chap. ix. and x.). The numbers of Daniel in chap. viii. are almost completely restored in the *Ascensio Jesajæ*, which also paints the coming of the Lord with Daniel's colors," etc.

The apocryphal additions to Daniel are found also in the ancient Coptic version, which is not without importance for textual criticism. They have been published by Henry Tattam, in vol. II., p. 270 ss. of his *Prophetæ majores in linguæ Ægyptiacæ dialecto Memphitica s. Coptica* (Oxon, 1852).

§ 12. THEOLOGICAL AND HOMILETICAL LITERATURE ON DANIEL.

I. *Ancient Period.*—1. *Christian expositors.* (1.) Church fathers: Hippolyti *Commentar. in Danielis et Nebuchadnezaris visionum solutiones* (capp. 7–12), editus e cod. Chisiano in Danielem sec. LXX. interpretes, Romæ, 1772 (see also the fragment in Greek of a commentary on Daniel in the *Opp. Hippolyti*, ed. J. A. Fabricius, Hamb., 1716). Ephræmi Syri *Commentar. in Dan.*, in his *Opp. Gr. et Syr*, ed. Assemani, Rom., 1740 et seq., tom. II., p. 203 et seq. Hieronymi *Explanatio in Danielem prophetam*, in his *Opp.* ed Vallars., Venet., 1768, tom. v., p. II. Theodoreti *Commentar. in visiones Danielis prophetæ* (Ὑπόμνημα εἰς τὰς ὁράσεις τοῦ προφήτου Δανιήλ), in his *Opp.* ed. Schulze, Hal., 1768 et seq., t. II., p. II., p. 1063 et seq.* Polychronii (a brother of Theodore of Mopsuestia) *Commentarius in Danielem*, in A. Mai, *Nova Collect*, I. B, p. 155. [Chrysostomi *Interpretatio in Danielem*, in his *Opp.* vi. 228 et seq.] (2.) During the middle ages: Joachimi *Expositio in Daniel.*, Venet., 1519. Thomas Aquinas, *Comm. in Daniel.*, separ. ed. Paris, 1640. [Rupertus Tuitiensis, *In Danielem*, liber i. (in his *Opp.* i., 520 et seq.) Albertus Magnus, *Comment. in Danielem* (in his *Opp.*, p. 8 et seq.)] 2. *Jewish expositors* (Rabbins): R. Saadia Hag-Gaon († 924), in the *Rabbin. Bibles* by Bomberg (Venet., 1526 et seq.) and Buxtorf (Basil, 1618). Rashi (*i.e.* R. Shelomoh ben-Jizchak, † 1105), *ibid.*, and also in J. F. Breithaupt's *Commentt. R. S. Jarchi in Prophh., Job, et Psalmos in Lat. vert.*, Goth., 1713. Ibn-Ezra († 1167), in the *Rabbin. Bibles.* Abarbanel († 1508), מַעְיְנֵי יְשׁוּעָה (*i.e.* "wells of salvation," Isa. xii. 3), Neap., 1497; also Amsterd., 1617, 4. R. Joseph Teitzack (about 1500), לֶחֶם סְתָרִים (panis absconditus, Prov. ix. 17—a commentary on Daniel and the 5 Megilloth), Venet., 1608, 4. R. Mosheh Alshech (about 1560), חֲבַצֶּלֶת הַשָּׁרוֹן (Cant. II., 1), Zaphat, 1568; Venet., 1592. R. Shamuel b.-Jeh. Valeri (16th cent.), חָזוֹן לַמּוֹעֵד (visio temporis statuti), Venet., 1586. R. Joseph ben-D. David ben-J. Jachim (usually Jacchiades, † 1559), *Paraphrasis in Dan. proph.*, Heb. et Lat., ed Const. L'Empereur, Amstel., 1633, 4to; [new ed., by Philippson, Dessau, 1808, 4to and 8vo. Jud. Löw Jeitteles, a Heb. Commentary on Dan., Ezra and Neh., Vienna, 1835, 8vo.]

II. *Modern period.* 1. *Protestant expositors.* (a) In the 16th century: Luther, *Der Prophet Daniel deutsch*, Wittenb., 1530, 4 (dedicated to duke John Fred.); *Vorrede über den Proph. Daniel, nebst Auslegung des XI. und XII. Kap.*, Wittenb., 1546, 4; *Disputation über den Ort Dan.* iv. 24;—the three works collected under the title *Auslegung des Proph. Daniel*, in vol. vi. of Walch's ed. Melancthon, *Comment. in Daniel. proph.*, Vitemb., 1543, 8 (in his *Opp.*, tom. II., p. 410); [*Exposition of Daniel*, gathered out of P. Melancthon, by G. Joy, Geneva, 1545, 16mo, Lond., 1550, 8vo]; in German, by Just. Jonas, 1546. Joh. Draconitis *Comment. in Daniel. ex Ebræo versum, cum oratione in Danielem*, Marburg, 1544, 8. Victorin. Strigel, *Danielis prophetæ concio, ad Ebraicam et Chaldaicam veritatem recognita et argumentis atque scholiis illustrata*, Lips., 1565, 1571. Joh. Wigand, *Explicatio brevis in Danielem*, Jen., 1571. Nik. Selnekker, *Erkl. des Proph. Daniel und der Offenbarung Johannis*, Jen., 1567, 1608. Phil. Heilbrunner, *Danielis proph. vaticinia in locos communes theologicos digesta et quæstionibus methodice illustrata*, Lauing., 1587. J. Œcolampadius, *In Danielem ll. II., omnigena et abstrusiore cum Ebræorum tum Græcorum scriptorum doctrina referti*, Basil., 1530, 1543, and often. J. Calvin, *Prælectiones in Danielem*, a Joa. Budæo et Car. Jonvillæo collectæ, Genev., 1563, 1576, and often (also in his *Opp.*, tom. v., Amstel., 1667 [*Commentary on Daniel*, tr. by T. Myres, M.A., Edinb., 1852, 2 vols. 8vo.]). Fr. Junius, *Expositio proph. Danielis*, a Jo. Grutero excepta, Heidelb., 1593; Genev., 1594. Rob. Rollock, *Comm. in libr. Dan. prophetæ*, Edinb., 1591; Basil, 1594; Gen., 1598. Hugh Broughton, *Danielis visiones Chaldaicæ et Ebrææ, ex originali translatæ et illustratæ*, London, 1596 (Engl. ed. [also in *Works*, p. 164 et seq.]), Basil., 1599 (Lat. ed. J. Boreel). A Polanus a Polansdorf, *In Danielem prophetam, visionum amplitudine difficillimum, vaticiniorum majestate augustissimum, commentarius, in quo logica analysi et theologica ἐκθέσει, tradita in publicis prælectionibis in vetusta Basileensi academia, totius libri, ad hoc ævum calamitosum saluberrimi, genuinus sensus et multiplex usus ostenditur*, Basil., 1599, 1608.

(b). In the 17th century: S. Gesner, *Daniel propheta disputationibus XII., et prefatione chronologica breviter explicatus*, Vitemberg., 1601, 1607, and often. Polyc. Leyser, *Commentarius in Dan. cap. I.-VI.*, Francof. et Darmst., 1609 et seq.† J. C. Rhumelius, *Liber Danielis paraphrasi recensitus*, Norimb., 1616. Mart. Geier, *Prælectiones academicæ in Danielem proph.*,

* The fragments of several other patristical expositors of Daniel, *e.g.* Ammonius, Polychronius, Apollinaris, Eudoxius, may be found in the commentary of H. Broughton, mentioned below (*Danielis visiones Chald. et Ebr.*, Basil., 1599), in connection with the expositions of Hippolytus and others.

† This work of Leyser's has been published in six parts under various titles: (1) *Scholia Babylonica, h. e. ecclesiastica commentationes in cap. I. Danielis*, Francof., 1609; (2) *Colossus Babylonicus quatuor mundi monarchias repræsentans, s. eccl. expositio cap. II. Danielis*, Darmst., 1609; (3) *Fornax Babylonica, sinceræ religionis confessores probans, s. eccl.*

Lips., 1667 and often. Abrah. Calov, *Annotata Anti-Grotiana in Jeremiam et Daniele n proph.*, Vitemb., 1664. A. Varenius, *Collegium canonicum quatuor novissimorum V. Ti. prophetarum, Danielis, Haggæi, Zachariæ, Malachiæ*, Rostochii, 1667. G. Meissner, *Der Prophet Daniel, sowohl geschehene Dinge ausredend, als künftige weissagend, durch kurze Anmerkungen erläutert;* with a preface by J. Fr. Mayer, Hamburg, 1695, 12. J. H. Alsted, *Trifolium propheticum, i.e. Cant. Canticor. Salom., prophetia Danielis, Apocalypsis Joannis, sic explicantur, ut series textus et temporis prophetici, e regione posita, lucem menti et consolationem cordi ingerant*, Herborn, 1640. Constantin L'Empereur (Professor controversiarum Judaicarum at Leyden, † 1648), *Paraphrasis Jos. Jachiadæ in Danielem cum versione et annotationibus*, Amstel., 1633 (see supra I., 2). Thom. Parker, *Expositio visionum et prophetiarum Danielis*, Lond., 1646. J. Cocceius, *Comment. in Danielem*, Lugd. Bat., 1666. H. Wingendorf, *Prophetia Danielis paraphrasi reddita et cum profanæ historiæ monumentis collata*, Lugd. Bat., 1674. J. H. Jungmann, *Propheta Daniel novo modo et hactenus inaudito reseratus*, etc., etc., Casselis, 1681. Balth. Bekker, *Uitlegginge van den Prophet Daniel*, Amsterd., 1688, 1698.

(c). In the 18th century: J. Musæus, *Scholæ propheticæ continuatæ, ex prælectionibus in prophetas Danielem, Micham, et Joelem collectæ*, ed. J. E. de Schulenberg, Quedlinb., 1719. Chr. Bened. Michaelis, *Adnotationes philologico-exegeticæ in Danielem*, Hal., 1720 (also in Vol. III. of the *Annotatt. uberiores in Hagiogr.*). J. W. Petersen, *Sinn des Geistes in dem Propheten Daniel*, Frankfort a. M., 1720. J. Koch, *Entsiegelter Daniel, d. i. richtige Auflösung der sämmtlichen Weissagungen Daniels, nach ihrem wahren Inhalt, unzertrennl. Verbindung, einhelligen Absicht, und genauen, sogar auf Jahre und Tage mit der Chronologie zutreffenden Zeitrechnung auf den Messiam*, Lemgo, 1740. M. Fr. Roos, *Auslegung der Weissagungen Daniels, die in die Zeit des Neuen Testaments hineinreichen, nebst ihrer Vergleichung mit der Offenb. Joh. nach der Bengel'schen Erklärung derselben*, Leips., 1771 [in English, by G. Henderson, Edinb., 1811, 8vo.]. J. Chr. Harenberg, *Aufklärung des Buches Daniel aus der Grundsprache, der Geschichte und übrigen rechten Hülfsmitteln, zum richtigen Verstand der Sätze, zur Befestigung der Wahrheit, und zur Erbauung durch die Religion*, Blankenburg and Quedlinburg, 1773, 2 parts. Chr. S. Benj. Zeise, *Uebersetzung und Erklärung des Buches Daniel*, Dresden, 1777. J. D. Lüderwald, *Die sechs ersten Kapitel Daniels, nach historischen Gründen geprüft und berichtigt*, Helmstädt, 1787. J. C. Volborth, *Daniel aufs neue aus dem Hebräish-Chaldäischen übersetzt, und mit kurzen Anmerkungen für unstudirte Leser und Nichttheologen begleitet*, Hanover, 1788. C. G. Thube, *Das Buch des Propheten Daniel, neu übersetzt und erklärt*, Schwerin and Wismar, 1797. Wm. Lowth, *Commentary upon the prophecy of Daniel and the twelve Minor prophets*, Lond., 1726, 2 vols. Isaac Newton, *Observations upon the prophecies of Daniel and the Apocalypse of St. John*, Lond., 1733, 2 vols. (a posthumous work, published six years after the death of the author; afterwards published in Latin by W. Südemann, Amstel., 1737, and in German, with notes, by C. F. Grossmann, Leips., 1765.—Cf. supra § 5.). H. Venema, *Dissertationes ad vaticinia Danielis emblematica, cap. II., VII. et VIII. de quatuor orientis regnis, ordine sibi successuris et quinto Messiæ; in quibus illa novâ viâ demonstrantur et illustrantur, aliisque prophetis lux affunditur*, Leovard., 1745. The same, *Comment. in Dan. cap.* XI. 4–XII. 3, ibid., 1752. R. Amner, *An essay towards an interpretation of the prophecies of Daniel*, Lond., 1776; also in German, *Versuch über die sämmtlichen Weissagungen Daniels, nebst Anmerkungen über die berühmtesten Erklärer derselben*, von Rich. Amner, Halle, 1779. T. Wintle, *Daniel, An improved version attempted, with a preliminary dissertation and notes, critical, historical, and explanatory*, Lond., 1792.

(d). In the 19th century: Leonh. Bertholdt, *Daniel aus dem Hebräish-Aramäischen neu übersetzt und erklärt, mit einer vollständigen Einleitung und einigen historischen u. exegetischen Exkursen*, 2 parts, Erlangen, 1806, 1808. G. F. Griesinger, *Neue Ansicht der Aufsätze im Buch Daniel*, Stuttg. and Tübingen, 1815. E. F. C. Rosenmüller *Danielem Lat. vertit et annotatione perpetua illustravit* (part X. of the *Scholia in V. T.*), Lips., 1832. H. A. Ch. Hävernick, *Kommentar über das Buch Daniel*, Hamb., 1832. Cäs. v. Lengerke, *Das Buch Daniel*, Kön-

---

exp. cap. III. Dan., Francof., 1610; (4) *Cedrus Babylonica, potentes docens humilitatem et detestans superbiam, s. eccl. exp. cap. IV. Dan.*, Francof., 1610; (5) *Epulum Babylonicum, in quo causæ interitus imperiorum et regnorum spectandæ ob oculos proponuntur, s. eccl. exp. cap. V. Dan.*, Darmst., 1619; (6) *Aula Persica, ostendens pietatem ab invidia aulica premi, sed nequaquam opprimi, s. eccl. exp. cap. VI. Dan.*, Darmst., 1610.

igsb., 1835. F. J. V. D. Maurer, *Commentar. gramm. crit. in V. T.*, vol. II, fasc. 1 (Ezech. et Dan.), 1836. F. Hitzig, *Kurzgefasstes exeget. Handbuch zum A. T.*; 10th pamphlet, *Das Buch Daniel*, Leips., 1850. C. A. Auberlen, *Der Prophet Daniel und die Offenbarung Johannis, in ihrem gegenseitigen Verhältniss betrachtet und in ihren Hauptstellen erläutert*, Basle, 1854, 1857 [in English, by Rev. A. Sophir, Edinb., 1856, 8vo.]. J. M. Gärtner, *Erklärung des Propheten Daniel und der Offenbarung Johannis, sowie der Weissagung von Hesekiel's Gog, in genauer Uebereinstimmung mit den Haupterscheinungen der Welt- und Kirchengeschichte seit der Gründung des babylonischen Weltreichs*, 606 *v. Chr., bis auf unsere Zeit und bis zur Wiederkunft Christi um das Ende unseres Jahrhunderts;* 6 numbers, Stuttgart, 1863 et seq. Rud. Kranichfeld, *Das Buch Daniel erklärt*, Berl., 1868. Kliefoth, *Das Buch Daniels übersetzt und erklärt*, Schwerin, 1868. Ad. Kamphausen, in Bunsen's *Bibelwerk*, 6 half vols., 1st half, Leips., 1867. H. Ewald, *Die Propheten des Alten Bundes*, 2d ed., vol. 3, Gött., 1868 (the first ed. contained merely a monograph exposition of chap. ix. 24–27—see infra). E. B. Pusey, *Lectures on Daniel the Prophet*, Oxford, 1864. [Füller, *Erklärung des P. Daniel*, Basle, 1868.]

(2) *Roman-Catholic expositors since the Reformation.* Arias Montanus, *Comment. in Dan.*, Antwerp, 1562. Hector Pintus, *Commentarii in Danielem, Lamentationes Jeremiæ et Nahum, divinos vates*, Coimbra, 1582; Venet., 1583; Colon., 1587. Bened. Pererius, *Commentariorum in Danielem proph.*, *ll. xvi.*, Rom., 1586; Lugd., 1588; Antv., 1594. Casp. Sanctius, *Comment. in Dan. proph.*, Lugd., 1612, 1619. Joh. Maldonatus, *Comment. in Jerem., Ezech., Dan.*, Leyd., 1611; Par., 1643. Jacob Veldius, *Comment. in Dan. proph. cum Chronologia ad intelligenda Jeremiæ, Ezech., et Dan. vaticinia*, Antv., 1602. Fabricius Paulitius, *Comm. in Dan.*, Rom., 1625. Ludov. ab Alcazar, *Comm. in varios locos l. Dan.*, Lugd., 1631. Cornelius à Lapide, August. Calmet, and Dereser-Scholz in their comprehensive Bible-works. G. K. Mayer (Prof. at Bamberg), *Die messianischen Prophezien des Daniel*, Vienna, 1866.

MONOGRAPHS.—For the *critical* and *apologetical literature*, or the principal monographs aiming to attack or defend the genuineness of the book (Bleek, Kirmss, Hävernick, Hengstenberg, Zündel, Füller, Volck, etc.), see supra, § 5.

Exegetical monographs: H. Venema, *Dissertationes* (see supra, II. 1 c). Thomas Newton, *Abhandlungen über die Weissagungen, welche merkwürdig erfüllt sind und noch bis auf den heutigen Tag in Erfüllung gehen;* from the English, Leips., 1757 (containing, on p. 304 et seq., an apologetical discussion of the visions concerning the world-kingdoms, chap. II. and VII., which is directed against Collins, Grotius, and others). J. G. Scharfenberg, *Specimen animadversionum, quibus loci nonnulli Danielis et vett. ejus interpretum, præsertim Græcorum, illustrantur et emendantur*, Lips., 1774. S. Th. Wald, *Curarum in historiam textus Danielis specim. I.*, Lips., 1783. Compare the essay by the same: *Ueber die arabische Uebersetzung des Daniel in den Polyglotten*, in Eichhorn's *Repert. für bibl. u. morgenl. Literatur*, part XIV., Leips., 1784. Laur. Reinke, *Die messian. Weissagungen bei den grossen und kleinen Propheten des A. T.*, vol. iv. 1, p. 167 et seq. (chiefly an exposition of chap. ix. 24–27), Giessen, 1862. H. Ewald, *Die Propheten des Alten Bundes*, 1st ed., Stuttgart, 1841, vol. II., appendix (likewise confined to the exposition of chap. ix. 24 et seq.) J. Chr. Hofmann, *Weissagung und Erfüllung im A. und N. T.*, I., p. 276 et seq., Nörd., 1841. The same, *Die 70 Jahre Jeremias und die 70 Jahrwochen des Daniel*, Nuremberg, 1836. K. Wieseler, *Die 70 Wochen und die 63 Jahrwochen des Propheten Daniel*, Götting., 1839. The most complete record of the older exegetical literature on Dan. ix. 24–27, or on the 70 weeks of years, may be found in Abrah. Calov's *Bibl. illustr.*, tom. I., p. 119 et seq., and in his monograph, *De LXX. septimanis mysterium*, Vitemb., 1663. Compare also Bertholdt, *Daniel*, etc., vol. II., p. 563 et seq.; Danko, *Historia revelationis divinæ Novi Testamenti*, p. lxxiii. et seq.; Ranke, as above, p. 211 et seq., and also Reusch, *Die patristischen Berechnungen der 70 Jahrwochen Daniels*, in the *Tübinger Theol. Quartalschrift*, 1868, No. IV., p. 535 et seq. [See also the monographs cited by Danz, *Wörterbuch*, s. v.; and Darling, *Cyclopædia*, ad loc.]

[III. *Additional exegetical works on Daniel in the English language.* 1. COMMENTARIES *on the entire book:* A. Willett, *A Six-fold Commentary on Daniel*, etc., Lond., 1610, fol. E. Huit, *The whole prophecies of Daniel explained*, etc., Lond., 1643, 4to. T. Parker, *The Visions and prophecies of Daniel expounded*, etc., Lond., 1646, 4to. H. More, *Exposition of the Prophet Daniel*, Lond., 1681, 4to; the same, *Answers to Remarks*, ibid., 1684, 4to; the same, *Supple-*

ment and Defences, ibid., 1685, 4to; the same, *Notes on Daniel and the Apocalypse*, ibid., 1685, 4to. Anon., *The visions and prophecies of Daniel explained*, etc., Lond., 1700, 12mo. E. Wells, *The Book of Daniel explained*, etc., Lond., 1716, 4to. R. Amner, *An Essay towards the interpretation of Daniel*, etc., Lond., 1776, 8vo. J. H. Frere, *A combined view of the prophecies of Daniel, Esdras, and St. John*, etc., Lond., 1815, 8vo. W. Girdlestone, *Observations on the visions of Daniel*, etc., Oxf., 1820, 8vo. J. Wilson, *Dissertations on the book of Daniel*, Oundle, 1824, 8vo. F. A. Coxe, *Outlines of lectures on Daniel*, 2d ed., Lond., 1834, 12mo. T. Wintle, *An improved Version of Daniel, with Notes*, Lond., 1836, 8vo. L. Gaussen, *Lectures on the Book of Daniel*, Lond., 1840, 12mo. C. P. Miles, *Lectures on Daniel*, Lond., 1840–41, 2 vols., 12mo. B. Harrison, *Prophetic Outlines of the Christian Church*, etc. (Warburton Lectures), Lond., 1849, 8vo. M. Stuart, *A Commentary on the Book of Daniel*, Andover, 1850, 8vo. A. Barnes, *Notes on Daniel*, N. Y., 1850, 12mo. J. Cumming, *Lectures on the Book of Daniel*, Lond., 1850, 8vo. W. Ramsay, *Exposition of the book of Daniel*, Lond., 1853, 12mo. J. Bellamy, *New Translation of the book of Daniel*, etc., Lond., 1863, 4to. W. Shrewsbury, *Notes on the book of Daniel*, Edinb., 1865, 8vo. P. S. Desprez, *The Apocalypse of the Old Test.*, Lond., 1865, 8vo. H. Cowles, *Ezekiel and Daniel, with Notes*, N. Y., 1867, 12mo. W. H. Rule, *Historical Exposition of the Book of Daniel*, Lond., 1869, 8vo. (adopts the year-day theory, and applies the little horn to the papacy). W. Kelly, *Notes on the Book of Daniel*, Edinb., 1870, 12mo. C. F. Keil, *The Book of the prophet Daniel* (being part of Keil and Delitzsch's *Commentary on the Old Testament*), Edinb., 1872, 8vo., from the German. L. Strong, *Lectures on the Book of Daniel*, Lond., 1872, 8vo. Prof. Gaussen, *The Prophesies of Daniel Explained*, translated by Blackstone, Lond., 1873, 8vo (makes the fourth kingdom Rome).

2. MONOGRAPHS.—T. Brightman, *Exposition of the last part of Daniel*, Lond., 1644, 4to. Anonymous, *An Essay on Scripture Prophecy*, s. l. [probably Lond.], 1724 (makes the fourth beast Rome). Z. Grey, *Examination of Sir Isaac Newton's Observations upon Daniel*, etc. (treats only of the special points named in the title), Lond., 1736, 8vo. G. Burton, *An Essay on the Numbers of Daniel and St. John*, Norwich, 1766–68, 2 vols., 8vo. Anon., *Seven prophetical periods*, etc., Lond., 1790, 4to. G. S. Faber, *Dissertation on Daniel's 70 Weeks* (makes them extend from the 17th of Artaxerxes to the 15th of Tiberius), Lond., 1811, 8vo. See also his *Sacred Calendar of Prophecy*, Lond., 1828, 3 vols. 8vo., in which he argues at length for the year-day theory. E. Irving, *Babylon and Infidelity foredoomed*, etc. (adopts the year-day theory with its consequences), Glasgow, 1826, 2 vols. 8vo.; ibid, 1828, 8vo. J. Tyso, *An elucidation*, etc., *showing that the Seventy Weeks have not yet taken place*, Lond., 1838, 8vo. J. Farquharson, *Illustrations of Daniel's last vision and prophecy*, Lond., 1838, 8vo. N. S. Folsom, *Interpretation of the prophecies of Daniel* (against Millerism, and of course rejects the reference of the fourth kingdom to Rome), Boston, 1842, 12mo. I. T. Hinton, *Prophecies of Daniel and John* (applies the third empire to the Turks, and the fourth to Rome), St. Louis, 1843, 12mo. I. Chase, *Remarks on the Book of Daniel* (applies the "little horn" exclusively to Antiochus Epiphanes), Boston, 1844, 12mo. G. Junkin, *The Little Stone of the Great Image* (interprets the "little horn" of the Papacy), Phila., 1844, 8vo. T. R. Birks, *The two later visions of Daniel* (makes the fourth kingdom Rome), Lond., 1846, 12mo. S. Lee, *Events and Times of the Visions of Daniel and St. John* (makes the "little horn" exclusively *heathen* Rome), London, 1851, 8vo. A. M. Osbon, *Daniel verified in History*, etc. (makes the fourth kingdom Rome), N. Y., 1856, 12mo. J. Oswald, *The kingdom which shall not be destroyed*, etc. (makes the fourth kingdom Rome), Phila., 1856, 12mo. S. Sparkes, *A Historical Commentary on Daniel xi.* (adopts the year-day theory, and applies the whole chapter to modern times), Binghamton, 1858, 8vo. W. R. A. Boyle, *The Inspiration of the Book of Daniel* (applies the fourth kindom to the Roman Empire), Lond., 1863, 8vo. S. P. Tregelles, *Remarks on the Visions of Daniel*, etc. (rejects the year-day theory with its conclusions), Lond., fifth ed., 1864, 12mo. R. Phillips, *On Daniel's Numbers*, Lond., 1864, 12mo. L. A. Sawyer, *Daniel with its apocryphal additions* (a new translation), Bost., 1864, 12mo. R. A. Watkinson, *The End as foretold in Daniel*, etc. (adopts the year-day theory), N. Y., 1865, 12mo. F. W. Bosanquet, *Messiah the Prince*, Lond., 1866, 8vo. H. W. Taylor, *The Times of Daniel* (adopts the year-day theory), N. Y., 1871, 12mo. H. Loomis, *The Great Conflict* (makes the little horn the Papacy), N. Y., 1874, 12mo.]

THE

BOOK OF THE PROPHET DANIEL.

FIRST (HISTORICAL) PART.

CHAPTERS I.–VI.

1. *Introduction. The Early History of Daniel and his Three Associates.*

I. 1–21.

1 In *the* third year of *the* reign of Jehoiakim king of Judah came Nebuchad-
2 nezzar king of Babylon *unto* Jerusalem and besieged it.[1] And *the* Lord gave
Jehoiakim king of Judah into his hand, with [and] part of *the* vessels of *the* house of
God, which [and] he carried [them] *into the* land of Shinar, *to the* house of his god;[2]
and he brought the vessels *into the* treasure-house[3] of his god.[2]
3 And the king spake[4] unto Ashpenaz the master[5] of his eunuchs, that he should
bring [to bring] *certain* of *the* children of Israel, and of the king's seed,[6] and of the
4 princes;[7] children[8] in whom *was* no blemish, but [and] well-favoured,[9] and skilful[10]
in all wisdom, and cunning[11] in knowledge, and understanding[12] science, and such
as had ability[13] in them [in whom *was* ability] to stand in the king's palace, and
whom *they might* teach[14] *the* learning[15] and the tongue of *the* Chaldæans.
5 And the king appointed them a daily provision[16] of the king's meat,[17] *and* of
the wine *which* he drank; so nourishing [, and to make grow] them three years,
that [; and] at the end thereof they might [should] stand before the king.
6 Now [And] among these [them] were of the children of Judah, Daniel, Hana-
7 niah [Chananyah], Mishael, and Azariah; unto whom [and to them] *the* prince
of the eunuchs gave [assigned] names: for he gave [and he assigned] unto Daniel,
the name of Belteshazzar; and to Hananiah, *of* Shadrach; and to Mishael, *of*
Meshach; and to Azariah, *of* Abed-nego.
8 But [And] Daniel purposed in[18] his heart that he would not defile himself with
the portion of the king's meat,[17] nor [and] with *the* wine *which* he drank: there-
fore [and] he requested of the prince of the eunuchs that he might not defile
9 himself. Now [And] God *had* brought [gave] Daniel into favour and tender
10 love[19] with [before] the prince of the eunuchs. And the prince of the
eunuchs said unto Daniel, I fear my lord the king, who hath appointed your
meat [food] and your drink:[20] for why should he see your faces worse liking
[more gloomy] than the children[8] which *are* of your sort?[21] then shall [, and
should] ye make *me* endanger my head to the king?
11 Then [And] said Daniel to [the] Melzar, whom the prince of the eunuchs
12 had set over Daniel, Hananiah, Mishael, and Azariah: Prove thy servants, I
beseech thee, ten days; and let them give us pulse to eat,[22] and water to drink.
13 Then [And] let our countenances be looked upon before thee, and the counte-
nance of the children[8] that eat of the portion of the king's meat;[17] and as thou
14 seest [shalt see], deal [do] with thy servants. So he consented [And he
15 hearkened] to them in [as to] this matter, and proved them ten days. And at
the end of ten days their countenances appeared [countenance was seen *to be*
good] fairer and [they were] fatter in [of] flesh than all the children[8] which did

16 eat *the portion of* the king's meat.[17] Thus [And the] Melzar took away *the*
portion of their meat,[17] and *the* wine *that* they *should* drink and gave them pulse.[22]
17 [And] *As for* these four children,[8] God gave them knowledge and skill in all
learning[15] and wisdom: and Daniel had understanding in all visions [every
vision] and dreams.
18 Now, [And] at the end of the days that the king had said[4] he should [to]
bring them *in*, then the prince of the eunuchs brought them *in* before Nebuchad-
19 nezzar. And the king communed [spake] with them: and among them all
was found none like Daniel, Hananiah, Mishael, and Azariah: therefore
20 [and] stood they before the king. And in all matters [every matter] of wisdom
and understanding, that the king inquired of them, [then] he found them ten
times better than[23] all the magicians[24] *and* astrologers[25] that *were* in all his
realm.
21 And Daniel continued[26] *even* unto *the* first year of king Cyrus.

GRAMMATICAL AND LEXICAL NOTES.

[[1] וַיָּצַר עָלֶיהָ, *and pressed upon it*, namely, with the usual military appliances.—[2] אֱלֹהָיו, *his gods*, probably referring to the Babylonian polytheism, in contrast with the true God above, הָאֱלֹהִים.—[3] בֵּית אוֹצַר, *store-house*, some room connected with the temple of Belus.—[4] וַיֹּאמֶר, *and said*, in the Chaldaïzing sense of *commanded*.—[5] רַב, *chief*, principal or head man.—[6] זֶרַע הַמְּלוּכָה, *seed of the kingdom*, namely, of Judah.—[7] הַפַּרְתְּמִים, *the nobles*, a Persic word denoting *the aristocracy*.—[8] יְלָדִים, *youths*, or lads, between infancy and adolescence.—[9] טוֹבֵי מַרְאֶה, *good of appearance*, *i.e.*, *handsome*.—[10] מַשְׂכִּלִים, *intelligent*, *i.e.*, of quick natural parts.—[11] יֹדְעֵי, *knowing*, *i.e.*, by acquired information.—[12] מְבִינֵי, *considerate*, *i.e.*, of attentive habits.—[13] כֹּחַ, *vigor*, *i.e.*, physical strength, and perhaps including mental energy.—[14] וּלְלַמְּדָם, *and to teach them*, *i.e.*, cause them to be instructed. This clause is to be connected in construction with the preceding לְהָבִיא, ver. 3.—[15] סֵפֶר, *book*, *i.e.*, the formularies or written mysteries.—[16] דְּבַר יוֹם בְּיוֹמוֹ, *a word* (or *matter*) *of a day in its day*, a regular ration from day to day.—[17] פַּתְבַּג, *delicacy*, a Persian word denoting *luxurious viands*.—[18] וַיָּשֶׂם עַל, *assigned upon*, *i.e.*, imposed this as a conscientious duty.—[19] רַחֲמִים, *mercies*, *i.e.*, kind consideration of his scruples.—[20] מַשְׁתֵּיכֶם, is regarded by the Grammarians as an instance of an epenthetic י in the *sing.*, or perhaps an older form of the construction in which the final ה has given place to a cognate letter.—[21] כְּגִילְכֶם, *according to your circle*, *i.e.*, in point of age and rank. There is, however, possibly an allusion to their emasculated condition. Eunuchs are constantly represented on the Assyrian monuments as being of fuller habit than other men.—[22] מִן־הַזֵּרֹעִים וְנֹאכְלָה, *of the seed*-fruits, *and we will surely eat*, *i.e.*, exclusively vegetable diet.—[23] עֶשֶׂר יָדוֹת עַל, *ten hands* (*parts*) *above*, ten-fold superior to.—[24] חַרְטֻמִּים is generally explained by the lexicographers as derived from חֶרֶט, *a style*, hence *scribes*, the Magian ἱερογραμματεῖς. Perhaps it signifies *horoscopists*.—[25] אַשָּׁפִים, from אָשַׁף, to whisper incantation, hence are *magicians* in the broad sence.—[26] וַיְהִי, *was* alive and influential in that official capacity.]

EXEGETICAL REMARKS.

Verses 1, 2. *The transportation to Babylon, by Nebuchadnezzar.*—**In the third year of the reign of Jehoiakim.** We have already shown, in the Introd., § 8, note 2, that this does not conflict with Jer. xxv. 1, 9.—**Came Nebuchadnezzar, king of Babylon, unto Jerusalem, and besieged it**, i. e., he departed for Jerusalem, in order to besiege it; he *began* his expedition against Jerusalem, which resulted in the siege of that city. For the view that בּוֹא is here to be taken in the sense of "departing," see the Introd., § 8, 2, a.—Instead of הֵצַר עַל, *to straiten*, besiege, we generally find elsewhere הֵצַר with the dative, e. g., Deut. xxviii, 52; 1 Kings viii. 37.—The form of the name נְבוּכַדְנֶאצַּר is the one in general use among the later Hebrew writers (cf. 2 Kings xxiv. 1; xxv. 1; Ezra ii. 1; v. 12, etc.). Jeremiah (xxv. 1; xxxix. 1, 11; xliii. 10) and Ezekiel (xxix. 18) have נְבוּכַדְרֶאצַּר, which corresponds more exactly to the older rendering *Nabukudurr-usur*, as found in the Babylonian cuneiform inscriptions, and also to the nearly identical Persian form *Nabukhadraçara*, which occurs at Behistun (see Oppert, *Journ. Asiat.*, 1851, p. 416; *Expédit. en Mésopotamie*, ii. 257 ss.). The name certainly comprehends, as its first element, the name of the Chaldæan god *Nebo*, = Mercury (נְבוֹ, Isa. xlvi. 1), and it seems also to include the terms *kadr*, "might," and *zar* = שַׂר, "prince" (compare Gesenius, *Thesaur.*, p. 890; Oppert, l. c.). The name is rendered with either *n* or *r* by Greek authors; for while Strabo (15, i. 6) writes Ναβοκοδρόσορος, Berosus (in Josephus *contr. Ap.*, i. 20, 21) has Ναβουχοδορόσορος, and the Sept.

Ναβουχοδονόσορ. Instead of נְבוּכַדְנֶאצַּר, however, our book elsewhere has uniformly ־נֶצַּר, omitting the euphonic א; cf. גּוֹ, chap. iii. 25; vii. 15, instead of גּוֹא, chap. iii. 6, 11, etc.; iv. 7.

[According to Ptolemy's chronological *canon* of the reigns of the Babylonian kings, Nebuchadnezzar became king near the close of B.C. 605, whereas his expedition in question, falling in the third year of Jehoiakim, occurred late in B.C. 607, and the capture of the city, in Jehoiakim's fourth year, fell about the middle of B.C. 606. It appears, however (Josephus *Antiq.* x. 11, 1), that his father, Nabopolassar, during his own lifetime, and near the close of his reign, had sent him to repel Pharaoh-Necho at Carchemish, and on his way back, Nebuchadnezzar captured Jerusalem, as related by Daniel. While he was engaged in this campaign, his father died, and he hastened back to Babylon in order to assume the reins of government. By the Jews, therefore, his reign is naturally reckoned from the date of this conquering expedition, although he did not actually become full king at Babylon till a year or more later.]

Verse 2. **And the Lord gave . . . into his hand,** *i.e.*, into his power. Compare Gen. ix. 2, 20; Ex. iv. 21; 2 Sam. xviii. 2; also Ps. xcv. 7, etc. The designation of Jehovah simply as "Lord" (אֲדֹנָי) is not confined to later writers, *e. g.*, Ezra x. 3; Neh. i. 11, but occurs as early as Gen. xviii. 27; Judges xiii. 8; Psa. xvi. 2; xxxv. 23, etc.—**Jehoiakim, king of Judah.** Jehoiakim reigned eleven years, according to 2 Kings xxiii. 36; 2 Chron. xxxvi. 5, while the conquest by Nebuchadnezzar here referred to can hardly have taken place later than the fourth year of this reign (see Introd. § 8, Note 2, and particularly what is there remarked in opposition to Kranichfeld). Hence it is impossible to consider the passage before us as describing a conquest which put an end to the rule of Jehoiakim, but rather an event which resulted in his becoming the vassal of Nebuchadnezzar; or, more correctly, of Nabopolassar, who was yet living. Similarly, what follows does not assert an actual banishment of Jehoiakim, but merely his temporary removal to Babylon, and perhaps not even this.—**And a part of the vessels of the house of God,** *i.e.*, of the sacred vessels of the temple, which are again mentioned in chap. v. 2 et seq.*—מִקְצָת, instead of which several manuscripts have מִקְצַת (cf. Theodotion's ἀπὸ μέρους), is compounded of קְצָת "end," and the preposition מִן, and, therefore, its literal meaning is "from the end," "on expiration," in which sense it occurs in vs. 5, 15, and 18 of this chapter. In this place, where it serves to designate a quantity instead of denoting time, it evidently expresses the idea of an integral part, a considerable part, like the Chaldee מִן קְצָת in chap. ii. 42, and like מִקְצָת in Neh. vii. 70. In explaining this meaning it is not necessary to assume (with Hitzig) that קְצָת may here be equivalent to "a part," for the word bears this sense in no other instance. The word, rather, indicates that the store in question, *from end to end*, has contributed a share, and throughout its extent some portion has been taken away. Hence "from the end of the vessels of the temple" signifies merely a portion of all its vessels. Cf. Kranichfeld on this passage; Gesen.-Dietrich s. v. קצת. [Fürst, however (*Heb. Lex.* s. v.), adopts the simple explanation that מִקְצָת is merely an alternative form of קְצָת, and this is certainly corroborated by the form וּלְמִקְצָת, chap. i. 18, where two prepositions cannot be tolerated.] This view is also essentially established by 2 Chron. xxxvi. 7: וּמִכְּלֵי בֵּית יְהוָה הֵבִיא נְבוּכַדְנֶאצַּר לְבָבֶל.—**Which he carried into the land of Shinar;** rather, "And he caused them to be brought to the land of Shinar,"—to Babylonia, which province is here called by the ancient name that occurs outside of Genesis (see Gen. x. 10; xi. 2; xiv. 1), only in the elevated language of the prophets, *e.g.*, in Isa. xi. 11; Zech. v. 11.—The suffix in וַיְבִיאֵם "and he caused them to be taken away," can hardly be taken (as do Hävern. and others) as referring exclusively to the sacred vessels, the mention of which immediately precedes this sentence; for the following words refer to them again, and thus distinguish them as a particular of the collective object of the verb הֵבִיא.* We are not obliged, however, to include the king Jehoiakim among those who were carried away with the sacred utensils; for while the narrative in its progress postulates the presence in Babylon of Jewish youths belonging to the royal and to noble families, it never implies the presence of the king himself (cf. vs. 3, 6; also v. 13); and while it is related in 2 Chron. xxxvi. 6, that Nebuchadnezzar bound Jehoiakim "in fetters, to carry him to Babylon," it is not expressly stated that he executed that purpose. The Sept. (καὶ ἔδησεν αὐτὸν ἐν χαλκαῖς πέδαις καὶ ἀνήγαγεν αὐτὸν εἰς Βαβυλῶνα) first imposed this sense on the passage, because they felt compelled to assume an actual deportation of Jehoiakim, followed by his return to Jerusalem at a later period—an opinion which was shared by the writer of the 3d Book of Esdras and the Vulgate, and by several rabbins of the Middle Ages, *e.g.*, Ibn-Ezra. While the passage before us does not directly contradict this assumption, which represents the fate of Jehoiakim as very similar to that of Manasseh (2 Chron. xxxiii. 13), it does not necessarily compel its adoption.

* ["Daniel is careful to say (with historical accuracy) that at this time the king of Babylon took away only a part of the vessels of the temple. Many more were taken during the short reign of Jeconiah (see 2 Kings xxiv. 13), and yet some were left behind even then, to be taken at the final destruction of the city in the reign of Zedekiah (Jer. xxvii. 19-22)."—*Cowles.*]

* [Stuart, on the contrary, insists that the following clause compels us to understand the same object of הֵבִיא in both cases; but he overstrains the particle אֵת by the rendering "*the same.*" The English Auth. Version interprets in a similar manner. But the latter clause certainly implies a distinction between the objects carried away, some of which were deposited in a particular spot. The author is, therefore, correct in understanding the *associates* of the king to be included generally under the mention of his name, but not himself particularly; he is inconsistent, however, a little farther on, as we shall see, in destroying the whole foundation of this distinction, in the interpretation of the last clause of the verse.]

Jehoiakim may be included among the transported Jews who are designated by the plural suffix in ויביאם; but, on the other hand, the suffix may, in addition to the temple-vessels, simply designate a band of noble Jews, whom the conqueror carried away as hostages, and to which the youth referred to in v. 3 et seq. belonged—hence those יְהוּדִים, whose presence may be gathered from the collective singular יְהוּדָה, to which reference has already been made (Kranichfeld; cf. Ibn-Ezra, Maldonat, Geier, and others; also Bertheau in *Kurzgefasstes exeg. Handbuch zur Chronik*, p. 427).—**To the house of his god**—rather "to the dwelling-place of his gods." בֵּית־אֱלֹהָיו is probably to be regarded as in opposition with אֶרֶץ שִׁנְעָר; for the sacred vessels of the temple at Jerusalem, as has been shown, formed only a part of the object in וַיְבִיאֵם; and, besides, if בֵּית־אֱלֹהָיו in this place were intended to designate the temple of Nebuchadnezzar's god (or gods), usage would require the particle אֶל in order to manifest the object towards which the motion is directed (see Gen. xxxi. 4; Isa. xxxvii. 23; Zech. xi. 13). The correct view is stated by Hitzig and Kranichfeld, who refer to Hos. viii. 1; ix. 15; Ex. xxix. 45; Num. xxxv. 3, etc., in support of the tropical signification, which takes בַּיִת in the sense of "land or dwelling-place." [Keil, however, shows the inaccuracy of this criticism, on grammatical grounds. Moreover, in this way the distinction evidently intended between the different classes of objects transported, is wholly taken away; the *persons* were merely removed to Babylon, but the utensils were lodged in a heathen temple, as they before had belonged to Jehovah's. The parallel history, 2 Chron. xxxvi. 6, 7, states all this explicitly. Daniel here merely rehearses the facts in a general way, but is nevertheless careful to mention the disposal, both of the captives, of whom he was himself one (chap. ii. 25), and the vessels, which afterwards became so important in his narrative (chap. v. 2, 23).] Whether the genitive אֱלֹהָיו be translated "of his gods" (cf. chap. ii. 47; iii. 29; iv. 6, 15) or "of his god," is unimportant. In the latter case, the reference is to Bel, the chief divinity of the Babylonians; cf. Isa. xlvi. 1; Jer. l. 2; li. 44.—**And he brought the vessels into the treasure-house of his gods** (or "his god," viz.: Bel). On בֵּית אוֹצָר, treasure-house γαζοφυλάκιον, compare Mal. iii. 10; Neh. xiii. 5, 12, 13, where the treasury of the second temple is the subject of remark. There is no contradiction between this passage and chap. v. 2 et seq. where the sacred vessels are profaned by Belshazzar, and thus appear to have been stored in his palace. Belshazzar was not Nebuchadnezzar, and it is conceivable that the son could trample in the mire what his father and predecessor had valued and reserved (cf. Ephr. Syr. on this passage). Nor is there a contradiction of 2 Chron. xxxvi. 7; the statement in that passage: "And he put them in his palace" (בְּהֵיכָלוֹ; A. V. "temple"), is merely less exact than the one before us; [or rather, perhaps, הֵיכָל is then used in its frequent signification of *temple*, as all the older versions render, and the suffix "*his*" designates it as that of his favorite deity].

Verses 3, 4. *The selection of youthful Jews of noble rank for service at the royal court.* **And the king spake unto** (commanded) **Ashpenaz, the master of his eunuchs.** אַשְׁפְּנַז, a name, whose formation is very similar to that of אַשְׁכְּנַז, Gen. x. 3, but not to be identified with it on that account (as Hitzig suggests) without further inquiry. It appears to be of Indo-Germanic origin, and, according to Rödiger, is compounded of the Sanscrit *açva*, "horse," and *nasa*, "nose." It is, therefore, equivalent to "horse-nose."—רַב סָרִיסִים, the chief of the eunuchs (Sept. ἀρχιεύνουχος; Vulgate, *præpositus eunuchorum*), an important and influential officer of the palace at Oriental courts, as may be shown from the position of the *Kislar-Aga* at the Turkish court in our day. However, neither he nor his subordinates are to be regarded as actual eunuchs, but rather as ordinary chamberlains (Luther: "*oberster Kämmerer*"). Compare Gen. xxxvii. 36; xxxix. 1, 7, where Joseph's master at the court of Pharaoh is called סָרִיס, although he was married; also 1 Sam. viii. 15; 1 Kings xxii. 9; xxv. 19, etc., in all of which the rendering of סָרִיס by "chamberlain" or court-official is adequate. However, the subordinates of Ashpenaz, mentioned in the passage under consideration, may be regarded as actual eunuchs (as also those in Esth. i. 10, 12, 15; ii. 3, 14; iv. 5), without necessitating the conclusion that Daniel and his associates also became eunuchs, on their being placed under his supervision. Only a grossly carnal conception of the facts narrated in this chapter, and of Isaiah's prophecy, Isa. xxxix. 7 (where סריס likewise means [or may mean] an official generally) could lead to this opinion, which is entertained by a number of Jewish and older Christian commentators, *e.g.*, Josephus, *Antiquit.*, x. 11; the Targum, on Esther iv. 5; Rashi, on Dan. i. 21; Origen *Homil.* iv. on Ezek.; Jerome, *adv. Jovin.* i. 1; and Joh. Damascenus, *De fide orthod.* iv. 25.* It is not even possible to argue from the relations of Daniel to the master of the eunuchs, as indicated in this passage, that the prophet always remained unmarried (as Pseudo-Epiphanius *De vit. prophet.*, c. 10, Cornelius a Lapide, Huetius, and others, suggest). See the Introd., § 2.—**That he should bring certain of the children of Israel**—*i.e.*, to choose of the children of Israel, viz.: of the Jews, who had been carried to Babylon as hostages, cf. v. 2. The more comprehensive phrase, "the children of Israel," is justified by the fact that the theocratic state under Jehoiakim included all of the tribes of Benjamin and Levi, and at least fragments of several other tribes, especially of Simeon (2 Chron. xv. 9), in addi-

* [Rather, a strictly literal interpretation of Isa. xxxix. 7, as well as all the probabilities and analogies of the case, requires this view, which the majority of commentators have accordingly taken. The case of Joseph's master affords no difficulty, for eunuchs of high rank are often married (cf. Ecclus. xx. 4; xxv. 20); indeed the supposition of his impotence affords some explanation of his wife's solicitation of Joseph.]

tion to the leading tribe of Judah.—**And of the king's seed, and of the princes**—rather, "of the royal seed, as well as of the number of nobles." Instead of this correlative view of the two ו's—the only correct view—which is found in Von Lengerke, and in Hitzig, and others, Bertholdt, without reason, adopts the designative (*either—or*), while a majority, including Hävernick, take the first ו (before זֶרַע, which, however, is wanting in several of Kennicott's and De Rossi's manuscripts,—but the authenticity of which is not, on that account, to be questioned) in the sense of "and indeed," "namely,"—hence as marking the use of an emphatic apposition. Our view is supported by parallel passages, such as chap. vii. 20; viii. 13, etc.—The term הַפַּרְתְּמִים, "nobles," "magnates," which occurs only here and in Esth. i. 3; vi. 9, seems to be borrowed from the Persian, and to be equivalent to the Pehlevi *pardom*, "the first," "the noble;" cf. the Sanscrit *prathama*, Zend *frathema*, Greek πρῶτος. Its derivation from the Greek πρότιμοι, essayed by Bertholdt, as well as the opinion which prevailed among older expositors, that the word is of Hebrew origin, and perhaps related to פרח, *invaluit*, are to be decisively rejected. The corresponding term in Hebrew is אֵילִים, the strong or powerful ones: Ex. xv. 15; Ezek. xvii. 13; 2 Kings xxiv. 15.—Verse 4. **Children in whom was no blemish,** *i.e.*, no physical fault; hence, of faultless beauty; compare 2 Sam. xiv. 25. (Cf. the form מאוּם in the Kethib in this place with Job xxxi. 7.) Corporeal soundness and a handsome form were considered indispensible among the ancient Orientals (cf. Curtius, vi. 5, 29), for those who were destined for court service,—a view which is still shared by the Turks; see Ricaut. *Gegenwärt. Zustand des türk. Reiches*, i. 13.—The indefinite יְלָדִים does not admit of a definite conclusion respecting the age of the youths, and particularly of Daniel. The remark in Plato, *Alcib.* i. § 37, however, according to which the training of the Persian youth by the παιδαγωγοὶ βασίλειοι began with the 14th year, has a certain importance for speculations on this question, which is enhanced by the statement of Xenophon, *Cyrop.* i. 2, that none of the ἔφηβοι might enter the service of the king before they attained their 17th year. What is said in v. 5 concerning a period of three years during which Daniel was in training, corresponds remarkably with these statements. —**Skilful in all wisdom.** The intellectual qualifications are immediately connected with the physical. Hävernick, Hitzig, and others, are correct in taking מַשְׂכִּילִים in the sense of "discerning, understanding," rather than "versed, or experienced,"—as denoting aptitudo rather than habitus. "חכמה, as כל indicates, is the objective wisdom, which is displayed in the various fields of knowledge, and, according to v. 17, is contained in books" (Hitzig)—hence scientific, as distinguished from the purely practical wisdom, which elsewhere is generally referred to.—**Cunning in knowledge, and understanding;** literally "knowing knowledge" (יֹדְעֵי דַעַת) and "understanding thought" (וּמְבִינֵי מַדָּע). On מַדָּע "thought" (elsewhere "knowledge"), compare Eccles. x. 20, and on both phrases compare chap. ii. 21; Neh. x. 29.—**And such as had ability in them to stand in the king's palace,** literally "who had power (כֹּחַ, here [perhaps] *ability, talent;* compare viii. 7; xi. 15) to stand in the king's palace" (לַעֲמֹד בְּהֵיכַל הַמֶּלֶךְ,—for which לַעֲבֹד בה is not to be substituted). "To stand in the king's palace" is the same as "to stand before the king" (cf. Gen. xviii. 8; xli. 46; Deut. i. 38, etc.), *i.e.*, to await his commands, to serve him. See below, v. 17, and compare the absolute הָעֹמְדִים, *the servants*, in Zech. iii. 7; also Esth. v. 2.—**And whom they might teach the learning and the tongue of the Chaldæans;** literally, "and to teach them the learning," etc. וּלְלַמְּדָם depends on the verb וַיֹּאמֶר v. 3, and is co-ordinate with לְהָבִיא in the same verse, as the preceding *athnâch* indicates.—ספר, "writing," does not in this place denote the art of writing, but the learning of the Chaldæans; compare כָּל־סֵפֶר v. 17, which can only be equivalent to *all learning*, "all literary knowledge." Further, לְשׁוֹן כַּשְׂדִּים can hardly signify the Aramæan idiom which begins with chap. ii. 4, but designates the original Chaldee, which was of Japhetic origin, or tinctured with Japhetic elements—as Michaelis, Bertholdt, Winer, Hävernick, Lengerke, Hengstenberg, and others, hold.* That the noble Jewish youths should be compelled to learn the Aramæan dialect, which, according to 2 Kings xviii. 26 et seq. (Isa. xxxvi. 11), was the official language both at the Assyrian and the Babylonian courts, admits, indeed, of an easy explanation; since the Jews of that time were but slightly acquainted with that dialect (cf. 2 Kings, in the above mentioned place), and since youth especially, of whatever rank, could not have been instructed in this language, which was indeed related to the Hebrew, but was nevertheless a foreign tongue. The view which identifies the "tongue of the Chaldæans" with the official Aramæan of the court, is untenable because of the circumstance that the latter is introduced in chap. ii. 4 by the term אֲרָמִית (cf. Isa. xxxvi. 11; Ezra iv. 7), and is thus clearly distinguished from the ordinary language of the כַּשְׂדִּים. (See notes on that passage, and compare Introd. § 1, note 3.)

Verse 5. *The provision for the selected youth, and their training.* **And the king appointed them a daily,** etc. "Them," *i.e.*, those who should be selected, but whom the king did not yet know. מִנָּה, *to ordain*, appoint, *assignare*, compare v. 10.—דְּבַר יוֹם בְּיוֹמוֹ, literally, "matter of the day in its day," *i.e.*, *a daily supply*, or ration. Compare Jer. lii. 34, where the same expression is used with reference to the daily food of the captive Jehoiachin; also Ex. v. 13, 19; Lev. xxiii. 7, etc.—**Of the king's meat,**—of which, according to Oriental custom,

*[Others, however, maintain that it was of Hamitic affinity. The subject of the origin of the כַּשְׂדִּים is very difficult. See the note in Keil ad loc.]

not only noble guests (cf. Jer. as cited above), but also all the servants and officials were accustomed to partake, compare 1 Kings v. 2, 3; and concerning the custom in question at the Persian court, see Athenæus, iv. 10, p. 69; Plutarch, *Probl.* vii. 4.—פַּתְבַּג "meat," really *delicacies*, luxurious food, is of Persian origin,—a composite word formed out of *bag*, "tribute" (cf. Sanscrit *bhaga*, "allowance," "ration"), and the preposition *paiti*, "towards, to," (= Sanscrit *prati*, Greek προτί, πρός)—and hence is equivalent to "apportioned food," which sense is also expressed by the Sanscrit *pratibhaga*, which designates the daily proportion of fruits, flowers, etc., required by the rajah in his household. Cf. Gildemeister in the *Zeitschrift für Kunde des Morgenlandes*, iv. 214.—**And of the wine which he drank**, properly "of the wine of his drinking," his banquet. מִשְׁתָּיו is to be taken in the singular in this place, as well as in vs. 8 and 10.—**So nourishing them three years**, rather, "and (commanded) to instruct them three years"—properly "educate," "bring up" [but literally, "to make great"—perhaps referring primarily to their physical culture]. The infinitive וּלְגַדְּלָם with a copulative ו certainly does not depend on וַיֹּאמֶר in v. 3; but rather is to be regarded as governed by וַיְמַן, from whose signification the idea of *commanding*, *ordaining*, is zeugmatically derived. Compare מִנָּה in v. 11; also Jonah ii. 1.—**That at the end thereof they might stand before the king**, *i.e.*, after the three years had expired. "To stand before the king" is "to serve him," cf. v. 3. ["*Standing* was the position of waiters in readiness to do their master's will."—*Stuart.*]

Verses 6, 7. *The names of Daniel and his associates, and their changing.*—**Now among these were of the children of Judah**, hence, belonging to the most prominent tribe, after which the entire nation was usually called, even at that early period. The four youths are here shown to be Jewish פַּרְתְּמִים (v. 3); but it does not follow from this passage that all of them, and Daniel in particular, were, in addition, of royal family (מִזֶּרַע הַמְּלוּכָה, v. 3).* The royal descent of Daniel can only be conjectured; that Zedekiah was his father, as is stated by Josephus, is a mere supposition. Compare Introd. § 2, where the names Daniel, Hananiah, Mishael, and Azariah have been sufficiently considered (cf. also note 1 to that §). Verse 7. **Unto whom the prince of the eunuchs gave** (other) **names**, rather, "and the prince . . . gave them." The changing of names as a sign of entrance into the condition of subjection to a ruler, is a frequently attested custom of Oriental and classical antiquity. Compare Gen. xli. 45 (Joseph); 2 Kings xxiii. 34 (Eliakim); 2 Kings xxiv. 17 (Matthaniah = Zedekiah); the re-naming of pupils by their preceptors, *e.g.*, 2 Sam. xii. 25 (Solomon = Jedediah); Mark iii. 16 (Simon = Peter); and respecting this custom among the Greeks and Romans, Theodoret, on our passage; Chrysostom, *Opp.* v. 286, etc. ["But while the kings referred to only had their paternal names changed for other Israelitish names, which were given them by their conquerors, Daniel and his friends received genuine heathen names in exchange for their own significant names, which were associated with that of the true God."—*Keil.*] **For he gave unto Daniel the name of Belteshazzar**, etc.; rather, "and he called Daniel Belteshazzar." The four new names of the youths doubtless contain, without exception, a reference to the divinities of Babylon. This is apparent in the name בֵּלְטְשַׁאצַּר (cf. chap. iv. 5),—with which the royal name בֵּלְשַׁאצַּר is probably identical—whether, as a majority hold, we find the name of the god בֵּל in it, and explain its composition perhaps by *Beli princeps* (which the expression of Nebuchadnezzar himself in chap. iv. 5 seems to endorse), or prefer Hitzig's more artificial interpretation = *Pâlâ tschâçara*, "nourisher and devourer." עֲבֵד נְגוֹ likewise (for which the scriptio plena, chap. iii. 29, is ע' נְגוֹא) is certainly equivalent to "adorer of Nego," which divinity is probably not the same as Nebo (Saadia, Hitz., Kranichf., and others), but a reptile god, and perhaps the familiar dragon of the apocryphal book *Bel and the Dragon*—since the comparison of the Sanscrit *nâga*, serpent, with this name, which was first essayed by Rödiger, affords a more likely conception than the transmutation of ב into ג. But שַׁדְרַךְ, which may be identical with חַדְרָךְ, Zech. ix. 1 (cf. Köhler, *Sacharia*, 2d pt., p. 18) also seems to designate a divinity, and possibly, in case it is based on the root חדר or הזר, "to move in a circle," the *sun-god*. מֵישַׁךְ may be the same as the Sanscrit *mêschach*, "stag," and therefore denote a god likewise belonging to the siderial domain; whether the sun-god be again intended, as Hitzig supposes, must remain doubtful (but see Hitzig on this place).

Verses 8-10. *Daniel's request, and the refusal of the master of the eunuchs to entertain it.* **But Daniel purposed in his heart.** So the A. V. and Luther, literally, but less agreeable to the sense of וַיָּשֶׂם עַל לִבּוֹ than "he was concerned," as Bertholdt properly renders it. **That he would** (better "should") **not defile himself with the king's meat.** The Sept. renders אשר לא יתגאל by ὅπως μὴ ἀλισγηθῇ; cf. ἀλισγήματα, Acts xv. 20. The reason for the refusal of the פַּתְבַּג, *i.e.*, the ordinary food of the king, as well as of the wine from his table (cf. v. 5), by Daniel and his associates, arose doubtless from the heathenish custom of consecrating each meal, by offering a portion to the gods.* In order to prevent their being involved

* [Much less does it follow "that the other youths of noble descent, who had been carried away along with them, belonged to other tribes" (Keil ad loc.), for (as the same commentator immediately adds), "the names of Daniel and his three companions only are mentioned, because their history recorded in this book brings them specially under our notice."]

* [That the special reason for their abstinence was not the Levitical distinction of "clean" and "unclean" animals, is evident from their rejection of the wine likewise, which the Mosaic law allowed. In addition to the reason assigned by our author, we suspect some sanitary

in idolatry by partaking of food which had been thus dedicated to the gods (cf. 1 Cor. x. 18–20), they avoided especially those kinds of food which were commonly offered to the gods, hence those prepared from flesh, wine, or flour. The vegetables, such as pulse, cabbage, etc., of which alone they were willing to partake, were indeed also prepared by the heathen cooks of the king, and were even unclean in themselves, as having been grown on heathen soil (Am. vii. 17; Hos. ix. 3, 4); but, since offerings or libations were never taken from them, they were not specially sacred to the gods, and hence, might be used by pious Jews, without any essential defilement of conscience. Compare Hävernick and Hitzig on this passage, and against Von Lengerke especially, who thought to find here the χορτώδης τροφή, 2 Macc. v. 27; and, therefore, a proof of the composition of the book in the time of the Maccabees; see Hävernick, *Neue krit. Unters.*, p. 47. ["Daniel's resolution to refrain from such unclean food flowed from fidelity to the law, and from steadfastness to the faith that 'man liveth not by bread only, but by every word that proceedeth out of the mouth of the Lord' (Deut. viii. 3)."—*Keil.*] Verse 9. **Now God had brought Daniel into favor and tender love with the prince of the eunuchs**; literally, "and God gave *into* favor . . . before the prince," etc. נתן לחסד is exactly the Greek ἔδωκεν εἰς ἔλεος καὶ οἰκτιρμόν (Theodot.). On this subject compare Gen. xxxix. 21; also Neh. i. 11; 1 Kings viii. 50.—Verse 10. **I fear my lord. the king**, etc. The prince of the eunuchs does not, in these words, positively refuse the favor which Daniel seeks, but intimates that in order to avoid the royal displeasure, he must render at least a formal and apparent obedience to the command he had received; aside from this, he shows his readiness to exercise every possible forbearance towards his wards. The remark in verse 9 that God had brought Daniel into the favor of the prince is, therefore, by no means in conflict with the tenor of this reply.—**For why should he see**, etc. The same turn as in Cant. i. 7, where the poetical שַׁלָּמָה stands for אֲשֶׁר לָמָּה, and where, similarly, the question expresses the sense of an emphatic negation (cf. 2 Chron. xxxii. 4; Ezra vii. 23).—**Your faces worse liking**, etc. זֹעֲפִים, properly "*sad*, lowering, of a peevish appearance" (Gen. xl. 6; cf. רָעִים, xl. 7), here implying a meager and decayed appearance, exactly like the Greek σκυθρωπός, Matt. vi. 16. ["פְּנֵי is to be understood before הַיְלָדִים, according to the *comparatio decurtata* frequently found in Hebrew; cf. Psa. iv. 8; xviii. 34, etc."—*Keil.*]—**Then shall ye make me endanger my head to the king**; properly, "and ye shall endanger." וְחִיַּבְתֶּם [*and ye cause to forfeit*, a Chaldaizing Piel from חוּב], is coordinated with יִרְאֶה, and like it depends on אֲשֶׁר לָמָּה; therefore: "for why should he see . . . and ye endanger my head," etc. On the phrase "to endanger the head," compare *Iliad.* iv. 162, ἀποτίσαι σὺν κεφαλῇ, and the German, "*den Kopf verwirken.*"

Verses 11-16. *Daniel's abstemiousness, and its consequences.* **Then said Daniel to Melzar.** הַמֶּלְצַר, as the prefixed article shows, is not a proper name, but an appellative, and probably designates an official. It can, however, scarcely mean a pedagogue or president of alumni, as Hitzig suggests, but rather a "butler" or "steward," as appears from the nearly identical Persian *melsar*, "vini princeps" (according to Haug a compound word from the Zend. *madhu* =μέθυ, "drink," and *çara*=κάρα, "head"); compare ἀρχιτρίκλινος, John ii. 8, 9),—[and רַבְשָׁקֵה, Isa. xxxvi. 2]. Verse 12. **Prove thy servants, I beseech thee, ten days.** The number *ten*, which was constantly employed as a *round number* (cf. verse 20; Zech. viii. 23; 2 Kings xx. 8, et seq.; and generally my *Theologia Naturalis*, i. 713 et seq.), was the more suitable in this case, as it was "sufficiently large to leave traces of the change of food in the appearance of the young men, yet not too great for a mere experiment" (Hitzig).—**Give us** (only) **pulse to eat.** Concerning זֵרֹעִים, *vegetables*, pulse, see on verse 8.—Verse 13. **And as thou seest, deal with thy servants**; *i.e.*, according to the result of thy observations. On תֵּרָאֶה with *tsêrê*, see Ewald, *Lehrbuch*, § 224, c.—Verse 15. **Fatter in flesh.** The youth themselves, and not merely their faces, are the subjects of this predicate; for neither מַרְאֵיהֶם nor מַרְאֵינוּ can be regarded as plurals. The plural מַרְאִים can nowhere be pointed out, and finds no support in Ecc. xi. 9 (cf. the exegetical notes on that passage, and also Hävernick on Daniel, p. 36).—Verse 16. **Thus Melzar took away the portion of their meat, and the wine that they drank**; better, "and the steward (henceforth) took away their appointed food and wine." וַיְהִי is "not introductory, but in connection with the participle expresses the duration" (Hitzig). The continuation of their treatment on this wise by the steward is remarked in order that the improvement in the condition of the youth, already mentioned as apparent in verse 15, may be more strikingly brought out.—On the question whether the narrative aims to represent this fact as *miraculous*, as well as concerning its ethical importance, see the dogmatico-ethical considerations [below].

Verse 17. *The great endowments of Daniel and his companions.*—**As for these four children, God gave them knowledge and skill**, etc.; properly, "And God gave . . . to these four," etc. Luther's rendering, "And the God of these four gave them," is inexact. On the precedence of the remote object in the nominative, followed by a personal pronoun in the dative (here לָהֶם), compare the examples adduced by Ewald, § 309, a, b.—**In all learning and wisdom.**—סֵפֶר, as in verse 4, "literary knowledge, acquaintance with literature, erudition" (Theodotion, γραμματική).—**And Daniel had understanding in all visions and dreams.** It was,

cause, arising from an apprehension of the stimulating effect of the highly-seasoned food, especially if they were under surgical treatment.]

therefore, his acquaintance with oneirocritics that distinguished him above his companions, who must also be regarded as wise and highly cultured. This was clearly a miraculous gift, which was intimately connected with his *χάρισμα προφητικόν*, but must not be confounded with it; for the skill to interpret the dreams and visions of others, is certainly different from the gift of seeing prophetical dreams and visions in person. Still, as the second half of the book shows, the possession of the latter faculty by our prophet presumed the existence of the former; just as in the New Testament the divinely-bestowed power to interpret tongues and prove spirits goes hand in hand with the power to speak in tongues and prophesy, in the case of the truly great bearers of the Divine Spirit, *e.g.*, St. Paul (1 Cor. xiv. 6 et seq.), St. Peter (Acts v. 3; viii. 20; x. 10, etc.).—הֵבִין בְּכָל־חָזוֹן is the same construction as in verse 4: מַשְׂכִּילִים בְּכָל־חָכְמָה, compare Ewald, § 217, 2. כֹּל, however, does not belong only to חָזוֹן, but also to וַחֲלֹמוֹת following. "All visions and dreams" are all possible ones, of every imaginable kind.

Verses 18–20. *Favorable issue of their examination before the king.* **Now at the end of the days.** Von Lengerke's rendering, "and toward the end of the time," is incorrect.—לַהֲבִיאָם, "to bring them," viz.: into the presence of the king. Hence not the same as הָבִיא in verse 3.—**The prince . . . brought them in before Nebuchadnezzar.** *Them*—not merely the four (verse 17), but, as may be inferred from ver. 19, all those Israelitish youths, verse 13.—**And among them all was none found like Daniel,** etc., either in physical beauty, or in marked mental excellencies.—**Therefore stood they before the king,** *i.e.*, they became his servants. "עָמַד is inceptive; they entered the royal service, and continued in it afterwards" (Hitzig).—Verse 20. **And in all matters of wisdom and understanding;** literally, "the discernment of wisdom" (חָכְמַת בִּינָה, something like חֻקַּת מִשְׁפָּט, Num. xxvii. 11; cf. Psa. lv. 24). חָכְמָה, however, is here, as in verse 4, employed exclusively in the sense of *objective wisdom*, which is essentially the same as *science*; while בִּינָה is "the subjective interior of this wisdom, the *mind* which shines through it." דְּבַר is here equivalent to a special point, *matter*, object; cf. Psa. xxxi. 9; Judg. xix. 24; Jer. xliv. 4, etc.—**That the king inquired of them.** בִּקֵּשׁ, not יְבַקֵּשׁ. The perfect refers back to the examination instituted by the king, verse 19, not forward to later questions, which he addressed to them.—**Found them ten times better.** Compare Gen. xxxi. 7, 41; Lev. xxvi. 26; Zech. viii. 23; Ecc. vii. 19.—**Than all the magicians and astrologers that were in all his realm;** rather, "than all the learned (in literature) magicians that were," etc. חַרְטֻמִּים, by reason of the probable derivation of the word from חֶרֶט, *stylus*, represents those who are versed in writings, scribes (scarcely persons who are clever, discerning, as Hitzig prefers, because of its assumed derivation from the Zend *khratumat*, the Rabbinical קוּרְטְמָן). The learned Egyptian priests were designated by this term (Gen. xli. 8, 24; Ex. vii. 11, 22, etc.), while Herodotus (ii. 36) calls them *ἱερογραμματεῖς*, and the Sept. sometimes terms them *ἐξηγηταί* (Gen. xli. 8, 24), and again *σοφισταί* (Ex. vii. 11). Unlike chap. ii. 2, 27; iv. 4, etc., where the Chartummim are mentioned as a special class beside the Ashaphim and other wise men, the word, though not connected with the following, serves in this place merely to enlarge the conception of the predicate. אַשָּׁפִים, the more special term designates (in virtue of the undeniable sameness in sense of its root שׁף ; with שׁאף and נשׁף) "breathers, whisperers," *i.e.*, *conjurers*, who murmured their magic formulas in an aspirated whisper. Whether they are to be specially regarded as "snake-charmers" must remain undecided, in view of the fact that the relation of this word to the term *ἀσπίς* is not established, and is possibly no more than an accidental similarity in sound. Compare, on the other hand, the Arabic *naphatha*, "to breathe mysteriously on coiled knots" (Freytag, *Lexic. Arab.* s. v.).

Verse 21. *Preliminary conclusion of the introduction.* **And Daniel continued** (thus) **even unto the first year of king Cyrus.** הָיָה, which is neither to be identified with, nor exchanged for חָיָה (the latter is advocated by Kirmss and Hitzig among others, who substitute וַיְחִי for וַיְהִי), expresses, in connection with עַד, the sense of *attaining to*, or of existing until the inauguration of an event. But "to live until the first year of the reign of Cyrus" is by no means equivalent to dying in that year. In this case the passage would contradict the statement found in chap. x. 1, and, therefore, would be in evidence against the original unity of this book (compare Introd. § 4). It is clear that the particle עד in this place does not refer to the close of the prophet's life, but simply designates a highly important period of time, up to which he lived and approved himself as the possessor of the exalted gifts of wisdom, prophecy, and interpreting dreams (verse 17). The special mention of the first year of Cyrus as such a period, "has, on the one hand, the objective reason that a really new æra, for the Jews especially, and one to which the most remarkable prophecies (Isa. xliv. 28; xlv. 1) referred, began with him; and, on the other, the subjective reason, that this sharp separation into great historical periods is general in Daniel, and, in addition, that a longing for the deliverance of his people must be regarded as a controlling disposition of his nature" (Hävernick). Compare Hengstenberg (*Beitr.*, p. 65, 314 et seq.), and Maurer on this passage, who regards וַיְהִי עַד, etc., correctly, as simply showing that Daniel lived through the whole period of the exile as a highly esteemed wise man at the Chaldæan court.* We need not, however, adopt Ewald's

* ["Compare the analogous statement, Jer. i. 2 et seq., that Jeremiah prophesied in the days of Josiah and Jehoiakim

view, who assumes that the words בְּשַׁעַר הַמֶּלֶךְ have been lost after דָנִיאֵל; "Thus Daniel lived at the royal court until," etc., with which he connects the venturesome hypothesis that Daniel and his companions dwelt in a separate building of the palace, which was specially intended to serve as "the royal academy (!)."—The Hebrew form of the name כּוֹרֶשׁ evidently corresponds better with the ancient Persian in the cuneiform inscriptions (*Qurus*, *Qurus*), than the Greek κῦρος. Its interpretation by "sun," which is found as early as Ctesias (*Plut. Artax.* i. p. 1012) and in the *Etymol. M.* (cf. the Sanscrit *sûra*, *sûrja*; Zend *hvare*; modern Persian *khur*), is not entirely certain. See the *Zeitschrift für Kunde des Morgenl.* vi. 153 et seq.; 350 et seq.

ETHICAL DEDUCTIONS CONNECTED WITH THE SCHEME OF REDEMPTION, APOLOGETICAL REMARKS, AND HOMILETICAL HINTS.

1. The dogmatic and ethical significance of the early history of Daniel and his companions consists chiefly, and it may even be said exclusively, in the proof of resolute faith and obedient devotion to God, which they displayed by abstaining from the royal provision at the Babylonian court. Our admiration is not enlisted in behalf of the abstinent diet, the fasting, the mortification of self, on the part of these youth, but finds something grand and morally important in the active trust in God, and the faithful obedience to God, that are displayed in those self-denials. They did not abstain from the use of the delicacies of the royal table, during the whole period of their training, from a spirit of desperate ascetic bravado, or because of a super-legal dread of God's creatures, which, in themselves, are not objectionable (1 Tim. iv. 4); nor yet because, like the Buddhists of India, they scrupled to destroy animal life in any form; but from the truly religious motive of remaining faithful and devoted to their covenant God Jehovah (see above, verse 8), and to avoid their being implicated, to any degree whatever, in the idolatrous practices of their heathen masters. Their abstemiousness has, therefore, essentially the same ethical value as that of the Rechabites, who refused to drink wine, from motives of religious obedience to the vow of their ancestor (Jer. xxxv.); or, as the conscientious abiding of the Nazarite by his sacred vow, which imposed similar denials on him, and which might cover the whole period of life (Samson, John the Baptist), or a definite time of longer or shorter duration (St. Paul, Acts xxi. 24 et seq.; Aquila, Acts xviii. 18). A further analogy to the course of these youth in Babylon will be found in the case of the Jews at Rome, whom Flavius Josephus mentions in chap. 3 of his autobiography. Our wonder and emulation are not excited in any of these instances by the avoiding of certain indulgences, but rather, by the disposition of faithful submission to the wholesome discipline of God. This it is, that marks their course as the effect of a strong, rather than weak faith, which thus becomes an example for the Christians of all ages. Several of the older expositors already recognized this, on the whole, although their extravagant estimate of the value of ascetic self-denial of any sort, prevented them from reaching a really unprejudiced and truly evangelical conclusion upon the subject. On the request of Daniel to Melzar, verse 12, to prove him and his companions during ten days with pulse and water, Jerome remarks, that it was a striking evidence of his faith: "*Incredibilis fidei magnitudo non solum sibi corpulentiam polliceri esu vilioris cibi; sed et tempus statuere. Non est ergo temeritatis, sed fidei, ob quam regias dapes contempserat.*" Similarly Theodoret on that passage: Οὐδὲν τῆς εἰς θεὸν πίστεως ἰσχυρότερον, καὶ δὴ τοῦτο πολλαχόθεν καὶ ἀλλαχόθεν ἐστὶ μαθεῖν, οὐχ ἥκιστα δὲ καὶ ἐκ τῶν τοῦ θεσπεσίου Δανιὴλ ῥημάτων· τὸ γὰρ πιστεῦσαι τε καὶ θαῤῥῆσαι, ὡς τῆς θείας ῥοπῆς ἀπολαύσεται, καὶ μὴ ἐσθίων — — εὐπρεπέστερος καὶ περικαλλέστερος φανήσεται καὶ μείζων· ποίην εὐσεβείας ὑπερβολὴν καταλείπει.—Among later writers, see especially Melancthon, who remarks correctly: "*Danielis temperentiam fuisse opus confessionis, et quidem hanc abstinentiam præceptam fuisse lege Dei, non humanis traditionibus. Ergo abstinebat Daniel, ut testaretur se non abjicere doctrinam, in qua sola exstabat verbum Dei, et abhorrere ab aliarum gentium traditionibus;*" also Calvin, who remarks on the words of Daniel, verse 11 et seq.: "*Tenendum est etiam illud, nempe non temere, neque proprio motu hæc dixisse, sed instinctu Spiritus Sancti. Fuisset enim non solertia, sed temeritas, si Daniel sibi fabricasset hoc consilium, et non fuisset certior factus a Domine de felici eventu Non est igitur dubium, quin hoc habuerit ex arcana revelatione, feliciter et ex voto cessurum, si permitteret minister ipsum et socios vesci leguminibus.*" And further: "*Sciamus, hoc esse verum experimentum frugalitatis et temperentiæ, si possimus esurire, ubi Deus nos ad inopiam et egestatem cogit, immo etiam si sponte possumus abjicere delicias, quæ nobis essent ad manum, sed nostro exitio. Nam hic subsistere in leguminibus et aqua esset valde frivolum, quia major interdum in emperentia se prodit in leguminibus, quam in optimis quibusque et lautissimis cibis.*" Note further, what Chr. B. Michaelis says concerning the contrast, indicated in verse 13, between the majority of the youth designed to be pages to the king, who partook unhesitatingly of the prescribed fare, and the strict abstinence of Daniel and his three friends: "*Hi ergo, licet et ipsi Judæi essent* (verses 3, 4, 6), *tamen in observanda lege divina minus religiosi fuerunt. Tanto laudibilior fuit Danielis sociorumque ejus pietas et in patria religione constantia.*"

2. The course of the self-denying youth will also appear as an effect of faith, from what is said in verse 15 respecting their surprisingly robust and handsome appearance. Whether this consequence of their vegetable diet is to be regarded as something miraculous, or as a purely natural result, may be questioned. The phenomenon can hardly pass for absolutely miraculous; for the traveler Chardin, in a manuscript remark on that verse, observes, "I have noticed that the Kechichs (*i.e.*, monks) have by far a fresher and more healthful color than others, and that the Ar-

to the end of the eleventh year of Zedekiah, although his book contains prophecies also of a date subsequent to the taking of Jerusalem."—*Keil.*]

menians and Greeks, though they frequently fast, appear healthy, lively, and handsome" (compare Burder, in Rosenmüller's *Alt- u. Neu-Morgenland*, iv. 340; also Harmer, *Observations in the East*, i. 357); and it is conceivable that an unrestrained indulgence in luxurious food might rather detract from the beauty of the remaining youths, than enhance it, especially if it were accompanied by the debaucheries and excesses which are so common among the pages at Oriental courts (Lüdecke, *Beschreibung des türk. Reichs*, i. 52 et seq.; Hävernick, *Komment.*, p. 37). Still, there is something extraordinary, indicative of Divinely supernatural co-operation, in the fact that at the end of three years the appearance of Daniel and his companions excelled that of *all* the other youths in fullness and beauty, and not less in the additional fact that they excelled these latter in point of intellectual qualities and scientific acquirements. Cf. Hävernick, "At the same time, it would be partial to ignore the Divine assistance; it was God who enabled his servants to find favor with their overseer, who gave them progress in Divine wisdom and understanding, and who did not forsake them in this instance. Only by this reference to God, which is certainly found in our narrative, can the believer comprehend its true bearing. Hence it is unwise, and the mark of a merely carnal exposition, to become involved in far-fetched and physiological explanations and calculations, such as are found in Aben-Ezra, no less than to ignore the Higher power, from which come all good and perfect gifts."

3. As an *apologetical* question of some importance, it must be remarked that what is related in this chapter concerning the abstinence and strict observance of the law at the heathen court of the Chaldæan king, by Daniel and his associates, is but poorly adapted to stamp the narrative as a fiction of Asmonæan times, in which the author seeks to beget trust in God on the part of his readers (Hitzig), or to warn them against partaking of unclean food (Bertholdt, Von Lengercke, etc.). The pious Jews of the Maccabæan period not only scrupulously avoided the flesh which was sacrificed to idols by their heathen oppressors, but everything that emanated from them, even to their arts and sciences. Daniel, Hananiah, etc., are, on the contrary, represented as distinguished adepts in all the wisdom of the Chaldæans, and at the same time, as filling official stations at the court of the Babylonian king, or even as members of the order of the magi (cf. chap. ii. 13, 48 et seq.). But while this latter feature shows a striking resemblance between the experience of the leading character and that of Joseph in Egypt; while especially the patronage of the youth Daniel by the prince of the eunuchs, as well as his high endowment as an interpreter of dreams, reminds us strongly of Joseph; we are yet compelled to reject the opinion that the whole is merely an artificial copy of the early history of that patriarch, because nothing is recorded, either of an ascetic refusal of food or drink on the part of Joseph, nor yet of his being trained with especial reference to service at the court of Pharaoh, or of a careful instruction in foreign wisdom and learning. With respect to the latter point, indeed, Moses, rather than Joseph, would serve as an example (see Acts vii. 22). Compare also Jerome (on verse 8): "*Qui de mensa regis et de vino potus ejus non vult comedere, ne polluatur, utique si sciret ipsam sapientiam atque doctrinam Babyloniorum esse peccatum, nunquam acquiesceret discere, quod non licebat. Discunt autem non ut sequantur, sed ut judicent atque convincant. Quomodo si quispiam adversus mathematicos velit scribere imperitus* μαθήματος, *risui pateat, et adversum philosophos disputans, si ignoret dogmata philosophorum. Discunt ergo ea mente doctrinam Chaldæorum, qua et Moyses omnem sapientiam Ægyptiorum didicerat.*"

4. The *Homiletical* treatment will, of course, seize on the chief and fundamental ethical principle of the section, as indicated above, under 1, without regard to subordinate details. Thus, perhaps: "Not dainty food, but the blessing of God develops beauty and strength. All wisdom, even in worldly concerns, is a gift of God, and the fear of the Lord is the beginning of this wisdom also" (Starke, after the *Bibl. Tübing.*).—Or: "Man shall not live by bread alone, but by every word that proceedeth out of the mouth of God" (Deut. viii. 3; Matt. iv. 4).—Or: "It is a good thing that the heart be established with grace; not with meats" (Heb. xiii. 9), etc. Compare Melancthon: "*Daniel in aula nec minis nec contemptu, nec illecebris voluptatem aut potentiæ victus est, ut deficeret a vero cultu. Hanc constantiam pauci imitantur, sed qui imitantur habebunt ingentia præmia corporalia et spiritualia, sicut inquit textus: Glorificantes me glorificabo, etc.* (2 Sam. ii. 20)."

---

2. *The vision of the monarchies, or Nebuchadnezzar's dream concerning the four world-kingdoms, and its interpretation by Daniel.*

II. 1–49.

1 And in the second year of the reign of Nebuchadnezzar, Nebuchadnezzar
dreamed dreams, wherewith [and] his spirit was troubled,[1] and his sleep brake
2 from him.[2] Then [And] the king commanded [3] to call the magicians, and the
astrologers, and the sorcerers, and the Chaldæans, for to shew [tell] the king
3 his dreams. So [And] they came and stood before the king. And the king
said unto them, I have dreamed a dream, and my spirit was troubled [1] to know
the dream.

4 Then spake the Chaldæans to the king in Syriac [Aramaic], O king, live
for ever! tell thy servants the dream, and we will shew the interpretation.
5 The king answered and said to the Chaldæans, The thing [word] is gone
from me: if ye will not make known unto me the dream, with [and] *the* inter-
pretation thereof, ye shall be cut in pieces,[4] and your houses shall be made a
6 dunghill [sink]. But [And] if ye shew the dream, and *the* interpretation
thereof, ye shall receive of [from before] me gifts and rewards [largess], and
great honour: therefore shew me the dream and *the* interpretation thereof.
7 They answered again, and said, Let the king tell his servants the dream,
8 and we will shew the interpretation *of it.* The king answered and said, I know
of certainty that ye *would* gain the time, because ye see the thing [word] is
9 gone from me. But [, that] if ye will not make known unto me the dream,
there is *but* one decree for you; for [and] ye have prepared lying and corrupt
words [a lie and a corrupt word] to speak before me till the time be changed;[5]
therefore tell me the dream, and I shall know that ye can shew me *the* inter-
pretation thereof.
10 The Chaldæans answered before the king, and said, *There* is not a man upon
the earth[6] that can shew the king's matter: therefore *there is* no king, lord, nor
ruler, *that* asked such things [a matter] at any magician, or astrologer, or Chal-
11 dæan. And *it is* a rare thing [And the matter] that the king requireth [asketh
is weighty]; and *there* is none other that can shew it before the king except
the gods, whose dwelling is not with flesh.
12 For this cause the king was angry and very furious, and commanded[8] to
13 destroy all the wise *men* of Babylon. And the decree went forth that [, and]
the wise *men* should be slain [were about to be killed]; and they sought Daniel
and his fellows to be slain.
14 Then Daniel answered with[7] counsel and wisdom to Arioch *the* captain of the
15 king's guard,[8] which was [who had] gone forth to slay the wise *men* of Babylon:
he answered and said to Arioch the king's captain, Why *is* the decree *so* hasty
16 from the king? Then Arioch made the thing known to Daniel. Then [And]
Daniel went *in,* and desired of the king that he would give him time, and
that he would shew [even to show] the king the interpretation.
17 Then Daniel went to his house, and made the thing known to Hananiah,
18 Mishael, and Azariah, his companions; that they would desire [even to request]
mercies of *the* God of heaven [the heavens] concerning this secret, that Daniel
19 and his fellows should not perish with *the* rest of the wise *men* of Babylon. Then
was the secret revealed unto Daniel in a night-vision. Then Daniel blessed *the*
20 God of heaven [the heavens]. Daniel answered and said, Blessed be *the* name
of God[9] for ever and ever [from everlasting and to everlasting]; for wisdom
21 and might are his.[10] And he[11] changeth the times and the seasons: *he* removeth
kings, and setteth up kings: *he* giveth wisdom unto *the* wise, and knowledge to
22 them that know understanding. He[11] revealeth the deep and secret *things: he*
23 knoweth what *is* in the darkness, and the light dwelleth with him. I thank
thee, and praise thee, *O thou* God of my fathers, who hast given me wisdom and
might, and made known unto me now[12] what we desired of thee: for thou
hast *now* made known unto us the king's matter.
24 Therefore Daniel went *in* unto[13] Arioch, whom the king had ordained
[appointed] to destroy the wise *men* of Babylon: he went and said thus unto
him, Destroy not[14] the wise *men* of Babylon: bring me *in* before the king,
25 and I will shew unto the king the interpretation. Then Arioch brought *in*
Daniel before the king in haste, and said thus unto him,[15] I have found a man of
the captives [children of the captivity] of Judah that [who] will make known
26 unto the king the interpretation. The king answered and said to Daniel,
whose name *was* Belteshazzar, Art thou able to make known unto me the
dream which I have seen, and *the* interpretation thereof?
27 Daniel answered in *the* presence of [before] the king, and said, The secret
which the king hath demanded [asked], cannot the wise *men,* the astrologers, the
magicians, the soothsayers, shew [the wise *men*. . . . cannot show] unto the king;
28 but [yet] *there* is a God in heaven [the heavens] that revealeth secrets, and

maketh known to the king Nebuchadnezzar what shall be in the latter days
[what *is it* that shall be in *the* end of the days]. Thy dream, and the visions
29 of thy head upon thy bed, are these [is this]; (*as for* thee, O king, thy thoughts
came *into thy mind* upon thy bed what should come to pass [what *it is* that
shall be] hereafter; and he that revealeth secrets maketh known to thee what
30 shall come to pass [what *it is* that shall be]: but [and] *as for* me, this secret
is not revealed to me for *any* wisdom that I have [is in me] *more* than any
living, but for *their* sakes that shall make known the interpretation [but in
order that the interpretation may be made known] to the king, and *that* thou
mightest know *the* thoughts of thy heart:)
31 Thou, O king, sawest, and, behold, a [16] great [17] image. This great image,
whose brightness *was* excellent, stood [a great image—this image *was* large, and
its brightness excessive—rising] before thee,[18] and the form thereof was terrible.
32 This image's head [This *was* the image: Its head] *was* of fine [19] gold, his breast
[its breasts] and his [its] arms of silver, his belly [its bowels] and his thighs
33 [its thighs] of brass [copper], his [its] legs of iron, his [its] feet part [of them]
34 of iron and part [of them] of clay. Thou sawest till that a stone was cut *out*
without hands, which [and it] smote the image upon his [its] feet, *that were*
35 of iron and clay,[20] and brake them to pieces [crushed them]. Then was [were]
the iron, the clay, the brass, the silver, and the gold, broken to pieces together,[21]
and became like *the* chaff of [from] *the* summer threshing-floors; and the wind
carried them *away*, that [and] no place was found for them: and the stone
that smote the image became [was for] a great mountain, and filled the whole
[all the] earth.
36 This *is* the dream; and we will tell *the* interpretation thereof [its interpretation we will tell] before the king.
37 Thou, O king, *art* a king of kings [the kings]: for *the* God of heaven [the heavens] hath given thee a [the] kingdom, [the] power, and [the] strength, and [the]
38 glory.[22] And wheresoever the children of men dwell [in every *place* that *the*
sons of man *are* dwelling], *the* beasts [living thing] of the field, and the fowls
[bird] of the heaven [heavens], hath he given into [in] thy hand, and hath
39 made thee ruler [rule] over them all. Thou *art* this [the] head of gold. And
after thee shall arise another kingdom inferior to [earthward from] thee, and
another third kingdom [a kingdom the third another] of brass,[23] which shall
40 *bear* rule over all the earth. And the fourth kingdom [a kingdom the fourth]
shall be strong as iron: forasmuch as iron breaketh *in pieces* and subdueth all
things [the whole]; and as iron that breaketh all these, shall it break *in pieces*
41 and bruise. And whereas thou sawest the feet and [the] toes part [of them]
of potter's clay and part [of them] *of* iron, *the* kingdom shall be divided [a
divided kingdom it shall be]; but [and] *there* shall be in it of the strength of the
42 iron, forasmuch as thou sawest the iron [24] mixed with miry clay. And *as the*
toes of the feet *were* part [of them] *of* iron and part [of them] *of* clay; *so* the
43 kingdom shall be partly [25] strong, and partly [*part* of it shall be] broken. And [26]
whereas thou sawest iron mixed with miry clay, they shall mingle themselves
with the seed of men [man]; but [and] they shall not cleave one to another
44 [this with this], even as iron *is* not mixed with clay. And in the [their] days
of these kings shall *the* God of heaven [the heavens] set up a kingdom, which
shall never be destroyed; and the kingdom shall not be left to other [another]
people, *but* it shall break *in pieces* and consume all these kingdoms, and it [27] shall
45 stand for ever. Forasmuch as thou sawest that the [a] stone was cut out of
the mountain without [upon not with] hands, and *that* it brake *in pieces* the
iron,[24] the brass,[24] the clay,[24] the silver,[24] and the gold;[24] *the* great God
hath made known to the king what shall come to pass hereafter [what *it is* that
shall be after this]: and the dream *is* certain, and *the* interpretation thereof
sure.
46 Then the king Nebuchadnezzar fell upon his face, and worshipped Daniel, and
commanded that they should offer [to offer] an oblation and *sweet* odours unto
47 him. The king answered unto Daniel, and said, Of a truth *it is* that your God
is [28] a God of gods, and a Lord of kings, and a revealer of secrets, seeing [that]

48 thou couldest reveal this secret. Then the king made Daniel a great *man* [29] and
gave him many great gifts, and made him ruler over the whole [all the]
province of Babylon, and chief of *the* governors over all *the* wise *men* of Bab-
49 ylon. Then [And] Daniel requested of the king, and he set Shadrach, Meshach,
and Abednego, over the affairs of *the* province of Babylon; but [and] Daniel
sat in *the* gate of the king.

GRAMMATICAL AND LEXICAL NOTES.

[[1] וַתִּתְפָּעֶם, *beat itself to and fro*, was agitated with conflicting thoughts and feelings.—[2] נִהְיְתָה עָלָיו, *was become upon him*, a Chaldaizing sense of the verb, like our colloquial "was all over with him".—[3] וַיֹּאמְרוּ, *said*, in the Chaldee sense.—[4] הַדָּמִין תִּתְעַבְדוּן, *bits ye shall be made*, *i.e.*, "chopped into mince meat;" probably a Babylonian form of punishment like "killing by inches."—[5] יִשְׁתַּנֵּא, *be turned*, *i.e.*, pass by.—[6] יַבֶּשְׁתָּא, *the dry ground*, an emphatic term for the world.—[7] הֲתִיב, *returned* in answer.—[8] טַבָּחַיָּא, *the executioners*, such being in Oriental courts an important part of the royal body-guard.—[9] אֱלָהָא, *the God*, like הָאֱלֹהִים, *i.e.*, the true God.—[10] דִּי־לֵהּ הִיא, *for* (I say) *his it* is, *i.e.*, each of the preceding qualities.—[11] וְהוּא, is emphatic, *and He*. The pronoun is understood with the following clauses.—[12] וּכְעַן, *and now*; the position makes these terms emphatic; *q. d.*, *at once*, promptly in this emergency.—[13] עַל, *upon*, seems here to denote the abruptness of the interview, *q. d.*, *came upon*.—[14] אַל־תְּהוֹבֵד, the deprecatory form, *mayest thou not destroy!*—[15] The דִּי following is expletive, like ὅτι before direct quotations.—[16] חַד, *one*, *i.e.*, a single one, standing alone and conspicuous.—[17] שַׂגִּיא, *huge* or colossal; a different and stronger term than the רַב immediately following.—[18] לְקָבְלָךְ, *in front of thee*; a stronger term, like the Heb. נֶגֶד, than קֳדָם, so frequently used in the context.—[19] טָב, *good*, *i.e.*, pure.—[20] פַּרְזְלָא וְחַסְפָּא, *the iron and the* clay, *i.e.*, the materials just described. The art. is emphatic, as in the following verse.—[21] כַּחֲדָה, *like one* thing, all at once; denoting suddenness as well as simultaneousness.—[22] With these epithets compare the similar terms in the (spurious or late) doxology at the close of the Lord's Prayer.—[23] נְחָשָׁא is rather *copper*, the simple metal; for zinc, which is a component of brass, was anciently unknown.—[24] פַּרְזְלָא. The *article* here, though present, as in all the preceding verses, should not be expressed in English, as it merely indicates the *material*.—[25] מִן־קְצָת, *in part* (lit. *from* the *end*); a different expression from the partitives elsewhere used in this connection.—[26] The וְ connective is wanting in the text, but is supplied in the Masoretic margin.—[27] The הִיא, *it*, is emphatic=*itself*.—[28] The הוּא is an emphatic copula=*he is*.—[29] לְדָנִיֵּאל רַבִּי, lit. *magnified Daniel*, *i.e.*, *promoted* him.]

EXEGETICAL REMARKS.

Verses 1-3. *Nebuchadnezzar demands an interpretation of his dream by the Magi.* **And in the second year of the reign of Nebuchadnezzar,** *i.e.*, in the second year of his sole reign, which, as remarked in § 8, note 2, of the Introduction, must have commenced some time after the fourth—perhaps in the sixth—year of the reign of Jehoiakim. The time, therefore, is about four years later than that mentioned in chap. i. 1, and soon after that designated in chap. i. 18. The three years of the training of Daniel and his companions had expired, perhaps by only a few weeks or months, and their reception into the number of the royal officials, as well as among the magicians, in the broader sense of the term, was of recent occurrence, when the remarkable event transpired which is here recorded, and which raised the four Jews to a far more exalted position in the royal favor. There is, therefore, no conflict, either with those passages of chap. i. nor with Jer. xxv. 1, where "the first year of Nebuchadnezzar," does not designate the first year of his sole reign, but of his joint rule. Compare Hengstenberg, p. 60 et seq., who is correct, in opposition to those who find here essentially a chronological error (Berth., Bleek, Hitz., etc.); and also, as compared with the less suitable modes of reconciliations attempted by several, *e. g.*, Wieseler (*Die 70 Wochen*, etc., p. 8 et seq.), who places the event narrated in this chapter *before* the expiration of the three years of Daniel's training, and therefore *before* chap. i. 18-20, thus regarding it as a supplementary attestation and illustration of the statement in chap. i. 20 (also Füller, p. 33 et seq.); Hävernick (*Neue krit. Unters.*, p. 64), who places the facts stated in chap. i. 1 et seq. altogether at the beginning of the third year of Jehoiakim, and assumes in addition, that Nebuchadnezzar became king a whole year later; from which it follows that 38-39 months may have elapsed between the taking of Jerusalem and the transportation of Daniel (chap. i. 1 et seq.), and the time of Nebuchadnezzar's dream. Ewald's opinion that עֶשְׂרֵה has been lost from after שְׁתַּיִם, which would give the *twelfth* instead of the second year of Nebuchadnezzar, is likewise superfluous.*—The copula in

* [It would be very natural for a Jewish writer, looking at events from the Palestinian point of view, as Jeremiah, to date occurrences according to the actual arrival of Nebuchadnezzar as apparent sovereign in Syria, although in reality only a viceroy in place of his father. A precisely parallel reckoning occurs in Luke iii. 1, with reference to the *associate* instead of the sole reign of Tiberius, as chronologers are now

וּבִשְׁנַת שׁ׳ probably indicates that verses 1–4*a* were written immediately after chap. i. and doubtless for the purpose of connecting this introductory section more closely with the Chaldaic fragment, chap. ii. 4*b*–49, which, together with the narratives in Chaldee that follow, may have already existed in manuscript form. Compare the Intr. § 4.—**Nebuchadnezzar dreamed dreams.** ["It has justly been regarded as a significant thing, that it was Nebuchadnezzar, the founder of the world-power, who first saw in a dream the whole future development of the world-power (and even its final overthrow) . . . . This circumstance also is worthy of notice, that Nebuchadnezzar did not himself understand the revelation which he received, but the prophet Daniel, enlightened by God, must interpret it to him."—*Keil.*] The plural חֲלֹמוֹת is used in this place with reference to the several contents of the dream, which, according to verse 31, comprises a number of scenes: (1) The sight of the great image; (2) its destruction; and (3) the growth of the stone which caused its ruin, until it became a gigantic mountain. The dream thus manifested its confused, mysterious character, that dissolved into indefiniteness. The plural may, therefore, with a certain propriety be taken as a plural of unlimited universality, which serves to prepare the way for the singular that follows in verse 3, in so far as it designates the whole of the confused and complex nature of the dream, among whose visions the image of the monarchies and its fate, were prominent in importance and in the impression they produced (cf. Hävern. and Maur. on the passage). The rabbinical interpretation, which refers the plural to the dream and its explanation, is certainly to be rejected (*e. g.*, Jos. Jacchiad.); and also the unauthorized identification of חֲלֹמוֹת with חֲלוֹם (Sept., Vulg., Luther, etc.; and also Hävernick, who endeavors to define this as a *plural of intensity*, supporting his view by a comparison with חָכְמוֹת, Prov. i. 20; ix. 1, which is certainly not plural).—**Wherewith his spirit was troubled.** Verse 3, and also Gen. xli. 8 (where the awaking of Pharaoh from his dream is described) employ the Niphal וַתִּפָּעֶם in the same sense that the Hithpael in this place bears, viz.: as indicating the alarm of one who has been frightened by a dream; compare Psa. lxxvii. 5, נִפְעַמְתִּי "I am so troubled" (properly, "I am bruised, beaten," *contundor*). and also the Greek *ταράττεσθαι*. "The Hithpael intensifies the conception of internal disturbance contained in the Niphal, so that it implies that its outward expression could not be mistaken" (Kranichf.).—**And his sleep brake from him,**" or "and his sleep was over for him." So, properly, the Sept., Vulg., Luther, Berth., etc., and, in general a majority of expositors. On the Niphal נִהְיָה, in the sense of being *past* or completed, compare chap. viii. 27, and especially Mic. ii. 4. The phrase "His sleep went from him" (chap. vi 19; Est. vi. 1) conveys a somewhat different idea. עָלָיו, "over him," or "for him," expresses, as frequently with conceptions of emotional activity, the sense of the dative in a more circumstantial and emphatic manner; cf. chap. iv. 24; vi. 19; x. 8, and see Gesenius' *Thesaurus*, p. 1027, 3, e. Hävernick renders it incorrectly: "His sleep came on him heavily;" for the statement that the king was greatly troubled does not admit of the other, that a heavy slumber had seized on him. Rather verse 3 shows clearly that the desire to recall his dream, hence such an effort to recollect as would necessarily banish sleep, formed the real cause of his disturbance.—On the phenomenon that Nebuchadnezzar should have a dream of prophetic significance, and then forget it (with reference to many of its details, if not entirely) consult the dogmatico-ethical considerations, No. 1.—Verse 2. **And the king commanded to call the magicians,** etc. This is exactly similar to Gen. xli. 8, to which record the writer seems designedly to have conformed in expression. Of the four classes of wise men here remarked (חַכִּימִין, verse 27), the Chartummim and Ashaphim have already been mentioned, chap. i. 20 (see on that place). The מְכַשְּׁפִים, mentioned as a third class, are clearly "enchanters;" cf. כִּשֵּׁף (properly "to mutter words of incantation;" Sept., *φαρμακεύεσθαι*) 2 Chron. xxxiii. 6, and מְכַשֵּׁף (*φαρμακός*) Ex. vii. 11; Deut. xlviii. 10. The term designates, in correspondence with its harsher formation, a stronger and more passionate mode of incantation than אשׁם—an apparent and observable enchantment, as distinguished from the mere breathing of magical formulas. The further mention of the כַּשְׂדִּים, Chaldæans, in connection with the Chartummim, etc., and therefore, as a special class of wise men coördinate with the others, involves no abuse or carelessness of expression, but rather corresponds fully with the statement of Herodotus (I. 181), that the Chaldæans were the priests of Bel, and with that of Diodorus (II. 24), that the Babylonians termed their priests *Χαλδαῖοι*. Those designated in this place as כַּשְׂדִּים are therefore the sacerdotal wise men (cf. Hesychius, s. v. Χαλδαῖοι, where the Chaldæans are distinguished as a *γένος Μάγων*), who, it is probable, were specially occupied with astronomy, the aboriginal science of the nations about the Euphrates and the Tigris, whose founder was supposed to be Belus, the chief divinity of the Chaldæans (Pliny, *H. N.*, vi. 30: "*Belus—inventor sideralis scientiæ*"). As astronomers, they were probably classed with the *astrologers*, the גָּזְרִין, who are mentioned in connection with them in chap. iv. 4; v. 7, 11, and instead of them in verse 27 of this chapter (see on that passage). The nationality of these Chaldæans was clearly different from that of the great mass of the Babylonian populace; for while these, the original inhabitants of Shinar, were pure Shemites, the former had adopted many Aryan elements into their language and customs. The Chaldæans, after inhabiting Babylonia for centuries, as a kind of priestly caste, attained to political supremacy through Belesys or Nabopolassar, whom Diodorus, II. 26, designates as

pretty well agreed. Daniel on the other hand, writing at Babylon, although by courtesy he applies the general title "king" to Nebuchadnezzar, while yet but a deputy, is exact in his statement of the years of the reign itself.]

ἐπισημότατον τῶν ἱερέων οὓς Βαβυλώνιοι καλοῦσι Χαλδαίους, hence through one of their superior priests (about B. C. 637). They retained this pre-eminence until the taking of Babylon by Cyrus, hence, about a century; but this probably did not exclude the primitive Babylonian priesthood from its place beside the sacerdotal class of the dominant nationality, either in regard to office, or to consideration. Thus we may explain why the Chaldæans are only co-ordinate with the other classes of magicians in this place and in the passages of chap. iv. and v. which have been mentioned, and also understand the fact that the official language (according to verse 4) was not the Chaldee, but continued to be the Aramæan (primitive Babylonian). The Chaldæans, Nabopolassar and Nebuchadnezzar did not, therefore, found a one-sided, intolerant, sacerdotal dynasty; they had rather, so far as this was possible, become thorough Babylonians, or, in other words, Aramæans. The Chaldæans, however, must have formed the *potior pars* of the whole body of the wise men at the court, for no other supposition will explain why the entire corps are designated sometimes as הַכַּשְׂדִּים, and at others as חַכִּימֵי בָבֶל, in the following account (verses 4, 5, 10, cf. verses 11, 12, etc.). Compare Hitz. and Kranichf. on this passage, and see infra, on verse 4.—**For to show the king his dreams.** All of the four classes of wise men just mentioned were therefore to co-operate in interpreting the dream, "because in this important matter the facts and opinions were to be settled by various methods, and possibly, to be placed on record. The several classes of wise men supplemented each other on such occasions, and assisted each other mutually by their peculiar methods. Thus, the priests might propitiate the gods and invoke their aid, by sacrifices; the conjurers might contribute to the increase of prophetic ability, as might also the enchanters, *e.g.*, by the use of narcotics, etc. In this way the Egyptian wise-men were constantly employed in individual cases as a σύστημα, according to Diodorus, II. 30." (Kranichf.)—Verse 3. **My spirit was troubled to know the dream.** A *constr. prægnans*, which signifies, "My spirit has become troubled (cf. on verse 1), and desirous to know the dream." The king clearly desires to have his dream rehearsed, and not merely to learn its meaning. The words לְדַעַת אֶת־חֲלוֹם may certainly imply the latter, but it appears definitely from verses 5 et seq., 9 et seq. 26, and 36, that he is more immediately concerned to recover the dream itself. The reason was, without doubt, that he had really forgotten it, or, as is frequently the case with intricate dreams, many of its particulars had escaped his memory, and he retained only a general undefined impression of having seen something fearful, monstrous, and alarming, in his dream. A total forgetting of the dream cannot be supposed in this case, since it was not possible for the king to be so greatly troubled as to lose his sleep about a dream which he had forgotten entirely (verse 1). Nor can it be assumed that he really recollected the dream, and had merely pretended that he no longer remembered it (R. Gaon in Ibn-Ezra, Hengstenberg, Hävernick); for the writer would hardly have left unnoticed a representation of this nature, which aimed to test the magicians; and, in addition, the rage of the king, as described in verse 12 et seq., is too furious to be pretended. [On the other hand, Keil justly contends (with the majority of interpreters) that he had not essentially forgotten his dream. "It is psychologically improbable that so impressive a dream, which, on awaking, he had forgotten, should have yet sorely disquieted his spirit during his waking hours. 'The disquiet was created in him, as in Pharaoh (Gen. xli.), by the specially striking incidents of the dream, and the fearful, alarming apprehensions with reference to his future fate connected therewith' (Kran.). According to verse 9, Nebuchadnezzar wished to hear the dream from the wise men that he might thus have a guarantee for the correctness of the interpretations which they might give. He could not thus have spoken to them if he had wholly forgotten the dream, and had only a dark apprehension remaining in his mind that he had dreamed. In that case he would neither have offered a great reward for the announcement of the dream, nor have threatened severe punishment, even death, for failure in announcing it. For then he would only have given the Chaldæans the opportunity, at the cost of truth, of declaring any dream with an interpretation. 'The Magi boasted that by the help of the gods they could reveal deep and hidden things' (Hengst.)." It is very probable, however, that while the king retained a lively recollection of the main features of the dream, he might have forgotten some of the particulars, which, if rehearsed again, he would be able to recognize. This justifies the whole proceeding.]

Verse 4. *The reply of the magicians.* **Then spake the Chaldæans to the king in Syriac,** *i.e.*, Aramaic. אֲרָמִית, the Aramaic dialect of the Babylonians, which was still prevalent at the court of the Chaldæan rulers, Nabopolassar, Nebuchadnezzar, etc., and which was distinguished from their Chaldee idiom, including numerous non-Shemitic elements, by its purely Shemitic character, and especially by its near relationship to the Aramæan of the Syrians. Hence, the Sept. and Theodotion translate Συριστί, the Vulg. *Syriace*, and Xenophon (*Cyrop.* VII. 5, 31) states directly that the Babylonians spoke Syriac. The reason for Daniel's express statement that the Chaldæans addressed the king in Aramaic (note the verb דִּבֵּר, corresponding to the adverb; cf. Isa. xxxvi. 11) consists simply in the fact that he desired to call the attention of his Hebrew readers to the contrast between the nationality of the כַּשְׂדִּים, *i.e.*, the majority of the wise men who were summoned before the king, and the purely Shemitic language, which they were obliged to employ (cf. on verse 2). It is wrong to look for the reason of their use of Aramaic, with Palmblad, Hävernick, and others, in their desire to hide the confession of their ignorance from the *turba adstantium*. This might rather have been accomplished by the use of Chaldee, while the Aramæan was familiar to all present as the language of the court and nation. Compare supra on chap. i. 4, and also the correct remark of Füller (p. 37): "While the language of the Chaldæans was the *language of science*, this (the Aram.) was the *language of popular intercourse.*"—**O king, live for ever.** This was an introductory formula of the address to the king (cf. chap. iii. 9; v. 10; vi. 7, 22), attested as a general Oriental formula of greeting by 1 Sam. x. 24 (Saul); 1 Kings i. 31 (David); Neh. ii. 3 (Artaxerxes); Ælian, *V. H.*, I. 31 (βασιλεῦ Ἀρταξέρξη, δι' αἰῶνος βασιλεύοις); Curtius, *R.*, VI. 5 (Alexander the Gr.); Judith xii. 14 (Holofernes).—On the Keri לְעַבְדָךְ, and similar omissions of י in the Keris, verse 26; iv. 16; v. 10, etc., see Hitzig and Kranichf. on this place.

Verses 5, 6. *Renewed demand by the king, connected with a stern menace.* **The king . . . said to the Chaldæans,** לְכַשְׂדָּיֵא. The uncontracted form כַּשְׂדָּאֵיא, a *stat. emphat. plur.*, from כַּשְׂדָּאִין, lies at the foundation of this Kethib, as well as of the Keri לְכַשְׂדָּאֵי; compare Winer, *Gramm. des bibl. und targum. Chaldaism.*, § 32, No. 3.—**The thing is gone from me,** rather, "the decree is made known by me," *i.e.*, it is my settled purpose, I say it with all emphasis. The words מִלְּתָא מִנִּי אַזְדָּא should probably be rendered in this way, as Hitz. and Kranichf. suggest; for (1) this view only is consistent with the repetition of the formula in verse 8, as well as with the parallel מִנִּי שִׂים טְעֵם, chap. iii. 29; iv. 3; (2) אַזְדָּא, which is found only here and in verse 8, is most readily explained by comparison with the Persian *azdâ* or *azanda*, which is found in inscriptions, and is equivalent to *publication*, science, what is known; (3) the rendering which makes אזדא correspond to קַיְּמָא, תּוּקְפָּא, "standing fast" (Pesh., Ibn-Ezra, the rabbins in Saadia, Winer, Hengstenb.), which is closely related to the one under consideration, is untenable from the fact that an assurance of the fixed and irrevocable character of the royal decree would here be out of place, and that an identification of the root אזד with the Arabic *vazada*, "to be firm," seems rather precarious; (4) the identification of אזד with אזל, *abiit* (verses 17, 24; vi. 19, 20), from which arises the sense, "the word has gone out from me" (Gesen., Hävern., Von Lengerke, etc.) is opposed by the extreme improbability that the two forms are identical in meaning, since an interchange of ל and ד is exceedingly rare, and especially because Daniel always employs the form with ל in other places; (5) finally, the view, "the word has escaped my recollection," which was formerly common, and which is found as early as Theodotion and the Sept. (*cod. Chis.*) (ὁ λόγος ἀπ' ἐμοῦ ἀπέστι), the Vulgate (*sermo recessit a me*), Luther, Dereser, and others, but which here, and much more in verse 8, contradicts the whole context, and does not consist with the only admissible sense of מִלְּתָה = word, command, is wholly untenable; for the term nowhere in this chapter, not even in verse 23, signifies the dream of the king, but always his decree, his demand. [Moreover, "the punctuation of the word אַזְדָּא is not at all that of a verb, for it can neither be a participle, nor the 3d pers. præt. fem." (Keil), but it is the fem. of an adj. אַזָד, or (as Fürst thinks), an adverbial form of the same. The meaning *firm*, however, which the author rejects, seems to us more suitable and better corroborated than any other.] — **Ye shall be cut in pieces.** אתעבד הדמין, *to be made pieces* (Sept. διαμερίζεσθαι; cf. μέλη ποιεῖν, 2 Macc. i. 16, and διχοτομεῖν, Matt. xxiv. 51); a cruel punishment in vogue among all the nations of antiquity, and especially among the Chaldæans (Eze. xvi. 40; xxiii. 47); compare chap. iii. 29.—**And your houses shall be made a dunghill.** Similarly chap. iii. 29, and also Ezra vii. 11, where the form נְוָלוּ is used instead of Daniel's נְוָלִי. This term, derived from the Pael נַוֵּל = נַבֵּל, *to soil*, defile, indicates the extremely disgraceful nature of the threatened penalty; the houses are to be changed into dunghills, by being razed to the ground and covered with animal and human ordure—just as Jehu turned the temple of Baal into a sink, 2 Kings x. 27. See the proofs of the frequent use of this method of disgrace and punishment in the East, adduced by Hävernick.—Verse 6. **Ye shall receive of me gifts and rewards, and great honors;** rather, "great treasures." The second of the terms here employed, נְבִזְבָּה, "reward" (compare the plural נְבִזְבְּיָן, "gifts," chap. v. 17, and the *Targ.* Jonath., Jer. xl. 5; Deut. xxxiii. 24) is satisfactorily explained by its derivation from בזז, and specially from a Palpel form בַּזְבֵּז, *facultates suas contemsit, prodegit.* It is not necessary, therefore, to refer with Berth., Eichhorn, etc., to the Greek νόμισμα in its elucidation, nor with Haug (in Ewald's *Jahrb. d. bibl. Wissenschaft*, 1853, p. 160), Gesen.-Dietr., etc., to institute a comparison with the old Persian *ni-bag-vâ*, "presentation," nor, above all, with the Sanscrit *namas*, "present, gift," as Hitzig attempts. Ewald prefers נִבְזְבָּה, and the translation of this term by *official stations*, or promoting to office (for which he refers to the old Persic and also to chap. v. 16)—which, however, is opposed to the entire body of exegetical tradition.—**Therefore shew me the dream,** etc. לָהֵן, *therefore* (composed of the demonstrative adverb הֵן and the preposition לְ), is found in this signification in verse 9, and chap. iv. 24, and in the Hebrew of Ruth i. 13. On the other hand it signifies "but rather" in verse 30, and "but" in Ezra v. 12.

Verses 7–9. *Repeated refusal of the Chaldæans, and renewed threatening of the king.* **They answered again.** תִּנְיָנוּת, an adverb from תִּנְיָן, "the second one," chap. vii. 5.—**And we will shew the interpretation,** וּפִשְׁרָה נְהַחֲוֵה. The form פִּשְׁרָה is not to be changed into פִּשְׁרֵהּ, as Hitzig suggests, but must rather be regarded simply as a Hebraized *stat. emphat.* for פִּשְׁרָא, just as (verse 5) מִלְּתָה is used for מִלְּתָא (verse 8, etc.), or כְּתָבָה (chap. v. 7, 15) instead of כְּתָבָא (ibid., verses 8, 16, etc.). Whether the Hebraizing orthography apparent in this and other similar instances is to be placed to the account of Daniel, and to be considered as a peculiar feature of the Chaldee in his time (Pusey, *Daniel*, p. 46), or whether it originated with later transcribers of Daniel's text, cannot be definitely decided; compare Kranichf. on this passage.—Verse 8. **I know of certainty.** מִן יַצִּיב, equivalent to מִן קְשׁוֹט, *ex veritate*, assuredly, verse 47.—**That ye would gain the time**; literally, "that ye *purchase* time" (Sept. and Theodotion: καιρὸν ἐξαγοράζετε); compare ἐξαγοράζεσθαι τὸν καιρόν, Eph. v. 16; Col. iv. 15; also *tempus emere*, Cicero, *Verr.* I. 3. The time, *i.e.*, the favorable juncture, the opportunitas, which the magicians sought to buy, *i.e.*, to improve, consisted in the fact that the king *had forgotten his dream*; they aim to improve this circumstance in such a way as eventually to avoid the interpretation altogether.* Their design is therefore properly "to gain time," to postpone the decision. Thus Gesen., De Wette, Von Leng., Hävernick, and still earlier, Luther, are correct: "That ye seek delay." Entirely too artificial is the view of Hitzig and Kranichf., that the favorable circumstances, of which the magicians hoped to avail themselves, consisted in the king's desire to learn the interpretation of the dream; and that they speculated on this desire, in the hope that the king might ultimately be persuaded to disclose to them the dream, etc.—**Because ye see that the thing has gone from me**; rather, "that my decree is published," *i.e.*, because ye observe that I am in earnest about the command; compare verse 5. כָּל־קֳבֵל דִּי does not, in this nor any other place, not even in chap. v. 22, signify "despite that," as Hitzig suggests, but "because," properly "because that," *propterea quod*. The king evidently aims to point out the motive for the artful temporizing and delay of the magicians, namely, the menace with which he has intimidated and frightened them.—Verse 9. **But if ye will not make known . . . the dream.** דִּי הֵן, Heb. אֲשֶׁר אִם, *quodsi*. The דִּי, properly "since," "therefore," takes up the subject of the preceding conditional clause, and places it in emphatic correlation to that clause (Kranichf.).—**There is but one decree for you**; *i.e.*, one and the same sentence of condemnation shall come on all of you (Vulg. correctly, *una est de vobis sententia*; cf. Luther, "*so ergeht das Recht über euch*"). דָּת, the sentence of condemnation in this passage, is clearly the same in substance as מִלְּתָא in verses 5 and 8; the suffix plainly indicates this (דָּתְכוֹן, "*your* sentence," *i.e.*, that which comes upon you, which concerns you). Von Leng. and Hitzig (following Theodotion) are wrong: "But one thing forms your object," ye entertain but one design; for דָּת never designates a subjective personal opinion or aim, but rather always an objective norm, which is binding on the individual.—**For ye have prepared lying and corrupt words to speak before me.** כִּדְבָה, "falsehood," and שְׁחִיתָה, properly, "corruption," "baseness," are in apposition with מִלָּה. The entire object is, however, placed before the infinitive לְמֵאמַר which governs it, on account of emphasis; compare verse 18; iii. 16; iv. 15. —The principal verb is הִזְמִנְתּוּן in the Kethib, the Aphel of זְמַן. This form, which does not occur in the Chaldee or Syriac, but is found in the Samaritan, expresses the sense of "conspiring" which is here required, as well as the Ithpa. הִזְדְּמִנְתּוּן substituted for it in the Keri (cf. the συνέθεσθε of Theodotion and the *composueritis* of the Vulg.).—**Till the time be changed**, *i.e.*, until by the aid of some hoped-for circumstance ye ascertain something more definite concerning the subject of the dream; or, also, until my anger ceases, and I withdraw the demand altogether.—**And I shall know that ye can show . . . the interpretation thereof.** The future תְּהַחֲוֻנַּנִי expresses the idea of ability, competency; compare Winer, *Gramm.*, § 44, 3, c. (p. 107).

Verses 10, 11. *The magicians attempt to establish their declaration respecting the impossibility of gratifying the king's desire.* **Therefore there is no king, lord, nor ruler, that asked such things**; rather, "since no great and mighty king (ever) asked," etc. כָּל־קֳבֵל דִּי is to be taken here, as in verse 8, in its usual sense of "since," not as drawing a conclusion, in the sense of "wherefore, for which reason" (Gesen., Von Leng., etc.). It does not, indeed, adduce the actual reason for the assertion that no one could satisfy the royal demand; but it refers to the subjective ground that in all human experience, no king, however great, had imposed such a demand. Compare the similar *probatio a posteriori*, or *a gnorismate*, in the familiar passage, Luke vii. 47.—The predicates רַב וְשַׁלִּיט are not empty titles after the manner of the Orient (Berth., Von Leng., Häv.), but imply that while the most extreme demands might be expected from precisely the most powerful kings, nevertheless, etc.—Verse 11. **Except the gods, whose dwelling is not** (to be found) **with flesh**, or "with men." בְּשַׂר, *flesh*, indicates the frailty of created man, encompassed by earthly limitations, as contrasted with the uncreated and divine, which is not confined within these perishable bounds; compare Isa. xxxi. 3; Jer. xvii. 5; Zech. iv. 6; Job v. 4; also John i. 14; 1 Tim. iii. 16, etc. The Chaldæans include themselves in the term *flesh*, in order to refer excusingly to their imperfection and the limitation of their knowledge, as in no wise deserving of censure.—The fact that the dwelling of the gods is not with men, prevents such intercourse with them, as would admit of man's instruction in their superior knowledge. This is certainly a truly heathenish, but not a specifically Babylonian thought (as Hävernick supposes). Von Lengerke's supposition that the king must already at this juncture have re-

* [But it is difficult to see how the supposed circumstance that the king *had forgotten* the dream can here be called "a favorable *time*." אִדָּנָא here is evidently to be taken in the sense of *delay*. The Magians are charged with trying to postpone the matter indefinitely, by the plea of requiring the statement of the dream by the king himself, which they presume cannot be done.]

marked the prophetic rank of Daniel (cf. Ex. viii. 15) is too far-fetched. On the other hand, the appeal of the wise men to the gods, becomes significant for the progress of the scene, as it might suggest to the king the consideration, so damaging to themselves, that the gods could not conceal their superior knowledge of important secrets from them, of all others, who were professional priests, in case they were not pretended, but real priests of the gods. In other words, the appeal of the magicians hastens the denunciation of the sentence with which they had been threatened.

Verses 12, 13. *The decree for the execution of the appointed penalty.* **And commanded to destroy all the wise men of Babylon;** naturally only those belonging to the capital city, who alone are to be regarded as summoned before the king (verse 2); not those of the whole realm, nor even of the province of Babylon (verse 49; iii. 1). Those remaining magicians, or wise men, who were not inhabitants of Babylon itself, formed, according to Strabo xvi. 1; Pliny, *H. N.* vi. 26, separate colleges, *e.g.*, in Borsippa, Urchoe, Hipparenum. They differed in certain principles and customs from the Babylonian college, as well as from each other, and therefore, could not be held directly responsible for a mistake or a crime committed by their colleagues in the capital.—Verse 13. **And the decree went forth.** דָּת, the decree in proper form, the *firman* (cf. *δόγμα*, Luke ii. 1); compare verse 9.—**That the wise men should be slain.** וְחַכִּימַיָּא מִתְקַטְּלִין probably expresses no more than this; the form of the imperf. partic. מִתְקַטְּלִין seems to be used as a gerundive, "they were (persons) to be slain, devoted to death;" or—of which, however, there is no other example—the וְ coupled with the participle, seems exceptionally to express the sense of design: "sapientes ut interficerentur" (cf. Kranichf. and Maurer on this passage, the one of whom prefers the former explanation, and the other the latter). The execution of the sentence is not to be regarded as having actually begun,* as appears sufficiently from what follows, especially in verses 14 and 24 (contra Hitzig, etc.).—**And they sought Daniel and his fellows to be slain;** evidently because they were regarded as belonging to the חַכִּימִין or מְגֻרִם in the broader sense, which could only be the case after they had passed the examination before the king mentioned in chap. i. 19—hence, after completing the three years of their training. It follows from this that the event here recorded did not transpire during that period (cf. on verse 1), as Wieseler holds. At the same time the statement before us indicates that Daniel was not entirely unknown to the king at this time, as might appear from verse 25 et seq. The fact that Daniel and his three fellows had not appeared in person before the king, but were sought for, is easily explained by the consideration that Nebuchadnezzar did not, by any means, summon *all* connected with the class of magians in the capital before him (cf. verse 2, where Luther's "*all* star-gazers and wise men" is decidedly inexact), but assuredly only the presidents of the several chief classes, the notables and representatives of the whole body.—On the apologetical significance of the circumstance that Daniel and his companions seem, in this place, to be at least connected or affiliated with the order of magians, if not formal members of it (as Von Lengerke, evidently going too far, supposed) see above, *Dogm.-eth. considerations on* chap. i., and also Kranichf. on this passage.

Verses 14–16. *Daniel prevails on the king to delay the execution of the sentence.* **Then Daniel answered with counsel and wisdom to Arioch,** etc. עֵטָא וּטְעֵם, *counsel and wisdom*, *i.e.*, words of counsel (cf. עֵצָה Isa. xi. 2; Jer. xxxii. 19, etc.) and of wisdom, namely, as concerning the difficult position in which he was placed with the rest of the wise men, and in regard to the proper way to relieve the difficulty (טְעֵם, *ratio*, similar to chap. iii. 12). On הֲתִיב "to reply," compare chap. iii. 16; Ezra v. 11. The connection הֲתִיב טְעֵם reminds us of מְשִׁיבֵי טַעַם, Prov. xxvi. 16.—The name אַרְיוֹךְ occurs as early as Gen. xiv. 1, as the name of a king of Ellasar. The leading element in its composition seems to be אֲרִיֵה, אֲרִי = Sanscrit *arja*, "lord," and, possibly, it may even be directly identified with the Sanscrit *ârjaka*, "venerabilis." This person was, therefore, a noble, of decidedly Indo-Germanic race, filling an important office at Nebuchadnezzar's court. His title רַב־טַבָּחַיָּא, *chief of the slaughterers* (*i.e.*, the executioners), is the Shemitic designation of the same official who was known in the Roman empire as the *Præfectus prætoris*, and in Turkey bears the title of *Kapidshi-pasha*, hence a chief of the life or body guards. Besides the execution of capital punishments, warlike functions, up to those of a commander-in-chief, might occasionally be devolved on this officer, as appears from the instance of Nebuzaradan, 2 Kings xxv. 8 et seq. The office existed, however, even at the court of the Egyptian Pharaohs (see שַׂר הַטַּבָּחִים, Gen. xxxvii. 36; xxxix. 1; xl. 3 et seq.). His extensive influence at the Chaldæan court is indicated elsewhere than here (see especially the predicate "the powerful one of the king," שַׁלִּיטָא דִּי־מַלְכָּא verse 15), in 2 Kings viii. 10; Jer. xxxix. 9 et seq.; xl. 1 et seq.; xli. 10; xliii. 6; lii. 12 et seq.—Verse 15. **Why is the decree so hasty from the king?**—rather, "why this furious decree on the part of the king?" or literally, "why the decree which furious from before the king?" מְהַחְצְפָה, the participle of אַחְצֵף, which, according to the Targ. Prov. vii. 13; xxi. 29, is equivalent to הֵעֵז, "to rage," is here in the *stat. absol.* instead of *emphat.*, just as the Hebrew participle when in apposition is sometimes without the article, *e.g.*,

* [Keil, however, insists that this must be the meaning of the passive participle here, and renders "the work of putting to death was begun." This is a straining of the sense. The execution being ordered, and preparations going on for it; it was regarded as virtually, but not actually in progress.]

Cant. xii. 5; Am. ix. 12; Jon. iv. 17. Some, as Hävernick, and others, prefer to translate "hurried," "hasty," in analogy with chap. iii. 29, where מַחְצְפָה seems to bear that sense (?); but the ancient versions support the rendering "furious, raging" (Sept. πικρῶς, Theodot. ἀναιδής, Vulg. *crudelis*), and the entire situation substantiates this meaning.—The writer, however, does not mention everything that Daniel must have said to Arioch on this occasion; but rather contents himself with faintly indicating that only which served to manifest his counsel and wisdom. The author employs an abbreviated style, as in chap. i. 9, 10 (see on the place); he is not, therefore, to be charged with incongruity (Hitzig), nor is the point in question to be strained by an artificially interpolating exegesis, and perhaps (with Kranichf.) to be regarded as particularly surprising and remarkable.—Verse 16. **And Daniel went in**, namely, to the king in the palace (cf. 2 Sam. xix. 6), naturally not until announced by Arioch (cf. verse 25), for none were admitted to the kings of the East without such announcement, see Esther iv. 11; Herodotus, I., 99; III., 110, 118. Hence, another abbreviating statement by the author, as also in what immediately follows.—**That he would give him time, and that he would show the king the interpretation**—and naturally, first of all, the contents of the dream itself. He hopes that God will impart both to him, during the respite that is to be granted. In the construction וּפִשְׁרָא לְהַחֲוָיָה לְמַלְכָּא the copula is explicative, "and indeed, to," etc., or "namely, to," etc. The change of construction here is analogous to that in chap. i. 5, where the verb וַיְמַן first governs a simple accusative of object, and afterward a telic infinitive clause with לְ (וּלְגַדְּלָם).

Verses 17–19. *God reveals the secret to Daniel.* Then **Daniel went to his house**—evidently because the king had granted the desired respite, which must be assumed in verse 16, without further question. This favor will not seem strange, nor inconsequent (Hitz.), when we reflect that Daniel and his three friends had secured the favor and good-will of the king but recently, on the occasion of their first appearance in his presence (chap. i. 19 et seq.). None were better adapted to soothe the angry king and obtain at least a postponement of the impending punishment, than the handsome and richly endowed Hebrew youth, who had already made so favorable an impression on the monarch, and who probably would have arrested the publication of the decree of punishment, had he been among those magians that were summoned before the king, according to verse 2; compare on verse 13.—Daniel's house may probably be considered as an official or servant's dwelling, as well as the houses of the other wise men mentioned in verse 5; and moreover, as the context shows, as a residence which he shared with his companions, Hananiah, etc.—Verse 18. **To desire mercies of the God of heaven**; more accurately, "*and indeed* in order to implore mercies." The clause וְרַחֲמִין לְמִבְעֵא depends on the last preceding verb הוֹדַע, "he made the thing known to them;" hence the construction is the same as in verse 16 *b*. The design of the הוֹדַע was to impress the exigency on the prayerful consideration of his friends, and, in fact, a united prayerful consideration in which Daniel himself participated (cf. verse 23). That the execution of the design to pray is not expressly mentioned, and that we have merely Daniel's offering of praise after the secret has been Divinely imparted to him, instead of the supplication of the friends, are additional illustrations of the abbreviating style with which our chapter abounds (cf. verses 14 and 16). A New-Testament parallel is found in the Johannean narrative of the raising of Lazarus, John xi. 40, 41 et seq., where the supplication of Jesus is likewise omitted, and only his thanksgiving after his prayer is heard, is recorded.—The designation of Jehovah as the "God of heaven," which occurs as early as Gen. xxiv. 7, is very general with Old-Testament writers after the captivity, probably in contradistinction from the custom of the Asiatic Orientals of deifying the several stars or zodiacal regions; cf. verses 19, 44; Neh. i. 5; ii. 4; Ezra i. 2; vi. 10; vii. 12, 21; also the related phrase "King of heaven," chap. iv. 34 (A. V., verse 37), and συνάστης οὐρανῶν, 2 Macc. xv. 23. In general see Hävernick, *Theologie des Alten Testaments*, 2d ed., p. 49.—Verse 19. **Then was the secret revealed unto Daniel in a night vision.** חֶזְוָא דִי־לֵילְיָא, as well as חֶזְיוֹנוֹת לַיְלָה, Job iv. 13, is probably not a *dream*-vision, but a vision generally, and properly a vision seen by night. On the influence of night to promote the higher range and prophetic elevation of spiritual meditation, by which it readily arrives at visions, consult Tholuck, *Die Propheten und ihre Weissagungen*, p. 52.—Compare also the dogmat.-eth. deductions, No. 2 [below].

Verses 20–23. *Daniel's praise and thanksgiving.* Hitzig observes correctly, "The leading thought which Daniel wishes to express is placed first, verse 20 *a*; next the exclamation is justified in *b*, by the attributes which belong to God, and in verses 21 and 22, by the manner in which they are displayed; finally, verse 22 shows why Daniel felt a desire to utter the specific thought of verse 20 *a*. Those attributes themselves, verse 20 *b*, return in verse 23 as belonging to Daniel, conferred on him by God; and thus the prayer is rounded into unity."—[**Daniel answered and said,** "The word עֲנֵה retains its proper meaning. The revelation is of the character of an address from God, which Daniel answers with praise and thanks to God."—*Keil.*]—**Blessed be the name of God for ever and ever.** The form לֶהֱוֵא, like the related לֶהֱוְיָן, לֶהֱוֹן, is to be explained, either by assuming that the particle לְ used as a conjunction (*that*) has excluded the prefix י (Gesenius, *Abhandlung zur hebr. Gramm.*, p. 180–194), or that the preformative י passes over into לְ, as in the later Syriac it passes into נ (Beer, *Inscriptiones et papyri vet. Semitici*, I., 19 et seq.; Maurer, Hitz., Kranichf., etc.). The latter assumption seems the more trustworthy. On the phrase, "for ever and **ever**" (**from** eternity to eternity) compare the similar doxologies, Psa. xli. 14; cvi. 48.—**For wisdom and might are his.** This is almost verbally the same as Job xii. 13. The דִּי in דִּי־לֵהּ הִיא is an emphatic repetition of the former conditional דִּי.—Verse 21. **He changeth the times and seasons.** Theodotion and the Sept. correctly render καιροὺς καὶ χρόνους, for which Acts i. 7; 1 Thess. v. 1, have the inverse order. עִדָּן is *time* in general; זְמַן, the *determined* time, the appointed period or point of time. Both terms are also connected in chap. vii. 12. The thought that God determines and conditions the change of times refers, like the following ("he removeth kings, and setteth up kings"), to the prophetic subject of Nebuchadnezzar's dream-vision, which had just been revealed to Daniel.—**He giveth wisdom unto the wise, and knowledge to them that know understanding.** Although Daniel includes himself among these wise and understanding ones, and even has special reference to himself while mentioning them, he utters no offensive sentiment, but expresses essentially the same thought as St. Paul when he writes, "By the grace of God I am what I am" (1 Cor. xv. 10). He traces the wisdom and understanding with which he had just been endowed back to its Divine source, and places himself, as the bearer of such wisdom graciously bestowed by God, in contrast with the heathen magians, who are without it.—Verse 22. **He revealeth the deep and secret things,** etc. Compare 1 Cor. ii. 10; iv. 5; Psa. cxxxix. 12.—**And the light dwelleth with him,** has made its abode with him, as a visiting personage of celestial race; compare the Johannean ἐσκήνωσεν ἐν ἡμῖν of the Logos, as well as what is stated in Prov. viii. 30, respecting the Divine wisdom. שְׁרֵא (for which, with Hitzig, we are perhaps to read שְׁרָא) is often used in the Targums instead of נוּחַ or שְׁכַן. Instead of the Kethib נְהִירָא, *illuminatio*, intellectual light, the Keri has נְהוֹרָה, physical light (compare perhaps Psa. civ. 2; 1 Tim. vi. 16). The Kethib, however, is sustained by the corresponding Syriac word, and also by the form נַהִירוּ, chap. v. 14.—Verse 23. **God of my fathers.** Daniel addresses Jehovah in this manner, because in contrast with the idols of the heathen, he has just revealed himself again as the same true God, who was known to the patriarchs of his nation.—**Who hast given me wisdom and might;** namely, *wisdom* in regard to the understanding of the king's dream and its interpretation, and *strength* with reference to the danger of impending death, which he was enabled boldly to face.—**And hast made known unto me now.** וּכְעַן, the Chaldee וְעַתָּה, "and now," connects the requisite special proof with the general statement just made. On the etymology of כְּעַן, probably a contraction of כְּעִדָּן, "at the time," see Gesenius, s. v.

Verses 24–26. *The announcing of Daniel to the king.* **Therefore Daniel went in unto Arioch.** עַל shows the direction, like the Hebrew אֶל; cf. chap. iv. 31; vii. 16. The Hebrew, however, also employs עַל occasionally in this sense, *e.g.*, 2 Sam. xv. 4.—**He went and said thus unto him.** The עַל, "he went in," which is cut off by the insertion of a lengthened clause, is resumed by אֲזַל in an anacoluthic way.—Verse 25. **Then Arioch brought in Daniel before the king in haste.** בְּהִתְבְּהָלָה, "hastily," properly, "in hasting;" cf. chap. iii. 24 and בִּבְהִילוּ, Ezra iv. 23, which has the same meaning.—The form הַנְעֵל, which occurs also in chap. iv. 4; vi. 19, neutralizes (like אַנְדַּע, verse 9) the harshness of the Daghesh (required by the omission of a radical) by the substitution of an epenthetic נ; cf. Winer, § 19, 1. In sense הַנְעֵל does not differ from הַעֵל, verse 24. Concerning Arioch as the εἰσαγγελεύς of Daniel, see on verse 16.—**I have found a man of the children of the captivity of Judah** (margin), *i.e.*, of the Jewish captives. Arioch here certainly speaks of Daniel as wholly unknown to the king, but this is sufficiently explained by the conceited pride and sovereign contempt, with which he, the dignified Indo-Germanic (verse 14) minister of police, believed himself compelled to look down upon the poor Shemitic prisoner. The etiquette of the Babylonian court, so to speak, and particularly of its military or police division, forbade the leader of the body-guard from recognizing Daniel as one known to the sovereign. The compiler can, therefore, by no means be charged with mentioning in this place what contradicts his former statements, and especially with having already forgotten the fact recorded in verse 16 (Hitz., Von Leng.). The manner in which, for instance, David is introduced as a shepherd totally unknown to Saul and Abner, 1 Sam. xvii. 33, 55, might much more readily lead to the conclusion that the narrative there did not originally consist with that recorded in 1 Sam. xvi., which had brought David into closer relations with Saul at an earlier period (cf. even Keil, on 1 *Sam.*, p. 129 et seq., who admits the strangeness of this contradiction). The marked difference between the discrepancy in that case and the far lighter one in the passage under consideration, shows of itself how little reason there is to assume a multiplicity of compilers, or even a want of skill on the part of the sole author.—Verse 26. **The king answered and said to Daniel, whose name was Belteshazzar.** This Babylonian name, which the king himself had caused to be conferred on Daniel (chap. i. 7), would naturally be the only one to claim the notice of Nebuchadnezzar.—["The question, **Art thou able?** *i.e.*, 'Hast thou ability?' does not express the king's ignorance of Daniel's person, but only his amazement at his ability to make known the dream, in the sense, 'Art thou really able?'"—*Keil.*]

Verses 27–30. *Introductory to the statement and interpretation of the dream.* **The secret . . . cannot the wise men, the astrologers, the magicians, the soothsayers, show unto the king.** (On אָשְׁפִין and חַרְטֻמִּין, A. V. "astrologers" and "magicians," see on chap. i. 20.)

Concerning the גָּזְרִין, "star-gazers," who are for the first time expressly mentioned in this place, see notes on verse 2. The word (from גְּזַר, "to cut in," "incise;" cf. גְּזֵרָה, chap. iv. 14) primarily denotes "deciders," viz.: deciders of fate, dispensers of decisive oracles concerning the fortunes of men, hence *astrologers*. Compare chap. iv. 4; v. 7, 11; also Isa. xlvii. 13, from which passage it appears that the office of the Babylonian astrologers was not confined merely to horoscopy, but extended to every kind of fortune-telling founded on the study of the stars. The Vulg. *haruspices* is incorrect; for the signification of the Hebrew (and Arabic) גְּזַר, "to cut in pieces," is foreign to the Aram. גְּזַר; and haruspicy as a specifically priestly function would seem rather to belong to the Chaldæans.—Verse 28. **But there is a God in heaven that revealeth secrets.** These words imply the total inability of the heathen gods as well as of their priests and wise men, to reveal secret things; compare Isa. xli. 22 et seq.; xliii. 8; xlviii. 3, etc.; Am. iii. 7; Hos. xii. 11.—**And maketh known to the king Nebuchadnezzar**—though that monarch is a heathen; compare the instances of Pharaoh (Gen. xx. 3 et seq.; xli. 16 et seq.), Balaam (Num. xxii. et seq.), the Eastern Magi (Matt. ii. 1 et seq.). The ו in וְהוֹדַע is explicative or particularizing. It serves to introduce the transition from the general truth to the special case in question.—**What shall be in the latter days.** בְּאַחֲרִית יוֹמַיָּא = Heb. בְּאַחֲרִית הַיָּמִים, is neither, directly and without qualification, "in the last time" (Hitzig), nor yet "in the course of time, in the future" generally (Maur., Häv.), but, as everywhere in the prophetic language of the Old Testament (not excepting Gen. xlix. 1; Num. xxiv. 14), "in the Messianic future,"—in the future theocratic period of salvation. Kranichfeld remarks correctly: "The writer at the outset of his prophetic announcement characterizes, by the use of באחרית יומיא, the whole matter as in relation to the Messianic destiny of his people."—**Thy dream, and the visions of thy head.** חֶזְוֵי רֵאשָׁךְ (cf. chap. iv. 2, 7, 10; vii. 1) here designate the dream-visions of the king, not because they were begotten by his head or brain in a purely subjective manner, but because God had originated them in connection with the meditations of his head. The phrase is synonymous with "thy dream," and with the latter forms a hendiadys, by virtue of their connection by ו; the plural is used because the king had seen a multiplicity of dreams (cf. verses 1, 2), but is subordinated to the singular חֶלְמָךְ as the leading conception, so that the following דְּנָה הוּא is exclusively conformed to this; cf. Winer, § 49, 6.—Verse 29. **As for thee, O king, thy thoughts came into thy mind** (marg. "came up") **upon thy bed**, *i.e.*, presented themselves, uncalled for as it were;—a strikingly expressive personifying phrase. On the form סְלִקוּ compare chap. iii. 8; vi. 13; Ezra iv. 12.—The רַעְיוֹנָךְ, "thoughts," are by no means to be directly identified with the "visions of thy head" in the preceding verse; they are, rather, merely the psychical substratum of those visions, the *natural soil*, as it were, from which the Divine communication sprang forth during the dream (correctly Ephraem, Maurer, Von Lengerke, Kranichf.). The רַעְיוֹנֵי לִבְבָךְ at the close of the following verse, again, are probably something different from both the רעיונך here mentioned, and from those "visions of the head." They are, most likely, as the context indicates, the disquieting thoughts which occupied the king after his dream, according to verse 1 (cf. chap. v. 6). The pronoun of the second person אַנְתָּה (for which the Keri substitutes the later form אַנְתְּ), which precedes in the nominative absolute, is repeated by the suffix in רַעְיוֹנָךְ, in a manner similar to that by which the introductory absolute וַאֲנָה, "and I," is resumed by לִי, in the next verse; cf. the same construction, chap. i. 17.—Verse 30. **Not for any wisdom that I have more than any living.** This denies every human agency in the imparting of such superior knowledge to Daniel, and at the same time refers to the design which governed it, concerning which the latter half of the verse is more explicit.—**But for the intent that the interpretation may be made known to the king** (margin); properly, "that they should make known to the king." The indefinite, impersonal plural יְהוֹדְעוּן (Winer, § 49, 3) was probably used with design, that the person of Daniel might be as little conspicuous as was possible, in accordance with the thought in the former half of the verse. Compare also chap. iv. 28.

Verses 31–35. *The subject of the dream, and, more immediately, the general description,* in verse 31, *of the image observed by the king.* **Thou, O king, sawest, and behold a great image.** "Sawest,"—literally, "wast seeing," wast in the condition of one who beholds a vision; cf. Winer, § 47, 1.— אֲלוּ, "behold," is a modification of אֲרוּ (chap. vii. 5, 6), which, according, to some, = the imperative רְאוּ, "behold," but seems rather to be a pronominal form from the demonstr. אַר = אל; see Hupfeld in the *Zeitschr. für Kunde des Morgenl.*, II., 133,163. The Talmud generally substitutes הֲרֵי for either of these forms.—The "image" (צְלֵם), as the context shows, designates a statue in the human form, an ἀνδριάς; also, in chap. iii. 1; cf. Isa. xliv. 13.—**This great image, whose brightness was excellent.** In the Chaldee the words "this image great and its brightness magnificent" are inserted as a parenthesis into the sentence, "and behold a great image stood before thee." The exceeding brightness of the image results naturally from the metals which compose it.—**The form** (rather "appearance") **thereof was terrible**; this on account of its brightness as well of its greatness; compare Cant. vi. 4.—Verse 32. **This image's head was of fine gold.** Literally, "this image, its head," etc. The position of the absolute הוּא צַלְמָא at the beginning of the sentence, is similar to verses 29, 30, and verses 33 *b*, 37, 42, etc.—The *stat. constr.* רֵאשׁ ought properly to be repeated before דִּי, the sign of the genitive; cf. vii. 7, 19; also Psa. xlv. 7; Ezra x. 13, etc.—Verse 33. **His legs of iron.** On שָׁקוֹהִי, "shanks," compare Cant. v. 15.—**His feet part of iron and part of clay;** literally, "of them of iron, and of them of clay." In the Kethib the masculine suffix is appended to the partitive מִן, מִנְּהוֹן; likewise in verses 41 and 42. The Keri employs, in each of these cases, the form מִנְּהֵן which the fem. רַגְל might lead us to expect, but which must probably be regarded as an easier reading. The masculine suffix in מִנְּהוֹן, like הִמּוֹן in verse 34, for example, and like the suffix הוֹן in chap. vii. 8, 19, must either be regarded as a common gender (Hitzig), or these masculine forms must be explained by a more general conception of the subject, or by one modified according to the sense,—in this case by transferring the thought from the figure to the fact to which it relates, *i.e.*, the conception "foot" to the other idea "kingdom," which is symbolized by it (so Kranichf., following Ewald, *Lehrb.*, p. 784, § 318,a).—Verse 34. **Till that a stone was cut out.** Naturally a stone that lay on the side of a mountain, from whence it rolled. This stone enters suddenly and unannounced into the transaction; as often happens in dreams.—**Without hands,** *i.e.*, without human, but solely through a supernatural and Divine agency; compare viii. 25, בְּאֶפֶס יָד; also Job xxxiv. 20; Lam. iv. 6; Heb. ix. 11.—Verse 35. **Then was the iron, the clay, etc., broken to pieces together.** דָּקוּ instead of דַּקּוּ; the lengthening of the preceding vowel compensates for the *Dag. forte.* The impersonal subject in the plural ("they broke in pieces," cf. verse 30) refers to the invisible supernatural powers, who effected the appearance of the stone itself and the consequent destination. The several component parts of the image, iron, clay, etc., are in this place recited from below upward, because the stone smote and crushed the feet first.—**And became like the chaff of the summer threshing-floors;** hence were totally demolished, annihilated without leaving a vestige. Compare Hos. xiii. 3; Mic. iv. 13; Isa. xli. 15,16; lvii. 13; Psa. i. 4; xxxv. 5; Job. xxi. 18.—**And the stone . . . became a great mountain.** טוּר, *mountain*, is the Heb. צוּר, *rock.* On the hyperbolical phrase "to fill the whole earth" (not merely "the whole land," as Van Ess, and others) compare John xxi. 25, and also the apocryphal parallels in Fabric., *Cod. Apocr. N. T.*, I., 321 seq. The exaggeration, however, holds with regard to the figure only, not to the symbolized reality, see verse 44.

Verse 36. *Transition to the interpretation of the dream.* **We will tell the interpretation thereof to the king.** נֵאמַר, in the plural, is used because Daniel classes himself among the worshippers of Jehovah, all of whom, as such, have access to the mysteries of Divine revelation. It is therefore an expression of modesty, similar to that contained in verse 30. [Daniel seems specially to refer to his three companions, who had been associated with him in prayer for the Divine aid in recovering and expounding the dream, verses 17, 18, 23.]

Verses 37–45. *The interpretation.*—**Thou, O king, art a king of kings.** מֶלֶךְ מַלְכַיָּא, the general title of Oriental sovereigns, *e.g.*, according to the cuneiform inscriptions, among the Persians (cf. Ezra vii. 12); among the Ethiopians of modern Abyssinia (*Inscr.*, 5138); and especially among the Babylonians; compare Ezek. xxvi. 7, where, as here, Nebuchadnezzar is termed a king of kings. For the rest, the form "Thou, O King" is taken up again below, in verse 38 *b*, by אַנְתְּה הוּא; for which reason מֶלֶךְ מַלְכַיָּא is really to be regarded as in apposition, and the period extended to the close of verse 38; for verse 37 *b* (דִּי to יְהַב־לָךְ) is merely a relative clause, and verse 38 *a* (וּבְכָל־דִּי to בְּכָלְּהוֹן) is a parenthetical supplement to it.*—**The God of heaven hath given thee a kingdom** (or dominion), **power, and strength, and glory.** For the connection of the relative דִּי with the pronoun of the second person לָךְ, compare, *e.g.*, Ecc. x. 16. On the idea, chap. iv. 19; v. 18.—Verse 38. **And wheresoever the children of men dwell,** etc. On וּבְכָל־דִּי, "and wheresoever," compare the essentially equivalent בַּאֲשֶׁר, Judg. v. 27; Ruth i. 17; Job xxxix. 30. The inserted adverbial כָּל strengthens the idea of the relation, as in כָּל־קֳבֵל דִּי, etc.—Instead of דָּאֲרִין "dwelling" (part. of דּוּר; cf. the Heb. דּוֹר, "race, generation") the Keri has here and in chap. iii. 31; iv. 32; vi. 26, דָּיְרִין, which form is usual in the Targums.—**Beasts of the field and fowls of the heaven.** This mention of the animals as also subject to the great monarch, serves to enforce and strengthen the corresponding statement with reference to men; similarly Jer. xxvii. 6; xxviii. 14—which passages Daniel probably had in view; also Bar. iii. 16; Judith xi. 7, etc.—["Nebuchadnezzar's dominion did not, it is true, extend over the whole earth, but perhaps over the whole civilized world of Asia, over all the historical nations of his time; and in this sense it was a world-kingdom, and as such, 'the prototype and pattern, the beginning and primary representative of all world-powers' (Klief.)."—*Keil.* "That this method of describing extensive dominion was common to the Shemitic dialects, is evident from Gen. i. 26; Psa. viii. 6–8; comp. Heb. ii. 7. 8."—*Stuart.*]—**Thou art this head of gold.** [In אַנְתְּה הוּא the הוּא is an emphatic copula, as in verse 47. "It carries a kind of demonstrative force with it, like that of the Greek οὗτος, and is equivalent to *Thou art the very* or *that same.*"—*Stuart.* Strictly,

*[Keil takes the same view of the construction, *Commentary*, p. 104. The rendering of the whole clause would then be as follows: "Thou, O King, the king of kings (for the God of heaven hath given to thee the kingdom, the power, and the strength, and the glory; and wherever the sons of man dwell, the beast of the field, and the fowl of the heavens hath he given into thy hand, and hath made thee ruler over them all)—thou art the head of gold."]

the clause might be rendered, "*Thou art it, the head of gold*," and this would yield the exact force of the expression.] Read רֵאשָׁה; the form רֵאשָׁה (or רֵאשֵׁה, as Hitzig prefers) seems to have been taken from verse 32. Still, שְׁמֵה, verse 20, might perhaps be adduced in support of this reading; see Hitz. on the passage.—The reason why Daniel designates Nebuchadnezzar himself as the golden head, instead of his kingdom, lies simply in the fact that the first (even though he were yet co-regent with his father Nabopolassar) gave to the Chaldæan empire its glory and world-wide greatness and importance; so that he could not only be considered the founder of this first world-monarchy, but might also, in a measure, be identified with it. Especially might this occur in the address of a speaker, who would ex-officio be compelled to magnify his fame, because he stood before the king in person, and in the presence of his court. How easily our author could identify a realm (מַלְכוּ) with its sovereign (מֶלֶךְ) is shown by chap. vii. 17, where "four kings" is almost exactly synonymous with "four kingdoms."—Verse 39. **And after thee shall arise another kingdom inferior to thee.** אַרְעָא probably does not signify "earthward, toward the earth," as is generally assumed; nor can we, with the Keri, consider אֲרַע as an adverb.* It may be taken instead as a *casus adverbialis* from עֲרַע (= Heb. שְׁפַל), "a low object,"—analogous to the adverbial עֵלָּא, "above, upward," from עֵל, "height," chap. vi. 3; and as there עֵלָּא מִנְּהוֹן signifies "higher than they, above them," so here אַרְעָא מִנָּךְ may mean "below, inferior to thee." The characterizing of the second kingdom as inferior to the first, which Nebuchadnezzar represented, does not, however, relate to its external power; for it is certainly also conceived of as a world-controlling kingdom, a universal monarchy, as appears abundantly from chap. vi. 26. Its inferiority to the former kingdom can only consist in a lower standard of morals, as also the third and fourth kingdoms can only be regarded as below their immediate predecessors in an ethical sense, but not physically or politically. This follows with the utmost clearness from the descending gradation of gold, silver, brass, and iron, as compared with the increasing magnitudes of the corresponding parts, the head, breast, belly, and legs of the image, a thought which lies at the foundation of the whole description (cf. on verse 40, and especially Dogmat.-eth. deductions, No. 3). Considering all this, it seems decidedly superfluous and inappropriate to refer the second kingdom to Belshazzar, as the successor of Nebuchadnezzar, and reserve the third for Medo-Persia (Hitzig, *Heidelberg. Jahrb.*, 1832, p. 131 ff., and Redepenning, *Stud. und Krit.*, 1833, p. 863). The suffix in בָּתְרָךְ and in מִנָּךְ does not at all compel us to assume that only Nebuchadnezzar's reign is designated by the golden head, and that therefore the breast of silver must refer to his successor on the throne of Babylon. Daniel probably conceived of the first and second kingdoms as monarchies under the rule of a succession of kings, as well as the fourth (see verses 43, 44); and the courtesy simply, which he was obliged to observe toward the great monarch who was personally before him, led him, in this and the preceding verses, to mention Nebuchadnezzar only as the representative of the first kingdom (see above).—**And another, third kingdom of brass, which shall bear rule over all the earth.** Its ethical inferiority to both its predecessors is indicated by the brass, while the relative clause דִּי תִשְׁלַט בְּכָל־אַרְעָא (compared with verse 38 *a*) seems to imply that the extent of its power should even exceed theirs. It may be remarked, in passing, how clearly this indicates the Macedonian world-monarchy.—Verses 40–43. *The fourth kingdom, corresponding to the fourth beast*, chap. vii. 7 et seq., *and like it signifying the divided Greek supremacy under the successors of Alex. the great.* **The fourth kingdom shall be strong as iron.** On the relation of the form רְבִיעָיָא in the Kethib, which is analogous to the usage of the Syriac, to the purer Chaldaic Keri רְבִיעָאָה (here and chap. iii. 25; vii. 7, 23), see Kranichfeld on the passage. The following explains the meaning of the predicate "strong as iron.—**Forasmuch as iron breaketh in pieces and subdueth all things;** rather, "crusheth all things." כָּל־קֳבֵל דִּי is clearly not to be taken in its usual signification, "since," but comparatively, "just as;" compare chap. vi. 11. The opinion that it stands here in its usual sense as = *because* (Kranichf., etc.), is opposed by the Athnach under the preceding כְּפַרְזְלָא, which shows that "to break in pieces and crush everything" is not merely stated to be a constant property of iron, but has its application to the nature of the fourth kingdom. [Keil labors at length to sustain this *illative* rather than *illustrative* sense of כָּל־קֳבֵל דִּי, but the arguments on both sides are very trivial, and the difference is not important.]—**As iron that breaketh in pieces all these, shall it break in pieces and bruise.** The וּכְפַרְזְלָא דִּי־מְרָעַע is no "offensive and dragging repetition of the already completed comparison," but rather serves to powerfully emphasize the iron-like destructive character of the fourth kingdom. The hardness and firmness of iron, however, and still more its solidity and durability, are not involved in the comparison, so much as its *destructive power*, as appears from the multiplication of verbs that express the idea of destroying (הדק, to *divide*. חשל, to *crush*, רעע, to *break* in pieces—the first and last of which are repeated). כָּל־אִלֵּין, "all these," an individualizing resumption of the more general כֹּלָּא, does not belong to the relative clause וּכְפַרְזְלָא דִּי־מְרָעַע (Kranichf.), but to תַּדִּק וְתֵרֹעַ, which verbs would otherwise stand too disconnected at the close of the verse.

*[Yet the author's explanation below amounts to this interpretation of אַרְעָא, which is substantially adopted by Gesenius and Fürst as being the most natural and agreeable to the form of the word.]

There is nothing suspicious in the fact that, by this construction a breaking to pieces of "all these,"—*i.e.*, the materials already mentioned, gold, silver, etc.—by the fourth kingdom, is stated; for it does not assert the destruction of all *former kingdoms as such*, but only the increasing diminution and shattering of their politico-ethnological material. The passage thus merely represents, in general, the separating and destructive influence which, naturally to its own injury, emanates from the fourth kingdom. The way is thus paved for the description which follows, of the divisions, internal confusion, and weakness of that kingdom (verses 41–43).—Verse 41. **And whereas thou sawest the feet and toes, part of potter's clay.** מִנְּהוֹן as in verse 33. The addition of דִּי־פֶחָר, "of the potter," to חֲסַף, "clay," strengthens the conception of weakness and lack of power which is implied in that term. The same idea results from the genitive combination חֲסַף טִינָא, "miry clay, potsherds," which occurs at the end of the verse; it designates the finished work of the potter (Vulg. *testa*), which, as sherd, is capable of being easily broken.—**The kingdom shall be divided**, *i.e.*, a kingdom that contains in itself the principle of an increasing disruption and self-division. The dual number of the legs, which might have been made to indicate such division (especially if the colossus were conceived as standing with widely-extended legs), is, evidently, not regarded by the composer. Nothing but the mixture of iron and clay forms the symbol of division in his view; and this mixture, according to him, pertains *only to the feet*, and does not extend to the legs, which are represented in verse 33 *a*, as composed entirely of iron. This indicates that the division, although its principle was inherent in the iron-kingdom (see on the preceding verse),* should only be thoroughly manifested, and its ruinous consequences become apparent in the course of the development of this kingdom; facts which were very fully realized in the history of the Macedonian empire after Alexander, whose rulers endeavored to maintain the unity of the realm down to the battle of Ipsus, although engaged in many conflicts and bloody quarrels with each other, and which only, from the period of that event, permanently dissolved into a number of kingdoms (originally four, from which, however, a constantly increasing number of smaller independent states was developed). Compare infra.—**But there shall be in it of the strength of iron.** Luther renders "of the iron's *plant*," corresponding to נִיצְבָא in the Targums, and to the Syr. *nezbeto* (cf. also Theodot. ἀπὸ τῆς ῥίζης, and Vulg.: *de plantaris*). But נִצְבְּתָא is probably derived from יְצַב in Pa. "to fortify, strengthen,"—and therefore to be rendered *firmness*, strength (cf. יַצִּיב, firm, certain, vs. 8 and 45; also chap. iii. 24; vi. 13, etc.), rather than from נְצַב, to *plant*.—Verse 42. **And as the toes of the feet were part of iron, and part of clay.** The nominative which precedes is really disconnected (cf. verse 32), but, since it is in comparison with the latter half of the verse, "as," or "just as," it may properly be supplied. The composition of even the toes out of the fatal mixture of iron and clay, indicates the weakness of the feet which support the great colossus, despite the fact that iron enters into its constitution throughout, as a principal element. That Daniel, while mentioning the toes, already refers to the ten kings of the Seleucidæ, who are represented later (chap. vii. 7, 24) as the ten horns of the fourth beast, cannot be certainly shown. At any rate, he follows this thought no further, as will be seen from the fact that while he mentions the toes, he does not premise their tenfold number (cf. Hitzig on this passage, against Hengstenb., p. 211. The latter clearly forces the symbol of the toes too far).—**So the kingdom shall be partly strong, and partly brittle** (margin). Concerning מִן קְצָת, "chiefly, partly," see on chap. i. 2.—Verse 43. **They shall mingle themselves with the seed of men**; *i.e.*, the several kingdoms, or rather their rulers, shall seek to establish harmony by means of marriage and voluntary relationship (hence in this way of sexual propagation).* On the expression, compare Jer. xxxi. 27; on the subject, chap. xi. 6 et seq. and 17, where the prophet enters more fully into the subject here referred to, of the adoption of the marriage policy, and of its failure.—**But they shall not cleave one to another, even as iron is not mixed with clay**; properly, "does not mingle itself with clay." The reflexive Ithpaal of עֲרַב designates the process of mixing or uniting itself, while the Pael, employed above in verse 41 *b*, expresses a passive sense. This involves the idea that the elements of iron and clay might be externally mixed, but could not be internally united, because their qualities do not blend, *i.e.*, they contribute nothing themselves to their coherence and permanent union.—Verses 44, 45. *The fifth, or Messianic kingdom.* **And in the days of these kings**; hence, while these kings, the Seleucidæ, Lagidæ, and the other Diadochi, are still reigning; and therefore not without being involved in strife and conflict with them: cf. *b*, and chap. vii. 13, 25 et seq.; viii. 10 et seq.; ix. 24 et seq.—**Shall the God of heaven set up a kingdom.** On "God of heaven," compare on verses 18 and 37. The highest and only true God appears there as the originator and supreme lord of *all* kingdoms (cf. verse 21); but this fifth and last kingdom alone, is, in the full sense of the word and with unqualified truth, a kingdom of specifically divine and heavenly character. This implies its miraculous origin as well as its never-ending duration.—**The kingdom** (rather, "its dominion"†) **shall not be left to other**

* ["פְּלַג always in Hebr., and often in Chald., signifies the unnatural or violent division arising from *inner disharmony or discord*; cf. Gen. x. 25; Psa. iv. 10; Job xxxviii. 25; and Leng., *Chald. Wörterb.*, s. v."—*Keil.*]

* [Keil, however, contends, with Klief., that the *mixing* is not solely nor properly on the part of the kings, but is only spoken of the vain efforts of the heterogeneous elements of the fourth kingdom to coalesce by juxtaposition or even by intermarriage among themselves. The general character of מִתְעָרְבִין, and especially the fact that *no subject* for it is expressed in the text, favor the opinion that both references are intended, namely, to the rulers as well as the people.]

† [The authorized rendering, however, is correct, if, with

people. This had occurred at the end of each of the former kingdoms; compare Ecclus. x. 18. The cessation of such transfers of dominion circumscribes the idea of eternal duration in a realizing manner. The term מַלְכוּ in וּמַלְכוּתָהּ is evidently no longer used in the same sense as before, but signifies "dominion," "government." The suffix does not refer to the God of heaven as the founder of the kingdom (Theodotion, ἡ βασιλεία αὐτοῦ), but to the kingdom itself. —**It shall break in pieces and consume all these kingdoms.** וְתָסֵף is literally, "and bring to an end"—annihilate them. The Divine kingdom is not merely to destroy the fourth world-kingdom, but also the three that preceded it, inasmuch as all had been incorporated with the former; which is shown by the figure of the stone that crushes the legs of the colossus, and thereby destroys the whole image. All these kingdoms are thus described as arrayed in hostile opposition to the divine kingdom, and as objects of its destructive influence; but this does not prevent the existence of certain gradations in their hostility to God and in their untheocratic tendencies; nor that, for instance, the golden head (Babylon) and the breast of silver (Medo-Persia) show greater favor and ethical approximation to God's people, than the brazen belly, etc. Compare supra, on verse 39.—Verse 45. **Forasmuch as thou sawest that the stone was cut out of the mountain,** etc. כָּל־קֳבֵל דִּי is employed here as in v. 40, in a comparative sense, like כַּאֲשֶׁר, "accordingly," or "forasmuch." From this usage results a closer connection of the former half of this verse (as far as וְדַהֲבָא) with what precedes it. The somewhat loosely connected and abrupt position which the second period, beginning with אֱלָהּ רַב, is thus made to occupy, need not deter us from this construction (against Hitzig and Kranichf.), which was employed by all the old translators (and also by Luther, Dereser, Von Leng., Maur., etc.).—On the subject compare Matt. xxi. 44; Luke xx. 18, where Jesus clearly refers this Messianic prophecy to himself and his kingdom. —**The** (rather "a") **great God hath made known to the king,** etc. "A great God," says Daniel, because he desires to refer to the infinite power of that God, who is not only able to disclose wonderful revelations respecting the future. but also to bring his promises to pass. The mode of expression is not exactly poetical, as Kranichfeld supposes, but generalizing. But compare אֱלָהָא רַבָּא, with the article, Ezra v. 8. [On the contrary, Keil more justly remarks, "That אלה רב means, not 'a (undefined) great God,' but *the great God in heaven*, whom Daniel had already (verse 28) announced to the king as the revealer of secrets, is obvious." The sign of definiteness (as the art. in Heb.) is omitted on the general principle that the construction by a qualifying adjective renders the term sufficiently definite, inasmuch as there could be no doubt what deity is referred to.]—**What shall come to pass hereafter.** אַחֲרֵי דְנָה, "after this, hereafter," refers specially to the time of Daniel and Nebuchadnezzar (cf. v. 29), and not merely to the incident in the former half of the verse, as Hitzig contends, in order to find here an additional trace of the composition of this book in Maccabæan times.—**And the dream is certain, and the interpretation thereof sure.** This is an emphatic affirmation at the close of the truly prophetic character of the dream and of the interpretation that had been submitted. The predicate יַצִּיב with חֶלְמָא hardly refers, as Kranichfeld supposes, to the fact that the king had forgotten the particulars of his dream, and now recovered them accurately and perfectly. It is better to hold, in harmony with the preceding context, that Daniel aims to set forth the trustworthiness and prophetic force of the dream, as he afterward certifies the correctness of the interpretation by מְהֵימַן, "faithful, trustworthy."

Verses 46–49. *The influence of Daniel's interpretation.* **Then the king Nebuchadnezzar fell upon his face, and worshipped Daniel.** Evidently סְגִד does not here signify a mere προσκύνησις, such as was sometimes offered to *men* (cf. Gen. xxxiii. 7; 2 Sam. xxv. 23; 1 Kings i. 16; Est. iii. 2), but rather a properly divine adoration (λατρεία), as is shown by the connected religious acts of sacrifice and burning incense. This he offers to Daniel as a great prophet of the highest God (see v. 47), and not because he considered him a god in human form, as the inhabitants of Lystra regarded Paul and Barnabas (Acts xiv. 13 et seq.). For this reason the course of Daniel is unlike that of the apostles on the latter occasion. He no more rejects the homage of the heathen king, than did the high-priest Jaddua, when Alexander the great bowed himself to the earth before him, in order to honor the God of Israel (Josephus, *Anti.* XI. 8, 5); at any rate, he has not definitely recorded that he protested against it and pointed from himself, the human instrument, to his God—which might, however, be explained on the ground of his abbreviating style (cf. on v. 15 et seq.). [We must not forget that Daniel had already explicitly disclaimed before the king the possession of supernatural powers as of himself (verse 36), and had repeatedly ascribed foreknowledge to God alone (verses 28, 45).] The opinion of Geier, Calov, and others, that Nebuchadnezzar merely worshipped *in the presence* of Daniel, without addressing his homage to the prophet (—as if סְגִד לְ were synonymous with קֳדָם ס׳), must be rejected; and no less the assertion of Hitzig, that the objective aim of the Maccabæan compiler is again betrayed in this instance, by the "highly improbable behavior of the king" (! ?).*—**And commanded that they**

most editions of the Masoretic text, we read וּמַלְכוּתָה, as the *emphatic state* simply; but if with others, we read וּמַלְכוּתֵהּ, as the *suffixed state*, we must translate *its realm* or *dominion*. We may adduce, as an objection to the latter, such a variation in the sense of מַלְכוּת in the same verse, as well as the unusual and somewhat tautological application of the pronominal suffix to its own noun as an antecedent, *i.q.*, *the kingdom's kingdom*.]

* Porphyry early took offence at this passage, but his objection was properly dispatched by Jerome in a pointed manner: "*Hunc locum calumniatur Porphyrius, quod*

should offer an oblation and sweet odours unto him. נְסַךְ, in the Pael "to pour out, deal out, *libare*" (not "to dedicate, offer," as Hitzig, with an unnecessary reference to the corresponding Arabic verb, prefers), is zeugmatic in this place, and relates not only to the bringing of the מִנְחָה, "meat-offering," which included an actual *libare*, but also the נִיחֹחִין, *i.e.*, sweet-smelling savors,—offerings of incense, which were connected with all meat-offerings. The offering of incense, therefore, which was really implied in the מִנְחָה (Lev. ii. 1, 15, etc.), is again explicitly noticed, in like manner as the קְטֹרֶת is specially mentioned beside the עֹלָה and the מִנְחָה, in Ex. xxx. 9. On the term נִיחוֹחַ (literally "satisfaction, pleasantness"), here used elliptically without רֵיחַ, which is constantly joined to it in the Hebrew (cf. Ezra vi. 10, Chaldee text), see Gesenius-Dietr. in the *Handwörterbuch.*—The tropical conception of the offering of sacrifice and incense as a purely civic testimonial of honor (Bertholdt) is decidedly improper, and leads to a rationalizing of the passage hostile to both the language and the context. Compare the well-known Persian custom of offering sacrifices to kings as the representatives of Ormuzd, which is mentioned in Curtius, VIII. 5, 6; VI. 6, 2; Arrian, VI. 27.—Verse 47. **Of a truth it is, that your God is a God of gods.** On מִן־קְשֹׁט see above, on v. 8; compare בִּקְשׁוֹט, Judg. ix. 15; also Jer. xxii. 13.—דִּי stands emphatically before the remark, similar to ὅτι in the Greek, but has greater significance than the latter. "God of gods" does not, in the mouth of the heathen Nebuchadnezzar, designate the only true God (Von Leng.), but the mightiest of all gods. The phrase here expresses a different sense from chap. xi. 36; Psa. cxxxvi. 2; Deut. x. 17.—Verse 48. **Then the king made Daniel a great man.** רַבִּי the Pael of רְבָה, "to become great" (chap. iv. 8), hence, "to make great, *exaltare*." ["It is more fully defined by the following clauses."—*Keil.*]—**And made him ruler over the whole province of Babylon**; not as Von Leng. supposes, over the whole kingdom, but simply over the province, מְדִינָא, therefore, as in chap. iii. 2. The bestowal of a formal governorship or satrapy is not implied in the verb השׁלטה here, or in v. 38. What really was conferred on the prophet, was probably merely a decisive influence over the administration of the province of Babylon, as is illustrated by v. 49. [Still this civil appointment, in distinction from the literary or professional one immediately added, was tantamount to an official position as recognized vice-regent over the province in which the capital was situated.]—**And chief of the governors over all the wise men of Babylon.** וְרַב־סִגְנִין still depends on הַשְׁלְטֵהּ, which verb therefore zeugmatically designates, first his elevation to political power, and then to the dignity of chief priest. סְגַן (related to סכן, *periclitari*, *tentare*, in the Heb. *utilitati esse, officia praestare*; cf. סֹכֵן, minister) is equivalent to "business-manager, president, overseer;" a רַב־סִגְנִין is therefore a superintendent or chief præfect, and the "Rab-Signin over all the wise men of Babylon" accordingly seems to have been identical with the רַב־מָג or "chief magian" mentioned in Jer. xxxix. 3. On the probable identity of the terms חַרְטֻמִּין and מָגִים and the relation of both to כַּשְׂדִּים, see above on v. 2.—Verse 49. **Then Daniel requested of the king, and he set, etc.** וּמַנִּי properly, "and (so) he set;" for ו must be joined to the imperfect, in order to express the sense of "that" (Winer, § 44, 4). בְּעָא therefore signifies an *effectual* asking in this passage, a prevailing with the king.—**Over the affairs of the province of Babylon.** עֲבִידְתָּא, "management of business, administration" (cf. עֲבֹדַת הַמֶּלֶךְ, 1 Chron. xxvi. 30). The effect of this "placing over the administration of the province of Babylon," was, evidently, to include the three friends of Daniel among the כֹּל שִׁלְטֹנֵי מְדִינָתָא, chap. iii. 2, whatever may have been their official title. But their elevation to the rank of Shiltonim to the king involved no receding on the part of Daniel from the political dignity conferred on him, according to v. 48 (Porphyry, Berth., Hitz., etc.). It rather serves to illustrate the powerful influence of the new royal favorite and councillor. But Daniel was only this, not an actual chief satrap of Babylon, to whom the three friends might have been subordinate. See v. 48, and compare chap. iii. 12, which clearly indicates that Daniel did not belong to the number of prominent civil functionaries of the province of Babylon. [On the contrary, the passage here referred to only shows that Daniel's three friends were, as here stated, the persons directly responsible for the civil functions in a certain district; evidently as subordinates under some single higher officer, who in this case could be no other than Daniel himself—a personage too high for direct impeachment by these officious underlings.]—**But Daniel sat in the gate of the king**, *i.e.*, within the bounds of his palace, at his court. Compare שַׁעַר הַמֶּלֶךְ Est. ii. 1, 9, 21; iii. 2 et seq.; also αἱ πυλαί (of the Medo-Persian court), *Cyropædia*, VIII. 1, and the Turkish "Porte,"—and generally, Rosenmüller, *Altes u. Neues Morgenland*, III. 399 ff. Incorrectly Bertholdt and Gesenius (*Jesaias*, i. 697), "He became intendant of the royal castle,"—on which Hävernick remarks, with justice: "It is hardly conceivable how such nonsense could be imputed to our book." ["The chief ruler of the province had a number of ὕπαρχοι, *under-officers*, in the province for the various branches of the government. To such offices the king appointed Daniel's three friends at his request, so that he

numquam superbissimus rex captivum adoraverit: quasi non et Lycaones ob signorum magnitudinem Paulo et Barnabæ noluerint hostias immolare. Error ergo Gentilium, qui omne quod supra se est Deos putant, Scripturæ non debet imputare, quæ simpliciter refert universa quæ gesta sunt."

might himself be able as chief ruler to reside continually at the court of the king."—*Keil.*]

ETHICO-FUNDAMENTAL PRINCIPLES RELATED TO THE HISTORY OF SALVATION, APOLOGETICAL REMARKS, AND HOMILETICAL SUGGESTIONS.

We are compelled, in view of the great importance of the image of the monarchies for a correct estimate of the Messianic and practical bearing of all that follows, to separate our dogmatical and ethical observations on this vision into several sections. Accordingly, we treat first of its *form* ; next of the *circumstances of the times*, which afforded suitable analogies for its prophetico-historical composition ; in the third place, of the *symbolism* of the image as a whole ; fourthly, of the *interpretation* of the four world-kingdoms, and especially of the second, third, and fourth ; and finally, of the relation of the prophetic vision to the history of the founding and development of the Messianic kingdom—the whole to be followed by practical homiletical remarks.

1. *The form of Nebuchadnezzar's vision* is distinguished from that of almost all the other prophetic visions of the Old Testament, by the peculiarity, that it is a *dream*-vision, under which mysterious form its highly important prophetic contents are revealed first to a powerful *heathen* monarch. The dreams of certain heathen princes of patriarchal times, *e.g.*, of Abimelech, Laban, and Pharaoh (Gen. xx. 3 ; xxxi. 24 ; xli. 1 et seq.), present the only analogy to this fact, so far as they were divinely occasioned, and had a direct reference to the fortunes of God's people. But their contents lack the rich, lively dramatic and symbolic character of this vision ; and in the double dream of Pharaoh, the single instance where this approximately exists (Gen. xli.), we miss the far-reaching vision that covers all history, and the wealth of Messianic references, by which the dream-vision under consideration is so remarkably distinguished. The observation of Hävernick (*Komm.*, p. 42 et seq.) respecting the dreams of heathen persons in the Scripture history, although instructive and worthy of approval in other respects, has only a *partial* application in this case : "We often (?) make the observation in the Scriptures, that whenever it became necessary to magnify the theocracy and the kingdom of God on earth—which could only be aided to accomplish its final destiny by means of miracles,—and whenever the welfare of the faithful required a special interference, revelations were imparted to heathen and unbelievers, and generally by means of dreams. Compare Gen. xx. 3 (where it is expressly stated, with reference to Abimelech, ויבא אלה־ם וגו'), xxxi. 24 ; xli. ; Judg. vii. 13, 14. At the same time, the Scriptures assign as the reason for such revelations the *subjective* aim, 'to withdraw man from his purpose, and hide pride from man,' Job xxxiii. 17. This Divine purpose was directly favored by the solemn awe with which the heathen world regarded dreams (ὄνειροι θεῖοι, θεόπεμπτοι), as is proven by the characteristic and probably proverbial expression of Homer: καὶ γάρ τ' ὄναρ ἐκ Διός ἐστιν (*Il.* I. 63) ; cf. further, *Il.* II. 26 et seq. ; *Odys.* VI. 13 et seq. ; xxiv. 11, 12 ; Herod. VII. 16 ; also Knapp, *Scripta varia arg.*, p. 103 ss. ; Rosenmüller, *A. u. N. Morgenl.*, III. 33 et seq. ; Jahn, *Einl. ins A. T.*, II. 391 et seq."—An instructive article in the *Evangel. Missions-Magazin*, 1863, No. 1, which was written by Ostertag and entitled *Der Traum und seine Wirkung in der Heidenwelt*, treats of the important part which dreams continually play in the religious life of heathendom, and more especially, when it is aroused and influenced by Christian missionary efforts. Cf. also Delitzsch, *Bibl. Psychologie*, § 14, p. 283 et seq., and Splittgerber, *Schlaf und Tod, nebst den damit zusammenhängenden Erscheinungen des Seelenlebens* (Halle, 1866), p. 144 et seq. The two latter distinguish more carefully than Hävernick, in the above passage, the dreams inspired merely by conscience and those of a divinely caused and presaging character, which were more frequent within the domain of heathendom, from the dreams of revelation in the proper sense, whose occurrence was much less common among gentile nations, being generally limited in the Old and New Testaments to the people of God. Among the former class they reckon, *e.g.*, the dreams of Pharaoh ; among the latter, the dreams of Nebuchadnezzar, in chap. ii. and iv. of our prophet.

The important circumstance must be observed, in this connection, that Nebuchadnezzar's dream-vision relating to the four world-kingdoms was evidently imparted to this heathen monarch while in a state of violent and guilty terror, but in so confused and indefinite a form as to exceed his understanding, and as even to prevent a clear reproduction of its nature by the unaided efforts of his memory. In both respects he was compelled to seek the aid of an Israelitish prophet, as an instrument of the only true God to make known the purport of His revelation (cf. supra, on vs. 1 and 3). This feature is certainly remarkable, but by no means incomprehensible. The heathen experienced but a single impulse in the direction of prophecy ; the clearly connected description and analysis of the image of the future which he had seen were reserved for the spiritual art of the theocratic seer. The startling impression which had been made on the mind of the king while dreaming, by the appearance of the bright colossus, its sudden fall, and its total destruction and annihilation predominated to an extent that destroyed his recollection, and left him, on awaking, with a mere sense of having seen something highly important and of great significance for his own future and for that of his kingdom. It was natural that this should at once give rise to the wish to recall the vision clearly, in order to ascertain more fully what it might portend ; and that this desire should finally excite such alarm as to banish sleep. His condition is not without many parallels in the history of man's spiritual life. The Egyptian ruler had, indeed, retained the contents of his prophetic dreams, and required Joseph for the purpose merely of interpreting their meaning ;—in connection with which the much less startling character of the dreams must be regarded. But in more recent times many instances have been recorded, in which significant dreams were forgotten,—either wholly, or so far as details were concerned,—while they left a powerful impression in the mind of the dreamer (cf. Reitz, *Historie der Wiedergeborenen*, I., p. 132 et seq.; Schubert, *Symbolik des Traums*, p. 211 [3d ed.]; by the same, *Geschichte der Seele*, II., p. 94 et seq.; Splittgerber, as above, p. 118 et seq.). And the ancient Roman poet Attius (Cicero, *de divinitat.*, II. 21) has at least described the alarm produced, on the sudden awaking of the subject, by an impressive dream, in a manner which thoroughly recalls the behavior of Nebuchadnezzar as described in this chapter:

> "*Rex ipse Priamus somnio mentis metu*
> *Perculsus, curis sumptus suspirantibus*
> *Exsacrificabat hostiis balantibus.*
> *Tum conjectorem postulat, pacem petens,*
> *Ut se edoceret, obsecrans Apollinem,*
> *Quo sese vertant tantæ sortes somnium.*"

In view of all this there is nothing in the external form and dress of Nebuchadnezzar's vision that removes it materially beyond the influence of conditioning circumstances, such as are elsewhere apparent in the surroundings of prophetic dream-visions. Consequently the credibility of the narrative cannot be assailed on psychological grounds, nor on any other; and the attempt of Von Lengerke, Bleek, Hitzig, and others, to stamp it as an imitation of the history of Pharaoh and Joseph, designed to encourage and strengthen the faith of the Israelites in the time of Antiochus Epiphanes, must especially be rejected, as being decidedly arbitrary, since the peculiarities in the conduct and character of Nebuchadnezzar by far exceed the traits he manifests in common with his precursor Pharaoh, and also with his alleged imitator Antiochus.

2. In regard to *the points of connection which existed in the state of the world for the prophetic image of Nebuchadnezzar's dream*, see Kranichfeld's observation on v. 10: "It is not recorded, as being unessential, how much information, in regard to his *spiritual state* at the time of the dream, the king imparted to the wise men, nor yet how much they were able to apprehend themselves in view of the political aspect of the times. The historical point of departure for the knowledge of the dream as a revelation, is found in a consideration that must pre-eminently concern a king as such, at the beginning of a newly-founded realm, and in the presence of a powerful and threatening contiguous state, viz.: the question respecting the fate of his dynasty and of his kingdom." Cf. page 120: "But the political constellation, even in the early years of Nebuchadnezzar's reign, was not of a nature to prevent the writer from recognizing a powerful rival of the Chaldæan empire in the Median kingdom. Isaiah and Jeremiah had already pointed to the nations of the *north*, or specifically to *Persia* (Elam) and *Media* as the executors of the judgment that should come upon Babylon, cf. Isa. xiii. 17; 21, 2; Jer. l. 3, 9, 41; li. 11, 28.—Above all, Media stood as a powerful rival to the Chaldæan kingdom upon the historical arena, at the time of Nebuchadnezzar's entrance. The Medes were allied with the Babylonians in the destruction of Nineveh, and in that joint undertaking of an earlier period were already able to render powerful assistance; there are even indications that on that occasion the Babylonians saw the direction of their military enterprises principally in the hands of the Medes. They shared with the Babylonians in the possession of the Assyrian empire—the latter taking the western portion, while the former claimed chiefly the regions east and north-east of the Tigris. How greatly Nebuchadnezzar was obliged to dread the power of his neighbor is shown by his fortifications in the north, which were begun soon after his accession to the throne, and prosecuted with vigor during the greater part of his reign (cf. Niebuhr, *Gesch. Assurs und Babels*, p. 218 et seq., p. 223); an Elamitic-Median war against Babylon appears to have transpired as early as the 11th or 12th year of his reign."—If to these observations on the relations of Babylon to Medo-Persia, we add the remarks of the same exegete in relation to Javan, *i.e.*, Greece, which was looming up in the distant political horizon of Nebuchadnezzar, and remember, that his western rival and probable successor to the power and greatness of Medo-Persia might be well known to a Chaldæan king about B. C. 600—since Sennacherib had already been engaged in a warm contest with an army of Greek mercenaries in Cilicia, about a century before; since further, such mercenaries were accustomed to serve in the Assyrian armies from the time of Esar-haddon, and in the Egyptian from the time of Psammetichus, and since the Lydian kings were involved in exhaustive and bloody wars with the Ionians, Dorians, and Æolians of Western Asia from about B. C. 610 (see *Herod.*, I. 6; II. 152, 163, 169; Abydenus, in Euseb. Armen. ed. Aucher, I., p. 53; Berosus, *Fragm. hist. Græcæ*, II., 504 ed. Müller;—cf. supra, Introd. § 7, note 2),—it will be evident that all the conditions were present which could possibly be required for the originating of a dream-vision, by which a Chaldæan monarch about B. C. 600 was forewarned of the future overthrow of his dynasty through the agency of warlike neighboring states. More than an external historical occasion or impulse for the dream-vision, was not probably derived by the king from the peculiar state of existing political affairs. All that bears a really prophetic character in his vision is to be traced back to the direct agency of God, which was able to construct a majestic and united vision of the deepest prophetical significance, out of the extremely sporadic and imperfect natural materials that were provided in the range of the king's political observation. Left to himself, Nebuchadnezzar, whether awake or dreaming, could merely have originated certain presentiments, or combinations of political wisdom, which at the best, must remain mere images of the fancy, or acute speculations. If his dream became a picture of the future that embraced the world and displayed the profoundest prophetic truths, a vision that was "certain, and the interpretation thereof sure" (see above, v. 45), this was entirely owing to the all-enlightening and revealing influence of the Divine Logos (John i. 9), who sought to glorify Himself and His prophet at the court of the powerful heathen king, in order thereby to kindle a shining light of Messianic consolation for His faithful ones of that age, as well as for those of the still darker periods of the future. Cf. infra, Ethico-fundamental principles, etc., on chap. viii., No. 3.

3. *The symbolism of the image of the monarchies in general*, namely, the succession of the

four metals, gold, silver, brass, and iron, as also the distribution of these metals over the several parts of a colossal idol or statue in the human form, the contrast between the brittleness and weakness of this image and the world-filling greatness and solidity of the stone which takes its place, etc.; all these, like the fundamental conditions of the vision itself, may find their point of departure, or so to speak, their root, in certain relations and estimates of the time that naturally prevailed in Nebuchadnezzar's kingdom, while the peculiarity of their arrangement is doubtless, as before, to be traced back to the revealing influence of God. An underlying natural basis cannot be mistaken.

a. In the symbolizing of a succession of four world-kingdoms by a connection of four metals of steadily decreasing value. "A comparative view of the idea of a separation of the course of temporal development into four world-periods, which occurs elsewhere also, is instructive in this connection. We meet it in the Indian transformations within the limits of the four *Yugs*, in the Græco-Roman conception of four metallic *æons* (the ages of gold, silver, etc.), and also in the Parsee idea of four trees that have sprung from a single root, composed respectively of gold, silver, steel, and iron.* Hesiod indeed, destroys the number four, by introducing a fifth kingdom between the kingdoms of brass and of iron, which is not of metal, and thus corresponds, in a measure, to the Messianic kingdom of Daniel, namely, the *δικαιότερον καὶ ἄρειον, θεῖον γένος* of the heroes; but irrespective of this feature, the constant and decided combination of the idea of world-periods with the precise number *four*, remains a noteworthy fact. And although the correspondence that has been indicated, for instance, in the case of Ovid as coming under the influence of Greek conceptions, must in all probability be regarded as based on that idea, and moreover, although the Persian idea of the four metallic trees, which has been referred to, may not have been uninfluenced by the representations of Daniel,—it will still be apparent, that the natural application of the number four to the ages of the world rests upon a profounder reason that inheres in the nature of things, and evidently, upon a natural and simple association with *the four stages of human life*. This connection of the number four with the periods of human life is especially easy in Daniel, since the four phases of development are illustrated by *the image of man*, as a personification of heathendom" (Kranichfeld, p. 118 et seq.). To what extent the application, in this case, of the idea of four ages of the world to the succession of Asiatic monarchies, is to be placed to the account of the natural or political meditations of Nebuchadnezzar, and how far it is of supernatural suggestion or positively revealed, cannot, of course, be definitely decided, especially in view of our extremely fragmentary knowledge respecting the scope of religious thought and the philosophy of human life among the Babylonians.

b. The comparison of the successive kingdoms with the several parts of a colossal human or idol image is also probably based on some heathen mode of conceiving and representing things, with which the dream-originating Divine principle of revelation may have connected itself. Daniel himself, indeed, indicates nothing whatever, either in his recapitulation of the dream or in the interpretation, that can show that the form, size, and natural dignity of the several parts (head, breast, belly, legs), contained any special symbolical reference to the character of the four world-kingdoms; and any attempt to construct such relations between the image and the objects symbolized is exposed to the danger of being involved in useless interpretations and idle pastimes, as may be seen in many older expositors, and even as late as in Starke (on vs. 39 and 41). But at any rate the size and position of the various parts merit consideration as a *tertium compar.*, so far as the first kingdom, which is represented by the head, as the highest and most important, but also the smallest organ, may be conceived of as intensively more, but extensively less considerable, than the succeeding ones; as also each successive organ may signify an aggregation of peoples or states (cf. supra, on v. 39), which becomes steadily more worthless and degraded, from an internal (ethical) point of view, but as regularly increases in size and extent. In one respect, therefore, namely, so far as the decrease of internal moral worth (or dignity, according to the theocratic standard) among the four successive kingdoms is concerned, the symbolism of the various bodily parts yields the same result as that of the metals; while in another respect it leads to a contrary result, inasmuch as it represents these kingdoms as constantly extending their boundaries.

c. The final consideration,—whether the mysterious stone, that descends from the mountain and shatters the metallic image, representing Messiah's kingdom or the fifth world-monarchy, also contains features that may be traced back to the religio-political ideas of the ancient Babylonians, or whether, on the other hand, this closing incident of the whole vision must be regarded as purely supernatural in its character,—can hardly lead to a definite conclusion. Some approach to Messianic ideas and expectations, however, may have been contained in the religious estimate of the world current among that people, as well as in that of the Persians, the Greeks (compare what was remarked above concerning Hesiod and the Zoroastrian myth of the

* Cf. Wollheim da Fonseca, *Mythologie des Alten Indien*, p. 26 et seq.; Hesiod, Ἔργα καὶ ἡμέραι, 106 ss.; Ovid, *Metam.* I., 89 ss.; and in relation to the old-Persic doctrine of four ages of the world, especially *Genesis und Avesta* in *Ausland*, 1868, Nos. 12 and 28, and also Delitzsch, Art. *Daniel*, in Herzog's *Real-Encyklop.*, p. 276. According to the two latter, the book *Bahman Jesht*, for instance, contains the following remarkable statement of the myth respecting the four ages of the world: ". . . Zerdusht demanded immortality from Ormuzd, then Ormuzd showed to Zerdusht the all-embracing wisdom; whereupon he saw a tree having such a root that four trees had sprung from it, one of gold, another of silver, another of steel, and the fourth of iron. . . . Ormuzd said to the holy Zerdusht: 'The root of this single tree, which thou hast seen (is the world), and these four trees are the four times which shall come; this golden one, when I and thou entertain each other, and Cstasp-Shah accepts the law, and the body of the Deos is broken and they conceal themselves; this silver one is the reign of the royal Artashir; the steel one is the rule of Anosheveran-Chosru, the son of Kobat; that of iron the evil reign of the Deos'" (on which, according to the Parsee teaching, the time of the Saviour Sofiosh is finally to follow).

four trees), the ancient Germans and Scandinavians, etc. The stone that crushes the image of the monarchies or world-periods may, therefore, have been a conception taken from the Chaldæan or Babylonian circle of ideas, similar in its nature and tendency to those remarkable mythological approximations to the fundamental dogma of Christianity, which have justly been characterized as "mythological foreshadowings of the great truth: 'The word was made flesh'" (Kahnis, *Lutherische Dogmatik*, III. 334; cf. v. Osterzee, *Das Bild Christi nach der Schrift*, p. 69 et seq.; J. P. Lange, *Das Apostolische Zeitalter*, I., p. 237 et seq.).

4. *The historical interpretation of the four kingdoms*, or the application of the image of the monarchies to the facts of history in detail, involves no really serious difficulty upon the symbolic principles that have been established, in view of the definite statement by the prophet in verses 37, 38, by which the golden head designates the *Chaldæan* empire of Nebuchadnezzar. The three succeeding kingdoms may therefore be discovered, without leaving room for doubt. They necessarily represent the three phases of development in the great Oriental universal monarchy, which followed next after the Chaldæan period; for the prophetic horizon, whether of the king or Daniel, did not embrace the Occident. The four world-kingdoms are developed without exception on one and the same geographical stage, on the soil of the *Orbis orientalis*, thus harmonizing with the Biblical representation under the symbol of a *single* colossal human image; and the only world-kingdoms of the Orient that arose after the overthrow of Babylon, and that equalled it in importance, were the Medo-Persian founded by Cyrus, and the Macedonian-Hellenistic, originated by Alexander the Great, the latter of which passed through two stages, viz.: the period of its undivided existence, and that of its constantly increasing division and disintegration under the post-Alexandrian Diadochi. These two, or, by a more correct enumeration three, final forms of the Oriental universal monarchy, are represented with the utmost clearness by the silver breast, the brazen (copper) belly, and the nether extremities which are at first of iron and then of intermingled iron and clay. The breast of silver designates the Medo-Persian kingdom, which first succeeded the golden head, or Babylon. It does not signify Media simply, for (1) at the time when the Median king Cyaxares (=Darius the Mede, see Introd. § 8, note 4) and his nephew and son-in-law Cyrus overthrew Babylon, the Persian tribe had already become so prominent within the Median realm as to warrant the designation of the whole kingdom by the names of both tribes, the Median, which was formerly predominant, and the Persian which had now become its equal. (2) Daniel accordingly refers to the whole world-kingdom which succeeded Babylon as a kingdom of "the Medes and Persians" (chap. v. 28; cf. the exposition of that passage), and even in the section relating to the reign of Darius the Mede (chap. vi. 9, 13, 16) he designates the religious code, which was in force throughout the kingdom, as "the law of the Medes and Persians," thus characterizing it as a sacred ordinance that rested on the common consent of both the nationalities that had united under a single government.* (3) In exact correspondence with this is his representation of the Medo-Persian kingdom, in chap. viii. under the figure of a warlike ram, and his designation of a succession of two dynasties—a Median and a Persian—simply by the growth of two horns from the head of the ram, of which the smaller comes up first (verse 3; cf. verse 20). (4) Consequently, the instances in which he distinguishes Darius, or Cyrus, or succeeding kings, by the titles, respectively, of "king of the Medes," or "king of the Persians," must be regarded as referring, not to a diversity of realms, but simply to a difference of tribal relations among these rulers. (5) Further, the vision of the four successive beasts, which is described in chap. vii. and which is doubtless parallel to that of the four elements in the image of the monarchies, does not accord with the assumption, on which the second beast, a carnivorous bear, represents the kingdom of the Medes, while the third, a leopard with four wings, designates the Persian monarchy, which fact was scarcely distinct from the former (see infra on that passage). (6) Nor does Zech. vi., which is an alleged parallel to the vision before us, warrant a conclusion in favor of the opinion that distinguishes between the Median and Persian kingdoms; for the red, black, white, and grizzled, and bay horses, mentioned in that place, do not designate various lands or kingdoms any more than do the horses with similarly varied colors, which are introduced by the same prophet in chap. i. 7 et seq. (see Köhler, *Die Nachexilischen Propheten* ii. 1, 69 et seq., 189 et seq.). (7) Finally, no conclusion in favor of the Median hypothesis can be deduced from the remark by Daniel in verse 39 *a*, that the second kingdom should be inferior to that of Nebuchadnezzar; for an ethical inferiority of the Persian kingdom to that of the Chaldæans might be readily asserted from a theocratic point of view, inasmuch as it clearly displayed a greater moral and social depravation under its later kings, than the former. Only Cyrus excelled the Chaldæan rulers in friendly and benevolent conduct toward the theocracy, while his immediate successors, Cambyses and Pseudo-Smerdis, treated the people of God with greater severity than had any Chaldæan king whatever (cf. also the sufferings inflicted on the Jews by Xerxes, according to the book of Esther, and also by Artaxerxes I., according to Ezra and Nehemiah).

But if, in view of these considerations, the

---

* The force of the expression "the law of the Medes and Persians" (דָּת מָדַי וּפָרַס), in chap. vi. as an evidence of the union of the two neighboring Iranian nations in a single state as early as the period of the Chaldæan supremacy, and perhaps earlier still, has been recognized, *e. g.*, by Kranichfeld, despite his preference for the interpretation which refers the second world-kingdom to Media, and the third to Persia. In a note on page 123 et seq. he contests the assertion of Von Lengerke, that this formula really originated after the time of Cyrus, and is therefore a gross anachronism in the mouth of Daniel, by arguing that the union of the two peoples in a single nation, or at least under a single government, dates considerably beyond the time of Cyrus, and accordingly, that an exclusively Median realm was never in existence. The conformity of this view to the actual historical development of the ancient Iran is shown by Niebuhr, *Gesch. Assurs und Babels*, p. 186; cf. Spiegel in *Ausland*, 1866, p. 355 et seq.

second kingdom of the image of the monarchies represents Medo-Persia, there can be no further doubt as to the interpretation of the third, which is symbolized by the brazen belly. It must necessarily designate the *Macedonian world-kingdom of Alexander the Great*, whose grand and rapid introduction, as if borne on the wings of the tempest, is represented in the parallel vision of chap. vii. by the figure of a leopard with four wings, but which receives consideration in this case (chap. ii.), only so far as its ethical and religious inferiority in relation to its predecessors is concerned, and as the remark that it should "bear rule over all the earth" (verse 39 *b*) characterizes its external greatness. The kingdoms of the Hellenistic Diadochi, which arose from the universal monarchy of Alexander the Great, cannot be included in the third or brazen kingdom, since they present a picture of internal disruption, such as is clearly symbolized by the fourth monarchy of Daniel. The nether extremities of the colossus only, which were at first (in the legs) of iron, but afterward (in the feet and toes) a mixture of iron and clay, can be made to harmonize with the period of the Diadochi. In their interpretation, the legs, which are yet of iron, will probably refer to the time during which the immediate successors of Alexander endeavored at least to maintain the unity of the realm, despite their incessant quarrels and bloody conflicts,—hence down to the battle near Ipsus (B. C. 323–301); while the feet, which are in part of iron, and in part of clay, represent the succeeding state of growing dismemberment and hostile divisions (in which the kingdom of the Seleucidæ in Syria, and that of the Lagidæ in Egypt, were alone able to maintain, during a considerable period, a position of commanding power); cf. above, on vs. 41–43. That this torn and corrupted state of the post-Alexandrian Hellenistic empire, so analogous to a putrefying gigantic carcass, and also that the vain attempts to heal the sores by means of intermarriages among the contending princely families, etc., should be already described and prefigured in the visions of a Chaldæan king about B. C. 600, can, of course, find an explanation only in the direct operations of the Divine Logos, by which the future is revealed (cf. No. 3). To base these features on a reference to the historical condition of Hellenism during the Chaldæan period, to its internal divisions and incurable discords, which were, at that early day, as apparent as was their warlike bravery, and further, to the custom of political marriages among princes, which was already frequently observed (Kranichfeld), seems inadequate, and involves the danger of an exaggerated naturalizing of the prophetic process in question. Nor can the custom of political marriages be shown to have existed in the time of Nebuchadnezzar among the Greeks (with whom we have chiefly to do, in this connection), although it prevailed in Medo-Persia and Egypt.

Finally, the fourth kingdom was, at an early period, made to signify the Roman universal dominion, so that its first stadium of unimpaired strength (the legs of iron) represented the period of the republic and the first emperors, and the second, divided and powerless stage (the feet of iron and clay) referred to the later empire, or even to the middle ages and more recent times (in which, according to Auberlen's exposition of v. 43, the German and Sclavic nationalities were intermingled with the Roman); but this interpretation is opposed by many considerations. (1) It ascribes a range of vision over the future to the dreaming king and the prophetic interpreter, which lacks every support based on the actual condition of the times, since, as is well known, the greatness and world-historical importance of Rome were unknown until four hundred years after the captivity. Unlike the sections of the prophecy which relate to Persia and Javan, this would have no foundation in existing relations, but rather, would be of an abstractly supernatural character. (2) The כִּתִּים mentioned in chap. xi. 30, although already identified with the Romans by the Septuagint and the Vulgate, must rather be regarded as a race of *Greek* islanders, in view of the constant usage of the word elsewhere in the Old Testament, and more especially, because there is no indication of the identity of these Chittim with the fourth world-kingdom, either in chap. xi., or elsewhere. They are simply noticed in that connection, like the northern and southern kingdoms, as a constituent part of the Javanic or Hellenistic empire. (3) The symbolic details comprehended in the fourth or lowest world-kingdom according to Nebuchadnezzar's vision—the legs of iron, the feet and toes part of iron and part of clay, etc., appear natural and suitable when applied to the development of Hellenism after Alexander, and particularly in the era of the Seleucidæ and the Ptolemies, while they lead to results of a more or less arbitrary character, with every attempt to demonstrate the Roman hypothesis; *e.g.*, the view of Buddeus, Hengstenberg, and others, by which the two legs of iron designate the eastern and western empires after Honorius and Arcadius, and that of Cocceius, which regards the iron and the clay as indicating the separation of the Roman power into a spiritual and a material kingdom (papacy and empire), etc. (4) That the collocation of the world-monarchy of Alexander and the kingdoms of the Diadochi as forming one and the same מַלְכוּ, a position that becomes necessary on this view, although supported by chap. viii. 21 (where a grouping into a מַלְכוּת יָוָן has actually come to pass), is yet shown by chap. xi. 4, to be decidedly opposed to the real meaning of the prophet (cf. 1 Macc. (i. 1 and 7 et seq.). (5) Finally, the figure of a stone, that destroys the image, is positively false as a representation of the triumph of Christianity over the world-power, if the Roman power be regarded as the fourth and final phase of the development of the latter; for this was not overthrown and destroyed suddenly and at a blow by the kingdom of Christ, like the statue by the stone, but instead, it incorporated Christianity with itself, and continued, as Christianized Rome, to bear rule over the earth during more than a thousand years. It might, therefore, be more properly identified with the stone, than described as a potency inimical to it; but it can, in any case, find no place in the series of pre-Messianic world-kingdoms that were hostile to His reign. [To these arguments we add the marked coincidences between the several visions of Daniel respecting these four great world-powers, as exhibited in the harmonic table inserted in the introduction; and we call especial attention to the almost perfect parallel between the two "little horns" in each case. Now as one of these is admitted on all hands to refer to Antiochus Epiphanes, the other, if identical, is, of course, a constituent likewise of the Syrian empire of the Seleucidæ, as the fourth Oriental monarchy. The discrepancies alleged by Keil, p. 258 et seq., as arguing a different interpretation of the little horns respectively, will be duly noticed in the exposition of the passages themselves.]

For these reasons we adopt that exposition of the four kingdoms which Bertholdt (*Daniel*, I. 192 et seq.) has recently advocated with penetration and fairness, after Polychronius, Grotius, Tossanus, Zeltner, and others, had asserted its principal features. We differ from Bertholdt, however, in failing to deduce anything that argues the composition of Daniel's prophecy in the period of the Seleucidæ and Asmonæans, from the reference of the feet of iron and of clay to the times of the later Diadochi, since, as will be shown more in detail hereafter, we regard the reference of passages like chap. vii. 8 et seq.; ix. 24 et seq. to Antiochus Epiphanes as not conflicting with the authenticity of the book. We accordingly reject the following interpretations, which differ from ours in various particulars:

(*a.*) That of Bunsen (cf. Introd. § 4, note 1), which applies the golden head to Assyria, in harmony with the alleged original interpretation by Daniel, the breast of silver to Babylon, the brazen belly to Media, and the iron legs to Persia, but which is thus guilty, not only of a direct contradiction of v. 38 ("thou art this head of gold"), but also of a misconception that conflicts with history, in relation to the intimate connection, and even essential identity of the kingdoms of Assyria and Babylon, which could never have been contrasted as gold and silver, or the lion and the bear (cf. chap. vii. 5 et seq.)*

(*b.*) That of Hitzig and Redepenning (see above, on v. 39 *a*), which refers the head and breast to Nebuchadnezzar and Belshazzar, as the only Babylonian kings whom the author is said to have known, and which is therefore, at least, a partial reproduction of the scheme formerly attempted by the Swede, H. Benzel (*Dissert. de quatuor orbis monarchiis*, 1745), and by Harenberg, Dathe, and Hezel, to personify the four kingdoms (regarding them as metonymies for four Babylonian kings).

(*c.*) The view of Ephraem Syrus, Venema, Eichhorn, V. Lengerke, Bleek, de Wette, Kirmss, Hilgenfeld, Delitzsch, Kranichfeld (and conditionally, *i.e.*, so far as it conforms to the views under *a* and *b*, also of Ewald, Bunsen, and Hitzig), that the head represents Babylon, the breast Media, the belly Persia, and the legs Greece and the Diadochian kingdoms (see for the contrary, above, No. 4).

(*d.*) The "orthodox" view, which refers the first three kingdoms to Babylon, Medo-Persia, and Greece, but the fourth to Rome and the states which have sprung from it since the empire; early represented by Josephus (*Ant.* x. 10, 4), by a majority of church-fathers—especially by Jerome, Orosius, and Theodoret; also by all the expositors of the Middle-age church after Walafrid Strabo, and by a majority of moderns, of whom we mention Buddeus (*Hist. eccles.* p. ii. sect. 5, p. 619 ss.), Joach. Lange, Starke, Zeis, Velthusen (*Animadversiones ad Dan.* II. 27-45; Prag, 1783), Menken (*Das Monarchienbild*, Brem, and Aurich, 1809), Hengstenberg, Hävernick, Caspari (*Die vier daniel. Weltmonarchien*, in the *Zeitschrift für luth. Theologie und Kirche*, 1841, No. 4), Hofmann (*Weissagung und Erfüllung*, I. 276 et seq.), Keil (*Einl. ins A. T.* § 134, p. 443, [also in his *Commentary on Daniel*]), Gaussen (*Daniel le Prophète*, 2d. edit. 1850, I. 250 ss.), Auberlen (*Daniel*, etc., p. 42 et seq.), Zündel (*Krit Unterss.* etc., p. 74 et seq.), Kliefoth, Füller, Gärtner (in their expositions), Pusey (p. 58 ss.), Volck (*Vindiciæ Dan.*, p. 7 ss.), [and the monographs added in the Introduction].—For the history of this orthodox-churchly interpretation of the image of the monarchies in older times, see *Antiquæ et pervulgatæ de quatuor Monarchiis sententiæ plenior et uberior assertis*, auct. J. G. Jano, 1728 (also in Breyer's *Histor. Magazin*, vol. I., p. 114 et seq.); and in relation to its influence on the conception and representation of universal history during the 16th and 17th centuries, see Meusel, *Bibliotheca historica*, vol. I., pt. 1, p. 176 ss.*

* Cf. Zündel. *Krit. Unterss.*, p. 82; and generally as respects the continuity of the Assyrian and Babylonian empires and their inseparable connection in point of nationality, religion, and civilization, see the valuable sketch of the results achieved by the latest efforts of Assyriologists: *Ninive et Babylone*, in the *Revue des deux Mondes*, 1868, March 15, by Alfred Maury. The old-Babylonian (Chaldæan), the Assyrian, and the later Babylonian empires, are in fact but three successive phases of the development of one and the same world-kingdom, despite their changes of dynasties and capitals, as also the Median, the Persian (Achæmenidian), the Parthian, and other kingdoms, are successive phases in the manifestation of a single national empire on Iranian soil. Cf. G. Rawlinson. *The Five Great Monarchies of the Eastern World, or the History . . . . of Chaldea, Assyria, Babylon, Media, and Persia.* London, 1867, 4 vols. Also A. Scheuchzer's *Assyrische Forschungen* in M. Heidenheim's *Deutsche Vierteljahrschrift für engl.-theol. Forschung*, Vol. IV., No. 4 (1868), p. 4 et seq.

* [Justice to this popular view of the fourth kingdom of Daniel's prophecies, which applies it to the Roman empire, either as a pagan or a papal tyranny, seems to require a statement here of the principal arguments in its favor. Other considerations will be examined, as well as some of these more in detail, in the exposition of the passages under which they arise.

1. The prominence of the Roman dominion, as being the only really world-wide government after that of Alexander, certainly lends great probability to its selection as the culmination of the previous world-monarchies in comparison with the territorially insignificant realm of the Seleucidæ. But this argument seems to us to be neutralized by indications in the text itself, especially the fact that Daniel's prophecies in this matter are bounded by the Orient as to their arena of dominion, the chosen people of God and their local heritage being the stand-point from which their influence is measured. The Jews did not come into any severe contact with Rome till after the dawn of the Messianic era, and (as the author observes above) Rome itself did not then succumb under the collision. The note of time "in the days of these kings" (ver. 44) cannot be pressed into a corroboration of this synchronism, for then it would cover the whole range of the previous dynasties likewise (see the exposition of that verse). But a most decisive prohibition of the allusion to Rome appears in the continual degeneration of the successive empires from the head downwards, till the fourth has deteriorated into a base metal and even a maudlin alloy. It is true the epithet "strong as iron" well applies to Rome, but it attained its culmination both of force and culture under the early emperors, and there was no subsequent change of government in its decay corresponding to the distinction between the unadulterated metal of the legs and the

5. *The relation of the image of the monarchies*, when correctly interpreted, *to the history of the founding of Christianity*, must be found, in view of the foregoing considerations, in the assumption that the destroying stone represents the kingdom of Christ at the time of its introduction on the historical arena, while the growth of the stone until it fills the earth, indicates its gradual extension over all the countries of the earth. The fulfillment of this closing incident of the prophetic vision as a whole, is therefore not confined exclusively to the initial period of the history of Christianity —as if the stone represented the pre-Messianic Israel, or any other historical agency preparatory to the advent of Christ; nor is it to be referred entirely to the future of Christianity—as if the destruction of the colossus of world-powers had not yet transpired, and the overthrow of the fourth monarchy were reserved for the final judgment or some other eschatological event. The descent of the stone and the overthrow of the image were rather realized in the history of salvation, when Christ, the stone that was rejected by the builders, ground His enemies to powder, and became the elect and precious corner-stone in Zion, upon which all the foes of God's kingdom are henceforth to fall, and by which they are to be shattered and put to shame (Matt. xxi. 42–44; 1 Pet. ii. 6–8; cf. Isa. viii. 14; xxviii. 16). This closing scene of the vision is in the course of being steadily and increasingly fulfilled, inasmuch as, on the one hand, the destruction and dissolution of the world-powers, and on the other, the growth of the stone into a mighty mountain that fills the whole earth, are yet far from their Divinely appointed goal—however surely the world, together with Satan, its head, may have been long since judged in principle by the Spirit of Christ, and however clearly the only true God, who is declared in Christ, may have demonstrated, in a certain measure, his nature as the all-supporting rock, from all eternity in the congregation of His faithful ones (as the "Rock of Israel," Gen. xlix. 24; Deut. xxxii. 4 et seq.,

crumbling mixture of the feet and toes. In the case of the Syro-Greek monarchy, on the other hand, all these particulars have their exact counterpart.

2. The difficulties attendant upon the effort to identify with the history of the Seleucid succession the particulars elsewhere given in connection with the fourth empire, especially the list of ten kings and the fall of three of them before the successful one (chap. vii. 24) have been urged in favor of the "orthodox" view. But the Roman interpretation, on the other hand, seems to be beset with equal if not greater difficulties in this point, as will be seen in the exposition of that passage. Chap. xi. of this book is acknowledged on all hands to be a detailed account of the dynasty of the Seleucidæ, showing that the prophetic ken had it prominently in view; and the little horn of the he-goat (chap. viii. 9) is generally admitted to be Antiochus Epiphanes. It is therefore hard to resist the conclusion that the little horn of the fourth beast (chap. vii. 8) is the same king, and the fourth section of the colossal image (chap. ii. 40 et seq.) the same dynasty. The characteristics make the parallel complete.

3. The violent persecution experienced by the saints under Roman power, particularly in the days of papal supremacy, has been especially thought to justify this scheme of interpretation. But it must be remembered that the Seleucidæ were the first kings who really oppressed the people of God on account of their religion, and the efforts of Antiochus to exterminate their faith were of the most extraordinary character, not exceeded by the virulence of the Inquisition itself. Moreover, the attempt to apply the prophecies in question to both pagan and papal Rome, weakens the force of the whole interpretation. The effort to find in the pope, as such, an emphatic and direct fulfillment of the "little horn" is indeed sustained by the striking analogy of *blasphemous* atrocity, but fails to find an equal agreement with many other features of the picture, *e.g.*, the "mingling themselves with the seed of men" (chap. ii. 43; absolutely forbidden by the celibacy of the pontiffs and clergy), the origin in dynastic and territorial revolution ("the sea," chap. vii. 3, and "earth," chap. vii. 17), the pointed reference to the Mosaic cultus and temple (chap. viii. 11), and the whole tenor of the overthrow by civil and military convulsion (chap. xi. 40 et seq.). We may also adduce the gross incongruity of representing any branch of the Christian Church, however corrupt, under these heathen symbols, and as the final foe of God's people.

4. The marked similarity between the visions of Daniel and those of John in the Revelation, extending to details of phraseology as well as of emblem, has naturally led to the belief that they coincide in application. This, however, is a superficial view of their import. In the New Testament we everywhere find the symbols and even the terms of the O. T. used conventionally with a different application and in a wider sense. Thus, in our Lord's eschatological discourse (Matt. xxiv.), the symptoms of the dissolution of Judaism are made premonitions of the end of all things; the whole of Ezekiel's wail over the queen of ancient commerce (chap. xxvii.) is transferred almost literally to the apocalyptic overthrow of the later mistress of the world (Rev. xviii.); the very names, Babylon, Gog, etc., are applied to new places and persons, just as Sodom, Egypt, Zion, etc., had long been current with a metaphorical meaning. It is a great mistake, however, to infer that these N.-T. adaptations of types and imagery and language, familiarly drawn from the O. T., necessarily denote the same objects or events. They are rather related as common types of some recurring Antichrist, as extensions of one general world-power ever inimical to the cause of spiritual religion. To identify them is to destroy the significance and beauty of the conventional signs by which they are expressed. The shallowness of this method of exposition, as applied to St. John's Apocalypse, has been demonstrated by the futile attempts to make them quadrate with the facts of history.

5. Lastly, the periods assigned in Daniel for the fulfillment of the various prophecies, are appealed to in support of their application to Rome. This seems to us, on the contrary, a fatal argument against the view in question. It is true the same numbers are often used by the Revelator for the length of "the times and seasons" prefigured in his visions, but we have never yet seen any satisfactory adjustment of them to the history of the Roman empire or the papal church. We are strongly inclined to that view which regards them as being conventionally adopted by St. John as representations of longer or shorter periods of indefinite length. But in Daniel they unquestionably denote determinate spaces of time, and for that very reason —as they are all periods of comparatively brief extent (some three and a half years, with the exception of the notable term of 70 weeks, or rather hebdomads; see the exposition of that passage)—they must be limited by the history of the Antiochian persecution and the Maccabæan revolution. The only escape from this conclusion is by a resort to what is termed the "year-for-a-day hypothesis," which consists in understanding the *days* in each of the periods in question as put for so many *years*. It is sufficient to say of this somewhat popular and certainly convenient theory, that it is a conjecture devoid of countenance in Scripture. True, the prophets occasionally make a literal day the type of a literal year, but they never do so without immediately adding the explanation, for the express purpose of preventing such a generalization of the rule. Besides the passages in Gen. i. 5 et seq.; ii. 4; 2 Peter iii. 8 (which would prove too much), the only instances of this usage adduced are Num. xiv. 34; Ezek. iv. 1–6; Dan. ix. 24 (but this is not in point); Rev. ii. 10 (but here the application is a pure assumption); Rev. xi. 3–11 (an equally imaginary case); Rev. xi. 2, 3, and xii. 6, 14 (to include which is a simple *petitio principii*); Rev. xx. 6 (a rather difficult case—think of a millennium of 365,000 years!). See the exhaustive list by Dr. Pond, in the *Meth. Quar. Rev.* for Jan., 1874, p. 116 sq.; where the learned writer argues that if one part of a vision be a symbol so must the rest, *e.g.*, if the locusts in Rev. ix., be symbolical (which is probably true only so far as they are a type of *ruin* in general, not any particular form or agency), so must the accompanying number be; *ergo*, the "5 months" of ver. 5 must denote 150 years—just as if the number might not be symbolical of an indefinite period, as it no doubt is. We conclude, therefore, by reiterating that no clear instance can be adduced of the use of a "day" in Scriptural prophecy for an exact year, *where the typical character of the time is not immediately expressed* as being limited to that particular case, much less is there any intimation that such a rule is to apply to prophecy in general. To admit such a principle in Biblical interpretation is to abandon all precision in the use of language.]

Isa. xxx. 29; xliv. 8; 1 Sam. ii. 2, etc.; cf. the "rock of strength," Isa. xvii. 10; "rock of eternities," Isa. xxvi. 4; "rock of refuge," Psa. xciv. 22, etc.).—Here again we are compelled to reject several partial conceptions:

(*a.*) The identification of the stone or fifth monarchy with the Roman dominion (Grotius), which clearly leads to an improper naturalizing of the passage, so far as it confines itself simply to the earthly relations of the historical Roman empire; but which certainly includes an important measure of truth in so far as it regards the Roman world-power as a Divinely chosen and sanctioned bearer and promoter of the royal Messianic cause at the stage of its introduction (cf. supra, No. 4).

(*b.*) The one-sided and exclusive reference of the stone to the people of Israel (older Jewish expositors; Porphyry;—see, on the other hand, Jerome on the passage).

(*c.*) That interpretation of the stone by which it symbolizes merely the *person of the Messiah*, as distinct from the kingdom founded by Him (Cosmos Indicopleustes, and several rabbins, as Saadia, Ibn-Ezra, etc.; and, after them, especially J. Chr. Beermann, *De monarchia quarta*, in his *Meditatt. politicæ*, 1679, where he submits an interpretation of the several kingdoms that is otherwise entirely correct; cf. Bertholdt, as above, p. 215 et seq., in relation to Beermann, and partially against him).

(*d.*) The reference of the stone, not to the first, but to the second advent of Christ, and also to the erection of the Apocalyptic millennium, which is said to constitute the "fifth monarchy," according to the true and actual meaning of the prophet. This view was held by the Chiliasts (Enthusiasts, Anabaptists) of the 16th and 17th centuries, and especially by the fanatical sect of Quintomonarchists or Fifth-monarchy men in England at the time of Cromwell (see Weingarten, *Die Revolutionskirchen Englands*, Berlin, 1868, p. 180 et seq.); also by several recent expositors of a subtile-chiliastic tendency, especially Auberlen (p. 42 et seq.; 248 et seq.;—in opposition to him see Kranichfeld, p. 113 et seq.). Several earlier exegetes of pietistic-chiliastic or theosophic temper, *e.g.*, Joach. Lange, Starke, M. Fr. Roos, Mencken, etc., contented themselves with finding a prophetic reference to the millennium in the final destiny of the stone, hence in its development to a greatness that fills and controls the earth, which is entirely admissible in view of the above.

6. *The practical and homiletical treatment* of this chapter will dwell predominantly on either its historical or its prophetic features. The leading subjects for consideration will be either the answer to Daniel's prayer and his promotion above the heathen wise-men, or the triumph of the kingdom of God over the world-powers.

a. The former theme is immediately connected with the subject of the preceding chapter, since Daniel's promotion and honor were merely additional fruits of the faithful obedience, which had already in that connection been praised as the source and basis of his greatness. Especially suitable texts may be found in the prayer of Daniel and his friends, vs. 16–23, and in the closing verses 46–49. Compare Calvin's observation on v. 16: "*Videmus, quo consilio, et qua etiam fiducia Daniel postulaverit, tempus sibi dari. Consilium hoc fuit ut Dei gratiam imploraret . . . . Non dubium est, quin speraverit Daniel, quod adeptus est, nempe somnium regis sibi revelatum iri. Exponit ergo sociis suis, ut simul postulent misericordiam a Deo.*" Also Chr. B. Michaelis on the same passage: "*Daniel eadem fide, qua postmodum ora leonum obstrinxit* (Heb. xi. 3), *hic solutionem somnii, quod necdum noverat, Nebuchadnezari promittit, certus jam de exauditione precum, quas super hac re ad Deum fusurus erat* (Jas. i. 6)."—On v. 19 cf. Jerome: "*Somnium regis suo discit somnio; immo et somnium et interpretationem ejus Dei revelatione cognoscit, quod dæmones ignorabant, sapientia sæculi scire non poterat. Unde et Apostoli mysterium, quod cunctis retro generationibus fuerat ignotum, Domino revelante cognoscunt* (Eph. iii. 5)."*—On v. 22 see Starke: "If many things in the Word of God are too deep and hidden for thee, the fault is not in the Word, but in thyself. Beseech God to enlighten thy dark heart, and thou shalt understand the depths of God's Word with ever-increasing clearness."—Notice also the evidence of Daniel's profound humility and modesty in v. 23 *b*: Thou "hast made known unto me now *what we desired* of thee;" on which Jerome (and after him Theodoret, Calvin, etc.) correctly observes: "*Quod quatuor rogant, uni ostenditur, ut et arrogantiam fugiat, ne solus impetrasse videatur, et agat gratias, quod mysterium somni solus audierit.*"—In treating the closing paragraph, vs. 46–49, notice particularly that it is a *heathen* ruler, a worshipper of idols, who is compelled to exalt and glorify Daniel and his God. Calvin (on v. 47): "*Profani homines interdum rapiuntur in admirationem Dei, et tunc large et prolixe fatentur, quicquid posset requiri a veris Dei cultoribus. Sed illud est momentaneum: deinde interea manent impliciti suis superstionibus. Extorquet igitur illis Deus verba, quum ita pie loquuntur, sed intus retinent sua vitia, ut facile postea recidant ad pristinos mores, quemadmodum memorabile exemplum postea sequetur. Quicquid sit, voluit Deus ore profani regis gloriam suam promulgari, et illum esse præconem suæ potentiæ et sui numinis.*"

b. With regard to the prophetic contents of Nebuchadnezzar's dream as brought out in Daniel's interpretation, vs. 37–44, Melancthon justly comprehends that the political element must in this connection be decidedly subordinate to the religious and Messianic factor, and observes: "*Hæc enarratio non tantum est politica de imperiis, sed præbet etiam occasionem Danieli concionandi de toto regno Christi, de novissimo judicio, de causa peccati, de redemptione et instauratione humani generis; cur sit tanta mundi brevitas; quale sit futurum perpetuum regnum, utrum in hac natura immunda vel alia; qualis sit futurus Redemtor, et quomodo ad hoc regnum perveniatur. Ita hæc brevis narratio complectitur summam Evangelii.*"—Cf. Calvin (on v. 44):

* Tertullian's assertion (*de jejun.*, c. 7), with reference to vs. 1–19, that Daniel and his friends *fasted* during three days, and that for this reason their prayer was heard, has its foundation in the fact that he (or rather the pre-Jeromian Latin version of the Bible used by him) followed an ancient ascetic interpolation of the passage, which is still found in the Septuagint: καὶ παρήγγειλε νηστείαν καὶ δέησιν, καὶ τιμωρίαν ζητῆσαι.—Cf. the similar ascetic extension which the passage 1 Cor. vii. 5 experienced at an early day, by the interpolation of the words τῇ νηστείᾳ before τῇ προσευχῇ.

"*Summa igitur est: quamvis visuri sint Judæi potentissima imperia, quæ malum et terrorem ipsis incutiant, immo reddant fere attonitos, tamen nihil in illis fore stabile vel firmum, quod scilicet contraria sint regno filii Dei. Atqui maledictionem denuntiat Jesaias* (c. lx. 12) *omnibus regnis, quæ non servierint ecclesiæ Dei. Quum ergo omnes illi monarchæ diabolica audacia erexerint cristas adversus filium Dei, oportuit deleri, et in illis conspicuam fieri Dei maledictionem, quæ habetur apud prophetam. Sic ergo contrivit Christus omnia mundi imperia.——Hortatur propheta* (Psa. ii. 12) *omnes reges terræ, ut osculentur Filium. Quum neque Babylonii, neque Persæ, neque Macedones, neque Romani Christo sese subjecerint, immo omnes suas vires contulerint ad ipsum oppugnandum et fuerint hostes pietatis, opportuit deleri a Christo regno, ... Neque etiam hic Daniel ea tantum attingit, quæ patent oculis hominum, sed altius attollit mentes nostras, nempe ut sciamus, non alibi veram fulturam, in qua quiescamus, posse reperiri, quam in imo Christi* (1 Cor. iii. 2). *Extra Christum ergo pronuntiat quicquid splendoris et potentiæ est in mundo et opulentiæ et roboris, hoc esse caducum et invalidum et nullius momenti.*"—Starke (after Geier, on v. 44): "All the kingdoms of earth are subject to change, but Christ's kingdom shall endure for ever, and no violence can accomplish its overthrow" (Matt. xiv. 19).—Id. (on v. 37 et seq.): "If God foreknows so exactly all changes in the world-kingdoms, and if He governs them all by His wisdom, should He not know the changes which are to transpire in His church? Should He not control them for good?" (Matt. x. 29, 30).—Menken (*Das Monarchienbild*, p. 82): "The object for which God created the world, and the end for which He governs it, is the kingdom of God. The kingdom of God is the invisible root which holds and sustains the world-kingdoms, the invisible power which smites and destroys them. Their more or less intimate connection with the kingdom of God decides the duration, the importance, the significance of world-kingdoms. The fate and the history of all the kingdoms of earth, that have no important connection with the kingdom of God, or no connection at all, would be of no value. Whatever may be their history, it is always unimportant, because they exert no influence whatever, or at best a very limited influence, upon the postponing or hastening of the final development of things, upon the supplanting of the world-kingdoms by the kingdom of God."

---

3. *The test of the faith of Daniel's three friends in the fiery furnace.*

CHAP. III. 1–30.

1 Nebuchadnezzar the king made an image of gold, whose [its] height *was*
threescore cubits, *and the* breadth thereof [its breadth] six cubits: he set it up in
2 *the* plain of Dura, in *the* province of Babylon. Then [And] Nebuchadnezzar
the king sent to gather *together* the princes [satraps], the governors, and the
captains [pashas], the judges, the treasurers, the counsellors, the sheriffs
[lawyers], and all *the* rulers of the provinces,[1] to come to *the* dedication of the
3 image which Nebuchadnezzar the king *had* set up. Then the princes, the gov-
ernors, and captains, the judges, the treasurers, the counsellors, the sheriffs, and
all *the* rulers of the provinces, *were* gathered *together* unto *the* dedication of the
image that Nebuchadnezzar the king *had* set up; and they stood [*were* standing]
4 before the image that Nebuchadnezzar *had* set up. Then [And] a herald cried
aloud [with might], To you *it is* commanded [*lit. they are* saying], O [*lit.* The]
5 people, nations [nations, peoples], and languages,[2] *That* at what time [the time
that] ye hear [shall hear] *the* sound of the cornet [horn], flute, harp, sackbut,
psaltery, dulcimer [symphony], and all kinds of music, ye fall *down* and
6 worship *the* golden image that Nebuchadnezzar the king hath set up: and
whoso [*lit.* who that] falleth not [*lit.* shall not fall] *down* and worshippeth, shall the
same hour [*lit.* in it the moment] be cast *into the* midst of a [*or,* the] burning
7 fiery furnace [*lit.* oven of fire the blazing]. Therefore at that [*lit.* in it the] time,
when [*lit.* as that] all the people heard [nations *were* hearing] the sound of the
cornet, flute, harp, sackbut, psaltery, and all kinds of music,[3] all the people, the
nations, and the languages, fell [*were* falling] *down and* worshipped [worshipping]
8 the golden image that Nebuchadnezzar the king *had* set up. Wherefore at
that time *certain* Chaldæans [*lit.* men Casdim] came near and accused the
9 Jews. They spake [*were* answering], and said [*were* saying] to the king
10 Nebuchadnezzar, O [*lit.* The] king, live for ever. Thou, O king, hast made a
decree, that every man that shall hear the sound of the cornet, flute, harp,
sackbut, psaltery, and dulcimer, and all kinds of music, shall fall *down* and
11 worship the golden image; and whoso falleth not *down* and worshippeth,

12 *that* he should be cast *into the* midst of a burning fiery furnace. *There* are
certain Jews, whom thou hast set over *the* affairs [work] of *the* province of
Babylon, Shadrach, Meshach, and Abed-nego: these men, O king, have not
regarded thee [set account upon thee]; they serve not thy gods, nor worship
13 *the* golden image which thou hast set up. Then Nebuchadnezzar, in *his* rage
and fury, commanded [said] to bring [cause to come] Shadrach, Meshach, and
Abed-nego. Then they brought these men [these men were brought] before
14 the king. Nebuchadnezzar spake, and said unto them, *Is it* true [*of* purpose],
O Shadrach, Meshach, and Abed-nego? do not ye [, *that* ye do not] serve my
15 gods, nor worship *the* golden image which I have set up? Now, if ye *be* ready,
that at what time [the time that] ye hear *the* sound of the cornet, flute, harp,
sackbut, psaltery, and dulcimer, and all kinds of music, ye fall *down* and wor-
ship the image which I have made, *well:* but [and] if ye worship not, ye shall
be cast the same hour [moment] *into the* midst of a burning fiery furnace; and
16 who *is* that [he] God that shall deliver you out of my hands? Shadrach, Me-
shach, and Abed-nego answered and said to the king, *O* Nebuchadnezzar, we *are*
17 not careful [needing] to answer thee [return thee answer] in this matter. If *it*
be *so*, our God [If *it* be *that* our God] whom we serve, is able to deliver us
from the burning fiery furnace; and he will deliver *us* out of thy
18 hand, O king.[4] But [And] if not, be it known unto thee, O king, that
we *will* not serve [are not serving] thy gods, nor worship *the* golden image
19 which thou hast set up. Then was Nebuchadnezzar full of fury, and *the* form of
his visage was changed against Shadrach, Meshach, and Abed-nego: *therefore*
he spake, and commanded that they should heat [to heat] the furnace one seven
times more than it *was* wont to be heated [*lit.* above that *any one was ever* seen
20 to heat it]. And he commanded *the* most mighty men [*lit.* men, heroes of might]
that *were* in his army to bind Shadrach, Meshach, and Abed-nego, *and* [*so as*] to
21 cast *them into* the burning fiery furnace. Then these men were bound in their
coats [shirts, *or* trowsers, *or* mantles], their hosen [coats, *or* tunics], and their
hats [cloaks, *or* turbans,] and their *other* garments, and were cast *into the* midst
22 of the burning fiery furnace. Therefore, because [*lit.* from that] the king's com-
mandment [word] *was* urgent, and the furnace exceeding hot, the flame of the
23 fire slew those men that took up Shadrach, Meshach, and Abed-nego.[5] And
these three men, Shadrach, Meshach, and Abed-nego, fell *down* bound *into the*
24 midst of the burning fiery furnace. Then Nebuchadnezzar the king was astonished,
and rose *up* in haste, *and* spake and said unto his counsellors, Did not we cast
three men bound *into the* midst of the fire?[6] They answered and said unto the
25 king, True,[7] O king. He answered and said, Lo, I[8] see four men loose [loosed],
walking in *the* midst of the fire, and they have no hurt [harm is not with them];
and *the* form [appearance] of the fourth *is* like *the* Son of God [a son of *the*
26 gods]. Then Nebuchadnezzar came near to *the* mouth [door] of the burning fiery
furnace, *and* spake, and said, Shadrach, Meshach, and Abed-nego, *ye* servants
of the most high God, come [go] forth, and come *hither*. Then Shadrach,
Meshach, and Abed-nego, came [went] forth of [from] *the* midst of the fire.
27 And the princes, [the] governors, and [the] captains, and the king's counsellors,
being gathered *together*, saw [*or*, were gathered *and* saw] these men, upon [over]
whose bodies the fire had no power [did not rule], nor was a [*the*] hair of their
head singed, neither were [had] their coats changed, nor *the* smell of fire had
28 passed on them. *Then* Nebuchadnezzar spake and said, Blessed *be the* God of
Shadrach, Meshach, and Abed-nego, who hath sent his angel, and delivered his
servants that trusted in him, and have changed[9] the king's word, and yielded
their bodies, that they might not serve or worship any god except their *own*
29 God. Therefore I make a decree [And from me *is* a decree made], That
every people, nation, and language, which [shall] speak anything amiss[10] against
the God of Shadrach, Meshach, and Abed-nego, shall be cut [made] *in* pieces,
and their houses[11] shall be made a dunghill [*or*, sink]; because there is no other
30 god that can deliver after [like] this *sort*. Then the king promoted Shadrach,
Meshach, and Abed-nego, in the province of Babylon.

CRITICAL NOTES.

1 [These are apparently technical terms for various classes of officers, who are carefully distinguished and graded, and may be represented as follows:

I.	*Satraps*, *Præfects*, *Pashas*.	Governmental,	Provinces. Districts. Metropolis.
II.	*Viziers*, *Treasurers*.	Courtly,	Executive. Financial.
III.	*Judges*, *Lawyers*.	Legal,	On the bench. At the bar.

IV. —*Superintendents*.—Functional—General.]

2 [There is in these three terms likewise clearly a gradation downwards: *nations, tribes, dialects*.]

3 [In these names of musical instruments, some borrowed from foreign languages, and all more or less uncertain of import, there are nevertheless traces of classification:

I.	*Cornet*, *Flute*.	Wind,	Simple. Keyed.
II.	*Guitar*, *Lyre*, *Harp*.	String,	Gradually more complex.

III. —*Bagpipe*.—Wind—Compound.
IV —*All sorts*.—General.]

4 [אֲכַלוּ קַרְצֵיהוֹן דִּי, lit., *ate their pieces of, i.e., slandered;* conf. English "backbite."]

4 [The Masoretic interpunction requires us to punctuate thus: *to deliver us; from the burning fiery furnace and from thy hand, O king, he will deliver.*]

5 [The position of the term for the executioners is very emphatic in the original: literally, *those men, who lifted ......, the flame of the fire killed them.*]

6 [The order of the words in the original is emphatic: "Was it *not three men we cast* into [to] the *midst of the fire—bound?*" This last was an additional circumstance of wonder.—[7] יַצִּיבָא may be the fem. or the "definite state;" in either case it is emphatic, *i. q.*, "the truth."—[8] The pronoun, being expressed, is emphatic, *i. q.*, "I myself." The others appear to have been so situated as not to observe this fact, or did not notice it.—[9] שַׁנִּיו, being in Pael, so far as the form is concerned, is simply transitive; but the context gives it the sense of *contravene*, common in the cognate Syriac.—[10] שָׁלָה, Keri שָׁלוּ, something astray, an *error* or wrong word, *i. e.*, detraction.—[11] בַּיְתֵהּ, *his house, i. e.*, the house of any individual so doing.]

EXEGETICAL REMARKS.

Verses 1, 2. *The erection of the image, and the command to attend its dedication.* **Nebuchadnezzar the king made** (had made) **an image of gold.** Properly "made" (עֲבַד), similar to the repeated phrase in the following: "he set it up," instead of "he caused it to be set up" (verses 1 *b*, 2, 3, 5, 7, 12, etc.), or to verse 24, "we cast three men into the fire," instead of "had them cast in."—The Heb. text does not state *when* the image was made. According to the Septuagint and Theodotion, who are followed by the Syriac hexaplar version, it was prepared ἔτους ὀκτωκαιδεκάτου Ναβουχοδόνοσορ, hence at about the time of the destruction of Jerusalem (cf. 2 Kings xxv. 8; Jer. lii. 12), and after the accomplished subjection to Chaldæa of all the nations from India to Ethiopia (cf. the additions in the Sept. to verses 2 and 3). The incident appears at all events to belong to this later period of Nebuchadnezzar's reign, since verses 4 *b*, 7 *b*, 29 *a*, mention many "peoples, nations, and languages," as being subject to him, and it was possibly a feature connected with a feast in commemoration of his victories (cf. Herodot. IV. 88). The impression of Jehovah's power and greatness which he had formerly received in consequence of Daniel's interpretation of his dream, appears therefore to have been long obliterated. He not only causes the colossal image subsequently described to be erected in honor of some Babylonian national god, but with arrogant presumption he challenges a conflict (see verse 15).—**An image of gold.** צְלֵם certainly designates in this place, as well as in chap. ii. 31, a statue in the human form, and more particularly, the image of a god, as appears from verses 12, 18, 28. It was not therefore a statue of Nebuchadnezzar himself. A marked disproportion seems to have existed in its dimensions, on the supposition that it represented an upright human form, since its height is given at sixty cubits, and its breadth or thickness at only six cubits, while the normal height and breadth of a person in an upright posture are as 6 : 1, not as 10 : 1. For this reason the צְלֵם has been held to have been in part a mere idol column, similar to the Egyptian obelisks, or, which is certainly more appropriate, analogous to the Amyclæan Apollo, which formed, according to Pausanius (*Lacon.* III. 19, 2), a slender column provided with head, arms, and feet, in the human form. So Münter, *Relig. der Babylonier*, p. 59; Hengstenberg, p. 95; and more recently Kranichfeld, who refers to the colossus of Rhodes, the height of which was seventy cubits, also to the Egyptian κολλοσσοὶ μεγάλοι and ἀνδρόσφιγγες mentioned by Herodotus (II. 175), and to the image of the sun mentioned by Pliny (*H. N.* xxiv. 18), which reached a height of 110 feet, in addition to the Apollo of Amyclæ. ["צְלֵם is properly *an image in human likeness*, and excludes the idea of a mere pillar or obelisk, for which מַצֵּבָה would have been the appropriate word. Yet . . . . as to the upper part—the head, countenance, arms, breast—it may have been in the form of a man, and the lower part may have been formed like a pillar."—*Keil.*] We might be content with this, or refer in addition to the remarkably tall and slender forms of individual persons on Egyptian wall-paintings and also on Assyrian and Babylonian sculptures (cf. the copies in Wilkinson's *Manners and customs of the ancient Egyptians*, and Layard's works on Nineveh and Babylon [German by Th. Zenker]—in the latter, *e.g.*, the colossal sitting figure on plate XXII. A), if it were not still more suitable to regard the statement of the height of sixty cubits as a synecdoche, designating both the image and its pedestal, and to allow to the latter perhaps twenty-four, and to the former thirty-six cubits, which assumption clearly results in an entirely well-proportioned shape of the statue. If therefore, the צְלֵם proper was limited to a height of about thirty-six feet, it would compare with the statue of Belus, which, according to Diodor. II. 9, was erected by Semiramis on the summit of the great temple of Bel at Babylon (probably the present "Birs Nimroud"), and attained a height of forty feet; but it can hardly be directly identified (with Bertholdt) with that statue of Bel, nor yet with the one mentioned by Herodotus (I. 183), which measured twelve cubits in height. Not only was it erected outside of the temple area of Babylon, and possibly even at a considerable distance from the city itself (see infra), but it is also extremely questionable whether an image of Bel must be assumed in this case, since the Babylonians were devoted to the zealous worship of numerous gods. Entirely too artificial is the opinion of Hofmann (*Weiss. und Erfüllung*, I. 277), Zündel, and Kliefoth, that the image was designed by Nebuchadnezzar to represent the world-power he had founded, in harmony with the religious (cosmical) conceptions of heathenism—as indicated (according to Kliefoth) particularly by the numbers six and sixty. —The expression דִּי־דְהַב does not compel us to assume that the image was composed throughout of solid gold; for in Ex. xxxvii. 25 et seq. an altar of wood, and merely covered with plates of gold, is designated simply as מִזְבַּח־הַזָּהָב; and Isa. xl. 19; xli. 7; Jer. x. 3–5 indicate plainly that the images of Babylonian idols especially were usually composed of wood with an outside covering of gold. The construction of this image by no means, therefore, involved an immoderate expenditure, as J. D. Michaelis supposed; and the gold required to cover its surface may have been less, in weight and value, than the amount required (800 talents) for the construction of the statue of Bel already referred to as mentioned by Herodotus, whose height was twelve cubits, and for the tables and chairs which accompanied it; and also less than the amount expended on the statue of Bel mentioned by Diodorus, which reached a height of forty cubits, and cost, as is reported, 1,000 talents. The relative unimportance of this image, which is thus so easy to conceive, deprives the *argumentum ex silentio* of all its force, as against the credibility of the narrative, which Von Lengerke and Hitzig have assigned to it, on the ground of its not being mentioned by profane authors. Finally, it is thoroughly inconsequent and ridiculous to discover, with Bleek (in Schleierm., Lücke, etc.; *Theol. Zeitschr.*, 1822, III., p. 259; cf. *Einl. ins A. T.*, § 265), an imaginary prototype of the βδέλυγμα ἐρημώσεως of Antiochus Epiphanes, which was assigned by pseudo-Daniel to the æra of the captivity; for according to 1 Macc. i. 54, 59, this βδέλ. was not a statue at all, but an altar of small size, erected on the altar of burnt offerings at Jerusalem (cf. Hengstenberg, p. 86).—**Whose height was threescore cubits, and the breadth thereof six cubits.** פְּתָיֵהּ, properly "breadth," but here signifying both breadth and thickness, cf. Ez. vi. 3. The cubits (אַמִּין) were probably the royal cubits of the Babylonians (Herod. I. 178), and not *smaller* than the ordinary cubits (Gesen., *Thesaur.*, p. 112 s.). Instead of πήχεων ἑξήκοντα as a statement of the height, the Septuagint has πήχεων ἕξ, which reading some have endeavored to defend, *e. g.*, Michaelis, Eichhorn, etc.; but is it probably not even an ancient attempt to provide an easier reading, and must be considered merely as the error of a copyist, if not as a typographical error of the *Ed. princeps* of Simon de Magistris; see Bugati, in Hävernick on this passage.—**He set it up** (caused it to be set up) **in the plain of Dura, in the province of Babylon.** בִּקְעָא, like the corresponding Hebrew term, does not designate a narrow valley enclosed by mountains, but a low and level tract, a *plain;* hence a majority of moderns read "in the plain of Dura." The location of this plain is not entirely certain; but it was probably east of the Tigris and near Apollonia in the province of Sittacene, where a town by the name of Dura was situated, according to Polyb. v. 52, and Ammian, xxv. 6, 9. The Δοῦρα (otherwise Dor) near Cæsarea Palæst. on the Mediterranean, mentioned in Polyb. v. 66, and the town of that name situated, according to Polyb. v. 48; Ammian, xxiii. 5, 8, near Circesium at the entrance of the Chaboras into the Euphrates, which was too far northward to have been included in the province of Babylon,* cannot possibly be intended here. ["We must, without doubt, much rather seek for this plain in the neighborhood of Babylon, where, according to the statement of Jul. Oppert (*Expédit. Scientifique en Mésopotamie*, I. 238 ff.), there are at present to be found in the S.S.E. of the ruins representing the former capital a row of mounds which bear the name of *Dura;* and at the end of them, along with two larger mounds, there is a smaller one named *el-Mohattat* (= *la coline obliquée*), which forms a square six metres high, with a basis of fourteen metres, wholly built of unburned bricks, and which shows so surprising a resemblance to a colossal statue with its pedestal, that Oppert believes this little mound to be the remains of the golden image erected by Nebuchadnezzar."—*Keil.*] The Sept., which probably regarded the plain here referred to as identical with the plain of Shinar, Gen. xi. 2, and which could find no town bearing the name of Dura within its limits, has conceived the name דּוּרָא to be an appellative, and rendered it by ἐν πεδίῳ τοῦ περιβόλου (cf. דּוּר, *circumire, in orbem ire*); in which, however, they were more nearly correct than is Hitzig, who assumes that his pseudo-Daniel adopted the name of the *plain* from the earlier designation (chap. ii. 45) of the *mountain*, טוּרָא.—Verse 2. **Then Nebuchadnezzar the king sent to gather together,** etc. This service was probably performed by couriers (רָצִים), who were doubtless employed in similar duties at the Babylonian court, as well as at the Persian (Esth. x. 15; viii. 14), and even at the courts of Saul (1 Sam. xi. 7) and of Hezekiah (2 Chron. xxx. 6, 10).—**The princes, the gov-**

* Cf. generally, Rawlinson, *Journal of the R. Geogr. Society*, x., p. 93.

ernors, and the captains. Among the seven classes of officials enumerated, these three are shown to have been more immediately related to each other by the וּ before פַּחֲוָתָא. Their members were executive officers of superior rank, who combined both civil and military functions in their range of duties, and who may have been substantially on a par with the executive officials connected with the ministry of the interior in a modern state, while the four succeeding classes were probably connected with the departments of finance and justice. (1) The אֲחַשְׁדַּרְפְּנִין were naturally *satraps* (cf. *kshatrapâwan* on the cuneiform inscriptions at Behitun, which, according to Haug [in Ewald's *Bibl. Jahrb.*, v. 153] is equivalent to "protector of the country," and according to Lassen [*Zeitschr. für Kunde des Morgenl.*, VI. 1, 18] is synonymous with "guardian of the warriors of the host;" cf. also the Zend *shôithrapaiti* and the Sanscr. *kshathrapa*)—the superior executive officers of the several provinces, vice or sub-kings to the sovereign (cf. the מַלְכִין, Isa. x. 8; Gen. xiv. 1, 2, with the מֶלֶךְ מַלְכַיָּא, Dan. ii. 37, Ezra vii. 12), and therefore mentioned at the head of the body of officials. The fact that the title of these chief administrators of provinces is Persian does not demonstrate that their office was entirely confined to the time of the Achæmenidian Persian empire, or that it was even created by Darius Hystaspis (Herod. III. 89 ss.); for Xenophon (*Cyrop.* viii. 6, 1) dates its existence back to the time of Cyrus, and Berosus (in Josephus, *c. Apion*, 1, 19; *Ant.* X. 11, 1) designates Necho already as a τεταγμένος σατράπης of Nabopolassar, which is hardly to be considered a gross anachronism, but rather as an indication of the relation of Necho as a vassal to Babylon. Consequently, the author cannot be charged with a historical error, either in this connection, or in chap. vi. 2 et seq., where he refers to the satraps of Darius the Mede. The אחשדרפנין must be regarded rather, as one of the Persian elements of the writer's Chaldee idiom, the number of which, according to the Introd. § 1, note 3, must have been considerable, even at an early period (cf. on chap. ii. 4); and the early intrusion of such into the language and range of conception among the Chaldæans, is no more remarkable than is the mention of the רַב־מָג, Jer. xxxix. 3, as a Chaldæan officer. The Septuagint, however, renders the term by σατράπαι only here and in chap. vi. 2, 4, while in vs. 3 and 27 it has ὕπατοι, in Ezra viii. 36 διοικηταί, in Esth. viii. 9 οἰκονόμοι, and in Esth. ix. 3 τύραννοι. These variations indicate that the conception of a definite office was no longer connected with the title, at the time when that version was made.—(2) According to the observations on chap. ii. 48, the סִגְנִין were "superintendents, administrators" generally; in this case naturally not endowed with spiritual functions, but rather performing secular duties under the satraps, and finally employed chiefly in military rather than in civil offices (cf. the סְגָנִים of Babylon, mentioned together with the גִּבּוֹרִים, Jer. li. 57). The Septuagint appears to have conceived of these *Signin*, in harmony with this view, as being "præfects of the host, or commanders of the provinces;" for they render the term in this instance by στρατηγοί (as in v. 3 and often, twelve times in all), while they translate it elsewhere by τοπάρχαι (chap. iii. 27), ἡγούμενοι (chap. ii. 48), or ἄρχοντες.—(3) פַּחֲוָתָא (Heb. פַּחוֹת, from פֶּחָה). In view of the probably Indo-Germanic derivation of this term (cf. Sanscr. *paksha*, "side," Prakr. *pakkha*, modern Persian and Turkish *pasha*) it properly designates "those who are stationed on the sides or flanks, adjutants," and then governors, or the representatives of a sovereign in a designated field of administration, provincial præfects. The governors whom Solomon placed over his provinces outside of Palestine, already bore this title (1 Kings x. 15; 2 Chron. ix. 14), also the governors of the Syrian king Benhadad (1 Kings xx. 24); the corresponding officers among the Syrians (Isa. xxxvi. 9; 2 Kings xviii. 24), Chaldæans (Ezek. xxvi. 6, 23; Jer. li. 23) and Persians (Esth. viii. 9; ix. 3); and especially the Persian governors of Judæa subsequent to the captivity (Hag. i. 1, 14; ii. 2, 21; Neh. v. 14, 18, etc.) Among the nations last mentioned, who employed satraps as the chief præfects of provinces, the פֶּחָה was merely a subordinate to those officers (and more purely civil than military in his official character, as appears from the position of Zerubbabel and Nehemiah, according to Haggai and Neh. l. c.); but in the kingdoms of Solomon and Benhadad the פַּחוֹת seem to have been equal in rank to the later satraps, and therefore were chief governors. In this place and v. 3 the Septuagint translates τοπάρχαι; in v. 27, ἀρχιπατριῶται (*i.e.*, chief of a nationality).—(4) According to the Sept. the אֲדַרְגָּזְרַיָּא are "overseers" generally (ὕπατοι), while most moderns regard them as "chief judges or discerners." Ewald defines them as "chief star-gazers, or augurs of the first-class" (!), and Hitzig, as "directors, upon whom devolves the decision of matters, or magistrates." The term, which occurs only in this place, appears to be a genuine Aramaic compound, from אֲדַר, glory, dignity, and גְּזַר, to decide (cf. chap. ii. 27), and therefore probably designates a class of officers with whom rested the final decision, particularly in regard to the economical or financial administration of the provinces [possibly = the modern Oriental *viziers*]. The class which follows next in order obliges this restriction of the offices of the אֲדַרְגָּזְרַיָּא.—(5) גְּדָבְרַיָּא, "the treasurers." These officers do not probably differ from the גִּזַּבְרִין, Ezra vii. 21 (cf. i. 8), which term signifies γαζοφύλακες, "managers of the public treasury" (cf. Sept. διοικηταί), and is possibly related to the Pers. *gaitha*, modern Pers. *genj*, "treasure" (cf. *gaza*). Ewald's assertion that גְּדָבַר is synonymous with הַדָּבַר, vs. 24, 27, and signifies a "bearer of power," or "exalted prince of the empire" (analogous to the old-Pers. *chudvâr*, from *chad*, "God, authorization"), is without adequate support.—(6) The דְּתָבְרַיָּא

are clearly the "learned in the law," or the "guardians of the law." The first element of the word is evidently דָּת, "the law" (cf. Pers. *data*, from *da*, "to give"), to which the Pers. ending *vâr* is annexed. Cf. the Pehlvi word *datouber* (Armen. *datavor*), "judges."—(7) The unmistakable connection of תִּפְתָּיֵא (like No. 4, a *hapax leg.*) with the Arab. *ftah* (cf. the Turkish *mufti*, chief judge) marks this class of officers as "dispensers of justice, lawyers, judges" in the strict sense (not "præfecti" as the Vulgate has it, or "οἱ ἐπ' ἐξουσιῶν," as it is rendered by Theodotion, in each case because of a failure to apprehend the true meaning.—**And all the rulers of the provinces;** *i.e.*, all the remaining officials who administrated the affairs of provinces. On שִׁלְטוֹן, "ruler, high official," cf. Eccles. viii. 4, and also the verb אשלט, chap. ii. 48. The præfect of the bodyguard, mentioned in chap. ii. 14, is not necessarily included among these remaining rulers, since only the officers of the provinces are more immediately referred to in this connection (against Kranichfeld). Von Lengerke is guilty of a gross impropriety, when he finds here "another extravagance, since the empire could not in the meantime be left without an administration." It is not necessary to stretch כֹּל so unreasonably in this case, as to make it indicate the presence of *all* the government officials without exception (cf. 1 Sam. xxviii. 4, and generally Kranichfeld on the passage).—**To come to the dedication of the image, etc.** חֲנֻכָּה, the *feast of dedication*, religious dedicatory services, with which were connected sacrifices, the burning of incense, sacrificial feasts, etc. Cf. Ezra vi. 16, where the same expression is employed with reference to the dedication of the second temple.

Verses 3–7. *The dedication.* **And they stood before the image that Nebuchadnezzar had** (caused to be) **set up.** The Keri has קָיְמִין instead of קָאְמִין, as it substitutes דָּיְרִין for דָּאְרִין in chap. ii. 38, according to the usage of the Targums.—לָקֳבֵל, "before, opposite," which is employed here and in Ezra iv. 16, instead of the usual Chaldee form לְקֳבֵל (chap. v. 1, 4, 10; Ezra vi. 13), is a Syriasm in the pronunciation, similar to that in וּצְרִי, Gen. xxxvii. 25, which is used instead of וּצֳרִי.—Verse 4. **Then a herald cried aloud.** כָּרוֹז and the corresponding verb כְּרַז "to proclaim publicly" (v. 29), are not exactly Aramaic adaptations of the Greek terms κῆρυξ, κηρύττειν (Bertholdt and others), but are without doubt radically related to them, and also to the Sanscr. *krus*, old-Pers. *khresio*, "one who calls or screams" (mod. Pers. *gris*-ten; cf. the German *kreischen*); while on the other hand, they are also related to קרא "to call."—בְּחַיִל, *mightily*, with a loud voice, as in chap. iv. 11; v. 7, and as in the Heb. בְּכֹחַ, Psa. xxix. 4; Isa. xl. 9.—**To you it is commanded, O people, nations, and languages.** אָמְרִין, properly "they say" (*are saying*), a very common idiom in the Chaldee, expressing an impersonal sense, or more directly, serving as a substitute for the impersonal passive construction (Winer, § 49, 3). The collocation of עַמְמַיָּא ("peoples, nations"), אֻמַּיָּא ("tribes," a more limited conception than the preceding; cf. also in the Heb., *e.g.* Psa. cxi. 6 with Gen. xxv. 16), and לִשָּׁנַיָּא ("tongues," "peoples having a common language;" cf. the Heb. לָשׁוֹן Isa. lxvi. 18; Zech. viii. 23), recurs again in vs. 7, 29, and 31, and, indeed, often in the book of Daniel (v. 19; vi. 26; vii. 14). This formula, which combines in a solemn triad "all the nations in the empire, however distantly related they may be, or however great may be the diversity between themselves or their constituent elements," and which exhorts them to give attention, was probably stereotyped in the official edicts of the Chaldæan realm, whose motley aggregate of languages and nations would give rise to such comprehensive phrases more readily than would the character of any other empire of antiquity. The proclamation, of course, is not addressed to all the individuals of the various nations, tribes, etc., but only to their representatives who were actually present. ["The proclamation of the herald refers not only to all who were present, since besides the officers there certainly was present a great crowd of people from all parts of the kingdom, as M. Geier has rightly remarked, so that the assembly consisted of persons of various races and languages. אֻמַּיָּא denotes *tribes* of people, as the Hebr. אֻמָּה, אֻמּוֹת, Gen. xxv. 16, denotes the several tribes of Ishmael, and in Num. xxv. 15, the separate tribes of Midianites; and is thus not so extensive in its import as עַמְמִין, *peoples*. לִשָּׁנַיָּא, corresponding to הַלְּשֹׁנוֹת, Isa. lxvi. 18, designates (see Gen. x. 5, 20, 31) *communities of men of the same language*, and is not a tautology, since the distinctions of nation and of language are in the course of history frequently found. The placing together of the three words denotes all nations, however they may have widely branched off into tribes with different languages, and expresses the sense that no one in the whole kingdom should be exempted from the command."—*Keil.*]—Verse 5. **At what time ye hear the sound of the cornet, flute, etc.** As in the case of religious dedicatory festivals among the Israelites (Psa. xxx. 1; Neh. xii. 27; 1 Macc. iv. 54), so at the dedication of this heathen statue, there was no lack of music and song (cf. Ex. xxxii. 18 et seq.). This is an especially natural feature, since the Babylonians, as well as the ancient Assyrians, appear, as a people, to have been unusually addicted to music, in view of the testimony afforded by numerous historical records of a positive character; cf. Isa. xiv. 11; Psa. cxxxvii. 2; Herodotus, I. 191 (the χορεύειν of the Babylonians during the capture of their city by Cyrus); Curtius, V. 3 (Alexander welcomed on his entrance into Babylon, by "*artifices cum fidibus sui generis—laudes regum canere soliti*"). Additional evidence is found in the representations of musicians with various instruments, on the monumental edifices of Nineveh and Babylon.—The names of the six instruments here enumerated are in the singular, not as indicating that only one of each kind was at hand, but as a generic designation of the entire class to which it belonged. Hence, there is no impropriety in rendering them in the plural "the cornets, flutes," etc. ["קַרְנָא, *horn*, is the *tuba* of the ancients, the קֶרֶן or שׁוֹפָר of the Hebr.; see Josh. vi. 5. מַשְׁרוֹקִיתָא, from שְׁרַק, to *hiss* or *whistle*, is the reed-flute, translated by the Sept. and Theodotion *σύριγξ*, the *shepherd's* or *Pan's pipe*, which consisted of several reeds of different thickness and length bound together, and according to a Greek tradition (Pollux, IV. 9, 15), was invented by two Medes."—*Keil.* "It is uncertain whether the horn intended was straight, like the Assyrian, or curved, like the Roman *cornu* and *lituus*. The pipe was probably the double instrument, played at the end, which was familiar to the Susianians and Assyrians. The harp would seem to have resembled the later harp of the Assyrians; but it had fewer strings, if we may judge from a representation upon a cylinder. Like the Assyrian, it was carried under the arm, and was played with both hands, one on either side of the strings" (Rawlinson, *Five Monarchies*, III. 20).] —**The harp, sackbut, psaltery, dulcimer.** For the opinion that of the names of the four instruments here mentioned, which several expositors hold to be derived without exception from the Greek, probably but two are really taken from that language, see the Introd. § 7. See ibid. note 2. concerning the possibility of an importation of musical instruments and their names from Greece, even prior to the time of Daniel. It is yet to be noticed in this connection: (1) that instead of the Kethib קִיתְרֹס, which is to be pronounced either as קִיתְרֹס or קִיתָרֹס, the Keri has the shortened form קִתְרֹס, which appears to have been in general use in later times. The Syriac affords repeated examples of the conversion of the Greek ending *ις* into וֹס (Gesen. *Thes.*, p. 1215), so that in this direction the derivation of the term from the Gr. *κίθαρις* seems certainly to be secured. However, see the Introd., as above.—(2) The *σαμβύκη*, which Strabo notices (X. 3, 7) as being of foreign origin, and whose invention is attributed by Clemens Alex. (*Strom.* I. 76) to the Troglodytes, might possibly be explained in analogy with the Sanscrit *çambuka*, "bivalve, muscle." The form סַבְּכָא, however, appears rather to point to the Shemitic root סבך, "to weave."—(3) The orthography of פְּסַנְתֵּרִין is not fixed; in v. 7 the name is written with ט instead of ת, and in vs. 10 and 15 it is pointed with ֵ under תּ. The numerous changes of the Greek ending *ιον* into ־ִין which are found in the later Chaldee, and of which סַנְהֶדְרִין = *συνέδριον* is the most familiar (Gesen. *Thesaur.*, p. 1116), indicate the identity of this instrument with the *ψαλτήριον*. ["It was an instrument like a harp, which, according to Augustine (on Psa. xxxii. [xxxiii.] 2 and Psa. xlii. [xliii.] 4) was distinguished from the *cithara* in this particular, that while the strings of the *cithara* passed over the sounding-board, those of the *psalterion* (or *organon*) were placed under it. Such harps are found on Egyptian (see Roselini) and also on Assyrian monuments (cf. Layard, *Ninev. and Bab.*, plate XIII. 4)."—*Keil.* "In Egypt they have an instrument, evidently of the same name, *santir* (Lane, *Mod. Eg.*, p. 77), which is a species of dulcimer, is stringed, and is beaten with two small sticks."—*Stuart.*]—(4) V. 10 has the softer סִפֹּנְיָה instead of סוּמְפּוֹנְיָה; a form which points back no less certainly than does the more usual term, to the Greek *συμφωνία*, since the sound *υ* is intermediate between ־ִ and ־ֻ. Its rendering by "bagpipe" (Germ. *Sackpfeife*, *Dudelsack*) has a sufficient support in Polyb. XXXI. 4, in Saadias on this passage, and in the Italian *sampogna*. In addition, the name *συμφωνία* (Jerome, "consonantia") is exceedingly suitable for an instrument consisting of two pipes which are passed through a leathern bag, from which their ends protrude equally above and below—the lower of which pipes, when played with the fingers like a flute, emits in screaming tones the sounds breathed into the upper and increased in force by passing through the bag (cf. Winer, *Realw.* II., p. 123). We must therefore reject its interpretation by עוּגָב, "Pandean pipes" in the Heb. translation of the passage; further, its rendering as "a drum" by Isidore (*Origg.* III. 21); the derivation of the word by Hävernick from סוּף, "a reed;" that by Paulus from סְפִינָה, "a ship," "the covering of a ship" (cf. *a resonant frame*), etc. [Stuart adduces the instrument called *summarah*, described and figured by Lane (*Mod. Eg.*, II. 81, 82), still commonly used in Egypt by the boatmen, and giving two symphonious sounds, being double.]—**And all kinds of music.** A comprehensive supplemental phrase, similar to that which follows the names of the officers in v. 2. [By the addition "this pompous language of the world-ruler and of the herald of his power is well expressed."—*Keil.*] זְמָרָא does not designate either instrumental music or "song" (Hitz.) as distinct from each other, but music in general; cf. the Sept. and Theodotion: *καὶ παντὸς γένους μουσικῶν*. The expression therefore does not refer to various melodies, nor to different parts of vocal music; but it does not, on the other hand, exclude such music from the ceremony; cf. the Targ. Gen. iv. 21; Ez. xxxiii. 22.—**Ye** (shall) **fall down and worship the golden image**, etc. Kranichfeld observes correctly (on v. 6): "The homage which the king required to be rendered to his *god* (cf. on v. 14) on the occasion of this great national festival in honor of their victories (cf. on v. 1), was regarded as a test of the loyalty of the officers to the *king* himself, and especially in the case of those who belonged to subjugated nations. The victory of a heathen king over other tribes and nations was considered a triumph of his gods over their gods (1 Kings xx. 23, 28; 2 Chron. xxviii. 23; Isa. xxxvi. 18–20, etc.); and hostile kingdoms included the gods of their opponents among their foes, and in contrast with the usual tolerance and indifference of heathenism in regard to the worship of the gods, they refused them reverence, so long as neither party believed that its cause was lost. Thus, for instance, the different foes of the Assyrian empire are characterized on an inscription of Tiglath-pilesar as those who 'refuse to reverence' the god of Asshur, as the lord of Tiglath-pilesar. *Opposition to the gods of a kingdom was therefore equivalent to hostility against the realm.* The same inscription represents Tiglath-pilesar, for this reason, as directly *imposing* on the conquered nations the worship of Asshur's god; they must prostrate themselves before this offended god, and thus render their tribute (Pusey, *Daniel*, p. 444 ss.). This will illustrate the baselessness of Von Lengerke's assertion that religious compulsion was unknown among the ancient Asiatic nations, and that they never enforced a recognition of the gods from unwilling persons. What has been remarked, serves to show that, on the contrary, an expression of homage toward the national divinity was always required, and even insisted on, whenever the political supremacy of a realm was in question; and this would be observed especially in the case of officers, upon whose loyalty the security of the realm of such divinity might depend. If Nebuchadnezzar was concerned, on the celebration of the nation's triumph before us, to secure a recognition of his right, as the supreme ruler, to the allegiance of his subjects, and especially to the homage of the officials to whom was entrusted the administration of his empire, it follows that the compulsory requirement to do homage to the national god of his kingdom, was, in this instance, a necessary measure, aiming simply at the preservation of the realm."—Verse 6, **And whoso falleth not down. . . . shall the same hour be cast into the midst of a burning fiery furnace.** מַן־דִּי, *quicunque*, synonymous with מַה־דִּי, chap. ii. 28 (cf. v. 11; chap. iv. 14). — בַּהּ־שַׁעֲתָא, *in the same hour*, literally "in it, the hour;" the suffix, which anticipates the connected noun, is annexed to the preposition; cf. vs. 7, 8, 15; iv. 30, 33, and also the instances in which, additionally, the preposition is itself repeated before the noun, *e.g.* בַּהּ בְּלֵילְיָא, chap. v. 30; cf. chap. v. 12. ["The frequent pleonastic use, in the later Aramaic, of the union of a preposition with a suffix anticipating the following noun, has in the Bibl. Chald. generally a certain emphasis, for the pronominal suffix is manifestly used demonstratively, in the sense, '*even* this.'"—*Keil.*] שָׁעָה, after the Arabic, is literally, "the quickly expiring, the quickly passing," hence *a moment*, in which sense the term is often found in the Targums (= Hebr. רֶגַע). In Daniel it always has the meaning of "hour," as appears especially from chap. iv. 16 [19]. [The passage here referred to, however, does not support this later or Rabbinical import to the word, which is therefore here, as elsewhere in Daniel, to be rendered *moment.*] The word does not seem to be related to the verb שָׁעָה, "to see;" the root from which it is derived signifies in the Arabic "*celeriter ire, currere*."—אַתּוּן, according to the Arabic, literally, "a furrow, excavation" (whence probably: *a lime pit*), designates an excavated *smelting furnace* in the form of a pit, a *fire pit*, which sense is also expressed in the corresponding Ethiop. אַתּוּן, and by the originally synonymous, but not essentially related Heb. תַּנּוּר. The smelting furnace here referred to, however, being designed for the infliction of the death penalty on criminals by means of fire, was arranged according to vs. 22 and 26, so that at least one, if not more of its sides, rose as perpendicular (or inclined) surfaces above the earth, analogous to the construction of our lime-kilns and furnaces, and probably also to the brick-kiln (מַלְבֵּן) at Tahpanhes in Egypt, which is referred to in Jer. xliii. 9 et seq. The principal opening, by which fuel and other materials designed for burning (or smelting) were introduced into the furnace, was above (see v. 22); a second, for the removal of slag, cinders, etc., or the molten metal, was arranged below, in one of the sides, and permitted persons standing before the furnace to observe the material in its interior (the תְּרַע, v. 26; cf. vs. 24, 25). The passage Jer. xxix. 22 ("The Lord make thee like Zedekiah and like Ahab, whom the king of Babylon roasted in the fire") attests that the Babylonians were accustomed to burn condemned criminals, and perhaps prisoners of war in such furnaces, even prior to the time of Daniel. The Moabites employed the same method of inflicting capital punishment, according to Am. ii. 1, as did also the Israelites, according to the Keri of 2 Sam. xii. 31. ["That burning was not an unusual punishment in the East is sufficiently known. As to the Persians, see Brissonius, *De Reg. Pers.*, II. cap. 216. . . . . . Chardin (who was in Persia A. D. 1671–7) relates that in a time of scarcity, two furnaces were kept burning a whole month, in order to consume such as exacted more than the lawful price of food (*Voyages*, VI. p. 118)."—*Stuart.*] The genitive clause נוּרָא יָקִדְתָּא, "of the burning fire," exemplifies the terribly cruel and frightful character of the threatened punishment.—Verse 7. **Therefore at that time when all the people heard the sound of the cornet,** etc. ["בַּהּ זִמְנָא (cf. also v. 8) is interchanged with בְּעִדָּנָא, *at the time* (verses 5 and 15); but it is to be distinguished from בַּהּ־שַׁעֲתָא, *at the same moment*, verses 6 and 15, for שְׁעָא, or שָׁעָה has in the Bib. Chald. only the meaning *instant, moment* (cf. chap. iv. 16, 30; v. 5), and acquires the signification *short time, hour,* first in the Targ. and Rabbins."—*Keil.*] Only five, instead of six, sorts of musical instruments are here mentioned; but the omission of the סוּמְפֹּנְיָא can hardly be designed, as appears from vs. 10 and 15. It is probably to be attributed to the haste of the writer, which also caused the orthography of פסנטרין, with ט instead of ת, in this passage, and only here.

Verses 8–12. *The companions of Daniel charged with transgressing the royal command.* **Wherefore at that time certain Chaldæans came near,** etc. "Wherefore," *i.e.*, in view of the worship rendered by all the people, excepting only the Jews, to the idol image. Daniel does not mention that it was refused by the

Jews, leaving it to be inferred, as a matter of course.—**And accused** (or slandered) **the Jews** (cf. chap. vi. 25); literally, "and ate the pieces (of flesh) of the Jews"—a phrase found also in the Arabic and the Syriac, which expresses both the murder caused by the slanderous tongue, and the gloating over the fragmentary remains of the victim. Cf. the German "*Jemanden kurz und klein machen, an ihm kein gutes Haar lassen.*" It appears from the indefinite "Chaldæan men" that the malicious informers were not specifically Chaldæan priests or wise men (this would have been indicated by כַּשְׂדָּיִן merely, cf. chap. ii. 2), but people generally, who were of Chaldæan descent. ["That which was odious in their report was, that they used the instance of disobedience to the king's command on the part of the Jewish officers as an occasion of removing them from their offices,—that their denunciation of them arose from their envying the Jews their position of influence, as in chap. vi. 5 (4), ff."—*Keil.*]—Verse 9. **O king, live for ever.** Cf. chap. ii. 4.—Verse 12. **There are certain Jews whom thou hast set over the affairs of the province of Babylon.** A clear reference to the close of the preceding section (chap. ii. 49). The mention of their exalted official rank was designed to emphasize the dangerous feature connected with the disobedience of *such men* to the royal command, and also to direct attention to the blackness of their ingratitude toward their royal benefactor.—**These men, O king, have not regarded thee**; *i.e.*, thy commands, אִלֵּךְ, "these," is peculiar to the *Biblical* Chaldee of Daniel and Ezra, and is not found in the Targums, which have אִלֵּין or אֵלֶּה instead (Winer, § 9, p. 29).—**They serve not thy gods, nor worship the golden image,** etc. The former of these charges is related to the latter as the general to the particular; the general lack of reverence for the gods of Babylon on the part of the three men, which had been formerly observed, was now demonstrated by a flagrant example. Because of this evident relation to each other between the two clauses—a relation that is again brought out in the parallel verse 18 (and possibly in verse 14; see on the passage)—the Kethib לֵאלָהָיךְ, "thy gods," must be preferred to the Keri לֵאלָהָךְ, "thy god;" which has been the case accordingly, in Theodotion and the Vulgate. Compare, although it is superfluous, verse 28 *b*, where לְכָל־אֱלָהּ shows clearly that a number of gods were in question. ["The Chaldæans knew the three Jews, who were so placed as to be well known, and at the same time envied, before this. They had long known that they did not worship idols; but on this occasion, when their religion made it necessary for the Jews to disobey the king's command, they made use of their knowledge."—*Hitzig.* It is barely possible that the proposal of erecting such an idolatrous image and requiring the whole realm, and especially the public officials to adore it, originated, as in chap. vi. with some such malicious and envious enemies of Judaism.]—Why was not Daniel included in this charge of the Chaldæans? To this question that so readily presents itself, no answer can be given that will be sufficiently assured to exclude all others; but we are not on that account compelled (with v. Lengerke) to find here a new improbability, and a testimony against the credibility of the book. Daniel might be omitted from the number of the accused, (1) because he was too firmly established in the favor of the king, to justify the attempt of a slanderer to destroy him (Calvin, Hävernick, etc.); (2) because he was absent on business, or sick (Lüderwald, Jahn); (3) because his position, as chief of the magian caste, would remove him from the gaze of the multitude, and would also relieve him from the obligation of prostrating himself before the idol, which more immediately affected the secular officials (see on verse 2, Kranichfeld). All of these explanations are admissible; and very possibly any two of the reasons adduced might combine to cause his absence, *e. g.* Nos. 1 and 2, or 2 and 3. The opinion of Hengstenberg however (with whom Hitzig agrees), that according to chap. ii. 49, Daniel filled no office of superior power and influence in the state, but that he at once transferred to his three friends the dignity of a viceroy which was offered to him, and contented himself with the spiritual rank of chief of the Magi, cannot be entertained. See to the contrary chap. ii. 48, 49, where it was shown that, together with this spiritual dignity, Daniel must have possessed considerable influence in the political field, although not bearing the title of a recognized officer of the state. ["But the circumstance that Daniel, if he were present, did not exert himself in behalf of his three friends, may be explained from the quick execution of Babylonian justice; provided some higher reason did not determine him confidently to commit the decision of the matter to the Lord his God."—*Keil.*]

Verses 13-15. *The accused summoned to renounce Jehovah.* **Then Nebuchadnezzar in rage and fury commanded to bring,** etc. בִּרְגַז וַחֲמָא. The use of the synonymous terms expresses the violence of the king's rage. The Inf. Aphel לְהַיְתָיָה, "to let them be brought," is found also in chap. v. 2, 13.—**Then they brought these men before the king**; rather, "Then these men were brought before the king." הֵיתָיו is not to be taken transitively, "they brought these men" (Chr. B. Michaelis, etc.); nor is it to be explained as a Hebraizing Hophal form (Buxt., Hävernick, v. Lengerke). It is rather a passive form of the Aphel after the manner of the Hebrew [Hophal], of which the 3d pers. masc. sing. is הֵיתַי, the fem. הֵיתָיִת (chap. vi. 18), while the regular participle with a passive signification would be מְהֵיתַי, and the active partic. Aphel מְהֵיתֵי (cf. Hitzig and Kranichfeld on this passage).—Verse 14. **Of purpose** (marg.); **O Shadrach . . . . do ye not serve my god?** The plural לֵאלָהַי, "my gods," is perhaps admissible here, in analogy with verses 12 and 18 (Hitzig); but in this instance the singular is especially suitable, as referring directly to the image of the idol immediately before them; and there is no Keri, in this case, recommending the plural.—הַצְדָּא,

literally, "Was it design?"—a combination of the interrogative הֲ with צְדָא, a noun that occurs in no other place, but which may be explained by "fraudulent design, evil purpose" [contumacy] on the analogy of the Hebrew צְדִיָּה (Num. xxxv. 20, 21). The question, "Does an evil purpose lead you to refuse to serve my god"? evidently has a substantial basis in the situation as described; for these men had by no means presented themselves at once in the festive assembly, as is shown by the command to "bring them." Despite their official station, they had rather endeavored to avoid any participation in the ceremonies. Nothing could therefore be more natural than the question of the king, as to whether their absence was grounded on an actual disobedience or evil design, or not. The usual interpretation of הַצְדָא is therefore to be retained, and the departures from it must be rejected; *e. g.*, the rendering of Hävernick ("Is it because ye *mock*, or despise my gods, that ye do not worship them?"), and by Fürst and Kranichfeld (who conceive הצדא as an adverbial Aphel noun, from צְדָא, and thus avoid the interrogative sense of the clause entirely: "In mockery ye not serve my god!"). [The interpretation of the Engl. Bible. "Is it *true*," is not only unsustained by the etymological signification of the word, but at variance with the circumstances of the case; for their absence was a matter of fact, and their declining to worship was only a question of inadvertence or setted determination. "The king, seemingly with more than usual moderation, first inquires into the truth of the accusation." (Rather he first opens the way for the most favorable construction of the omission.) "He probably suspected the accusers of envious motives, and was desirous of sparing these Hebrews on whom he had bestowed special favors."—*Stuart.*] —Verse 15. **Now if ye be ready that at what time . . . . ye worship;** *i.e.* "at the time . . . to worship. This conditional clause of a positive character may be readily completed from the negative conditional clause which immediately follows, whose apodosis involves the contrary of the thought here required; hence, *e.g.*, "nothing shall be done to you; ye shall escape the death by fire." The same construction [aposiopesis] occurs in Ex. xxxii. 32; Luke xiii. 9. It is also frequent in the classics, *e. g.*, Homer, *Il.* I. 135; Plato, *Protag.* 15; and likewise in the Arabic.— כְּעַן, at the beginning of the sentence, corresponds to the Heb. וְעַתָּה; the Vulgate renders it correctly by "*Nunc ergo.*" —**And who is that God that shall deliver you out of my hand?** Not exactly a direct blasphemy of the God of the Jew (Hitzig), but still a challenge addressed to Him in a presumptuous spirit and with a haughty sense of superior power; cf. Isa. xxxvii. 10; and supra, on verse 1.

Verses 16–18. *The steadfast confession of the three Jews.* **Shadrach . . . . answered and said to the king, O Nebuchadnezzar,** etc. Thus the Masoretic punctuation, which, however, is departed from by all the ancient translations. The Septuagint introduces a βασιλεῦ, "O king," before the vocative Nebuchadnezzar, and Theodotion and the Vulgate connect the name of the king with the preceding dative case, and therefore place the Athnach under נְבוּכ׳. But there is no ground for either of these variations: for while on the one hand, the boldness of the reply is indicated at the beginning by the word לְמַלְכָּא, the direct address by name, on the other hand, conveys an emphasis and solemnity that fully comport with the situation. The vocative מַלְכָּא in v. 17 shows that the form of this address, which contains merely the name of the king, and omits the royal title, was not designed as an expression of contempt. Cf. v. 14, where Nebuchadnezzar likewise addresses the three Hebrews simply by name.—**We are not careful to answer thee in this matter,** *i.e.*, *it is not necessary.* The primary emphasis falls on אֲנַחְנָא, as appears from the words הֵן אִיתַי אֱלָהַנָא at the beginning of the next verse. Hence the sense is, "It is not *we* that are compelled to answer thee (*i.e.*, to manage our case before thee), but if our God can deliver us," etc. On חַשְׁחִין cf. chap. iv. 16; v. 25. The root חֲשַׁח is foreign to the language of the Targums, but is found in the Syriac, where it signifies "to be useful, suitable," while in the Bibl. Chaldee it expresses the idea of being necessary (*e.g.*, Ezra vi. 9; cf. חַשְׁחוּת, "need," Ezra vii. 20), or of standing in need of (as in this place).—עַל־דְּנָה, "upon this," is connected with the following פִּתְגָם, by the Sept., Theodotion, Vulgate, Hävernick, etc.: "to answer thee upon this word (or matter);" but in that case פתגם must be in the *stat. emphaticus*, despite the preceding demonstrative; cf. chap. iv. 15; ii. 32; Ezra vi. 11.—פִּתְגָם is a word unquestionably borrowed from the Persian (cf. the Introd. § 1, note 3), but found also in the later Hebrew of the book of Ecclesiastes (see on Ecc. viii. 11). It is compounded from the Zend preposition *paiti* (= *prati*, πρός) and the verb *gam*, "to go," and accordingly, signifies "what is going forward, a message" (cf. mod. Pers. *paiam*, "a messenger," and the Armen. *patgam*, "a message"), from which results the further meaning of "a command, edict, word." The latter is the sense in this place. The idea of "answer" results from its connection with the verb הֲתָבָה, "to give back." —Verse 17. **If it be so, our God whom we serve is able to deliver us;** rather, "If our God whom we serve, can save us." הֵן is not the Heb. הֵן or הִנֵּה, and cannot be rendered by *ecce enim*, with the Vulgate, nor by a causal γάρ, with the Sept. It corresponds rather, as always in Daniel, to the Heb. אִם, "if," and is here, as in v. 15, in contrast with a הֵן לָא (see v. 17). In this case, however, the conditional clause is followed by its apodosis, which begins, as the *athnach* correctly indicates, with the words יָכִל, מִן־אַתּוּן, "to be able," does not, of course, refer to the ability of God, as limited by any bounds whatever, but as ethically conditioned (cf. Gen. xix. 29). The pious Jews were not probably concerned to maintain the perfection of the Divine power in opposition to the king, but at the most, their own worthiness to find mercy at the hands of the Almighty (cf. chap. ii. 18; vi. 22; ix. 15-19),—and perhaps not even this,—for the whole may have been spoken from the point of view occupied by the heathen hearers of the three Hebrews, who certainly doubted Jehovah's ability to save His servants. In order to refer these opponents, and above all the king himself, with all possible emphasis to the test of experience, upon which everything depended, the Jews employ the words, "If our God—*can* save" (thus corresponding to v. 17), although it would have been more in harmony with their Israelitish consciousness to say, "If He *will* save" (cf. Hitzig on this passage). ["There lies in the answer, 'If our God will save us, then . . . . and if not, know, O king, that we will not serve thy gods,' neither audacity, nor a superstitious expectation of some miracle, (ver. 17), nor fanaticism (ver. 18), as Berth., v. Leng., and Hitz. maintain, but only the confidence of faith and a humble submission to the will of God."—*Keil.* In the most extreme event they prefer death to idolatry.]

Verses 19-23. *The execution.* **Then . . . . and the form** (the expression) **of his visage was changed against Shadrach,** etc. The A. V. is literal. The Kethib אֶשְׁתַּנּוּ is conformed to the Genit. אַנְפּוֹהִי, while the Keri אֶשְׁתַּנִּי agrees with the Nom. sing. צְלֵם. The former construction, as being more rare and difficult, is to be considered genuine.—**Seven times more than it was wont to be heated;** thus Bertholdt, Gesenius, and others, in agreement with the A. V. But חֲזֵי, passive part. of חזה, "to see," is constantly used in the Targums in the sense of "suitable, appropriate" (literally, "what has been selected as appropriate," *quod conveniens visum est*), and the construction with לְ, c. Infinit., shows that the same signification is required here. Therefore, "seven times beyond its appropriate heating;" *i.e.*, seven times more than was necessary (παρ' ὃ ἔδει, Sept). [The sense thus yielded, however, is more inept than the other, and the impersonal construction of the former verb (חזה), together with the active form of the latter (למזיה), rather favors the same rendering. In either case the ultimate thought is the *unusually* intense fire.]—The command to heat the furnace exactly *seven* times beyond its proper measure, has a parallel in judicial procedures and limitations, where seven as a number indicates a full atonement or satisfaction, cf. Lev. xxvi. 18-24; Deut. xxxviii. 7 et seq.; Prov. vi. 31; Matt. xviii. 21 et seq.; and perhaps passages like Isa. xi. 15; xxx. 26; Psa. xii. 7, etc. This judicial bearing of the number seven, which was familiar to all the ancient Oriental nations and current among them, is the only respect in which the number is here employed, and it affords the only explanation of the phrase as used by the Babylonian king. Kranichfeld's remark is less appropriate, when he observes that the number seven serves in this instance to express the idea of intensity, because here, "where a notorious injury had been inflicted on the national divinity," no other than a pre-eminently sacred number would be adequate; but this may be admitted rather than the general opinion that in this case seven was "merely the indefinite expression of a round number" (Hävernick, etc.)—Verse 20. **And he commanded the most mighty men . . . in his army.** בְּחַיְלֵהּ must not be limited to the life or body guards, against which view the comprehensive and indefinite signification of the term חיל is, in itself, a sufficient testimony; but in addition, the selection of executioners from the *army* is seen to be well grounded and capable of an easy explanation, in view of the fact that the task was not without danger, and would require the services of especially trustworthy men; and the presence of the troops at a religious ceremony is not strange, since a great festive procession was one of its features.—**To bind Shadrach . . . . and to** (rather "in order to") **cast them into the burning fiery furnace.** The second inf. לְמִרְמֵא is subordinated to the first, לְכַפָּתָה, as more directly pointing out the special design.—Verse 21. **Then these men were bound in their coats, their hosen,** etc; rather, their undergarments, coats, etc. The haste, as here implied, with which the sentence was executed, is in strong contrast with the direction given immediately before, to heat the furnace more intensely than usual; for the newly added fuel would require time before it could burn with sufficient force, in a furnace of considerable size. But the rage of an inflamed Oriental despot allows itself no time in which to quietly consider all the circumstances connected with any given case.—Three articles of clothing are specified as belonging to the costume of the three Hebrews, which may have constituted the distinguishing features of their official dress; and upon these follows the generalizing וּלְבוּשֵׁיהוֹן, "and their (other) garments" (cf. vs. 2 and 5) [as "coverings for the feet and the head" (Keil)]. There would be no need to mention such a variety of garments in the case of men of inferior rank.—(1) The סַרְבָּלִין were probably long and closely-fitting under-garments, that covered the whole body (*shirts, tunics*); for the word is most readily explained by comparison with the Chald. quadril. verb סַרְבֵּל, *texit, operuit.* It occurs in the Syriac and the Talmuds, with the signification of *pallium* (hence "mantles"—Luther, Gesenius, and many others); and in the Arabic, where it becomes *serbal*, it designates a long under-garment for females, *indusium mulieris.* Others, among moderns, especially Hävernick, v. Lengerke, and Hitzig, identify סַרְבָּל with the Pers. *shalwâr*, Chald. שְׁרָוַל, and therefore translate it by "hosen," justifying this opinion by an appeal to Symmachus, the Vulgate, and also to Hesychius, Suidas, etc. (who explain the later Greek σαράβαρα by τὰ περὶ τὰς κνημῖδας ἐνδύματα, βρακία, σκελεαί). But the Pers. *shalwâr* appears to differ fundamentally from our word, and to be related to *shul*, "the hip" (Sanscr. *khura*, Latin *crus*), while it bears no relation to the Zend *sáravâro*, "covering for the head" (from *sára*, "head," and *vri*, "to cover") in either sound or signification. The Greek σαράβαρα (Mid. Age *saraballa*), in the sense of "hosen," seems, on the other hand, to owe this interpretation to the Arabic *sarawîl* "a covering for the thighs," and also to the Pers. *shalvár;* but this sense was not attributed to it by the earliest Greek translators. Theodotion, indeed, renders סַרְבָּלֵין by σαράβαρα, but reserves the interpretation by "hosen" for the third garment, כַּרְבְּלָן, which he translates περικνημῖδες; while the Sept. (and Aquila) evidently failed to comprehend the meaning of סרבלין, since it renders it in this place by ὑποδήματα, but adopts σαράβαρα in v. 27. Upon the whole, the first named garment in this passage is probably identical with the κιθὼν ποδηνεκὴς λίνεος, which Herodotus (I. 195) describes as the innermost garment worn by the Babylonians.—(2) The פַּטִּישֵׁיהוֹן, or, as the Keri prefers, פַּטְּשֵׁיהוֹן, were not "hammers," of course, although the root פטש, "to spread, extend" (cf. פשט, "to spread out"), is probably the same from which פַּטִּישׁ, "a hammer," is derived; cf. the Gr. πατάσσω, "to strike." According to the Hebrew translator of the Chaldee sections of Daniel, פַּטִּישׁ in this place corresponds to the Heb. כְּתֹנֶת, and therefore designates a wider and more flowing under-garment than the סַרְבָּל, which answers to the second, woolen tunic (εἰρίνεος κιθών), which the Babylonians wore, cf. Herod. l. c. The derivation from the Arabic *fuds*, "a spider, fine web," according to which the word would rather designate the innermost, closest, and finest garmant (Hitzig), seems too precarious, because of the harsh *t*-sound. The identification of the word with the Gr. πέτασος, "a hat, covering for the head" (Bertholdt), is entirely too far-fetched, since πέτασος was used by the Greeks exclusively to designate the head-covering of the ἔφηβοι, and since the Chaldee language was certainly able to command other than Greek terms with which to designate the Oriental turban (*e.g.*, in Ezek. xxiii. 15 we find טְבוּלִים). The same reference of פַּטִּישׁ back to πέτασος seems to underlie the τιάραις, by which the Sept., Theodotion, and Theodoret render the word in this passage.—(3) The כַּרְבְּלָא appears to have been the third Babylonian garment mentioned by Herodotus, the χλανίδιον λευκόν, which was worn over the two κιθῶνες; for this word is based on the quadril. verb כִּרְבֵּל, "to gird, wind about," which is also found in the later Hebrew, cf. 1 Chron. xv. 27, מְכֻרְבָּל בִּמְעִיל בּוּץ. [According to Rawlinson (*Five Monarchies*, iii. 2 sq.), the ordinary Babylonian dress of the lower orders of men, was "but one garment, a tunic, generally ornamented with a diagonal fringe, and reaching from the shoulder to a little above the knee. It was confined round the waist by a belt." The head and feet were bare. The richer persons are represented on the cylinders as having "a fillet or head-band, not a turban, round the head. They wear generally the same sort of a tunic as the others, but over it they have a long robe, shaped like a modern dressing-gown, except that it has no sleeves, and does not cover the right shoulder. In a few cases only, we see underneath this open gown a long under-dress or robe, such as that described by Herodotus." "In lieu of the long robe reaching to the feet, which seems to have been the ordinary costume of the higher classes, we observe sometimes a shorter but still a similar garment—a sort of coat without sleeves, fringed down both sides, and reaching a little below the knee." "With rare exceptions the Babylonians are represented with bare feet on the monuments." "The girdle was an essential feature of Babylonian costumes, common to high and low." "The dress of the priests was a long robe or gown, flounced and striped, over which they seem to have worn an open jacket of a similar character. A long scarf or ribbon depended from behind down their backs. They carried on their heads an elaborate crown or mitre" (*ib.*).]—The garments which are specially mentioned, are accordingly referred to in the order of their succession from within outward, "under-garments, coats, mantles"—a climax which serves to indicate that because of the excessive haste under which this transaction took place, the victims were not relieved of their under, nor even of their outer garments. [Or, as Keil suggests, "in the easily inflammable nature of these materials, namely, of the fine *long linen gown* (cf. Herod.), we have perhaps to seek the reason on account of which the accused were bound in their clothes."]—Verses 22, 23. **Because the king's command was urgent**, or furious. "Because" (כָּל קֳבֵל דְּנָה) refers to what has preceded, and the clause מִן־דִּי וגו׳ (= Heb. מֵאֲשֶׁר, "therefore") points out this reference more fully; "because" is therefore equivalent to "namely because," and the וְ before אַתּוּנָא expresses the consequence: "and because in consequence the furnace was in the mean time exceedingly heated up." With regard to מְהַחְצְפָה, "strict, raging" (not "hurried") see on chap. ii. 15.—**The flame of the fire slew those men that took up**, etc. It is not stated how and at what portion of the furnace the death of these executioners took place, nor could it be demonstrated with any degree of probability; but it is not difficult to assume that, owing to the excessive violence of the fire, a strong draught of air, while sweeping through the compressed flames, might blow them in the direction of the executioners on their issuing from the upper opening of the furnace, while leaving the three victims unharmed at the bottom of the furnace, and continuing to burn above their heads without attacking them. The deliverance of the condemned Hebrews is still *miraculous*, even on this assumption, and the contrast between the extraordinary strictness of the means employed, and the security of the followers of Jehovah in the face of the rage of men, which is so strongly emphasized by our book (and also by the "Song of the three children," vs. 46–50), is still a notable fact. Cf. the Dog.-ethical remarks, No. 3. ["If the three were brought up to the furnace, it must have had a mouth above, through which the victims could be cast into it. When heated to an ordinary degree, this could be done without danger to the men who performed this service; but in the present case the heat of the fire was so great that the servants themselves perished by it. This circumstance also is mentioned to show the greatness of the miracle by which the three were preserved unhurt in the midst of the furnace. The same thing is intended by the repetition of the word מְכַפְּתִין, *bound*, ver. 23, which, moreover, is purposely placed at the close of the passage to prepare for the contrast שְׁרַיִן, *at liberty*, free from the bonds, ver. 25."—*Keil.*]—The Sept., and also Theodotion and the Vulg., influenced probably by an already existing Hebrew or Greek tradition (see Introd. § 11), introduce after v. 23 the apocryphal fragment, "The prayer of Azariah and Song of the three children" (προσευχὴ Ἀζαρίου καὶ ὕμνος τῶν τριῶν), which is broken by a shorter narrative section (vs. 46–50, or also vs. 22–26), devoted to a detailed description of the subject of vs. 22, 23, and containing especially the statement, that the turning aside of the flames from the three men was due to an angel of the Lord.

Verses 24–26. *The liberation of the three men from the furnace.* **Then Nebuchadnezzar the king was astonished, and rose up in haste,** viz.: from the chair on which he had been seated opposite the side-door of the furnace, and from whence he had witnessed the execution. He did not seat himself in that position *after* the victims were cast into the furnace, for the purpose of gloating over their tortures (Hitzig); but, as a king, he was doubtless seated before (although all others might be standing), and his position probably enabled him to see the inside of the furnace, in whose immediate vicinity his chair was placed. It is not necessary to assume that his seat was so near the opening of the furnace, that he could view the interior perfectly, and thus observe the three men together with their heavenly protector; for his words in v. 25 may be readily explained on the hypothesis of a merely spiritual or visional sight.—**Spake, and said to his counsellors.** The הַדָּבְרִין are councillors of state or ministers, *consiliarii*, *socii in judicio* (Sept. φίλοι; Theodot. μεγιστᾶνες; Vulg. and Syr. *optimates*). The word is scarcely the Chaldee דָּבְרִין, "leaders," with the prefixed Hebrew article הַ, which in this instance, like the Arabic article in "Alcoran," "Almanac," has become inseparably united to the word (Gesenius); but the ה must probably be regarded as an organic element of the first half of this compound word (as it must be considered), whether that part be traced back to the Sanscr. *sahas*, "power" (Hitzig), or it be compared with the Pers. *hamd*, "judgment, counsel" (v. Bohlen, Kranichfeld). The second half בַּר is, without doubt, the Pers. *vār*, "possessor, owner," as in דְּבָרִין and גְּדָבְרַיָּא, v. 2. In regard to Ewald's attempt to identify the terms הַדָּבַר and גְּדָבַר directly, see supra, on v. 2. Compare generally the repeated mention of these prominent royal officials, in v. 27; chap. iv. 33; vi. 8.—Verse 25. **Lo, I see four men loose, walking in the midst of the fire.** מְהַלְּכִין is a regular part. Aphel, as in iv. 34; cf. the Chaldaizing מַהְלְכִים in the Heb. of Zech. iii. 7. In opposition to Hitzig, who regards the form as a metamorphosed part. Pael, basing his opinion on chap. iv. 26, see Kranichfeld on this passage.—**And the form of the fourth is like the son of God;** rather "like a son of the gods." It is by no means necessary to believe that this vision of the king which revealed to him this "son of the gods" (בַּר־אֱלָהִין, cf. the plural אלהין in vs. 12 and 18) in company with the three Jews, was an *objective* seeing. It must be observed, that here as well as in v. 28, where the son of the gods is designated as the "angel" of the God of the Jews, Daniel does not himself attest his appearance, nor does he refer to additional witnesses, but in each case mentions the king *only* as the authority for the occurrence of the event. Kranichfeld's hypothesis that the king employed the term "angel" (מַלְאַךְ) in the second reference to the son of the gods, in consequence of the instruction (which is to be read between the lines after v. 27) imparted to him meanwhile by the rescued Jews, is unnecessary, and without support in the context. From his heathen Babylonian point of view the king could readily characterize an appearance from the celestial world which he fancied he had seen, either as a "son" or a "messenger" of the gods (or of one of the gods—for only thus would he conceive of the national God of the Jews, despite v. 26). That *theogonic ideas* were unknown to the ancient Babylonians, and that the expression "a son of the gods" must therefore be regarded as a conception of Hellenistic origin, which was foreign to the Orient until after the march of Alexander, as Bertholdt asserts, is wholly untrue; and it is with entire justice that Hengstenberg (p. 159 et seq.) while opposing it, refers to the marriage between Bel and Mylitta and to their offspring. On the conception of a messenger of the gods, compare also the god Nebo, the "writer of the gods," who corresponds fully to the Greek Hermes. The Sept., however, renders even the בַּר־אֱלָהִין of this verse by ἄγγελος θεοῦ, and thus avoids all reference to heathen conceptions.—Verse 26. **Then Nebuchadnezzar came near to the mouth of the burning fiery furnace.** On תְּרַע, see on v. 6.—**Ye servants of the most high God.** The king thus designates the national God of the Jews from his heathen stand-point, because he has just received an overpowering impression of His greatness, and therefore regards Him as mightier than all his Babylonian divinities. Cf. אֱלָהּ אֱלָהִין, chap. ii. 47; also the Gr. ὕψιστος θεός, as applied to Zeus by Pindar, *Nem.* i. 90.—אֱלָהָא עִלָּיָא corresponds exactly to the Hebrew אֵל עֶלְיוֹן, Gen. xiv. 18. Instead of עִלָּיָא the Keri has עִלָּאָה in this place, chap. iv. 14, and nine times elsewhere in the book—substituting the later form, which is usual in the Targums, for the more ancient; cf. the similar Keris in chap. ii. 5 and 40.

Verses 27–30. *The effect of this incident.* **And the princes . . . . being gathered together, saw these men, upon whose bodies the fire**

had no power, etc. ; literally, *that* the fire had possessed no power over their bodies,—an *antiptosis*, like Gen. i. 3. The Chaldee of the Targums constantly substitutes גּוּשְׁמָא, a fuller form, and analogous to the Syriac, for the גְּשֵׁם, גִּשְׁמָא, "body," of Daniel.—**Neither were their coats** (under-garments) **changed.** The mention of this particular article of clothing only, as being uninjured, might lead to the conclusion that the remaining, or outer garments, had actually been harmed by the fire; but that the writer intended no such toning down of the marvelous nature of the event, is shown by the words, "nor the smell of fire had passed upon them." The pointing of the expression "on them" (בְּהוֹן) refers indeed, to the persons themselves, but it furnishes an *indirect* testimony to the preservation of their clothing that is unmistakable ; and the testimony of the passage as a whole, relating to their bodies, hair, and under-clothing, and also to the absence of any odor of the burning, constitutes a gradation analogous to that of v. 21. Only one of the four garments there referred to is here mentioned, and the *first* is selected, in order to recall that enumeration.—Verse 28. **Blessed be the God of Shadrach,** etc. The doxology corresponds in form with those recorded in chap. iv. 31 et seq. and vi. 26 et seq., but is addressed to Jehovah himself, in a precatory or explanatory form, cf. Gen. ix. 26; Luke i. 68.—**That trusted in Him, and have changed the king's word** ; rather, "and transgressed the king's command." The ו before מִלַּת is illative: "and in consequence," or, "and by reason of their trust, they transgressed the king's command;" cf. supra on v. 22. שְׁנָא מִלַּת מַלְכָּא is, literally, "to *change* the word of the king, to alter it (criminally)." The same idiom occurs in Ezra vi. 11; cf. חָלְפוּ חֹק, Isa. xxiv. 5.—**And yielded their bodies** ; cf. Acts xv. 26: ἀνθρώποις παραδεδωκόσι τὰς ψυχὰς αὐτῶν ὑπὲρ τοῦ ὀνόματος τοῦ κυρίου—Verse 29. **Therefore, I make a decree**; literally, "And by me is issued a decree." שִׂים טְעֵם as in v. 9, and also in Ezra vi. 11, which latter passage is upon the whole very similar to this (*e.g.*, because of its use of the phrase (שְׁנָא מִלַּת מ׳), but is not for this reason to be regarded as the model, from which the alleged pseudo-Daniel copied in this place (as Hitzig contends). The writer of this book displays too thorough an acquaintance with the Chaldee, to warrant the assumption of its composition by the process of a laborious and clumsy compilation of extracts taken from Ezra and other ancient documents ; and in addition, nothing is more probable than that royal edicts should employ stereotyped phrases to enforce obedience to law, threaten punishments, etc.—whether the respective kings were Chaldæans or Persians (cf. also Kranichfeld on this passage). —**Which speak anything amiss against the God of Shadrach,** etc. The Kethib שָׁלָה, a Hebraized form for שָׁלָא, is not to be changed, with Hitzig, into שָׁלָה (= שְׁאֵלָה = דָּבָר, "anything whatever"), nor to be replaced by the Keri שָׁלוּ, which is used in the Kethib of chap. vi. 5; Ezra iv. 22; vi. 9. שָׁלָה, "a fault, single error, offence," is rather a concrete term, which is related to the abstract שָׁלוּ, "error," precisely as the Heb. כְּלִמָּה, "a disgraceful thing," is to כְּלִמּוּת (Jer. xxiii. 40), "disgrace," or the Chaldee מַלְכָּה (Dan. v. 12) to מַלְכוּ, etc.—**Shall be cut in pieces.** This threat, which was evidently a stereotyped formula in royal edicts, and in view of the customs of Oriental despots might also be employed with reference to minor offences, has already been explained in chap. ii. 5.—**Because there is no other God that can deliver after this sort.** Thus also, among recent expositors, Kranichfefd, who takes כִּדְנָה = οὕτως, *ita ;* cf. Sept., Theodotion, Vulg., in a feminine sense. The masculine form, however, which accords better with the syntax and the context, is sufficiently supported by chap. ii. 43 ; vi. 29. Therefore, "that can deliver as He can."—**Then the king made Shadrach, ... , to prosper** (marg.) **in the province of Babylon.** הַצְלַח is not intransitive, as in chap. vi. 29, but has a transitive signification, "to bless," and is accompanied by לְ of the person prospered, as in the Heb. of Neh. i. 11 ; ii. 20 ; cf. Gen. xxxix. 23 ; 2 Chron. xxvi. 5. The reference to "the province of Babylon" indicates the nature of this blessing or prospering, viz. : as a repeated endowment with a position of exalted dignity and power; cf. chap. ii. 49. The expression "made to prosper" is therefore equivalent to "gave prosperity and great power."

ETHICO-FUNDAMENTAL PRINCIPLES RELATED TO THE HISTORY OF SALVATION, APOLOGETICAL REMARKS, AND HOMILETICAL SUGGESTIONS.

1. *General preliminary observation.*—A correct estimate of the foregoing section imperatively requires the recognition of the peculiarities of the style of writing employed. That style will serve in a greater degree than any other of the first six chapters, to exemplify the repeated observations in the Introduction respecting the "theocratic chronicling style" of our prophet (cf. Introd. § 4, note 2; § 9, note 1). The whole of the event described is considered emphatically in the light of *the strictest theocratic pragmatism.* It is Jehovah who preserves His devoted confessors in the midst of the flames. The heathen executors of the barbarous decree, and not *they*, are destroyed. The tyrant, at first blasphemous and presumptuously defiant, is compelled to humble himself, and reverently to acknowledge the superior power of the only true God, in the end. At the same time, the narrative possesses a peculiar breadth and minuteness of detail, combined with a condensed brevity and force that recall the lapidary style of records relating to the Assyrian and Babylonian empires. Observe the frequent repetition of identical formulas, and of changes and series of names (including both appellatives and proper names). The phrase, "The image

which king Nebuchadnezzar had caused to be set up," is found no less than ten times in the first fifteen verses; three times we meet the expression "not serve the gods (or "the god") of the king, nor worship the golden image erected by him," and the characteristic triad "peoples, tribes, and tongues" recurs as often, as does also the triad of officials, "satraps, governors, and præfects." The sounding list of official titles, "satraps, governors, præfects, chief-judges, treasurers, judges, lawyers," is repeated at least once; the names of the six instruments, "the cornet, flute, harp, sackbut, psaltery, and dulcimer" three times (on v. 6, where the "dulcimer" is omitted, see the exegetical remarks); while the proper names Shadrach, Meshach, and Abed-nego recur no less than thirteen times. The explanation of this extraordinary wealth in repetitions, is evidently not to be sought in the careless style of the writer, but in his well-defined intention to impart a solemn and weighty character to the narrative. This hypothesis, however, which is supported by the frequent use of a similar style by both earlier and later writers of the Old-Testament Scriptures,—*e.g.*, by the Elohist in the Pentateuch, among the former, and by the writer of the books of Chronicles among the latter—is not of itself sufficient to explain the numerous repetitions. It will be necessary to assume, in addition, a designed imitation of the solemn phrases and stereotyped formulas employed in the official documents and records of the Babylonian empire, on the part of our prophetic author. The propriety of this method was already apparent in the preceding chapter, in view of the repeated expression, "The decree has been published by me" (vs. 5 and 8); and also with regard to the triad "scribes, conjurers, and Chaldæans" (vs. 2 and 10), and in the phrases repeated in this chapter, although not found in the former: "O king, live for ever," and "ye shall be cut in pieces, and your houses be made dunghills" (cf. ii. 4 with iii. 9, and ii. 5 with iii. 29). The fact that such stereotyped formulas and repeated phrases in an unchanged form are considerably more numerous in this chapter, than in either the chapters that precede or the three narrative sections that follow, indicates that the writer preferred the documentary and chronicling style in this connection, because the subject-matter afforded greater inducements than any other for this choice, and possibly also because he had a special inclination to narrate the event in question in the manner of a theocratic chronicler. —The peculiar coloring of the style of narration in this section unquestionably affords an evidence of especial significance, for the hypothesis postulated in the Introd. § 4, note 2 (in agreement with Kranichfeld), which assumes that the writer recorded the events contained in chap. ii.–v. at different times (although not without regard to their relation to each other), and in the form of a diary.

2. *Apologetical.*—The foregoing remarks contain features that testify to the authenticity and historical accuracy of the narrative; but a far more forcible evidence is found in the strong *contrast between the situation and circumstances* of the persecuted Hebrews who steadfastly clung to their faith, as here related, and the similar fortunes of pious Jews in the Asmonæan age. According to Bertholdt, Bleek, v. Lengerke, Hitzig, etc., the motive that inspired the alleged historical fictions of the pseudo-Daniel, was derived from the tribulations of the latter period; but at that time Israel endured the barbarous persecutions inflicted on account of its faith in Jehovah while established on its own native soil; whereas here, the suffering is imposed while in a foreign land and in captivity, and merely upon three individual representatives, who are penally prosecuted on the ground of the slanderous accusations of envious persons or of politico-religious opponents, who charge them with hostility to the national gods of Babylon. In the former case the heathen despot attempted to carry into effect a general system of persecution which aimed at the extirpation of the worship of Jehovah (1 Macc. i. 41 et seq.); while here an *occasional* denunciation incites a single act of heathen intolerance, which is immediately followed by the recognition and adoration of the God of Israel as a pre-eminently powerful divinity, as in a former instance (cf. chap. ii. 46 with iii. 28 et seq.). In that case the furious religious intolerance of the persecuting tyrant is opposed by the fanatical defiance of the desperate Jewish confessors,* while the confession of the three persecuted Hebrews in this case, vs. 17 and 18, reveals no trace of fanatical excitement; it presents, on the contrary, "so moderate a reflection on the interference of God for the purpose of delivering His servants, that it concedes the possibility of a refusal, on the part of God, to deliver in the present exigency,—for which reason the Sept. felt constrained, in the spirit of its time, to guard against the possible mistake that a doubt of the Divine ability to save is here implied" (see on the passage). Finally, while the barbarous custom of inflicting the death-penalty by means of fire, and in large smelting-furnaces, prevailed at the period of the Chaldæan supremacy, as is certified by Jer. xxix. 22 (cf. xliii. 9 et seq.; cf. above, on v. 6), the books of the Maccabees, which describe so many modes of capital punishment as inflicted on the Jews of his time by Antiochus Epiphanes (see 1 Macc. i. 50, 57, 60 et seq.; ii. 38; 2 Macc. vii.), make no mention whatever of this. The burning of isolated fugitives in caverns, where they had concealed themselves in order to observe the Sabbath (2 Macc. vi. 11), was an unpremeditated device, and therefore entirely different from the predetermined punishment by means of the fiery furnace.—Even Hitzig recognizes the weight of the numerous differences in the situation, as here indicated—to which must be added the extreme contrast between the golden image on the plain of Dura, and the βδέλυγμα ἐρημώσεως of Antiochus (1 Macc. i. 54; see above, on v. 1)—but assumes that the compiler purposely avoided an exact adaptation of his types to the circumstances and facts of his time, in order to prevent any suspicion that his work was invented for a

* The martyrs in 2 Macc. vii. 9 address the Syrian king as: "Thou accursed man," and in v. 34 of the same chapter they denounce him thus: "Thou godless man, and of all others most wicked, be not lifted up without a cause, nor puffed up with uncertain hopes, lifting up thy hand against the servants of God; for thou has not yet escaped the judgment of Almighty God, who seeth all things." How different is the language of the three Hebrews, vs. 16 18, Cf. upon the whole, Zündel, *Krit. Unterss.*, p. 72 et seq.

purpose (p. 43, "Ought a type to correspond so exactly as to arouse suspicion?") He thus attributes to our author an art in concealing his aim, a gift of refined simulation, a practised cunning and adroitness, that might excel even the efforts of modern pseudological tendency writers. But while these, and similar charges of such a critical tendency in the book, are unworthy, and establish nothing, the manifold expositions of details of the narrative which have been deemed necessary by the modern criticism, are no less so. No improbability can be discovered in the statement of the dimensions of the golden image, giving its height at sixty cubits and its thickness at six (v. 1), or in the remark that *all* the high officials of the realm were summoned to the dedication of the image (vs. 2, 3), which is unquestionably to be taken in a relative sense; nor yet in the mention of certain Grecian instruments (vs. 5, 7, 10, 15), or in the occurrence of the title of "satrap" among those pertaining to political dignitaries (vs. 2, 3, 27). We have already furnished the necessary explanation of these features, and also have accounted for the circumstance that Daniel was *absent* from the ceremony (see on v. 12), that the garments of the three martyrs are referred to by names that belong, as is asserted, to a post-Babylonian (Persian or Greek) age, and finally, that the decree directed against the blasphemers of the God of these Jews (v. 29) is couched in terms that are considered extravagantly severe.

3. *The miracle.*—The strongest objections, of course, are raised by opponents against the deliverance of the three condemned Hebrews out of the fiery furnace, while at the same time the executioners are destroyed by the flames. Hitzig holds that "the claim of this narrative to a historical character is unworthy of consideration. Its correctness would not only involve that the nature of an element was changed, but also that the flames had at the same time demonstrated (v. 22) and denied (v. 27) their power to consume; and a reference to the angel (vs. 28, 25) does not improve the matter."—Our exegetical remarks have already pointed out that the case is not really so desperate. Traces of a certain co-operation of natural laws in the wonderful event are by no means wanting from the text, despite its evident aim to emphasize the extraordinary and supernatural features of the incident, rather than to modify them. The excessive heating of the furnace which the king had commanded, the reckless haste in executing his commands, which his rage demanded, and even the circumstances that the flames issuing from the upper opening should seize upon and destroy the persons employed in the execution—all these taken together make it possible, up to a certain point, to conceive how the condemned persons might remain uninjured, and afterward, on their leaving the furnace, be without even the odor of fire upon them. Nebuchadnezzar believed himself able to testify that the efficient or co-operating cause of this deliverance was the visible appearance of an angel which was observed at the same time by several witnesses, probably because, in his fearful excitement and conscientious terror, he really saw in vision a fourth person of celestial form in company with the three victims. The writer, however, does not personally assert such an objective entrance of an angel on the arena, because he neither aims to positively establish the fact, nor yet to explain the philosophy of the event taken as a whole. Without seeking out secondary causes of the deliverance of the Hebrews, he contents himself with simply certifying to the extraordinary event itself, which was probably reported to him, as absent at the time, by his delivered friends in person; and his added remarks, of a religious and practical nature, refer merely to the unmistakable interference of *his God*, whom he represents, after the manner of the *older* theocratic writers, as working directly and without the mediation of angels. A narrator of the Maccabæan period who possessed a mania for miracles, would exaggerate the marvelous element of the event far more conspicuously, would describe the terrible rage of the flames in colors much more glowing, and would introduce, not one, but a multitude of angels as instrumental deliverers. An approximate idea of the description of the event in question which such a writer would have furnished may be gained from a comparison of verses 46–50 of the apocryphal "Prayer of Azariah and song of the three children;" although the embellishment and description of the event attempted in that connection are still within the bounds of reason, and would doubtless be surpassed by a religious-tendency writer of the Maccabæan period. On the other hand, a writer at the beginning of the exile, although influenced by an extravagant mania for miracles and inclined to angelolatry, was not necessarily without a real belief in miracles, but rather, might possess a firm and living confidence in the power of God to work miracles for the deliverance and exaltation of His faithful ones. This is apparent in numerous expressions of the exilian Isaiah,* and of Jeremiah and Ezekiel, who assert miraculous displays of Jehovah's power and grace, in the proper sense, and also express conceptions of the Divine government of the world, and particularly of his direction of the theocratical people in the past, present, and future, which are, to say the least, decidedly supranaturalistic; cf. Introd., § 1, note 1; § 9, note 1. The shallowness and triteness of the reasoning is thus apparent, on which Hitzig, p. 44, formulates his conclusion: "A belief in miracles, such as the writer confesses, could not arise and flourish in the night of the exile, in the days of discouragement and despondency, nor yet in the centuries of servitude (Ezra ix. 9) subsequent to Cyrus. The deliverance from the fiery furnace expresses a supranaturalism entirely different from that manifested in the additions of the reviser in Lev. xxv. 21; xx. 20; Ex. xxxiv. 2, 4 (?), and seems to be indicative of the enthusiasm, the increased power of faith, and the boundless imagination of the Maccabæan epoch."

4. *The ethical and religious importance* of the miracle is found substantially in the consequent Divine confirmation and rewarding of the steadfast faith, by which the three Hebrews had glorified the name of God before the heathen

* [The author by this epithet probably refers to the pseudo-Isaiah assumed to have written the latter chapters of that book—an unnecessary and unwarranted distinction.]

monarch and his court. As they had confessed Him, so He now acknowledges them; as they had glorified His name by the confession of their faith, so He now magnifies Himself in them by a glorious display of His power, and of His infinite superiority over all the gods of the heathen. It is a miracle of deliverance, analogous to those witnessed by Noah at the flood, by Lot at the burning of Sodom, and by Israel at the passage of the Red Sea and of the Jordan; but it is none the less, on that account, a type of the deliverance which the recording prophet should himself experience when, at a much later period, his unwavering devotion to Jehovah had brought him to the lion's den, as well as of the rescue of a Peter from the dungeon of Herod, of a Paul from the jail at Philippi, and of other miraculous events of the Apostolic age. The writer of the epistle to the Hebrews therefore classes this event among the Old-Testament trials of faith that were followed by marvelous results, when, near the close of his glorious *Catalogus testium fidei Veteris Testamenti* (chap. xi. 33), and immediately after the allusion to Daniel in the lion's den, he refers to his three companions with the words, they "quenched the violence of fire" (ἐσβεσαν δύναμιν πυρός). In the same sense, and in a similar connection, the first book of the Maccabees had already adduced the wonderful occurrence, observing with reference to Hananiah, Azariah, and Mishael, that they πιστεύσαντες ἐσώθησαν ἐκ φλογός,—a primitive attestation of the fact, with which, as has been indicated in a former connection, the assumption of its invention in the Asmonæan period can hardly be made to consist (Introd., § 6). The dogmatic importance of this miraculous event is, however, decidedly overestimated, when it is assumed, with several church fathers, *e.g.*, Tertullian, Irenæus, Hilary, Augustine, etc., and also with Carpzov, Joh. Gerhard (in the *Bibl. Vimar.*), Joach. Lange, etc., that the appearance in company with the three men was an actual objective fact, and further, that it was not merely an angel, but the personal Logos that was made flesh in Jesus Christ. Jerome is far more correct when he rejects, as being improbable, the idea that the Son of God should have appeared to the godless king Nebuchadnezzar, and therefore assumes that the appearance of the delivering angel was only a typical prefiguration of the Redeemer: "*Cæterum in typo præfigurat iste angelus sive 'filius Dei' Dominum nostrum Jesum Christum, qui ad fornacem descendit inferni, in quo causæ peccatorum et justorum animæ tenebantur, ut absque exustione et noxa sui eos, qui tenebantur inclusi, vinculis mortis liberaret.*" His remark (on v. 1) on the relation of this event to the Messianic mission of Israel in the midst of the pre-Christian world of nations, is also worthy of note: "*Datur autem per occasionem captivorum barbaris nationibus salutis occasio; ut qui primum per Danielis revelationem potentiam cognoverant unius Dei, in trium puerorum quoque fortitudine discant mortem contemnere et idola non colere.*"

5. *Homiletical suggestions.* Melancthon has correctly specified the points of practical importance in his observations: 1, on v. 1: "*Exemplum humanæ cæcitatis et audaciæ instituentis novos cultus sine verbo Dei, quos hic ostendit se Deus reprobare;*" 2, on v. 12: "*Quod oporteat mandatum Dei anteferre omnibus rebus humanis, potestati, legibus humanis, paci, tranquillitati vitæ nostræ;*" 3, on vs. 16-18: "*Qualis debeat esse fides de corporali liberatione, videlicet cum conditione, si Deo placet;*" 4, on v. 22 et seq.: "*Glorificatio piorum contra blasphemiam, et pœna impiorum, præsertim satellitum, qui alieni furoris ministri sunt;*" 5, on v. 25 et seq.: "*Conversio regis, sequens concionem et glorificationem piorum.*" He also finely develops several of these points. Thus, he remarks on v. 1 et seq.: "Consider that not only the one Nebuchadnezzar is here intended, but all idolaters in general. As Nebuchadnezzar, with fearful temerity, but still under the impression that he was acting religiously, establishes a new cultus, so have many acted at other periods. A majority of states protect idolatry; and even within the church godless popes found dynasties, and seek to confirm them by the successive introduction of new forms of worship. . . . . Consider, therefore, how great is the guilt of the popes and princes, who defend ceremonies and traditions that contradict the Word of God, such as the Mass, monasticism, etc." Cf. M. Geier: "The great lords often put forth greater efforts to introduce false religions than to protect the true. . . . It is a false opinion that all the subjects of a state must adhere to one and the same religion. Thence result so many bloody plans to effect by force what cannot be required with a good conscience." Melancthon observes, on vs. 17, 18: "All the Divine promises require us to believe both that God *can* and that He *will* aid; but with reference to His will the following distinction must be observed; God *will* bestow on us the forgiveness of sins, justification, and eternal life, for He has positively declared His readiness to do this (John iii. 36; 1 John v. 11). Faith in this must therefore shine everywhere upon our pathway before us, and govern our expectations of various external blessings and supports. But the latter must ever be subject to the condition, 'If it *please* God, He will now deliver me,'—a condition that in no wise conflicts with the essence of faith, but that exhorts us to obedience, to prayer, to patient waiting for aid, and to humble submission to the only wise decree of God." Cf. Starke: "In need and danger men are cheerfully to submit to the will of God, and are not to prescribe to Him in relation to His aid and deliverance. Their motto must always be, 'Thy will be done' (Matt. xxvi. 39; cf. Jas. iv. 15")." On v. 23 et seq., cf. Melancthon: "Though the deliverance be long delayed, in order that we may be tried, we dare not cease to call upon the Lord, because supplication is never in vain. For . . . God always aids, either by immediately imparting comfort and diminishing the evil, or by granting a fortunate escape from the tribulation" (1 Cor. x. 13). Cf. Osiander: "God has assigned a limit to all tribulations and persecutions. If it appears to be too distant, consider that the affliction is light and but for a moment, yea, that it secures an eternal glory" (2 Cor. iv. 17). On v. 28 et seq., Melancthon: "Learn from this that it is the office of princes to suppress godless teaching and customs, and to provide for truly pious instruction and worship. For the government is the guardian and protector of the whole moral law; it cannot change

and renew men's hearts, but it must forbid and prevent idolatry, blasphemy, immoral religious services, etc., as well as murder, theft, and the like. For, although a civil government is not enrolled in the service of the Holy Spirit, it is nevertheless the servant of the external moral law, and the responsibility rests upon it, as a distinguished member of the church (*membrum præcipuum Ecclesiæ*), to aid and protect the other members in maintaining the true faith." ["The moral effect of this transaction must have been all the greater because it was the final outcome of a public conflict between the king's god and Jehovah of Hosts. Nor let us fail to note that here, as usual, an unseen hand made the wrath of man work out the praise of God."—*Cowles*].

---

4. *The royal report concerning Nebuchadnezzar's dream relating to his unfitness to govern, and its fulfillment.*

CHAP. III. 31–IV. 34 [English Bible, Chap. IV.].

1 Nebuchadnezzar the king, unto all people, nations [tribes], and languages,
2 that dwell in all the earth;[1] Peace be multiplied unto you.[2] I thought it good[3]
to shew the signs and wonders that the high God hath wrought toward [with]
3 me. How great *are* his signs![4] and how mighty *are* his wonders! his kingdom
is an everlasting kingdom,[5] and his dominion *is* from generation to generation
[with age and age].
4 I Nebuchadnezzar was at rest [tranquil] in my house, and flourishing [green]
5 in my palace. I saw a dream which made [, and it would make] me afraid,[6]
and *the* thoughts upon my bed [*came*], and *the* visions of my head troubled
6 [would trouble] me. Therefore [And] made I a decree[7] to bring in all *the*
wise *men* of Babylon before me, that they might make known unto me [make
7 me know] *the* interpretation of the dream. Then came in the magicians, the
astrologers, the Chaldæans, and the soothsayers;[8] and I told the dream before
them; but [and] they did not make known unto me *the* interpretation thereof.
8 But [And] at *the* last Daniel came in before me, (whose name *was* Belteshazzar,
according to *the* name of my god, and in whom *is the* spirit of *the* holy gods),
9 and before him I told the dream, *saying*, O Belteshazzar, master of the magi-
cians, because I[9] know that *the* spirit of *the* holy gods *is* in thee, and no secret
troubleth [is burdensome to] thee, tell *me the* visions of my dream that I have
seen, and *the* interpretation thereof.
10 Thus [And *these*] *were the* visions of my head in [on] my bed: I saw, and,
11 behold, a tree in *the* midst of the earth, and *the* height thereof *was* great. The
tree grew, and was strong, and *the* height thereof reached [would reach] unto
12 heaven [the heavens], and *the* sight thereof to *the* end of all the earth. *The*
leaves thereof *were* [Its foliage *was*] fair, and *the* fruit[10] thereof much, and in it
was meat [food] for all [the whole]: *the* beasts [living *creature*] of the field had
[might have] shadow under it, and the fowls of the heaven dwelt [might dwell]
13 in *the* boughs thereof, and all flesh was [might be] fed of it. I saw in *the* visions
of my head upon my bed, and, behold, a watcher and a holy *one* came down
14 from heaven [the heavens]. He cried aloud [with might], and said thus, Hew
[cut] *down* the tree, and cut [lop] off his [its] branches, shake off his leaves
[its foliage], and scatter his [its] fruit: let the beasts get away [living *creature*
15 flee] from under it, and the fowls from his [its] branches. Nevertheless, leave
the stump of his [its] roots in the earth, even [and] with a band of iron and
brass in the *tender* grass of the field; and let it [him] be wet with *the* dew of heaven
[the heavens], and *let* his portion *be* with the beasts [living *creature*] in *the* grass
16 [herbage] of the earth. Let his heart be changed[11] from man's [mankind], and
let a beast's heart[12] be given unto him: and let seven times pass over him.
17 This matter [The rescript] *is* by *the* decree [decision] of *the* watchers, and the
demand by *the* word of *the* holy *ones*; to the intent that the living may know
that the *Most* High ruleth in *the* kingdom of men [mankind], and giveth [will
give] it to whomsoever he will [may please], and setteth [will set] up over it *the*
basest [low] of men.
18 This dream I king Nebuchadnezzar have seen. Now [And] thou, *O* Belte-
shazzar, declare *the* interpretation thereof; forasmuch as all *the* wise *men* of my

kingdom *are* not able to make known unto me [make me know] *the* interpreta-
tion: but [and] thou *art* able [capable]; for *the* spirit of *the* holy gods *is* in thee.
19 Then Daniel (whose name *was* Belteshazzar) was astonished for [as] one
hour, and his thoughts troubled [would trouble] him. The king spake and said,
Belteshazzar, let not the dream, or [and] *the* interpretation thereof, trouble thee.
Belteshazzar answered and said, My lord, the dream *be* to *them that* hate thee,
20 and *the* interpretation thereof to thine enemies. The tree that thou sawest,
which grew, and was strong, whose height reached [would reach] unto the
21 heaven, and *the* sight thereof to all the earth; whose leaves *were* [and its foliage
was] fair, and *the* fruit thereof much, and in it *was* meat for all [the whole]; under
which [it] the beasts [living *creature*] of the field dwelt [might dwell], and upon
whose [its] branches the fowls of the heaven had their habitation [might abide]:
22 it *is* thou, *O* king, that art [hast] grown and become strong: for [and] thy
greatness is [has] grown, and reacheth unto heaven [the heavens], and thy
23 dominion to *the* end of the earth. And whereas the king saw a watcher and a
holy *one* coming down from heaven [the heavens], and saying, Hew [cut] the
tree *down*, and destroy it; yet leave *the* stump of *the* roots thereof in the earth,
even [and] with a band of iron and brass in the *tender* grass of the field; and
let it be wet with the dew of heaven [the heavens], and *let* his portion *be* with
24 *the* beasts [living *creature*] of the field, till seven times pass over him; this *is*
the interpretation, *O* king, and this *is the* decree [decision] of the *Most* High,
25 which is [has] come upon my lord the king: That they shall drive thee from
men,[13] and thy dwelling shall be with the beasts [living *creature*] of the field,
and they shall make thee to eat grass [the herbage] as oxen, and they shall
wet thee with [from] the dew of heaven [the heavens], and seven times shall
pass over thee, till thou know that the *Most* High ruleth in *the* kingdom of men
26 [mankind], and giveth [will give] it to whomsoever he will [may please]. And
whereas they commanded [said] to leave *the* stump of the tree roots [roots of
the tree]; thy kingdom shall be sure [standing] unto thee, after that thou shalt
27 have known that the heavens *do* rule. Wherefore, O king, let my counsel be
acceptable unto thee, and break off thy sins by righteousness, and thine iniqui-
ties by shewing mercy to [pitying] *the* poor; if it may be a lengthening of [to]
thy tranquillity.
28 All this [The whole] came upon the king Nebuchadnezzar. At the end of
29 twelve months he walked in [was walking on] the palace of the kingdom of
30 Babylon. The king spake and said, Is not this [the] great Babylon that I[9] have
built for *the* house of *the* kingdom,[14] by *the* might of my power, and for *the* honour
31 of my majesty? While the word *was* in the king's mouth, *there* fell a voice from
heaven [the heavens], *saying*, *O* king Nebuchadnezzar, to thee *it is* spoken,[15]
32 The kingdom is [has] departed from thee. And they shall drive thee from
men,[16] and thy dwelling *shall be* with *the* beasts [living *creature*] of the field:
they shall make thee to eat grass [the herbage] as oxen, and seven times shall
pass over thee, until [that] thou know that the *Most* High ruleth in *the* kingdom
of men [mankind], and giveth [will give] it to whomsoever he will [may
33 please]. [In] The same hour was the thing [word] fulfilled upon Nebuchad-
nezzar: and *he was* driven from men [mankind,], and did [would] eat grass
[the herbage] as oxen, and his body was [would be] wet with [from] the dew
of heaven [the heavens], till [that] his hairs [hair] were [had] grown like eagles'
feathers, and his nails like birds' *claws*.
34 And at the end of the days, I Nebuchadnezzar lifted *up* mine eyes unto heaven
[the heavens], and mine understanding [knowledge] returned [would return]
unto [upon] me; and I blessed the *Most* High; and I praised and honoured *him*
that liveth *for* ever, whose dominion *is* an everlasting dominion, and his kingdom
35 *is* from generation to generation [with age and age]: and all *the* inhabitants
of the earth *are* reputed as nothing; and he doeth according to his will in *the*
army of heaven [the heavens], and *among the* inhabitants of the earth; and
[*there* is] none [who] can stay [lay hold of] his hand, or say unto him, What
36 doest thou? At the same time my reason [knowledge] returned [would
return] unto [upon] me; and, for [*as* to] *the* glory of my kingdom, mine honour

and brightness returned unto [would return upon] me; and my counsellors and
my lords sought [would seek] unto me; and I was established in [upon] my
37 kingdom; and excellent majesty was added unto me. Now[17] I Nebuchad-
nezzar praise and extol and honour *the* King of heaven [the heavens], all whose
works *are* truth, and his ways judgment: and *those* that walk in pride *he is* able
to abase.

CRITICAL AND GRAMMATICAL NOTES.

[The numerical division of the verses in chap. iv. differs in the English Bible from that in the original text, as the latter annexes the first three verses of this narrative to chap. iii., and consequently begins its chap. iv. with ver. 4 of the English Bible.]

[[1] The customary phrase: *sends this greeting*, is to be mentally supplied.—[2] Literally, *May your peace* (*i. e.*, prosperity) *be increased*.—[3] Literally, *It has seemed good before me*. The order in the original is also emphatic: *The signs and wonders. . . . . I (have) thought it good to show*.—[4] The same emphatic order is observed in this and the following clause: *His signs how*, (literally, *as what*) *great* (literally, *very great*, a reduplicated form)! etc.—[5] Literally, *a kingdom of eternity*.—[6] וִידַחֲלִנַּנִי is the fut. Pael, with נ epenthelic, as usual in these forms. The *tense* seems to express the continued effect on the speaker's mind.—[7] Literally, *From me* was *made a decree*.—[8] The terms employed for these various classes of conjurers are the same as those in chap. ii. 2, except the last, but they are named in a somewhat different order.—[9] The pronoun, being expressed, is somewhat emphatic.—[10] אִנְבֵּהּ from אֵב by resolution of the dagesh.—[11] Literally, *Let them change his heart from the man*.—[12] Literally, *a heart of the living* creature.—[13] Literally, *And thee* they are *driving from mankind* (the man).—[14] Both nouns being anarthrous, the meaning is *a royal residence*.—[15] Literally, they are *saying*.—[16] Literally, *and from mankind* (the man) *thee* they *are driving*.—[17] The particle כְּעַן is emphatic=*At this time*, in contrast with his former impiety.]

EXEGETICAL REMARKS.

Chap. iii. 31–33 [Engl. iv. 1–3]. *The introduction to the edict*. **Nebuchadnezzar the king unto all the people, nations, and languages,** etc. On the triad "people, tribes, and tongues," see on chap. iii. 4. As it there occurs in the public proclamation of a herald, so here in a royal edict in writing, and at the very beginning. This probably induced the persons who in a former age arranged the division [of the Hebrew text] into chapters, to include the introduction of this edict in the preceding section; but such an arrangement is obviously inadmissible and incorrect, in view of the evident relation of verses 31–33 to the statements commencing with chap. iv. 1, and in view also of the considerable interval of time that appears to have elapsed between the events of the third and those of the fourth chapter (cf. on chap. iii. 1, and see chap. iv. 26 et seq.). A certain relation, however, exists between the subject of the present section and that of the preceding, inasmuch as both record experiences of the exalted greatness and power of God, such as had come to the king in the course of events that partook of the supernatural to a greater or smaller extent.—Like this edict of the Babylonian king Nebuchadnezzar, so an open letter (manifesto) of the Persian king Artaxerxes, in Ezra vii. 12, begins with a solemn wish for the welfare of the people, immediately after the names of the king and of the person addressed.—Is Nebuchadnezzar in person to be regarded as the immediate composer of the proclamation? Such a conclusion is opposed (1.) by the frequent indications of an intimate acquaintance with theocratic modes of thought and expression which are found in the document, and especially in the beginning and the end (cf. *e.g.*, the doxology in chap. iii. 33; iv. 31; with Psa. lxxii. 4 et seq.; Psa. cxlv. 13, and also with Dan. vii. 14, 27; cf. further, the description of the infinite greatness of God in chap. iv. 32, with Isa. xxiv. 21; xl. 17; xli. 12, 24, 29; xliii. 13; xlv. 9; Job ix. 12; xxi. 22, etc.); (2.) by the broad and circumstantial character of the narrative, resulting from the many repetitions (cf. *e.g.*, the repetition of identical or entirely similar turns in the sentences of chap. iv. 6, 15 and of v. 5; in iv. 17–23 and in vs. 17–23; in iv. 30 and in vs. 12 and 22; in iv. 31 and in iii. 33, etc.), which it has in common with the remaining narrative sections, thus indicating by its style that Daniel was its author; (3.) by chap. iv. 25–30, where the king is referred to in the third person, while elsewhere the first person is constantly employed; (4.) by the designation of the palace as being located "at Babylon," chap. iv. 26, which is positively inconsistent with the assumption that Nebuchadnezzar composed the proclamation in person, but indicates, as clearly as could possibly be required, that the writer was not a Babylonian, or, at least, that he wrote chiefly for other than Babylonians, and that he even adopted their modes of thought. No substantial difficulty can be raised against the hypothesis that Daniel was the writer, and that he composed the proclamation by direction of the king soon after the conclusion of the events to which it refers. The peculiarly heathen forms of thought and expression which occur beside the Jewish-theocratic (especially in chap. iv. 5, 6, 10, 14, 15, and 20), find a sufficient explanation in the consideration that the writer employed, although a decided theocrat, would be obliged to adhere as closely as possible to the king's habits of thought and the range of his conception in the framing of an official document to be published in the royal name—otherwise it would fail to receive his approval. This view, which has recently been represented by Kranichfeld especially, is at any rate more simple and natural than the assumption, which becomes necessary on the supposition that Nebuchadnezzar in person composed the writing, that its theocratic coloring resulted from the instruction derived by the king from his intercourse with Daniel (Calvin, Hävernick, Hengstenberg, etc.). Upon our hypothesis, moreover, it becomes easy to comprehend why the writer should occasionally pass from the first to the third person (vs. 25–30). If Nebuchadnezzar be conceived as the author, the explanation of this feature can only be found in the supposition that the report of the king is interrupted to admit of an abbreviated statement by Daniel (Calvin), or in the assumption that "Nebuchadnezzar considered it improper to report his insanity in person" (Hengstenberg, Maurer, etc.), or finally, in the admission that verse 25 is still due to Nebuchadnezzar, while verses 26–30 are regarded as a parenthesis inserted by Daniel (Hävernick; see to the contrary infra, on ver. 25).*—**Peace be multiplied to you**; literally, "increase richly, be richly imparted to you;" cf. Ezra iv. 22. יִשְׂגֵּא corresponds exactly to πληθυνθείη in the analogous formulas of greeting, 1 Pet. i. 2; 2 Pet. i. 2; Jude 2; Clem. Rom. 1; 1 Cor. i. 1.—Verse 32 [iv. 2], **I thought it good to show** (to you) **the signs and wonders**, etc.; *i.e.*, "it pleases me."—אָתַיָּא וְתִמְהַיָּא, in the Heb. trans., אותות וְנוֹרָאוֹת; cf. the well-known similar combination אותות וּמוֹפְתִים, Isa. viii. 18 (Greek σημεῖα καὶ τέρατα). The somewhat indefinite and general term אָת, "a sign, token," receives the special signification of "miraculous sign" (*portentum*) from its combination with תְּמַהּ, "a wonder, wonderful thing." The same combination occurs in v. 33 [iv. 3], and also in chap. vi. 28.— שְׁפַר קֳדָמַי, *pulcrum est coram me, i.e., visum est mihi, placuit mihi* (Vulg.); cf. iv. 24; vi. 2.—Verse 33 [iv. 3]. **How great are His signs**, etc. כְּמָה, *quantopere*, a strengthening of the simple כְּ, *quam*. The exclamation does not by any means deny that signs and wonders were also performed by the Babylonian gods, but asserts the incomparable greatness of the miracles of Jehovah—a thought which Daniel might express as well as Nebuchadnezzar.—**His kingdom is an everlasting kingdom**, etc. The same doxology occurs also at the close of chap. iv. 31, with but little change. Cf. Psa. cxlv. 13.

Chap. iv. 1–6 [4–9]. *The king's dream. Inability of the Magians to interpret it.* **I Nebuchadnezzar was at rest in mine house.** "At rest," *i.e.*, in the undisturbed possession of my kingdom, which, according to v. 19, extended to the end of the earth; "in my house," *i.e.*, in the abode of peace, not in the field in order to prosecute warlike enterprises. Both expressions therefore refer to the *later period* of Nebuchadnezzar's reign, when his wars (probably including that against Tyre, Ezek. xxix. 17) were ended, and he was able to devote himself to the affairs of peace, and especially to the erection of the great edifices at Babylon, to which v. 27, and also Berosus, in Josephus, *c. Apion*, I. 19, refer. The time of this dream is therefore still later than that indicated by chap. iii. 1.—**And flourishing in my palace.** רַעֲנַן, "green," not שַׁלְאֲנַן, "quiet" (as the analogy of Job xxi. 23 might perhaps lead us to expect), is the term employed by Nebuchadnezzar, perhaps because he already recalls at this point the fresh and strongly flourishing tree (v. 7 et seq.), by which he was symbolized in the dream-vision. Such a prefatory use of a characteristic feature in the symbolic vision was the more appropriate, since the comparison of fortunate and healthful conditions in life with the verdure of trees was exceedingly common throughout the Orient, and especially so in the Old-Testament usage of language; cf. Psa. i. 3; xxxvii. 35; lii. 10; xcii. 13 et seq.; Prov. xi. 28; Hos. xiv. 7; Ezek. xlvii. 12 (see upon this thought, my *Theologia naturalis*, p. 495 et seq.). For the rest, רַעֲנַן belongs to the somewhat numerous class of words which fell into disuse in the later Aramæism; cf. Pusey, *Daniel*, p. 599–606.—Verse 2 [5]. **I saw a dream which made me afraid.** The abrupt connection, without ו or בֵּאדַיִן indicates the alarming influence which the suddenly transpiring dream exercised over the king, who had previously spent his time in peace; cf. Job iv. 20, and also the numerous antithetic asyndeta in the Proverbs (Introd. to Prov. of Sol., § 14).—**And thoughts upon my bed**, viz.: "came to me, arose in me;" an independent clause, which must not be connected with the final verb יבהלנני, but which is rather to be regarded as a parallel to חֵלֶם חֲזֵית, exactly as וְחֶזְוֵי וגו׳ is parallel to וִידַחֲלִנַּנִי in the former half of the verse. The assumption of such a parallelism is not, however, to be strained to the point of regarding (with Kranichf.) the "thoughts" as the details of the vision itself; for they, like the רַעְיוֹנֵי לִבְבָךְ in chap. ii. 29, were probably the troubled reflections of the king on awaking from his slumber, and while meditating on the nature of his dream (Von Lengerke; cf. supra, on chap. ii. 29).—The הַרְהֹרִין (= the הרהורין of the Targums) seem, however, to be identical with the Armen. *chorhurd*, "a thought," and the word, therefore, is perhaps of Indo-Germanic derivation (thus Hitzig, at any rate; but Ewald, p. 477, objects; cf. also Gesenius and Dietrich, s. v. הרר).—**And visions of my head troubled me.** Exactly similar to chap. vii. 15 *b*. The "visions of the head" are the several fancies or images of the dream, as in chap. ii. 28.—Verse 3 [6]. **Therefore made I a decree.** The same words occur in chap. iii. 29; cf. chap. ii. 5.—In regard to

* [The author's arguments for the original composition of this passage by Daniel are plausible, but not quite conclusive. It would seem that all the Chaldee portions of this book are substantially extracts from the archives of the Chaldæan realm, and this portion has more than ordinary marks of having been such a document. The record of the facts would doubtless be made as a part of the annals of the empire, such as we know were wont to be preserved by the monarchs of the great East (Esther vi. 1). written doubtless by the official scribe or historiographer in the vernacular or court language. This account we may readily conceive Nebuchadnezzar on his recovery from insanity would be anxious to revise, and he would naturally select Daniel as his secretary in publishing an authorized statement of the matter. This view accounts for the mixture of theocratic and heathen sentiments contained in this extraordinary *confession* of royal humiliation. Well might Daniel recur to this scene in his bold rebuke of Belshazzar's impiety, chap. v. 18 et seq. The explanation of the Jewish coloring of parts of this chapter by the hypothesis of a later interpolation of the Maccabæan age, is amply refuted by Stuart and Keil (see likewise our author's apologetical remarks [No. 3] appended to this chapter). These writers both adduce, as corroboration of the account of Nebuchadnezzar's madness, the statement of Abydenus in the fragments preserved by Eusebius (*Præp. Evang.*, IX. 42, and *Chron. Armen.*, ed. Aucher, I. p. 59), that the Chaldæan monarch was seized with a preternatural frenzy (κατασχεθείη θεῷ ὅτεω δὴ . . . . θεοπίσαι) while walking on the top of his royal tower at Babylon.]

לְהַנְעָלָה, see on ii. 25.—Observe that, in this instance, where the contents of the dream were not forgotten by the king, nor regarded as being especially marvellous, the condition of the king while demanding an interpretation of the dream is very different from that described in chap. ii. 5—a circumstance that strongly endorses the credibility of the narrative.—Verse 4 [7]. **Then came in all the magicians,** etc. Concerning the various classes of the wise men of Babylon, four of which are here specially referred to, see on chap. ii. 2.—Instead of עָלְלִין (read עָלִּין), the participle of עָלַל, "to go in," the Keri in this place has עָלִּין (cf. chap. v. 8), which is contracted from עָלְלִין, a form that shortens the initial ְ to ַ ; with the latter cf., *e.g.*, חַשְׁחִין, chap. iii. 16.—Verse 5 [8]. **But at the last Daniel came in before me.** The Kethib אחרין is a form with an undeniably adverbial signification (= "at last, *postremo*"—not adjective: "the last, *postremus*," as Hitzig prefers); that does not occur in the later Chaldee, and is replaced by the Keri אָחֳרֵן (or אָחֳרֵין). It is rather to be regarded as an extension of the sing. adjective formation אחרי, than as an irregular plural in which the *e*-sound has taken the place of ־ֶי (see Olshausen, *Lehrb. der hebr. Sprache*, p. 208).—The עַד preceding is the familiar conjunction "until" (Ezra iv. 21; v. 5); the whole expression ועד אחרין, "until at last," is an adverbial phrase similar to מִן־יַצִּיב, chap. ii. 8. —**Whose name is Belteshazzar, according to the name of my god.** Cf. on chap. i. 7. This thoroughly heathen reference to the name of Daniel is immediately followed by a reference to his person, which indicates the feature that had inspired the heathen king with confidence in his superior power and understanding, and, through this, with a faint conception of the nature of that Deity to whom he owed such power and wisdom. From this affirmation "that the spirit of the holy gods is in thee," which is repeated in vs. 6 [9] and 15 [18], it follows that Nebuchadnezzar had by no means forgotten what he had learned upon two previous occasions respecting the eminent prophetic gifts of Daniel, and his direct intercourse with the only true God. The expression does not, indeed, have an orthodox look from a theocratic or Old-Testament point of view; but it is only to the half a heathen sentiment, similar to the remarks by Pharoah in praise of Joseph, Gen. xli. 38.—קַדִּישִׁין is probably not an *epitheton ornans* of the gods in general, but rather a special designation of the ἀγαθοδαίμονες in distinction from the destructive divinities (Kranichf.).—Verse 6 [9]. **O Belteshazzar, master of the magicians,** רַב חַרְטֻמַיָּא. This title differs only in form and not in substance from that of "chief president of all the wise men of Babylon," which dignity was conferred on Daniel, chap. ii. 48. It was by no means necessary that Daniel, as the possessor of this exalted dignity, should at once and without ceremony present himself before the king with the remaining חכימין. The *more independent* position which he occupies, according to this passage, is rather in entire harmony with chap. iii., where he is absent from a large assembly of the officials of the royal court, and also with chap. v. 10 et seq., where it is represented that his character as the chief magian was lost sight of by Nebuchadnezzar's successors, but not that he had been deprived of that dignity. Among the various answers to the question as to why Daniel was not at once summoned before the king to interpret the dream, instead of being subsequently introduced, the one here indicated, which refers to the freedom of his official station, is certainly the most simple and appropriate, since various features of our book appear to conflict with the assumption that he occupied a political or priestly station in the proper sense (cf. on chap. ii. 49; iii. 12; and on viii. 2). Consequently we prefer this explanation to the many which have been attempted, *e.g.*, that of Jahn, that "*custom* required that the chief of the magians should not be summoned at the first;" that of Füller, which considers Daniel as being, in fact, an officer of the state (chief satrap) rather than a magian; that of Hävernick, that "the *haste* with which the terrified king caused the wise men to be summoned" caused the overlooking of Daniel at the outset; that of Kranichfeld, which argues that Nebuchadnezzar, who already surmised the relation of the image of the fallen tree in his dream to his royal person, dreaded the harsher judgment and sterner prophecy of evil to be expected from Daniel, the prophet of Jehovah, exactly as Ahab, in 1 Kings xxii. 8 et seq., summoned the heathen wise men and seers into his presence, before he turned to the proper source, etc. J. D. Michaelis, however, observes with entire correctness, that a certain and trustworthy answer to that question would require a more exact acquaintance with all the facts of the history than we are able to command.*—**And that no secret troubleth thee.** אָנֵס signifies in the Targums "to sweep away, to apply force," but here "to cause difficulty or trouble;" cf. the Heb. אָנַס, "to compel," Esth. i. 8.

Verses 7–14 [10–17]. *Subject of the king's dream.* **Thus were the visions of my head,** etc.; literally, "And (concerning) the visions of my head upon my bed; I saw;" an abrupt and detached clause similar to chap. vii. 17–23.—In relation to "vision of my head," see on v. 2.—**And behold, a tree** (stood) **in the midst of the earth.** אִילָן, unlike the corresponding Heb. אֵלוֹן, does not signify an "oak" in particular, but "tree" generally; cf. δρῦς and *robur*. The position of this tree, "in the midst of the earth," indicates its great importance for the whole earth, and its destiny to develop an unlimited growth in every direction (cf. v. 8). The tree thus occupies a central position that corresponds

* [Keil reviews at length the various reasons assigned for not summoning Daniel at first, and concludes that it must have been because the king had in the lapse of time and varied successes meanwhile totally forgotten the former prophetical powers of the Hebrew captive. This would be natural and entirely satisfactory, but for the fact that on his very introduction into the royal presence he is here designated as one possessing divine foreknowledge, an evident allusion to his former services in that relation.]

to its exceeding height. The symbolizing of the mighty Babylonian king by a tree recalls the description by Ezekiel, chap. xxi. 3 et seq., which was probably not known to Nebuchadnezzar, but with which Daniel, the narrator of his dream, must have been acquainted. It also suggests a reference to Ezek. xvii. 22; xix. 10 et seq.; and, among the earlier prophets, to Isa. ii. 13; vi. 13; xiv. 12; Jer. xxii. 15; Am. ii. 9 (cf. also the passages cited above, on v. 1). The especial fondness of the ancient Orientals for the illustration of the growth or decline of human greatness and power by the figure of a growing or fallen tree, is shown by Hävernick in the parallels he adduces from Herodotus (iii. 19; the dream of Xerxes; vi. 37; the threat of Crœsus to destroy the town of Lampsacus like a pine tree; cf. also i. 108; the dream of Astyages respecting his daughter Mandane), from Arabic writers (Antara's *Moallaka*, V. 51, 56; Reiske on *Tarafa*, proleg., p. xlvii.); from the later Mohammedan traditions (Mohammed's comparison of a Moslem to an evergreen palm in Sunna, according to v. Hammer, *Fundgruben des Orients*, I. 152), and from Turkish history and literature (the prophetic dream of Osman I., according to Murajea d'Ohsson, *Allgem. Schilderung des ottoman. Reichs*, p. 273 et seq.). Cf. further, with reference to the general use of this tree-symbolism among the Greeks, the interesting work of Bötticher: *Baumkultus der Hellenen* (Leips., 1858).—Verse 8 [11]. **The tree grew and was strong,** "became great and strong;" thus, correctly, Chr. B. Michaelis, Hitzig, and Kranichfeld. The finite verbs רְבָה and תְקִף do not designate a fixed, but a becoming state; hence Nabuchadnezzar sees the tree growing and becoming greater than it was in v. 7 [10].—**And the height thereof reached unto heaven,** like the tower of Babel, Gen. xi. 4, or the δένδρεα οὐρανομήκεα, Herod. II. 138. Observe the imperfect יִמְטֵא, which here takes the place of the perfect, and indicates the heaven-aspiring tendency of the slowly developing tree.—**And the sight thereof to the end of all the earth;** rather, "its extent," or circumference. חֲזוֹתֵהּ does not signify "its visibility" (Vulg., Syr., de Wette, and many moderns), but "its *outlook*, its circumference, its extent" (the Sept. and Theodotion are correct, so far as the sense is concerned: τὸ κύτος αὐτοῦ, its bulging, extension); the contrast with רוּמֵהּ would itself require this interpretation.—Verse 9 [12]. **The leaves** (branches) **thereof were fair, and the fruit thereof much.** עָפְיֵהּ, properly its branching, its *crown*, as אִנְבֵּהּ is the aggregate of its fruit. Bertholdt, von Lengerke, and others, render incorrectly "and its fruit was *large*" (*i.e.*, it bore a large, thick kind of fruit); for there was no reason to mention such a quality of the tree. The immediate connection shows that the great quantity of fruit, instead of its size, was here referred to.—**And it was meat for all,** rather, "and food for all (was found) on it." לְכֹלָּא, "for all," *i.e.*, for all who lived under its shelter—an exemplification and more circumstantial exposition of שַׂגִּיא. It is, however immaterial to the sense of the passage as a whole, whether בֵּהּ be construed with מָזוֹן by neglecting the *makkeph* between לְכֹלָּא and בֵּהּ, as a majority of expositors, including ourselves, translate, or whether we translate, as Kranichfeld [and Keil], with regard to the *makkeph*: "and food was found for *all on* it," *i.e.*, for all the birds that nestled on it. The *masora* evidently requires this rendering here, while in ver. 18 [21], where the *makkeph* is wanting from between לְכֹלָּא and בֵּהּ, it observes the other construction.—**The beasts of the field had shadow under it.** תַּטְלֵל, *umbram egit*, spent in the shadow. The aphel of טלל ("*obumbrare*, to overshadow, protect"), which, in the language of the Targums, is generally transitive, like the Heb. הֵצַל, 1 Chron. iv. 3, is here intransitive by virtue of its Niphal signification.—**And the fowls of the heaven dwelt in the boughs thereof;** cf. Matt. xiii. 32, and the parallel passages. The masculine יְדֻרוּן has its explanation in the fact that צִפְּרִין is of the common gender; the Keri יְדֻרָן construes the word in the feminine, in analogy with יִשְׁכְּנָן, v. 18 [21].—**And all flesh was fed of it.** "All flesh," *i.e.*, not merely all the birds, but also all the beasts of the field, and, in short, all the animals living on and under the tree, thus imaging all of the human race that were united under the sceptre of Nebuchadnezzar; cf. v. 19 [22].—Verse 10 [13]. **I saw in the visions of my head upon my bed;** a formula designed to prepare for the new and remarkably sudden turn of the hitherto quietly transpiring dream.—**A watcher and holy one came down from heaven.** עִיר וְקַדִּישׁ, obviously a *hendiadys* for "a holy watcher, a watcher who is holy." עִיר, the pass. part. of עוּר, *expergefieri*, designates a "watchful one, one who watches" (cf. עֵר, Cant. v. 2; Mal. ii. 12), in this place more particularly a celestial watcher, an angel who from heaven watches over the fortunes of men. Thus Aquila, Symm., and the Sept.: ἐγρήγορος; also a scholium in the Cod. Alex. on the εἰρ [a transfer of עִיר] of Theodotion (ἐγρήγορος καὶ ἀγρυπνῶν); also Polychronius: τὸ ἄγρυπνον καὶ ἄγγελος, and Jerome: "*Significat angelos, quod semper vigilent et ad Dei imperium sint parati.*" By the addition of the modifying וְקַדִּישׁ the עִיר mentioned in this place is expressly classed with the good or holy watchers of heaven, and thus is distinguished from the κακοδαίμονες, in which light the Babylonians regarded a number of their astral gods (see Gesenius *on Isa.*, II. 334 et seq.), and also from the ἐγρήγοροι of the book of Enoch, who are described as bad angels and as inimical to men. The expression "decree (determination, counsel) of the watchers" points strongly to the conclusion that the עִירִין of our book are identical with the θεοὶ βουλαῖοι of the Babylonians in Diodor., ii. 30—*i.e.*, with the thirty-six inferior gods associated as counsellors (*deos*) with the five superior planetary gods; but the entire correspondence of this feature to the

Babylonian doctrine of the gods does not exclude the existence, at the same time, of a certain analogy or essential relation of the "watchers" with the *Amesha-çpenta* of the Parsees, nor even that the supposed etymology of Amesha-çpenta = *non connivens sanctus* (thus Bopp, who is, however, contradicted, *e.g.*, by Burnouf) might be asserted in its support. But that עִיר וְקַדִּישׁ is "merely a translation of Amshaspand" is an arbitrary dictum of Hitzig, which is opposed by the possibly post-Babylonian age of the name Amesha-çpenta (this does not occur at all in the oldest portion of the Zendavesta), and which lacks all scientific support, to an extent equal to the identification of עִיר with צִיר, "a messenger" (Isa. xviii. 2; lvii. 9), as was attempted by several older expositors, *e.g.*, Michaelis (in Castell. *Lex. Syr.*, p. 649), cf., however, Hävernick and Kranichfeld on this passage, and also Hengstenberg, *Christologie des Alten Testaments*, III. 2, 74 et seq.—Verse 11 [14]. **He cried aloud and said thus.** "Aloud," exactly like the royal herald, in chap. iii. 4; cf. x. 16; Isa. lviii. 1, etc.—**Hew down the tree and cut off its branches.** The command is addressed to the servants of the angel, who were perhaps inferior angels, and whose presence the rapidly transpiring dream presumes without further explanation; cf. Matt. viii. 9, and the parallel passages. Isidorus Pelusiota already is correct (*Epp.* l. II. n. 177): *ἁγίους δὲ ἔφησεν τοὺς τὸ δένδρον ἐκτέμνειν προσταχθέντας ἀγγέλους.* [Perhaps Keil rather is correct, who suggests that "the plur. is to be regarded as impersonal: *the tree shall be cut down.*"]—**Shake** (strip) **off its leaves**, literally, "cause them to fall off." אַתַּרוּ (instead of אַתְּרוּ after the analogy of verbs third gutt.), the aphel of נְתַר, which designates the falling of faded leaves or blossoms from the tree, in the Targums, Psa. i. 3; Isa. xl. 8; Joel i. 10.—**Scatter its fruit**; contemptuously, as if it were of no value, and as if it were not worth the trouble of gathering. The consequence, that the animals, who were hitherto sheltered by the tree, were now likewise scattered, and driven far asunder—a lively image of subjects alarmed by the fall of their sovereign—is indicated in what follows.—Verse 12 [15]. **Nevertheless, leave the stump of its roots in the earth.** עִקַּר, the still thrifty stump, like מַצֶּבֶת, Isa. vi. 13, or גֵּזַע, Isa. xi. 1; Job xiv. 8. The ultimate sprouting of this root-stump (cf. Job xiv. 7–9), which was allowed to remain in the earth, typified, as appears from verse 23 [26] compared with verse 33 [36], the restoration of Nebuchadnezzar from his sickness; but not the continued supremacy of his dynasty, as Hävernick interprets, since עִקַּר in this passage obviously designates an individual, Nebuchadnezzar himself, instead of the whole race of Chaldæan rulers.—**Even with a band of iron and brass**; rather, "but in fetters of iron and brass." Supply "shall he lie, or be;" or even "shall he be left" (שְׁבֻקוּהִי). The figure of a tree is now dropped; in the stead of a vegetable organism that necessarily clings to the ground there is presented, obviously with regard to the bestializing of Nebuchadnezzar, an animal organism, which, while naturally capable of unimpeded motion and of an individual and independent participation in life, is for the present forcibly restrained. There is thus a partial transition from the figure to the fact (as is frequently the case in the comparisons and allegories of our Lord, *e.g.*, Mark iv. 28; Luke xii. 46; Matt. xxii. 13; John x. 11 et seq.), or at least an approximation of the figurative representation to the actual conditions of the event typified. This fact is misunderstood as soon as the attempt is made, with Von Lengerke, to conceive of the fetters of iron as fastened on the root-stump, "in order to prevent it from cracking and splitting," and also when it is assumed, with Jerome and others, that an actual binding of Nebuchadnezzar as a *furiosus*, who required to be fettered like all maniacs, is asserted at this early stage. The literal conception of the idea "to fetter" is inappropriate on either method. The "fetters of iron and brass" symbolize the chains of darkness and coarse bestiality in which the mind of the king was held during an extended period. Cf. expressions like "chains of darkness," Wisd. xvii. 17; 2 Pet. ii. 4, and figurative descriptions, such as Psa. cvii. 10; cxvi. 16; cxlix. 8; Job xxxvi. 8. Kranichfeld observes correctly: "A more forcible binding of his sovereign aims for himself, exceeding the disgrace of that which might be applied to a prisoner of war, could scarcely happen to the king, than was that to which he was compelled to submit according to verses 22 [25] and 29 [31], in the form of a beastly restraint on his understanding, and of an actual expulsion from the society in which he moved. And since binding in fetters of iron and brass is a metaphor as common as it is in this instance a striking figure of the deplorable condition to which the Babylonian universal monarch was reduced; since, moreover, the towering height of the tree in the dream is of itself sufficient to establish the selection of an expression to indicate the corresponding contrast of a severe and servile compulsion, the explanation of the figure does not require the combination of this expression proposed by Hitzig with an assonant *kedan*, Syr., 'to bind,' taken from the name of Nebuchadnezzar. This is the more obvious because of the consideration that no reference is made to the name in other portions of the description, although, by a repeated use of the *k* in *nebuk* (Nebuch), it might to the Hebrew sound portentously like the Arabic *inbaka*, "*turbata mente fuit.*" For the Talmudic animal with an ingrown tree which resembled man in form and language, *adne sadeh* (Buxt. *Lex. Chald.*, p. 34), may be explained, as by Hitzig, without any doubt whatever, from the אַדְנֵ of the name Nebuchadnezzar much more readily than that really fabulous creature would have allowed itself to be fabricated, had not the self-authenticated description of Daniel (verses 12, 13 [15, 16], in connection with the otherwise familiar אַדְנֵי, the *heliotropum* which moves its leaves (see Buxt. l. c.), furnished the material."—**In the tender grass of the field,** etc. This lying in the grass and being exposed to the dews of heaven is as applicable to the stump of the tree as to Nebuchadnezzar, the maniac; cf. verse 20 [23] et seq.—

Concerning the reading דִּתְאָא, for which verse 20 [23] substitutes דִּתְאָה (corresponding to the Hebraizing Keris in chap. v. 39; vi. 1), cf. Hitzig and Kranichfeld on this passage.—**And let his portion be with the beasts in the grass of the earth.** Cf. verse 30 [33], "and did eat grass as oxen." The figure has been departed from entirely in this place, and a feature of the interpretation is anticipated. חֲלָק, "portion," occurs also in verse 20 [23] and Ezra iv. 16. The Targums have חוּלָק instead. Concerning the not local, but telic signification of בְּ, "*in* or *of* the grass," cf. *e.g.*, Joshua xxii. 25; 2 Sam. xx. 1.—Verse 13 [16]. **Let his heart be changed from a man's;** literally, "they shall change from (that of) a man" (מִן־אֱנָשָׁא = מִלְּבַב אֱנוֹשׁ, as Ibn-Ezra correctly adds). Cf. the similar *breviloquentiæ* in chap. i. 10; vii. 20, etc., and concerning the active signification of יְשַׁנּוֹן (for which the angels addressed in שְׁבֻקוּ serve as an indefinite subject), cf. supra, on chap. iii. 4. "His heart," *i. e.*, his faculties of conception and desire, or, if it be preferred, his consciousness; cf. verses 29, 30 [32, 33]. The Hebraizing form אֱנוֹשָׁא here and in verse 14 [17] is perhaps to be rejected in favor of the more correct Chaldee אֱנָשָׁא; cf. verses 22, 29, 30 [25, 32, 33]; chap. v. 21; vii. 13, etc. [—**And let a beast's heart be given unto him.** "The heart of a man is dehumanized when his soul becomes like that of a beast; for the difference between the heart of a man and that of a beast has its foundation in the difference between the soul of a man and the soul of a beast (Delitzsch, *Bibl. Psych.*, p. 252)."—*Keil.*]—**And let seven times pass over him,** properly, "change over him;" יַחְלְפוּן, a select word for "to pass over, expire," *præterire*, *præterlabi*. It may be seriously doubted whether the term עֲלוֹהִי, "over him," was chosen with a special reference to "the stars succeeding each other in the heavenly heights above the tormented one, which were to indicate the duration of his affliction" (Kranichfeld), although the mystical phrase "seven times" may contain a certain reference to the astrology of the Chaldæans. The seven עִדָּנִין are seven *years*, as appears from chap. vii. 25, compared with xii. 7 (thus the Sept., Josephus, Ibn-Ezra, Rashi, etc.),—not seven months (as Saadia Gaon, Dorotheus, Pseudo-Epiphanius, etc., held) or seven half-years (Theodoret). עִדָּן, in itself equivalent to "juncture, emergency," receives in this place and chap. vii. 25, the sense of מוֹעֵד or זְמַן, "a point of time," from the context. The duration of the king's punishment as extending over *seven* years is explained here, as in chap. iii. 19, by the fact that a *judicial* retribution is concerned; and the heavy weight of punishment which Jehovah caused to be announced with solemn emphasis to the king was accordingly inflicted, verses 25, 29 [28, 32]. The number seven is, however, not to be pressed literally, to the extent of assuming that the duration of the king's sickness covered exactly seven times 365 days, which would do violence to the always prophetically-ideal pragmatism of the history. Cf. infra, on chap. vii. 25.*—Verse 14 [17]. **This matter (message) is by the decree of the watchers, and the demand by the word of the holy ones.** The *parallelismus membrorum* in which the solemn and elevated speech proceeds, shows that the קַדִּישִׁין are here also, as in verse 10 [13], identical with the עִירִין. The terms פִּתְגָם and שְׁאֵלָא are likewise synonymous, but do not, as Hitzig holds, signify "matter" (concern) and "circumstance," but, in harmony with their etymology and the sense of פתגם in chap. iii. 16, must be rendered "word" (message, announcement) and "demand" (command); cf. the Heb. שְׁאֵלָה, "a request, desire," Judg. viii. 24; 1 Kings ii. 16; Job. vi. 8; Esth. v. 6, 8, etc. Entirely too artificial and contradictory of the unquestionable sense of גְּזֵרָא, "a decision, resolution" (and also of מֵאמַר, "a decree, decision"), is the attempt of Kranichfeld to vindicate the signification "a request, petition," for שְׁאֵלָא, which is based on the idea of a petition such as the watchers, as inferior θεοὶ βουλαῖοι (see on verse 10 [13]), were obliged to address to their superiors, the five planetary gods. But the עִירִין appear nevertheless to be *advisory* deities, inasmuch as they are only עִירִין, and not אֱלָהִין, and inasmuch as the supreme decision in their college rests, according to verse 21 [24], with the "Most High"

* [Keil, on the other hand, contends that "from ver. 26 the duration of the עִדָּנִין cannot at all be concluded, and in chap. vii. 25, and xii. 7, the *times* are not years. עִדָּן designates generally a definite period of time, whose length or duration may be very different. "Seven is the 'measure and signature of the history of the development of the kingdom of God, and of all the factors and phenomena significant for it" (Lämmert's *Revision of the Biblical or Symbolical Numbers*, in the *Jahrb. f. deutsche Theol.*, IX. p. 11), or as Leyrer, in Herzog's *Realencykl.*, XVIII. p. 366, expresses himself, 'the signature for all the actions of God, in judgment and in mercy, punishments, expiations, consecrations, blessings, consecrated with the economy of redemption, perfecting themselves in time.' Accordingly, 'seven times' is the duration of the divine punishment which was decreed against Nebuchadnezzar for purposes connected with the history of redemption. Whether these times are to be understood as years, months, or weeks is not said, and cannot at all be determined. The supposition that they were seven years 'cannot well be adopted in opposition to the circumstance that Nebuchadnezzar was again restored to reason, a thing that very rarely occurs, after so long a continuance of psychical disease' (J. B. Friedrich, *Zur Bibl. Naturhist., anthrop. u. med. Fragmente*, I. p. 316)." This last argument, however, is of little force, in view of the evidently miraculous, or at least specially providential, character of the entire event. "C. B. Michaelis, Gesenius, Rosenmüller, Winer, Lengerke, and nearly all the critics agree that *year* is the probable meaning."—*Stuart.* The supposed difficulty of the management of the empire during so long a period of the king's incapacity is fairly disposed of by Stuart, by a reference to Berosus, who states that on Nebuchadnezzar's return to his capital, after his protracted absence during his wars in Western Asia, upon his father's death, "he took upon himself the affairs which had been managed by the Chaldees [Magi], and the royal authority *which had been preserved for him by their chief*" (Josephus, *Antiq.*, X. 11, 1.) Geo. Rawlinson was inclined to find a trace of this interruption of Nebuchadnezzar's government in the period of *four* years' inactivity noted in his annals (*Historical Evidences*, p. 137) on the "Standard Inscription" (Herodotus, II. 485); but he has since doubted the reference (*Five Monarchies*, III. 60).]

(עִלָּיָא). Cf. the representation of a great subordinate council of the Deity as composed of angels in 1 Kings xxii. 19 et seq.; Job ii. 1 et seq.; and also, with reference to the specifically Babylonian idea of a *decision* in the council of the deity, Diodor. ii. 30: *οἱ δ᾽οὖν Χαλδαῖοι—φάσιν τὴν τῶν ὅλων τάξιν καὶ διακόσμησιν θείᾳ τινὶ προνοίᾳ γεγονέναι, καὶ νῦν ἕκαστα τῶν ἐν οὐρανῷ γινομένων οὐχ ὡς ἔτυχεν οὐδ᾽ αὐτομάτως, ἀλλ᾽ ὡρισμένῃ τινὶ καὶ βεβαίως κεκυρωμένῃ θεῶν κρίσει συντελεῖσθαι*; further, the familiar picture near Kazwini, which represents Bel as a judge and surrounded by genii (Gesen., *on Isa.*, ii. 337). Before מֵאמַר, "a decree," the instrumental בְּ must be supplied from the preceding. The variation וּבְמֵאמַר is, therefore, correctly supplied in the interpretation.—**To the intent that the living may know that the Most High ruleth,** etc. עַד־דִּבְרַת דִּי is to be rendered, either "until, to the circumstance, that" = "until that" (*donec*, Vulg.); or, with Hitzig, in harmony with chap. ii. 30, and with the *ἵνα γνῶσιν* of Theodotion, עַל־דִּבְרַת דִּי, "to the end that." The latter may perhaps be preferred, because of the ease of mistaking עַל for עַד, and because of the fact that עַד־דִּבְרַת does not occur elsewhere.* Verse 22 [25], which directly substitutes תִּנְדַּע for the יִנְדְּעוּן of this verse, shows that Nebuchadnezzar, the ruler of the earth, is not excluded from the number of the "living" who are to recognize the authority of the Most High, but rather, that he especially is included.—**And setteth up** (rather, "can set up") **over it the basest of men.** שְׁפַל אֲנָשִׁים, "the humblest of men," is grammatically a general conception conveying the idea of the superlative, as in 2 Chron. xxi. 17, the Heb. קְטֹן בָּנָיו; cf. Winer, *Chald. Gramm.*, § 58, 2. The assertion of Hitzig, that by this humblest of men, an Israelite, or even the Israelitish Messiah (בַּר אֱנָשׁ, chap. vii. 13), is designated as successor to the great world-monarch, is without support from the context. The thought of a person of the lowest rank, rather, was naturally suggested to the mind of the dreaming king, because the fall of himself, the most exalted man, was concerned.—For the opinion that the imperfects יִתְּנִנַּהּ and יְקִים in this place express the idea of ability—"*is able* to confer, *can* exalt"—cf. chap. ii. 47, where גָּלֵה רָזִין also designates that Being who *is able* to reveal secrets. [—"The Kethib עִלָּיָה is shortened from עִלָּיָא, and in the Keri is yet further shortened by the rejection of the י; cf. chap. v. 21; vii. 4 sq., etc."—*Keil.*]

Verse 15 [18]. *Daniel required to interpret the dream.* **This dream I king Nebuchadnezzar have seen.** The demonstrative דְּנָה is placed first for emphasis, thus corresponding to the disturbing and exciting subject of the dream. The predicative rendering, "This is the dream, which," etc., is opposed by the rule that the relative cannot be omitted after the designated noun (Winer, § 41, 4).—**Declare the interpretation thereof.** פִּשְׁרֵא, is a softened form for פִּשְׁרֵהּ, "its interpretation," in this place, v. 16 [19], and chap. v. 8. This view is confirmed by the Peshito, while Theodotion and the Vulgate have פִּשְׁרָא, which reading is still represented among moderns, *e.g.*, by Hitzig.—On the close of the verse, cf. 6 [9].

Verses 16–24 [19–27]. *The interpretation.* **Then Daniel . . . . . was astonished for** (about) **one hour.** On the reading אֶשְׁתּוֹמַם instead of אִשְׁתּ׳, cf. Winer, § 25, 2. Several MSS. have בִּשְׁעָה instead of כְּשָׁעָה, but this reading conflicts with the usage of the context, and also with the testimony of the ancient translators (Theodot., Vulg., Syr., and probably with the Sept.). Concerning the etymology of שָׁעָה, "hour," which is certainly to be taken here in the literal sense, cf. on chap. iii. 6.* That the astonished gazing of Daniel continued "about an hour," is mentioned by the author from a motive (viz., in order to indicate the greatness of his astonishment) similar to that from which the book of Job records the sympathetic mourning and silence of the three friends during seven days (Job ii. 13). Hitzig observes correctly: "He meditates on the interpretation, and is astonished when he perceives it, because he wishes well to the king, and probably, also, because Nebuchadnezzar might receive the prophecy ungraciously, and might take vengeance on him (as Ahab did on Micaiah, 1 Kings xxii. 26, 27). His confusion is depicted on his countenance; which causes the king to observe that he has found the interpretation, and to invite him in encouraging terms to impart it freely." It cannot really be comprehended how it is possible, in the face of so unsought-for, and, in itself, probable a historical situation, to establish the hypothesis of a conventional forgery in the Maccabæan age.—["That Nebuchadnezzar (ver. 16 [19]) in his account speaks in the third person does not justify the conclusion either that another spoke of him, and that thus the document is not genuine (Hitzig), nor yet the conclusion that this verse includes a historical notice introduced as an interpolation into the document; for similar forms of expression are often found in such documents; cf. Ezra vii. 13–15; Esth. viii. 7, 8."—*Keil.*]—**My lord, the dream be to them that hate thee, and the interpretation thereof to thine enemies!** *i.e.*, Would that the dream concerned thine enemies, and that its interpretation related

* [Keil, however, justly claims that "the change of עַד to עַל is unnecessary and arbitrary. The expression is general, because it is not yet said who is to be understood by the tree that is to be cut down. This general expression is in reality correct; for the king comes by experience to this knowledge, and so all will attain to it who consider this."]

* [Keil, however, insists that the term here means "as it were an instant, *a moment*." But so brief a delay would seem altogether insignificant, and could have excited little surprise, or called for any urging on the part of the king. Stuart, on the other hand, regards so long a hesitation as an hour as "very improbable," and therefore adduces the derivation of שָׁעָה (*a look*, Germ. *augenblick*, Heb. רֶגַע) as favoring the signification *an instant*; and in this interpretation Gesenius and Fürst both coincide.]

to thy foes rather than to thee! Instead of the Kethib מָרְאִי (a regular formation from מָרֵא, chap. ii. 47; v. 23), the Keri has, here and in v. 21 [24], the shorter form מָרִי, which corresponds to the usage of the later Chaldee. The following עָר, "an enemy," is likewise peculiar to the pre-targumistic Chaldee.—Verse 17 [20]. **The tree that thou sawest, which grew, and was strong**; rather, "of which thou sawest that it was great and strong." The second דִּי is subordinated to the first in דִּי חֲזַיְתָ, and is therefore to be rendered as a conjunction, not as a relative pronoun coordinated with the first. The ensuing description of the tree, in vs. 17 and 18 [20 and 21], and likewise of the Divine sentence of judgment pronounced on it in v. 20 [23], are repeated verbally from vs. 7 and 13 [10 and 16], although with abbreviations and unessential variations.—Verse 19 [22]. **It is thou, O king, that art grown and become strong**, etc.; *i.e.*, "that art become great and strong." The following וּרְבוּתָךְ רְבָת, etc., is loosely connected with the relative clause דִּי רְבַיְתְּ וְגו׳. The Keri offers the smoother form רְבַת instead of רְבַיְתְּ, and in the following, the third pers. fem. מְטַת instead of מְטָאת = מְטַאת; cf. also v. 21 [24].—Concerning the remarkable addition by the Sept. to v. 19 [22], cf., *e.g.*, Eth.-fund. principles, No. 3 [below].—Verse 21 [24]. **This is the interpretation (of it), O king**;—the conclusion to the lengthy antecedent clause, v. 20 [23].—**And this is the decree of the Most High which is come (determined) upon my lord the king.** In regard to מְטָא עַל, cf. the Heb. בּוֹא עַל, Gen. xxxiv. 27; Job ii. 11. The preterite מְטָת represents the decree as already decided on, and, therefore, as unavoidable, and certain to be executed on the king.—Verse 22 [25]. **They shall drive thee from men**, literally, "and thee shall they drive," etc. The וְ in וְלָךְ is consecutive: "*and thus* shall they drive thee." The impersonal active טָרְדִין is exactly similar to אָמְרִין, chap. iii. 4, and infra, v. 28 [31]. The agents of the punishment, who are not designated, are the inferior angels, as with יְשַׁנּוֹן, v. 13 [16], and as in v. 28 [31].*—Verse 23 [26]. **And whereas they commanded to leave the stump of the tree roots**; "they" = the heavenly watchers, of whom one only spoke, vs. 10–14 [13–17]; but that *one* was the representative of the entire community of angels.—**Thy kingdom shall (again) be sure unto thee, after that thou shalt have known**, etc. קַיָּם neither signifies "to continue" (Theodotion, Vulg., Dereser, von Lengerke, etc.), nor "to be preserved" (Bertholdt), but rather, "to arise, stand, be firm," and here, in view of the context, "to again be firm" (Hitz., Kranichf.). מִן־דִּי in this place is not inferential—"since, because,"—as in chap. iii. 22, but instead relates to time, "as soon as," and designates a juncture following the period included in עַד דִּי, vs. 21, 29 [24, 32]—hence at the close of the seven years.—**That the heavens do rule**, viz.: over the kingdoms of men, cf. vs. 14 [17] and 22 [25]. "The heavens" is here used to designate God, instead of "the Most High." The expression must be regarded as an abbreviation of the phrase "the God of heaven," which was employed on former occasions (chap. ii. 18, 37, 44), or of "the King of heaven" (iv. 34), which is synonymous with the former, or also of "the Lord of heaven" (v. 23). There is nothing untheocratic and polytheistic in the expression, even though the Chinese designate their god as heaven, and though the same usage prevailed among the ancient Persians (Herod. i. 131), the Greeks (Ζεύς = Sanscr. *jâus*, "heaven"), and the Romans (*Deus*; Divus, Jovis, etc.). Even in the New Testament the *βασιλεία τῶν οὐρανῶν* is identical with the *βασιλ. τοῦ θεοῦ*, and the Talmudists (*e.g.*, *Nedarim*, IX. 10; X. 12, etc.; Buxtorf, *Lex. Chald.*, col. 2440), as well as the Jews of a much earlier period (according to Juvenal, *Sat.*, XIV. 96 et seq., and Diodorus in Photius, *Bibl.*, XL.), generally designated God directly as "heaven," indicating thereby that they attributed to Him the sole dominion over the heavenly world, and denied that other gods were associated with Him (cf. Psa. cxv. 16).—Verse 24 [27]. **Wherefore, O king, let my counsel be acceptable unto thee.** לָהֵן, "wherefore," as in chap. ii. 6. In regard to שְׁפַר, cf. on chap. iii. 32. The term is here construed with עַל, as in that passage and chap. vi. 2, with קֳדָם, by which the persuasiveness of the remarks is increased (cf. טָב with עַל, Ezra v. 17), and by which the desire of Daniel to aid the king, if possible, in averting the impending danger and punishment, becomes more apparent than would be the case if the more courteous phrase שְׁפַר קֳדָמָיךְ had been employed. From this truly theocratic standpoint, the prophet persists in holding it possible to turn aside the punishment threatened in the dream, similar to Isaiah (xxxviii. 1 et seq.) and Jeremiah (xviii. 7 et seq.) in analogous cases; cf. Joel ii. 12 et seq.; Am. vii. 3, 6; Jonah iii. 5 et seq.; 2 Kings xx. 1 et seq.*—**And break off thy sins by righteousness**; rather, "purchase thy deliverance from thy sins," etc. The ancient translators justly regard חֲטָיָךְ as plural; cf. the parallel עֲוָיָתָךְ. The suffix in חֲטָיָךְ, instead of חֲטָיָיךְ, is defective, similar to that in רַעְיוֹנָךְ, chap. v. 10. The word is derived from the Stat. emphat. חֲטָיָא of a singular חֲטָי (=

* [We prefer to say, with Keil, that "the indefinite plur. form טָרְדִין stands instead of the passive, as the following יְטַעֲמוּן לָךְ and מְצַבְּעִין, cf. under chap. iii. 4. Thus the subject remains altogether indefinite, and one has neither to think of men who will drive him from their society, etc., nor of angels, of whom perhaps the expulsion of the king may be predicated, but scarcely the feeding on grass and being wet with dew."]

* ["Daniel knew nothing of a heathen *Fatum*, but he knew that the judgments of God were directed against men according to their conduct, and that punishment threatened could only be averted by repentance."—*Keil.*]

Heb. חֵטְא, cf. Olshausen, *Lehrb.*, p. 283).—פְּרֻק, properly "to break" (cf. Sanscr. *prak*, Lat. *frango*, Germ. *brechen*), designates, similar to the Heb. פרק in passages like Psa. cxxxvi. 24; Sam. v. 8, etc., a "tearing out" of a matter from its former position or relations, and hence, a "liberating, redeeming, or purchase" (cf. 2 Sam. vii. 23; Isa. xxxv. 9, 10, where פרק is used for גאל or פדה, *exsolvere, redimere*). The Sept. and Theodot. therefore render it correctly by λύτρωσαι, the Vulg. *redime*, and Syr., Saad., Ibn-Ezra, Berth., de Wette, Hitzig, etc., in a similar manner. On the other hand, Rashi, Geier, Starke, Dereser, Hävernick, von Lengerke, Kranichfeld, etc., prefer the idea of casting off, casting away, as it is found in Gen. xxxvii. 40, and accordingly interpret: "lay off thy sins" (Häv.), or "break off thy sins, give them up" (Kranichfeld). But in the usage of the Chaldee language, and especially in that of the Targums, פרק constantly and undeniably bears the sense of redeeming by purchase (*e.g.*, a birthright, a field, the daughter of Jephthah, Judg. xi. 35); and the rather broad conception, admitting, as it does, of an application to many and diverse relations, by no means requires that the object to be redeemed should be desirable to the purchaser, and possess value for him. Rather, the remark of von Hofmann (*Schriftbeweis*, I. 519) is correct: "The sins are not under restraint, but, instead, they enslave. The idea of Daniel, therefore, is that the king should deliver himself from the sins that involve him in guilt and slavery, by practising righteousness and mercy for the future, instead of persisting in the arbitrary and tyrannical course to which he had hitherto been addicted." * Cf. Melancthon also, in the *Apology* (Art. III., p. 112), where the "redime" of the Vulgate is retained, but the supposed interpretation is decidedly rejected, as favoring the doctrines of work-righteousness insisted on by the Jewish and Roman Catholic exegesis (see Eth.-fund. principles, etc., No. 2 [below]). This interpretation, however, does not result from any possible rendering of the imper. פְּרֻק, but from the incorrect explanation of צִדְקָה by "doing good, alms," which is found in numerous expositors, from Jerome to Hitzig; and the latter rendering is not justified, either by Psa. xxxvii. 21, nor by a comparison with extravagant laudations of works of mercy in Ecclus. iii. 28; xxix. 12; Tob. iv. 10; xii. 9, etc. The only interpretation of צִדְקָה allowed by the context and general usage is "righteous deportment" to be observed by the king toward his subjects, in contrast with his former tyranny and arbitrary domination. In the parallel member, "mercy toward the poor" is intimately connected with this, as being the second leading virtue in rulers, which virtue the king is exhorted to cultivate (cf. Hofm., as above). The historical situation, rather than the usage, indicates that, in connection herewith, the עֲנָיִן are to be sought for principally in the number of the poor Israelites, the theocratically wretched (עֲנָוִים), who were languishing in exile and captivity. The usage would admit of a different rendering of the עֲנָיִן.*—**If it may be a lengthening of thy tranquility**; rather, "if thy prosperity shall be durable." This is the external motive addressed to the king, to induce him to heed the warning of the theocratic seer. The conditional language is very decided; הֵן, "if," is no more to be taken in the dubious sense of εἰ ἄρα (Acts viii. 22) in this passage than in chap. iii. 17.—אַרְכָּא is not "forbearance, forgiveness," but "duration, continuance;" cf. Jer. xv. 15; Ecc. viii. 12.

Verses 25–30 [28–33]. *The fulfilment.* **All this came upon the king Nebuchadnezzar.** Hävernick regards these words as still belonging to the royal proclamation, while all that follows, to v. 30 [33], is a parenthesis inserted by the prophet (see supra, on chap. iii. 31). But this hypothesis renders it impossible to observe unity of the report, which must obviously be preserved, since the theocratic coloring apparent in these verses may elsewhere be frequently noticed (supra), and since a detailed statement of the infliction of the threatened punishment is required in order to give point to the report. This does not make it inconceivable that Daniel, the writer of the report as a whole, should in this connection relegate the royal subject, who had hitherto been spoken of in the first person, to the background, and that he should describe the Divine judgment executed on the king from his own theocratic point of view.†—Verse 26

* [This interpretation of פְּרַק, however, is hardly satisfactory, for, as Keil urges, it "means to break off, to break in pieces, hence to separate, to disjoin, to put at a distance, see under Gen. xxi. 40. And though in the Targums פרק is used for גְּאַל, פְּדָה, *to loosen, to unbend*, of redeeming, ransoming the first-born, an inheritance, or any other valuable possession, yet this use of the word by no means accords with *sins* as the object, because sins are not goods which one redeems or ransoms so as to retain them for his own use." Rosenmüller likewise notes this incongruity, and adduces Exod. xxxii. 2, as an instance, where Onkelos retains the word in the sense of *breaking off* (the earrings). He even declares that "Chaldee writers employ פרק simply for *laying aside* as in Num. i. 51."]

* [Daniel prudently alludes to the king's moral obliquities only in general terms. Impiety was doubtless his most heinous offence (see verses 27 [20], 37 [40], and compare chap. v. 22, 23), and it was indeed his failure to remember Jehovah, whom he had once been brought to recognise (chap. iii. 28), that bred and fostered his heaven-insulting arrogance. Yet Daniel doubtless hinted also at some special sins of Nebuchadnezzar as a wilful despot. Stuart thinks "he means to designate his capricious and tyrannical behavior on some occasions when he fell into a rage; perhaps also to remind him of the heavy hand that pressed on all the captives whom he had led into exile" and still retained. This last seems especially probable from the particulars specified immediately.]

† [Keil thus aptly refutes the view of Bertholdt, Hitzig, and others, who "find here that the author falls out of the role of the king into the narrative tone, and thus betrays the fact that some other than the king framed the edict. But this conclusion is opposed by the fact that Nebuchadnezzar from ver. 31 [34] speaks of his recovery again in the first person. Thus it is beyond doubt that the change of person has its reason in the matter itself. Certainly it could not be that in this Nebuchadnezzar thought it unbecoming to speak in his own person of his madness; for, if he had had so tender a regard for his own person, he would not have published the whole occurrence in a manifesto addressed to his subjects. But the reason of his speaking of his madness in the third person, as if some other one were narrating it, lies simply in this, that in that condition he was not *Ich* = *Ego* (Kliefoth). With the return of the *Ich*, *I*, on his recovery from his madness Nebuchadnezzar begins again to narrate in the first person."]

[29]. **At the end of twelve months he walked upon** (marg.) **the palace of the kingdom of Babylon;** rather, "the royal palace at Babylon." In relation to the time indicated, "at the end of twelve months," Kranichfeld observes: "When the important incident of the dream was a year old, and on that account its recollection naturally exercised the imagination of the king with special force, he gave himself up, despite the Divine warning, to the proudest exaltation of self, which indicated that he was neither controlled by religious piety in general, nor by reverence for the God of the Jews in particular," etc. It appears to us that this is seeking too much in that designation of time. It is simply a historical circumstance that exactly twelve months elapsed between the dream and its fulfilment, and at the same time an illustration of the simple accuracy and concrete truth of the narrative.* — "Upon the royal palace," *i.e.*, upon its flat roof; cf. 2 Sam. xi. 2. The proud king, who has employed the respite of twelve months in nursing his tyrannical superciliousness, instead of improving it by repenting and working righteousness, wishes, by actual observation from this elevated spot, to assure himself of the condition of his royal power, and to feast himself with looking on the gigantic metropolis of the world which *he* had created. His thoughts are similar to those of another, in Schiller's *Glocke* (the Bell):

> "The splendor of the house
> Stands firm as earth's foundations
> Against the power of evil," etc.

The "walking along" (מְהַלֵּךְ הֲוָא; cf. מַהְלְכִין בְּגֵוָה, v. 34 [37]) likewise indicates his conceited arrogance and pride; cf. the Germ. "*einherstolziren*" (strutting along).—The mention of the location, "at Babylon," does not at all compel the assumption of a Palestinian origin of the book, or of any particular part of it, as even Hitzig acknowledges. It merely indicates that the author was not a constant resident in the *city* of Babylon, and that his narrative was composed for readers who were chiefly, or without exception, strangers in Babylon (however long they might have been detained in that city against their will). These features are suited to the view that Daniel was the writer of the document before us, as thoroughly as they militate against the idea that Nebuchadnezzar was its immediate author; cf. supra, on chap. iii. 31.†—Verse 27 [30]. **Is not this** (the) **great Babylon that I have built,** etc. "The great" (רַבְּתָא) was evidently a standing title of Babylon, with its circumference of 480 stadia (Herod. i. 191), its colossal walls, its 25 gates on either side of the immense square, its 676 districts filled with houses of several stories each, its hanging gardens on the Euphrates, its gigantic temples and palaces, etc. Cf. Herod., l. c.; Diodor. ii. 5 et seq.; Aristotle's *Polit.*, III. 2; Philostratus, i. 18; Curtius, VI. 1 et seq.; also Starke's *Synopsis* on this passage; Wattenbach, *Nineve und Babylon* (Heidelberg, 1868); and Alfred Maury, *Nineve et Babylone*, in the *Revue des deux Mondes*, 1868, March 15, p. 470 ss.; [also Rawlinson's *Five Ancient Monarchies*, I. 510 et seq.]. For this reason many other authors apply the predicate ἡ μεγάλη to that city; *e.g.*, the Apocalyptist John, Rev. xiv. 8; xvi. 19 (cf. also Isa. xiii. 19; xiv. 4; xlvii. 3, 4); and Strabo (l. xvi.), who applies to it the stanza: ἐρημία μεγάλη ἐστὶν ἡ μεγάλη πόλις, cf. Pausanius, *Arcad.*, p. 509, who describes Babylon as a city ἥντινα εἶδε πόλεω τῶν τότε μεγίστην ἥλιος. Nebuchadnezzar's Babylon might certainly be designated as "the great city" with as much propriety as formerly Nineveh (cf. Gen. x. 11, 12; Jonah i. 2; iii. 2; iv. 11), and far more justly than, *e.g.*, Hamath (see Amos vi. 2; חֲמַת רַבָּה), or Diospolis (Διόσπολις ἡ μεγάλη, Inscr. 4717), or Ephesus, Smyrna, Pergamos, Nicomedia, and other cities of a later period in Asia Minor (cf. Rheinwald, *Komment. zum Br. an die Philipper*, p. 3 et seq.).—**That I have built for the house** (or seat) **of the kingdom.** The A. V. is literal. The expression is equivalent, in modern idiom, to "the royal capital and seat of government." The מַלְכוּ of the whole empire was to have its seat, its residence, in that metropolis (Kranichf.). Cf. the reference to Bethel as a מַמְלָכָה, in Am. vii. 13. "That I have built;" *i.e.*, that I have developed and completed. On בְּנָא, otherwise בָּנָה, in this signification, cf. 2 Kings xiv. 22; 2 Chron. xi. 5, 6; and see the Chaldæan historians Berosus, Abydenus, and Megasthenes, in Josephus, *Ant.*, X. 11, 1; *c. Apion*, I. 19; and in Eusebius, *Chron.*, I. 59, with reference to the numerous edifices erected in Babylon by Nebuchadnezzar; also Bochart, *Phaleg*, p. 263 et seq., where Nebuchadnezzar's services in beautifying the city and increasing its architectural greatness are compared with those of Augustus in Rome, which justified his well-known remark, "*se marmoream relinquere, quam lateritiam accepisset*" (Suetonius, *Aug.*, c. 29).*—**For the honor of my majesty;** לִיקָר הַדְרִי; cf. the similar constructions in Deut. v. 33, 17; Zech. xi. 13; and with reference to the preceding expression, "by the might of my power," cf. passages like Isa. xl. 26; Eph. i. 19; Col. i. 11, etc.—Verse 28 [31]. **While the word was in the king's mouth.** The Divine punishment follows closely after the vain and presumptuous exclamation (cf. Isa. xxviii. 4); exactly as in the poem by Schiller quoted above, where it is added:

---

* [Keil will have it that "עֲנֵה here means not simply *to begin to speak*, but, properly, *to answer*, and suggests to us a foregoing colloquy of the king with himself in his own mind." He prudently refrains, however, from inferring that Nebuchadnezzar was thinking of the very dream in question at the time.]

† [Rather, as Keil suggests, "the addition at Babylon does not indicate that the king was then living at a distance from Babylon, as Berth., von Leng., Maurer, and others imagine, but is altogether suitable to the matter, because Nebuchadnezzar certainly had palaces outside of Babylon; but it is made with reference to the language of the king which follows regarding the greatness of Babylon."]

* [Abundant confirmation has been found of these enlargements and reconstructions of the edifices of Babylon by Nebuchadnezzar in the excavations carried on there by Botta, Layard, and others. Most of the ancient bricks are stamped with the name of that monarch. See Rawlinson's *Herodotus*, I. 412 (Am. ed.).]

> "For no eternal bond can be
> With the fates that rule our destiny,
> And misfortune's pace is swift."—

There fell a voice from heaven. Observe the agreement between the prophetic description in the dream, vs. 10 [13] and 11 [14], and the fulfilment twelve months later. The words נְחַת מִן שְׁמַיָּא, which are employed in the former passage, are here echoed by נְפַל (cf. Isa. ix. 7), which still more strongly emphasizes the suddenness with which the judicial sentence is promulgated; and קָרֵא בְחַיִל in that place is here repeated by the characteristic קָל, which recalls the analogies in Deut. iv. 33, 36; Matt. iii. 17; John xii. 28; Acts ix. 4; x. 13, etc. The record, although sufficiently circumstantial, is but a summary, and affords no trustworthy indications to show whether this φωνὴ ἐξ οὐρανοῦ was produced by the mediation of psychological or of physical causes. The leading fact to be observed is merely that the powerfully excited king was compelled to recollect the warning formerly conveyed in the dream, by what he now heard, whether by a purely subjective mode of perception, or whether objective agencies were at the same time employed.—**O king Nebuchadnezzar, to thee it is spoken; The kingdom is departed from thee.** The perf. עֲדָת is employed, because he who was degraded to the level of the brute by the most fearful of mental maladies, was at once and directly incapacitated for his position and office as ruler as a matter of course. In regard to אָמְרִין, "they say," see on v. 22 [25]; concerning v. 29 [32] see ibid., and on v. 14 [17].—Verse 30 [33] **The same hour** (hence immediately; cf. on chap. iii. 6) **was the thing** (or word) **fulfilled upon Nebuchadnezzar.** סָפַת, literally, "came to end;" for the end of a prophecy is its coming to pass, by which it ceases to be prophecy (Hitzig); cf. כְּלָה, chap. xii. 7; Ezra i. 1, etc.—Concerning the lycanthropy of Nebuchadnezzar, see Introd., § 8, note 1, and the literature there adduced.—**Till his hairs were grown like eagles' feathers, and his nails like birds' claws;** literally, "like eagles—like birds" (כְּצִפְּרִין—כְּנִשְׁרִין), a *comparatio compendiaria*, with which the Stat. const. after the particle of comparison has been omitted, as with מִן in v. 13 [16], and as in Isa. ix. 3; Joshua v. 36, and also in the classics (*e.g.*, *Il.*, 17, 51; Juvenal, *Sat.* 4, 71, etc.).

Verses 31–34 [34–37]. *The restoration of Nebuchadnezzar, and his ascription of praise to God.* **And** (rather "but") **at the end of the days,** *i.e.*, of the period of seven years, vs. 13, 22, 29 [16, 25, 32].—**I . . . . lifted up mine eyes unto heaven,** namely, as seeking help from thence, as supplicating the God of heaven (see on v. 23 [26]; cf. Psa. cxxiii. 1 et seq.; xxv. 5, etc.*—**And mine understanding returned unto me;** or, taking the ו as illative, "*so that* mine understanding returned." The prayer of the hitherto maniac king was thus shown to be anything rather than a "flagrant inconsequence," as Von Lengerke, Hitzig, and others characterize it. On the contrary, it produced the beneficial effect of delivering the penitent king from his disease, and of restoring him to the society and the mode of life of civilized people. Cf. Pusey and Kranichfeld on this passage, in relation to the inclination to prayer, or to other religious manifestations and observances, which has frequently been observed in the case of maniacs afflicted with lycanthropy. In the case before us, where the period of insanity and punishment imposed by God had, at any rate, expired, the prayerful looking up to heaven by the humbled king could not possibly result in less than the elevation of the sufferer from his brutal condition to manhood—from the state of one lying helplessly on the ground, and looking earthward in his debasement, to the dignity and bearing of man, who is formed in the image of God, that is to say, to the normal form of man, of which Ovid sings (*Metam.*, I. 85 ss.):

> "*Pronaque cum spectent animalia cætera terram,*
> *Os homini sublime dedit, cœlumque videre*
> *Jussit, et erectos ad sidera tollere vultus.*"—

And I praised and honored him that liveth forever. Cf. vi. 27; xii. 7; and also, in relation to the latter half of the verse, chap. iii. 33. ["The first thought he entertained was to thank God, to praise him as the ever-living One, and to recognize the eternity of His sway. Nebuchadnezzar acknowledges and praises God as the 'ever-living One,' because He had again given to him his life, which had been lost in his madness."—*Keil.*]—Verse 32 [35]. **And all the inhabitants of the earth are** (to be) **reputed as nothing,** that is, "in comparison to Him." The partic. חֲשִׁיבִין must be regarded in this place as the part. fut. pass., and is not, therefore, to be explained (in analogy with Isa. xl. 17) by, "are reputed as nothing by Him" (Hävern., Kranichf., etc.). ["The eternity of the supremacy of God includes His omnipotence as opposed to the weakness of the inhabitants of earth" (Keil).] כְּלָה instead of כְּלָא may be regarded as the error of a copyist, who thought to correct a supposed כְּלָא (that is, אַרְעָא) by substituting כְּלָה. Or "לָה for לָא, is an archaism, conforming to the pregnant character of the negation, similar to לֹה for לֹא, Deut. iii. 11" (Kranichf.). [The final ה seems to be a mere Chaldaic interchange for א in the ordinary כְּלָא, *as not.*] The rabbinical assertion, found in Rashi and Saadia, that לָה signifies "an atom of solar dust," is at all events to be rejected.—**And he doeth according to his will in the army of heaven,** etc. Cf. Isa. xxiv. 21, a passage that evidently lies at the foundation of the one before us, in which "the host on high" presents the same idea as is contained in "the army of heaven" in this place. Both refer to the innumerable companies of angels who inhabit heaven (Gen. xxxii 2 et seq.; Heb. xii. 22 et seq.; cf. Dan. vii. 10).—**And none can . . . . say unto him, what doest thou?** Cf. Isa. xliii. 13; and in relation to the phrase, "to stay one's hand —

* [This raising of his eyes to heaven was "the first sign of the return of human consciousness; from which, however, we are not to conclude, with Hitzig, that before this, in his madness, he went on all-fours like an ox."—*Keil.*]

to oppose him," see the Targ. on Eccles. viii. 4; Tr. *Sanhedr.*, c. 2; also the Arabic of Hariri, p. 444.*—Verse 33 [36]. **And the glory of my kingdom, mine honor, and my brightness returned unto me.** The ל before יְקָר serves to introduce that word as a new subject, after the former, מַנְדְּעִי (cf. Isa. xxxii. 1; xxxviii. 16; Psa. lxxxix. 19). יְקָר, "station, majesty, dignity," such as is manifested in the look, bearing, and manners of a princely personage. הֲדַר, "splendor," A. V. "honor" (cf. v. 27 [30]; chap. v. 18), is here contrasted with his former appearance and condition, which denied his royal state, and even his nature as a man, v. 30 [33]. זִיו is properly "brightness," and here refers to the beauty or beaming freshness of the human countenance (cf. chap. v. 6, 9; vii. 28), while הדר refers more particularly to the splendor of his robes (cf. Psa. cx. 3; xxix. 2; xcvi. 9; 2 Chron. xx. 21).—**And my counsellors and my lords sought unto me,**—they, who had formerly avoided and deserted me! That בְּעָא signifies a search for one who is believed to have disappeared without leaving a trace by which to discover him, is an assumption made by Hitzig and also by a number of earlier expositors, such as Geier, Michaelis, Bertholdt, etc., which, however, is without any support whatever. The expression rather designates "a search conducing to the honor of the king, which was instituted by his former counsellors and magnates in their capacity as the council of the regency during the interim, for the purpose of officially requesting the king on his restoration to health, to resume the control of the government." The terms הדברין (see on iii. 24) and רברבנין do not, however, designate different subjects, but the same ones with reference to their several powers and dignities; cf. שַׂר וְגָדוֹל, 2 Sam. iii. 28; μέγας καὶ δυνάστης, Job. ix. 22.—**And I was (again) established in my kingdom.** הָתְקְנַת instead of הָתְקְנֵת, because of the following *accent. distinct.*—**And excellent majesty was added unto me;** "I received still greater power" than I had formerly enjoyed; cf. Job xlii. 10. There are no historical authorities to show in what the additional power consisted which came to Nebuchadnezzar toward the end of his life; but the truth of this statement cannot on that account be questioned.—Verse 34 [37]. **Now** (or therefore) **I, Nebuchadnezzar, praise, and extol, and honor,** etc. By this doxology the close of the royal proclamation returns to the thought of the introduction, chap. iii. 32 et seq.—**All whose** (rather, "for all His") **works are truth, and his ways judgment.** קְשׁוֹט, literally "firmness, immutability," and hence, "faithfulness, truth" (= Heb. אֱמֶת). דִּין, literally "judgment," procedure strictly conformed to justice (= Heb. מִשְׁפָּט); cf. Jer. ix. 23; xxii. 13.—**And those that walk in pride, he is able to abase.** Cf. Isa. x. 33; xiii. 11; xxv. 11; 1 Sam. ii. 7; Psa. xviii. 28; Luke i. 51 et seq.—In relation to the enlargement of this doxology of Nebuchadnezzar which is found in the Sept. in this place, see the Eth.-fund. principles, etc., No. 3 [below].

* [מְחָא בִידֵהּ in the Pael, *to strike on the hand, to hinder*, is derived from the custom of striking children on the hand in chastisement (Keil), or in order to check them from a proceeding.]

ETHICO-FUNDAMENTAL PRINCIPLES RELATED TO THE HISTORY OF SALVATION, APOLOGETICAL REMARKS, AND HOMILETICAL SUGGESTIONS.

According to the remarks on chap. iii. 31 [iv. 1], the authorship of this section is divided between Nebuchadnezzar and Daniel, with the distinction that the former is conceived as the moral originator and ordainer of the edict, while the latter is its writer. But, at the same time, both the heathen king and the theocratic prophet are so exclusively the active (or suffering) characters of the narrative, that every observation of dogmatic or apologetical importance must be derived from the conduct of one or the other of these two persons. We therefore direct our attention

1. *To Nebuchadnezzar*, — with reference to whose seizure by lycanthropic mania, as being credible on general grounds, and also as being attested by extra-biblical authorities, the necessary explanation has been given in the Introd. (§ 8, note 1). We now direct attention to the act of profound self-abasement which the king performed by publishing, of his own impulse, a report respecting his protracted disease of several years' duration, and also respecting its causes and his final cure. This involves no improbability on psychological, political, or religious grounds. (1.) From a *psychological* point of view, the report became necessary, because a spirit of repentance and of sincere self-abasement had really come over the proud monarch, and because he had been led to recognize with all emphasis that the humiliation, as wearisome as it was deeply painful to his consciousness, was a righteous punishment inflicted on him by the only true God, even though a genuine, durable, and fruit-bearing conversion might not have been accomplished in his case. On the nature of this sincere and profoundly realized humiliation of the king, which, however, was inadequate to secure his admission to a gracious state, or to formal membership in the congregation of God's people under the Old Covenant, cf. Calvin on chap. iv. 34: "*Hic est modus omnis humiliationis; sed careret profectu illa humiliatio, nisi Dominus postea regeret nos spiritu mansuetudinis. Et ita Nebucadnezar hic non complectitur gratiam Dei, quæ tamen digna erat non vulgari elogio et prædicatione; sed non descripsit etiam in hoc edicto quicquid posset requiri ab homine pio et qui edoctus fuerit diu in schola Dei, sed tamen ostendit se multum profecisse sub Dei ferulis, quum tribuit illi summam potentiam* (c. iii. 32, 33; c. iv. 31 ss.), *deinde conjungit justitiæ laudem et rectitudinis* (c. iv. 34) *et sese interea fatetur reum et testatur justam fuisse pœnam, quæ divinitus irrogata fuit.*"—(2.) In a *political* aspect, also, the edict became necessary, since, as appears from v. 33, circumstances required that at the end of the king's illness a proclamation should be issued, certifying that the monarch in person

was about to resume the government, and to supersede the regency of the interim, composed of his "counsellors and lords," who had hitherto administered the affairs of the state. The king had no need to dread the effect of such an explanation on his people, even though it involved much that was humiliating to him; but it is by no means recorded that he caused it to be promulgated in the public places and on the streets by the lips of a herald (as was the case with the edict in chap. iii. 4 et seq.), nor even that it was at any time brought into public notice in writing. (3.) Finally, the document involves no considerable difficulty in a *religious* point of view, inasmuch as the partly heathen and partly Israelitish faith of the Babylonian king, in other words, that syncretism which amalgamated all religions, and which so frequently appears in the history of the rulers of the period of the captivity, is clearly manifested, as has already been shown on chap. iii. 31 [iv. 1]. Accordingly, even Hitzig finds it to be entirely credible that Nebuchadnezzar as a newly or only partially converted person should "acknowledge a god as his god (v. 5), and even other holy gods (vs. 6, 15), in addition to the Highest God." The statement by the same critic that it is strange that "after this stern experience Nebuchadnezzar should not have liberated the Jews, the captive servants of the Highest God, as the history shows he did not," is without any foundation; for, according to chap. iv. 1 compared with vs. 27 and 31, the event did not transpire until near the close of Nebuchadnezzar's reign, and we cannot tell what he would have done had he lived any considerable time after his recovery (which was certainly *not* the case, according to Berosus, in Josephus, *c. Apion*, I, 20), nor yet what political relations, combinations, or considerations may have prevented the immediate execution of a plan to restore the Jews to their country, which may already have been prepared.

2. *So far as the conduct of Daniel is concerned*, the characteristic feature of the two-fold position which he occupied at the Chaldæan court as a prophet of Jehovah and chief of the Magians, is prominently exhibited in a manner that affords a highly favorable testimony for the credibility of the narrative as a whole. The Jewish wise man, who is dignified by an honorary office rather than burdened with definite official functions, *e. g.*, with sacerdotal duties, is permitted to be absent at first, on the occasion when the interpreters of dreams or Magians were summoned before the king, because he was allowed a greater freedom of action in general (see on v. 6). It was not, probably, without producing a feeling of profound injury that when he finally appeared the king addressed the servant of the living God (vs. 5, 6) in a thoroughly heathen manner as "Belteshazzar," after the name of *his* god (*i. e.*, the idol Bel), according to Calvin's just remark, "*Non dubium est, quin hoc nomen graviter vulneraverit animum prophetæ.*" He did not, however, renounce his allegiance and devotion to the royal personage who was his benefactor, and who, in case he would receive and be guided by the prophet's counsel, might so easily become the benefactor and liberator of the entire people of God. When the king had related to him the dream, so prophetic of misfortune, he gave way to trouble and sympathetic sorrow "about an hour" (v. 16), and the words by which he at length introduced the interpretation, invoked a blessing on the king coupled with the wish that the fate which threatened the monarch might rather overtake his foes. Cf. Calvin again: "*Daniel exponit* (v. 16), *cur ita fuerit attonitus, nempe quia cuperet averti tam horribilem pœnam a regis persona. Etsi enim merito eum potuit detestari, tamen reveritus est potestatem divinitus ei traditam. Discamus igitur exemplo prophetæ, bene precari pro inimicis nostris, qui cupiunt nos perdere, maxime vero precari pro tyrannis, si Deo placeat subjici nos eorum libidini;—alioquin non tantum illis, sed etiam Deo ipsi sumus rebelles. Cæterum altera ex parte ostendit Daniel, se non frangi ullo misericordiæ affectu, neque etiam molliri, quominus pergat in sua vocatione.*"—The manner in which Daniel succeeded in uniting the strictest theocratic fidelity towards God with this devotion to his sovereign, is seen partly in the unconcealed directness and the categorical plainness with which he announced the most degrading and humiliating punishment to the king, in v. 22 [25], and partly in the warning or epilogue, v. 24 [27], with which he concluded his interpretation. In this epilogue the fundamental dogmatic and ethical ideas of the entire section concentrate and crowd together in pregnant significance. The exposition of this passage has shown that the course which Daniel here recommends, with a noble frankness and an impressive fervor, is none other than that which should be followed by every pious ruler who is faithful in his office, and in brief, that it comprehends the sum of princely virtues. Hence, those expositors who find that this passage recommends and prescribes work-righteous conduct, and especially the giving of alms, as in itself meritorious, do violence to the words. Such expositors are the Rabbins, who generally ascribe an almost magical virtue to alms-giving, and who press every possible passage of Scripture to support their view, especially those containing the term צְדָקָה, which is by them rendered "well-doing, alms-giving" (cf. Buxtorf, *Lex.* p. 1,891 et sq.); further, the Roman Catholic exegetes, who are accustomed, since Bellarmine's detailed exposition of this passage (l. II. *pœnitentia*, c. 6; cf. l. iv. c. 6), to employ it as one of the principal proof-texts for their anti-evangelical theory of justification and sanctification (in connection with which they declare, of course, that the rendering of the Vulgate: "*peccata tua eleemosynis redime*," is the only correct translation); finally, nearly all the *rationalistic* expositors, from Griesinger and Bertholdt down to Gesenius, de Wette, and Hitzig, who, while defending the translation by Jerome above referred to, and while referring to apocryphal passages like Ecclus. iii. 28; xxix. 12; Tob. iv. 7 et seq.; xii. 9 et seq.; xiv. 10 et seq., endeavor to find here a work-righteous "morality of the later Judaism," and therefore a certain indication of the composition of the book subsequent to the exile. Grotius already pointed out that even on the adoption of the faulty Vulgate exegesis, which makes צדקה equivalent to *eleemosynæ*, the passage does not necessarily yield a sense favorable to Pelagianism: "*Neque*

offendere quemquam potest, quod operibus pœnitentiæ, in quibus excellunt eleemosynæ, tribuatur id, quod pœnitentiæ proprie convenit; est enim talis metonymia aut synecdoche frequens." Still better Melancthon, in the *Apolog. Conf. Aug.* art. iii. p. 112 R: "*Non volebat Daniel regem tantum eleemosynam largiri, sed totam pœnitentiam complectitur, quum ait: 'Redime peccata tua eleemosynis,' i. e.: redime peccata tua mutatione cordis et operum. Hic autem et fides requiritur . . . . . Ac verba Danielis in sua lingua clarius de tota pœnitentia loquuntur et clarius promissionem efferunt: 'Peccata tua per justitiam redime, et iniquitates tuas beneficiis erga pauperes.' Hæc verba præcipiunt de tota pœnitentia; jubent enim, ut justus fiat, deinde ut bene operetur, ut, quod regis officium erat, miseros adversus injuriam defendat. Justitia autem est fides in corde,*" etc. He expresses himself similarly in his comment on the passage (*Opp.* ed. Bretschneider, vol. xiii. p. 843 ss.), where he pays no attention to the false rendering of צדקה in the Vulgate; as does also Calvin in his commentary and the *Inst. rel. Chr.*, III. 4, 31, 36, and among the later Protestant expositors especially Carpzov, *De eleemosynis Judæorum* (in his *Apparat. historicus* in the *Critica Sacra*, p. 726 ss.). In all the conduct of Daniel, therefore, as described in this section, nothing can be discovered which is at variance with the proper deportment of a witness to the faith and a highly enlightened seer of the Old Covenant in the presence of a heathen ruler of the world. To this deportment in practical life corresponds also the tone observed by him in the composition, under the king's direction, of the document before us, whose agreement with the theocratic modes of thought and conception has already been pointed out.

3. In an *apologetic* respect the disharmony must be noticed, which exists between what might have been expected from the art of a pseudological tendency-writer of Asmonæan times, and the conditions of place and time as indicated in our narrative. A careful and unbiased examination of the document with reference to the conditions of the Maccabæan period, reveals at once how empty and arbitrary is everything that has been said by Bertholdt, Bleek, Von Lengerke, Hitzig, and others, respecting the parenetic aim, calculated for the time of Antiochus Epiphanes, with which they allege it was written. "The sinner Nebuchadnezzar, who was punished for his pride and folly, was a type of the presumptuous Ἐπιμανής, who in like manner sought improper associates, denied the kingly character, and had but recently issued a circular letter, although of an entirely different character." This brief extract from Hitzig (p. 58) contains a whole brood of tendency-critical assumptions and captious perversions of the actual historical facts, based on the erection of false parallels. It is impossible to understand why precisely Nebuchadnezzar, the Chaldæan king whose presumption was punished with lycanthropy, should be selected as a type of the proud Seleucidian Ἐπιμανής (cf. 1 Macc. i. 21, 24), when, *e.g.*, Sennacherib (2 Kings xviii. 19), Saul (1 Sam. xvi. 14; xviii. 10 et seq.), or Pharaoh (Ex. 14), would have furnished a far more suitable parallel to the tyrant of the Maccabæan period, who was to be punished for presumptuous fury against God, and since, moreover, there is no lack, upon the whole, of historical examples to illustrate the proverb, "A haughty spirit goeth before a fall" (Prov. xvi. 18). The fact recorded by Polybius xxvi. 10 (to which passage Hitzig explicitly refers), that Antiochus Epiphanes was a lover of improper, *i.e.*, immoral, coarse, and riotous gatherings, certainly finds but a clumsy illustration and an exceedingly vague foreshadowing in Nebuchadnezzar's association with the beasts of the field. The analogy is merely superficial, and that to a degree in which it dissolves into incongruity and even absurdity, whenever it is submitted to a careful examination (cf. Kranichf. p. 174 et seq.). With reference to the third parallel, that both tyrants issued circular letters, Hitzig himself concedes that the circular mentioned in 1 Macc. i. 41 et seq. was "really of a nature entirely different" from that of Nebuchadnezzar's edict. The mere fact, therefore, that Nebuchadnezzar addressed a circular to his subjects, convinces him that it was typical of the other fact, that Epiphanes also issued such a document—as if any king whatever could reign but a single year, without publishing some manifesto, or edict, or circular, etc.! Hitzig's treatment of chap. iv. 28 [31], (the sentence of Divine punishment denounced on Nebuchadnezzar, "The kingdom is departed from thee"), by which he endeavors to demonstrate the special time in the Maccabæan epoch during which this section originated, results in similar absurdities. He holds that the threat of an immediate overthrow, or rather of a ruin already in progress, clearly indicates that the document was "composed at a time when the Asmonæans had already taken up arms and had gained the upper hand," hence in the period designated in 1 Macc. ii. 42–48; as if any real analogy existed between the punishment of a presumptuous spirit by means of a severe mental disease, and the political and religious revolt of an oppressed nation against their persecutors! and further, as if the syncretistic Chaldæan king, who admitted all religions, could by any means be placed in comparison with Antiochus, the fanatically intolerant worshipper of Zeus! How can Nebuchadnezzar, who was exhorted to mercy toward the "poor" (עֲנָיִן, v. 24 [27], be brought into parallelism with the Syrian king, who was engaged in an open conflict with the representatives of the Theocracy (*i.e.*, with the armed bands of Israelitish heroes inflamed with rage, who, moreover, could at that time hardly be termed the poor)?—the world-monarch of the captivity, who was punished indeed, but whose punishment led him to repent and be converted, with the incorrigibly hardened and diabolized antichrist upon the throne of the Seleucidæ, whc for that very reason was regarded as hopelessly lost, and as the certain prey of eternal damnation, from a theocratic point of view? And in relation to the conduct of Daniel—where, in the theocratic state, and especially among the apocalyptists of the Maccabæan period who were enthusiasts for God, could a parallel to the prophet of this chapter be found? What servant of Jehovah in that age can be mentioned, who, like our prophet, and in analogy with the

course of the Syrian captain Naaman (2 Kings v. 18), would quietly sojourn at the court and in the immediate presence of a heathen ruler; who would have counselled the king in friendship, warned him in loving earnestness, supported and comforted him, as Daniel actually did in his intercourse with the Chaldæan monarch, according to the statements of our section? Certain passages of the Talmud, (*Hilchot Rozeach*, xii. 15; *Baba Bathra*, f. 4, p. 1) may serve to indicate the kind of description which the Maccabæan age would probably have given of the ancient Daniel. It is there asserted that God afterwards punished that prophet, because he had wasted good advice and instruction on the heathen Nebuchadnezzar, such as are found in chap. iv. 24! In addition, cf. the doxology appended by the Sept. to chap. iv. 34, for an illustration of the manner in which that age would have described a Nebuchadnezzar who should actually repent and turn to God. In that passage the restored king is represented as renouncing forever the heathen gods as being utterly powerless, as promising to dedicate himself and his people to the constant service of Jehovah, and as honoring and exulting the Jewish people with excessive praise!—Upon the whole cf. Kranichfeld, p. 170 et seq. and p. 203. See also Ibid., p. 175: "The situation, however, becomes no more conceivable, if, for the purpose of demonstrating the invention of this section as a sketch copied from the circumstances of the reign of Antiochus Epiphanes, its composition be placed prior to the armed revolt mentioned in 1 Macc. ii. 42 et seq. and consequently in a time when Antiochus raged in unresisted power against the helpless Jews. In this case it must be allowed indeed, that the writer possessed considerable prophetic gifts, so that even Hitzig ascribes prophecy to him in relation to the final fate of Epiphanes, without characterizing it as prophecy *ex eventu*. The definite and unconditional prediction concerning the loss of the kingdom by means of force, v. 28 et seq., would thus be fully realized; and likewise that foretelling of a peculiar disease by which he should be brought to a humble recognition of the God of the Jews, even though it were not a disease of the mind (cf. 2 Macc. ix. 5 et seq.). The total desertion to which he was actually exposed during the progress of his disease (cf. 2 Macc. ix. 9) *ἐπὶ ξένης ἐν τοῖς ὄρεσιν* (ibid. v. 28) would have reflected honor on the prophetic threat of the alleged forger (cf. Dan. iv. 22, 29 et seq.). But besides mistaking the nature of the disease, he has unfortunately erred with reference to the recovery, and on that very account he is compelled, according to Hitzig, to renounce the honor of composing a prophecy *after the event* had transpired, and that without compensation for the otherwise really wonderful prediction of the three circumstances mentioned above, whose combined fulfillment of itself assuredly deserves the distinguishing attribute of pseudo-prophecy. But there still remains the oracle of chap. iv. 23 [26], an expression on the part of a Jew regarded as a model of the patriot who is jealous because the law of his God is trodden under foot, and which is *ambiguous* when compared with the circumstances of the period of persecution under Antiochus Epiphanes, and therefore *inconceivable* in a historical point of view, since that period preceded the armed rising. Moreover, it must seem strange at the least, that the writer should content himself at the time of Epiphanes with assigning such very ordinary limits to the sinfulness and presumptuous pride of Nebuchadnezzar, while the violence done to the sanctuary of Israel is not mentioned with a single word, for instance, in v. 24 [27]; and yet it was this very act which ranked chief in importance in the eyes of Antiochus himself (cf. i. Macc. 21–24, 36 et seq., 44 et seq.; v. 1 et seq.), and which was regarded as the most heinous crime of that tyrant, and as the principal ground for the lamentations of pious Jews in the Maccabæan period, as well as of the Divine vengeance visited on him; cf. 1 Macc. ii. 8–13; iii. 55, 51, 58 et seq.; iv. 36 et seq.; vi. 12 et seq. Such a silence in this connection with regard to so scandalous a deed is the more remarkable, since the historical books expressly record the robbery of the sanctuary perpetrated by Nebuchadnezzar, which action was known to our author, according to chap. i. 2; cf. v. 3, as well as to his compatriots. He was not obliged therefore, as a *cautious* forger, to fear that he should betray his pseudonymity by the mention of the sacred edifice. How greatly the Sept. animated by the spirit and views of the Maccabæan time, must have desired to find in the words of Daniel v. 19, a condemnatory mention of the violence done to the temple by Nebuchadnezzar, and how appropriate it would seem to them, may appear from their addition to v. 19, which is certainly significant for the Asmonæan period, and for that reason has unjustly been eliminated by Tischendorf without ceremony: *ὑψώθη σοῦ ἡ καρδία ὑπερηφανίᾳ καὶ ἰσχύϊ ὑπὲρ τὰ πρὸς τὸν ἅγιον καὶ τοὺς ἀγγέλους αὐτοῦ. Τὰ ἔργα σοῦ ὤφθη καθότι ἐξηρήμωσας τὸν οἶκον τοῦ θεοῦ τοῦ ζῶντος ἐπὶ ταῖς ἁμαρτίαις τοῦ λαοῦ τοῦ ἡγιασμένου.*"—The *exact acquaintance* of the writer with the architectural condition of Babylon (cf. the exegesis) which is apparent in vs. 26 [29], and 27 [30], and is as unlooked for as it is evident, deserves to be mentioned as a circumstance of especial force as bearing against the hypothesis of a fiction in the interests of a tendency of the Maccabæan period. A Maccabæan author would scarcely have represented that his typical pseudo-Antiochus was overtaken by a fearful visitation of Divine justice in the form of an unusual disease, while walking on the roof of his own palace and within the limits of his capital. The temptation to let him encounter this fate in the place where Epiphanes succumbed to his, "in a strange land and in the desert," would have been almost irresistible (cf. 2 Macc. ix. 3, 28).

4. *Homiletical suggestions.*—The features of practical importance in this section are concentrated in v. 24 [27], the same passage in which Daniel's words of exhortation and warning to the king furnish the leading elements of dogmatic significance. Not merely is the counsel of Daniel, recommending the practice of the virtues belonging to a ruler who pleases God, such as the doing of works of righteousness and mercy (cf. supra. No. 2), worthy of notice and of thorough homiletical treatment; but equally so the impulse which constrains and encourages him to venture this exhortation—his faith in the willingness of God to avert the threatened punishment from the king, in case he should

repent and be converted while it was yet time; his truly prophetic and theocratic conviction that God might possibly repent of His purpose, on the fulfilment of the proper conditions by the threatened person. In this connection see the prophetic parallels adduced above, and compare the remarks of Jerome on this subject: "*Si prædixit sententiam Dei, quæ non potest immutari, quomodo hortatur ad eleemosynas et misericordias pauperum, ut Dei sententia commutetur? Quod facile solvitur Ezechiæ regis exemplo, quem Isajas dixerat esse moriturum, et Ninivitarum, quibus dictum est: Adhuc quadraginta dies, et Ninive subvertetur. Et tamen ad preces Ezechiæ et Ninive Dei sententia commutata est; non vanitate judicii, sed illorum conversione qui meruere indulgentiam. Alioquin et in Jeremia loquitur Deus se mala minari super gentem; et si bona fecerit, minas clementia commutare. Rursum bona agenti se asserit polliceri, et si mala fecerit, dicit se mutare suam sententiam; non in homines sed in opera, quæ mutata sunt. Neque enim Deus hominibus, sed vitiis irascitur; quæ quum in homine non fuerint, nequaquam punit quod mutatum est.*" Cf. also Melancthon, Calvin, Geier and Starke, on this passage, and further, the expositions of Biblical theologians on the Old-Testament teaching concerning the *repentance* of God, *e.g.*, Steudel, *Theologie des A. Ts.*, p. 181 et seq.; Hävernick, *Vorless.*, p. 65 et seq.; F. Majer, *Was hast du wider das Alte Testament?* (Stuttgart, 1864), p. 118 et seq., and Kling, in Herzog's *Real-Encykl.*, art. *Reue*, vol. xii. p. 764.—The theme derived from v. 24 [27] might therefore be formulated: "Repent of thy sin, and God will repent of the punishment threatened against thee;" or, "The aim of Divine punishment is the conversion of men; if this be attained, how gladly will He cause the punishment to cease" (Starke); or, "Be ye therefore merciful, as your Father also is merciful" (Luke vi. 36).*

Additional points of departure for homiletical discussion and observation are afforded in chap. iii. 31–33 [iv. 1–3], and chap. iv. 31–34 [34–37], the introductory and closing doxologies of the report. These are particularly adapted to serve as points of connection for sermons upon the entire narrative, having the theme, "All the works of God are truth, and His ways judgment" (iv. 34 [37]); or, "Humble yourselves in the sight of God, and He shall lift you up" (Jas. iv. 10); or, "God puts down the mighty from their seats, and exalts them of low degree" (Luke i. 52), etc. Cf. especially what Theodoret observes, on chap. iv. 31: *Τοσαύτην ὠφέλειαν ὁ Ναβουχοδονόσορ ἐκ τῶν συμφορῶν ἐδέξατο, ὅτι προφητικῶς περὶ τοῦ θεοῦ καὶ φρονεῖ καὶ φθέγγεται, καὶ ὡς ἐκ συμφωνίας τινὸς ἀπὸ τῆς κτίσεως πάσην τὴν ὑμνῳδίαν ὕφαινει.* Another homiletical text is contained in chap. iv. 3 [6] et seq., on which Cramer (in Starke) observes correctly, "If human wisdom cannot interpret and explain a dream, it is much less able to discover the secrets of God. Human reason should therefore not be permitted to be master in Divine things; for none can know what is in God, except the Spirit of God." A still further passage of homiletical bearing is chap. iv. 26–30 [29–33], a powerful and awfully impressive illustration of the proverb, "Pride goeth before destruction" (Prov. xvi. 18). Cf. Starke: "When a man permits the time for repentance to pass without a change of disposition, the Divine punishment overtakes him in the midst of his sins. He then learns that the threatenings of God were not idle words" (Num. xvi. 12, 31 et seq).

* ["This noble example of manly and Christian fidelity to his sovereign is worthy of all admiration, and of course *imitation*. Prompted by such manifest love and in manner so respectful to the king, and yet with so much personal dignity, it must have fallen upon the king's mind with great force.—The sin specially indicated here, unrighteous oppression of the poor, looks very probably toward the terrible exactions of labor imposed upon his defenceless subjects (some of them captives of war) in those immense public works which were, in the eyes of men, the glory of his reign. The eye of man, dazzled with so much architectural splendor, commonly fails to look down through to the crushed bodies and broken hearts, and to the hopeless, never-lifted pressure of woe which such a mass of coerced labor always signifies. Human eyes rarely see it, still more rarely make any account of it, but the Great Father sees it and can never fail to take it into most solemn account."—*Cowles.*]

---

5. *Belshazzar's feast, and Daniel's foreshadowing of the downfall of the Chaldæan Empire, based upon the mysterious handwriting on the wall.*

CHAP. V. 1–30.

1 Belshazzar the king made a great feast to a thousand *of* his lords, and drank
2 wine[1] before the thousand. Belshazzar, while he tasted [in *the* taste of] the
wine, commanded to bring *the* golden and silver vessels which his father[2]
Nebuchadnezzar had taken out *of* the temple which *was* in Jerusalem; that
[and] the king and his princes [lords], his wives and his concubines, might drink
3 therein. Then they brought *the* golden vessels that were taken out of the temple
of *the* house of God which *was* at [in] Jerusalem; and the king and his princes
4 [lords], his wives and his concubines, drank in them. They drank wine[1] and
praised the gods of gold, and *of* silver, *of* brass, *of* iron, *of* wood, and *of* stone.
5 In the same hour came forth fingers of a man's hand, and wrote over against
the candlestick upon the plaster of *the* wall of the king's palace; and the king
6 saw *the* part of the hand that wrote. Then the king's countenance *was* changed,[3]
and his thoughts troubled [would trouble] him, *so* that [and] *the* joints of his
loins [loin] *were* loosed, and his knees smote one against another [this to that].

7 The king cried aloud [with might] to bring in the astrologers, the Chaldæans
and the soothsayers. *And* the king spake, and said to *the* wise *men* of Babylon
Whosoever [That any man that] shall read this writing, and shew me *the* inter
pretation thereof, shall *be* clothed *with* scarlet [put on the purple], and *have* a
[the] chain of gold about [upon] his neck, and shall be *the* third ruler [rule
8 third] in the kingdom. Then came in all *the* king's wise *men:* but [and] they
could not read [call] the writing, nor [and] make known *to* the king [make the
9 king know] *the* interpretation thereof. Then *was* [the] king Belshazzar greatly
troubled, and his countenance *was* changed in him,[4] and his lords *were* aston-
ished.
10 *Now* the queen, by reason of the words of the king and his lords, came into
the banquet-house [house of the drinking]; *and* the queen spake and said, O
11 king, live for ever; let not thy thoughts trouble thee, nor let thy countenance
be changed.[5] *There* is a man in thy kingdom, in whom *is the* spirit of *the* holy
gods: and, in *the* days of thy father, light, and understanding, and wisdom,
like *the* wisdom of *the* gods, was found in him; whom [and] the king Nebu-
chadnezzar thy father, the king, *I say*, thy father, made [appointed him] master
12 of the magicians, astrologers, Chaldæans, *and* soothsayers; forasmuch as an
excellent spirit, and knowledge, and understanding, interpreting of dreams, and
shewing of hard sentences [riddles], and dissolving of doubts [knots], were
[was] found in the same [in him] Daniel, whom the king named [put his
name]Belteshazzar: now let Daniel be called, and he will shew [*or*, and shew]
the interpretation.
13 Then was Daniel brought in before the king. *And* the king spake and said
unto Daniel, *Art* thou that Daniel, which *art* of the children of the captivity of
14 Judah,[6] whom the king my father brought out of Jewry [Judah]?[6] I have
even heard of [upon] thee, that *the* spirit of *the* gods *is* in thee, and *that* light,
15 and understanding, and excellent wisdom, is [was] found in thee. And now
the wise *men*, the astrologers, have been brought in before me, that they should
read [call] this writing, and make known *unto* me [make me know] *the* inter-
pretation thereof: but [and] they could not shew *the* interpretation of the thing.
16 And I[7] have heard of [upon] thee that thou canst make [interpret] interpreta-
tions and dissolve doubts [knots]: now, if thou canst read [call] the writ-
ing and make known to me [make me know] the interpretation thereof, thou
shalt *be* clothed *with* scarlet [put on the purple], and *have* a [the] chain of gold
about [upon] thy neck, and shalt be the third ruler [rule the third] in the
kingdom.
17 Then Daniel answered and said before the king, Let thy gifts be to thyself
[thee], and give thy rewards [largesses] to another; yet I will read [call] the
writing unto the king, and make known to him [make him know] the interpre-
18 tation. O thou king, [Thou O king—] the *most* high God gave [to] Nebuchad-
nezzar thy father a [the] kingdom, and majesty [greatness], and glory, and
19 honour. And, for [from] the majesty [greatness] that he gave him, all people,
nations [the nations, peoples], and languages, trembled and feared [were trem-
bling and fearing from] before him: whom he would he slew, and whom he
would he kept alive, and whom he would he set up, and whom he would he
20 put down.[8] But [And] when his heart *was* lifted *up*, and his mind [spirit]
hardened in pride [to act proudly], he was deposed from his kingly throne [the
throne of his kingdom], and they took [caused to pass away] his glory [the
21 dignity] from him. And *he was* driven from *the* sons of men [mankind]; and
his heart *was* made like [with] the beasts [living *creatures*], and his dwelling
was with the wild-asses: they fed him *with* [would make him eat] grass [herb-
age] like oxen, and his body was [would be] wet with [from] *the* dew of heaven
[the heavens]; till [that] he knew that the *most* high God ruled in the kingdom
of men [mankind], and *that* he appointeth [will set up] over it whomsoever he
22 [may] will. And thou[9] his son, *O* Belshazzar, hast not humbled thy heart,
23 though [because] thou knewest all this; but [and] hast lifted *up* thyself
against *the* Lord[10] of heaven [the heavens]: and they have brought the vessels
of his house before thee, and thou and thy lords, thy wives and thy concubines,

have drunk [*are* drinking], wine[1] in them: and thou hast praised *the* gods of
silver and gold, *of* brass, iron, wood, and stone, which see not, nor hear, nor
know; and the God in whose hand thy breath *is*, and whose *are* all thy ways,
24 hast thou not glorified: Then *was* the part of the hand sent from [before]
him; and this writing *was* written [signed].
25 And this *is* the writing that *was* written [signed], MENE, MENE, TEKEL,
26 UPHARSIN. This *is the* interpretation of the thing [*or*, word]: MENE
27 [NUMBERED]; God[11] hath numbered thy kingdom, and finished it. TEKEL
28 [WEIGHED]; Thou art weighed in *the* balances, and art found wanting. PERES
[DIVIDED]; thy kingdom is divided, and given to *the* Medes [Media] and Per-
sians [Persia].
29 Then commanded [said] Belshazzar, and they clothed Daniel *with* scarlet [the
purple], and *put* a [the] chain of gold about [upon] his neck, and made a pro-
clamation concerning [upon] him, that he should be the third ruler in the king-
30 dom. In that night *was* Belshazzar the king of the Chaldæans slain.

GRAMMATICAL NOTES.

[[1] The emphatic state in חַמְרָא, like the art. in Heb. and Gr., is equivalent to the pers. pron. *his wine*.—[2] אַב frequently used, in all the Shemitic tongues, of a forefather, whether immediate or remote.—[3] Literally, *the king—his bright* looks *changed* for *him*.—[4] Literally, *his bright* looks were *changing upon him*.—[5] Literally, *and let not thy bright* looks *be changed*.—[6] The form יְהוּד, apocopated for brevity's sake from יְהוּדָה, is exclusively applied in Biblical Chaldee to *Judæa*.—[7] The pronoun is emphatic, being expressed.—[8] The participial form of these verbs (*whom he was willing he was killing, and whom he was willing he was making live, and whom he was willing he was raising, and whom he was willing he was depressing*) indicates the continued as well as absolute power of the autocrat.—[9] The pronoun here is resumptive of that which stands absolutely in verse 18.—[10] מָרֵא is the Chaldee equivalent of אָדוֹן.—[11] אֱלָהָא is significant of the *true* God, like הָאֱלֹהִים].

EXEGETICAL REMARKS.

Verses 1–4. *The desecration of the sacred vessels of the temple at the royal feast.* **Belshazzar the king made a great feast.** The name of the king בֵּלְשַׁאצַּר differs in its orthography merely from the Chaldee name בֵּלְטְשַׁאצַּר, which Nebuchadnezzar, according to chap. i. 7 (cf. infra, v. 12 of this chapter), had conferred on Daniel, as it omits the *t*-sound between the letters *l* and *sh*. It is therefore a softened form, having the same etymological significance in its elements, and both are equivalent to *Beli princeps*, = the *Bel-sarussur* of the Babylonian inscriptions (cf. Introd., § 8, note 3). According to Hitzig (on i. 7, and on this passage), *Bel-tsh-âzar* is synonymous with the Sanscrit *Pâla-tshâçara*, "provider and devourer," while in *Bel-shazzar* the middle member of this compound, the Sanscr. and Zend copula *tsha*, "and," has been dropped out and replaced by the Heb. relative שֶׁ, so that the shortened form signifies, "provider, *who* (is) devourer." This hypothesis appears altogether too artificial, and, like the direct derivation of the word from the Aryan, is doubtful, especially as the Bel-sarussur of the inscriptions on the Babylonian monuments favors it but little. Ewald's assumption that the royal name בֵּלְשׁ׳ comprehends the name of the male god Bel, while that of Daniel, בֵּלְטְשׁ׳, includes that of the goddess Belt, is likewise without sufficient proof, and is opposed by chap. iv. 5 [8], and also by the orthography with ט instead of ת.—Concerning the hypothesis that Belshazzar was the same as Evil-merodach, the son and immediate successor of Nebuchadnezzar, see the Introd., § 8, note 3.—**Made a great feast,** *i.e.*, caused it to be made. עֲבַד, "he had prepared," as in chap. iii. 1. לְחֶם, "bread, food," comprehends the beverages (מִשְׁתְּיָא, v. 10) also, as the second half of the verse shows; cf. in the Heb., Gen. xxvi. 30; 1 Sam. xxv. 36; Ecc. x. 19.—**And drank wine before the thousand.** This does not probably mean that he "vied with them in drinking" (Hävernick), but that he "drank in their presence, while seated at a separate table,"—as was the custom of the Persian kings on the occasion of their great banquets, according to Athenæus, *Deipnos*, iv. 10. On the expression, "to eat and drink before others," cf. Jer. lii. 33; it differs materially from "to eat and drink *with* others," Ex. xviii. 12; Acts x. 41, etc. The number of the king's guests, a *thousand* lords (grand-officers, mighty ones, cf. iv. 33 [36], which the Sept. doubles, διαχίλιοι), is not remarkable, when it is remembered that, according to Ctesias (in Athen., l. c.), the Persian king provided daily for fifteen thousand persons at his table; that, according to Curtius, Alexander the Great invited ten thousand to a wedding feast; and that Ptolemy Dionysius (according to Pliny, *H. N.*, XXXIII. 10) supported a thousand soldiers of the army of Pompey the Great from his kitchen. ["The number specified is evidently a round number, *i.e.*, the number of the guests amounted to about a thousand" (Keil).] However, according to the genuinely Oriental custom, which is attested, *e.g.*, by Herodotus, II. 78, in the case of the Egyptians, and by Ælian, *V. H.*, XI. 1, among the Persians, the wine-drinking or carousal *follows* upon the feast proper. At such times, and especially at a court like the Babylonian immediately prior to the Persian period, the banqueters may have given way to all the excesses of their dissolute frivolity, in the manner described in the ensuing narrative. In relation to the drunkenness and wantonness of the Babylonians, cf. Isa. xiv. 11; xlvii. 1; Jer. li. 39; Herod., I. 193, 195; Athenæus, XIV. p. 601; Curtius, V. 1 etc.—Verse 2. **Belshazzar, while he tasted the wine, commanded,** etc. בִּטְעֵם חַמְרָא, "while tasting, while enjoying the wine," therefore, while under its influence; cf. Prov. xx. 1; Acts ii. 13; and in regard to טעם, cf. Job vi. 6. [It "does not mean merely *sipping* in order to determine the flavor, or as a prelude to drinking more freely, but *drinking with relish*, and therefore plentifully" (Stuart).]—**To bring the golden and silver vessels,** namely, out of the "treasure-house of the gods," in which they had been deposited by Nebuchadnezzar, according to chap. i. 2. The etymology of the name Belshazzar invented by Saadia and favored by Hitzig, by which it is derived from this very act of causing the vessels to be brought from the treasure-house (בְּלַשׁ, "to seek" and אוֹצָר), is an idle vagary that never entered into the mind of the writer.—**That the king . . . . and his concubines might drink therein.** The ו in וְיִשְׁתּוֹן is expressive of the design; cf. chap. i. 5 *b.* שְׁתָה with בְּ, "to drink *from* a vessel," occurs also in vs. 3 and 23; cf. Winer, § 51, 1.—**His wives and his concubines.** שֵׁגַל designates the legal consort as contrasted with the concubine (לְחֵנָה), as in the Hebrew (Psa. xlv. 10; Neh. ii. 6). The Sept. represents only the concubines as present at the feast (both here and in vs. 3 and 23), being apparently governed in this by what is described in Esther i. 9 et seq. (cf. Josephus, *Ant.*, XI. 6, 1) as the court custom of the *ancient* Persians; but even with reference to them, Herodotus (v. 18) testifies that their wives (κουρίδιαι γυναῖκες) were admitted to banquets (cf. also Plutarch, *Sympos.* I. 1 and Macrob. vii. 1, who represent that at least concubines were present at the Persian feasts). It is clear that the luxurious Babylonians were even more lax in the observance of a strict etiquette, from Herod. i. 191; Xenophon, *Cyrop.*, V. 2, 28, and especially from Curtius, V. 1, 38. From this may appear the propriety with which Bertholdt (p. 366), on the strength of v. 10 of this chapter, which he misunderstood, charges ignorance of the Babylonian custom in question on the prophet.—Verse 3. **Then they brought the golden vessels that were taken out of the temple of the house of God which was at Jerusalem.** Merely the *golden vessels* are here mentioned, while the silver ones are omitted, on the principle *a potiori fit denominatio.* The temple" (הֵיכְלָא) in this place, as in 1 Kings vi. 3; Ezek. xli. 4, is the temple proper, consisting of the holy and the most holy place, and is here distinguished from the "house of God," *i.e.*, the whole of the sacred area of the temple.—Verse 4. **They drank wine, and praised,** etc. אִשְׁתִּיו (with א prosthet., Winer, *Gramm.*, § 23, note 1) resumes the וְאִשְׁתִּיו of the preceding verse supplemented by חַמְרָא, "wine," in order to connect immediately with it the praising of the gods, and thus to present in a striking manner the profanity and lasciviousness of the scene.*—On the six-fold number of the materials from which the idols were constructed, "gold, silver, brass, iron, wood, and stone," compare the similar number ("gold, silver, precious stones, wood, hay stubble") in 1 Cor. iii. 11; also Psa. cxv. 5–7; Bar. vi. 7 et seq.; Wisd. xv. 15.† On the number itself, as the number of the world amenable to judgment because of its hostility to God, cf. Auberlen, *Dan.*, p. 304 et seq.; and my *Theologia naturalis*, p. 816 et seq.—The aggravated feature of this profanation of the sacred vessels of the temple does not consist in the "placing of Jehovah and the idols of the king upon the same level" (Hävernick), but in the fact, which Daniel mentions with censure in v. 23, that Belshazzar proudly exalted himself above the God of Israel, and in mockery employed the vessels stolen from His sanctuary to drink wine while singing the praises of the victorious gods of Babylon. It was thus essentially *an exaltation of the idols above Jehovah*, who had succumbed to them in battle, and whom they had despoiled (cf. Kranichf. on this passage).

Verses 5, 6. *The finger on the wall, and the consequent terror of the king.* **In the same hour,** therefore while the sacrilegious act was in progress; immediately and suddenly. Cf. chap iii. 6.—**Came forth fingers of a man's hand.** The Kethib נְפַקוּ (3 plur. masc.) is sufficiently explained by its position before the feminine subject אֶצְבְּעָן, or also by the supposition that the mind of the writer reverted in an indefinite manner to the Divine powers here engaged. The feminine plural נְפַקָה, substituted for it by the Keri, is therefore to be rejected, as an easier reading (similar to that in chap. ii. 33). The participle וְכָתְבָן ("and writing," instead of "and wrote"), which follows the verb נְפַקוּ, has a realizing effect, as in chap. ii. 7 *a*; iii. 9 *a*.—**Over against the candlestick on the wall of the king's palace.** The wall of the banquet-hall was not panelled nor draped, but rather a simple, light-colored "wall of lime or plaster" (כְּתַל = the כּוֹתֶל of the Targums), such as the ruins of the palaces at Nineveh still exhibit in great number, according to Layard (*Nin. and Babylon*, p. 651). Upon a spot of this wall that was especially exposed to the light from the lamp above the king, he suddenly beheld the mysterious and terrifying phenomenon of the hand engaged in writing.—**And the king saw the part** (the extremity) **of the hand that wrote.** פַּס יְדָא properly designates here and in v. 24 the "extremity of the hand," probably

* ["As the city was already besieged, and the real king Nabonned had gone into the field against the armies of the Medes and Persians under Cyrus, the sense of security which this feast implied must be accounted for by their confidence in the assumed strength of the city. Plainly it was supposed to be absolutely impregnable.—It may be added that God had given up the king and the princes to a blind infatuation, of such sort as usually precedes destruction."—*Cowles.*]

† ["The six predicates of the gods are divided by the copula ו into two classes: gold and silver—brass, iron, wood, and stone, in order to represent before the eyes in an advancing degree the variety of these gods."—*Keil.*]

including the fingers, hence what the first sentence describes by אֶצְבְּעָן. The rendering of Gesenius and Dietrich in the *Handwörterbuch*, "palm of the hand, *palma*," is hardly correct; nor is that of Hitzig, who, in connection with Saadia, takes יְדָא in the wider sense of "the lower arm, including the hand," and hence explains פס־ידא by "the whole hand." The writer appears rather to have employed the words "fingers" and "extremity of the hand" interchangeably, with design, —"in order to excite more effectually the conception of a mysterious person in the background, by the observation that only the extremity of the organ employed in writing was visible" (Kranichfeld). Whether the phenomenon of the mysterious hand is to be placed solely to the account of "the fancy of the king under the influence of wine," and therefore to be reduced (with Kranichfeld) from an objective and actually transpiring miracle to a merely subjective apprehension (similar to the perception of the fourth person in the fiery furnace—see on chap. iii. 24), or otherwise, depends entirely on the other question, whether the mysterious writing on the wall, which certainly was visible to others as well as to Belshazzar (cf. vs. 7, 8, 16, 25), is to be regarded as having been previously carved or painted in a natural way and by human agency, or whether it is to be accepted that the inscription was made by supernatural intervention at the time of the banquet and before the eyes of the terrified king. In support of the former theory reference might perhaps be made to the distinction between an older and a later cuneiform writing among the Babylonians, the former of which differed materially from the latter, or even to the hieroglyphics which the primitive Babylonians are said to have employed (cf. Spiegel, Art. *Nineve u. Assyrien*, in Herzog's *Real-Encykl.*, vol. xx. p. 234 et seq.), but with which the later ages were entirely unacquainted. It is conceivable that the king may suddenly have noticed an inscription in characters of that former time, that were traced on bricks and inserted in the wall, and that such characters were not intelligible to the ordinary magians of the time, but required the all-surpassing knowledge of Daniel to decipher. But, aside from the evident design of the narrator to report a positively miraculous incident, this theory is militated against and positively overthrown by the *nature of the writing*, which does not bear the character of the primitive oracles of the kind represented by the Sibyllines, but is a Divine sentence of destruction upon the king and his people, that was called forth by the insolent presumption of the present ruler, and is adapted to the circumstances of his time (cf. on v. 25 et seq.). The theory of an actual miracle is therefore to be received, and the psychological explanation cited above, as well as every other naturalistic theory, must be rejected.*—**Then the** (color of the) **king's countenance was changed;** literally, "Then the king, his color was changed to him." ["מַלְכָּא (*the king*) stands absolutely, because the impression made by the occurrence on the king is to be depicted" (*Keil*).] The intransitive שְׁנָא ("to change") has the accusative suffix in שְׁנוֹהִי, instead of the dative; cf. בְּשׁוּבֵנִי in the Heb. of Ezek. xlvii. 7. However, the more circumstantial expression זִיוֹהִי שְׁנַיִן עֲלוֹהִי, v. 9, has substantially the same signification, as is the case also with the somewhat different expressions in v. 10 and chap. vii. 28. On זִיוִין, see on chap. iv. 33.—**And his thoughts troubled him;** רעיונין, the uncomfortable and terrifying thoughts concerning the meaning of the writing, which sprang from the guilty conscience of the king. Cf. chap. ii. 30.—**The joints of his loins were loosed, and his knees smote one against another.** The tremulous knocking together of the knees is a consequence of the yielding of the joints of the loins, and this again, like the change of color in the countenance, is the natural effect of terror.* Cf. with חֲרַץ, "hip, loin," the etymologically equivalent Heb. חלץ (only in the dual, חֲלָצַיִם). אַרְכֻּבָא, "knee," appears not to be etymologically related to בְּרַךְ, ברכים, but rather to signify originally "combination, *commissura;*" cf. *commissura genu*, Plin., *H. N.*, XI. 103.

Verses 7–9. *The useless consultation with the Magians.* **The king cried aloud;** בְּחַיִל, "with power," as in chap. iii. 4; iv. 11.—**To bring in the astrologers** (soothsayers), **the Chaldæans, and the soothsayers** (astrologers). Several classes of wise men are here mentioned to designate the entire number, as in chap. ii. 2 (cf. 27) and in iv. 4; and among them the *Chartummin* or learned class (see on chap. ii. 2), whose wisdom would be especially required in the present instance, are not even mentioned by name. This is evidently an oversight on the part of the writer, which is paralleled in the somewhat more complete enumeration of the principal classes of Magians in v. 11, and also in the abbreviated expression, "the wise men, the soothsayers," in v. 15. The indefinite חכימי בבל in this verse, and the expression כֹּל חַכִּימֵי מַלְכָּא in v. 8, show clearly that the author always refers to *all* the wise men, without excluding any of the chief classes, and especially so in this instance. But it cannot be required here, any more than in the similar case mentioned in the preceding chapter, that Daniel should have at once presented himself among *all* these wise men of Babylon (see on iv. 5). The position of the great Jewish wise man under Nebuchadnezzar's reign, which was not official in the more limited sense, was probably continued to him under Belshazzar; and, moreover, the latter, who, according to v. 11 et seq., knew little or nothing about Daniel, would be far more likely than was his father to ignore the prophet of Jehovah, and to

* [The appearance of the fingers "immediately awakened the thought that the writing was by a supernatural being, and alarmed the king out of his intoxication."—*Keil.*]

* ["It is an appalling scene when a sinning mortal knows that the great God has come to meet him in the very midst of his sins!—How changed the scene from the glee of his blasphemous revelry to this paleness of cheek, convulsion of frame, remorse of conscience, and dread foreboding of doom! Many a sinner has had a like experience, and other thousands must have it!"—*Cowles.*]

seek the counsel of the heathen wise men at the outset. The words of the queen in v. 11 et seq. by no means indicate that the king was wholly unacquainted with Daniel, but merely that up to that time no personal or official intercourse had taken place between them. This circumstance also finds a sufficient explanation in the greater freedom of action incident to the partly official and partly private station of Daniel, which devolved on him the obligation to attend to certain portions of "the king's business" indeed (see chap. viii. 27), but released him from the duty of frequently presenting himself before the king. The assumption of Hengstenberg and Hävernick, that on the accession of Belshazzar Daniel was formally deprived of his office as the chief Magian, is a very doubtful supposition, and stands in direct contradiction to chap. viii. 27 (cf. viii. 1).—**Whosoever shall read this writing,** etc. כְּתָבָה (here and v. 15), for כְּתָבָא, v. 8, 16, 25, appears to be the orthography of a later copyist, as in the case of כִּלָּה, chap. iv. 32, and of פִּשְׁרָה in v. 12, below.—**Shall be clothed with purple** (marg.) **and have** (rather "with"*) **a chain of gold about his neck.** אַרְגְּוָן here, and in the Chaldaizing Heb. of 2 Chron. ii. 6, equivalent to the Heb. אַרְגָּמָן (Ex. xxv. 26, 27, and often), the "red or genuine purple," πορφύρα, was probably more costly and brilliant than the violet or blue purple תְּכֵלֶת, from which it must be distinguished. It formed the distinguishing feature of clothing among the Persian kings (Pollux, VII. 13), and was by them occasionally bestowed on high officials, as a mark of especial favor and exalted dignity; *e.g.*, on Mordecai, Esth. viii. 15; and on the *purpurati*, *i.e.*, persons who were adorned with the purple κάνδυς, whom Xenophon (*Anab.*, I. 5, 8), Curtius (III. 2, 10; VIII. 3, 15; XIII. 13, 14), and others mention (cf. Xenophon, *Cyrop.*, I. 3, 2; II. 4, 6; Herodotus, III. 20, etc.). Purple was probably the badge of distinguished rank at the Babylonian as well as at the Persian court, especially as Babylon, like Tyre, was celebrated among the ancients for its manufacture of purple goods. Cf. Philostratus, *Ep.*, 27; Ezek. xxvii. 24; Josh. vii. 21; and generally, Heeren, *Ideen*, etc., I. 2, 205 et seq. With respect to their etymology, both forms, ארגמן and ארגון, may be most readily derived from the Sanscrit, in which both *râgaman* and *râgavan* occur as adjectives derived from *râga*, "red," and signify "red-colored;" cf. Gesen., *Addit. ad Thesaur.*, p. 111. Hitzig however refers to the Sanscr. *argh* = "to possess value, be costly," and most of the older expositors prefer a Shemitic root, *e.g.* רגם.—הַמְנוּכָא, "chain, necklace" (Sept. and Theodot., μανιάκης; also Aquil. and Symm. on Gen. xli. 42), seems not to have been changed to הַמְנִיכָא (= Gr. μανιάκης), the form which is here and in vs. 16 and 29 preferred by the Keri. As among the early Egyptians (Gen. xli. 42), so also among the later Persians the golden necklace served as the ornament of princes and as the mark of special favor from the king, cf. Herod., III. 20; Xenophon, *Anab.*, I. 2, 27; 5, 8; 8, 29.—**And shall be the third ruler in the kingdom**; rather, "shall have power in the kingdom as a triumvir." תַּלְתִּי, not the same as תַּלְתָּא, vs. 16 and 29, is generally regarded as an ordinal number, "the third," formed after the Heb. analogy, and is compared with the more usual תְּלִיתַי; but it may perhaps, and with greater probability, be regarded, with Kranichfeld, as a feminine adverbial formation after the analogy of adverbs like אֲרָמִית, אֲחֹרַי, etc., and be rendered accordingly, by *like*, or *as a triumvir*; while תַּלְתָּא in vs. 16 and 29 is the corresponding masculine noun "triumvir" (formed from תְּלָתָא, "three"). There is therefore no difference in sense between the term employed in this passage and those found in the parallel verses cited above; but it is unnecessary and arbitrary to declare, with Hitzig, that the two forms are identical, and on that account to substitute תַּלְתִּי in this place. The dignity of triumvir which is here promised to the fortunate interpreter of the mystery is probably not identical with the office of one of the three governors of the province of Babylon mentioned in chap. ii. 49, but designates the position of one of the three chief governors over the whole kingdom. The latter office is noticed in chap. vi. 3, as established by Darius the Mede; but that statement may be regarded as merely indicating the restoration of a feature in the administration of government which had already existed under the Babylonian regime. The Sept. presents the correct idea: ἐξουσία τοῦ τρίτου μέρους τῆς βασιλείας; but the Peshito is less correct in its rendering by "the third rank in the kingdom," which results in the idea that the recipient should immediately succeed in rank the king, who was supreme, and the prime minister or grand vizier, who filled the second place in the kingdom. This thought was certainly foreign to the author, and would be expressed as indefinitely as is possible by וְתַלְתִּי וגו׳. The evident meaning of these words is rather that the person concerned should be placed over the kingdom αὐτὸς τρίτος, or the third beside two other grand officials or שַׁלִּיטִין (cf. chap. vi. 3).—Verse 8. **Then came in all the king's wise men.** On the Keri עָלִּין see on chap. iv. 4. The כֹּל חַכִּימֵי מַלְכָּא are evidently the same as those mentioned separately (although not exhaustively, and merely by way of indicating their office) in v. 7. Kranichfeld is exceedingly arbitrary when he assumes a gradation between the three classes of wise men who are specially mentioned in v. 7, and the summoning of *all* the wise men related in this passage, and consequently finds between the lines and preceding the אֱדַיִן, "then," a series of incidents that are not expressly noticed (after the manner in which many expositors treat the καὶ εἶπεν ὁ δοῦλος, Luke xiv. 22). Instead of this compare the relation of the general expression כֹּל חַכִּימֵי

* [The phrase וְהַמְנוּכָא דִי דַהֲבָא וגו׳ "does not depend on יִלְבַּשׁ, but forms a clause by itself; *and a chain of gold shall be about his neck.*"—*Keil.*]

בָּבֶל in chap. iv. 3, to the special classes of wise men which are immediately referred to (ibid. v. 4), and also what has been observed above, on v. 7, in relation to the careless style of the author.—**But they could not read the writing,** etc. Kranichfeld supposes that the reason for this was, that the mysterious inscription was written in the old Phœnician characters, which Daniel, being a Hebrew, would have recognized, while the Chaldæan *Chartummin*, who were acquainted only with the character in use among the ancient Babylonians, which corresponded to the later Syriac or Palmyrene, would naturally be unable to understand them. But in this instance we are probably to conceive of cuneiform writing, or of hieroglyphic characters (see on v. 7), because the brick walls of the palaces in ancient Babylon generally contained only such. Prideaux, however, preceded Kranichfeld in the opinion expressed in the *Universal History*, part III. p. 755, that the writing was not composed of the square characters in use among the Chaldæans, but of the ancient Arabic (?), which preceded the modern Samaritan.*—Verse 9. **Then was king Belshazzar greatly troubled . . . and his lords were astonished.** The unusual, and even unique and incomprehensible characters in which the suddenly apparent writing was composed, increased the alarm produced by the apparition, and filled the king and his guests, now thoroughly aroused from their wild debauch, with anxious dread in relation to the misfortunes predicted by the supposed oracle. If, with Hävernick, and many earlier expositors, we could believe that Belshazzar's feast was held during the siege of the city by the Medo-Persians, and with a design to ridicule the danger from that source, it would be still easier to explain so general an alarm, and it would not even be necessary, in that case, to allude to the fear of the many officials that their own deposition from office might be connected with the king's impending fall; but that conclusion does not necessarily result from v. 30 et seq.—Hitzig remarks on the Ithpael Part. מִשְׁתַּבְּשִׁין, and probably with justice, that "it not only comprehends the idea of alarm, but also that of confusion and excited movement." "None retained their places; a general uproar ensued; groups were formed; and the people talked, and ran hither and thither to no purpose."

Verses 10–12. *The queen-mother refers Belshazzar to Daniel.* **Now** (or "then") **the queen . . . came into the banquet-house.** מַלְכְּתָא can only be the *queen-mother* (גְּבִירָה, 1 Kings xv. 13; 2 Chron. xv. 16; cf. Jer. xiii. 18)—not one of the king's wives; for, according to vs. 3 and 23 these were already in the banquet-hall among the carousers. Hence, if Belshazzar was the same person as Evil-merodach, the son and successor of Nebuchadnezzar, this queen-mother, who here evidently displays a dignity and authority such as belonged to the *gebiroth* at the Israelitish courts (cf. the passages adduced), was probably the *Nitocris* whom Herodotus celebrates in I. 185. Cf. the Introd., § 8, note 3.*—Instead of the Kethib עַלְלַת, the Keri, conforming to the usage of the later Chaldee, has עַלַּת; cf. on chap. iv. 4.—לָקֳבֵל מִלֵּי מַ׳ וגו׳, "by reason (on account) of the words of the king and his lords." So the majority of moderns, correctly; for a confused, excited talking, whose sound possibly penetrated to the apartments of the queen-mother, is implicitly included in משתבשין, v. 9. The plural מִלִּין, as well as the complementary genitive, is opposed to the version of the Vulg.; Luther, Bertholdt, Dereser, von Lengerke, etc.: "by reason of the *matter*, or the *affair*."—**O king, live for ever.** Cf. on chap. ii. 4, where also the defective רַעְיוֹנָךְ וְזִיוָךְ has been noticed.—Verse 11. **And in the days of thy father light** (נַהִירוּ, cf. on chap. ii. 22), **and understanding, and wisdom, like the wisdom of the gods, was found in him.** Cf. 1 Kings iii. 28; Wisd. viii. 11.—**King Nebuchadnezzar, the king, thy father.** The subject is briefly repeated at the close of the sentence, because its first position was somewhat distant from the verb, similar to Cant. v. 7.—Verse 12. **Forasmuch as an excellent spirit . . . were found in the same Daniel.** The wisdom of Daniel, which had been extolled in v. 11, is again mentioned as the reason for the distinction conferred on him by Nebuchadnezzar, for the purpose of preparing Belshazzar to listen to the counsel which follows.—**Interpreting of dreams, and showing of hard sentences, and dissolving of doubts**; rather, "to interpret dreams, show riddles, and loosen knots." This triplicate circumstantial clause,—the first and third of whose members are expressed in the Heb. [Chald.] by participles, and the second by the infinitive אַחֲוָיַא—is a genitive, depending on וְשָׂכְלְתָנוּ, which closes the series of objects governed by the principal verb הִשְׁתְּכַחַת in the manner of a parenthesis. Hitzig holds differently, taking the three terms מְפַשַּׁר, אַחֲוָיַא, and מְשָׁרֵא, under the precedence of the Vulgate, as three nouns of action, coördinated to the preceding ones ("an excellent spirit, knowledge, and understanding"), and consequently assuming *six* subjects to הִשְׁתְּכַחַת בֵּהּ. But מְפַשַּׁר and

* ["But this interpretation of the miracle on natural principles is quite erroneous. First, it is very unlikely that the Chaldæan wise men should not have known these old Shemitic characters, even although at that time they had ceased to be in current use among the Babylonians in their common writing. Then, from the circumstance that Daniel could at once read the writing, it does not follow that it was the well-known Old-Hebrew writing of his fatherland. 'The characters employed in the writing,' as Hengstenberg has rightly observed (*Beitr.*, I. p. 122), 'must have been altogether unusual, so as not to be deciphered but by Divine illumination.' Yet we must not, with M. Geier and others, assume that the writing was visible only to the king and Daniel. This contradicts the text, according to which the Chaldæan wise men, and, without doubt, all that were present, also saw the traces of the writing, but were not able to read it."—*Keil.*]

* ["The 'queen' in this passage is the queen-mother, as may be inferred from the fact that the king's (Belshazzar's) wives and concubines are with him in his carousals, while this woman was not; and also from her intimate acquaintance with Daniel and the incidents of Nebuchadnezzar's life. She was probably the daughter of Nebuchadnezzar, and the mother of Belshazzar."—*Cowles.* If Rawlinson's conjecture (*Herodotus* i. 424) be correct, that the real king Nabonadus had left his son Belshazzar temporarily in charge of Babylon, this woman may have really been the consort of the actual king.]

מְשַׁרֵא are clearly Pael participles, and they cannot be taken as *nomina actionis*, even under reference to the Heb. מְכַסֶּה, "a covering," or to מְשֹׁמֵם, chap. ix. 27. It is exceedingly doubtful whether the figurative expression "to loosen knots" (cf. the Lat. *nodos solvere*; and also Seneca's "*nodosa sortis verba*," *Œdip.*, 101) contains an illusion to the "loosening of the loins," in v. 6 (as Hitzig, Kranichfeld, etc., assert), or not, in view of the merely superficial relation between משרא and משתרין.—**In . . . Daniel whom the king named Belteshazzar;** בֵּהּ בְּדָנִיֵּאל (cf. v. 30), an emphatic pleonasm. The giving of the name is referred to, as in chap. iv. 5, as something honorable to the prophet.—**Now let Daniel be called, and he will show the interpretation.** Concerning the form וּפִשְׁרָה, see above, on v. 7. ["The tone in which this last clause is spoken betokens that the speaker herself is conscious of an elevated rank and a kind of authority, or, at least, a right to give advice; a tone which only such a woman as stood in the relation of a *mother* (not a wife) could assume in the East before a king" (*Stuart*).]

Verses 13–16. *Daniel's appearance before the king.* **Then was Daniel brought in before the king.** הֻעַל and הֻעַלּוּ are Hebraizing Hophal-forms, like הוּסַק, chap. iv. 33, or like הָנְחַת in v. 20.—**Art thou that Daniel, which art of the children of the captivity of Judah,** etc. ["The question did not expect an answer, and has this meaning: *Thou art indeed Daniel.*"—*Keil.*] This question clearly indicates that no direct intercourse had hitherto taken place between the king and Daniel (see on v. 7), but also, on the other hand, that the former had some knowledge of the prophet. The use of the name Daniel instead of Belteshazzar, in the king's address, was probably dictated simply by a desire to avoid the use of a name so nearly identical in sound to his own—although it certainly belonged to the prophet in the official language of the Babylonian court. Hitzig therefore commits a decided error, when he assumes a historical improbability in this place, suggestive of a later Jewish authorship.—**Whom the king . . . . brought from** (rather "hitherto, out of") **Jewry?** דִּי הַיְתִי is probably to be referred to the captives, as Theodotion, the Sept., Luther, Hitzig, etc., hold, and not specially to the person of Daniel, which is the view of the Vulgate, Kranichfeld, etc. On the form אֲבִי for אַבִי (cf. the voc. אַבָּא = Ἀββᾶ, Rom. viii. 15), see Hitzig, Kranichfeld, and others, on this passage. —On v. 14 cf. v. 11; on v. 15 cf. v. 8. ["It is not to be overlooked that here Belshazzar leaves out the predicate *holy* in connection with אֱלָהִין, *gods*" (*Keil*).]—**The wise men, the astrologers** ("soothsayers"). On this combination cf. on v. 7. —**That they should read this writing, etc.** דִּי, as the accompanying imperfect indicates, is in this place the *telic* conjunction "that, in order that." Upon this clause which indicates the design, depends that which follows, construed with לְ c. Inf. (cf. ii. 16). Concerning the form כְּתָבָה see supra, on v. 7.—**But they could not shew the interpretation of the thing** (or "word"). מִלְּתָא cannot be rendered by "matter, thing," any more than מִלִּין in v. 10; it rather signifies, collectively, the words written on the wall (against Hitzig and others).—Concerning תִּלְתָּא v. 16 b., see supra, on v. 7.

Verses 17–24. *Daniel's censuring address to the king, as the prologue to the interpretation of the writing.* **Let thy gifts be to thyself.** This refusal of the royal presents was designed merely to decisively reject, at the outset, and in a manner becoming the prophet of Jehovah, any influence that might be brought to bear on him. It is not, therefore, a pert expression, which the king might justly punish, nor is it inconsistent with the fact that Daniel ultimately accepted the reward offered for the interpretation, v. 29, since he regarded it as a recognition of his God. The assertion of v. Lengerke, Hitzig, etc., that we should expect either that the enraged king would punish the prophet who bears evil tidings and couples them with threatenings and censure, or that, in v. 29, Daniel would despise the royal purple and the golden necklace, all this is simply adapted to afford a conception of the manner in which a Maccabæan tendency-writer would have treated this history, and of the probable issue to which he would have conducted it.—Verse 18. **O thou king, the most high God,** etc. The absolute position of the vocative אַנְתְּה מַלְכָּא at the beginning of the sentence, places the king rhetorically in a living relation with the facts reported in the following clause, with regard to his father Nebuchadnezzar.—Verse 19. **And for the majesty** (or "power") **. . . . all people, nations** ("tribes"), **and languages trembled and feared;** properly, "were trembling and fearing," were in a state of fear and trembling. The Keri has זָיְעִין instead of זאעין, similar to דָּיְרִין (chap. ii. 38; iii. 31; iv. 32) instead of דָּארִין; see on ii. 38. Concerning the triad, "people, tribes, and tongues," see on chap. iii. 4.—**Whom** (-soever) **he would** (cf. Winer, *Gramm.* § 47, 1, a) . . . . **he kept alive.** מַחֵא is derived by Theodotion (ἔτυπτεν) and the Vulgate (*percutiebat*; cf. Luther, "*er schlug*") from מְחָא "to smite;" but the parallelism requires the Aphel partic. of חֲיָא, "to live," and מַחֵא must either be considered as such (namely, as a peculiar, old-Chaldaic contraction of מַחְיֵא, which is generally contracted to מַחֵי, *e. g.*, Targ. Deut. xxxii. 39), or, with Saadia, Rashi, Buxt., Bertholdt, Gesenius, Fürst, Hitzig, etc., the usual contracted form מַחֵא must be substituted for מַחֵא. ["The brilliant description of Nebuchadnezzar's power in ver. 18 and 19 has undesirably the object of impressing it on the mind of Belshazzar that he did not equal his father (that monarch) in power and majesty . . . . The last clause in ver. 19 reminds us of 1 Sam. ii. 6, 7" (*Keil*).] Verse 20.

But when his heart was lifted up. רָם = רִים, is a preterite with intransitive signification, not a passive partic., as v. Lengerke suggests. Cf. Winer, § 22, 4.—**And his mind hardened in pride.** רוּחַ, the nearest synonym to לְבַב, is also frequently used interchangeably with it in the Hebrew, *e. g.*, Psa. li. 12, 19. תְּקֵף, in this place, is about equivalent to the Heb. חִזֵּק in Ex. vii. 13.*—**He was deposed . . . , and they took his glory from him**; or, "his glory was taken from him." Instead of וִיקָרָא the best MSS. have ויקרה, which is possibly to be read as וִיקָרֵהּ (Hitzig); but on the other hand the case may be analogous to פִּשְׁרֵא, supra, v. 8 and chap. iv. 15.—Verse 21. **And his heart was made like the** (heart of) **beasts.** Read שַׁוִּי, not שַׁוִּיו (Keri) or שֻׁוִּי (v. Leng., Hitzig), or even שַׁוִּי (Ewald). The 3d sing. active שַׁוִּי is used, instead of the more usual 3d plural active, to express an impersonal sense. There are thus three several modes of indicating that sense employed in vs. 20 and 21: *a*, the passive (הָנְחַת v. 20, טְרִיד v. 21); *b*, the 3d plural active (הֶעְדִּיו v. 20, יְטַעֲמוּנֵּהּ v. 21); *c*, the 3d sing. active (שַׁוִּי v. 21)—a rapid change, that is conditioned by the rhetorical, or if it be preferred, the poetical elevation of Daniel's remarks. — [**And his dwelling was with the wild asses.** This "circumstance is added by the speaker, and not found in chap. iv. 29 (32). It is added for the sake of stronger impression" (*Stuart*).]—**Till he knew that . . . God . . appointeth over it** (or "them") **whomsoever he will.** Cf. chap. iv. 14, at the close of which, as here, the Keri substitutes עֲלַהּ for the Kethib עֲלֵיהּ.—Verse 22. **And thou . . . . hast not humbled thine heart, though thou knewest all this.**† Properly, "*precisely because* (כָּל־קֳבֵל דִּי) thou knewest all this," hence, because of a defiant opposition to the well known design and will of the Highest. The words indicate the reason not for what Belshazzar should have done, but for what *he did not perform* (thus Kranichf. correctly, against v. Lengerke, Hitzig, etc.).—Verse 23. **And thou has praised the gods of silver, and gold,** etc., cf. v. 4. The descriptive addition in this case, "which see not, nor hear, nor know," is based on Deut. iv. 28; cf. Psa. cxv. 5 et seq.; cxxxv. 15 et seq.—**And** (rather "but") **the God in whose hand thy breath is.** Cf Job xii. 10; Num. xvi. 22. On the following, "whose (or "with whom") are all thy ways" (אֹרְחָךְ ways = experiences, Targ. Job viii. 13), cf. Jer. x. 23.—**Hast thou not glorified**; a litotes for, "hast thou dishonored, disgraced." ["This is surely plain and faithful admonition; and probably the king's conscience was smitten by it."—*Stuart.*] —Verse 24. **Then** (or "therefore") **was . . . . . sent from him.** בֵּאדַיִן, properly "then," namely at the time when thou didst thus exalt thyself against God. The *post hoc* in this instance is really a *propter hoc.* — שְׁלִיחַ does not, as, *e.g.*, in Ezra vi. 12 (cf. the Heb. Dan. xi. 42), designate the stretching forth of the hand, as if God Himself were the writer; but rather indicates the emanation of the hand from God in a general way, and therefore, so as not to exclude the intervention of angels, but rather to presume it. Hitzig remarks correctly: "The hand that writes is that of an angel who stood before God (chap. vii. 10), and received the commission to write this."

Verses 25–28. *The reading and interpretation of the writing.* **Mene, Mene, Tekel, Upharsin** = *numbered, numbered, weighed, and-dividers.* The forms מְנֵא, תְּקֵל, and also פְּרֵס, which in v. 28 takes the place of פַּרְסִין, are unmistakably passive participles Peal, by which the *surely-impending future* is expressed in the manner of a *Præteritum propheticum*, but with greater brevity and emphasis. The forcible laconic utterance of a mysterious oracle sounds forth from these disconnected consecutive passive participles; and this tendency and signification appear also in the unusual and antique form of the participles, of which only the first, מְנֵא, has a somewhat regular formation (analogous to קְרֵב, chap. iii. 26, or to שְׁכֵב, for שְׁכִיב, in the later Chaldee), while the *e*-sound in תְּקֵל and פְּרֵס is decidedly abnormal, and conflicts with the ordinary usage. תְּקֵל appears to have been selected as an equivocal mediating form between תְּקִיל, the regular passive participle of תְּקַל, and תְּקַל (from קָלַל, "to be light;" cf. v. 27); מְנֵא was possibly chosen because of its assonance to מָאנַיָּא, vs. 2 and 23; and in like manner פְּרֵס = פְּרִיס may contain an amphibole, by way of an allusion to the name פָּרָס—hence a reference to the world-power which was chiefly instrumental in the "division," *i.e.*, the overthrow of the Chaldæan empire. Kranichfeld rejects, but without any reason, this assumption of a designed two-fold sense of the terms, and especially of תְּקֵל, which is adopted by Hitzig and others; although Hitzig is probably in error when he assigns to פרס (upon the ground of Isa. lviii. 7, and in connection with Ibn-Ezra and Rashi) the meaning of the Heb. שָׁבַר or פָּרַק, "to break."* As v. 28 shows, the writer repre-

* ["The perpetual incense of flattery, coupled with the daily experience of being dependent on no one, and of having every one dependent upon himself, tempts an absolute monarch to feel himself almost a god.—It is fully time for the Almighty to hurl such a hardened sinner down."—*Cowles.*]

† [Keil argues that these words "place it beyond a doubt that Belshazzar knew these incidents in the life of Nebuchadnezzar, and thus that he was his son, since his grandson (daughter's son) could scarcely have been so old that the forgetfulness of the Divine judgment could have been charged against him as a sin." Most readers, however, will regard this as a strained argument, for surely Belshazzar had ample means of knowing what his grandfather had set forth by a royal proclamation, and these events are here not merely alluded to as aggravating his sin, but rather by way of contrast, and possibly for an incitement to similar repentance.]

* [Keil regards פַּרְסִין as "a noun-form, and plur. of

sents the destruction of the Chaldæan empire, which is foretold in פְּרֵס (פָּרְסִין), precisely as a *division* between the allied nations of the Persians and *the Medes*, although he might properly have mentioned the Persians only, as effecting the destruction of the kingdom. The substitution of the plural active partic. פָּרְסִין for the abnormal passive partic. פְּרֵס in the written oracle itself, which results in a change of construction similar to that observed in vs. 20 and 21 (cf. also chap. ii. 7; iii. 9; vi. 14, and the remarks on אָמְרִין, chap. iii. 4), appears to have been made for the sake of clearness. The unusual פְּרֵס would have accorded more exactly with the two preceding terms, but would scarcely have been intelligible; while the plur. וּפַרְסִין, "and dividers," or, "and they divide," could not be misunderstood. (Ewald's interpretation: "and in pieces and in ruins," is without any linguistic proof.) However, the expressions "to number" or "count," and "to weigh" are found elsewhere also, as figures to designate a final judicial determination; cf. Psa. lvi. 9; lxii. 10; Job xxxi. 4, 6. The repetition of מְנֵא as indicating the character of the entire sentence, is designed merely to add a solemn emphasis to the words; cf. the frequent ἀμήν, ἀμὴν λέγω ὑμῖν in the New Testament, and O.-T. passages like Gen. xiv. 10; Deut. ii. 27; xiv. 22, etc.; and, generally, Ewald, *Lehrb.*, § 313 *a*.—Verse 26. **God hath numbered thy kingdom.** מַלְכוּתָךְ is not "thy kingdom," but "thy *kingship*," the duration of thy reign, the days of thy sovereignty.* The verb מְנָה is written with ה probably with design, in order to indicate the change of the vowel as compared with מְנֵא.—**And finished it.** הַשְׁלְמַהּ, literally, "has made it complete," or "has fully numbered it;" *i.e.*, has brought it to the end of the time assigned to it. Cf. תַּשְׁלִימֵנִי, Isa. xxxviii. 12.—Verse 27. **Thou art weighed in the balances, and art found wanting.** "Thou," *i.e.*, thy moral personality, thy moral character and worth; cf. Job xxxi. 6: "Let me be weighed in an even balance, that God may know mine integrity."—Thou "art found wanting" seems to refer to the threatening כִּי קַלּוֹתָ, "for thou art vile" (or "too light"), which the prophet Nahum (i. 14) hurls at the Assyrian king; and in so far may serve to substantiate what has been observed above on the two-fold sense of תְּקֵל. חַסִּיר, properly "wanting" (= חָסֵר), namely in moral worth or capacity.—Verse 28. **Thy kingdom is divided, and given to the Medes and Persians.** In regard to the abnormal form פְּרֵס, which is followed by the regular fem. pass. part., פְּרִיסַת, see above, on v. 25. God is naturally conceived of as the divider; the related tribes of the Medes and the Persians are named as the recipients, although the latter clearly appears as the principal power. The oracle contains an etymological allusion to פְּרָס only, and none to מָדַי, an assonance to which might have been readily found in the root מדד, "to measure" (cf. מִדָּה, מִנְדָּה, Ezra iv. 20; vi. 8; vii. 24). The evident design with which the Persians, as the preponderating power in the Medo-Persian kingdom (for only thus was it known to the author, as the comprehensive וּפַרְסִין indicates cf. on chap. ii. 39), are thus brought into prominence, is not contradicted by chap. vi. 1, where Darius the Mede is mentioned as the first foreign ruler over Babylon after the Chaldæan dynasty was overthrown. The actual state of affairs compelled the author to represent that at that time Media still held the same rank as Persia, at least formally and officially, and at first even gave a dynasty and name to the whole empire; and this was done with sufficient clearness by the mention of the Medes *before* the Persians in this verse.*

Verses 29 and 30. *The consequences.* **Then commanded Belshazzar, and they clothed Daniel;** rather, "and caused Daniel to be clothed." The literal rendering is, "Then said Belshazzar, and they clothed," etc.; a similar construction as in chap. ii. 49; iv. 17, 25. In the Heb וְהַלְבִּשׁוּ (fut. with *vav* convers.—cf. Neh. xiii. 9; 2 Chron. xxiv. 8; Jon. ii. 11), rather than וְהַלְבִּישׁוּ would have corresponded to וְהַלְבִּשׁוּ. The enrobing is therefore to be regarded as immediately succeeding the command, and Hävernick's opinion, that "the sudden death of the king prevented the execution of his design," is evidently wide of the narrator's meaning. The opinion that the prophet was invested with the royal insignia of the purple and the necklace on the same evening, involves no questionable feature, which could lead us to refer the execution of the king's command to the following day (Dereser), or even to regard the whole incident as improbable (Hitzig, etc.); but rather, the *immediate* bestowal of the promised marks of favor and honor harmonizes fully with the oriental despotic methods of administering government and justice, which under different circumstances observed the most rapid modes of executing punishment (see chap. iii. 6, 20 et seq.). The "public announcement" of the promotion which had taken place (the verb כְּרַז = Sanscrit *krus*, κηρύττειν, signifies to proclaim *publicly*, as was shown on chap. iii. 4), in the same night and in every street by means of heralds, is however an unjustified demand which the closing words of v. 29 by no means involve. The solemnity in question may have been confined to the range of the royal palace, and even

פְּרֵס = Hebr. פֶּרֶס (cf. פַּרְסֵיהֶן, Zech. xi. 16), in the sense of broken pieces, fragments." He adds that מְנֵא "is twice given perhaps only for the sake of the parallelism, so as to maintain two members of the verse, each of two words."]

* [The author is led to this forced interpretation by his attempt to identify Belshazzar with Evil-merodach, and consequently to defer the capture of Babylon beyond the night under consideration.]

* ["In the naming of the Median before the Persian there lies a notable proof of the genuineness of this narrative; for the hegemony of the Medes was of a very short duration, and after its overthrow by the Persians the form of expression used is always '*Persians and Medes*,' as is found in the book of Esther."—*Keil.*]

to the banquet hall (which, according to v. 1, must be regarded as an extended building, and as filled with an extraordinary multitude).—Concerning the probable motive (namely, because his *God and Lord* was thus honored) which induced Daniel, despite his former refusal, to accept the expressions of the royal favor, see on v. 17. In connection with this, the assumption is still admissible, that any protest which the prophet may have offered, remained without effect, in view of the stormy haste of the king in his alarm, and was lost amid the acclamations and the noisy conversation of the excited throng. Cf. Jerome: "*Accepit autem* (*Daniel*) *insigne regium, torquem et purpuram, ut Darius, qui erat successurus in regnum, fieret notior et per notitiam honoratior. Nec mirum, si Baltasar, audiens tristia, solverit præmium, quod pollicitus est. Aut enim longo post tempore credidit ventura, quæ dixerat, aut dum Dei Prophetam honorat, sperat se veniam consecuturum.*"—Verse 30. **In that night was Belshazzar, the king of the Chaldæans, slain**—evidently through a conspiracy of a number of his magnates, which may have existed previously, but which did not attempt the execution of its design, until the interpretation of the mysterious writing by Daniel gave the conspirators courage. Only this opinion seems to be justified by the language of this passage and by the context,* to the exclusion of the more general view, by which the king was slain at the hands of the victorious Medo-Persians, who are supposed to have taken the city on that night, and by which Belshazzar is in consequence identified with Nabonidus, the last Chaldæan king—all of which is based on a combination of Isa. xvi.; xxi. 5; Jer. li. 39; and of Xenophon, *Cyrop.* vii. 5, 15 et seq.; Herodotus, I. 190, etc., with this narrative. The latter view has recently been defended, especially by Hengstenberg (p. 325 et seq.), Keil (*Einl.*, p. 457), Hävernick, etc., and also by nearly all the rationalistic expositors and critics (also by Stähelin, *Einl. ins A. T.*, p. 350 et seq.), and is certainly supported by the opening verse of chap. vi., in case it be immediately connected with the one before us, as is done by the writers named. It is however more than questionable whether this arrangement corresponds to the conception and design of the author; for (1) the words, "And Darius the Median took the kingdom," together with the subjoined reference to his age, "being about threescore and two years old," seems intended to *introduce* the narrative concerning Darius and his relations to the Babylonian dynasty; much rather than to close that relating to Belshazzar. (2) Berosus and Abydenus *relate nothing* of a taking of Babylon while a luxurious banquet, held by the last Chaldæan king and his magnates, was in progress, as the tradition of Xenophon and Herodotus asserts (cf. Introd. § 8, note 3, and especially the extracts from Kranichfeld on this question there adduced). (3) Berosus, in Josephus, *Ant.* x. 11, 1, does not, indeed, state that Nabonidus, the last Babylonian king, became the victim of a conspiracy, but he does ascribe that fate to Evil-merodach, the immediate successor of his father Nebuchadnezzar (cf. vs. 11, 13, 18, 22). The conspiracy in the case of the latter was headed by Neriglissar, the brother-in-law of the king, and removed the latter under circumstances entirely similar to those under which Belshazzar is said by our passage to have been slain, by murderers whose names are not given. The identity of the latter with Evil-merodach thus becomes highly probable (cf. Introd. l. c.). (4) Finally, the prophecy of the mysterious writing in v. 25, which transfers the Chaldæan empire to the hands of the Medes and Persians, does not *oppose*, but it rather *favors*, the mode of division we advocate, on which an entirely new section begins with chap. vi. 1. For precisely as in chap. ii. 38, 39, Nebuchadnezzar, the head of gold, appears first as an individual, and then as identified with his dynasty and as the representative of the Babylonian world-kingdom, so Belshazzar appears first under the conception of a single person—in the words, "numbered, numbered, weighed"—but afterward as identified with his kingdom, in the closing prediction expressed by פְּרֵס or פַּרְסִין.* The interval of perhaps 22–24 years which thus falls between his own destruction and that of his kingdom, will, in view of the recognized perspective character of all prophecy, appear no more questionable than the still greater number of years which, according to that earlier prediction, were to elapse between the death of Nebuchadnezzar and the ruin of his dynasty. Similar groupings of immediate with more distant events are frequent in the O.-T. prophecies; a particularly noteworthy and instructive instance of which fact may be found in the remarkable prophecy to the wife of Jeroboam by Ahijah of Shiloh in 1 Kings xiv., that comprehends three distinct events, between which extended intervals intervene: (1) The death of the sick prince, Abijah (vs. 12, 13); (2) the overthrow of Jeroboam's dynasty, more than 28 years later (vs. 10, 14; cf. 1 Kings xv. 29 et seq.); (3) the ruin of the kingdom of Israel, which did not transpire until two centuries afterward (v. 15 et seq.; cf. 2 Kings xvii.). The fundamental law of all Messianic typology, by which later events are grouped organically with earlier ones, and by which one and the same guilty act conditions a succession of Divine judgments in the course of developments, underlies this collocation in the perspective vision of a single prophecy. "The cause of the sad end of the kingdom of the ten tribes existed already in the beginning made and cultivated by Jeroboam, two and a half centuries before; the fate that extinguishes the house of Jeroboam is at bottom the same which destroys the kingdom of the ten tribes. Jeroboam's sin destroys his dynasty and his kingdom; for this reason the destruction of both is comprehended in the same prophecy, and not merely because the destruction of the dynasty coincides with that of the kingdom" (Kranichfeld; cf. also Bähr, on 1 Kings chap. xiv. p. 149

*[The requirements of the language are obviously met quite as well by the presumption that the king fell that same night together with his empire, and so the author candidly admits a little further on, although himself driven to another view by his preconceived theory of the identity of Belshazzar with Evil-merodach.]

* [The weakness of these arguments is obvious, and indeed seems to have been apparent to the writer himself. The collateral considerations which he adduces below are too vague to support a theory so plainly at variance with the tenor of the text and its connections.]

of vol. 7 of the *Bibelwerk*). Substantially the same principles apply to the predictions of evil denounced by our prophet against Nebuchadnezzar and his kingdom, and against Belshazzar and his kingdom. The connection of widely separate events which they embody, is natural and organically necessary; and therefore the reference to *two* events of fulfilment, although separate in point of time, upon which we insist, involves no arbitrary features.—The assertion of Keil (*Einl.* l. c.) that if the two events were not coincident, the author would have been required to state, in chap. vi. 1, how the second fact in the fulfilment stands related to the first, or, in other words, "when and how the transmission of the kingdom to the Medes and Persians came to pass," is entirely uncalled for, and is opposed by the analogy of Ahijah's oracle, whose final and complete realization by the overthrow of Israel, is likewise *not expressly* noticed; and in addition the *mere mention* of the taking of Babylon by Darius is a sufficient indication of the anti-typical relation of that event to chap. v. 25–28. The annexed reference to the age of Darius seems rather to indicate a reference to a period considerably later, than a design to designate the particular night in which Belshazzar was slain as falling in the sixty-second year of Darius. There was certainly no apparent motive for the author to make a chronological statement of this sort.—In relation to the peculiar opinion of Ebrard (*Die Offenbarung Johannis erklärt*, p. 55 et seq.), that chap. v. 30 together with chap. vi. 1, refers to the overthrow of Laborasoarchad, the grandson and third successor of Nebuchadnezzar, by Nabonidus (= Darius the Mede), see on chap. vi. 1 et seq. (cf. supra Introd. § 8, notes 3 and 4).

Ethico-fundamental principles related to the history of salvation, apologetical remarks, and homiletical suggestions.

1. The principal object in an apologetic point of view will have been realized in this section, whenever the identity of Belshazzar with Evil-merodach is established, and when, in consequence, the repeated designation of Nebuchadnezzar as his father (vs. 11, 13, 18, 22), the correspondence of the mode of his sudden and violent death (v. 30) with that attested by Berosus with regard to Evil-merodach, and the accession of Darius the Mede to the throne of Babylon at a period considerably later, shall have been properly substantiated. After what has been observed upon this question on v. 30, and also in the Introd. (§ 8, note 3), it only remains to examine the question, "In how far does the narrative yield to the tendency-critical attempts to represent it as a romantic fiction of the Maccabæan age?"—According to Bleek (*Einl.* § 266), v. Lengerke (*Daniel*, p. 241 et seq., p. 256) and others, the story was inspired by the plundering of the temple at Jerusalem by Antiochus Epiphanes in the year B. C. 168, and above a year before the Maccabæan revolt. The brutal manner in which the Syrian king at that time penetrated into the temple of Jehovah, and seized, with polluted hands, the golden lavers and other sacred vessels (1 Macc. i. 21 et seq.; 2 Macc. v. 15 et seq.), is said to have led the pseudo-Daniel to compose this history, and "by the fate of Belshazzar to warn the Syrian monarch, that a similar Divine judgment would be visited on him, because of his sacrilege." But the narrative concerning the Seleucidæ and the Maccabees makes no mention of a luxurious banquet, such as a sacrificial feast, at which anything transpired that would at all compare with the profanation of the sacred vessels, as described in this chapter; and the only remaining parallel between the passages cited from 1st and 2d Maccabees, and Dan. i. 2 (cf. v. 2), is surely insufficient to justify the adoption of the charge that the history was invented to further a tendency! Any other embellishment of the sacrilege that took place at that time would certainly have been more appropriate than the one here offered, which does not charge the insolent spoiler of the temple with venting his frivolous pride on the stolen relics, but reserves this *for his son and successor!* The tendency-narrator might well be charged with clumsiness, if he had represented his Epiphanes-Belshazzar as not merely easy to be excited and capable of contrition and repentance while influenced by terror, but also as promising and conferring the highest dignities and honors of his kingdom upon a zealous theocrat and prophet of Jehovah. The circumstance that such a theocrat is permitted to accept such honors and rewards (v. 29) without further question, is likewise in strange contrast with the rigid monotheism and anti-Hellenistic fanaticism of the Judaism of Maccabæan times, as whose representative the author is said to have written, and for which his work is alleged to have been designed (cf. 1 Macc. i. 24; Dan. xi. 28).—In no wise superior to this theory of the date of the history, as advocated by Bleek and v. Lengerke, is the assertion of Hitzig, that although this section was not composed before the revolt of the Asmonæans, it yet originated in the first year after that rising took place, immediately after and in consequence of the magnificent feasts which Antiochus Epiphanes held in B. C. 166 near Daphne, when, besides splendid games and luxurious banquets, there was a solemn procession in the presence of many ladies of the highest, as well as of lower rank, in which "the images of all conceivable gods were carried, together with an incredible number of golden and silver vessels." If the report by Polybius (l. 31, cp. 3, 4) respecting those festivities be carefully examined, it will reveal a most marked discrepancy between the historical original and the supposed copy, which was framed after it by the alleged pseudo-Daniel. Polybius does not mention the sacrilegious use during those feasts of sacred vessels belonging to the temple with a single syllable. He states indeed that the expense connected with those festivities was chiefly met out of the treasures stolen from various temples —but from *Egyptian* temples, which the pseudo-Daniel would assuredly have placed in the category of the vain "gods of gold, silver, brass, iron, wood, and stone" (vs. 4, 23), and whose desecration he would have been more ready to applaud than to censure. But beyond all this, Polybius reveals no trace of a knowledge that the wild festivities were interrupted by a terrifying incident, which compelled the proud Syrian king to recognize the judicial interference of superior Divine power; nor of any inclination on the part of that prince to honor and promote the prophet who opposed him with earnest censure, despite his boldness; nor yet of a course on the part of the heroic Jewish defender of his faith towards the heathen ruler, which, although not slavishly subservient, was yet courteous, and mindful of the obedience due from a subject to his superior. But if such a meeting between a Jewish zealot and the proud Antiochus, who was fanatically devoted to his Hellenistic faith in the gods, had transpired during a public feast in the Maccabæan age, a materially different kind of incidents might have been looked for, from that described in this chapter. Both the ὑπερηφανία and φρονοκτονία of the bloodthirsty tyrant, and the defiance inspired by faith, prepared for conflict, and careless of death, which was characteristic of the martyr of the theocracy who was engaged in an open revolt against the despot, would have been brought into collision in a manner entirely different from anything found in the report of Polybius—which contains no mention whatever of such an interruption during the feasts of Daphne—and also from the description found in our alleged tendency-forgery. The latter, if it were really the work of a pseudological apocalyptist of the Maccabæan times, would, without any doubt whatever, have presented to our notice persons of the stamp of Matthias (1 Macc. ii. 2, 18 et seq.), Judas and Simon Maccabæus (ibid. chap. iii. 1 et seq.), and Eleazar (2 Macc. vi.) as opponents of the raging heathen, instead of a man like Daniel. A narrative of the kind before us, as respects its contents and progress, would be wholly inconceivable as a product of the orthodox Palestinian Judaism of the year B. C. 166, and would rank as an unequalled historical monstrosity.

2. Accordingly, if confidence may be placed in the pre-Maccabæan, and, what amounts to the same thing, in the Babylonian origin of the history during the captivity, it will be possible for that very reason to examine the miracle of the mysteriously introduced hand which traced the writing, as here recorded, without being restrained by sceptical considerations. It will not be necessary to inquire in this connection, *how* such a thing could take place, but merely, *whether* and *why* such an event was *necessary.*—The necessity for a miraculous announcement to Belshazzar of the impending judgment was conditioned by the fact that his impious conduct had reached an intolerable height when he desecrated the sacred vessels of Jehovah's temple to a common use, and exposed them to the ridicule of a besotted heathen mob, and also that it threatened danger to the faith in Jehovah of the community of exiles. If such an act of presumption was permitted to pass without being Divinely censured and punished, it might certainly be expected that not only the last spark of reverence for the mighty God of the Jews would fade from the consciousness of the royal officials and the Babylonian population, but that the faithful adherence of the Jewish captives to their confession would gradually lose its firmness, and give way to a tendency to favor the idolatrous worship of the Babylonians, and to adopt their luxurious, dissipated, and immoral mode of life. Dangers such as these are described, in a realizing manner, in the second part of Isaiah (see xlvi. 6 et seq.; lvii. 5 et seq.; lxv. 3 et seq.; lviii. 2 et seq.; lix. 3 et seq. Cf. supra, Introd. § 1, note 1); and it appears from the penitential prayer of our prophet in chap. ix., that they existed for his people, and threatened the continuance of the theocracy and its Messianic faith, while in the land of exile. With regard to them it became imperatively necessary that a stern example should be made of the presumptuous king, while giving utterance to his witticisms and blasphemies, and while surrounded by the sycophants of his court and the women of his harem, that thus the name of the only true God might be brought powerfully to the recollection of all, and that an emphatic testimony, coupled with an immediate execution of the threat, might be borne against the impious conduct of the idolaters. Such a testimony, however, could only possess sufficient weight if it were demonstrated to be absolutely miraculous, admitting of no natural explanation (*i.e.*, for the purpose of destroying its supernatural force), and transpiring under the observation of *all* who were present. For this reason all the various attempts to limit the incomprehensible character of the incident, that have been made by modern expositors since M. Geier, are to be rejected, without exception; *e.g.*, the assumption of Geier, which decidedly conflicts with v. 8, that the writing was visible to the king and Daniel, but to no others (similarly Calvin remarks that the Chaldæans were all smitten with blindness—"*ita excæcatos fuisse, ut videndo non viderint*"); the coarsely naturalistic attempt at explanation made by Bertholdt, that the hostile party of the king's courtiers, who were in league with the Medo-Persian besiegers of the city, produced the writing in a purely natural manner, but gave a mysterious appearance to the transaction, in order "to gratify their malice and over-confidence, by announcing his last hour to the victim of their treason;" and finally, the psychological-visionary mode of interpretation, advocated in the last century by Lüderwald, and more recently by Kranichfeld—the latter by means of an attempt to transfer the miraculous feature to the imagination of the king (cf. his observation on v. 8, p. 221: "How and when during the hilarious banquet the writing itself was traced on the wall, was of no importance to the author, as the wonderful feature was alone significant for his purpose, that the king should observe, at the moment of the blasphemous act by which he ridiculed the God of Israel, the hand which wrote the sentence that changed the confident humor of the idolater into anxious fear"). In opposition to these naturalizing interpretations, and especially to the one last mentioned, see the remarks on v. 5, and compare Buddeus, *Hist. eccl. V. Test.*, II. p. 508: "*Verum quis non videt, hæc omnia ad meras conjecturas redire, quæ eadem rejiciuntur facilitate, qua afferuntur. Satius itaque fuerit, in iis acquiescere, quæ Daniel ipse de hac re tradiderit, scripturam scil. ita comparatam fuisse, ut sapientes et magi, etsi eam viderent* (v. 8), *non tamen legere, multo minus interpretari potuerint; Danielem autem eam ita et legere et interpretari potuisse, ut rex ipse statim*

convinceretur, lectionem istam atque interpretationem veram esse." Also cf. Pfeiffer, *Dubia vexata*, p. 503 ss., and Starke, *Synops.* on the passage.

3. In accordance with this, the homiletical treatment of the section is chiefly concerned with the miracle of the writing and its mysterious origin and contents, as the central point of the narrative, and also of its theological and ethical importance. As in the preceding chapter the object of the narrative was to show that "pride goeth before destruction," so the aim here is to illustrate the "judgments that are prepared for scorners" (Prov. xix. 29), the "snare" into which "they bring the whole city" (Prov. xxix. 8), the "non-immunity from punishment of the blasphemers of the Divine Wisdom" (Wisd. i. 6). Cf. Psa. i. 1; Jer. xv. 17; Prov. xiii. 1; xiv. 6; xxiv. 9; also Ecclus. xxvii. 28: "Mockery and reproach are from the proud; but vengeance as a lion shall lie in wait for them;" Psa. lxxii. 4: "He shall break in pieces the oppressor" (or blasphemer); 1 Cor. v. 10: "Nor revilers . . . shall inherit the kingdom of God,"—and other oracles directed against the reviling and blaspheming of the Holy One, which may afford a theme for a homiletical treatment of the section as a whole. Starke is therefore correct in designating as the leading features of the narrative "Belshazzar's transgression and his punishment." Cf. Geier's arrangement of subjects in this chapter: "(1) *Regium flagitium* (v. 1–4); (2) *subsequens portentum* (v. 5, 6); (3) *portenti interpretamentum, partim ut profanis impossibile* (v. 7–6), *partim ut Danieli expeditum ac facile* (v. 10–28); (4) *interpretamenti complementum* (v. 29, 30)."—With reference to the relation of the fundamental idea in this narrative to that of the preceding section, cf. Melancthon: "*Supra proposuit regem agentem pœnitentiam et propagantem veros cultus, quem Deus etiam ornavit præmiis. Nunc addit contrarium exemplum regis impii, restituentis idolatriam, non agentis pœnitentiam, quem Deus punit et regno exuit . . . Has blasphemias enim cito sequuntur pœnæ, juxta secundum præceptum: 'Non habebit Deus insontem,' etc.* (Ex. xx. 7)."

Upon separate points the following passages may be used, as furnishing suitable matter for homiletical discussion.

Verses 2–4. Luxurious banquets and carousals are dangerous precipices, even for the pious and unsuspecting (cf. Jude v. 12); at them Satan himself is the host and master (Cramer, in Starke, under reference to 1 Cor. x. 20), and there religion, the fear of God, brotherly love, uprightness, morality—and, in short, everything is forgotten (Starke).

Verse 17. Daniel's disinterestedness and modesty. On these Jerome observes: "*Æmulemur Danielem, regis dignitatem et munera contemnentem, qui absque pretio proferens veritatem jam illo tempore præceptum evangelicum sequabitur: 'Gratis accepistis, gratis date'* (Matt. x. 8). *Alioquin et tristia nuntiantem indecens erat libenter dona accipere.*"

Verses 25–28. The oracle against Belshazzar, whose spirit is: "If thou wilt neglect to *number* thy days, to *weigh* thyself in the balance of divine righteousness (Job xxxi. 6), and to *measure* thyself by the rule of the Divine law, thou shalt be weighed by God in the scale of His judgment, and—*be found wanting.*" Cf. the figure of farming grain, Am. ix. 9; Isa. xxx. 24; Jer. xv. 7; Matt. iii. 12; Luke xxii. 31, etc.; and also Joachim Lange: "Outside of Christ we are always wanting in the scales of God, and are lighter than nothing," Psa lxii. 10, and Starke: "The duration of every kingdom is pre-determined by God; without the permission of God, no monarch is able to extend or limit it," etc.

---

6. *The deliverance of Daniel from the lion's den.*

CHAP. VI. 1–29.[1] [English Bible, v. 31–vi. 28.]

31 Darius the Median took [received] the kingdom, *being* about three score and
two years old [as a son of sixty and two years].
1 It pleased [seemed good before] Darius to set over the kingdom a hundred
and twenty princes [satraps], which should be over the whole [in all the] king-
2 dom; and over[2] these [them], three presidents, of whom Daniel *was* first
[one]; that the [these] princes might give accounts [the reason] unto them,
and the king should have no damage [not be damaged].
3 Then this Daniel was preferred [made eminent] above the presidents and
princes, because an excellent spirit *was* in him; and the king thought to set
4 him over the whole realm [all the kingdom]. Then the presidents and princes
sought [were seeking] to find occasion against [cause *as* to] Daniel concerning
[from *the* side of] the kingdom; but [and] they could find none occasion nor
fault [corrupt *thing*]; forasmuch as he *was* faithful, neither was there any error
[wrong] or fault [corrupt *thing*] found in him.
5 Then said these men, [That] We shall not find any occasion against [cause *as*
to] this Daniel, except we find *it* against him concerning [in] *the* law of his God.
6 Then these presidents and princes assembled [crowded] *together* to [upon] the
7 king, and said thus unto him, King Darius, live for ever. All the presidents of

the kingdom, the governors, and the princes, the counsellors, and the captains
[pashas], have consulted together to establish a royal [*or*, for the king to establish
a] statute [an established *act* of the king], and to make a firm decree [confirm an in-
terdict], that whosoever [any *one* that] shall ask a petition of [an asking from]
any god or man for [till] thirty days, save of [except from] thee, O king, he
8 shall be cast *into the* den of [the] lions. Now, O king, [mayest thou] estab-
lish the decree [interdict], and sign the writing, that it *be* not changed [change
not], according to [like] *the* law of *the* Medes [Media] and Persians [Persia],
9 which altereth not [will not pass away]. Wherefore [Therefore the] king
Darius signed the writing and the decree [interdict].
10 Now when Daniel [And Daniel, as *soon* as he] knew that the writing *was*
signed, *he* went into his house; and, his [its] windows *being* [*were*] open in his
[its upper] *chamber* toward [in front of] Jerusalem, [and] he[3] kneeled upon his
knees three times a day [in the day], and prayed [*was* praying], and gave
thanks [thanking] before his God, as he did aforetime [because he was doing
11 *so* from before that *time*]. Then these men assembled [crowded *in*], and found
Daniel praying [asking] and making supplication before his God.
12 Then they came near, and spake before the king concerning [upon] *the* king's
decree [interdict]; Hast thou not signed a decree [an interdict], that every
[any] man that shall ask *a petition* of [from] any god or man within [till] thirty
days, save of [except from] thee, O king, shall be cast *into the* den of [the]
lions? The king answered and said, The thing *is* true [word *is* firm] accord-
ing to [like] *the* law of *the* Medes [Media] and Persians [Persia], which altereth
13 not [will not pass away]. Then answered they, and said before the king,
That[4] Daniel, which *is* of [from] the captivity of the children of Judah, regard-
eth not [has not put attention upon] thee, O king, nor [and] the decree [inter-
dict] that thou hast signed, but [and] maketh his petition [*is* asking his asking]
14 three times a day [in the day]. Then the king, when he heard *these* words
[this word (thing)], *was* sore displeased with [it greatly offended upon] him-
self, and [he] set *his* heart on Daniel to deliver him; and he laboured [was
exerting himself] till *the* going down of the sun to deliver [rescue] him.
15 Then these men assembled [crowded] unto [upon] the king, and said unto the
king, Know, O king, that the law of the Medes and Persians *is* [*it is* a law to
Media and Persia], that no decree nor statute [interdict and established *act*]
16 which the king establisheth [shall establish] may *be* changed [change]. Then
the king commanded [said], and they brought Daniel, and cast *him into the* den
of [the] lions. *Now* the king spake and said unto Daniel, Thy God, whom
thou[3] servest continually [*art* serving in continuity], he[3] will [may he] deliver
17 thee. And a stone was brought, and laid upon *the* mouth of the den; and the
king sealed it with his *own* signet, and with *the* signet of his lords, that *the*
purpose [(will) matter] might not *be* changed [change] concerning [in *respect to*]
Daniel.
18 Then the king went to his palace, and passed [lodged] *the night* fasting:
neither were instruments of music brought [and concubines he did not bring]
19 before him, and his sleep went from [fled upon] him. Then the king arose very
early in the morning [in the dawn would rise in the *early* light], and went in
20 haste unto the den of [the] lions. And when he came [near] to the den, he
cried with a lamentable [pained] voice unto Daniel: *and* the king spake and
said to Daniel, *O* Daniel, servant of the living God, is thy God, whom thou[3]
servest continually [*art* serving in continuity], able[5] to deliver thee from the
21 lions? Then said [talked] Daniel unto [with] the king, O king, live for ever.
22 My God hath sent his angel, and hath shut *the* lions' mouths, that [and] they
have not hurt me: forasmuch as before him innocency was found in [to] me;
and also before thee, O king, have I done no hurt.
23 Then *was* the king exceeding glad [it greatly rejoiced] for him [upon him-
self], and commanded [said] that they should take Daniel up out of the den.
So [And] Daniel was taken up out of the den, and no *manner of* hurt was
found upon [in] him, because he believed in his God.
24 And the king commanded [said], and they brought those men which [who] had

accused[6] Daniel, and they cast *them into the* den of [the] lions, them, their children, and their wives; and the lions had *the* mastery of them, and brake all their bones *in pieces* or ever [ere] they came at *the* bottom of the den.[7]
25 Then [the] king Darius wrote unto all people, nations, and languages,[8] that
26 dwell in all the earth; Peace be multiplied unto you.[9] I make[10] a decree, That in every dominion of my kingdom *men* tremble and fear[11] before *the* God of Daniel; for he *is* the living God, and steadfast for ever, and his kingdom *that*
27 which shall not be destroyed, and his dominion *shall be even* unto the end. *He* delivereth [delivering] and rescueth [rescuing], and *he* worketh [working] signs and wonders in heaven [the heavens] and in [the] earth, who hath delivered Daniel from *the* power of the lions.
28 So [And] this Daniel prospered in *the* reign of Darius, and in *the* reign of Cyrus the Persian.

GRAMMATICAL NOTES.

[[1] As Chap. vi. in the original begins with verse 31 of the A. V., there is a difference of *one* in numbering the verses of this section.—[2] The form עֵלָּא, followed by מִן, seems like a noun in the emphatic state, and may not inaptly be rendered, "*as the chief above.*"—[3] The pronoun, being expressed, is emphatic.—[4] דִּי here = ὅτι expletive.—[5] The order of words is emphatic: *Thy God . . . . has He been able.*—[6] Literally, *that ate his pieces of, i. e.*, backbit, as in chap. iii. 8.—[7] The order and style of the original are very emphatic: *and they did not reach to the earth of the den till that* (before) *the lions ruled over them*, etc..—[8] The terms in the original are the same as in chap. iii. 4, *the nations, the peoples, and the tongues.*—[9] Literally, *May your peace be great.*—[10] *From me is made.*—[11] *They shall be trembling and fearing from.*]

EXEGETICAL REMARKS.

Verse 1 [v. 31]. *Transitional introductory observations.* **And Darius the Median took the kingdom**, etc. The copula before דָּרְיָוֶשׁ serves, indeed, to connect the present section closely with the preceding one, and indicates that its subject is more intimately related to the foregoing, than is the case in chapters iii., iv., and v., which begin without any copulative particle whatever. The ו however, does not compel the assumption that chapters v. and vi. were properly a unit in their plan and the time of their composition (Hitzig, Kranichfeld); for (1) chap. ii., although forming a decidedly independent whole, likewise begins with the copula, as do also numerous sections in the historical and prophetical portions of the Old Testament, whose subjects are independent of what precedes them. (2) Kranichfeld's opinion (p. 210) that chap. v. ought to conclude with a "theocratic panegyrical closing sentence" similar to chap. vi. 27, 28, if it were to rank as an independent and complete section in itself, is apparently confirmed, indeed, by the closing verses of chaps. ii., iii., and iv., but is decidedly opposed by chap. i.; which has no such doxology at the close. (3) Chapters v. and vi. are distinguished from each other by several unmistakable differences in the mode of expression and representation, which indicate the composition of these sections at different times. Notice especially the character of the descriptions in chap. v., which are more circumstantial and full of repetitions than those in chap vi. (cf. vs. 2, 3, 4 with v. 23; v. 7 with v. 12; v. 12 with v. 16; v. 16 with vs. 7 and 29, etc.). (4) The transactions recorded in the two sections are separated by an interval of at least twenty-two years (cf. supra, on chap. v. 30) since the events of chap. v. transpired under the fourth reign before the close of the Chaldæan dynasty, while chap. vi. falls in the reign of Darius the Mede,—which covered about two years and a half—and probably not in its opening period (see vs. 15, 17); and chap. v. creates the impression that it was composed immediately after the events which it records transpired, and that, like all the narratives in the historical part of the book, it originated while they were still fresh in the recollection of the writer (cf. Introd., § 4, note 2). The connection of the two sections by means of a copulative ו, despite the difference in the time of their composition, is probably owing to the circumstance that at the close of chap v. only the beginning of the fulfilment of the oracle addressed to Belshazzar had been noticed, while the principal fact, which concludes the fulfilment, is reserved for the narrative in the present section; cf. on chap. v. 30.—For the view that "Darius the Mede" can only designate Cyaxares, the son of Astyages and father-in-law of Cyrus, see Introd., § 8, note 4. Perhaps the Sept. also referred to this Cyaxares, when it translated this passage Καὶ Ἀρταξέρξης ὁ τῶν Μήδων παρέλαβεν τὴν βασιλείαν καὶ Δαρεῖος πλήρης τῶν ἡμερῶν καὶ ἔνδοξος ἐν γήρει; by Ἀρταξέρξης they may have intended Astyages, the father of Darius Medus, and by the predicate πλήρης κτλ., which they applied to Darius, they may have attempted to repeat the כְּבַר שְׁנִין of the second half of the verse (cf. Michaelis, *Oriental. Bibl.*, iv. 20). Despite the marked ignorance of history which the Alexandrians occasionally reveal, they can hardly be presumed to have been guilty of the gross anachronism of confounding the Median Darius with Darius Nothus, the son of Artaxerxes I. Longimanus (against Hävernick).—Ebrard (*Die Offenbarung Johannis* [in Olshausen's *Bibl. Kommentar*], p. 55 et seq., and in a review of Füller's *Prophet Daniel* in the Güterslohe *Allg. literar. Anzeiger*, October, 1868, p. 267), attempts, in harmony with his assumption that Belshazzar was identical with Laborasoarchad, to identify Darius the Mede with Nabonidus, whom the conspirators who slew Laborasoarchad elevated to the throne (similarly Syncellus, Scaliger, Petavius and Buddeus). In this way he certainly succeeds in removing every difference between the time of chap. v. 30 and vi. 1; but he neglects to notice (1) that Laborasoarchad was a grandson of Nebuchadnezzar, instead of being his son, as chap v. 11 et seq. requires; (2) that Nabonidus, according to the express statement of Berosus, was not of Median, but of Babylonian descent, although not of royal blood; (3) that according to vs. 9, 13, and 16 (the "laws of the Medes and Persians") the administration of the king in question is characterized, in the plainest manner, as modelled and organized after the Medo-Persian code, rather than the Babylonian; (4) that the system of espionage and denunciation (vs. 12, 14, 16), the barbarous custom of executing the families of criminals (v. 25) together with the culprit, and also the aristocratic constitutional procedure connected with the promulgation of the prohibition and with the sealing of the stone (vs. 8, 18), all likewise refer to specifically Medo-Persian arrangements, such as could not yet have been introduced under Nabonidus. These arguments will also hold good against A. Scheuchzer, of Zurich, who, without reference to Ebrard, and to some extent basing his views on different grounds, has recently likewise attempted to identify Nabonidus with Darius the Mede (*Assyrische Forschungen*, in Heidenheim's *Vierteljahrsschrift für engl.-theolog. Forschung*, vol. IV., No. 1, p. 17 et seq.).—["The addition of מָדָיָא (Kethib) forms on the one hand a contrast to the expression, 'the king of the Chaldæans' (chap. v. 30), and on the other hand it points forward to פָּרְסָיָא, ver. 29 (28); it, however, furnishes no proof that Daniel distinguished the Median kingdom from the Persian; for the kingdom is not called a Median kingdom, but it is only said of Darius that he was of Median descent, and, ver. 29 (28), that Cyrus the Persian succeeded him. In קַבֵּל, *he received* the kingdom, it is indicated that Darius did not conquer it, but received it from the conqueror" (*Keil*).]—**Being about threescore and two years old.** This precise and concrete designation of his age was hardly designed to note that he had overthrown the Chaldæan empire after attaining to old age and when he was no longer competent to the personal conduct of warlike operations (Kranichfeld); for such a purpose is not expressed with sufficient clearness, and moreover, the implied reference to the weakness and defenceless condition of the declining Babylonian empire would involve a historical inaccuracy which cannot well be charged against the author. The real motive that led him to mention the age of Darius can only consist in the design to refer to the considerably later time of the taking of Babylon, in its relation to the events that had just been described (cf. supra, on chap. v. 30).*

Verses 2, 3 [1, 2]. *The new constitution of the empire under Darius, and the position assigned to Daniel.* **It pleased Darius to set over the kingdom a hundred and twenty princes.** The Sept. increases this number to 127, probably with a reference to Esth. i. 1. Josephus' *Ant.* X. 13 multiplies it by three (ἑξήκοντα καὶ τριακόσιοι σατράπαι), perhaps because he believed each of the three chief præfects to have been placed over 120 satraps, or because he believed himself obliged to make the number of satrapies equal to that of the days in the year. The number 120 is to be retained, in opposition to both these uncritical attempts to enlarge it, although no other authorities mention so large a number of satrapies or provinces in the Medo-Persian empire at the time of its first organization under Darius-Cyaxares and Cyrus, and although according to both Herodotus and Xenophon their number seems to have been considerably smaller at that period. The former of these authors mentions no definite organization of satrapies by Cyrus whatever, and remarks of Darius Hystaspis that he founded *in all only twenty* of such provinces for the whole empire (III. 89); the latter notices satraps under Cyrus as well, but mentions only nine, eight of whom were appointed for Asia Minor and one for Arabia—from which it might be concluded that the aggregate number of such officials did not much exceed twenty, and perhaps, did not even reach that number (*Cyrop.* VII. 4, 2; VIII. 6). The statements of these Greek historians do not, however, compel us to doubt the accuracy of Daniel's report, or to reduce the number from 120 to 20; for various indications lead to the conclusion that the number and boundaries of the satrapies varied exceedingly in different periods of the Persian empire. The three lists of Persian provinces, for instance, which are found among the inscriptions of Darius (at Persepolis, at Behistun, and at Nakshi Rustam) enumerate on the whole thirty-three satrapies or provinces, without permitting us to regard the number as exhaustively complete. The opinion that such changes among the satrapies actually occurred is further supported by Ezra viii. 36, where *several* satraps beyond the Euphrates are mentioned as holding office under Artaxerxes, while Herodotus, III. 91, knew of but one; and also by Esth. i. 1, where the whole number of the Persian satrapies is fixed at 127, etc. Hence, it must probably be assumed that at different times the arrangement of provinces varied in the Persian empire, and that a subdivision of the realm into numerous smaller sections (whose number, 120, may have been symbolically significant, and relating to astronomical conditions) existed already under Darius-Medus and Cyrus, but in such a manner that in addition a reckoning by larger, and consequently less numerous provinces, was customary. The division into 120 smaller satrapies may have descended to the Medo-Persians from the Chaldæo-Babylonian world-kingdom, in which, according to chap. iii. 2, 27, the title of satrap had long been known, and on account of its almost sacred astronomical importance, they may have gladly admitted it into the constitution of their realm. The enumeration by larger and less numerous (20–30) satrapies may have been chiefly in use in the official language of the court and the arts in the kingdom of the Achæmenidæ, as being

* [Rather it may have been as a premonition of the short interval during Darius's rule before the full assumption of dominion by Cyrus in person at Babylon.]

a national Medo-Persian institution, and for that reason may have been principally or exclusively observed by the Greeks. The Biblical enumeration, having a Babylonian origin, may therefore be properly designated as the *esoteric* or *hieratic*, and the ancient Aryan division, supported by the classics, as the *exoteric* or *demotic*. Nor is it a questionable feature that on this explanation the title *kshatrapa* (*shôitrapaiti*, *achashdarpan*) was applied interchangeably to the administrators of both larger and smaller divisions; since this harmonizes well with the fluctuations of later Hellenistic writers in rendering the word and especially with the indecision of the Sept. On this question, and in relation to the origin and significance of the title of satrap, cf. the exeg. remarks on chap. iii. 2.—Verse 3 [21]. **And over these three presidents, of whom Daniel was first**; rather, "was one." [The following verse, however, shows that he was the principal one]. The סָרְכִין (in the Targ. equivalent to שׁוֹטְרִים, "arrangers, overseers") were certainly "chief-præfects, princes, ministers," whether the סרך is regarded as related to שַׂר, *i.e.*, as derived, by means of the Pers. particle of derivation ךְ, from the Zend *sara* (Gr. κάρα, Pers. *ser*), "head," or as related to the Sanscr. *çarana*, "protector," or also to *târaka*, "steersman" (the former according to Gesenius, the latter, to Hitzig). The dignity of these *Sarekin* was doubtless identical with that of the *Taltaïn* or "triumvirs," who are mentioned in the preceding chapter (vs. 7, 16, 29) as the superior princes of the realm, or heads of the government under Belshazzar. Accordingly, like the 120 satraps, they were a class of dignitaries in the Medo-Persian kingdom, whose office was modelled after the Babylonian precedent, but was discontinued at a later period, or perhaps, was developed into the institution of the *seven counsellors* of the Persian kings (corresponding to the seven Amshaspands—cf. Esth. i. 14; Ezra vii. 14; Herod. III. 31). Daniel owed his elevation to this rank to the circumstance that he had already been raised to the dignity of a triumvir by Belshazzar, and had probably remained in that office until the overthrow of the Chaldæan kingdom; as also Nebuchadnezzar, according to chap. ii. 48, 49, had already conferred on him a position of distinguished political and priestly power and eminence.—**That the princes** (satraps) **might give accounts to them, and the king should have no damage,** *i.e.*, not suffer loss in his revenues (cf. נְזִק Ezra iv. 13, 15, and נֵזֶק Esth. vii. 4). The satraps are thus designated more particularly as officers of *finance*, which doubtless constituted one of their chief functions; cf. Herod. III. 89 et seq.

Verses 4, 5 [3, 4]. *The ill-will of the other grand officials of the realm against Daniel.* **Then this Daniel was preferred above** (showed himself superior to) **the presidents, etc.** מִתְנַצַּח, "distinguished himself, outshone them." The demonstrative דְּנָה, "this," which is connected with the name of Daniel only here and in v. 20, is conceived and spoken from the standpoint of his opponents, who look with envy on him (*istum*) whom God has hitherto so highly favored with His assistance. In this way the succeeding remark, "because an excellent spirit was in him" (cf. chap. v. 12), may likewise be explained without involving any suspicion of self-laudation on the part of the narrator.—**And the king thought to set him over the whole realm,** hence, to promote him to the office of grand-vizier or prime minister—the superior of the "triumvirs" or Sarekin. The Targums always employ the Ithpael for the intransitive עֲשִׁית, "to be inclined, to purpose." ["This intention of the king stirred up the envy of the other presidents" (*Keil*)].—Verse 5 [4]. **Then the presidents . . . . sought to find occasion against Daniel concerning the kingdom,** *i.e.*, they sought to assail his official character; and only after frequent proofs that their efforts in this direction were futile, did they direct their attention to his religious standpoint (v. 6 et seq.). *—**But they could find none occasion nor fault.** עִלָּה, as before, is an "occasion, opportunity, pretext," upon which the accusation might be based ["as αἰτία, John xviii. 38; Matt. xxvii. 37, *an occasion for impeachment*" (Keil)]. This more general term may be co-ordinated with שְׁחִיתָה, "wickedness," because it is conceived concretely or objectively; and hence also with the following שָׁלוּ, "fault, inadvertence." (from שׁלה, the probable primitive form for שׁנה; cf. in the Gr. μόλις and μόγις). Fidelity is the leading political virtue of the servant or officer of a government (cf. 1 Cor. iv. 2), in like manner as justice and mercy should be the ornament of rulers (chap. iv. 24).

Verses 6–10 [5–9]. *The procuring of a governmental edict pertaining to religion, directed against Daniel.* † **We shall not . . . . against this Daniel, except we find it against him concerning the law of his God.** דָּת אֱלָהֵהּ, the law of Daniel's God, is the theocratic law, considered as the rule of his religious life, and especially of his devotional exercises. Cf. דָּת in Ezra vii. 6, 12, 14, 21, 25, 26; and supra, chap. ii. 9.—Verse 7. **Then these presidents** (princes) **and princes** (satraps) **assembled together to the king**; rather (as marg.), "ran in stormy haste." "*These* princes and satraps" (cf. "these men," v. 6 [5]) were not, of course, *all* of them, without exception, but only those who envied and sought to calumniate Daniel, since only such are here concerned; cf. v. 25 [24]. The idea that *all* the satraps participated is the more improbable, in view of the fact that the possible presence of all in the metropolis is nowhere indicated (not

* ["Such a model of excellence, so far surpassing and so uncomfortably eclipsing themselves, was keenly cutting to these corrupt officers, and aroused their bitterest hostility." —*Cowles*.]

† ["With Satanic cunning the princes shaped this proposed law to take with the king by a bait for his low vanity, and to entrap Daniel through his known decision and firmness in the worship of his God. It was the best compliment they could pay to Daniel that they assumed so confidently that he would pray to God none the less for this monstrous law. It was the keenest reproach to their king that they should anticipate his ready assent to such a law under the impulses of his excessive vanity. Darius was a weak and vain king, else he would have asked, What can be the motive of these men in proposing such a law? Plainly the appended exception, 'Save of thee, O king,' was so grateful to his vanity that it blinded his dull eye to the monstrous nature and possible bearings of this law."—*Cowles*.]

even in v. 8 [7]).—On הַרְגִּשׁוּ, "to rush anywhere in stormy haste, to rush anywhere frequently" [rather, *tumultuously*] (Luther, "came *often*"), cf. the German "*jemanden die Thüre stürmen*" ("to storm somebody's door"); see infra, vs. 12 [11] and 16 [15].—Verse 8. **All the presidents** (princes) **of the kingdom, the governors, and the princes** (satraps), **the counsellors, and the captains** (præfects) **have consulted together**; rather, "have considered it advisable." סָרְכִין seems here to be employed in a more extended sense than heretofore (vs. 3 [2], 5 [4], and 7 [6]), where it designates the chief-præfects who were placed over the satraps; * for the four classes of officials which follow—the same as in chap. iii. 27, but in a different order —are evidently intended to specialize the prefixed general idea of "princes" or "præfects" (thus Chr. B. Michaelis correctly, against Hitzig and others, who in this place also regard the Sarekin as the chief præfects who were Daniel's colleagues). In like manner the term Chaldæans was found to be employed above, at one time to designate a special class of wise men, and at another to denote the whole order of magians (see on chap. ii. 2).†—In relation to אִתְיָעַטוּ, "to determine or agree among themselves," compare the term יָעֵט, "a counsellor," *consiliarius*, as designating one of the principal officers of the Persian king, Ezra vii. 14, 15.—**To establish a royal statute**; rather, "that the king should establish a statute." In view of the accentuation, מַלְכָּא is not to be construed with קְיָם as a genitive ("to establish a royal statute," etc.), but must be regarded as the subject of the Inf. לְקַיָּמָה, so that the object קְיָם is placed between the infinitive and its noun, as in Isa. v. 24; xix. 8; xx. 1 (thus correctly Rosenmüller, Hitzig, Kranichfeld, [Keil], etc., against Theodotion, Vulgate, Luther, Bertholdt, and a majority of moderns).*—**And make a firm interdict** (marg.). The קְיָם which the king was to establish, is at the same time an אֱסָר, "interdict;" in the parallelism of the address it is at first designated generally as a "statute," and afterwards more especially as an "interdict." On אֱסָר, "to bind," in the sense of "to prohibit," see Num. xxx. 10, and also the N.-T. δέειν as the opposite of λύειν, Matt. xvi. 19; xviii. 18.—**That whosoever shall ask a petition . . . . for thirty days**; *i.e.*, during the thirty days next ensuing, from that time until the expiration of thirty days. Literally, "unto thirty days." This number, the triplicate of the ten days in chap. i. 12-15, is a round number, corresponding to the duration of a month, and employed otherwise also as a general period, during which an interdict was imposed on persons; *e.g.*, by the vows of Nazarites, Acts xxi. 26; cf. Tract. *Nasir*, I. 3; Joseph., *de B. Jud.*, II. 15, 1.—The command (or interdict) to pray † during one month only to the king was in this instance specially aimed at Daniel, the pious worshipper of Jehovah, for the purpose of entrapping him; but it was suggested by a national religious custom of older date among the *Medes*, by which Divine honors were rendered to the king. Herodotus, I. 199, refers to this custom, when he remarks that Deioces had introduced the περὶ ἑαυτὸν σεμνύειν for himself and his successors, by removing his person from the observation of his subjects, in order to persuade them that he was ἑτεροῖος (cf. also Xenophon, *Cyrop.*, I. 3, 18). The existence of this custom among the Medes is further substantiated by the fact that the Persians, who were intimately related to the Medes, observed it, as did several others of the Oriental nations of antiquity (*e.g.*, the Egyptians and Ethiopians, according to Diodor., *Sicul.*, I. 90; III. 3, 5)—the former from the peculiar religious reason that they considered the king as the "offspring of the gods" (ἔκγονος θεῶν) and the image of Ormuzd, and even addressed him directly as θεός; cf. Æschylus, *Pers.*, 157, 855; Plutarch, *Themist.*, 27; Cur-

* ["If we compare the list of the four official classes here mentioned with that of the great officers of state under Nebuchadnezzar, ch. iii. 2, the naming of the סִגְנַיָּא before the אֲחַשְׁדַּרְפְּנַיָּא (*satraps*, while in ch. iii. 2 they are named after them) shows that the סִגְנַיָּא are here great officers to whom the satraps were subordinate, and that only the three סָרְכִין could be meant to whom the satraps had to render an account. Moreover, the list of four names is divided by the copula ו into two classes. To the first class belong the סִגְנַיָּא and the satraps; to the second the הַדָּבְרִין, *state councillors*, and the פַּחֲוָתָא, *civil præfects of the provinces.* Accordingly, we will scarcely err if by סִגְנַיָּא we understand *the members of the highest council of state*, by הַדָּבְרַיָּא *the ministers* or *members of the (lower) state council*, and by the satraps and *pechas the military* and *civil rulers of the provinces.* This grouping of the names confirms, consequently, the general interpretation of the כֹּל סָרְכֵי מַלְכוּתָא, for the four classes named constitute the entire chief præfecture of the kingdom. This interpretation is not made questionable by the fact that the סָרְכִין had in the kingdom of Darius a different position from that they held in the kingdom of Nebuchadnezzar; for in this respect each kingdom had its own particular arrangement, which underwent manifold changes according to the times."—*Keil.*]

† ["The whole connection of the narrative plainly shows that the authors of the accusation deceived the king. The council of state, or chief court, to which all the satraps had to render an account, consisted of three men, of whom Daniel was one. But Daniel certainly was not called to this consultation; therefore their pretence that *all* 'presidents of the kingdom' had consulted on the matter, was false. Besides, they deceived the king in this, that they concealed from him the intention of the decree, or misled him regarding it."—*Keil.*]

* [But this construction is extremely harsh, and, as Lengerke remarks, opposed to the usage of אֱסָר מַלְכָּא in v. 13. Even Rosenmüller renders (apparently by inadvertence, however) *decreto regio.* The passages adduced by the author from Isaiah (xix. 8 is not correct) are not altogether in point, as the preposition there is not לְ, but כְּ or בְּ. Had the writer intended such a construction he would naturally have used דִּי with the fut. The Masoretic interpunction, however, undeniably favors it.]

† [The term "בְּעוּ" is here not any kind of request or supplication, but prayer, as the phrase, ver. 14 (13), בָּעֵא בָּעוּתֵהּ, *directing his prayer*, shows. The word וֶאֱנָשׁ does not prove the contrary, for the heathen prayed also to men (cf. ch. ii. 46), and here the clause, *except to the king* places together god and man, so that the king might not observe that the prohibition was specially directed against Daniel."—*Keil.*

tius, VIII. 5, 11; Isocrates, *Panegyr.*, in Brissonius, *de Persar. princ.*, p. 17, and generally, Hengstenberg, *Authentie des Daniel*, etc., p. 127 et seq.; Delitzsch, Art. *Daniel* in Herzog's *Real-Encykl.*, p. 278 et seq. See the Ethico-fund. principles, etc., against the assumption of the modern pseudo-Daniel tendency-criticism, on which the edict of Darius in question is a cunningly invented prototype, and at the same time an exaggerated caricature of the course of Antiochus Epiphanes as described in 1 Macc. i. 41 et seq.; 2 Macc. vi. 1 et seq.—Verse 9 [8]. **Now, O king, establish the decree and sign the writing**; rather, "and record the writing," for רשׁם always signifies to record, and not to sign; and moreover, the Persian edicts received their official stamp as laws from the royal *seal*, instead of the royal signature; * cf. Esth. iii. 10 et seq.; viii. 8.—**That it be not changed, according to the law of the Medes and Persians,** *i.e.*, according to that law of the united Medo-Persian realm, as is somewhat more fully described in v. 16 [15], by which every official edict from the king, issued with certain formalities, should possess *enduring force as law*, hence, "should not be changed" (לָא לְהַשְׁנָיָה, cf. Winer, *Gramm.*, § 46, 3); cf. Esth. i. 19; viii. 8. Against the opinion of Von Lengerke, that the writer here was guilty of an anachronism, since the phrase "the law of the Medes and Persians" must have originated subsequently to the time of Cyrus, cf. supra. Hitzig also rejects this position of Von Lengerke, inasmuch as he denies, for telling reasons, the presumption on which it rests, that דָּת in that formula designates the *whole body of laws* of the kingdom.—[Verse 10 (9). "The king carried out the proposal. וֶאֱסָרָא is explicative: *the writing*, namely, the prohibition (spoken of); for this was the chief matter, therefore אֱסָרָא alone is here mentioned, and not also קְיָם (edict), ver. 8 (7)."—*Keil.*]

Verses 11, 12 [10, 11]. *Daniel's protest, by his conduct, against the royal decree.*† **And, his windows being open in his chamber toward Jerusalem**; rather, "but he [it‡] had open windows," etc. The upper chamber, or attic, receives consideration as being more removed and less liable to be disturbed, hence as being particularly adapted to purposes of devotion; cf. 2 Sam. xix. 1; 1 Kings xvii. 20; Acts i. 13; x. 9.—"Opened windows," כַּוִּין פְּתִיחָן, are the opposite of such as are covered with lattice-work (כַּוִּין זְתִרְמָן, Ezek. xl. 16) by which the view is obstructed. These open windows were required to be "toward Jerusalem," because according to ancient custom the face of the worshipper must be turned towards the temple in that city; for as in Jerusalem the supplicant turned toward the sanctuary (Psa. v. 8; xxviii. 2 etc.), so he turned when abroad towards the "holy city" (Matt. iv. 5) as the site of the temple. This was the case long prior to the captivity; see 1 Kings viii. 33, 35, 38, 44, 48; 2 Chron. vi. 29, 34, 38. The corresponding custom among the Mahommedans (Kibla) with reference to Mecca, appears thus to be the imitation of a custom developed on the primitive soil of Bible lands; and for the earliest followers of Islam Jerusalem itself was Kibla. On the other hand, the ancient Jewish and the most ancient Christian custom prohibited, on the ground of Ezek. viii. 16, 17, the turning of the face in prayer towards the east, *i.e.*, towards the sun (cf. Clement, *Strom.* VII. 724; Origen, *Homil.* V. in Num.; Tertull. *Apol.* c. 16), while the later church, standing on the ground of Mal. iii. 20; Luke i. 78 et seq., zealously recommended that supplicants and houses for prayer should face towards the east, and introduced it into general use. Cf. Bingham, *Origines*, V. 275 ss.—**He kneeled upon his knees three times a day.** Kneeling is mentioned as the characteristic posture of supplicants in 1 Kings viii. 54; 2 Chron. vi. 12; Ezra ix. 5; Luke xxii. 41; Acts vii. 59; ix. 40; xxi. 5; Eph. iii. 14; Clem. Rom. 1 Cor. 48; Hermas, *Pastor, Vis.* I. 1, etc. Cf. O. A. Hubnerus, *de genuflexione* (Halle, 1741); Zöckler, *Krit. Geschichte der Askese* (Frankf. and Erlangen, 1863), p. 350 et seq.—["Daniel offered prayers not to make an outward show, for only secret spies could observe him when so engaged. כָּל־קֳבֵל דִּי does not mean *altogether so as* (Rosenmüller, Von Leng., Maurer, Hitzig), but, as always, *on this account* that, *because*. Because he always did thus, so now he continues to do it"—(*Keil*).]* The custom of praying three times in a day, which is attested for the first time in this passage, and which, according to the Talmudic tradition was first brought into general use among the Jews by the "men of the great synagogue," appears to have taken shape during the Babylonian captivity as a usage observed by pious individuals among the Israelites. The fundamental general idea of this custom is already expressed in Psa. lv. 18; but the desire to find a regular substitute for the morning and evening sacrifices, which were now interrupted, doubtless contributed towards originating the custom, since the Jews were accustomed, from an early period, to regard prayer as in itself a sacrifice with which God is pleased (Hos. xiv. 3; Psa. li. 17; cxvi. 17, etc.), and especially since they associated it in their minds with the evening sacrifice (Psa. cxli. 2; 1 Kings xviii. 36 et seq.;

* [This distinction is rather over-nice; for it was not the *engrossing* of the edict, surely, that the magnates desired, and this of course would not have been done by the royal hand, but his official approval and sanction, such as a signature—whether by writing or stamping the name—only could confer.]

† ["The satraps did not wait long for Daniel's expected disregard of the king's prohibition. . . . He continued this custom (of prayer) even after the issuing of the edict; for a discontinuance of it on account of that law would have been a denying of the faith and a sinning against God. On this his enemies had reckoned. They secretly watched him, and immediately reported his disregard of the king's command. In ver. 11 (10), the place where he was wont to pray is more particularly described in order that it might be shown how they could observe him."—*Keil.*]

‡ ["לֵהּ does not refer to Daniel ('he had opened windows'), but to לְבַיְתֵהּ, *his house had open windows.* If לֵהּ referred to Daniel, then the הוּא following would be superfluous."—*Keil.* The same remark of course will apply to בְּעִלִּיתֵהּ following.]

* ["Blessed man! How quietly, how calmly, how peacefully did thy heart repose on the enduring love and faithfulness of the never-failing power of thy fathers' God!"—*Cowles.*]

Ezra ix. 5; cf. Dan. ix. 21). The Parsee custom of rendering Divine honors to the three parts of the day themselves, has, of course, nothing in common with the habit of the Jews and primitive Christians (Acts iii. 1; x. 9, 30; cf. Pusey, *Daniel*, p. 554); nor has the custom of the Egyptian priests, who, according to Porphyry, *de abstinent.* IV. 8, sang daily four hymns of praise to the sun; nor yet the three daily sacrifices and hymns of the Pythagoreans, as mentioned by Jamblichus, *Vit. Pythag.* c. 149 ss. Cf. generally, Zöckler, l. c. p. 329 et seq.—Verse 12 [11]. **Then these men assembled** (rushed together), **and found Daniel praying and making supplication before his God.** Here, as in v. 7 [6], הַרְגִּשׁוּ is not a single rushing together, but a frequent* hasty gathering; the only difference is that in that passage the design was to obtain the decree from the king, while here it is to watch Daniel in order to denounce him. According to v. 11, the open windows in Daniel's upper chamber seem to have enabled them to execute their plan of espionage with success, either because they *saw* him while engaged in prayer (perhaps from a still more elevated room in the vicinity, cf. 2 Sam. xi. 2), or because they *heard* him from the street. At any rate, a repeated [?] approach and observation in secret must be assumed, instead of a single surprise; hence the question, "At which of his daily prayers was he surprised?" is inappropriate.—Concerning the thoroughly organized system of espionage and denunciation in the Medo-Persian kingdom, of which this passage affords a characteristic proof, see Max Duncker, *Geschichte des Alterthums*, II. 648.

Verses 13-15 [12-14]. *The denunciation.* **Then they came near and spake before** ("with") **the king**, etc., cf. chap. iii. 8, and for what follows, iii. 24.—**The thing is true, according to the law of the Medes and Persians**; rather, "the word is firm, according, etc. יַצִּיבָא מִלְּתָא does not affirm that the decree was published, but indicates the certain punishment of any who might transgress it.—Verse 14 [13]. **Daniel, which is of the children of the captivity of Judah.** Cf. chap. v. 13, and observe that the accusers do not mention the high official station of Daniel and his intimate official relations with the king, but merely refer to his foreign birth, ["in order that they may thereby bring his conduct under the suspicion of being a political act of rebellion against the royal authority." (*Keil.*)]—Verse 15 [14]. **Then the king . . . . was sore displeased.** בְּאֵשׁ is impersonal in בְּאֵשׁ עֲלוֹהִי, like יֵרַע in Gen. xxi. 12, and like טְאֵב below, in v. 24 [23]. Literally, therefore, it reads, "Then the king, when he heard the word—sorrow came on him" (and similarly v. 24 [23], "Then . . . joy came on him").†—**And set his heart on Daniel to deliver him.** בָּל, "heart," is not found in the later Chaldee, but occurs in the Syriac and Arabic. Compare, however, the phrase שׂם לִ׳ לְבָּא, Targ. Prov. xxii. 17.—**And he labored till the going down of the sun**, etc. On the form מֶעָלֵי (st. constr. plur. of מֶעָלָא, or also of the Inf. מֶעַל), cf. Hitzig and Kranichfeld on this passage. Instead of אִשְׁתַּדַּר, "he labored" (cf. ἀγωνίζεσθαι, Luke xiii. 24), the Targums have אִשְׁתַּדַּל, which, however, has a different meaning from that of אִשְׁתַּדַּר.

Verses 16-18 [15-17]. *The condemnation and execution.* On v. 16 cf. supra, on v. 9 b.—Verse 17 [16]. **Then the king commanded, and they brought Daniel, and cast him into the den of lions**; rather, "that they should bring Daniel and cast," etc. The construction is the same as in chap. v. 29 [but in neither this nor that passage is this rendering justified by the force of the text, וּרְמוֹ . . . . וְהַיְתִיו]. According to Oriental custom, the execution in this case, as in that under Belshazzar, chap. v. 29, and in that under Nebuchadnezzar, chap. iii. 19 et seq., was to follow immediately on the sentence. ["This does not, however, imply that it was on the evening in which, at the ninth hour, he had prayed, as Hitzig affirms, in order that he may thereby make the whole matter improbable." (*Keil*). The season of prayer at which Daniel was discovered would seem to have been at noon. This will allow ample time for the preparation of the edict the same morning, and the execution the same evening. The accusers were evidently in hot haste].—**Thy God, whom thou servest continually, he will deliver thee**; rather, "may thy God . . . . deliver thee." Pilate may have solaced himself with a similar confession of his own weakness and cowardice, when he delivered the Saviour into the hands of his mortal enemies (Matt. xxvii. 24; Luke xxiii. 25, etc.); or Herod, when he commanded to bring the head of the Baptist (Matt. xiv. 9). Verse 19 [18] et seq. shows that the exclamation was by no means intended to be ironical or malicious, as those in Psa. xxii. 9; Matt. xxvii. 43; but on the other hand, Josephus probably attributes too favorable a disposition to Darius, when he observes: ἐλπίσας δὲ ὁ Δαρεῖος, ὅτι ῥύσεται τὸ θεῖον αὐτὸν καὶ οὐδὲν μὴ πάθῃ δεινὸν ὑπὸ τῶν θηρίων, ἐκέλευσεν αὐτὸν εὐθύμως φέρειν τὰ συμβαίνοντα (similarly also Jerome et al.).—Verse 18 [17]. **And a stone was brought, and laid upon the mouth of the den.** הֵיתָיִת, a Hebraizing passive form of the Aphel; cf. on chap. iii. 13. שָׂמַת, Hebraizing passive partic. Peal, instead of שִׂימַת (cf. v. 27 [26]).—It is natural to suppose that the stone was of sufficient size to completely close the mouth of the den, and that it was at hand for that purpose, instead of

* [The idea of *frequency* insisted upon by the author as residing in הַרְגִּשׁ seems to have no good support. The sense is rather *rushed forward*, made their way in a body and eagerly.]

† ["The king is chagrined and ashamed of himself that he allowed himself to be caught in this snare. Now for the first time he sees the enmity and mean spirit of his officers in obtaining from him that decree, and bites his lips in shame that he could have been so beguiled and entrapped. No doubt he heartily esteemed Daniel, and probably loved him, and felt therefore the bitterest grief and shame that he should be made unwillingly the author of his destruction."—*Cowles.* He also felt intensely anxious for his fate, and doubtless cast about in his mind some method of extricating him, and at the same time of exposing and punishing his accusers.]

assuming, with Hitzig, that it was necessary to bring it from a distance. The den itself, corresponding to the sense of גֻּבָּא (גּוּבָּא), which is thoroughly identical with that of the Heb. בּוֹר, must not be conceived of as a cistern or funnel-shaped pit (Hitzig); but rather as having a capacity sufficient to hold several lions and permit them to move freely about (which involves no greater difficulty than that the גּוּבָּא in the Targ Jer. xli. 7, 9 should have contained the corpses of seventy slain persons; cf. also the Targ. Jer. xxxvii. 16; Isa. xvi. 15). In brief, it may be supposed to have been an actual lions' den, similar to those connected with the Roman amphitheatres, from which it probaby differed simply in having a horizontal opening in the flat or arched roof, through which the *ad bestias damnati* were thrown to the lions, in addition to the door at the side, by which the beasts were introduced into the den or removed from it. Its construction may therefore have been similar to that of the fiery furnace, upon the whole (see on chap. iii. 6)—an opinion which seems to derive additional support from the manner in which Darius was enabled to converse with Daniel while in the den, even before the stone was removed from its opening (v. 21 et seq.). The two lions' dens at Fez, belonging to the emperor of Morocco, which Höst describes in his *Nachrichten von Fez und Marokko* (pp. 77, 290) as being large rectangular and uncovered pits in the earth (whose wide opening was surrounded by a wall one and a half ells in height), were consequently constructed somewhat differently from that of the Medo-Babylonians under consideration, but are still interesting for comparison with the latter.—**And the king sealed it with his own signet, and with the signet of his lords.** On the custom of sealing cf. Matt. xxvii. 26. The two-fold sealing, with the ring of the king and with that of his grand officers, may have been designed to secure Daniel, for whose deliverance the king still hoped (see vs. 17 [16], 21 [20], against any violent assault, and also against any attempt to liberate him—hence, to insure a strict control of the prisoner. Cf. Jerome: "*Obsignavit annulo suo lapidem, quo os laci claudebatur, ne quid contra Danielem moliantur inimici . . . . Obsignat autem et annulo optimatum suorum, ne quid suspicionis contra eos habere videretur.*"—**That the purpose might not be changed concerning Daniel;** rather, "that the matter," etc.; that his situation might not be unlawfully altered. צְבוּ here is not "intention, purpose" (v. Leng. etc.)* but "affair, matter;" cf. the corresponding Syriac word.

Verses 19–23 [18–22]. *The king discovers the miraculous preservation of Daniel.* **Then the king went . . . and passed the night fasting.** טְוָת is properly a substantive with adverbial signification — "with fasting" — *i.e.*, supperless. Luther renders it forcibly, "and remained not eating."—**Neither wer instruments of music brought before him;** rather "concubines." Instead of "food," which is the interpretation assigned by Theodotion, the Peshito, the Vulgate, Luther, etc., the rendering of דַּחֲוָן by "concubines, women of the harem," is sufficiently supported by closely related terms in the Arabic; and the verb הַנְעֵל in connection with the prep. קֳדָם admits of no other interpretation. The bringing in of inanimate objects would have been expressed by הֵיתִי; cf. chap. v. 2 with ii. 24, 25; iv. 3; v. 13, 15.—**And his sleep went from him;** forsook him; cf. on chap. ii. 1.—Verse 20 [19]. **Then the king arose very early in the morning;** "with the dawn, when it became light." שְׁפַרְפָּרָא, "the dawn" (= שַׁחַר, Targ. Jon. on Isa. lviii. 8). The hypothetical rendering of the imperf. יְקוּם, for which Kranichfeld contends, is unnecessary. ["The future or imperfect is used instead of the perfect to place this clause in relation to the following, meaning: *the king, as soon as he arose at morning dawn, went hastily by the early light*" (*Keil*).] The Septuagint is [substantially] correct: ὤρθρισε πρωΐ; also Theodotion, the Peshito, etc.—בְּנָגְהָא, "with the twilight, with the dawn or break of day" ["serves for a mere determination of the בִּשְׁפַרְפָּרָא, *at the morning dawn*, namely, as soon as the first rays of the rising sun appeared" (*Keil*)]; cf. לָאוֹר, Job xxiv. 14.—**And went in haste.** בְּהִתְבְּהָלָה, as in chap. ii. 35, = μετὰ σπουδῆς; cf. Luke i. 39.—Verse 21 [20]. **And . . . . cried with a lamentable voice unto Daniel.** עֲצִיב = מַר; cf. Isa. liv. 6 with Prov. xxxi. 6.—**O Daniel, servant of the living God.** Darius was able to designate the God of Daniel as the *living God* (cf. v. 27) thus early, before his observation had convinced him of the prophet's safety, for the simple reason that during the intercourse consequent on their intimate relation, Daniel had instructed him concerning the nature and power of his God as the God of all gods, and also because the pangs of conscience endured by him during the night that had just elapsed, had produced a profound conviction of the truth of the prophet's testimony to Jehovah.*—Verse 23 [22]. **My God hath sent his angel, and hath shut the lions' mouths.** Cf. v. 28 [27]; Acts xii. 7. The summary conciseness of the statement forbids any conclusion as to whether Daniel had seen the angel who wrought his miraculous deliverance, as an objective fact, or whether he merely argued from the effect to the underlying invisible cause (cf. Psa. xxxiv. 8; xci. 11 et seq.; Matt. viii. 9, etc.). On the expression, "to shut the lions' mouths," cf. 2 Tim. iv. 17; Heb. xi. 33.—**And also before thee, O king, have I done no hurt.** "Before thee," קֳדָמַיךְ, *i.e.*, "in thine eyes, according to thy judgment" — a loosely connected supplemental proof of what he has just asserted, viz., that he is innocent. In

* ["This thought (would have) required the *stat. emphat.* צְבוּתָא, and also does not correspond with the application of a double seal."—*Keil.*]

* ["The predicate *the living God* is occasioned by the preservation of life which the king regarded as possible, and probably was made known to the king in previous conversations with Daniel; cf. Psa. xlii. 3; lxxxiv. 3; 1 Sam. xvii. 36, etc."—*Keil.*]

modern speech the connection might have been, "even as I was likewise found innocent by thee" (which was apparent to him from the king's anxious inquiries concerning his welfare).*

Verses 24, 25 [23, 24]. *The deliverance of Daniel and the punishment of his enemies.* **Then was the king exceeding glad** (cf. on v. 15) **for him,**† **and commanded that they should take Daniel up out of the den.**‡ הַנְסָקָה, the inf. Aphel of the root סְלַק, compensates for the doubling by נ, similarly to הַנְעָל in v. 19 [18] (cf. ii. 25). Cf. הַסִּיק, chap. iii. 22.—Verse 25 [24]. **And the king commanded, and they brought those men**; rather, "that those men should be brought." The same construction as in v. 17 [16].§—"Those men" are the same who are mentioned in vs. 6 [5] and 7 [6], viz.: the grand officers who were present in Babylon itself, and who had taken part in traducing Daniel. A number of them may have been in the king's train, when he commanded that the seals should be broken and the stone removed (v. 24 [23]), without venturing to protest, in the presence of the angry monarch, against the violation of the seal which belonged in part to them. The others were brought from their houses by the king's command. There is consequently nothing in the passage that involves a difficulty or that contradicts v. 18 [17] (against Hitzig).—**Which had accused Daniel.** Literally, "who had devoured Daniel's flesh;" cf. on chap. iii. 8.—**And they cast . . . into the den of lions, them, their children, and their wives.** Upon this point even Hitzig is compelled to remark: "To execute the familes of criminals together with themselves was eminently the Persian custom (Herod., III. 119; Ammian. Marcel., xxiii. 6, 81); Justin, in such an instance, makes especial reference to the wives and children (X. 2); cf. further, Justin, XXI. 4; Josh. vii. 24, 25." On the authority of the statements quoted from Herodotus and Justin (and also influenced by what Curtius, VI. 11, states with reference to the custom among the Macedonians), Hitzig contends that such fearfully bloody justice—whose barbarous severity our prophet seems to allude to when he mentions the *children* before the wives—was only inflicted on conspirators against the king. But Ammian. (l. c.) states no such limitation; and the malicious plot of these magnates against one of the chief officials of the kingdom, as well as intimate counsellor of the king, was almost equivalent to a conspiracy directed against the royal person.—**And the lions had the mastery of them** (or "fell upon them") **. . . or ever they came at the bottom of the den.** Literally, "and not came they . . . . *until that*," *i.e.*, when the lions already seized them. On the incident, cf. chap. iii. 22; concerning the form שְׁלִטוּ, see chap. ii. 29.

Verses 26–28 [25–27]. *The royal proclamation consequent on the miraculous deliverance of Daniel.* **Then king Darius wrote** (commanded to write) **unto all people, nations, and languages,** etc.; *i.e.*, to all the subjects of his realm, which was a world-kingdom like that of Nebuchadnezzar, chap. iii. 31.—Verse 27 [26]. **I make a decree.** Cf. iii. 29; iv. 3, where the shorter מִנִּי occurs instead of מִן־קֳדָמַי, which is found in this place.—**That . . . men tremble and fear before the God of Daniel.** Cf. chap. v. 19.—The theocratic phraseology of the royal edict admits of the same explanation as do the similar proclamations of Nebuchadnezzar, chap. ii. 47; iii. 28 et seq.; iii. 31 et seq.; iv. 31 et seq. It results in part from the extended intercourse of the king with Daniel, the representative of the theocratic faith of revelation; and in part from the profound influence of the experience of the immediate past.—**And his kingdom** (is one) **which shall not be destroyed**; a forcible ellipsis, similar, for instance, to that in chap. vii. 14; cf. also chap. ii. 44; and on the thought, iii. 33; iv. 31.—**And his dominion** (shall be even) **unto the end**; *i.e.*, "to the end of all earthly kingdoms, to the end of the world" (the *συντέλεια τοῦ αἰῶνος*), which coincides with the erection of the completed kingdom of Messiah or God; cf. vii. 14, 26 et seq.—Verse 28 [27]. **He delivereth and rescueth**; rather, "He is a saviour and deliverer." Cf. chap. iii. 29 *b.*, and for what follows cf. iii. 32; iv. 32.—**From the power of the lions**: literally, "out of the *hand* of the lions;" cf. Psa. xxii. 21, "out of the hand of the dogs."

Verse 29 [28]. *The epilogue.* **So this Daniel prospered in the reign of Darius.** "This Daniel," as in v. 4 [3].—הַצְלַח, "found prosperity, prospered;" similar to chap. iii. 30. Ewald's reading, הָצְלַח, which is designed to be equivalent to, "he was reinstated in his office" (?), is unnecessary.—On the subject cf. chap. ii. 48.—**And** (also) **in the reign of Cyrus the Persian.** This complementary closing sentence, like that in chap. i. 21, appears to have been added a considerable time after the preceding facts were recorded, for the purpose of closing the historical part of the book as a whole. But the objection that it is clearly a "bald and labored gloss in its appearance" (Kranichf.), is not therefore justified. The reign of Cyrus is merely mentioned, as having been reached by Daniel, for the same reason that dictated chap. i. 21.

ETHICO-FUNDAMENTAL PRINCIPLES RELATED TO THE HISTORY OF SALVATION, APOLOGETICAL REMARKS, AND HOMILETICAL SUGGESTIONS.

1. The similarity of the facts recorded in this section to those of the third chapter is certainly

* ["Daniel casts no severe reproach upon the king. Indeed the original rather expresses a genial and kindly feeling: Daniel 'talked with the king.' With beautiful modesty he ascribes his deliverance to God's own hand alone through his angel, and very properly asserts his innocence of any wrong in this matter.—We may suppose Daniel to have had a sweet sense of the presence of God by his angel while spending the night in the den with these hungry lions."—*Cowles.*]

† [עֲלוֹהִי does not refer to Daniel, but to the king himself. It denotes the reflexive sense of טְאֵב, which is here used impersonally: *gladness came over him.*]

‡ ["By this, however, we are not to understand a being drawn up by ropes through the opening of the den from above. The *bringing out* was by the opened passage in the side of the den, for which purpose the stone with the seals was removed."—*Keil.*]

§ [But the rendering proposed by the author is equally inadmissible here.]

evident and undeniable; but these analogies do not warrent the disregarding of the important *differences* between the incidents of the two sections. These differences, on the one hand, affect the disposition and the modes of action of the persons engaged in the various transactions, in which respect the king Darius especially observes from the beginning a more cordial bearing toward the worshipper of Jehovah than does Nebuchadnezzar; and, on the other, they relate to the miracle which forms the end and climax of the entire event. The deliverance of Daniel from the lions' den was a miracle differing materially in character from that of the deliverance of the three Hebrews from the fiery furnace; while the latter, as was intimated on chap. iii. 22, would admit of a natural explanation. To some extent at least, this is absolutely impossible with the event recorded in this chapter, as may be seen more particularly from the fact, noticed in v. 25 [24] *b*, that the same lions who spared Daniel during an entire night immediately seized on his accusers with a ravenous voracity in order to rend them. By this contrast between the subjection of the beasts to the prophet, and the outburst of their savage nature towards the guilty princes—a contrast which evidently constitutes the fundamental characteristic of the incident before us—this miracle takes its position among that series of marvellous events in Old and New Testament history in which the life and work of isolated distinguished messengers of revelation appear, by virtue of Divine grace, to have restored the paradisaical dominion of man over nature, so that the beasts of the desert yield him a ready obedience as their rightful lord. We class here, prior to the time of Daniel, the ravens of Elijah (1 Kings xvii. 4) and the bears of Elisha (2 Kings ii. 24); and in N. T. times, the sojourning of the Saviour with the beasts of the desert, immediately subsequent to his temptation (Mark i. 13), Paul's escape from injury by the viper on the island of Malta (Acts xxviii. 5; cf. Mark xvi. 18), and perhaps several incidents of a similar character in the history of the earliest monkish saints and missionaries of the Church down to the times of Columban and Gallus, so far as any faith may be placed on the statements in the generally fancifully distorted biographies of these saints which relate to their friendly intercourse with wild beasts (cf. Montalembert, *Les Moines d'Occident depuis St. Benoit jusqu'à St. Bernard*, vol. II.; and for a criticism of the often excessively credulous judgment of this author with reference to such miracles, see the review of his work in the *Jahrbücher für deutsche Theologie*, 1862, No. 2).—It is, however, precisely because the miraculous incident of this section belongs to the category of such facts, that it must rank as the greatest wonder recorded in the historical part of the book, as the climax in the series of mighty works by which God glorified Himself in His servants in the metropolis of the Chaldæan empire, and which, forming a gradation of miracles in certain aspects, and presenting a constantly-increasing manifestation of the supernatural element in them, from chap. i. 15 to the close of this chapter, excludes, with steadily-increasing emphasis, the possibility of tracing back the events to natural causes (cf. especially on chap. v. 5).

2. So far as the general situation is similar to that described in chap. iii., it accords well with the conditions of the captivity, in which the aim was *not*, as afterwards under Antiochus Epiphanes, to extirpate the Jewish worship, but where we find merely certain very natural and intelligible displays of grudging selfishness and envy on the part of individual native officials, as against a captive foreigner who was preferred above them in official stations; while the general condition of the captives was very tolerable, as a natural result of the lax administration of government which was usual among Oriental conquerors" (Kranichfeld). The assertion of the modern "tendency-critics" (Hitzig, p. 89 et seq.; Bleek, p. 604, etc.), that the edict of Darius which prohibited the rendering of Divine honors during one month to any but the king (v. 8 [7]) was invented for the purpose of exaggerating or caricaturing the proclamation of Antiochus Epiphanes, which prohibited the Jews from observing the Divine law and their worship of Jehovah (1 Macc. i. 41; 2 Macc. vi. 1–9), in order to incite them to steadfast endurance and to patient trust in God,—this assertion is decidedly nugatory, since the raging fanaticism of the Syrian king, which aimed at the total destruction of the Jewish worship and nationality, had nothing in common with the far milder disposition of Darius, and since the latter was merely concerned to bring about a temporary suspension of the religious observances in vogue, rather than to definitely extirpate the current systems of religion. Nor would it have been possible for the pious Jews of the Maccabæan period to recognize an edict, which amounted directly to the deifying of the king, as a prototype of the manifesto of the Syrian king, which differed materially from it, in respect both to its language and its character. For this reason Von Lengerke, more cautious than his compeers, rejects the assumption that the edict of v. 8 [7] was a conventional fiction framed on the model of that mentioned in the Maccabæan books, as being too artificial and unsupported a hypothesis, and contents himself with observing that "the proclamation of Darius on the religious question corresponds *in general* to that persecuting spirit which produced the measures of Antiochus." But it will be seen that even this is not correct, since the deportment of Darius towards Daniel, manifesting in every respect a mild, friendly, and benevolent spirit (vs. 14, 15 et seq.; 21 et seq.), presents the sharpest contrast to the senseless rage and blood-thirsty spirit of persecution displayed by the intolerant Syrian tyrant; and, moreover, since no reason whatever can be discovered that could induce the alleged Maccabæan-tendency writer to invent so weak, and in all respects so inappropriate, a counterfeit of Antiochus at the last, after having furnished in Nebuchadnezzar and Belshazzar far more suitable and tangible types of that despot. Nor does it appear why he should desire to conceal the person of Antiochus behind that of a jealous and scheming official under the Median king (vs. 4, 5 et seq.).—How much more simple and intelligible, in comparison with such hypercritical assumptions, does the narrative appear when its characteristic peculiarities are regarded as *historical* facts, such as were naturally to be expected in the scenes of a politico-

religious drama that transpired on the soil of the newly-founded Medo-Persian world-kingdom! The 120 satrapies instead of the former division of the kingdom into differently constituted provinces (cf. vi. 2 with iii. 2); the exceedingly independent course of the royal counsellors and officers, without whose consent no edict could be promulgated nor the royal seal affixed (vs. 8 [7], 18 [17]); the temporary deifying of the king as the son and image of the supreme God (v. 8 et seq.), so surprisingly in harmony with the fundamental principles of the Old-Persian state religion; the cruel procedure connected with the punishment of the offenders (v. 25 [24]) which bears, in an equal degree, the stamp of specifically Persian legal usage; and finally, the repeated reference to the "law of the Medes and Persians," as the original source and inviolable authority for the measures proposed and put in force—all these point, with all possible force and internal congruity, to a well-defined historical condition with which the writer was familiarly acquainted, an actual condition which was distinguished from the state existing in the Chaldæo-Babylonian kingdom in a manner that corresponds fully with numerous extra-biblical testimonies, and which indicates that the experience and personal observation of the author formed the only source of his descriptions. Cf. the observations made above on the several passages.

3. The homiletical treatment of this section will vary, according as the conduct and fate of Daniel, the man of God, receive attention, or as those of the other agents, viz.: of the good-natured but weak king and of the jealous accusers, are prominently considered. In the former case, the theme for the treatment of the subject as a whole might be: "We should obey God, rather than men" (cf. v. 5 with v. 11 et seq.); or, "Fidelity to God is a more precious virtue, and secures a more certain and precious reward, than fidelity to human authority;" or, "It is better to be the friend of God, even if the foe of the whole world." In the latter case: "Whoso digs a pit for others, shall fall into it himself;" or, "God knows how to use the plans by which men seek to destroy his faithful servants, for their deliverance and honor;" or "God has converted many a ruler, from being a persecutor of His church into its forwarder and zealous protector!"

In connection with the former class of meditations, cf. the following extracts from older practical expositors: Jerome (on vs. 11, 12): "*Daniel, regis jussa contemnens et in Deo habens fiduciam, non orat in humili loco, sed in excelso, et fenestras aperit contra Jerusalem, ubi erat visio pacis. Orat autem secundum præceptum Dei dictaque Salomonis, qui contra templum orandum esse admonuit.*" Melancthon (on v. 19 et seq.): "*Periculum Danielis pingit robur et violentiam hostium Christi. Sicut Daniel imbecillis objicitur leonibus, sic tota Ecclesia habet hostes validissimos, diabolum, reges, potentes, superbos, præstantes auctoritate et opibus in mundo. Liberatio Danielis est testimonium, quod Deus adsit sanctis et servet eos suo judicio, alias corpore, alias spiritu.*" Starke (on v. 29 [28]): "Whosoever does not permit himself to be driven by persecution and danger, either from the upright fear of God, nor, on the other hand, from his lawful obedience to earthly authorities, shall find at last that honor and glory follow upon fidelity" (1 Sam. xxiv. 11, 21).

With the second class of themes, cf.: Melancthon (on v. 5 [4]): "*Tales habet diabolus ministros, qui captatis occasionibus regum animos astute a veritate avertunt, ubi summa officii et virtutis specie insidiæ struuntur. Ita hic . . . bonus senex . . . non videt quantum admittat sceleris, quod in edicto etiam Dei invocatio prohibetur. Monet igitur hoc exemplum, ut cauti sint principes in observandis talibus insidiis, ac præsertim in legibus et edictis condendis.*" Id. (on v. 15 et seq.): "*Quamquam igitur peccavit Darius, tamen infirmitate lapsus est et contra furorem accusatorum sustentat se quadam scintilla fidei, quæ ostendit non ipsum, sed principes esse supplicii auctores, etiamsi ipsi non satis fortiter eos represserat . . . . Tales infirmos sublevat Deus, ut hic apparet. Sequitur enim statim acerbissima pænitentia regis, ac deinde tantum fidei robur, tanta animi magnitudo, ut puniat etiam accusatores.*" Geier (on v. 21 [20]): "*Hoc sensu Darium ex animi sui sententia adeoque ex vera fide compellasse Danielis Deum, verosimile non est; sic namque omnia Persarum Medorumque improbasset et abnegasset numina . . . . immo non vocat Deum suum, sed Danielis, neque ait se ipsum colere, sed: quem tu colis.*" Joh. Gerhard (*Weim. Bib.*, on v. 24 et seq.): "God is able to promote and extend the true faith by means of the very persecutions and other methods by which its enemies seek to destroy it."

SECOND (PROPHETIC) DIVISION.

CHAP. VII.-XII.

1. *The vision of the four world-kingdoms and of the Messianic kingdom.*

VII.

1 In the first year of[1] Belshazzar king of Babylon, Daniel had [saw] a dream,
and visions of his head upon his bed: then he wrote the dream, *and* told *the* sum
of *the* matters.[2]
2 Daniel spake[3] and said, I saw[4] in my vision by[5] night, and, behold, *the* four
3 winds of the heaven [heavens] strove upon [were *rushing to*] the great sea. And
four great beasts came up from the sea, diverse one from another[6]

4 The first *was* like a lion, and had eagle's wings: I beheld till[7] *the* wings there-
of were plucked, and it was lifted *up* from the earth, and made [to] stand upon
5 *the* feet as a man, and a man's heart *was* given to it. And, behold, another beast,
a second, like to a bear, and it raised[8] *up itself* [was made to stand] on one side,[9]
and *it had* three ribs in *the* mouth of it between *the* teeth of it: and they said
6 thus unto it, Arise, devour much flesh. After this I beheld,[4] and lo, another,
like a leopard, which, [and it] had upon *the* back of it four wings of a fowl [bird]:
7 the beast had also four heads; and dominion *was* given to it. After this I saw[4]
in the night visions, and, behold, a fourth beast, dreadful and terrible, and strong
exceedingly; and it had great iron teeth:[10] it devoured and brake *in pieces*, and
stamped the residue with *the* feet of it: and it *was* diverse from all the beasts
8 that *were* before it; and it had ten horns. I considered[11] the horns, and, behold,
there came up among them another little horn, before whom [and from before it]
there were three of[12] the first horns plucked up by the roots [were extirpated]:
and, behold, in this horn *were* eyes like the eyes of man, and a mouth speaking
great *things*.
9 I beheld till[7] *the* thrones were cast [set] *down*, and *the* Ancient of days did
sit, whose [his] garment *was* white as snow, and *the* hair of his head like *the*[13]
pure wool: his throne *was like the*[13] fiery flame [flames of fire], *and* his wheels *as*
10 burning fire. A fiery stream [stream of fire] issued [flowed] and came forth from
before him: thousand thousands ministered unto him,[14] and ten thousand times
ten thousand stood[15] before him: the judgment was set [did sit], and *the* books
11 were opened. I beheld[4] then, because of the voice of the great words which
the horn spake [*was* speaking]; I beheld, *even* till[7] the beast was slain, and his
12 [its] body destroyed, and given to the burning flame. As concerning [And]
the rest of the beasts, they had their dominion taken away:[16] yet their lives were
prolonged for[17] a season and time.
13 I saw[4] in the night visions, and, behold, *one* like the Son of man came [was
coming] with *the* clouds of heaven [the heavens], and came to [reached] the
14 Ancient of days, and they brought him near before him. And *there was* given
him [to him *was* given] dominion, and glory, and a kingdom, that all people,
nations, and languages,[18] should serve[19] him: his dominion *is* an everlasting
dominion, which shall not pass away, and his kingdom *that* which shall not be
destroyed.
15 I Daniel was grieved *in* my spirit [my spirit was grieved] in *the* midst of *my*
16 body [*its* sheath], and the visions of my head troubled[20] me. I came near unto[21]
one[12] of them that stood *by*, and asked him[22] the truth of[21] all this. So [And]
17 he told me, and made[23] me know *the* interpretation of the things.[24] These great
18 beasts, which are[25] four, *are* four kings, *which* shall arise out of the earth. But
[And] *the* saints of *the Most* High[26] shall take [receive] the kingdom, and pos-
sess the kingdom for ever, even for ever and ever.
19 Then I would *know* [wished] the truth of[21] the fourth beast, which was diverse
from all the *others* [of them], exceeding dreadful, whose [its] teeth *were of* iron,
and his [its] nails *of* brass; *which* devoured, brake [breaking] *in pieces*, and
20 stamped the residue with his [its] feet; and of[21] the ten horns that *were* in his
[its] head, and *of the* other which came up, and before whom [from before it]
three fell; even [and] *of* that horn that [and it] had eyes, and a mouth that
spake [speaking] *very* great *things*, whose [and its] look *was more* stout than his
21 [its] fellows. I beheld,[4] and the same [that] horn made war with *the* saints, and
22 prevailed[1] against them; until the Ancient of days came, and [the] judgment was
given to *the* saints of *the Most* High;[26] and the time came [arrived] that [, and]
the saints possessed the kingdom.
23 Thus he said, The fourth beast shall be the fourth kingdom[27] upon [the] earth,
which shall be diverse from all [the] kingdoms, and shall devour the whole
24 earth, and shall tread it *down*, and break it *in pieces*. And the ten horns out of
this[28] kingdom *are* ten kings *that* shall arise: and another shall rise [arise] after
them; and he shall be diverse from the first, and he shall subdue [abase] three
25 kings. And he shall speak *great* words against the *Most* High, and shall wear
out [afflict] *the* saints of *the Most* High,[26] and think to change times and laws

[law]: and they shall be given into his hand, until a time and times and the
26 dividing of [half a] time. But [And] the judgment shall [did] sit, and they
27 shall take away his dominion, o consume and to destroy *it* unto the end. And
the kingdom and [the] dominion, and the greatness of *the* kingdom under the
whole heaven [heavens], shall be given to *the* people of *the* saints of *the Most* High,[28]
whose [his] kingdom *is* an everlasting kingdom, and all [the] dominions shall
serve and obey him.
28 Hitherto *is* the end of the matter.[30] *As for* me[31] Daniel, my cogitations
[thoughts] much troubled[20] me, and my countenance[32] changed in[21] me: but
[and] I kept the matter[30] in my heart.

8

GRAMMATICAL AND LEXICAL NOTES.

[[1] *To.*—[2] Or, *chief of the words.*—[3] *Answered.*—[4] *Was seeing.*—[5] *With the.*—[6] *Changed this from that.*—[7] *Was seeing till that.*—[8] הקימת is evidently used here to correspond with the description of the preceding verse, and hence the pointing הְ to is preferred, as in the margin.—[9] לְשְׂטַר־חַד, *to one side*, sidewise, *i.e.*, *partially*, prob. on the fore or hind feet only; in a crouching or half-risen posture; thus contrasted with the erect attitude of the lion preceding on *both* feet עַל רַגְלִין.—[10] The position of the terms is emphatic, *teeth of iron* were *to it*, *great* ones.—[11] *Was occupying my attention with.*—[12] *Out of*, or *among.*—[13] The definite article is here injurious to the sense.—[14] *Would serve him* as attendants.—[15] *Myriad of myriads would stand.*—[16] Literally, *caused to pass away.*—[17] *And a lengthening in their lives was given them till.*—[18] As in chap. vi. 25: *All the nations, the peoples, and the tongues.*—[19] *Labor for.*—[20] *Would trouble.*—[21] *Upon.*—[22] *Would ask from him.*—[23] *Would make.*—[24] Or, *words.*—[25] *They.*—[26] In the plur., like most names of Deity.—[27] *A kingdom the fourth.*—[28] *It the.*—[29] To the *side of.*—[30] Or, *word.*—[31] *I.*—[32] *Looks would be.*]

EXEGETICAL REMARKS.

Verse 1. *Historical introduction.* **In the first year of Belshazzar;** hence, in the first year after the death of Nebuchadnezzar, the father and predecessor of Belshazzar; see on chap. v. 1.* This designation of the time "seems substantially to have furnished the occasion for renewed reflection on the part of the prophet, bearing upon the former series of prophetical meditations that had been called forth in him by an important event (the dream of Nebuchadnezzar concerning the image of the monarchies, which Daniel interpreted, chap. ii.). The idea of the four heathen kingdoms which were to precede the introduction of the Messianic kingdom of Israel, that was announced by the earlier prophets and believed by them to be near, is again brought out comprehensively in this place, with reference to the course observed by those kingdoms toward the theocracy" (Kranichfeld). — Concerning the chronological parallelism of the series of apocalyptic visions, opened by this new vision of the monarchies, with the series of historical events recorded in the former division of the book, and beginning with chap. ii., see the Introd., § 3.—**Daniel had a dream and visions of his head upon his bed.** Cf. chap. ii. 19; and with reference to the visions of his head, cf. ii. 28.—**Then he wrote the dream,** immediately or soon after it transpired; a note intended to strengthen the following statements concerning its nature (cf. chap. xii. 4). This note, however, as the change of person between vs. 1 and 2 indicates, was probably introduced by the author at a later time, in connection with his final revision of the whole book. The closing verse of the chapter, which likewise is merely important as a transitional passage, seems also to be a later addition.—**And told the sum of the matters;** gave the leading features. רֵאשׁ מִלִּין, the sum or substance of the words; cf. רֹאשׁ in passages like Lev. v. 24; Psa. cxix. 160; and also the Talmudic ראשי דברים (*Rosh hash.*, II. 6), and the Gr. κεφάλαιον, which is employed in this place by the Sept. The "sum" signifies, of course, the aggregate of all that is of Messianic significance. Cf. Ewald: "When it is said that Daniel merely recorded the leading features, or gave a mere summary, of the wonderful visions which he saw, the meaning becomes evident, when it is observed with what freedom the leading outlines of the visions are drawn in the first two turns of the description (vs. 1–14), and are afterward repeated for the purpose of interpretation. All the remaining prophetic sections of the book have the same plan in substance; but whenever it is attempted to record personal experiences and observations in writing, it is advisable to furnish the briefest outline consistent with clearness, on account of the readers, if for no other reason." *

* [This assumption rests upon the author's theory that Belshazzar is identical with Evil-merodach, which, as we have shown in the notes appended to the Introduction, is not sustained by the latest authorities on Babylonian history. If Rawlinson's conjecture is correct, that Belshazzar was the son of Nabouned, left in command of Babylon while his father threw himself into Borsippa, the date in question will relate to the viceroyship of the former, which may well have continued a year or more (or even into the third year, see chap. viii. 1), since the siege of Babylon lasted two years.]

* [" This vision accords not only in many respects with the dream of Nebuchadnezzar (ch. ii), but has the same subject. This subject, however, the representation of the world-power in its principal forms, is differently given in the two chapters. In ch. ii. it is represented according to its whole character as an image of a man whose different parts consist of different metals, and in chap. vii. under the figure of four beasts which arise one after the other out of the sea. In the former, its destruction is represented by a stone breaking the image in pieces, while in the latter it is effected by a solemn act of judgment. This further difference also is to be observed, that in this chapter, the first, but chiefly the fourth, world-kingdom, in its development and relation to the people of God, is much more clearly exhibited in ch. ii. These differences have their principal reason in the difference of the recipients of the Divine revelation: Nebuchadnezzar, the founder of the world-power, saw this power in its imposing greatness and glory; while Daniel, the prophet of God, saw it in its opposition to God in the form of ravenous beasts of prey. Nebuchadnezzar had his dream in the second year of his reign, when he had just founded his world-monarchy; while Daniel had his vision of the world-kingdoms

Verses 2, 3. *The entrance of the four beasts.* **Daniel spake and said.** The incoherence of these words with the statements of v. 1 seems to indicate that they no longer belong (as Kranichfeld believes) to the supplementary note, v. 1, but that they originally served to introduce the description of the vision.—**I saw in my vision by night;** עִם, "during, by," spoken of synchronous things; cf. chap. iii. 33.—**And behold, the four winds of the heavens strove** ("broke forth") **upon the great sea.** Concerning אֲרוּ, see on chap. ii. 31.—The fourfold number of the "winds of the heaven" (*i.e.*, the winds blowing from the different quarters of heaven, or, more simply, those blowing *under* heaven; cf. "the birds of heaven") has reference, of course, to that of the beasts in v. 3 et seq. It designates all the winds of the world (cf. chap. viii. 8; Zech. vi. 5; Jer. xlix. 36), and therefore indicates at the outset the universal importance of the following vision. Hence actual winds must be intended, and not "*angelicæ potestates*", as Jerome suggests, under reference to Deut. xxxii. 8 (Sept.).* It is not necessary to ask, in connection with a dream-vision, how all the four winds could arise together; nor how the great sea (*i.e.*, probably the Mediterranean, the ocean of the nations of hither Asia; cf. Josh. xv. 48) could enter into the dream of an Israelite who resided from his early youth at Babylon. The sea, as is frequent in prophetic figurative language of the Old Testament, represents the *heathen world* of nations, which unquestionably afforded a striking illustration in every case when they arose in hostility against the theocracy, in order to overwhelm and destroy the constantly-diminishing people of God, as the raging waves of the ocean break upon an insignificant island or coast. Cf. Isa. viii. 7 et seq.; xvii. 12; xxvii. 1; lvii. 20; Psa. xlvi. 4; also Rev. viii. 8; xvii. 15; and with reference to the *overflowing* (by hostile forces) see Dan. ix. 26; xi. 10, 22, 26.—מְגִיחָן לְיַמָּא may be properly translated "breaking forth *upon* the sea, breaking loose *against* the sea;" on גִּיחַ, cf. the corresponding Heb. word in Job xl. 23; Ezek. xxxii. 22, and also the Syr. and Targum. usage, which principally employs the word to represent the hostile irruption of warlike forces. Less natural is the factitive rendering of the partic., "*caused* the great sea to break forth" (Kranichf.), and the reciprocal, by Luther, "stormed against each other *on* the great sea (cf. Ewald's "swept through the great sea"); the prep. לְ seems not suited to either conception.†—Verse 3. **And four** (excessively) **great beasts came up from the sea.** The strengthening of the idea implied in the reduplicated רַבְרְבָן may be rendered, with Ewald, by "monstrous," or by an adverb of comparison prefixed to "great," as "very, excessively," etc.* Kranichfeld is incorrect and interpolating: "four ravenous beasts."—The rising of "the beasts from the sea" describes, figuratively, their rising out of the great undefined, and, so to speak, mist-enveloped sea of nations, and their more noticeable entrance into the range of the dreaming prophet's vision. There is therefore no allusion to a coming up out of the sea *to the land* (unlike Gen. xli. 2, 18 et seq.), especially since, in the parallel description in v. 17, four kings, corresponding to the four beasts, arise "out of the earth." ["These four fierce beasts arise, not all at once, but, as ver. 6 and 7 teach, one after another" (*Keil*).]—Concerning the representation of nations or kingdoms under the figure of certain beasts, especially ravenous beasts, monsters (cf. Isa. xxvii. 1; li. 9; Ezek. xxix. 3; xxxii. 2; Psa. lxviii. 31; lxxiv. 13), see Ewald: "It is an ancient habit to regard beasts as symbols of kings and empires; but it first became really significant through the custom of emblazoning them on standards and arms, especially on shields, and also on permanent monuments and works of art, as standing symbols. The most ancient picture-writing in Egypt and Assyria afterward contributed its part to introduce an intimate connection in thought between a figurative creature and a kingdom corresponding to it. It is now known that each of the twelve tribes of Israel bore the figure of an animal on its standard and its coat of arms; and likewise that every representative of a tribe could wear such a symbol, while a king could elevate the symbol of his tribe to the dignity of a national emblem" (*Geschichte des V. Israel*, III. 341, 849). Certain animals, such as the lion, panther, and ox, would naturally be suggested in any case; and others would be chosen by way of contrast. But nowhere would such animal-symbols be likely to become so significant as in the ancient Assyrian empire. This has become the more certain, since the frequent colossal animals scattered among the ruins of Nineveh and other places, which served as symbols of the power and greatness of that empire, *i. e.*, of its kings and gods, have been brought to light. Hence, after Assyria and the other great powers of the ancient world had, from the 8th and 7th centuries B. C., been opposed to the Israelites, whom the latter were continually less and less able to resist, their poets and orators adopted the custom of designating them on proper occasions by such symbols, *e. g.*, Assyria as a lion or as a "reed-beast," and Egypt as a crocodile or dragon. As a consequence, it is comprehensible why animals were chosen here and in chapters vii. and viii. as symbols of the great monarchies beginning with the Assyrio-Chaldæan, although these animals are selected independently, because an entirely new conception is here introduced. Since an increased spiritual significance was attributed to animals as the emblems of kingdoms, it would become possible for the imagination to extend such figures beyond the realm of actual creation, and to construct ideal forms; but our author clearly avoids the use of wholly imaginary animals for this purpose, as being inappropriate. His object is here to re-

---

and of the judgment against them in the first year of Belshazzar, when the glory of the world-monarchy began to fade, and the spirit of its opposition to God became more manifest."—*Keil.*]

* [Keil's remark, however, is apposite: "The winds *of the heavens* represent the heavenly powers and forces by which God sets the nations of the world in motion."]

† [We suggest that the preposition rather indicates the *direction* of the winds as converging to this one point as a scene of conflict.]

* [The reduplicated form, however, seems to be merely the usual one in Chaldee.]

present in a more striking and impressive manner the four successive changes of the great world-kingdom described in chap. ii. under the figure of a monstrous human image, which afforded but faint analogies; and for this purpose he selects four wild beasts, which differ among themselves respectively, and which overcome each other in succession.—**Diverse one from another,** for the reason that they represented distinct kingdoms, which differed from each other respectively, and were peculiarly constituted in respect to their national character and their political tendencies. These distinctions are now to be brought out as clearly and prominently as possible, thus indicating a different purpose from that connected with the image of the monarchies, which was chiefly designed to represent the perpetuation of the same heathen world-power throughout the four successive phases of its development.

Verses 4–8. *More detailed description of the four beasts, and especially of the fourth.* **The first was like a lion and had eagle's wings.** The emblem of a wonderful beast so constituted might be chosen with propriety to represent the Chaldæan, or, if it be preferred, the Assyrio-Chaldæan world-power (cf. supra, Eth.-fund. principles, etc., on chap. ii.), since the winged lions with human heads recovered at Nimrud (Layard, *Nineveh and Babylon*, p. 348) and also the similar images of winged animals at Babylon (Münter, *Religion der Babylonier*, pp. 98, 139) were doubtless designed as symbols of the power and glory of that empire or of its rulers. In addition, the description of Nebuchadnezzar as a lion in strength and an eagle in swiftness was familiar to his contemporaries, as may be seen on the one hand, in Jer. iv. 7; xlix. 19; l. 17, 44; on the other, in Jer. xlix. 22; Lam. iv. 19; Hab. i. 8; Ezek. xvii. 3, 12. Moreover, the rank of the lion as the king of beasts, and of the eagle as the king of birds, corresponds to that of gold, the most precious of metals, which had been in chap. ii. the symbol of the first world-kingdom. As in that instance (v. 38) the king was identified with his realm, and therefore was regarded as its representative, so here the fate of the first world-kingdom is illustrated by various traits taken from the history of Nebuchadnezzar in chap. iv.—**I beheld till the wings thereof were plucked,** *i.e.*, until its power and unrestrained motion were taken from it; cf. chap. iv. 28 et seq.—**And it was lifted up from the earth,** to which, after being deprived of its wings, it had been confined; compare chap. iv. 30 with iv. 33. The words, therefore, as well as those which follow, relate to the restoration from a state of beastly degradation to the upright posture and free dignity of man. Others, as Jerome, Theodoret, Rashi, Bertholdt, Hitzig, etc., render it, "and it was taken away from the earth," as if the sentence implied the destruction of the Chaldæan world-power; but neither its connection with the following context, nor the usual meaning of נְטַל, "to raise up, elevate,"—cf. iv. 31 and the corresponding Heb. verb, Gen. xxi. 18—will justify this reading.—**And made (to) stand upon the feet as a man;** cf. chap. iv. 13, 31, 33; v. 21. Notice the suffixless עַל רַגְלַיִן, "upon two feet," instead of "on *its* two feet," which (corresponding with 2 Kings xiii. 21) would have been employed if the description had from the first referred to Nebuchadnezzar in person. [The phrase "does not mean that the whole beast was lifted up into the air, but that it stood upon its hinder legs, taking the upright position of a man. The purpose of this is explained more fully by the clause that follows.—רַגְלַיִן is a Hebraizing *dual* form, only found in Biblical Chaldee. . . . .—**The heart of a man was given to it,** *i.e.* (in connection with the preceding clause), not only did it take the outward position of a man, but also partook of his internal mind and feelings. I understand the design here to be to characterize the greater moderation and humanity which the Babylonian dominion exhibited after Nebuchadnezzar's malady and restoration, or, to use the language of the prophet, after 'its wings were plucked.'"—*Stuart.*]—See Hitzig on this passage, with reference to the at times venturous explanations offered by exegetes who deny its relation to chap. iv. in any way whatever (*e.g.*, Bertholdt: "The writer designed to indicate in this place that *human* empires are symbolized;" J. D. Michaelis, Dereser: "The civilizing of the formerly barbarous Chaldæans, which was reserved until the Babylonian period, was to be described;" Jerome, Rashi, Ibn-Ezra, etc.: "The standing upon two feet of the hitherto four-footed beast was to symbolize the humiliation of the Chaldæans on the overthrow of their supremacy;" etc., etc.).—Verse 5. **And behold another beast, a second, like to a bear.** אָחֳרִי is the more extended, תִנְיָנָה the more definite idea; the former only is repeated in v. 6, and the latter in v. 7. The bear, considered as being second only to the lion in point of strength and savage disposition, is frequently mentioned in close connection with the latter; *e.g.*, 1 Sam. xvii. 34; Prov. xxviii. 15 (cf. xvii. 12); Wisd. xi. 17.—**And it raised up itself on one side;** or even, "it stood leaning to one side" (Hitzig), as it is to be rendered on the authority of the reading שְׂטַר, "side" (for which several MSS. substitute the usual Aram. form סְטַר.

The common reading שְׁטַר would require to be regarded as synonymous with the Heb. מִשְׁטָר, "dominion" (Job xxxviii. 33), but would thus lead to the vapid sense, "and it raised up one dominion," which is opposed by the context, and is questionable in every respect. This meaning, however, has recently been unsuccessfully advocated by Kranichfeld, who refers to the erection of a Median empire on the ruins of the Babylonian. Most expositors regard it correctly as indicating a *leaning* posture of the beast, an inclination to one side. Such a posture would naturally suggest a tendency to fall, an unsteady, vacillating character of the monarchy in question, verging upon ruin—and thus it has been interpreted by the Sept., Theodot., the Syr., and by many moderns, as Hitzig, Ewald, Kamphausen, etc., who find here a reference to the weakness and brief duration of the *Median* supremacy, which soon gave way to that of the Persians. The context, however, requires that a strong kingdom, animated with a lust for conquest—or, in the figurative language of the text, a "voracious" kingdom—should be understood, to which the words "arise, devour much flesh," are not spoken ironically and uselessly. For this reason we must suppose (with Hävernick; cf. also Bertholdt, Von Lengerke, and Maurer) that the beast inclined *forward*, *i.e.*, that it was prepared to spring and to attack; and this threatening, rapacious, and warlike posture of the beast shows clearly that not the weak and short-lived Median kingdom, but the powerful empire of the Medo-Persians, with its greed for lands and conquest, is intended.*—**And it had three ribs in the mouth of it between the teeth of it.** תְּלָת עִלְעִין evidently designates a prey that has already been seized by the beast, and which it is preparing finally to devour (cf. Num. xi. 33; Zech. ix. 7), and not (as Saadia, Bertholdt, and Hävernick suppose) parts of its own body, such as three *molar teeth*—an interpretation which עִלְעִין nowhere bears. The three states, or even cities, which became the prey of the Persian empire as symbolized by the "three ribs," can hardly be specified; perhaps three is used merely as a round and indefinite number. If, however, it is attempted to designate them more particularly, it will certainly be more appropriate to conceive of three countries, *e.g.*, Babylon, Egypt, and Lydia (or, instead of the latter, Palestine, including Syria), which were conquered by the Medes or Medo-Persians (with De Wette), than (with Hitzig) to think of the three great Assyrian cities on the Tigris, Nineveh, Calah, and Resen,—or Nineveh, Mespila (?), and Larissa, which, according to Xenophon, *Anab.*, III. 4, 10, the Medes are said to have destroyed (cf. Gen. x. 12; Jon. iii. 1 et seq.). —**And they said thus unto it, Arise, devour much flesh.** These words evidently refer to something in the history of the Median empire, that is subsequent to the devouring of the three ribs, and therefore to the later wars of that state for conquest and plunder, which followed after the subjugation of the three neighboring kingdoms. This clearly indicates that the beast described in this connection does not represent Media only, but the united Medo-Persian empire (against Ewald, Kranichfeld, etc.; and also against Hitzig, who applies this command to "devour much flesh" to the overthrow of the Chaldæan empire by the Medes, which he believes to have preceded the destruction of the three cities on the Tigris). The direction to devour much flesh is, however, an appropriate feature in the description of the voracity of this ζῶον πάμφαγον; cf. Micah iii. 2, 3; Isa. ix. 11; Jer. l. 17. The speakers who are implied (אָמְרִין, as in chap. iii. 4; iv. 28) are the angelic powers of God, who govern the world and especially watch over and guide the fortunes of the great world-powers.*—Verse 6. **After this I beheld, and lo another, like a leopard, which had upon the back of it four wings of (or "like") a fowl.** Ewald observes, with entire correctness: "This beast is already distinguished from the other in being less one-sided, and in having 'four wings of a bird'—*i.e.*, such as are large and capable of carrying it swiftly to any place—on its back. [It moves, however, "not so royally as Nebuchadnezzar—for the panther has not eagle's wings but only the wings of a fowl—yet extending to all the regions of the earth" (Keil).] Hence it can move with ease and freedom towards either of the four regions of the world, and therefore, in a sense, it possesses all the four regions of the world, *i.e.*, it is in the full sense a world-kingdom." Cf. Kranichfeld also: "The flashing swiftness of movement, the παρδάλεος ὀξύτης (Hab. i. 8), which is here specially indicated by 'four wings of a fowl on the back of it,' *i.e.*, in a condition for flying, is regarded as characteristic of this beast (the leopard) while lurking for its prey (Jer. v. 6; Hos. xiii. 7). Compared with the clearness and correctness of this interpretation there seems to be a strange lack of motive for the refusal of the two scholars to apply it to that world-kingdom, which more than any other was remarkable for its extension by leaps of panther-like swiftness, and by the lightning-like rapidity of its rise and fall—namely, the Macedonian empire of Alex. the Gr." Cf. the remark of Hitzig: "The special rapidity of the Persian movements to war and victory cannot be historically established"—certainly a correct remark, but one which ought not to have decided its author, who was likewise an opponent of the Macedonian hypothesis, to regard the four wings in this instance, not as symbols of rapid movement, but as "an emblem of the far-reaching protecting royal power from above" (after Lam. iv. 20; Psa. xxxvi. 8).—**The beast had also four heads,** *i.e.*, it extended its dominion in the four quarters of the earth, and governed the whole world. The words which follow, "and dominion was given unto it," are probably merely epexegetical of this symbolical description, in which the four heads have the same significance as the pushing of the ram towards the four quarters of the heavens in chap. viii. 4, or as the four faces of the cherubs which looked towards the four quarters of the earth in Ezek. i. 10 et seq. If it is desired to interpret the four heads more closely, they may be taken to represent the four principal divisions

* [Keil adopts a different, but, as it seems to us, far-fetched and over-ingenious interpretation: "This means neither that it leaned on one side (Ebrard), nor that it stood on its fore feet (Hävernick), for the sides of a bear are not its fore and hinder parts; but we conceive that the beast, resting on its feet, raised up the feet of the one side for the purpose of going forward, and so raised the shoulder or the whole body on that side. But with such a motion of the beast the geographical situation of the kingdom (Geier, Mich., Ros.) cannot naturally be represented, much less can the near approach of the destruction of the kingdom (Hitzig) be signified. Hofmann, Delitzsch, and Kliefoth have found the right interpretation by a reference to ch. ii. and viii. As in ch. ii. the arms on each side of the breast signify that the second kingdom will consist of two parts, and this is more distinctly indicated in ch. viii. by the two horns, one of which rose up after the other, and higher, so also in this verse the double-sidedness of this world-kingdom is represented by the beast lifting itself up on one side. The Medo-Persian bear, as such, has, as Kliefoth well remarks, two sides; the one, the Median side, is at rest after the efforts made for the erection of the world-kingdom; but the other, the Persian side, raises itself up, and then becomes not only higher than the first, but also is prepared for new rapine."—Stuart justly remarks that "the difficulty seems to have arisen from the fact that, until lately, we have been ignorant of a like symbol sculptured on the ancient monuments of Persia. Münter (*Rel. der Bab.*, p. 112) has given us a description (with an engraving) of an animal of the symbolic kind, in a group near the star of Belus, which, kneeling or lying on the right foot, has its left one erect. A sense of security, combined with watchfulness, seems to be the indication. Probably this symbol, now on the monuments of Persia and Babylon, was a part of what belonged to the *insignia* of the royal and national standards."]

* ["The plur. אָמְרִין *is impersonal*" (Keil); "it might be rendered passively" (Stuart).]

or aggregates of countries which the empire of Alexander embraced (cf. Hävernick on this passage), *e.g.*, Greece, Western Asia, Egypt, and Persia (including India). This is less arbitrary, at least, than the opinion of Jerome, that the heads represented the four leading generals of Alexander, viz.: Ptolemy, Seleucus, Philip, and Antigonus, or than the favorite assumption of many moderns after Von Lengerke (*e.g.*, Hitzig, Ewald, Kamphausen, etc.), that the author represents the four earliest Persian kings, from Cyrus to Xerxes, who alone were known to him as the four heads of the leopard. The advocates of the latter opinion refer for support to chap. xi. 2, which passage, however, does not even imply that Daniel knew of but four kings of Persia (see on that passage), to say nothing of its affording no proof whatever that the present passage is concerned with *any* Persian kings. Our apocalyptist does not represent kings by heads, but by horns (see vs. 8 and 24 et seq.); a feature which recurs in the apocalypse of St. John, where the ten horns of the beast (Rev. xvii. 13) symbolize ten kings, while the seven heads indicate seven mountains. This analogy seems to favor the view of Hävernick, which assumes that the four heads represent the four principal sections of the world-kingdom in question, but of course without demonstrating its correctness.—Verse 7. **After this I saw in the night visions, and behold a fourth beast, dreadful and terrible, and strong exceedingly.** Observe the solemn minuteness with which the fourth beast is introduced, and also the description as both "dreadful and terrible," דְּחִילָה וְאֵמְתָנִי; cf. Chr. B. Michaelis: "*Junguntur duo synonyma, ad intendendum rem significatam, ut hæc bestia non vulgariter, sed supra modum horribilis apparuisse videatur.*" *—**And it had great iron teeth.** Iron is mentioned as signifying firmness and incisive sharpness (cf. Jer. xv. 12; Mic. iv. 13), while the teeth symbolize its lust of conquest (cf. v. 5).—**It devoured and brake in pieces and stamped the residue with the feet of it.** Unlike the other beasts, it was not content with simply securing its prey, but, rejoicing in destruction, it stamped with its feet what it could not devour. This description evidently does not indicate that the conquests of the fourth world-kingdom were more extensive than those of its predecessors, but merely that its course was more devastating and destructive. This obviously alludes to the description of the legs of iron and clay (the organs employed in treading and stamping), which belonged to the colossus in chap. ii., and corresponds fully to the actual character of the empires of the Macedonian Diadochi, and particularly that of the Seleucidæ. Cf. Kranichfeld: "It is generally acknowledged that the description of the fourth beast agrees in its leading features with that of the fourth kingdom in chap. ii. 40; especially in regard to its rage for destruction, which crushed without pity and trode everything under foot. Even the iron, the medium of destruction in chap. ii. 23, 40, returns here in the large teeth of the monster. The terrible appearance of the colossus resulted primarily from its fourth constituent part, and corresponding to this, the qualities which produce a terrible appearance are here expressly connected with the form of the fourth beast."—**And it was diverse from all the beasts before it.** This does not assert that "it combined in itself all that was prominent in the three former beasts, the lion, bear, and leopard respectively" (Jerome, Hävernick, et al., under comparison with Rev. xiii. 2), but merely that it differed from them all, and displayed its nature in a way that could not be realized by a comparison with the lion, the bear, or the leopard. This difference of the fourth beast from all the others is chiefly suggestive of the *fragmentary* and *divided* character of the fourth world-kingdom, and consequently alludes to the composition of the feet of the colossus out of intermingled iron and clay.* The opinion of Hävernick and other advocates of the theory which regards the Roman empire as the fourth world-kingdom, that this description indicates the contrast between the character of that empire and that of the Oriental-Hellenistic monarchies which preceded it, is entirely too far-fetched; but that of Hitzig is no less so, when, in the support of his theory that the fourth beast represents Alexander the Great, he asserts that the contrast between the Hellenistic and the Oriental rule is here indicated—a contrast that was far greater than that between Rome and the world-kingdoms which preceded it.—**And it had ten horns.** According to v. 24 these ten horns represent "ten kings." Unlike ordinary animals, which have two horns, this monster representing the fourth world-kingdom has ten, being so many symbols of warlike power and dominion (cf. Deut. xxxiii. 17; 1 Sam. ii. 1, 10; Psa. xviii. 3; Job xvi. 15; Mic. iv. 13, etc.). The number ten is hardly to be strained, in this connection, to represent ten specified kings; but like the number four in v. 6, it is rather to be taken in a *symbolic* sense, and to be regarded as indicating a multiplicity of rulers, or an indefinitely large number of kings—in harmony with the usual significance of the number,

* ["The writer gives to this fourth beast no particular name. Plainly it was a peculiar monster. The reason why he omits a name seems to be, that in the world of nature no similitude could be found, for in no case of really-existing beasts are four of them united in one, so as to constitute an appropriate symbol for the four kingdoms of Alexander's successors. He classes these under the dynasty, comprehensively considered, which grew up out of the predominance or victories of the Greeks in the East. But when enough is introduced to designate the general nature of the dynasty, both here and in ch. viii. and xi., he goes over into a notice of only such kings as were in the neighborhood of Palestine, and had more or less to do with annoying it. As Antiochus Epiphanes was incomparably the most annoying and mischievous of them all, so a peculiar share of the prophecy respecting the fourth dynasty is allotted to him in each of the chapters named. It is evident from a comparison of historical facts as well as from the nature of the case, that a dynasty is spoken of by Daniel as more or less dreadful and destructive according to the measure in which Palestine was actually affected by it in this way."—*Stuart.* Keil, on the contrary, who adopts the common or "orthodox" interpretation of the fourth monarchy, gives a different explanation of this feature: "The fourth kingdom is represented by a nameless beast, because in Daniel's time Rome had not come into contact with Israel, and as yet lay beyond the circle of vision of Old-Testament prophecy." This candid admission one would think might have led the commentator to doubt any reference even here to Rome. He does not seem, moreover, to have perceived that, for precisely the same reason the Macedonian empire should have been represented by some nameless beast, as being hitherto unknown to the Hebrews.]

* [May not the diversity rather consist in the fact that, unlike all the former governments, the Seleucid dynasty began a systematic attack upon the *religious* institutions of the subject Jews?]

both in the Scriptures and elsewhere, as the symbol of earthly perfection.* Kranichfeld observes correctly, "It is clearly not in the nature of the prophetic idea, that the number ten, in addition to the value which it thus has for the writer, should be capable of being demonstrated on the analogy of ordinary numerals, in the realization of the picture of the future." The notes on chap. xi. will show that in the more detailed description of the development of the fourth world-power in that place, there is by no means an exact enumeration of ten kings on the throne of the Seleucidæ.—Verse 8. **And behold, there came up among them another little horn.** Concerning אָחֳרִי, and its relation to the succeeding modifying predicate, see supra, on v. 5.—The prophet observes the rising or springing up of this little horn, the eleventh one, as taking place between the ten which already existed (notice the idea of *continued* observation, so to speak, of *being lost* in observation, which is indicated by the expression מִשְׂתַּכַּל הֲוֵית, "I was engaged in considering, in observing"). The smallness of the new horn in this case, as in the parallel chap. viii. 9, refers merely to its original state, not to its later appearance when fully grown; for, according to v. 20, it was then greater than any of the other horns. Concerning the reading סִלְקַת, instead of סִלְקָת, see Hitzig on this passage.—**Before** (or "by") **whom there were three of the first horns plucked up by the roots**; *i.e.*, it grew so strongly, and through its growth exercised so disturbing an influence upon its neighbors, that three of them were uprooted and wholly destroyed. Here also the definite number "three" is hardly to be strained to signify precisely three kings, who were overthrown by the monarch represented by the eleventh horn.† The prophecy certainly had its more immediate Messianic fulfilment in the manner in which Antiochus Epiphanes rose from his originally obscure condition to the throne of the Seleucidæ, by removing two or perhaps three of his rivals (see infra); but from the prophet's point of view, involving substantially a merely ideal, or, more correctly, a dream-like indefinite view of the future, the idea of precisely this personage in future history, and of the political conjunctures preceding his accession to the throne, was assuredly excluded.—**And behold, in this horn were eyes like the eyes of a man.** Eyes like those of a man, human eyes (therefore *two* in number, despite the plural עַיְנִין, which is probably substituted for the dual for euphonic reasons merely, and by virtue of a usage that is frequent in the Chaldee), are borne by the horn in token that it represents a *man*,* and, moreover, a wise, judicious man; for here as elsewhere (*e.g.*, Ezek. i. 18; x. 12) eyes are the symbol of understanding; cf. שׂכל, "to look at, understand."—**And a mouth speaking great** (or "proud") **things**; a farther indication of the *human* nature and character of the historical personage prefigured by the horn. מְמַלִּל רַבְרְבָן, properly, "speaking great or monstrous things;" cf. supra, on v. 3, and also infra, v. 11; also the Heb. דִּבֵּר גְּדוֹלוֹת, Psa. xii. 4. The interpretation in v. 25 shows that blasphemies are meant by this "speaking of great things;" cf. xi. 36; Rev. xiii. 5.†

Verses 9–12. *The Divine judgment upon the world-powers.* **I beheld** (such things) **till the thrones were cast down** (or "set"). The A. V. is literal (רְמִיו). The chairs of the Orientals consist of cushions, which are not *set* down, but laid down, and, in case of haste, are *cast* down; cf. ἔκειντο, Rev. iv. 2. The place where the thrones are set is not in heaven, for according to v. 13 the Son of man descends to it from heaven; nor is it on the earth, but, as in chap. xii. 7, a locality intervening between heaven and earth. ["Seats, not merely a throne for God the judge, but a number of seats for the assembly sitting in judgment with God. That assembly consists neither of the elders of Israel (Rabbins), nor of glorified men (Hengstenb. on Rev. iv. 4), but of angels (Psa. lxxxix. 8), who are to be distinguished from the thousands and tens of thousands mentioned in ver. 10, for those do not sit upon thrones, but stand before God as servants to fulfil his commands and execute His judgments" (Keil).]—**And the** ("an") **Ancient of days did sit**; viz., on his throne, in order to preside at the judgment; cf. Psa. ix. 5; xxix. 10; Isa. xxviii. 6. The "Ancient of days" (עַתִּיק יוֹמִין), *i.e.*, the aged in days (πεπαλαιωμένος ἡμερῶν, Sus. 52), is doubtless the God of Israel, the same as the Most High, v. 25, who was blasphemed by the little horn. He is described as the "Ancient of days," probably not by way of comparison with the *younger* associated judges, nor yet with the "blasphemous upstart," the little horn (Kranichfeld), but in comparison with the more recent gods of the heathen; cf. Deut. xxxii. 17; Jer. xxiii. 23. This predicate therefore refers to that attribute of the God of the Old Covenant, which is designated in such expressions as אֱלֹהֵי קֶדֶם, Deut. xxxiii. 27, יֹשֵׁב קֶדֶם, Psa. lv. 20; *βασιλεὺς τῶν αἰώνων*, 1 Tim. i. 17; *ὁ πρῶτος καὶ ὁ ἔσχατος*, Rev. i. 17 (cf. Isa. xliv. 6; xlviii. 12). "He, who from primitive times has proven Himself a powerful judge, assumes the form of venerable age, in order to beget the confidence that He pos-

* See Leyrer, art. *Zahlen* in Herzog's Real-Encyklop., vol. 18, p. 378: also Zöckler, *Theologia naturalis*, I. 713 et seq. In both places the essentially *political* or *cosmical* significance of this number is pointed out, in opposition to Delitzsch, who regards it as the symbol of *Divine* perfection. Cf. further, Bähr. *Symbolik des mos. Kultus*, I. 175; Hofmann, *Weissagung und Erfüllung*, I. 75; Hengstenberg, *Beiträge z. Einl.*, III. 391, 605. [On the contrary, it seems to us that the definiteness of the numbers *four* and *three* in the same connection requires a similar definiteness in this number likewise. See our remarks in the Ethico-fundamental principles, etc., on this chap., No. 3, *a*.]

† [See, however, the remarks in the Ethico-fundamental principles, etc., below, 3, *a*.]

* ["The eyes of a man were not attributed to it (merely) in opposition to a beast, but in opposition to a higher celestial being, for whom the ruler denoted by the horn might be mistaken on account of the terribleness of his rule and government: '*ne cum putemus juxta quorundam opinionem vel diabolum esse vel dæmonem, sed unum de hominibus, in quo totus Satanas habiturus sit corporealiter*,' as Jerome well remarks; cf. Hofmann and Kliefoth."—*Keil.*]

† ["A mouth which speaketh great things is a vain glorious mouth. רַבְרְבָן are *presumptuous things*, not directly blasphemous (Hävr.). In the Apocalypse, xiii. 5, μεγάλα and βλασφημίαι are distinguished."—*Keil.*]

sesses the wisdom and power to bring the blasphemer to judgment."—**His garment was white as snow**; thus correctly Theodot., Vulg., Hitzig, under comparison with Mark ix. 3, but conflicting with the Masoretic accentuation, which requires " as the white snow." The white color of the garment is probably not designed " to increase the impression of awful majesty " (Kranichf.), but to symbolize the *purity* and *innocence* of the judge. He appears, " so to speak, robed in the צְדָקָה of the righteous judge;" cf. Isa. lix. 17; Job xxix. 14; 2 Chron. xix. 7, and also the passages which mention the light, the symbol of *holiness*, as the garment of God, *e.g.*, Ezek. i. 26; Psa. civ. 2; 1 Tim. vi. 16.—**And the hair of his head like the pure wool,** hence, likewise as white as snow, as in the case of a venerable sage. Cf. the parallelism of snow and wool in passages like Isa. i. 16; Psa. cxlvii. 16; Rev. i. 14.—**His throne like the fiery flame;** flashing like flaming fire, and apparently composed of it. The mention of the fiery appearance of the throne of God, does not of itself convey the conception of flaming vengeance on the part of the strict judge (Deut. iv. 24; ix. 3; xxxii. 22; Heb. xii. 29, etc.); for He frequently appears surrounded by fire in cases where His judicial character is not involved, *e.g.*, Gen. xv. 17; Ex. iii. 3; Psa. xviii. 9, etc. In the present instance, however, the judicial significance of the fire that emanates from God is clearly established by the connection, as in Ex. xix. 16; xx. 15; Psa. l. 3 et seq. (against Hitzig and Von Lengerke).—**His wheels as burning fire.** The throne of the universal judge is therefore mounted on wheels (cf. the cherubic chariot, Ezek. i. 12 et seq.; x. 13 et seq.; Psa. lxxvii. 19), whose swift revolutions are encompassed with flashing fire. This description of the Divine throne of judgment as mounted upon wheels leads Kranichfeld to the incongruous opinion that the " casting down of the thrones" was accompanied with noise (!).—Verse 10. **A fiery stream issued and came forth from him**; *i.e.*, from the Divine Judge, not from His throne; for the קֳדָמוֹהִי of the first sentence can hardly be construed with a different object from that of the second, which clearly relates to God. Nevertheless both the author of the book of Enoch (xiv. 19) and the writer of the Apocalypse (iv. 9) represent the fiery stream as issuing from the *throne*, in the descriptions copied by them from this passage. Ewald interprets the " stream of fire " as a " stream of light," and arbitrarily makes it the symbol of the *speech* which issues from God, that is, of His *command* to begin the judgment (in support of which he appeals to chap. ii. 15; vi. 27, etc., whose character is entirely different). Hitzig is no less arbitrary when he remarks that the stream must be conceived as flowing evenly over a smooth bottom (hence like liquid glowing lava!), and as constituting the floor for the entire scene of the judicial procedure, since without this "the whole apparition would float in the air without support"—an empty fancy, which the prophet's language in no wise favors.*—**Thousand thousands ministered unto him, and ten thousand times ten thousand stood before him.** The imperfect tense of the verbs indicates that a readiness to serve existed in the thousands as a constant and enduring quality. Concerning " to stand before one " as synonymous with " to serve," cf. chap. i. 4.—In relation to the plural ending ־ִים in אַלְפִּים, which the Keri rejects as a Hebraism, cf. chap. iv. 14; Ezra iv. 13.—The Kethib רִבְוָן (the plural of רִבּוֹ) immediately following is likewise to be retained, in opposition to the Hebraizing Keri רִבְבָן; Hitzig's suggestion, however, to write רִבּוּ (on the analogy of the corresponding Syr. word) instead of רִבּוֹ is unnecessary.—The " thousand thousands and ten thousand times ten thousand " are of course a host of ministering angels, which, standing in a wide circle, surrounds the council of the judges who are *seated* beside God (these are angels of a superior order, or perhaps " elders," cf. Rev. iv. 4). Cf. Deut. xxxiii. 2; 1 Kings xxii. 19; Neh. ix. 6; Psa. lxviii. 18; ciii. 20 et seq., and also the mention of the angelic hosts in Gen. xxxii. 3; 2 Kings vi. 17, etc. The numbers 1,000 and 10,000 are not to be regarded as definite; they indicate, in a symbolic manner, the impression of an innumerable multitude which was made on the prophet in his dream-vision, while he was naturally in no condition to overlook the whole of this immense host, to say nothing of counting its numbers exactly; cf. Psa. lxviii. 18; xci. 7.*—**The judgment was set.** דִּינָא is properly an abstract word, signifying "judgment;" here used concretely to designate the judicial conclave composed of the superior angels—the angelic princes or archangels (cf. Josh. v. 14; Tob. xii. 15, etc.); cf. the analogous use of *judicium* in the concrete by Cicero, *Verr.*, II. 18. Since chairs indeed were mentioned in the foregoing (v. 9 *a*), but nothing was said about the judges taking their seats, we must find it indicated in this place, and it is therefore not necessary to explain, with Dathe and Kranichfeld, that " He seated Himself in judgment " (the Ancient of days), as if this were merely a repetition of יְתִב in v. 9 (similarly also Syrus, who read דַּיָּנָא instead of דִּינָא, and therefore renders it, " the judge seated himself ").—**And the books were opened;** the books of record, in which the good and bad deeds of men were recorded, that they may serve as a basis of the sentence to be pronounced upon men by God, the heavenly judge. Cf. Rev. xx. 12, as well as the frequent mention of the " book of life " in which the names of the

* ["Fire and the shining of fire are the constant phenomena of the manifestation of God in the world as the earthly elements most fitting for the representation of the burning zeal with which the holy God not only punishes and destroys sinners but also purifies and renders glorious His own people; see on Exod. iii. 3."—*Keil.*]

* ["In the N. T. Christians are represented as sharing in the like solemnities, 1 Cor. vi. 2; Matt. xix. 28; Luke xxii. 30; Rev. iii. 21. Not improbably such expressions as 'Let *us* make man in our image,' 'Let *us* go down and see,' 'Who will go for us?' take their *plural* form from such views of the heavenly *Concessus*. The sum of the matter is that the prophet presents the Supreme Lord and Judge to our view by imagery borrowed from earthly sovereigns, *i.e.*, as having all the insignia of pre-eminence and supremacy around him."—*Stuart.*]

heirs of celestial glory, who have been reconciled to God, are inserted,—in Ex. xxxii. 32; Psa. lxix. 29; Isa. iv. 3; Dan. xii. 1 (see on that passage); Luke x. 20; Phil. iv. 3; Rev. iii. 5; xx. 15; also the "book of remembrance," in which God records the sufferings of His faithful servants, which is noticed in Psa. lvi. 9; Mal. iii. 16, etc. —Verse 11. **I beheld then, because of the voice of great words which the horn spake—I beheld even till the beast was slain.** An anacoluthon, in the second חָזֵה הֲוֵית repeats the first, which was separated from בֵּאדַיִן by the accent, but gives a somewhat different turn to the thought; cf. the similar constructions in Jer. xx. 5; Rev. xii. 9; 1 Macc. i. 1. עַד דִּי, "till that," indicates a protracted trial, which ends with the destruction of the beast, *i.e.*, with the judicial execution of the God-opposed world-power. The little horn, representing the last anti-christian king of the fourth monarchy, who brings ruin upon his whole empire by his insolent rebellion against the Most High, is designated as the cause for this destruction.—**And his body destroyed, and given to the burning flame**; rather, "and given for burning to the flame." The latter of these expressions illustrates the former; the destroying of the "body" of the beast, *i.e.*, of the entire edifice of anti-christian national power, is effected by burning, which burning (יְקֵדָא = Heb. שְׂרֵפָה in Isa. lxiv. 10) is of course to be taken figuratively, as in Isa. ix. 4; lxvi. 24; Rev. xix. 20; xx. 10; and the fiery nature of the Divine Judge of the world, as described in v. 9, unquestionably stands in a causal relation to the kindling of this devouring fire of judgment; cf. Isa. x. 17; xxx. 27; Zeph. i. 18, etc.—Verse 12. **The rest of the beasts: they had their dominion taken away**; rather, "and the power of the rest of the beasts was also taken away." The subjects of הֶעְדִּיו are the celestial powers, as in v. 5. Since the dominion of the three earlier beasts was destroyed before the rise of the fourth, so far at least as it was a dominion over the world in the proper sense, and since it does not seem admissible to take הֶעְדִּיו in the sense of the pluperfect, thus explaining the passage as a mere supplementary note (against Ephraem, Polychron., Kamphausen, C. B. Michaelis, etc.), the judgment inflicted on the "rest of the beasts" together with that visited on the fourth must be understood to signify that *utter destruction of the heathen world-powers which subjects the remnants of all the four world-kingdoms to the new all-embracing Messianic dominion, and incorporates them in its realm*; for as the characteristic expression שְׁאָר חֵיוָתָא, "the rest of the beasts" (instead of חֵיוְתָא אָחֳרָן or כָל־חֵיוָתָא דִּי קָדָמַיהּ, v. 7 *b*) indicates, certain fragments or remnants of the three former world-kingdoms are conceived of as continuing to exist beside the fourth, and as being involved in its destruction. The fall of the three earlier world-kingdoms is not regarded as complete by the prophet, inasmuch as larger or smaller portions of them continue to exist beside the last—perhaps temporarily incorporated into it as provinces, but not on that account assimilated to it—until the Messianic judgment involves them in a common destruction. That he refers only to such remnants, and not to *new* kingdoms essentially distinct from the former world-monarchies (as J. D. Michaelis, Von Lengerke, Hitzig, Ewald, etc., suppose), is evident (1) from the parallel description in chap. ii., where the destruction of the four constituent parts of the colossus results at the last and in the same moment through the agency of the stone which rolls from the mountain (see v. 34 et seq., and especially v. 44); (2) from the later parallel, chap. viii. 4, where all the beasts (כָּל־חַיּוֹת) with whom the Persian ram contends, are likewise only the constituent parts into which the latest world-kingdom had dissolved, and which are all overthrown and subjugated by the new dynasty (see on that passage, and compare Kranichfeld's remarks on this place, p. 265 et seq., which are certainly correct).—**Yet their lives were prolonged for a season and time**; rather, "for the duration of their life was fixed, to the season and time." This time (זְמַן, identical with זִמְנָא, v. 22, according to the correct opinion of Von Lengerke, Kranichfeld, etc.) has come, so far as the seer is concerned, with the judgment of the fourth beast and of the remnants of the other beasts, which has just been described. The duration of their lives (אַרְכָה בְחַיִּין, properly "respite, prolongation of life") finds its unalterable *terminus ad quem* in this period of Messianic judgment, beyond which, indeed, the various nations (v. 14) continue to exist, but not the *heathen world powers* formerly composed of them. Concerning זְמַן וְעִדָּן (= Heb. עֵת וּמוֹעֵד) see on chap. ii. 21.

Verses 13, 14. *The erection of Messiah's kingdom.* **I saw in the night visions, and behold**; again a solemn and circumstantial introduction, like that preceding the description of the fourth beast in v. 7. Cf. the minuteness with which the prophet dwelt on the description of the fourth world-power, and of the Messianic judgment which came upon it, in chap. ii. 40 et seq. —**(One) like the Son of man came with the clouds of heaven**; literally, "with the clouds of heaven (one) coming like a Son of man" (אָתֵה הֲוָא). The subject is omitted, and must be rendered indefinitely by "one," as in chap. viii. 15; x. 16, 18. "*With* the clouds of heaven," *i.e.*, together with them (Rev. i. 7), and therefore *in* them (Mark xiii. 26) or *upon* them, ἐπὶ τῶν νεφελῶν (Matt. xxiv. 30; xxvi. 64; Rev. xiv. 14). As the Messiah here comes to God upon the clouds of heaven and stands before Him, so God Himself rides, in poetical and prophetic descriptions elsewhere, upon the clouds as His celestial chariot, cf. Psa. civ. 3; Jer. iv. 13; also Psa. xviii. 10–18; xcvii. 2–4; Nah. i. 3 et seq.; Isa xix. 1 (cf. Isa. xiv. 14).—בַּר אֱנָשׁ, "son of a man, son of man," is a simple circumlocution to express the idea "man," which is found also in the Syr. and the Targums; and therefore = the Heb. אֱנוֹשׁ or אָדָם, for which the Heb. also occasionally substitutes בֶּן־אָדָם or בַּר־אֱנוֹשׁ (see Psa. viii. 5; cxliv. 3; and infra, chap. viii. 17; x. 16, 18). This combination serves to specially point out an organic connection with or membership in the human race. The personage whom Daniel saw coming with the clouds of heaven had the appearance, therefore, of being one of the human race—a man. The mention of the human appearance of the apparition certainly does not aim at contrasting it with the forms of the beasts before described (as Hofmann supposes, *Weissagung und Erfüllung*, I. 290); for these have passed from the prophet's vision in consequence of their destruction, which has already transpired (vs. 11, 12). The comparison with the human form of Him who comes with the clouds, which, although not expressed, is certainly implied, is to be found in the *super*-human—hence the *Divine*, or at least *angelic*—form, which the seer would naturally expect to behold in these exalted scenes (see Ewald on this passage). That he should observe a form similar to that of man, shining through the clouds, instead of a terrifying apparition that blinds and confuses his senses, produces on him an impression of wonder, but also of pleasure. Cf. Kranichfeld: "The case here is different from that of chap. iii. 25, where only ordinary *men* might be looked for in the fiery furnace, so that he who became the associate of the three Jews was at first regarded merely as partaking of *human* nature, and a comparison with *merely* human traits was necessary to lead the judgment to express the stronger utterance כְּבַר אֱלָהִין, without thereby denying the human appearance of the form. And as the judgment in iii. 25 rests in the conclusion that the personage in question belongs to the race of gods, although present in human form, so it here concludes that the object of notice is one *belonging to the human race, but wearing the form of God*." The prophet, however, holds fast to the distinction between a wholly human appearance and the vision he has seen, and indicates this by the particle of comparison כְּ, which points out that he intends to represent a *really supernatural*, but still human-like personage. (The correspondence with the כְּ in vs. 4 and 6, does not militate against this conception of the כְּ here—despite the assertion to the contrary by Richno, in the *Stud. u. Kritt.*, 1869, II., p. 255.) There cannot be the slightest doubt, in view of the entire description, particularly in v. 14, and also in view of the exactly corresponding signification of the destroying stone, in the parallel vision of the 2d chapter (see ii. 44 et seq.), that this superhuman form of a man represents the *Messiah*, the Divine-human founder of that fifth world-kingdom, which is at the same time a heavenly kingdom of eternal duration. The effort of Hitzig to refer the כְּבַר אֱנָשׁ to the people of Israel as the "personified community of saints, which rules over the heathen," is merely the product of a persistent and fundamental aversion to the idea of a personal Messiah, which results naturally from the extreme rationalistic position of that exegete. The interpretation which asserts a personal Messiah is advocated by nearly all expositors (with the exception of Ibn-Ezra, Jahn, Paulus, Baumgarten-Crusius, and Hofmann, who agree with Hitzig, but, in part, for very different reasons, and giving a more positive turn to the subject), and is removed beyond the region of doubt, (1) by vs. 18 and 21 of this chapter, in which an unbiassed exegesis is compelled to find the people of Israel clearly distinguished from the Son of man (see on v. 18); (2) by the undeniable reference of υἱὸς τοῦ ἀνθρώπου, the pre-eminently favorite Messianic designation of Himself employed by the Saviour, to this passage (Matt. viii. 20, etc.; John xii. 34); (3) by important testimonies of the Jewish-Hellenistic literature, such as Enoch (xlvi. 1-3; xlviii. 2 et seq.; lxii. 7, 9, 14; lxiii. 11; lxix. 27.—Cf. Hilgenfeld, *Jüdische Apokalyptik*, p. 155 et seq.), *Orac. Sibyll.* (III., 286 et seq., 653 et seq., ed. Friedlieb; cf. Zündel, *Kritische Untersuchungen*, p. 163 et seq.); * (4) by most of the rabbins (*e.g.*, R. Joshua in Ibn-Ezra, Saadia, Rashi, Ibn-Jahja, etc.), who frequently designate the Messiah simply as עֲנָנִי, "the beclouded one." Cf. the Eth.-fund. principles, etc., No. 4.—**And came to the Ancient of days**; *i.e.*, he was admitted to the immediate presence of God (cf. Ezek. xlii. 13), conducted before Him until he was placed as near as were the elders who sat on the right and left, and even still nearer.—**And they brought him near before him.** The subject of הַקְרְבוּהִי is probably not "the clouds," but rather thy ministering angels, v. 10. Thus Hitzig, Ewald, etc., correctly hold, in opposition to Kranichfeld, who construes the clouds as the subject, and to several others, as Kamphausen, etc., who prefer to leave the subject wholly undesignated, as with הֶעְדִּיו, v. 12.—That the Messiah was required to be brought before God and be presented to Him at this juncture, indicates that the prophet regards him as having previously existed while the beasts exercised their dominion—and therefore that he ascribes *personal pre-existence* to him. Daniel probably conceived of him as pre-existing among the thousands and tens of thousands of the saints of God, and as subduing and crushing the God-opposed world-powers at their head (vs. 11, 12); for only thus can be explained the investing of the Messiah with eternal dominion over the kingdom of God, which is evidently a reward for his valiant battling in the service of the Most High, as described in the next verse; cf. also the parallel description in chap. ii. 44 et seq.—Verse 14. **And there was given him dominion and glory, and a kingdom.** Instead of יְהִב Syrus and the Vulgate read יְהַב—"and He (the Ancient of days) gave him," etc.; likewise Luther in this place and the parallel v. 22, where also the Sept. and Theodot. interpret יְהַב. In the latter instance the active sense would certainly seem preferable, since the "Ancient of days" immediately precedes a different verb in the 3d sing. active as its subject; here, however, this subject is too distant, and the analogy of vs. 4 and 6 recommends the passive form יְהִיב.—The triad "dominion, glory, and kingdom" recalls chap. iii. 33; iv. 31; vi. 22, where at least "dominion" (שָׁלְטָן) and "kingdom" (מַלְכוּ) are given.

* Cf. also *Sibyll.*, l. II., p. 277, ed. Galland: ἥξει ἐν νεφέλῃ πρὸς ἄφθιτον ἄφθιτος αὐτὸς ἐν δόξῃ χριστὸς σὺν ἀμύμοσιν ἀγγελτῆρσι καὶ καθίσει, κτλ.

Upon it is based the ancient doxology at the close of the Lord's prayer: σοῦ γάρ ἡ βασιλεία καὶ ἡ δύναμις καὶ ἡ δόξα εἰς τοὺς αἰῶνας.—**And all people . . . . should serve** ("served") **him.** Concerning the triad "peoples, tribes, and tongues" see on chap. iii. 4. Von Lengerke and Ewald regard יִפְלְחוּן as future, "shall serve him," but thereby assume a rather harsh change of tense in the midst of the remarks which describe the objects seen in the vision. Hitzig, Kranichfeld, etc., are correct in considering the verb as logically dependent on the preceding principal verb יְהִיב, thus expressing design—"in order that," or, "so that all people, etc., should serve him." פלח in itself is certainly not to be limited to signify *religious* service (Divine adoration, *cultus*), for in the extra-Biblical Chaldee, *e.g.*, in the Targums, it signifies also a purely secular service, and in v. 27 of this chapter it is synonymous with אשתמע, "to obey;" but in point of fact it serves, both here and in that passage, to designate service rendered to a Divine person, which is also its bearing in chap. iii. 12 et seq.—**His dominion is an everlasting dominion, which shall not be destroyed.** Cf. chap. iii. 33; iv. 31; vi. 27; also Mic. iv. 7; Luke i. 33; Rev. xi. 15; xix. 16, etc.

Verses 15–18. *The interpretation of the vision in general, without special reference to the fourth beast.* The impression of alarm produced on Daniel by what he saw, led him to seek a further explanation of its meaning. He therefore mingles with the host that surrounds the Ancient of days, after having hitherto remained apart as a mere observer. A second act in the drama of the dream-vision, in which the prophet himself takes part, though merely as an inquirer, begins therefore at this point. Von Lengerke arbitrarily remarks: "The vision is now over (with v. 14); but the seer remains on the heavenly scene, and requests an angel to interpret the dream." That this is incorrect, appears from v. 16, where the ministering hosts of angels mentioned in v. 10 still appear, while on that assumption they must have disappeared with all the other features of the vision; and the character of what follows, to the end of the chapter, does not indicate that it is a mere interpretation as distinguished from the preceding dream.—**I, Daniel, was grieved in my spirit in the midst of my body;** properly, "within in the sheath" (בְּגוֹ נִדְנֶה), *i.e.*, in the body, which contains the spirit, as the sword is contained in its scabbard; cf. Job xxvii. 8; Pliny, *H. N.*, VII., 53. Ewald well remarks that "as the sword remains at rest as long as it is in its sheath, so the spirit of man is generally quiet while it feels itself enclosed by the coarse veil of the body; but there are still moments in which the spirit becomes restless while in its coarse tenement, and when it would break forth impatiently and venture all," etc. In relation to כְּרָא (properly "to abbreviate, contract, *torquere*") as designating an unusually bitter grief, cf. the corresponding Syr. and Arab. verbs. The feature that plunges the prophet into so severe and bitter sorrow is not so much the circumstance that he is unacquainted with the special meaning of the vision, as that a majority of its features, and particularly the four beasts and the dreadful fate imposed on them, were so prophetic of evil and misfortune. The end, indeed, toward which everything was tending, according to vs. 13 and 14, was glorious, but the way by which to reach it was painful, and opened a prospect of severe conflicts for the people of God; and the prophet must have suspected this, even before it was explained to him in detail.—אֲנָה, in the combination רוּחִי אֲנָה, is not the nominat. absol., as Bertholdt supposed, but is in apposition to the suffix in רוּחִי; cf. viii. 1, 15; Ezra vii. 21; also Winer, § 40, 4, and concerning the corresponding construction in the Hebrew, see Gesenius, *Lehrgeb.*, p. 728. The solemn emphasis which the prophet's language gains by this appositional supplement, corresponds to the importance of his vision; cf. chap. x. 1, 7; xii. 5.—Verse 16. **I came near unto one of them that stood by,** *i.e.*, one of those engaged in His service, who stood about God.—**And asked him the truth** (or "the true explanation") **of all this;** יַצִּיבָא properly "the firm, or certain;" here used of the trustworthy interpretation, conforming to the designs of God, for which Daniel asks. Kranichfeld interpolates: "He desires that nothing should be concealed because of a desire to spare the inquirer in his excited state." This additional idea of laying aside reserve, of disregarding considerations of pity, is not contained in the simple יַצִּיבָא.—**And he told me, and made me know the interpretation of the things** (or "words"), viz.: in the remarks which follow (vs. 17, 18). The clause "and made me to know" is therefore epexegetical to "and he told me;" the ו before פְּשַׁר is explicative, as in v. 1 *a*. Von Lengerke and Kranichfeld unnecessarily take יְהוֹדְעִנַּנִי in the telic sense, "He told me that he would make me to know," etc. The reason for such a *promise* to reveal the interpretation is not discoverable, since the interpretation itself immediately follows.—Verse 17. **These** (exceedingly) **great beasts, which are four—four kings—shall arise,** etc. With reference to the clause in the nom. absol., "these exceedingly great beasts, which are four" (or, "With reference to these . . . . beasts, concerning them," etc.), cf. vs. 23, 24, and also Isa. xlix. 49.—The four kings (מַלְכִין) whom the beasts are here said to denote, are unquestionably not regarded as four individuals, but as the *representatives of four kingdoms*, as appears from vs. 23, 24 (where the fourth beast is represented as a מַלְכוּ governed by a numerous succession of individual kings). Cf. the identifying of מַלְכוּ and מֶלֶךְ which appears already in chap. ii. 37 (as well as supra, v. 4) in the case of Nebuchadnezzar, and again in chap. viii. 21 et seq.; xi. 2.—The "arising of the kings will be מִן אַרְעָא, *i.e.*, not "*out of* the earth," but "from the surface of the earth," hence, in effect, "on earth" (Luther).—In the later Heb. parallels, viii. 22, 23; xi. 2, 3 et seq., קוּם is rendered by עֲמַד. The future יְקוּמוּן denotes the Divine decree, which limits the duration of the dominion of kings, as well as appoints their rise. Instead of "They shall arise," יְקוּמוּן may therefore be rendered modally, "They shall be compelled to arise." If the purely future sense be retained, it will be necessary to assume, with Von Lengerke, Kamphausen, etc., that the prophet carelessly, or by virtue of a *denominatio a potiori,* included the actually existing, and even partially superseded Babylonian world-kingdom among the future ones of his vision. This view is, however, more eligible than the strange assumption of Hitzig that the author does not in this connection regard the Chaldæan empire as the first of the coming monarchies, but assigns that position to the reign of Belshazzar merely, which opened shortly after the time of this vision; as if v. 1 did not expressly specify "the first year of Belshazzar" as the time of recording the vision, and as if it were at all certain that the author really regarded Belshazzar as the last Chaldæan king! Moreover, how can it be reconciled, that while formerly (chap. ii. 37) Nebuchadnezzar was selected as the representative of the Chaldæan monarchy, and this was to a certain extent repeated at the commencement of the present vision (see v. 4), the unimportant, listless, idle Belshazzar should here suddenly be installed in his place?—Verse 18. **But the saints of the Most High shall take** ("receive") **the kingdom.** The plural עֶלְיוֹנִין, which occurs here and in vs. 22, 25, and 27, serves, like עִלָּי in the Targums, as a *pluralis excellentiæ,* to denote the God of Israel, who in Gen. xiv. 18 is called אֵל עֶלְיוֹן. As similar plurals of excellence, cf. not merely אֱלֹהִים, but also קְדוֹשִׁים, Josh. xxiv. 19; Hos. xii. 1; Prov. ix. 10; xxx. 3.—The "saints of the Most High," or the "saints" simply (קַדִּישִׁין), as they are called in vs. 21 and 22, are not the angels, mentioned in vs. 10 and 16, who surround the throne of God, but the people of God on the earth, the "real members in the communion of the perfectly true religion" (Ewald), the members of the house of Israel in its ideal spiritual signification (Gal. vi. 16), the Israel of the Messianic time of fulfilment; cf. Isa. iv. 3; vi. 13; lxii. 12; Rom. ix. 6, etc.—The same expression is also found in vs. 22 and 25; cf. עַם־קְדוֹשִׁים, chap. viii. 24, and עַם־קֹדֶשׁ, chap. xii. 7 (also Ex. xix. 6; Deut. vii. 6; xiv. 21; Psa. xvi. 3; xxxiv. 10).—When it is said that these saints of the Most High "shall receive *the* kingdom," the reference is evidently to the transmission of the Messianic kingdom into the hands of the Son of man from the Ancient of days, as described in v. 14. The saints, however, are by no means to be regarded as identical with the Son of man, so as to make him a mere personification of the people of Israel. This view, which, besides being advocated by Hitzig and Hofmann (see supra, on v. 13), is adopted by Herzfeld in his *Geschichte Israels,* II., 381, is opposed by v. 21, where the saints are represented as a host of battling persons, and are clearly distinguished from the Messiah, who is exalted far above them, and at the time of their conflict with the anti-christ tarries in heaven with the Ancient of days—hence the relation between the Messiah and the Messianic people is represented to be such that he aids them in heaven and from heaven (strengthening, comforting, and supporting them in their conflicts and sufferings), and for that reason, as their representative, receives *for them* the dominion over the eternal kingdom from the hand of God, as was already indicated in the vision, v. 14. Cf. Auberlen, p. 51; also Von Lengerke, Kranichfeld, and Ewald on this passage. The latter correctly observes, p. 406: "If the language in this place and in vs. 22 and 27 refers at once to the genuine members of Messiah's kingdom instead of Himself, this is merely for the purpose of more fully explaining the great picture which has been given once for all. A kingdom and its sovereign cannot exist without subjects, and in fact, *they* only exist through the latter. . . . When such a people has really been found, it receives the power and perpetuity, the indestructible and eternal character, as well as the dignity and the pre-eminence which lie in the nature of that empire and its Messiah (cf. ii. 44). The language of this interpretation refers therefore to this *people,* and the subject of the vision in v. 13 et seq. derives therefrom a self-evident but not unimportant completion. This by no means implies, however, that the Messiah, who was already sufficiently characterized in that passage, is identical with the people who are now, at the final stage, included, any more than that the description of the Messiah in that place, whose majestic character is not easily repeated, has any analogy with the words here employed. The king and his people are associated only in the final results and end, in the eternity and glory of the kingdom itself, as is strikingly remarked in this passage and in v. 27; and yet even here the distinction is clearly observed that the three things, 'authority, glory, and dominion,' *i.e.,* majesty in its full activity and glorious recognition, are in v. 14 awarded only to the Messiah, and not to his people." Cf. also the same author's *Jahrbücher der biblischen Wissenschaft,* vol. III., p. 231 et seq.—**And possess the kingdom for ever,** etc. אחסן, "to possess," here denotes the continued possession, while in v. 22 it is inceptive, and signifies the assumption of the possession, or the entrance upon it. The superlative expression עַד עָלְם עָלְמַיָּא, "unto the eternity of eternities, unto all eternities," is exactly like the Hebrew עַד־עוֹלְמֵי עַד, Isa. xlv. 17; cf. 1 Tim. i. 17; Eph. iii. 21, etc.

Verses 19–22. *Daniel desires a certain explanation of the* FOURTH BEAST. He therefore briefly recapitulates the former description of its appearance and fate in vs. 7–14. In this recapitulation, which recalls to mind the similar ones in chap. ii. 45 (cf. v. 34), and especially in chap. iv. 17 et seq. (cf. v. 7 et seq.), we have the new features that *claws of brass* are noticed in addition to its iron teeth (v. 19), and that the *people* of God are mentioned as warring against the beast (aided by the Messiah, and under his protection) and overcoming it.—**Then I would know the truth of the fourth beast.** צְבִית לְיַצָּבָא עַל, I desired to be certain about this, ἐζήτουν ἀκριβῶς περί (Theodot.). The reading

לְיַצָּבָא, instead of לְיַצֵּבָא, which is found in three MSS. at Erfurth, probably owes its origin to the defective form, which in this place, unlike v. 16, seemed to indicate an Inf. Pael (which, however, is found in no other place). The rendering in the Vulgate: "*Post hoc volui diligenter discere*," may also have contributed to originate that reading.—**Whose teeth were of iron and its nails of brass.** The brazen claws are associated with the iron teeth, by virtue of the association of ideas, which frequently connects iron and brass in thought; see *e.g.*, Deut. xxxiii. 25; Jer. xv. 12; Isa. xlv. 2; Psa. cvii. 16, etc. —Verse 20. **And the other which came up, and before whom three fell.** Literally, "and they fell before him the three." The relative construction is dropped at this point, as well as the connection of the speech from וְעַל, at the beginning of the 20th verse, so that the discourse again assumes the character of description, especially from the beginning of the 21st verse.—**And** (of) **that horn that had eyes;** properly, "and that horn, and it had eyes," etc. The וְ before עַיְנִין is epexegetical or correlative, as in Isa. xliv. 12; Psa. lxxvi. 7.—The form מְמַלִּל with ַ occurs also in v. 25 and chap. vi. 22.—**Whose look was more stout than his fellows.** מִן חַבְרָתַהּ, a shortened expression for מִן חֱזוּ ה׳; cf. chap. i. 10; iv. 13, 30.—Verse 21. **I beheld, and the same horn made war with the saints,** etc. This war against the saints merely indicates a special feature connected with the "devouring, breaking in pieces, and stamping under foot" (v. 19), of which the beast was guilty, but precisely *that* feature which would especially arouse the attention and fears of the prophet. So far as the mode of expression is concerned, the writer here passes from figurative to literal language; cf. Rev. xi. 7; xiii. 7; xix. 19.—Verse 22. **Until . . . judgment was given to the saints of the Most High;** *i.e.*, "until justice was done to them." דִּינָא here signifies justice to be secured by law, equivalent to the Heb. מִשְׁפָּט, *e.g.*, Deut. x. 18; cf. Psa. cxl. 13. It cannot *here* be taken in the sense of judging or performing judicial functions; for according to vs. 9, 10, it is God, with whom are associated the elders of heaven, who sits in judgment and administers justice (cf. Psa. ix. 5). There is no design *here* to assign a participation in this judicial administration of the Almighty to the saints (thus differing from Matt. xix. 28; 1 Cor. vi. 2).—Instead of "*the* saints of the Most High," the original has "saints of the Most High," without the article, which is also the case in the latter half of the verse, and in v. 21. Concerning the omission of the article in solemn and poetic speech, cf. Ewald, *Lehrb.*, § 277 *b*, where Mic. vii. 11 et seq.; Isa. xiv. 32; Hab. iii. 16; Psa. lvi. 11, etc., are adduced as illustrations of the Hebrew usage.

Verses 23–27. *The explanation of the angel respecting the fourth beast and its judgment.* **The fourth beast shall be the fourth kingdom;** rather, "the fourth beast, a fourth kingdom shall be," etc. The same construction as in v. 17 *a*, and as in v. 24.—**And shall devour the whole earth.** The emphasis does not fall on "the whole earth," but on "shall devour" (תֵּאכֻל), which is not only placed first, but is also repeated by two synonymous terms following the object. כָּל אַרְעָא does not, therefore, as Hitzig supposes, signify "all the countries of the earth," for this would result in an unnecessary exaggeration of the hyperbole which, without question, really exists. Nor does the related אכל signify "to swallow up," which would be equivalent to "appropriating, or incorporating with itself" (as Hitzig asserts, appealing for proof to Deut. vii. 16; Isa. ix. 11; Jer. x. 25—which passages are, however, by no means convincing), but only "to devour," which, like the synonyms "to break" and "to stamp" (דוּשׁ and חֲדַק), indicates merely a devastating and destructive energy, without including the idea of *conquering*. The fourth world-kingdom, therefore, may be held to signify the empire of the Seleucidæ, in the light of this passage also; and there is no necessity to refer it to the Macedonian empire of Alexander, nor yet to that of the Romans.—Verse 24. **And the ten horns out of this kingdom are ten kings that shall arise;** rather, "And the ten horns; out of this kingdom shall arise ten kings." מִנַּהּ מַלְכוּתָה, literally, "out of this, the kingdom," *i.e.*, out of this same kingdom; cf. on chap. iii. 6. Concerning the form מַלְכוּתָה, for מַלְכוּתָא, see on chap. ii. 7. Hitzig prefers, needlessly, to substitute the ending הּ ָ, and refers the resulting "out of it, *his* kingdom" to the fourth beast, or even to the "other one" (antichrist) who is afterward mentioned, as its subject—which clearly is forced and arbitrary. Hengstenberg (p. 211 et seq.) attempts, contrary to the sense of the prophet, to make the "ten horns" represent *ten kingdoms*, *i.e.*, ten Christian German states which are developed out of the Roman world-empire. Bleek (*Jahrb. für deutsche Theol.*, 1860, I. p. 68) also inclines to this transformation of the "kings" into kingdoms, since he attempts to apply the fourth beast as a whole to the Macedonian-Hellenistic world-monarchy, the ten horns to the several kingdoms of the Diadochi which sprang from the former, and the eleventh horn directly to the dominion of the Seleucidæ, and at the same time to its characteristic leading representative, Antiochus Epiphanes. Since the ten horns correspond to the partly iron and partly clay toes of the colossus in chap. ii. 41 et seq.,* the assumption that "kings" are here really put for "kingdoms" might seem admissible; but in parallelizing the toes of the image with the horns of the beast, the prophet would hardly think of individual rulers, any more than of distinct states or kingdoms (see on ii. 42). A horn, as Hitzig justly observes, would not be especially appropriate as the symbol of a kingdom; and the attempts of

* [This correspondence, however, cannot be legitimately urged as an argument in favor of the contemporaneousness of the ten kings, for it is doubtful if the number of the toes has any special significance, and no stress is laid upon it in the explanation of the vision. Like the two legs, it forms but an accidental accessory in completing the figure. Otherwise we should be obliged to count the toes on *both* feet likewise, and this would be more than any interpreters are prepared to do.]

Luther, Melancthon, Geier, Ph. Nicolai (*De regno Christi*, l. I., c. 5 ss.), etc., to make the ten horns denote ten designated states which were formed out of the Roman world-monarchy—*e.g.*, Syria, Asia, Egypt, Africa, Greece, Italy, Germany, France, Spain, and England, or (as Nicolai, l. c., suggests) Syria, Egypt, Greece, Italy, Germany, Poland, Hungary, France, Spain, and England—can only produce absurd and arbitrary results. In v. 8 the horn is clearly represented as a person; and accordingly the numerous horns in this place are probably intended to denote individual royal personages. Cf. also chap. viii. 21, where the horn is said, in the plainest terms, to represent a personal king.* For the rest, see Ethico-fund. principles, etc., Nos. 2 and 3.—**He shall be diverse from the first.** "As the fourth kingdom differs (vs. 7, 19) from the other three, so he differs, and to his disadvantage, from his predecessors; this is true generally, but especially so in his conduct towards God and his saints, v. 25" (Hitzig).—**And he shall subdue three kings.** יְהַשְׁפִּל, the opposite of אֲקִים, as in chap. ii. 21. It does not denote a merely moral humiliation, but a complete degradation, and even a hurling down, a seizing of their dominion (cf. Ezek. xxi. 32; Isa. x. 33). This is also shown by v. 8, which speaks very plainly about a "plucking up by the roots" of three of the former horns by the "little horn," and thereby probably refers to a supplanting of three rulers of the Seleucidæ by the violence of a new sovereign (see on that passage).†—Verse 25. **And he shall speak—words against the Most High;** מִלִּין—יְמַלִּל, like the Heb. דַּבֵּר דְּבָרִים, Hos. x. 4; Isa. viii. 10; lviii. 13: It appears from vs. 8 and 20, and also from the later parallel, chap. viii. 25 *b*, that blasphemous words are meant. This prophecy was certainly fulfilled in a marked degree by the blasphemous words of Antiochus Epiphanes (1 Macc. i. 24, etc.), but by no means for the last time; cf. the N.-T. prophecies relating to antichrist, 2 Thess. ii. 4; Rev. xiii. 5 et seq. לְצַד עִלָּיָא, properly, "in the direction of the Most High," *i. e.*, *against* the Most High (who is personally near), "against the person of the Most High" (Kranichfeld).—**And shall wear out ("disturb") the saints of the Most High.** Hitzig's remark is too far-fetched: "יְבַלֵּא is assonant with the preceding parallel יְמַלִּל, and is not equivalent to 'disturb, wear out' (cf. בַּלּוֹת in 1 Chron. xvii. 9, and the Targ., Isa. iii. 15), but signifies 'to try, oppress, make wretched.'" (?).—**And think to change times and laws.** זִמְנִין does not signify "*statuta sacra*" (Hävernick), but = Heb. מוֹעֲדִים "festival seasons" (Lev. xxiii. iv.; Isa. xxxiii. 20), *i. e.*, determined, legally appointed times for religious celebrations in general, for the great annual feasts as well as for the weekly and monthly (Sabbaths and new moons); cf. Num. xxviii. 2. The following וְדָת, "and law, traditional usage," indicates that the impious king shall not merely endeavor to change the appointed *times* of these rites, but that he shall seek to abrogate the ceremonial observances of religion themselves; hence, what was formerly said in a good sense (chap. ii. 21) of God, the absolutely perfect and omnipotent "changer of times and seasons," is here predicated in a bad sense of His dæmoniacal adversary, the impious Ἀντίθεος. Cf. the attempts of Antiochus Epiphanes, recorded in 1 Macc. i. 45 et seq.; 2 Macc. vi. 2–7, to destroy the theocratic system by abrogating the daily sacrifices, the observance of Sabbaths and feasts, and by introducing the sacrifice of unclean beasts, and the worship of Jupiter and Bacchus—attempts in which the prophecy before us found its more immediate historical fulfilment, while its ultimate realization must be looked for in the last times, according to 2 Thess. ii. 4; Rev. xiii. 8, 12 et seq.—**And they shall be given into his hand until a time and** (two) **times and the dividing of** (or, "a half") **time.** The expression sounds, upon the whole, like Mic. v. 26; but the duration of the period of suffering imposed by the permission and pædagogic wisdom of God is somewhat more definitely fixed in this instance, without, however, omitting the mystical feature in this limitation which requires to be interpreted. The aggregate duration of this time of affliction is divided *into three distinct periods*, which, however, are sufficiently indefinite in themselves, and therefore in no wise indicate the real measure of time in the prophet's mind; for while it is entirely probable that עִדָּן has the same signification here as in chap. iv. 13, namely, "a year" (see on that passage), yet the duration of "a year" in a vision of the future, which constantly presents symbolic conceptions, is upon the whole extremely doubtful. It must remain an open question whether ordinary calendar years are intended, or, what is scarcely less probable in itself, whether mystical periods are referred to, which are measured by a standard not known to men, but only to God.* It may

* [Keil's reference to chap. viii. 20–22 is unavailing against this express statement of the text here, for not only is the great goat horn there undeniably a personal ruler, but so are likewise the "four notable horns" that succeed it as the founders of so many dynasties. His entire argument on this point is a perversion of the sense: "Since the ten horns all exist at the same time together on the head of the beast, the ten kings that arise out of the fourth kingdom are to be regarded as contemporary." On the contrary, they are explicitly said to "arise" in the sight of the prophet, as if they were not there originally, and this admits, if it does not require, the idea of their gradual and consecutive development. So in the case of the two-horned ram (chap. viii. 3) we might with equal reason have presumed both horns to have arisen simultaneously, but such was not the fact. Moreover, as they are stated in so many words to be kings of one and the same kingdom, they must in the nature of the case be successive; for ten simultaneous sovereigns in one dominion would be a palpable absurdity. In the case of the last three only, whose fall makes room for the eleventh, is there a partial simultaneousness.]

† [Keil contends that "the king coming after them can only overthrow three of the ten kingdoms when he himself has established and possesses a kingdom or empire of his own." But such is not the process represented in the vision. The little horn *in the act of arising* evidently usurps the room previously occupied by the three others. It is this expansion in their place that makes it become great. They must, therefore, have been themselves rivals at the time, and not well-established in their seat, when this fourth contestant arose in its first insignificance.]

* [Few readers, however, will be content with this indefinite exposition of these sharply defined and frequently reiterated statements of time with reference to the events predicted. The difficulties in the way of their literal application to the period of desecration of the Temple by Antiochus Epiphanes do not appear so formidable as to require such a vague interpretation. See under the Ethico-fundamental considerations below.]

be shown with more confidence how the three particular designations of time, עִדָּן, עִדָּנִין, and פְּלַג עִדָּן, are related to each other, and also why precisely these terms are employed in the prophecy, which are repeated in the Heb. of the parallel, chap. xii. 7, in the words מוֹעֵד, מוֹעֲדִים and וָחֵצִי. In harmony with a not infrequent Chaldee usage, the plural עִדָּנִין is put for the dual (cf. Targ., Am. iv. 6; Ex. xi. 5; Num. xix. 36; supra, v. 8 et seq., and, upon the whole question, Winer, § 55, 3), and therefore, like the corresponding Heb. מוֹעֲדִים, represents a double period, a pair of times, and, in case עִדָּן signifies a year, a period of *two years*. The converse holds with פְּלַג, which, though in itself denoting any fraction whatever, is shown positively by the parallel חֵצִי in xii. 7 to signify "a half." Hence a double year is at first added to the year which stands at the beginning, and afterward another half year. The period of 3½ years which thus results is symbolically significant, inasmuch as it forms the half of seven years, and therefore stands related to the prophetically significant "seven times" in chap. iv. 13, as the half to the whole. If, therefore, the sevenfold number of the years passed in lycanthropy by Nebuchadnezzar (which was not to be taken literally, but ideally and prophetically) denoted, in a general way, an extended duration of the sufferings imposed on him by God, it follows that the present figures indicate a period of affliction *that is shorter by one-half*. "A time, and times, and a half time" represents a time of suffering that is abbreviated by one-half, or that is interrupted at the middle, similar to that referred to in the prophetic words of Christ: εἰ μὴ ἐκολοβώθησαν αἱ ἡμέραι ἐκεῖναι, οὐκ ἂν ἐσώθη πᾶσα σάρξ, Matt. xxiv. 22; Mark xiii. 20. The same idea of a shortened or halved time of affliction is expressed by the "half-week" (*i.e.*, half week of years) in chap. ix. 27, which, like the 1,290 days in chap. xii. 11 (or the 1,260 days or 42 months of the Apocalypse, xi. 2 et seq.; xiii. 5), is merely a tolerably exact designation of the 3½ years, in different language. It will be shown hereafter that this prophecy of the affliction of Israel during 3½ years prior to its deliverance likewise had a typical fulfilment in the history of Antiochus Epiphanes, while its final realization is reserved for the eschatological future.* For the present it will be necessary to remember merely, as the result of an unprejudiced exegesis having a suitable regard for the prophetic usage of language in this book, that a strictly literal conception of the period of 3½ years will hardly conform to the sense of the prophecy, and that there is therefore no need to seek for a period of suffering in the history of the Jews, while subject to that Syrian despot, which shall cover precisely that length of time, for the purpose of demonstrating that first fulfilment of the prophecy.*—**But the judgment shall sit**; cf. v. 10 *b*, and also v. 22.—**And they shall take away his dominion, to consume and to destroy** (it) **unto the end.** שָׁלְטָנֵהּ is to be repeated, as the accusative of the object to the two infinitives. עַד־סוֹפָא, "unto the realized end," *i.e.*, to the end of the last God-opposed world-power, which marks the end of the heathen world-power as a whole. סוֹפָא therefore designates (unlike chap. vi. 27, where the never-accomplished end of God's kingdom is referred to) the goal at the end of the development of earthly dominion, which coincides with the erection of the kingdom of God (v. 13 et seq.).—Verse 27. **And the kingdom and dominion and the greatness of the kingdom** ("kingdoms"); a triad similar to that in v. 14, differing only in the substitution of רְבוּתָא, "the greatness" (Luther, "the power"), for יְקָר, "glory." דִּי מַלְכְוָת depends equally on all the three nouns as a subjective genitive, and therefore denotes that the dominion, power, and greatness possessed by *all* the heathen kingdoms is intended. On the meaning of the expression "of the kingdoms under the whole heaven," see supra, on v. 12.

Verse 28. *The impression made on Daniel by what he has seen and heard.* **Hitherto is the end of the matter** (or "remarks"), namely of the interpreter, the conclusion of which coincides with the end of the dream. De Wette, Hitzig, etc., render it inappropriately, and contrary to the sense of מִלְּתָא, "Thus far the history"—an interpretation which finds no support in chap. xii. 6.—**As for me, Daniel, my cogitations much troubled me,** namely, after awaking from his dream-vision; cf. ii. 1; iv. 2.—**And** (the color of) **my countenance changed in me.** Cf. chap. v. 9, where the same expression is found, and chap. x. 8, which is parallel in substance.—**But I kept the matter in my heart,** viz.: the remarks of the interpreting angel, v. 17 et seq., and consequently, the subject and signification of the dream-vision. Cf. Luke ii. 19.

ETHICO-FUNDAMENTAL PRINCIPLES RELATED TO THE HISTORY OF SALVATION, APOLOGETICAL REMARKS, AND HOMILETICAL SUGGESTIONS.

1. After what has been remarked, it is apparent that the principal force and the greatest interest of the prophetic descriptions of this chapter centre in the *fourth world-kingdom* and in its development as an anti-christian power, which immediately prepares the way for the judicial advent of Christ. In the parallel description in

* [Some of those modern interpreters who hold in part to the "year-for-a-day theory" make the little horn in this passage to be different from that in ch. viii., referring the latter to Antiochus Epiphanes, but the former to the papacy or else to Mohammedanism. Such as maintain that the days stand for years in both instances regard the difference in the periods between this passage and that (1,050 years here and 2,300 there) as caused by computing the period in the one case from the *rise of the power* to its downfall, and in the other from *Daniel's own time*. In either case the same fatal objection applies, that there is no good evidence of such a symbolic use of the word "day" by Daniel.]

* [Keil, in like manner, argues for the purely symbolical and indefinite import of this designation of time, being driven thereto by his theory that this whole prophecy applies to the duration of the Roman power, which he extends into the unknown future. He has all along contended against a literal interpretation of these chronological data as they seem to be.]

the second chapter,—where the series of world-kingdoms was represented by four metallic substances, respectively inferior to each other in value, in the order of their succession, and although together forming a great colossus, yet indicating its perishable nature by the weakness of the feet on which it rested—the observation of both the dreaming king and the interpreting prophet was fixed equally on all the four world-monarchies. Their intimate relations to each other, their separation, and their subjection to the same ultimate fate through the agency of the rock of Messiah's kingdom, formed the principal features of that prophecy, which, however, likewise dwelt more extensively upon the fourth kingdom than upon its predecessors (v. 40 et seq.); but the principal reason for the prominence thus given to the last kingdom in the series, existed substantially in the fact that the aim was to point out that its heterogeneous elements and its divisions laid the foundation for its own ruin, and, as a matter of course, for the fall and ruin of the former empires. The case is different with the present vision and its interpretation. Each of the four beasts which in this instance represent the world-kingdoms is indeed drawn with nervous and strongly characterizing strokes, that admit of no doubt respecting their identity with the four constituents of the image (v. 4 et seq); but the attention of the narrator is principally directed to the fourth beast, and to the horn which denotes the height of the development of the world-power (v. 7 et seq.; 11 et seq.), even during the dream-vision itself. The interpretation of the vision disposes of the first three beasts and their reference to the three earliest world-kingdoms very summarily (v. 17), but emphasizes the fourth beast and its "little horn which speaks blasphemous things," as symbols of the final phase of development on the part of the world-power, and of the reign of antichrist produced by it; for not only are the characteristic peculiarities of this beast noticed twice over, the second time in a recapitulation denoting the reflections of the prophet concerning its nature and appearance (vs. 18–22), but they receive a somewhat detailed explanation (vs. 23–26), which does not indeed display the clearness of the disclosures in chapters viii., xi., and xii. relating to the same events in the period immediately prior to the Messianic future, but which is nevertheless far superior to all the former prophetic sections of the book, and especially to that contained in chap. ii., in the precision and clearness of its expositions.

2. In order to a correct apprehension of the Messianic bearing of this prophecy, it is requisite before all else, that the identity of the monarchial relations and situations indicated in this chapter with those described in chapters viii., xi., and xii. should be carefully observed; or, in other words, that the common reference of the prophecies in all these chapters to Antiochus Epiphanes and the Maccabæan period, as marking their more immediate fulfilment, should be recognized. The following considerations will demonstrate that this reference is common to the prophecies mentioned (and also to that contained in chap. ix. 24–27), and that, consequently, the second part of the book of Daniel refers, as a whole, to that time as the epoch of its first and more immediate fulfilment:

a. The world-power in question is described as *divided and subject to dissensions in itself*, in all the parallel representations, especially in chap. ii. and vii. on the one hand and chap. xi. on the other. This agreement extends even to the point, that in both instances, chap. ii. 43 as well as chap. xi. 6, 17, the vain attempts to secure peace by means of intermarriages are noticed (see on ii. 43 and cf. infra, on chap. xi., l. c.).

b. The number *ten* is applied to the kings of the fourth monarchy, and receives prominent mention in at least two of the parallel descriptions (chap. vii. and xi.), although merely as a symbolic number, which finds its counterpart, in a general way, in the first ten possessors of the throne of the Seleucidæ. (It must be remembered, however, that [according to the author's view] neither the ten toes of the image of the monarchies, chap. ii. 42 et seq., nor the four horns of the Grecian goat, chap. viii. 7 et seq., refer to these ten predecessors of Antiochus Epiphanes, or to any individual kings whatever.)

c. The *blasphemous and sacrilegious course of the eleventh king*—symbolized by the "little horn"—towards the Most High, His law, and His saints, is described in chap. vii. (vs. 8, 11, 20–25), and more fully in chap. viii. 10, 24 et seq.; ix. 24 et seq. [?]; xi. 31, 36, in a manner that recalls the statements of the Maccabæan books relating to the abominable attempts of Epiphanes to profane the Jewish worship and oppress its adherents, with the liveliest and strongest emphasis.

d. Chapters vii. 25; ix. 27; xii. 7 et seq., agree in limiting the duration of the tribulation caused by the antichristian tyrant to 3½ years. (In relation to the merely apparent discrepancy in the duration of the suffering, as stated in chap. viii. 14 and chap. xii. 12, see on those passages.)

e. The several descriptions agree *in superseding and destroying* the antichristian supremacy by the *erection of a Messianic kingdom.* This is not only asserted in the chapter before us and in chap. ii. 44 et seq., but also in chap. viii., where the breaking of the foe *without hands* (v. 25) is evidently synonymous with the loosening of the destroying stone "without hand" in chap. ii. 34, 45, and where the "justifying" (v. 14) of the desolated sanctuary denotes nothing else than the introduction of the Messianic period of salvation. Further illustrations of this head appear in chap. ix. 24 and in xii. 1 et seq., 7 et seq., where the Messiah likewise is described as the direct opponent and victorious successor of antichrist and his abominations. Hengstenberg (p. 213 et seq.), Hävernick, Ebrard (*Offenb. Joh.*, p. 84 et seq.), Zündel (p. 119), and Auberlen (p. 197 et seq.) attempt in vain to deny the identity of the antichrist noticed in chapters ii. and vii. with the enemy of the people of God described in chapters viii. and ix., asserting that the former is to be looked for in N.-T. times immediately prior to Messiah's second advent, while the latter appeared and was destroyed during the Old Dispensation and before the first advent of Christ, and that the prophecies in chapters ii. and vii. relate to the eschatological antichrist. while those in viii. and xi. denote a typical per sonage!—as if the descriptions in chap. vii. 25 did not already indicate an opponent of the O.-T.

church and ceremonial! as if the "changing of (festal) times and laws," there referred to, could designate anything but the violent offences against the temple and the sacrifices of the Old Covenant, as described in chapters viii., ix., and xi. (see supra on v. 25, and also under c) ! and as if an Israelitish prophet could possibly suspect that the worship of Messianic times would differ from that of the former dispensation; and as if he had not, in chap. ix. 24, even expressly opened the prospect of a restoration of the O.-T. sacrifices and sanctuary services when Messiah should appear (see on that passage) ! An unprejudiced exegesis, governed by scientific principles, can discover but a single antichrist in all the parallel prophecies, and that one is clearly described as the immediate predecessor of the Messiah, who supersedes and destroys him.* The prophet, however, was evidently ignorant of the merely typical importance of this antichrist, as being only a forerunner of the antichrist of the last times (to whom refer the N.-T. descriptions of the future, which are based upon this book indeed, and which frequently recall its features—in 2 Thess. ii.; Rev. xi. 7; xiii. 1 et seq.; xvii.; xix. 19 et seq.); for instead of representing the former as merely an imperfect analogue of the incomparably more atrocious impiety, the far more concentrated and diabolical wickedness of the latter, as he must have done if he were actually conscious that the distinction between type and anti-type existed in this case, he everywhere presents the idea of a flagrant rebellion against the Most High, and of the desecration of the sanctuary, and the attempted extirpation of the true religion, in expressions of equal force. And instead of dwelling chiefly on the anti-type as the more important character, and as being more significant in his relations to Messiah's work, as might have been expected, he pursues a contrary course, and furnishes a far more thorough and realistic prophetic description of the type!—We are therefore obliged to conclude that, in harmony with the law of prophetic perspective, Daniel saw the type and anti-type, the vista of Old and New-Testament times, the scenes of the more immediate future and those of the eschatological period, as a *comprehensive whole*, and that from his point of view, as a captive in Babylon, he no more saw the interval between the two features in the history of the future, although it covered thousands of years, than the pilgrim who journeys toward a distant goal is able to observe the broad and depressed valley that intervenes between the mountain immediately before him and that which seems to rise in close proximity beyond it. Cf. Hofmann, *Weissagung und Erf.*, p. 313 et seq., where it is correctly remarked, with reference to the closing verses of chap. xi., which describe the terrible end of the typical antichrist, Antiochus Epiphanes, that "at a subsequent point he (the prophet, or rather the angel who speaks to him) observes *only the final end of national history*, the fear and tribulation which overtake the whole world, and the preservation of Israel in the midst of it, in addition to the final end of human history, the resurrection of the dead to life or to perdition (chap. xii. 1–3). . . . . The connection of these last things with the prospect of the end of that oppressor of Israel is not different, for instance, from that by which Isaiah speaks of the impending attack on Jerusalem by Assyria as the *final* alarm of that city, or which causes Jeremiah to regard the end of the seventy years as coinciding with the end of all the afflictions of his people." Similar views are advanced by the same author in his *Schriftbeweis*, II. 2, 547 et seq., and also by Delitzsch, p. 285: "It is a law of Messianic history that the fulfilment of a prophecy, if not completed by one event, must produce successive developments, until the actual state that has been realized shall correspond to the sense and word of the prophecy. The afflictions caused by Antiochus were *not the last* experienced by God's people; but the book of Daniel *predicts them as the last*, as Isaiah in the downfall of Assyria, chapter x., and Habakkuk in the destruction of Babylon, chap. ii. et seq., foretell the overthrow of the world-power. The range of the prophet's vision is decided by the border of the horizon where arises the glory of the congregation of God, but not the measure of the meaning which the Spirit of prophecy introduces into his words, and which history gradually unfolds." . . . .

3. While, however, the more immediate fulfilment of the predicted misfortunes of the dream-vision is to be chiefly, and even exclusively sought in the period of tribulation marked by the reign of the Seleucidæ and the revolt of the Asmonæans, it does not follow in any degree that a contemporary of that generation must be regarded as the composer of this vision, and that therefore it must be held to be a prophecy forged *ex eventu*. In opposition to this assumption of a pseudological conventional composition of the chapter by an apocalyptist of the Maccabæan period, it must be observed that discrepancies exist between several leading characteristic features of the prophecy and the facts connected with the history of the sufferings of Israel under Antiochus, and also the facts connected with the development of the empire, which are *unquestionably more marked than the origin of the chapter in the time of the Maccabees would justify in any way*. Above all we notice the following:

a. The difference between the ten horns of the fourth beast (v. 7 et seq., 20, 24) and the number of the predecessors of Antiochus Epiphanes on the throne of the Seleucidæ. The most plau-

* [Keil seeks (p. 258 et seq.) to make the most of the incidental variations in the description of the "little horn," in ch. vii. and viii.; but his points are minute and often far-fetched, whereas the coincidences are striking, numerous, and essential. Consult the harmonic table in the introduction. Lest we might be thought to treat the opposite view too lightly, we briefly note the differences adduced by Keil. 1. The little horn of ch. vii. rises out of one of the four horns without adding to their number or injuring them; that of ch. viii. arises *among* the ten as an additional or parallel element, and uproots three. This merely proves that the four powers are not identical with the ten horns, which is precisely our view. 2. The enemy in ch. vii. goes much farther in his violence than that in ch. viii.; but as the conduct is of the same general character, this is evidently but a fuller or more detailed description. Both certainly tallied with the behavior of Antiochus. It is vain to allege that in one chapter the persecutor is not an antichrist because he is not directly said to arrogate divinity as in the other chapter, but only to oppose the people of God; for these are everywhere in the Bible identified with God himself, and their cause and interests are his likewise. 3. The periods in the two cases are different (2,300 days, and a year and a half, or 1,290, or 1,335 days). This is readily explained as including in some passages more accessory circumstances than in others. See the exegetical remarks on each.]

sible method of reconciling the number of the horns with that of the early Seleucidæ—hence, of fixing the number of the latter at ten, while Antiochus follows as the eleventh—is that adopted by Prideaux, Bertholdt, Von Lengerke, Delitzsch, and Ewald, by which Alexander the Great is excluded from the series, and Seleucus Nicator heads the list. This certainly secures a succession of seven rulers down to Seleucus IV. Philopator, the brother and predecessor of Ant. Epiphanes (1. Seleucus Nicator, B. C. 312–280; 2. Antiochus Soter, 279–261; 3. Antiochus Theos, 260–246; 4. Seleucus Callinicus, 245–226; 5. Seleucus Ceraunus, 225–223; 6. Antiochus the Great, 222–187; 7. Seleucus Philopator, 186–176); but every attempt to designate the three missing monarchs, who should fill the brief interregnum and state of restless anarchy which preceded the accession of Antiochus Epiphanes, results in failure. The ordinary resource is to assume that these three kings, whom Antiochus dethroned and superseded, or, as the figurative language in v. 8 has it, "the three horns which were uprooted before the little horn came up," were (1) Demetrius, the eldest son of Seleucus Philopator, and therefore the nephew of Ant. Epiphanes, who was at Rome as a hostage when his father died, and whose crown was usurped in his absence by his uncle (who had just returned to Syria from an extended sojourn in Rome, where he had likewise been a hostage); (2) Heliodorus, the murderer of Seleucus Philopator (see chap. xi. 20), who occupied the throne for a short time after poisoning that king, until Epiphanes dethroned him; and finally (3) Ptolemy IV. Philometer, king of Egypt, a minor at the time, who was the son of Cleopatra, the daughter of Antiochus the Great and sister of Epiphanes. It is assumed that this queen laid claim to the throne of the Seleucidæ for her son, or at least to the provinces of Palestine and Phœnicia, which adjoined Egypt. In point of fact, however, none of these rivals of Epiphanes could be regarded as the king of Syria, for Heliodorus was a mere usurper, who was dethroned after a brief reign, and there is no record to show that either Demetrius or Ptolemy Philometer pretended to the throne with any degree of earnestness.* Hence a variety of different explanations have been attempted; as, for instance, Alexander the Great has been included in the series of the ten kings, as being the actual founder of the empire of the Seleucidæ (!), so that the line begins with him and closes with Seleucus Philopator as the eighth, Heliodorus as the ninth, and Demetrius as the tenth representative of that dynasty (thus Hitzig, on the passage, and Hilgenfeld, *Die Propheten Esra und Daniel*, 1863, p. 82); or again, attention is called to the fact that exactly that period in the history of Syria which immediately precedes the reign of Epiphanes, is known to be particularly obscure, uncertain, and defective in its records (Ewald, and also Hitzig and Kamphausen); or it is observed that on the analogy of the toes of the image, which were partly of clay and partly of iron, the requisite number of kings is probably to be found both among the Seleucidæ and the Ptolemies (Rosenmüller, Delitzsch, following Porphyry, Polychron, and other ancients); or the attempt to discover a succession of ten kings is wholly given up, and the ten horns are regarded as denoting ten *contemporary* rulers, *e.g.*, ten satraps or generals of Alexander the Great, among whom the three that Seleucus Nicator conquered, Antigonus, Ptolemy Lagus, and Lysimachus, were especially prominent (Bleek, p. 68). The uncertain and unsatisfactory nature of all these attempts at an explanation, which Delitzsch (p. 283) also acknowledges in substance, has finally led even several advocates of the theory of the Maccabæan composition of this section (*e.g.*, Hertzfeld, *Geschichte Israels*) to adopt the only correct view, on which the number ten as applied to the horns is a *round or symbolic* number, whose more specific interpretation it is useless to attempt. This view is also held in substance by a majority of the expositors who refer the fourth beast to the *Roman* world-power and the occidental-Christian kingdoms which emanated from it, although they hold fast to the really prophetic character of the vision, and therefore its origin with Daniel and during the captivity.* We have already shown that the advocacy of the genuineness of this prophetic book by no means involves, as a necessary consequence, the interpretation by which the fourth beast designates Rome. It has also been shown, on v. 8, that we must be content with a general and symbolic explanation of the subordinate three-fold number of the horns, as well as of the number ten. Cf. infra, on chap. xi. 2 et seq.

b. The statement in v. 25, according to which the period of tribulation, prepared for God's people by the eleventh king of the fourth monarchy, was to cover "a time, and two times, and a half time" (hence according to chap. iv. 13 was to extend over three and a half years and then to be ended by an act of Divine judgment), will likewise admit of no exact and thoroughly

* [Keil urges these objections with all their force to disprove any reference here to the time of the Seleucidæ; but they apply with equal and even greater force to the Roman list of emperors. It does not appear however, that the three horns in question represent actually reigning kings, nor do the terms "plucked up" and "fell" clearly mean dethronement. It is sufficient that they were royal personages who claimed or were entitled to the throne. One of them, at least, Heliodorus, actually occupied it, for a brief period, indeed, but long enough to come within the description. The other two, as being legitimate heirs, may fairly be designated as *princes*, and this is all that the figure requires. The partial and temporary royalty of all three is evidently denoted by their speedily succumbing to the upstart. It is difficult to imagine a case of four rivals to the same throne that would more accurately answer to the vision.]

* [So formidable is this difficulty on the Roman theory of interpretation that Keil, its last most noted advocate, takes refuge in a remarkable *postponement* of the solution. "The kingdoms represented by the ten horns belong still to the future. To be able to judge regarding them with any certainty, we must first make clear to ourselves the place of the Messianic kingdom with reference to the fourth world-kingdom, and then compare the prophecy of the Apocalypse of John regarding the formation of the world-power—a prophecy which rests on the book of Daniel." This is a virtual abandonment of the field. If all the other parts of this prophecy have their clear counterpart in history, why not this also? If, as Keil claims, these ten horns are found simultaneously on the head of the beast as it first arises, it is obviously inconsistent to refer their identification to the future. But the attempts made to distinguish the horns in question, in their literal application Rome, have signally failed, as the most cursory inspection of the schemes proposed in various commentaries on Daniel and the Apocalypse will abundantly show. The ten kings in Rev. xvii. 12 are there expressly assigned to the indefinite future; but the seven in ver. 10 are clearly characterized as belonging to proximate history, and the first six as having been at the time actually realized.]

satisfactory comparison with the periods of religious persecution under Antiochus and of the Maccabæan revolt. If the introduction of a sacrificial worship and the erection of an altar to the Olympic Zeus by Antiochus (1 Macc. i. 54) be taken as the *terminus a quo*, and the re-dedication of the desecrated sanctuary by Judas Maccabæus (1 Macc. iv. 52) as the *terminus ad quem* of that period of suffering, the result is merely three years and ten days, instead of three and a half years (cf. Josephus, *Ant.* XII. 7, 6); for the Maccabæan books fix the date of the former event on the 15th Chisleu of the year 145 of the æra of the Seleucidæ (= B. C. 167) and of the latter on the 25th Chisleu 148 æ. Sel. (B. C. 164). Hitzig attempts unsuccessfully to recover the five and two third months yet lacking by going back to the arrival in Judæa of Appollonius, the commissioner of tribute (which he asserts must have happened about three months before the 15th Chisleu 145, according to 1 Macc. i. 29 [cf. v. 19]), as the actual commencement of the æra of persecution. The result is still only three and a fourth years instead of the requisite three and a half; and a yet more unfortunate feature, which increases the difficulty of settling both the beginning and the end of the epoch of three and a half years in question, appears in the two-fold consideration, that on the one hand the real beginning of the Maccabæan persecution may be found in the barbarous attack on the life and religion of the Jews, which, according to 1 Macc. i. 22, took place fully *six* years prior to the re-dedication of the temple, while on the other hand it is by no means necessary to regard the dedication of the sanctuary on the 25th Chisleu 148 as marking the cessation of the persecution, which might rather be dated from the great victories of Judas Maccabæus over the Syrian generals Gorgias and Lysias (the one of which was gained during the year 147, and the other in the earlier months of 148 in the æra of the Seleucidæ), or on the contrary, from some event subsequent to the dedication, as the death of Antiochus Epiphanes (cf. infra, on chap. xii. 11). The theories which are admissible, therefore, vacillate between periods covering from three to six years, without being able, in any case, to demonstrate an æra of exactly three and a half years, such as v. 25 requires, and further, without presenting any evidence from the recorded history of the Maccabees of so sudden, complete, and wonderful a conclusion of the period of suffering (without being secured by repeated conflicts and successes), as the same passage and its parallels in chap. viii. 14 and chap. xii. 7 et seq. seem to require.* For this reason we are sometimes referred to the alleged insufficiency of our information respecting the various events connected with the Maccabæan history, which lacks certainty and thoroughness (Hilgenfeld, as above), and at others, the assumption has been adopted that the Maccabæan tendency-writer employed a designedly mystical and indefinite mode of indicating time, which cannot be accurately elucidated by a comparison with the facts of history (Von Lengerke). However conceivable and in itself probable the latter view may be, on the opinion that the prophet was drawing an apocalyptic picture of the distant future, which was necessarily ideal and indefinite so far as details were concerned, it is to the same degree improbable and incapable of being demonstrated, when the author is regarded as a conventional inventor of *vaticinia ex eventu*, who everywhere attempts to introduce allusions to the circumstances of the recent past or of the present. From such a writer we might assuredly have expected a more exact agreement and palpable correspondence between the prophecy and its fulfilling counterpart than results from the relation of the $1+2+\frac{1}{2}$ times to the period of the Antiochian persecution. "The alleged pseudo-composer of our chapter must accordingly have written for a time, with whose historical conditions he was unacquainted, *despite the fact that he was its contemporary;* and the entire condition of the theocracy, covered with shame and the want of success as it was, during the three and a half years of this chapter —before whose expiration this advocate of the actually victorious but not by him so-designated Maccabæan rebellion is said to have written— becomes historically inconceivable in the light of the pseudo-Daniel tendency-hypothesis" (Kranichfeld).

* [In this chronological examination the author does injustice to the data in question, as the following exhibit from Stuart's *Commentary* (p. 223) will render clear: "Is this expression of time poetical merely and figurative, consisting of round numbers (as they say), and comprising just half of the mystical number *seven*, which is so often employed in a kind of tropical way? *Historical facts* seem to speak for the *literal* interpretation. in the book before us. Yet, considering the nature of the case and of the number usually concerned with such reckonings (*i.e.*, the number *seven*), we surely need not be solicitous about a day, a week, or even a month, more or less. The convenience of the reckoning, when it is near enough to exactness, for all the purposes of prophecy, is very obvious, and will account for adopting it.

"In exhibiting the historical facts, we will begin with an æra which is certain. viz., the time when Judas Macc. expurgated the temple, and began the service of God anew. This was on the 25th of Dec. 148 ann. Sel. = 165 B.C., see 1 Macc. iv. 52. Counting back three and a half years, we come to June in 145 A.S. = 168 B.C. Livy has described the retreat of Antiochus from Egypt, in the *early spring* ('*primo vere*,' Liv. xlv. 11) of that year. While on that retreat, Antiochus detached Apollonius, one of his military chieftains, to lay waste Jerusalem (comp. 2 Macc. v. 11, which makes the time clear), for he had heard that the Jews exulted at his misfortune, in being obliged by the Romans to retreat from Egypt, and he was determined to wreak his vengeance on them. He did so effectually, as 1 Macc. i. 29 seq. fully shows; and vs. 29, 20, of the same chapter, compared together, show that the year was 145 A. S. as above stated. From June, when Jerusalem was probably taken, to December, is six months; and from December in 168 to December, 165, is three years. In the same way, as to time, does Josephus reckon *Proem. ad Bell. Jud.* § 7. But to avoid perplexity, it should be noted that a different mode of reckoning, viz., *three years*, is sometimes employed, *e.g.*, in 1 Macc. iv. 54, and 2 Macc. x. 5, such a method seems to be implied; and so in Jos., *Ant. Jud.* XII. 7, 6. An examination of the context in these cases shows, however, that this period designates only the time that intervened between the profanation of the temple by heathen sacrifices, 1 Macc. i. 54, and the consecration of it by Judas Maccabæus, 1 Macc. iv. 54. Some six months after capture of the city, during which all manner of cruelties and excesses were committed, appear to have elapsed before Antiochus began his *swinish* offerings in the temple. The consecration of the temple by Judas introduced regular Hebrew worship there: and the death of Antiochus happening shortly afterward, the period of his oppression was of course at its end. Thus did events correspond very exactly with the time designated in our text. We cannot indeed specify the exact *day*, because history has not done this; but it is enough, that we come so near to the time designated, as to remove all serious difficulty respecting it."

To this we may add that the period three and a half years may reasonably be taken as a somewhat round number, not only because of its being in itself a general and inexact expression, but more especially as being the half of the conventional term of seven years. See on ch. ix. 27.]

c. Intimately connected with this is the discrepancy between the picture of the Messiah drawn in our chapter, and the nature of the Messianic hopes entertained by the Jews of the Maccabæan period, as revealed in the books of the Maccabees, and also in the other products of Jewish apocalyptic literature of nearly the same date. These authorities are indeed able to refer to a final deliverance and re-union of the scattered tribes of Israel (see, *e.g.*, Ecclus. xxx. 11; l. 24; Tob. xiii. 13–18; xiv. 6), and also to a Divine visitation of judgment upon the heathen (Ecclus. xxxii. 18; Judith xvi. 17, etc.); but they nowhere base their theocratic expectations clearly on the appearance of a single Messianic personage, least of all, on one who is so positively characterized by traits belonging to both Divine and human nature as is the "Son of man" in v. 13 of this chapter. The *προφήτης πιστός* of 1 Macc. (xiv. 41) is a purely human prophet, devoid of all celestial, supernatural character; and the "poor righteous one" of the book of Wisdom (chap. ii. 10–20) can make no claim to recognition as an individual Messianic person, but is rather a mere personification of the class of suffering righteous men. The conception of a Messiah is very dim upon the whole in all the apocryphal literature of the two centuries immediately preceding the Christian æra; and in the cases, where the expectation of a personal Messiah, possessed of the Divine-human character to a greater or less degree, actually appears in several productions of this period, as in books II. and III. of the *Sibylline Oracles*, or in the book of Enoch (which at least some critics admit to have been composed as early as in the second century B. C., and possibly under John Hyrcanus—*e.g.*, Ewald, Dillmann, Jos. Langen), the dependence of such writings on this book must doubtless be assumed (cf. the passage from the *Orac. Sibyll.* l. II., cited above, on v. 8, and also Introd. § 6, note 3). This dependence, however, in no wise compels to the assumption that the prophecies of Daniel originated in the Asmonæan period; it is far more readily understood on the opinion that they originated during the captivity, but that they were recognized at their true value and introduced into general use in all the circles of pious Jewish apocalyptists in the Maccabæan age and as a result of its afflictions.

4. In support of the opinion that He who "came with the clouds of heaven" in v. 13 is no other than the *personal Messiah*, it has already been remarked among other things (see on that passage) that Christ preferably and frequently employed the phrase *ὁ υἱὸς τοῦ ἀνθρώπου*, as a testimony in favor of that view. It is now recognized by a majority of expositors and Biblical theologians that this designation, which is found in all eighty-one times in the New Testament, was intended to recall Dan. vii. 13, and to assert the identity of Jesus as the Messiah with the בַּר אֱנָשׁ who is there described, although several (*e.g.*, Von Hofmann, Delitzsch, Kahnis, etc.) still attempt to advocate the view formerly represented by Huetius, Harduin, Schleiermacher, Neander, Weisse, Baur, etc., on which the phrase was derived from Psa. viii. 5, and designates Jesus, not as being the Messiah, but as "the flower of humanity," as "the ideal and normal man," the "man of history, toward whom all human development tends." The former method of explaining the phrase does not exclude the latter, but is rather to be traced back to both these passages of the Old Testament, inasmuch as Dan. vii. 13 also expresses the sense of the ideal and normally human, of the perfectly human, and even of the *Divine human*, as will appear with special clearness from the manner in which the Saviour, in Matt. xxvi. 64, replies to the question of the High priest inquiring whether He were "the Christ, the Son of God," when, with an evident allusion to this passage, He declares Himself "the Son of man," who shall thereafter be seen sitting "on the right hand of power and coming in the clouds of heaven;" cf. also John xii. 35, 36, where in answer to the question of the unbelieving people, "Who is this Son of man?" the Lord declares, "Yet a little while is *the light* with you," and thus again identifies himself most clearly with the Messianic "Son of man" of this passage. Cf. Meyer and Lange on both these passages (and also on Matt. viii. 20); likewise Gess, *Lehre von der Person Christi* (1856) p. 7 et seq., 257; J.F Tafel, *Leben Jesu*, p. 127 et seq., and especially Nebe, *Ueber den Begriff des Namens υἱὸς τοῦ ἀνθρώπου*, Herborn, 1860; also Holtzmann, *Ueber den neutestamentlichen Ausdruck Menschensohn*, in Hilgenfeld's *Zeitschr. f. wissenschaftliche Theologie*, 1865, p. 212 et seq. (although the latter has so distorted a view of the reference of the name to Dan. vii. 13 that he chooses to entirely exclude that to Psa. viii. 5, thus approaching the opinion advocated by Strauss in his *Leben Jesu*).—In addition to this reference to our passage in the mouth of our Lord as directly testifying to a personal Messiah, and besides the possibly still more ancient references in the same spirit which are found in the Sibyllines and the book of Enoch (see supra), the substantial agreement of its description of Christ with that of the prophets prior to the captivity affords an important testimony in favor of the correctness of our view. Especially if the description of the "Son of man" in chap. vii. 13 et seq., to whom an eternal and all-embracing dominion over all nations is given, be compared with the designation מָשִׁיחַ נָגִיד, "an anointed prince," in chap. ix. 26, which, although primarily applicable to a typical forerunner of Christ (see on that passage), yet clearly indicates the character of the Messianic ruler as being at the same time priest and king, the result will be a demonstration of the close analogy and even identity of Daniel's description of the Messiah with those by which Isaiah (chap. ix. 5; xi. 1 et seq.) and his contemporary, Micah (chap. v. 1 et seq.), characterize the spiritually anointed ruler of the house of David who should introduce the period of the deliverance of Israel and all nations, and also with the Messianic prophecies of Jeremiah (xxiii. 5; xxx. 9) and Ezekiel (xxxiv. 23; xxxvii. 25) and even those of the time of David and Solomon together with the period immediately subsequent, *e.g.*, David himself (Psa. cx.), Nathan (2 Sam. vii.), Amos (ix. 11 et seq.), Hosea (iii. 5), etc. The Messiah of Daniel does not differ from Him to whom all the earlier prophets bore witness; the super-human glory and perfection of power of Him who nevertheless appears in human form, as described in

this vision, correspond exactly to the expectations which the prophetism of Israel in general, from the time of David, when the theocracy bloomed and shone in its splendor, had learned to connect with a later offspring of the house of David, as the restorer, endowed with Divine power and majesty, who should renew the glory of that house, and consequently the glory of the theocracy as a whole.

5. For the purpose of a practical homiletical treatment of the chapter it will of course be necessary to pay special regard to the shining clearness of this description of the Messiah, and through it to clear up the more obscure features of the prophetic vision, in so far as this may be possible and of practical utility. The Divine-human Messiah of Israel, the founder and ruler of the kingdom of God in the earth, the Saviour and Judge of the world (cf. John iv. 42; v. 27), is to be described in His relations toward the earthly world-power, which, passing through various forms and phases of development, finally reaches the diabolical rage of anti-Christianity, and rebels against Him; and his ultimate triumph over all His foes is to be displayed as a necessity, founded in the Divine economy of salvation. In this connection it will not be wise to enter upon a consideration of those phases in the development of the world-power, symbolized by the figure of the beasts, in their relation to the pre-Christian world-monarchies which are to be regarded as their historical counterparts, any farther than is imperatively necessary for the purpose of clearness. The ideal and fundamental thought of the prophecy, which substantially coincides with that of the image of the monarchies in chap. II. and may be expressed by the statement "that all the kingdoms of the earth must be put to shame" (cf. Rev. xi. 15; xii. 10) before the kingdom of the everlasting God (the Ancient of days, v. 9), and of His Anointed, must evidently be made prominent; but the details of its realization in the history of the world should receive only a subordinate attention, especially since none of the theories promulgated to the present time, which undertake to specify the particular kingdoms designated by the four beasts, can claim to be absolutely correct, and recourse must therefore be had to a choice between probabilities, or between interpretations, more or less plausible, of the mysterious hieroglyphic animal figures that "came up from the sea." For as merely the forms of the future world-monarchies were revealed to the prophet—sometimes indeed in surprisingly definite and exact outlines—but he was not made acquainted with their names; as their nature, but not their historic appearance was prefigured to him: so can no effort of scientific penetration on the part of exegetes succeed in establishing an exact correspondence between the character of these monarchies, as shadowed forth in prophetic images, and its actualization in the surging confusion of the life of nations during the course of the last pre-Christian century, and thus in stating, with mathematical exactness and certainty, *which* great world-kingdom subsequent to the captivity was intended by the Spirit of prophecy by each of the beasts seen by Daniel, *what* kings were represented by the ten horns of the fourth beast, what was the precise conception of the blasphemous course and anti-theocratic rage of the last horn, and whether, in point of fact, Antiochus Epiphanes conformed to it in all respects, or merely realized it generally and in substance. In view of these unavoidable obscurities and difficulties, the practical expositor, still more than the scientific exegete, is limited to a chaste, modest, and reserved course in the treatment of this prophecy as it applies to the history of nations and of the world. Instead of pursuing to particulars the interpretation of the series of monarchies in vs. 4–7, or even of the succession of kings in v. 8, in the details of history, he will be able to present only *examples* of the wonderfully exact correspondence between the type and its historical antitype, or *illustrative proofs* of the generally unquestionable congruity between the visional and the actual succession of monarchies; and especially, instead of treating the fourth beast and its eleventh horn (in which the idea of the fourth beast attains its complete development, and which may, therefore, to a certain extent, be identified with the beast itself) as referring solely to the anti-Christian world-power in pre-Christian times, or also to the Roman supremacy with Herod or Nero as the representative of its anti-Christian character * — which would be wholly impractical and a grave offence against all the rules of sound homiletics;—instead of so one-sided an Old-Testament or typical interpretation of this beast, he will doubtless be obliged to deal prominently with that more unfettered, spiritual, and ideal mode of treatment, by which the fourth beast represents at the same time both type and antitype, thus including the world-power of the last times, which is inimical to God and Christ. Here also every one-sided interpretation, centring in a definite point of the history of the past, must be avoided, and the antichrist must not be found specifically in the Turkish nation (so Luther, *Vorrede über den Proph. Daniel;* Melancthon in the *Kommentar*, where, however, he also associates the pope; Calov.; M. Geier, etc.); nor in the pope (Luther in his exposition of chap. xi. and xii. and elsewhere frequently; also Brentius, Calvin, Zanchius, Cocceius, Buddeus, Bengel, Roos, and recently, F. Brunn, in the little work, *Ist der Pabst der Antichrist?* Dresden, 1868), nor in Napoleon I. or III. (cf. Leutwein, *Das Thier war und ist nicht*, etc., Ludwigsburg, 1825), nor, most remarkable of all, in Count Bismarck as representing the Prussian State (thus, *e.g.*, Groen van Priesterer; many clergymen of Würtemberg in the year 1866, etc.), but his eschatological character as belonging to the final stage of mundane history must be retained. Cf. Lünemann, on 2 Thess. ii., p. 204 et seq.; Auberlen and Riggenbach on the same chapter, p. 117 et seq.; H. O. Köhler, *Die Schriftwidrigkeit des Chiliasmus*, in Guericke's *Zeitschr. für die luth. Theol. und Kirche*, 1861, No. III., p. 459 et seq. (where the numerous writers in the Middle Ages are mentioned, who declared the pope to be the antichrist, *e.g.*, bishop Arnulf of Orleans, 991; Honorius of Autun; John of Salisbury; Joachim v. Floris; Robert Grosshead; Joh. Milicz; Matth. v. Janow; Gregory of Heimburg; the Waldenses; many Hussites,

* Thus, *e.g.*, Beckmann, *Meditationes politicæ*, c. 26, and Koch (in Starke, on v. 8).

et.); S. Baring Gould, *Curious Myths of the Middle Ages*, London, 1866 (chap. 9, the Antichrist); H. W. Rinck, *Die Lehre der Heiligen Schrift vom Antichrist, mit Berücksichtigung der Zeichen unserer Zeit*, Elberfeld, 1867 [and many of the monographs cited at the close of the Introduction].

Since but few of the practical expositors of former times occupy the ground of this more free and spiritual interpretation, but rather are generally concerned to adapt the visions of the prophet to special events and appearances in modern history, or confine themselves to the work of disproving the interpretation which assumes that the chap. was a *vatic. ex eventu*, written by a pretended Daniel in the Maccabæan period (so many church fathers, *e.g.*, Jerome, whose observations on this section aim solely to resist the tendency-critical attacks of Porphyry; among moderns, *e.g.*, Hävernick), a thoroughly proper practical and homiletical treatment of the chapter, based on a solid exegetical foundation, can of course derive but little benefit from them. Nevertheless, we quote several observations on the more important passages.

On vs. 4-8, Melancthon: "*Mirabili Dei consilio et voluntate Ecclesia subjecta est cruci. . . . Prædicunt Prophetæ et Apostoli, mundum pœnas daturum esse, quod post sparsum evangelium tyranni sæviant in membra Christi, deinde et ab illis ipsis qui gubernant Ecclesiam, polluta sit Ecclesia idolis, falsis dogmatibus, paricidiis sanctorum libidinibus.*" (To this, however, is added the one-sided and arbitrary remark, "*Est ex his seminibus ortam esse pestam Mahometicam historia ostendit.*") On v. 9, Calvin: "*Sciamus non posse a nobis Deum conspici qualis est, donec simus plane similes ei. . . . Deus certe neque solium aliquod occupat, neque rotis vehitur, sed non debemus imaginari Deum in sua essentia talem esse, qualis prophetæ suo et aliis sanctis patribus apparuit; sed induit subinde varias formas pro captu hominum, quibus præsentiæ suæ aliquod signum dare volebat.*"

On vs. 11, 12, the *Tübinger Bibel*: "In His eternal decree God has fixed a limit to every kingdom; beyond this it cannot go, and the Divine providence exerts a special agency to this end (Isa. xxiii. 15)."

On v. 13 et seq., Luther (*Von den letzten Worten Davids*, in his *Werke*, vol. XXXI. p. 30 et seq.): "This eternity or eternal kingdom cannot be given to any evil creature, whether man or angel; for it is the power of God, and of God Himself. . . . Namely, the Father confers the everlasting power on the Son, and the Son receives it from the Father, and all this from all eternity. . . At the same time, the Son is also a child, *i.e.*, a real man and the Son of David, to whom such eternal power is given. Thus we see how the prophets properly regarded and understood the word 'eternal,' when God says to David by the mouth of Nathan, 'I will place my and thy son in my eternal kingdom' (2 Sam. vii. 13, 16)."

On v. 25, Starke: "When crowned heads assail God with impious hands, and are not content with the honor of earthly gods, their respect and honor, dominion and glory, are taken from them by a common stroke; cf. Acts xii. 22 et seq."

---

2. *The vision of the two world-kingdoms and their fall.*

CHAP. VIII. 1-27.

1 In *the* third year of[1] *the* reign of king Belshazzar a vision appeared unto me,
2 *even unto* me [I] Daniel, after that *which* appeared unto me at the first. And I
saw in a vision (and it came to pass, when I saw, that I *was* at [in] Shushan *in*
the palace [*or*, citadel], which *is* in the province *of* Elam); and I saw in a vision,
and I was by [upon] *the* river of Ulai.
3 Then [And] I lifted *up* mine eyes and saw, and, behold, *there* stood before the
river a [single] ram which [and he] had *two* horns, and the *two* horns *were* high;
4 but [the] one *was* higher than the other, and the higher came up last. I saw
the ram pushing[2] westward [sea-ward], and northward, and southward; so *that*
[and] no beasts might [could] stand before him, neither *was there any that could*
deliver out of his hand; but [and] he did according to his will, and became
great.[3]
5 And *as* I was considering [then], behold, a he-goat[4] came from the west,[5] on
the face of the whole earth, and touched not the ground [earth]: and the goat
6 *had* a notable [sightly] horn between his eyes. And he came to the ram that
had [master of the] *two* horns, which I *had* seen standing before the river, and
7 ran unto him in the fury of his power. And I saw him come close unto[6] the
ram, and he was moved with choler[7] against [towards] him, and smote the ram,
and brake his two horns; and *there* was no power in the ram to stand before
him, but he cast him down to *the* ground [earth], and stamped *upon* [trampled]
him: and *there* was none *that could* deliver[8] the ram out of his hand.

8 Therefore [And] the he-goat[4] waxed [became] very[9] great:[3] and when [as]
he was strong, the great horn was broken; and for it came up four notable
9 [sightly] *ones*,[10] *toward the* four winds of heaven [the heavens]. And out of [the]
one of them came forth a [single] little[11] horn which waxed [and it became]
exceeding great,[3] toward the south, and toward the east and toward the pleasant
10 *land*.[12] And it waxed [became] great,[3] *even* to *the* host of heaven [the heavens];
and it cast down[13] *some* of the host and of the stars to *the* ground [earth], and
11 stamped *upon* [trampled] them. Yea [And] he magnified *himself*[3] *even* to *the*
prince of the host, and by [from] him the daily [continual] *sacrifice* was taken
12 away,[14] and *the* place of his sanctuary was cast *down*. And a host was [would
be] given *him* against the daily [continual] *sacrifice* by *reason of* [in] transgression,
and it [would] cast *down the* truth to *the* ground [earth]; and it practised [did],
and prospered.
13 Then [And] I [quite] heard one saint [holy *one*] speaking, and another saint
[one holy *one*] said unto that certain *saint* which spake [to so-*and*-so the *one*
speaking], How long *shall be* the vision *concerning* [of] the daily [continual]
sacrifice, and the transgression of desolation [desolating *or* astounding trans-
14 gression], *to* give both *the* sanctuary and *the* host *to be* trodden *under foot?* And
he said unto me, Unto two thousand and three hundred days [evening-mornings];[15]
then [and] shall *the* sanctuary be cleansed [sanctified].
15 And it came to pass, when I, *even* I Daniel, had seen the vision, and sought
for the meaning [understanding], then, behold, *there* stood before me as *the*
16 appearance of a man [person]. And I heard a man's voice between *the banks of*
Ulai, which [and he] called, and said, Gabriel, make this *man to* understand the
17 vision [appearance]. So [And] he came near where I stood;[16] and when he
came, I was afraid, and fell [quite] upon my face: but [and] he said unto me,
Understand, *O* son of man; for [that] at [to] *the* time of *the* end *shall be* the
18 vision. Now [And], as he was speaking with me, I was in a deep sleep
[stunned] on my face toward *the* ground [earth]: but [and] he touched me, and
19 set me [made me stand] upright.[17] And he said, Behold, I *will* make thee know
what shall be in *the last* end of the indignation: for at *the* time *appointed the* end
shall be [*it is* to *the* time of *the* end].
20 The ram which thou sawest having [master of the] *two* horns *are the* kings of
21 Media and Persia. And the rough goat[19] *is the* king of Græcia [Javan]; and the
22 great horn that *is* between his eyes [, that] *is* the first king. Now that being
broken, whereas [And the broken *one*, and] four stood *up* for it, four kingdoms
23 shall stand *up* out of *the* nation, but [and] not in his power. And in *the* latter
time of their kingdom, when [as] the transgressors *are* come to the full [have
completed], a king of fierce countenance [strong (bold) of face], and understand-
24 ing dark sentences [stratagems], shall stand *up*. And his power shall be
mighty, but not by his *own* power: and he shall destroy [*or*, corrupt] wonder-
fully, and shall prosper, and practise [do], and shall destroy [*or*, corrupt] *the*
25 mighty [*ones*] and *the* holy people [people of the holy *ones*]. And through
[upon] his policy also [and] he shall cause craft to prosper in his hand; and he
shall magnify *himself*[3] in his heart, and by peace [in security] shall destroy [*or*,
corrupt] many: he shall also [and he will] stand *up* against *the* Prince of
26 princes; but [and] he shall be broken without[20] hand. And *the* vision [appear-
ance] of the evening and the morning which was told *is* true [, it *is* truth]:
wherefore [and thou] shut thou *up* the vision; for *it shall be* for many days.
27 And I Daniel fainted,[21] and was sick *certain* days: afterward [and] I rose *up*,
and did the king's business [work]; and I was astonished at the vision [appear-
ance], but [and] none understood *it*.

GRAMMATICAL AND LEXICAL NOTES.

[[1] *To*.—[2] מְנַגֵּחַ, *butting*, as rams are fond of doing.—[3] הִגְדִּיל, *acted proudly*.—[4] Literally, *a leaper of the goats*.—[5] מַעֲרָב, a different term from that used in ver. 4, יָם, *the sea*, *i.e.*, Mediterranean, which here might have been misunderstood as being literally the place of *origin*, whereas the idea of *direction* only is intended.—[6] Literally, *touching the side of*.—[7] Literally, *imbittered himself*, *i.e.*, was exasperated.—[8] Literally, *no deliverer for*.—[9] Literally, *till exceedingly*.—

[10] Literally, *a sight of four*.—[11] מִצְּעִירָה, *diminution;* the order too is emphatic, *one horn—a petty one*.—[12] הַצְּבִי, *the beauty* of lands.—[13] *Caused to fall*.—[14] According to the text הֵרִים, *one took away*.—[15] The original is exceedingly laconic and obscure, תֵּת וְקֹדֶשׁ וְצָבָא מִרְמָס, literally, *a giving and* the *sanctuary and* the *host a treading*.—[16] The original is very peculiar, *Till an evening-morning*, 2300.—[17] Literally, to the *side of my standing*.—[18] Literally, *upon my standing*.—[19] Literally, *hairy leaper*.—[20] Literally, *with a cessation of*.—[21] נִהְיֵיתִי, *q.d.*, "Was done up," was overcome.]

EXEGETICAL REMARKS.

Verses 1, 2. *Time and place of the vision.* **In the third year of the reign of king Belshazzar;** hence, shortly before the end of this king, who reigned but little more than two years (cf. Introd., § 8, note 3), and therefore not long after the incident recorded in chap. v., which revealed the Medo-Persian kingdom already rising with a threatening light above the political horizon of the Chaldæan empire, as the heiress of Babylonia. Nebuchadnezzar's vision of the image and that of the four beasts and the Son of man (seen perhaps two years before the present date), as well as the vision of the Medo-Persian ram and the Græcian goat, described in the following verses, had already prepared Daniel, before he interpreted the mysterious writing on the wall of Belshazzar's banquet-hall, to see Medo-Persia standing on the arena of history as the leading world-power instead of Babylonia in the not distant future The extent, however, to which recent political events, such as successes achieved by the Medes, or, what is more probable, the rise of the youthful Persian prince Cyrus and his victory over Astyages (B. C. 559, and therefore two years after the death of Nebuchadnezzar in 561, and shortly after the overthrow of his successor Belshazzar-Evilmerodach), may have been influential in inciting the prophet to the politico-religious meditations from which originated the vision of this chapter, cannot be positively decided, in view of the silence of the book with regard to such externally conditioning circumstances. The political situation must certainly not be apprehended as if the fall of the Babylonian empire were immediately impending, and the approach of the Medes under Darius were looked for shortly. Against this view, which is based on the familiar but incorrect interpretation of chap. v. 29 et seq., and which is still advocated by Hitzig, Ewald, etc., see supra, on that passage.*—**A vision appeared unto me . . . Daniel, after that which appeared unto me at the first;** *i.e.*, "after having seen, somewhat earlier, an important prophetic vision, another of a similar character appeared to me." This new vision, however, is not called a "dream" or a dream-vision, like that in chap. vii. 1, but simply a חָזוֹן, "vision, what has been seen;" cf. vs. 15, 26, and also מַרְאֶה (vs. 16, 27; chap. x. 7; also Ex. iii. 3; Ezek. xliii. 3), which is often substituted for חָזוֹן. It is evident that the prophet was awake and conscious during this vision, from the language of the verses at the beginning and end of the section (vs. 2 and 27), and also from a comparison with the vision in chap. x., which is analogous in form (see especially vs. 7–10).—הַנִּרְאָה, instead of הֶחָזוֹן אֲשֶׁר נִרְאָה. On this apparently relative use of the article, cf. Ewald, *Lehrb.*, § 335 *a*.—בַּתְּחִלָּה, properly, "in the beginning," is here and in chap. ix. 21 equivalent to "formerly, before," and therefore = בָּרִאשֹׁנָה, Isa. i. 26; Gen. xiii. 3, 4 (in both passages the two terms are employed as synonyms). The expression refers back to chap. vii., and especially to vii. 28.—Verse 2. **And I saw in a vision; and it came to pass, when I saw, that I was at Shushan in the palace.** וַיְהִי בִּרְאֹתִי indicates that he was merely visionally present at Shushan, or that in spirit he was transported to that Persian metropolis; but in the following words he describes its situation and locality in so realizing and exact a manner that his actual presence in or near that city becomes exceedingly probable. During his long official and semi-official service under Nebuchadnezzar he may have visited that region more than once (cf. supra, on iii. 12 and iv. 6). Like Josephus, a majority of the older translators, Luther, Grotius, etc., Bertholdt and Gesenius advocate the view that the words beginning with ויהי are in parenthesis; but this is contrary to the Heb. usage and to the expression of the author, and consequently the view adopted by nearly all the modern expositors, which finds only a presence of Daniel ἐν πνεύματι at Shushan indicated by this language, is preferable. This destroys all foundation for the charge of Bertholdt, that the writer is guilty of anachronism in this instance, since Shushan was no longer subject to the Babylonian empire in the reign of Belshazzar, *i.e.*, Nabonidus. Even prior to the fall of the Chaldæan world-power Daniel was able to speak of the palace (or castle) of Shushan (with regard to בִּירָה, Pers. *bāru*, "a castle," Sanscr. *bura*, Gr. βᾶρις, cf. Gesenius and Dietrich, s. v.) as a centre of Persian power, and *even, in a measure, as the heart of the Medo-Persian world-monarchy*, because the city of Susa (Old-Pers. probably *Shuza*, now *Shush*—see Lassen, *Zeitschr. für Kunde des Morgenl.*, VI. 47), together with its well-fortified castle, was, from the earliest times, a principal feature in the province of Elymaïs (which is indicated by the terms applied to it by Herodotus, *e.g.*, Μεμνόνιον ἄστυ, Σοῦσα τὰ Μεμνόνια, etc.; see Herod., V. 53, 54; VII. 151; cf. Strabo, XV. 52 et seq.; Pausan., IV. 31, 5), and because the prominent and all-controlling part which that city would take under the direction of a native Persian prince could readily be foreseen, even before Cyrus should have solemnly declared it the capital of his empire, and before Darius Hystaspis should have enlarged and splendidly ornamented it as such (cf. Hävernick, on this passage).—**Which is in the province of**

* [If, however, Rawlinson's identification of Belshazzar with Nabonned's son and viceroy be correct, the Medo-Persian army was at this very time besieging Babylon, though with apparently little prospect of success; and the fall of the city must have followed shortly after this vision. Hence the first monarchy, the Chaldæan, is here kept out of view, as if already a thing of the past.]

Elam. Kranichfeld observes correctly that "if this book had been written subsequent to the exile, Shushan would not have been located in Elam, but in Susiana" (cf. Füller, p. 190); for Elam (Gr. Ἐλυμαΐς, Sept. Αἰλάμ) is the old-Heb. designation of the countries situated east of Babylon and the lower Tigris, which were inhabited from the earliest times by Shemites (see Gen. x. 22; xiv. 19; cf. Isa. xi. 11; xxi. 2; xxii. 6; Jer. xxv. 25, etc.), and it was not till the period of the Persian supremacy that the extended province of Elam was limited to the narrow strip between the Tigris and the Eulæus, or between the Persian satrapies of Babylonia and Susiana, by which arrangement the river Eulæus (see the notes immediately following) became the boundary between Elymaïs and Susiana, and the city of Susa was assigned to the latter province. Cf. Strabo, XV. 3, 12; XVI. 1, 17; Pliny, *H. N.*, VI. 27: "*Susianam ab Elymaide disterminat omnis Eulæus.*" The expression עֵילָם הַמְּדִינָה, "the province of Elam," does not by any means convey the idea of a *Chaldæan* province of that name, whose capital was Susa, because the author conforms entirely to the ancient Heb. usage. Cf. Niebuhr, *Gesch. Assurs und Babels*, p. 198 et seq.; Vaihinger, in Herzog's *Real-Encykl.*, Art. *Elam.* —**And I was by the river of Ulai**, *i.e.*, on the banks of the Eulæus, which flowed on one side of the city of Susa, while the Choaspes (on which river the classics, as Herod., I. 188; V. 49, 52; Strab., XV. p. 728, etc., locate that town) probably bounded it on the other. Corresponding with this, the representation of a large city, lying between two rivers, on a bas-relief of Kuyunjik copied by Layard (*Nineveh and Babylon*, p. 452), was probably designed for Susa. The explorations of Loftus in the region of Shush in 1851 make it probable that the Eulæus itself was merely a fork or branch of the ancient Choaspes or modern Kerkhah, and that the latter stream was also occasionally called Eulæus (see Rödiger, *Zeitschr. f. Kunde des Morgenl.*, XIII. 715 et seq.; Rüetschi, in Herzog's *Real-Encykl.*, art. *Susa*). The peculiar name אוּבַל, "stream, water-course," which is applied to the Ulai in this place and in vs. 3, 6, 16, appears likewise to indicate that it was not so much a single river as a stream which divided into two forks. The same idea was probably intended by the expression "between the Ulai," v. 16 (see on that passage).*

Verses 3, 4. *The first leading feature of the vision: the Persian ram.* **And behold there stood before the river a ram.** "Before it," *i.e.*, probably, eastward from it, in case the branch of the river which flowed to the west of Susa is intended; for if Daniel did not stand *in* the castle of Shushan, he was at any rate close beside it, and therefore on the eastern bank of that branch of the stream. If from this position he saw the ram standing *before* the river, the latter must likewise have been on the eastern bank. ["Daniel first sees *one* ram, אַיִל, standing by the river. The אֶחָד (*one*) does not here stand for the indefinite article, but is a numeral in contradistinction to the *two* horns which the *one* ram has" (*Keil*). Rather it indicates a *solitary* ram, and not a member of a flock, as is usual with these gregarious animals. For every ram has of course two horns.] The vision symbolizes the Persian monarchy as a *ram* (and afterward the Græcian empire as a he-goat), in harmony with that mode of representation—which prevailed generally in the figurative language of O.-T. prophecy and accorded with Oriental modes of conception in general—by which princes, national sovereigns, or military leaders were typified under similar figures; cf. Isa. xiv. 9 ("all the great goats of the earth"), and as parallel with it, "all the kings of the heathen," Jer. l. 8; Ezek. xxxiv. 17; Zech. x. 3. From extra-Biblical sources, cf. *Zendav.*, part II., p. 273 et seq., in Kleuker (Ized Behram appears "like a ram with clean feet and sharp-pointed horns"); *Hamasa*, p. 482, ed. Shultens; also the *Iliad*, xiii. 491–493; Cicero, *de divinat.*, I. 22, 14; Plutarch, *Sulla*, c. 27.* It is especially significant that Persia is represented as a male sheep, while the Macedonian-Greek empire is symbolized as a he-goat, in view of the contrast between the solid prosperity and even abundant wealth of the Persian monarchy, and the combative, rampant, and warlike nature of Macedon. With similar propriety the preceding vision (chap. vii. 5 et seq.) employed the bear to represent the slow, clumsy, but enormous power of Medo-Persia, and the four-winged leopard to illustrate the fleetness and warlike spirit of the Macedonians. It is also possible that an indirect allusion to the *ethical* contrast between Medo-Persia, as a power which in a religious point of view approximated somewhat towards Shemitism and the Theocracy, and maintained friendly relations with them, and the Græcian empire, as being thoroughly heathen and fundamentally opposed to all monotheism, was implied in this representation; for the parallel descriptions in chapters ii. and vii. likewise describe the succeeding world-kingdoms as in every

* ["But why *such a locality?* Because the prophet's present vision begins with the Medo-Persian empire, and Shushan was to be its capital. And why on the *river's bank?* Not because the Jews were wont to build *prayer-houses* in such places, Acts xvi. 13; nor because Ezekiel had visions on the Chaborns, i. 1, 3; iii. 15, 25 *al.* (Leng.); nor because of the solitude of the place (Maurer); but simply, as I understand it, because the castle (בִּירָה) stood on the banks of the river. The mention of the river, however, would still be in a measure superfluous, were not this mention a preparation for what is said in ver. 16."—*Stuart.*]

* *Iliad*, l. c.:

Οἱ οἱ ἅμ' ἡγεμόνες Τρώων ἔσαν· αὐταρ ἔπειτα
Λαοὶ ἕπονθ', ὡσεὶ τε μετὰ κτίλου ἕσπετο μῆλα
Πιόμεν ἐκ βοτάνης· γάνυται δ' ἄρα τε φρένα ποιμήν.

Cf. the prophetic dream relating to the murder of a brother of Brutus by Tarquin Superbus, and to the vengeance inflicted by Brutus for that deed, as narrated by Tarquin in Cicero, *de divin.*, l. c.

"*Visus 't in somnis pastor ad me adpellere*
Pecus lanigerum eximia pulchritudine,
Duo consanguineos arietes inde eligi
Præclarioremque alterum immolare me;
Deinde ejus germanum cornibus connitier
In me arietare, eoque ictu me ad casum dari."

In Plutarch's *Sylla* the following is related, and treated as an omen of the defeat of the younger Marius and the consul Norbanus,' which occurred soon afterwards: ἐν Καμπανίᾳ περὶ τὸ Ἥφαιον (? read Τίφατον instead) ὄρος ἡμέρας ὤφθησαν δύο τράγοι μεγάλοι συμφερόμενοι, καὶ πάντα δρῶντες καὶ πάσχοντες, ἃ συμβαίνει μαχομένοις ἀνθρώποις.—Cf. additional extracts from the classics and from the oriental literature which bear on this point in Hävernick.

case more degraded and abominable, in a religious and ethical light, than their predecessors (see Eth.-fund. principles, etc., on chap. ii. No. 3, *a* and *b*). He-goats serve elsewhere also as symbols of a violent, savage, and obstinately hostile disposition, while sheep (and consequently rams also) are distinguished by being more governable, and by evincing a more peaceful and mild nature, and thus are better adapted to typify what is ethically good and attractive. See Matt. xxv. 31-46, and cf. Lange on that passage, who observes against Meyer, and certainly with justice, that in this description of the last judgment, Christ does not represent the wicked under the symbol of goats because of the inferior value of that animal (Luke xv. 29), but because of its "incorrigible obstinacy" and ungovernable temper (Vol. I. of the New-Test. portion of this Bible work). Cf. also Piper, *Christus der Weltrichter* in the *evangel. Kalender*, 1853, p. 25.—**Which had two horns; and the horns were high.** The ram was therefore not impotent and defenceless, since the tall horns which he bore are symbols of great power, being the natural weapons of rams, both for offence and defence; cf. on chap. vii. 7, 24.—**But one was higher than the other, and the higher came up last.** The vision therefore represents the horns as still growing, and fixes the prophet's attention on the fact that the horn which comes up last excels the other in its powerful growth—a striking illustration of the well-known process of development by which the Persian nation became the head of the Medo-Persian world-empire after the time of Cyrus, as being the more powerful element in the confederacy, and thus able to compel the Median branch, though older, to assume the second place in power and dignity. Theodoret thinks that this passage refers to the expulsion of the dynasty of Cyrus by the later, but more powerful family of Darius Hystaspis; the ram, however, does not represent Persia only, but the combined Medo-Persia, as the angel expressly states in the interpretation v 20, and as the parallel visions in chap. ii. 39 and vii. 5, when properly conceived and understood, compel us to suppose (see on that passage).—Verse 4. **I saw the ram pushing westward, and northward, and southward.** The "pushing" can only be intended to signify the assertion and extension of its power in a warlike manner; cf. chap. xi. 40; Psa. xliv. 6; Deut. xxxiii. 17; 1 Kings xxii. 11. In this place the pushing westward denotes more particularly the victories of Medo-Persia over Babylonia and the Lydian kingdom of Asia Minor; that toward the north, the expeditions for the conquest of Scythia, led by Cyrus and Darius; and that towards the south, the conquest of Egypt and Libya by Cambyses. The ram does not push eastward, because the east already belonged to the Medo-Persian empire, and no farther extension in that direction was to be expected. Hitzig remarks, with incredible absurdity: "The fourth quarter of the earth is here unnoticed. While the ram turns his head to the right or left, he may, without changing his position, push northward and southward, *but not backwards*; in that direction, moreover, he would assail Daniel himself, and afterward Susa"—as if there could have been any difficulty in the matter of changing the position of the ram, in case it became necessary to represent an extension of its power eastward, by the symbol of pushing in that direction!*—**So that no beasts might stand before him**; literally, "and all beasts—they stood not before him." The imperfect לֹא יַעַמְדוּ expresses here, as often, the sense of "*not being able* to resist" (cf. Gesen., *Lehrgeb.*, p. 772 et seq.). The verb in this place is masculine (unlike v. 22), because the writer has in his mind the kingdoms or monarchs symbolized by the חַיּוֹת. Cf. the similar *enallage gen.* in Job xv. 6; Hos. xiv. 1.—**But he did according to his will and became great.** וְהִגְדִּיל, properly, "and he made great," namely, his power, *i.e.*, he became strong, mighty. Not "and he *pretended to be* great, gave himself boastful airs" (de Wette, van Ess, Ewald, etc.); for, as v. 25 shows, הִגְדִּיל never expresses the sense of boasting or conceited superciliousness when standing alone, as it does here and in v. 8, but only when joined with the particularizing בִּלְבָבוֹ.† With regard to vs. 10 and 11 cf. infra, on those passages.

Verses 5-7. *The Græcian he-goat and its victory over the Persian ram.* **And as I was considering, behold, a he-goat**, etc. "Considering," מֵבִין, as in v. 27. The he-goat with a single notable horn between the eyes—hence in its general appearance resembling one of the *unicorns* which are prominent in the drawings on the monuments of Nineveh, Babylon, and Persepolis—symbolizes the Macedonian-Hellenistic world-monarchy founded by Alexander the Great (whom the single great horn more directly represents, see v. 21), and at the same time the kingdoms of the Diadochi which emanated from it, as v. 8 indicates with all possible clearness by the growth of four new horns in the place of the great horn which was broken. This comprehensive animal symbol accordingly includes all that had been characterized separately in the two former visions of the world-monarchies, chapters ii. and vii., at first by the figure of two different parts of the body of the colossus, and afterward by the symbol of two beasts appearing in succession. This departure from the former mode of representation involves no questionable features whatever, inasmuch as this chapter follows a different train of ideas in many other respects as well, and the advocates of the interpretation of the fourth beast in chap. vii. (and of the legs of clay and iron intermingled,

* ["He did push toward the east—not because . . . . the Medo-Persians themselves came from the east (Von Leng., Kran.); nor yet because the conquests of the Persians did not stretch toward the east (Häv.), for Cyrus and Darius subdued nations to the east of Persia, even as far as to the Indus, but because, for the unfolding of the Medo-Persian monarchy as a world-power, its conquests in the east were subordinate, and therefore are not mentioned. The pushing toward the three world-regions corresponds to the three ribs of the bear, ch. vii. 5, and intimates that the Medo-Persian world-kingdom, in spite of the irresistibility of its arms, did not extend its power into all the regions of the world."—*Keil.*]

† [Yet "the idea of insolence or arrogance is not absent from הִגְדִּיל used thus absolutely, see Sam. i. 9; Zeph. ii. 8. Flushed with success, we know from all quarters that the Persians assumed a haughty position; so Crœsus (in Herod. i. 89), Πέρσαι . . . . ὑβρισταί, and so Æschylus (*Pers.* 795) ὑπέρκομποι ἄγαν."—*Stuart*]

in chap. ii.), which differs from ours, must not be permitted to urge their view to the exclusion of our own, because they also are compelled to acknowledge that the present vision combines in one two features which are there found separately, so that the one Medo-Persian ram in this place corresponds to the *two* beasts in the former vision, which, in their judgment, represent Media and Persia (cf. supra).—**Came from the west on the face of the whole earth, and touched not the ground**; therefore, with great swiftness, as if flying, or as if borne on the wings of the storm. Cf. the description of the leopard in chap. vii. 6, and the statement respecting Alexander the Great, in 1 Macc. i. 3: *διῆλθεν ἕως ἄκρων τῆς γῆς*; also Isa. xli. 2 et seq.; Hos. xiii. 7; Hab. i. 6, 8, and other descriptions relating to conquerors of earlier times.—**And the goat had a notable horn between his eyes.** קֶרֶן חָזוּת does not signify a "horn of vision" (Hofmann, *Weiss. und Erfüllung*, I. 292), but rather a "*notable* horn," as the parallel גְּדוֹלָה in vs. 8 and 21 shows, and as the ancient versions already declare (Theod.: *κέρας θεωρητόν*; Vulg.: *cornu insigne*, etc.); cf. אִישׁ מַרְאֶה, 2 Sam. xxiii. 21; also Targ., Esth. ii. 2; Gen. xii. 11.—Verse 6. **And he came to the ram that had two horns.** The Arabs term Alexander the Great "the two-horned one," because he was represented on coins, etc., as the son of Jupiter Ammon, wearing two horns on his head. The fact that, on the contrary, the Medo-Persian empire which he conquered is represented as a double-horned ram, indicates with sufficient clearness that the symbolic visions of this chapter did not originate with a pseudo-Daniel, who prophesied subsequent to the event. Cf. Kranichfeld on this passage, where he justly rejects Hitzig's opinion that we have here merely an "accidental analogy" to the Arabian idea.—**And ran unto him in the fury of his power**; properly, in the heat of his power, *i.e.*, in the irresistible rage (חמה) of which he was capable by reason of his mighty power. Hävernick is not exactly correct when he reads "full of a fierce desire for battle;" nor are De Wette, Von Lengerke, etc., in their version, "in his mighty rage."—Verse 7. **And I saw him come close unto the ram.** The manner in which Alexander the Great, at the head of the Macedonian forces, put an end to the Medo-Persian empire, corresponds in the main with this description of the assault by the goat upon the ram, which resulted in the breaking of the two horns of the latter (*i.e.*, the power of Media and of Persia), but still not so exactly as to suggest a sketching *ex eventu* of that event. The figurative description is especially defective in not containing any tolerably clear indication of the fact that *several* vigorous blows by the ram, which were inflicted at different points (the first at Granicus, the next at Issus, and the final one in the neighborhood of Susa and the Eulæus river), were required to break and destroy the Persian power. A Maccabæan pseudo-Daniel would hardly have escaped the temptation to introduce more tangible allusions to these features.

Verses 8-12. *The little horn which grew from the goat, and its violence against the Most High and His sanctuary.* **And the goat waxed very great.** Here again הִגְדִּיל does not signify "to pretend to greatness," but "to become great, to develop mightily." * עַד מְאֹד, "unto excess," as in Gen. xxvii. 33; 1 Kings i. 4; Isa. lxiv. 8.—**And when he was** (or, "had become") **strong, the great horn was broken.** כְּעָצְמוֹ, when the height of his "becoming great" was reached, when his power was at its climax. Think of Alexander's expeditions to Bactria, Sogdiana, and India, which were soon followed by his death. The "breaking of the great horn," however, does not refer simply to Alexander's death, but also to the division of the dominion and disruption of the unity of the realm immediately consequent on the decease of that monarch.—**And for it came up four notable ones.** חָזוּת is properly in apposition with אַרְבַּע, "conspicuousness, four," or also an adverbial accusative, "in conspicuousness, in a notable manner;" cf. supra, on v. 5. Each of the separate powers is therefore still important, although each receives but a fourth of the power and greatness of the original collective empire.—**Toward the four winds of heaven.** This addition alludes to the centrifugal principle, tending to division and separation, which after Alexander's death (not after the battle of Ipsus, as Hitzig prefers) seized on the Macedonian-Hellenistic world-monarchy, in which the centralizing principle had hitherto prevailed. The number of the horns appears to be based on the number of the winds, and to be a standing symbolic expression which is found in other writers also (cf. Jer. xlix. 36; Zech. ii. 10; vi. 5; Job i. 19). It is at any rate of symbolic significance, referring to the separation and parting of the empire toward all quarters of the world; and it is therefore not admissible to seek four particular kingdoms which should be denoted by the four horns growing towards the four quarters of the earth, as those of Cassander (Macedon), Lysimachus (Thrace and Asia Minor), Seleucus (Syria, Babylonia, and Persia), and Ptolemy (Egypt).† Both the opponents and the advocates of the genuineness of this book, since Porphyry and Jerome, are agreed in this specializing interpretation of the four horns, by which the kingdoms of the four Diadochi, who have been mentioned, are obtained (cf. in addition Hävernick, Hitzig, Ewald, and Kamphausen, on the passage). But they do not consider (1) that not the battle of Ipsus, but the death of Alexander, the monarch who founded the empire, is given as the *terminus a quo* at which the growth of the "four horns" begins; (2) that in point of fact the number of the great empires of the Diadochi Cassander, Lysimachus, etc., was limited to four during a period even more brief than that during which the empire was a unit under Alexander; (3) that the enumeration of four such empires even immediately subsequent to the battle of Ipsus

* [The necessity for this limitation of the meaning of הִגְדִּיל here is not clear; it seems better to take it in the same sense of arrogance as the result of success which it bears in the remainder of the chapter.]

† [Yet Daniel says explicitly that the four horns are four *kingdoms* (ver. 22), and the coincidence is too striking and minute to be accidental. There were indeed originally five of the Diadochi, but they so soon resolved themselves into four that this temporary pentarchy is disregarded.]

might be assailed as being inexact, inasmuch as Demetrius, the son of Antigonus whom those kings had conquered, stood upon the scene of action (as ruler of the sea, and lord of Phœnicia, Cyprus, Athens, etc.), as well as the independent rulers of the Achæmenidæ who governed Pontus, Armenia, and Cappadocia; (4) that the parallel visions in chap. ii. and vii. appear to indicate a division of the original empire into *two* kingdoms (the "two legs" of the colossus, chap. ii. 33, 40 et seq.), or into *ten* (cf. Bleek's interpretation of the ten horns, chap. vii. 7) instead of four. Among modern expositors Kranichfeld advocates the correct view by laying the principal stress on the symbolic idea of a "dispersion to the four winds," and contenting himself with observing in relation to the bearing of this prophecy upon the four empires of the Diadochi in question, that "the prophetic idea is verified formally also, by events suggesting its fulfilment which were connected with the four kingdoms of the Diadochi in the Macedonian realm."—Verse 9. **And out of one of them came forth a little horn.** מִצְּעִירָה, literally, "out of littleness, in a small way," an adverbial conception of similar formation as מִן קְשׁוֹט, מִן יַצִּיב, in chap. ii. 8, 47 (see on those passages). On the masculine forms מֵהֶם and יָצָא cf. the similar constructions *ad sensum* in v. 4 (יַעַמְדוּ) and v. 11 (הִגְדִּיל). — The horn from which the horn "sprouting in a diminutive manner" comes forth has its historical counterpart in the kingdom of the Seleucidæ; the little horn which sprouts or branches forth from it—after the manner of the prongs in the antlers of a deer—finds, like that in chap. vii. 8, its most pregnant historical illustration in the most godless offspring of that dynasty, Antiochus Epiphanes. The little horn, however, was certainly not intended to represent Epiphanes only and exclusively, as the description shows that immediately follows, which relates to the predecessors of Epiphanes also, especially to Antiochus the Great, and perhaps even suggests a reference to Seleucus Nicator and his expeditions to Persia and India in search of conquest.— **Which waxed exceeding great toward the south and toward the east.** It is usual to apply this to the wars of Ant. Epiphanes against Egypt (1 Macc. i. 18 et seq.; cf. infra, Dan. xi. 22 et seq.), against the countries beyond the Euphrates, Armenia and Elymaïs (1 Macc. i. 31, 37; vi. 1 et seq.; cf. Appian., *Syr.*, c. 45, 66), and against the Jews under the leadership of the Asmonæans. But Syria derived no "exceeding greatness under that tyrant from these wars; the וַתִּגְדַּל־יֶתֶר may be far more appropriately applied to the former extensions of the power of the Seleucidæ under Sel. Nicator and Antiochus the Great (whose conquests toward the *west* are not noticed, probably because of their transient character). Moreover, in case the reference to the undertakings of Epiphanes that have been mentioned could be established, the prophecy would be so direct in its application, that it would be hardly possible to defend its origin during the captivity with Daniel.* It is better, therefore, to be content with the more general, and, so to speak, collective or genealogical interpretation of the "little horn," by which it signifies, *more immediately*, the anti-theocratic or anti-Christian governing power in the empire of the Seleucidæ merely, the power of the "transgressors," who are clearly distinguished in like manner in v. 23 from Ant. Epiphanes as the most concentrated expression of the anti-theistic principle (see on that passage). Cf. also Kranichfeld, who, while assenting to this general idea of the little horn, seeks to explain the circumstance that the growth of this horn toward the west is not mentioned, by assuming that "the Græcian horn as such is conceived as being *in the west* and as operating from thence," and that therefore the author "would naturally describe it as asserting its power only in the regions which lay southward and eastward from Javan."—**And toward the pleasant land.** הַצְּבִי, properly, "the ornament;" here equivalent to אֶרֶץ הַצְּבִי (chap. xi. 16, 41), *i.e.*, the valued, precious land, the blessed land, the land of Israel; cf. Jer. iii. 19; Ezek. xx. 6, 15; Zech. vii. 14; Psa. cvi. 24. "Palestine is here noticed as a third land between the south and the east, as, in a different connection, in Isa. xix. 23 et seq., it is located between the once hostile Egypt and Assyria."†—Verse 10. **And it waxed great, even to the host of heaven.** The "becoming great" is here no longer to be taken in the strict and proper objective sense, but is subjective, an impious presumption, a conceited pride whose greatness reached to the host of heaven; cf. v. 25. The "host of heaven," however, is doubtless a figurative expression, referring in strong eulogistic phrase to Israel, the community of saints, who contsitute "the Lord's host" on earth, even as the glittering stars form His host in the sky; cf. Gen. xv. 5; xxii. 17; Num. xxiv. 17; also Ex. vii. 4; xii. 41; and further, the name Jehovah Sabaoth, which probably designates God in a two-fold sense, namely, as the "Lord of hosts," with reference to the starry host, and also to people of Israel, the host of His earthly servants and elect ones. The figurative designation of Israel as the "host of heaven" was probably caused by the designed assonance between צָבָא and צְבִי, the latter of which had just been employed to characterize the *land* of Israel.‡—**And it cast down** (some) **of the host and of the stars to the ground.** The copula before מִן

* [The force of these arguments, especially the last, for extending the import of "the little horn" beyond Antiochus Epiphanes, it is very difficult for those who are wholly untinged with rationalistic sentiments to appreciate.]

† A later Rabbinical interpretation conceives צְבִי in the sense of "gazelle," and refers this designation partly to its beauty, and partly to its peculiarity to extend its borders, when inhabited, like the skin of a gazelle, but to shrink when uninhabited (*Taanith*, 69 *a*).

‡ ["The comparison of the saints to the host of heaven has its root in this, that God, the king of Israel, is called the God of hosts, and by the צְבָאוֹת (*hosts*) are generally to be understood the stars or angels; but the tribes of Israel also, who were led by God out of Egypt, are called 'the hosts of Jehovah' (Exod. vii. 4; xii. 41)."—*Keil.*]

הַכּוֹכָבִים **is** explicative (= namely), and serves **to** introduce an explanatory clause, intended to sustain the force of the figure presented in the preceding sentence while applying the term צָבָא—which is not metaphorical in itself—to the host of Israel, and thus to strengthen the conception of the impious character of the attempt.—**And stamped upon them,** namely, the members of the people of God; cf. v. 13 and chap. vii. 21, 25. The manner in which this part of the prophetic vision was fulfilled under Ant. Epiphanes is recorded in 1 Macc. i. 24, 30, 37; ii. 38. Cf. the reference expressly to this prophecy in 2 Macc. ix. 10.—Verse 11. **Yea, he magnified himself even to the prince of the host.** The masculine הִגְדִּיל is used because the foe who is typified by the horn is intended; cf. xi. 36.—The "prince of the host" is of course not identical with him who is mentioned in Josh. v. 14 (who is probably identical with Michael, Dan. x. 13), but the Most High God Himself, to whom v. 25 refers as the "Prince of princes." Cf. chap. vii. 8, 20, 25; xi. 36.—**And by him the daily sacrifice was taken away.** The enemy of God's people, who is symbolized by the horn, must be regarded as the agent of the two passive verbs הוּרַם and הֻשְׁלַךְ (for which Hitzig, following the Keri and the versions, unnecessarily desires to substitute the actives הֵרִים and וְהִשְׁלִיךְ). הַתָּמִיד, "the daily" (Gr. ἐνδελεχισμός), designates, as is shown by the mention of "the place of his sanctuary" immediately afterward, the *daily service* in the temple, and more particularly, probably the *daily morning and evening sacrifices*, the עֹלַת תָּמִיד, Num. xxviii. 3; 1 Chron. xvi. 40; 2 Chron. xxix. 7. Cf. the rabbinical usage which expresses this idea also by התמיד simply; cf. also infra, on v. 14.—The events in the history of the theocracy immediately prior to the Christian æra, which fulfilled this prophecy in a measure, are narrated in 1 Macc. i. 39, 45 et seq.; iii. 45.—Verse 12. **And a host was given him against the daily sacrifice by reason of transgression**; rather, "and war is raised against the daily sacrifice, with outrage." The imperf. verbs תִּנָּתֵן and תַּשְׁלֵךְ are not, indeed, præterites (Hitzig), but they are not used in a strictly future sense (Ewald, *Lehrb.*, p 829 et seq.). They denote, rather, the idea that the predicted course of conduct accords with the Divine decree, or that it is ordained or *permitted* by God, thus corresponding to chap. vii. 14, 17, or supra, v. 4. This sense is most readily expressed in the English by the present tense.—צָבָא תִּנָּתֵן does not signify "the host is given up, or devoted to ruin" (De Wette, Von Lengerke, Hävernick, Kranichfeld, etc.), but, "a war is carried on, a warlike expedition is begun, a campaign is undertaken" (cf. Isa. xl. 2). The correct view was already entertained by Jerome, Luther, etc., and among moderns by Hitzig, Kamphausen, and Ewald, the latter of whom justly notices the contrast between צָבָא here and the same word in v. 10, where it stands in a different sense, and therefore translates, "and *the compulsion of a host* is imposed on the daily." His idea is that *compulsion* is employed for the purpose of introducing idolatrous worship in place of the service of the true God, and particularly, *compulsion* to service in the host, so that "host stands opposed to host, serfdom to the true service (of God), coercion to freedom."—In imitation of Theodotion (καὶ ἐδόθη ἐπὶ τὴν θυσίαν ἁμαρτία), Bertholdt makes the very uncalled-for proposition of rejecting וְצָבָא from the text, and then reading הַפֶּשַׁע. בְּפָשַׁע unquestionably indicates the method of making war upon the daily sacrifice; it stands *sensu objectivo*, to designate the outrageous heathen idolatry or sacrificial service, which superseded the worship belonging to the true faith. The same feature occurs in v. 13, where שֹׁמֵם is added, to strengthen the idea.*—**And it cast** ("casts") **down the truth to the ground.** The subject of וְתַשְׁלֵךְ (for which Hitzig, following the Septuagint, Theodot., and Syr., prefers to read וְתִשְׁלַךְ) is the קֶרֶן, which is last mentioned

* [Keil thus reviews the various interpretations proposed of this difficult clause: "We must altogether reject the interpretation of the Vulgate, '*Robur autem datum est contra juge sacrificium propter peccata*,' which is reproduced in Luther's translation, 'There was given to him such strength against the daily sacrifice on account of sin;' or Calvin's, '*Et tempus datum est super jugi sacrificio in scelere*," whereby, after Rashi's example, צָבָא is interpreted of the *statio militaris*, and thence the interpretation *tempus* or *intervallum* is derived. For צָבָא means neither *robur* nor *tempus*, nor *statio militaris*, but only *military service*, and perhaps *military forces*. Add to this that צָבָא both in vers. 10 and 13 means *host*. If we maintain this, with the majority of interpreters, only two explanations are admissible, according as we understand צָבָא of the host of heaven, *i.e.*, of Israel, or of some other host. The latter interpretation is apparently supported partly by the absence of the article in צָבָא and partly by the construction of the word as fem. (תִּנָּתֵן). Accordingly, Hitzig says that a Hebrew reader could not understand the words otherwise than as meaning, 'and a warlike expedition was made or conducted against the daily sacrifice with wickedness' (*i.e.*, the impure service of idols): while others translate, 'and a host placed against the daily sacrifice on account of sin' (Syr., Grot., Harenb., J. D. Michaelis); or, 'a host is given against the daily sacrifice in wickedness' (Wieseler); or, 'given against that which was continual with the service of idols,' *i.e.*, so that, in the place of the 'continual' wickedness, the worship of idols is appointed (Hofmann); or, 'the power of an army is given to it (the horn) against the daily sacrifice through wickedness,' *i.e.*, by the evil higher dæmons (Ebrard). But the latter interpretation is to be rejected on account of the arbitrary insertion of לוֹ (*to it*); and against all the others it is to be remarked that there is no proof either from ver. 13, or from Ezek. xxxii. 23, or xxvi. 8, that נתן means to lead out, to bring forward, to give contrary to or against." Keil concludes by translating: "And (a) host shall be given up together with the daily sacrifice, because of transgression." Stuart renders, "And a host was placed over the daily sacrifice by wickedness," and remarks: "*Put* or *place* is a very common meaning of נָתַן, as also the kindred signification *to appoint*, *constitute*, see Lex.—עַל, *over*, in a hostile sense, implying that the *daily sacrifice* was subjected to oppression and impious supervision.—בְּפָשַׁע, *by the rebel*. Hence, in the N. Test., 2 Thess. ii. 3, ἀποστασία (an exact version of פֶּשַׁע), also ὁ ἄνθρωπος τῆς ἁμαρτίας; and in v. 8 (ib.), ὁ ἄνομος; expressions having their basis, as I apprehend, in the verse before us, and applied by Paul to some personage of a character similar to that of Antiochus."]

in v. 10; and which forms the principal feature of the entire description before us. The "truth" (אֱמֶת, Theodot., δικαιοσύνη) to be cast down by this "horn" is the true religion, the objective truth of God, which is revealed in the law and the prophets (cf. Psa. xix. 10; xxx. 10; also Dan. ix. 13). V. 14 shows that its being cast down, like that of the daily sacrifice, shall continue but for a brief period.—**And it practised and prospered**; rather, "and it accomplishes this, and prospers," namely, because of the Divine permission. The words, and indeed the verse as a whole, serve to recapitulate and gather together the preceding statements.

Verses 13, 14. *A question concerning the duration of the oppression of the truth, and the answer to this question.* **Then I heard one saint speaking.** This speaking angel (for קָדוֹשׁ here signifies an angel, cf. קַדִּישׁ, chap. iv. 10, and also, Deut. xxxiii. 2; Job v. 1; xv. 5; Psa. lxxxix. 6, 8; Zech. xiv. 1) enters into the vision here described without previous notice, because the prophet conceives of the whole scene as surrounded by angels, similar to chap. vii. 10; cf. v. 16, and analogous features (perhaps in imitation of this passage) in the night visions of Zechariah, *e.g.*, Zech. i. 9 et seq., 13 et seq.; ii. 2, 5, 7; iii. 1 et seq.; iv. 1 et seq. The prophet does not state *what* the angel, who is introduced in this mysterious and dream-like manner, said at first, evidently because he does not know, *i.e.*, because, although he has heard him speak, he has not understood his words. He saw, therefore, two angels, who were engaged in conversing with each other, and *heard* one of them say something which he failed to understand; the question, however, which the other addressed to the first speaker was so clearly apprehended by the prophet that he was able to repeat it in the latter half of this verse. Ewald puts it, correctly: "Thus, at the first moment of silence after that speech, he suddenly hears one angel ask another, *with whom he is conversing*," etc. Hitzig, Kamphausen, etc., on the other hand, are arbitrary: "The second angel addressed the speaker, by directing an inquiry in the interest of Daniel to him (v. 13 *b*), *by replying to which the other angel became for the first time a speaker*." According to this the greater part of v. 13 would be a logical parenthesis, and the words "and he said unto me" at the beginning of v. 14 would serve simply to resume the introductory words of v. 13; the language of the writer, however, does not accord with this view. His evident aim is to repeat what he has overheard of a conversation between two angels; otherwise the most simple course for him would have been to address the inquiry concerning the duration of the tribulation to the angel in person, as in chap. vii. 16, which is, in other respects, an analogous case. —**How long shall be the vision concerning the daily sacrifice.** "The vision," *i.e.*, the subject of the vision, which is here more specially indicated by the two genitives that follow, viz.: הַתָּמִיד and וְהַפֶּשַׁע שֹׁמֵם. The anxious question as to "how long?" (cf. Isa. vi. 11), is caused by the fearful and alarming character of the profanation and destruction, as seen in the vision of the prophet.—**And the transgression of desolation**; rather, "and the horrible transgression." שֹׁמֵם, the partic. of שָׁמֵם, "to be astonished," and then "to be desolate or laid waste," certainly expresses the idea of the "horrible or monstrous" (Lat. *horrendus*), whether the intransitive sense of "being astounded," or, in accord with Ezek. xxxvi. 3, the less general transitive sense of "laying waste," be regarded as the radical meaning; cf. on chap. ix. 27. In the latter case it would probably be necessary to translate the participle as a substantive in apposition; "and (of) the transgressor, the destroyer;" * but in the former case also, where the adjective sense "horrible" (Ewald) or "astounding" (Kranichfeld) is chosen, the participle must be regarded as a kind of appositional supplement to פֶּשַׁע, to which it is therefore added without the article (as in Ezek. xxxix. 27). The expression הַפֶּשַׁע שֹׁמֵם, instead of which פֶּשַׁע הַשֹּׁמֵם might have been expected (cf. xi. 31), produces a solemn emphasis, which warrants the urgent question that is proposed.—**To give both the sanctuary** (rather, "the most sacred thing") **and the host to be trodden under foot**, *i.e.*, to give both the holy sacrifice (the central point of worship) and the community of the saints of the Most High (cf. vii. 18, 22, 27), the partakers of the theocratic covenant, to be trodden under foot (thus Ewald, correctly). [The grammatical construction of the latter clause of the verse seems to be that תֵּת and קֹדֶשׁ and צָבָא are all in dependence upon חָזוֹן, like תָּמִיד and פֶּשַׁע preceding. "How long shall be . . . . (the) giving, and (the) sanctuary, and (the) host (to be) trampled." מִרְמָס thus qualifies all the last three nouns; the latter two directly as an adj., and the former as an equivalent for the infin.] "The expression adds nothing that is new to the former statements, but simply repeats the comprehensive estimate of the condition of the Jewish religion referred to, and the outrage committed against it, in the light of the idea that they are permitted by a superior Providence; and, in point of fact, the only object of the question is to recapitulate what has already been said. The asyndetic connection accords with the abrupt conciseness of the description, and the disjunctive וְ before קֹדֶשׁ and צָבָא, added to the lack of conjunctions, is suited to its poetic character (note also the omission of articles). Consequently, everything that Hitzig regards as objectionable in this place, and that he urges against the traditional pointing for the purpose of removing תֵּת to the preceding clause, arises naturally from the subject itself. Moreover, the explanation of נָתַן by Hitzig, 'to permit the horrible transgression to go on,' has no parallel, neither in v. 12, nor in Isa.

* [Stuart, on the other hand, strongly contends for the *passive* sense of שֹׁמֵם here, "equivalent to *which ought to be laid waste or destroyed*," as being sustained not only by the intransitive force of the root, but by the distinctive use of the transitive מְשֹׁמֵם in ch. ix. 27. Keil takes substantially the same view.]

x. 6, where, like the synonymous שׂוּם, 'to make into something,' it is joined to a double accusative; and when Hitzig takes נָתַן at first in the sense of 'to permit,' and immediately afterward makes it signify 'to make into something,' the artificial zeugma certainly does not diminish the imaginary difficulty which, in view of the disjunctive vav, he discovers in the vav that is not prefixed to תֵּת," (Kranichfeld.)—Verse 14. **And he said unto me.** Thus all the MSS., which read אֵלַי, while the ancient translators, and among modern expositors, Bertholdt, Dereser, Hitzig, Ewald, etc., prefer אֵלָיו. The latter form certainly seems to accord better with the contents of v. 13, since it is supposed that the פַּלְמוֹנִי הַמְדַבֵּר (cf. Ruth iv. 1) who says what follows, would address it to the other angel, who inquires of him; but it is conceivable, on both logical and psychological grounds, that the witness to the conversation of the angels would represent the information conveyed in the reply to the angel's question as *imparted to himself*, because he was still more interested in that information than was the inquirer. Accordingly, he substitutes himself for the angel, because the interest felt by him in equal measure justifies him in identifying himself to some extent with the questioner.—**Unto two-thousand and three-hundred days** ("evening-mornings"); **then shall the sanctuary be cleansed** (rather, "justified"). The "justifying of the sanctuary" is the re-consecration of the desecrated sanctuary and its services (which were permitted to be trodden under foot), which is accomplished by the renewal of the daily sacrifices. וְנִצְדַּק consequently denotes a being justified by that work, and, in its position at the head of the apodosis to the antecedent clause beginning with the connective עַד, expresses to some extent the sense of the *fut. exactum.* The material justification or renewal of the perfection of the *host*, according to v. 13, the second of the objects exposed to being "trodden under foot," is conceived of as essentially coincident with that of the sanctuary, or as immediately involved in it, and for that reason is not expressly mentioned. The neglect to mention the host does not warrant the conclusion reached by Hitzig, under reference to 1 Macc. v. 2 et seq., that the author intended to point out that *its* state of being trodden under foot was to be more protracted, while that of the sanctuary was to cease at an earlier date.—The duration of the period which is to precede the re-dedication of the sanctuary, is again indicated by a mystically indefinite and equivocal limitation of time, as in chap. vii. 25. The 2,300 evening-mornings (עֶרֶב בֹּקֶר) cannot be intended to signify so many *days* (as Bertholdt, Hävernick, v. Lengerke, etc., assume), for although the several days are, in Gen. i. 5 et seq., divided into the two parts which represent them, עֶרֶב and בֹּקֶר, they are not numbered accordingly; and the Gr. νυχθήμερον, which is often adduced in comparison, is the less adapted to serve as an analogy or ground of probability for the signification of evening-morning as synonymous with "day," as עֶרֶב בֹּקֶר can hardly be regarded as a compound word (on the analogy of מַסְגֵּר), but is, on the contrary, an asyndeton, arising from the poetic brevity of expression in this section (similar to וְהַפֶּשַׁע שֹׁמֵם in v. 13), which, so far from being a "current phrase" or "stereotyped formula," occurs *only in this place* as a designation of time. The limitation of the expression in this sense to this passage indicates, with an almost absolute certainty, that ערב and בקר do not signify the corresponding periods of the day, but rather the *sacrifices* required to be offered in them. The whole prophecy relates principally to the תָּמִיד, to which the passage under consideration assigns an especially prominent position; but as, according to Ex. xxix. 41 (cf. infra, chap. ix. 21), this consists of a מִנְחַת־עֶרֶב and a מ׳־בקר, the terms "evening" and "morning" in this place clearly denote the evening and morning *sacrifices*, or, if it be preferred, the *times* at which they were offered. "Morning" and "evening" are therefore to be counted *separately;* * and thus the period indicated by the author covers 1,150 days instead of 2,300. This period is *nearly* equivalent to the three and a half years in chap. vii. 25, while, on the other hand, the later numbers of 1,290 and 1,335 days (chap. xii. 11 et seq.) exceed the medium of three and a half years but little. How this discrepancy in the limits assigned to the duration of the time of anti-Christian persecution and oppression is to be explained, and, in particular, how the number in this place is to be interpreted, is of course very uncertain, and must always remain undecided. In general, those expositors of the truth who always come nearest to the sense of the prophetic author, will regard the present number 1,150 as a designed *narrowing*, and the numbers 1,290 and 1,335 as a designed *extension* or *overstepping* of the limit of three and a half years, and seek to establish a conformity to law both in the narrowing and the extension of that period. If it is assumed that this book limits the year to 360 days (or to twelve months of thirty days each) besides five intercalated days, amounting in all

* [This conclusion, however, is by no means certain, as the following considerations will serve to show: "עֶרֶב בֹּקֶר have no copula or conjunction between them; it would therefore seem to be a popular mode of compound expression, like that of the Greek νυχθήμερον (2 Cor. xi. 25), in order to designate *the whole of a day*. Compare Gen. i., where the evening and morning constitute respectively *day the first, day the second*, etc.; for it seems plain that the phraseology before us is derived from this source. In other words, עֶרֶב בֹּקֶר, as here employed, may be admitted to contain an allusion to the morning and evening sacrifices, and thus the phrase virtually becomes a kind of substitution for תָּמִיד, which is generic, and includes both the morning and the evening sacrifice."—*Stuart.* "That in ver. 26 הָעֶרֶב וְהַבֹּקֶר (*the evening and the morning*) stands for the phrase in question, does not prove that the evening and morning are reckoned separately, but only that evening-morning is a period of time consisting of evening and morning. When the Hebrews wish to express separately day and night, the component parts of a day of a week, then the number of both is expressed. Thus they say, *e.g.*, forty days and forty nights (Gen. vii. 4, 12; Exod. xxiv. 18; 1 Kings xix. 8), or three days and three nights (Jonah ii. 1; Matt. xii. 40), but not eighty or six days and nights, when they wish to speak of forty or three full days."—*Keil.*]

to 365 days, it will be found (1) that the whole number of 1,277 days, which are necessary to cover the period of three and a half years, is decreased by 127 days, or something more than four months, by the number 1,150; (2) that the number 1,290 adds twelve days or about half a month to 1,277 days or three and a half years; and (3) that the number 1,335 adds fifty-eight days, or nearly two months, to the period of three and a half years. A certain conformity to law is evident from these figures, inasmuch as the two months by which the three and a half years are extended in the last number, are added to the shorter period of three years in the first (*i.e.*, to 1,095 days); or, in other words, in the one case the prophet regards the period of three and a half years as *extended* by two months, in the other (in the present passage) as *shortened* by four months. *These prophetic limitations of time correspond generally* to the events of the primary historical fulfilment of this vision in the Maccabæan æra of oppression and revolt, *without being chronologically covered by them.* It has already been shown, on chap. vii. 25, that the interval between the abrogation of the daily sacrifices by Epiphanes (1 Macc. i. 54) and the reconsecration of the sanctuary by Judas Maccabæus (ibid. iv. 52) amounted to three years and ten days, or 1,105 days, thus covering forty-five days or one and a half months less than 1,150 days, as here stated. But if, on the other hand, the arrival in Judæa of Appollonius, the commissioner of tribute (1 Macc. i. 29), is taken as the starting-point of the calculation (as Hitzig does), a result of three and a quarter years to the rededication of the temple is obtained, with tolerable exactness, which amounts at least to from one to one and a half months more than 1,150 days. A comparison of the larger periods of 1,290 and 1,335 days with the circumstances of the æra of the religious persecution by Antiochus, as recorded in the books of Maccabees, leads to still more unsatisfactory results (cf. infra, on chap. xii. 11 et seq.). Hence, nothing more definite than a general or approximate correspondence between the predicted periods and their historical counterparts can be looked for; or, what amounts to the same thing, the *prophetically-ideal* value of the numbers in question must be recognized. Cf. the remarks in the Eth.-fund. principles, etc., No. 1, respecting the *necessity* that the predictions of any prophet which involve numbers should be only approximately fulfilled.—*All* the expositors of this passage, whether upholding or denying the composition of Daniel's prophecies during the captivity, are in the end obliged to assume a merely approximate correspondence of the number 1,150 to the periods of the Maccabæan æra of persecution. Among the former class, the view we have presented comes nearest to that of Delitzsch (p. 280), who holds that, "*for reasons which our knowledge of history does not permit us to recognize*," the prophet's estimate of the period of something more than three years, from the 15th Chisleu 145 æ. Sel. to the 25th Chisleu 148, is "somewhat inadequate;" and also to that of Kranichfeld (p. 300 et seq.), who diverges from us on the mode of estimating the duration of the years in question, but is wholly agreed on the general principle. His opinion is that here, as well as elsewhere in the book, Daniel estimated the year at twelve months of thirty days each, intercalating a month of thirty days every third year. This results in exactly 1,290 days for 3½ years, but leaves a discrepancy of forty days between 1,150 days and three years or 1,110 days. With regard to this difference he then observes: "It is equally in harmony with the very general employment of the number forty in theocratic representations of times of severe trial and sifting (*e.g.*, Gen. vii. 4, 12, 17; Num. xiv. 33, 34; Ezek. iv. 6; xxix. 11 et seq.; 1 Kings xix. 8; Matt. vi. 1 et seq.), and with the author's general usage which employs numbers in an ideal sense (cf. on iv. 13; vii. 25), as well as with the context more especially, that precisely this number should be found in combination with the final half-time. Consequently the amount 1,110 + 40 results as substantially identical with the more direct measurement of the three and a half times in chap. xii. 11; and this discrepancy within the book itself becomes no more strange than that, for instance, which represents the same kingdom at one time as divided into two parts, at another as falling into ten, and again (see supra, on v. 8) as separating into four, in all of which descriptions the same fundamental idea prevails, although presented under different forms." We cannot adopt this estimate of the 1,150 days, by which they are made to consist of 1,110+40 days, because it seems too artificial upon the whole, and because the opinion on which it rests, that Daniel added an intercalary month of thirty days to every third year of 360 days, seems to be untenable, and to conflict with the 1,260 days or forty-two months of the Apocalypse, which, beyond all question, are synonymous with the three and a half years of this book (cf. Auberlen, *Daniel*, etc., pp. 185, 286 et seq.).—Among those who deny the genuineness of this book, Ewald approaches our method of reckoning, upon the whole, inasmuch as he supposes that the author constantly assigns 365 days to the year; and he consequently extends the 1,290 days over three and a half years + one-half month, and the 1,335 days over three and a half years + two months; but he departs from our view in arbitrarily reducing the number 2,300 to 2,230, so as to obtain only 1,115 days, or three years + one month, instead of 1,150 (p. 468). In opposition to such critical violence, Hilgenfeld, Kamphausen, etc., retain the reading 2,300 in the text, reckon the 1,150 days backwards from the dedication of the temple on the 25th Chisleu 148, and accept some unknown event as marking the beginning of the 1,150 days, since they exceed the period to the 15th Chisleu 145 by forty days. Hitzig thinks that only 1,105 days elapsed between the 15th Chisleu 145 and the 25th Chisleu 148, instead of 1,110, and therefore forty-five less than 2,300 evening-mornings, and that this difference of one and a half months "belongs to the interval between the abrogation of the תָּמִיד (1 Macc. i. 45) and the introduction of the *βδέλυγμα ἐρημώσεως* (ibid. v. 54)." A hasty glance at the description of these incidents in 1 Maccabees will be sufficient to show that this interval of exactly forty-five days between the interdict of the daily sacrifices and the erection of the statue of Zeus in the temple is *wholly* imaginary. Moreover, the critic contradicts himself, since he employs all his acuteness to prove, on chap. vii. 25, that the Antiochian persecution began at least a quarter of a year, or more than three months, before the 15th Chisleu 145, while he finds it proper in this place to place the abrogation of the הַתָּמִיד, or the beginning of the same period of oppression, only one and a half months earlier than this date.—While the representatives of the opinion that the 2,300 evening-mornings are but half as many days, fail to establish an exact correspondence between the prophecy and its fulfilment, those expositors who regard the language as designating 2,300 days succeed no better. Bertholdt and Hävernick go three years beyond the time of Antiochus, to the defeat of Nicanor (1 Macc. vii. 43, 49), and assign to that period 2,271 days; the 29 days which, accordingly, are still lacking, are placed by Bertholdt at the close of the period, as an interval between that victory and the consequent celebration of the triumph; while Hävernick would prefer to assign them to the beginning, prior to the 15th Chisleu 145 (in opposition to both, see Hitzig, p. 136). On the other hand, Dereser, Von Lengerke, Wieseler (*Die 70 Jahrwochen*, etc., p. 110 et seq.), and Von Hofmann (*Weissagung und Erfüllung*, I., 295 et seq.) go back to the year 142 æ. Sel. in reckoning the entire period of about six years—Dereser and Hofmann calculating from the 25th Chisleu 148 (the day of the dedication of the temple), and Von Lengerke and Wieseler from the death of Ant. Epiphanes in the month of Shebat 148. The former are thus carried back to the summer of the year 142 in fixing the date of the beginning of the apostasy of the Jews who were seduced by Antiochus, Von Lengerke to Sivan, or the third month, and Wieseler only to the feast of tabernacles in the same year, 142. Wieseler himself afterwards recognized the untenable character of this method of reckoning, and therefore acknowledged his conversion to the exegetically more correct view entertained by a majority of moderns, which estimates only 1,150 days, in his subsequent essay in the *Gött. Gelehrten-Anzeigen*, 1846.* [The author, it will be perceived, ignores that class of interpreters, quite common in this country and Great Britain, but comparatively rare in Germany, who understand by the days in question so many *years*, and generally apply the prophecy to the continuance of the papal supremacy. There is, however, a great discrepancy among these interpreters as to the point of time from which to date the period spoken of, as well as some diversity as to its length, whether 2,300 years or only 1,150 years, although the majority prefer the latter. It would be a tedious, and, in our opinion, a bootless task, to follow them into all the details of their historical investigations, computations, and comparisons. Others, adopting the same substitution of *years* for "days," apply the prophecy to the rise and sway of Mohammedanism, and make out the requisite dates as best they can. It is an adequate answer to all these interpretations to say that such a meaning of the word *day* has no sufficient—if any—warrant in Scripture use, and certainly is not hinted at in this entire passage. A calm but fundamental refutation of the theory in question is given by Tregelles, *Remarks on Daniel* (Lond., 1864, 5th ed.), p. 110 et seq. It is also abundantly met by Stuart in his *Commentary on the Apocalypse*, II. 459 seq. Elliott, the strongest advocate of this theory, admits (*Horæ Apocalypticæ*, II. 965) that it was unknown till the close of the fourteenth century, when it was first broached by Walter Brute. It came into vogue with the Reformation, and owes its prevalence, not to any sound exegetical support, but to the

* [These difficulties in the way of the literal exactness of the period in question as applicable to the history of the persecution by Antiochus Epiphanes, are drawn out in detail by Keil, p. 302 et seq., who does not, however, add anything of importance to what the author adduces. They seem to us to be fairly met by the following explanation of Stuart in his *Commentary*, p. 238 et seq.: "*And then shall that which is holy be vindicated*, וְנִצְדַּק, *shall have justice done*, *i.e.*, the rights of the sanctuary shall be effectually restored, its claims shall be vindicated. This was done when Judas Maccabæus, after the three and a half years in which all temple rites had been suspended, and heathen sacrifices had been offered there, made a thorough expurgation of everything pertaining to the temple, and restored its entire services. This was on the 25th of Dec., 165 B. C., just three years from the time when swine's flesh was first offered there by Antiochus. We have then the *terminus ad quem* of the 2,300 days; and it is not difficult, therefore, to find the *terminus a quo*. These days, at thirty in a month (which is clearly the prophetic mode of reckoning), make six years, four months, and twenty days. Dec. 25th of 171 makes six years, and the four months and twenty days will bring the time to the latter half of July in the same year, *i.e.*, 171 B. C. During this year, Menelaus, the high-priest appointed by Antiochus on the ground of a proffered bribe, rifled the temple of many of the treasures to pay that bribe, and in this transaction he was assisted by his brother Lysimachus. The regular and lawful high-priest, Onias III., who had been removed, severely reproved this sacrilege committed by his brethren; and afterward, through fear of them, fled for refuge to Daphne, an asylum near Antioch, in Syria. Thence he was allured by the false promises of Menelaus, and perfidiously murdered by the king's lieutenant, Andronicus. See the whole story in 2 Macc. iv. 27 seq. The Jews at Jerusalem, incensed by the violent death of their lawful high-priest, and by the sacrilegious robberies of Menelaus and Lysimachus, became tumultuous, and a severe contest took place between them and the adherents of those who committed the robbery, in which the patriotic Jews at last gained the victory, and Lysimachus was slain at the treasury. This was the first contest that took place between the friends of Antiochus and the adherents to the Hebrew laws and usages. The whole of it was occasioned by the baseness of Antiochus in accepting bribes for bestowing the office of high-priest on those who had no just claim to it. The payment of the bribes occasioned the robbing of the temple and the sacrilege committed there; and this was the commencement of that long series of oppression, persecution, and bloodshed which took place in the sequel under Antiochus.

"We have, indeed, no data in ancient history by which the very day, or even month, connected with the transactions above related can be exactly ascertained. But the *year* is certain; and, as the time seems to be *definite* in our text, the fair presumption is, that the outbreak of the populace and the battle that followed constitutes the *terminus a quo* of the 2,300 days. See Frœlich, *Annales Reg. Syr.*, p. 46; and also Usher's *Chronol.* . . . . As to the difference between the time here, viz., 2,300 days, and the three and a half years in vii. 25, if the reader narrowly inspects the latter, he will perceive that the time there specified has relation to the period during which Antiochus entirely prohibited the Jewish religion in every shape. This period, as is well known, corresponds with historical facts. In the passage before us a more extensive series of events is comprised, as vs. 10-12 indicate. They begin with assaults on the priesthood (which we have seen to be matter of fact, as stated above), and end with the desecration and prostration of all that is sacred and holy. It is unnecessary to show that each of the things described belongs to each and every part of the 2,300 days. Enough that the events are *successive*, and spread over the time specified in our text. The *trampling down* or degradation of the priesthood and the sanctuary commenced the whole series of oppression and persecution, and this, with most aggravated acts of sacrilege and blasphemy, was also the consummation of the tyrant's outrages." Cowles gives a similar explanation in detail, *Commentary*, p. 378 et seq.]

polemical spirit of the times, which has seized upon it as a popular weapon against papacy.]

Verses 15–19. *Preparatory to the interpretation of the vision of the ram and the he-goat.* **And . . . when I . . . sought for the meaning,** namely, of the entire vision that was seen. The seeking was purely subjective, and not expressed in the form of a question addressed to the angel (Von Leng.), nor in a silent prayer to God (Hävernick).—**Behold, there stood before me** (one), **as the appearance of a man,** *i.e.*, appearing like a man. The expression "behold, there stood," etc., indicates the startling and extraordinary character of the apparition, which argued something terrible and superhuman (cf. Job iv. 16); the כְּמַרְאֵה גָבֶר then follows to denote the encouraging effect produced on the seer by the *manlike* appearance of the form. The term גֶּבֶר is employed instead of אָדָם or אֱנוֹשׁ, doubtless in allusion to the name of the angel, which is given below, in v. 16; see on that passage, and cf. chap. ix. 21, where the same angel is designated as "*the man* Gabriel," but where his super-human nature is also very clearly implied (in his "flying").—Verse 16. **And I heard a man's voice between** (the) **Ulai,** *i.e.*, between the two branches of the Eulæus; cf. supra, on v. 2. בֵּין does not stand for מִבֵּין, as if the voice only, and not also the listener, were stationed between the Ulai; nor does בֵּין אוּלָי signify "between the banks of the Ulai" (against Von Lengerke, Hitzig, etc.).—**Gabriel, make this man to understand the vision.** גַּבְרִיאֵל, *i.e.*, "man of God," or also "man-god" (according to Ewald, "a God who kindly condescends to man"), is the name of one of the principal angels or angel-princes (cf. Luke i. 19), one of the ἀρχάγγελοι or שָׂרִים (chap. x. 13 et seq.), whose number is fixed at *seven* in Rev. viii. 2 (οἱ ἑπτὰ ἄγγελοι, οἳ ἐνώπιον τοῦ θεοῦ ἑστήκασι), equal to that of the *amshaspands*, who stand beside Ormuzd as a divine council, according to the ancient religious books of Parseeism. The Scriptural archangels, however, of whom another, Michael, is mentioned hereafter in this book, are not to be regarded as identical with the *Amêshaspentas* of Parseeism; for (1) the number seven in the latter case is obtained only by adding Ormuzd himself to six others; (2) they are not represented as angels or servants of God, but as being themselves divine, and as governing determined portions of creation in that character, *e.g.*, *Bohumano* (Bohman) governs the sky, *Ardihesht* the fire, *Sapandomad* the earth, etc.; (3) the *names* of the *amshaspands* are as thoroughly Persian or Aryan in their character as those of the Scriptural archangel, so far as they occur in the Holy Bible (namely, Gabriel and Michael, and Raphael in the Apocrypha, Tob. iii. 25; xii. 12 et seq.) are specifically Shemitic, and bear, by virtue of the ending אֵל in each case, a thoroughly monotheistic character; (4) the attempts to establish the identity of individual *amshaspands* with individual archangels of the Bible must be regarded, without exception, as failures; *e. g.*, the supposed recognition of *Chordad* (Haurvatat) in the Apocalyptic "angel of the waters," Rev. xvi. 5 (Hitzig; also Hilgenfeld, *Das Judenthum im pers. Zeitalter*, in the *Zeitschr. f. wissenschaftl. Theologie*, 1866, No. 4), the proposed identifying of Gabriel with *Craosha* and of Michael with *Bohman* (by Alex. Kohut, "*Ueber die jüdische Angelologie und Dämonologie in ihrer Abhängigkeit vom Parsismus*," in *Abhandlungen der Deutsch. Morgenl. Gesellschaft*, vol. IV. No. 3). Cf. Haneberg, in Reusch's *Theolog. Literaturbl.*, 1867, No. 3, p. 72; also Döllinger, *Heidenthum und Judenthum*, p. 361; M. Haug, *Essays on the sacred language, writings, and religion of the Parsees*, Bombay, 1862.—Ewald appears inclined to regard Gabriel not as one of the superior angels, but as occupying an intermediate or inferior rank, since he designates the "man's voice" which calls to him as that of a *still higher* angel. This assumption, however, is unnecessary; it is conceivable that an angel of equal rank may have given him this direction, or, if this should not be preferred, that God Himself, giving a human sound to His voice that He might be heard by Daniel, addressed the angel.—It must remain undecided whether the "man's voice" is to be considered as belonging to the former of the קְדֹשִׁים who were speaking together in v. 13, while Gabriel is to be identified with the questioner in that place (as Hitzig supposes), since the author has not definitely indicated such an identity.—Verse 17. **So he came near where I stood**; literally, "beside my standing" (cf. v. 18). Luther renders it, "and he came hard by me."—**And when** (or "as") **he came, I was afraid, and fell upon my face.** Cf. chap. x. 9; Ezek. i. 28; xliii. 3; Rev. i. 17.—**Understand, O son of man** (—this address is probably modelled after Ezekiel—); **for at the time of the end shall be the vision**; rather, "for the vision is for the final time," *i.e.*, it refers to the final period of earthly history; cf. v. 19 *b*, 26. [But these verses do not warrant this interpretation. See below.] The words are not designed to comfort, but to direct attention to the impressive and alarming nature of the prophecy, in which, according to the following context, they are successful.—Verse 18. **Now as he was speaking with me, I was in a deep sleep on my face toward the ground**; rather, "and while he was speaking with me, I fell stunned upon my face to the ground." Not until this repeated falling down in terror did the "benumbing" or Divine ἔκστασις take place, as the immediate presence of God for the purpose of imparting to the prophet a highly important revelation, was not realized until then. Cf. the case of Moses (Ex. xxxiii. 20), Isaiah (Isa. vi. 5), Peter, John, and James, on the mount of transfiguration (Luke ix. 32), Paul and his companions near Damascus (Acts ix. 4; xxii. 7; xxvi. 12), etc.—**But he touched me, and set me upright.** Cf. x. 10 et seq.; Neh. ix. 3, etc.—Verse 19. **Behold . . . . what shall be in the last end of the indignation,** namely, of the Divine indignation upon the godless world (the ὀργὴ μεγάλη, 1 Macc. i. 64; cf. Rom. ii. 5; Isa. x. 5, 25; xxvi. 20; Jer. l. 5), which naturally will be manifested most strongly toward the close of human history, when the tares of wickedness shall flourish most luxuriantly (see v. 23 and

Matt. xiii. 30, 39; cf. Matt. xxiv. 9 et seq.). For this reason the last times shall constitute a period of great tribulation and woes (θλίψεις, ὠδῖνες—Matt. xxiv. 7 et seq.).—**For at the time appointed the end shall be**; rather, "for it relates to the point of time of the end." The subject here, as in v. 17 *b*, is the vision (הֶחָזוֹן), or rather its contents, which, according to this assurance from the angel, refers to the מוֹעֵד קֵץ, the determined point of time of the end." *

Verses 20–26. *The interpretation of the vision.* On v. 20, cf. supra, on v. 3; concerning v. 21, on v. 5.—**The king of Græcia**; properly, of Javan (יָוָן). By this term the Hebrews designated all the Hellenic lands and peoples, because the Ionians (Homer, Ἰάονες) dwelt in the eastern portions of Hellas, and through their colonies in Asia Minor were the first to become acquainted with the Asiatics. The Egyptians, ancient Persians, and Indians appear likewise to have constantly denominated the whole body of Græcian nations as Ionians or Jaonians; Æschylus and Aristophanes, at least, introduce Persians as employing the term Ἰάονες instead of Ἕλληνες. Cf. generally, Knobel, *Völkertafel*, p. 78 et seq. —Verse 22. **Now that being broken, whereas four stood up for it**; rather, "and that which was broken, and in whose stead four stood up." It should have read, properly, "and concerning this, that it (the great horn) was broken, and that in its stead four stood up;" but instead of this, וְהַנִּשְׁבֶּרֶת stands abruptly at the beginning (cf. vii. 17), and the ecbactic וַתַּעֲמֹדְנָה וגו׳, "and four stood up," etc., is *subordinate* to that term in its absolute position.—**Four kingdoms shall stand up out of the nation**; יַעֲמֹדְנָה, an archaism (Gen. xxx. 38; 1 Sam. vi. 12), that here seems to be renewed under the influence of the Chaldee element.—**But not in his power.** The suffix in בְּכֹחוֹ does not refer back to מִגּוֹי, but to הַמֶּלֶךְ in v. 21 *b*. The power of the first great Græcian conqueror shall not descend to the kingdoms which spring from his empire; they shall not equal him, neither singly, nor all taken together.—Verse 23. **And in the latter time of their kingdom, when the transgressors are come to the full**, namely, of the measure of their wicked plans and actions; cf. the same elliptic usage of הָתֵם in chap. ix. 24 Keri, and in addition Gen. xv. 16; 2 Macc. vi. 14; Matt. xxiii. 32; 1 Thess. ii. 16. The פֹּשְׁעִים who are here charged with "filling the measure of their sins" are not the Israelites who have forsaken Jehovah and His law (Dereser, Von Lengerke, Kranichfeld), but, without doubt, the enemies of God's people, the heathen oppressors of the saints of the Most High; for the term פֹּשְׁעִים alludes with sufficient clearness to פֶּשַׁע in vs. 6, 12, and 13. For the opinion that this does not probably refer to the servants and abettors of Antiochus Epiphanes, but rather to his predecessors, see supra, on v. 9.*—**A king of fierce** (rather, "insolent") **countenance, and understanding dark sentences, shall stand up.** עַז פָּנִים, properly, "of hard countenance" (cf. Deut. xxviii. 50; Isa. xix. 4). The predicate probably refers chiefly to the blasphemous sayings of the tyrant, see chap. vii. 3 et seq. The following predicate, מֵבִין חִידוֹת, "versed in riddles," denotes his art of cunning dissimulation, by which he is able to conceal his purposes from both friend and foe; cf. v. 25, and xi. 21, 27.—Verse 24. **And his power shall be mighty, but not by his own power.** The implied thought is, "but by Divine permission;" cf. vs. 12 and 13, and also Isa. x. 5 et seq.; 1 Sam. ii. 9, etc.—It is incorrect to supply, with Dereser, Von Lengerke, etc., an antithesis to "not by his own power," so that it will read "but by his *cunning*." לֹא בְּכֹחוֹ is a *litotes*, which, exactly similar to the expression "without hand" (chap. ii. 34 and infra, v. 25), alludes to the superhuman providence of God as compared to human power, which is never more than impotence.—**And he shall destroy wonderfully, and shall prosper**; נִפְלָאוֹת, an adverb, as in Job xxxvii. 5. For what remains, cf. supra, v. 12 *b*.—**And shall destroy the mighty** (ones) **and the holy people.** The וְ in וְהִשְׁחִית is explicative; it is designed to denote more particularly the respects in which the king shall prosper. The "mighty ones" are the warlike enemies over whom he shall triumph, and to them are added, by way of contrast, the

* [Keil, however, justly remarks: "But עֵת־קֵץ, *the time of the end*, and מוֹעֵד קֵץ, *the appointed time of the end*, is not the absolute end of all things, the time of the setting up of the *regnum gloriæ*, and the time of the tribulation preceding the return of the Lord; but the time of the judgment of the world-kingdom and the setting up of the everlasting kingdom of God by the appearance of the Messiah, the end of αἰὼν οὗτος and the commencement of the αἰὼν μέλλων, the time of the אַחֲרִית הַיָּמִים (chap. ix. 14), which an apostle calls (1 Cor. x. 11) τὰ τέλη τῶν αἰώνων, and speaks of as having then already come." Stuart still more correctly says: "*End* of what? Of Antiochus? or of a troublous state of things? or end of the world? Not merely of Antiochus; for his importance, as exhibited in the book of Daniel, arises principally from his power to annoy the people of God. Not the end of the world; for in chap. viii. no Messianic period is developed at the close of its predictions, and yet the Messianic reign is itself the end or last time of the world. Ver. 19 gives us perhaps more light; בְּאַחֲרִית הַזָּעַם, *in the latter time of the indignation*, *i.e.*, the latter time of afflictions permitted to be brought upon Israel, because of the divine indignation against their sins. The vision itself in fact reaches only to *the end* of those special afflictions that are to come on the people of the Jews *before* the Messianic period, and which are made the subject of prophecy because of their importance. The warning to *mark well* or *consider* the vision, because it discloses these afflictions, connects itself of course with a supposed importance attached to the knowledge of the final special troubles of the Jews before the coming of the Messiah. The Rabbins call these troubles חֶבְלֵי מָשִׁיחַ." In other words, as Keil presently says more distinctly, "הַזַּעַם is *the wrath* of God against Israel, the punishment which God hung over them on account of their sins, as in Isa. x. 5; Jer. xxv. 11; Ezek. xxii. 24, etc., and here the sufferings of punishment and discipline which the little horn shall bring over Israel."]

* [Stuart and Keil, on the contrary, strongly maintain that "the transgressors" here are not the heathen, but the apostate Jews, whose sin will be visited by the indignation of God; and this seems to be more appropriate to the whole connection.]

"nation of saints" (cf. vii. 18, 22), as unwarlike opponents. In the opinion of Hitzig, Ewald, etc., the עֲצוּמִים are the three pretenders to the crown whom Epiphanes was compelled to depose; but not one of these deserved to be called a mighty one, not even the usurper Heliodorus; see supra, on chap. vii. 8, 25.*—Verse 25. **And through** (rather, "according to") **his policy he shall cause craft to prosper in his hand.** עַל־שִׂכְלוֹ is probably not "by reason of," but "according to his cunning;" cf. Psa. cx. 4; Esth. ix. 26, etc. This expression, in an absolute position at the beginning, is connected with the principal sentence which follows by an emphatic וְ; cf. Gesenius, *Thesaur.*, p. 396 *a*. הִצְלִיחַ is not transitive (Hitzig, et al.), as if the following מִרְמָה were its accusative, but probably intransitive, despite the fem. מִרְמָה; cf. Isa. liii. 10.—"In (or with) his hand" (cf. Isa. xliv. 20), considered as the outward sphere of action, seems intended to form an antithesis to the following "in his heart." Concerning בִּלְבָבוֹ and the signification of יַגְדִּיל which results from it, cf. supra, on v. 4.—**And by peace shall destroy many;** rather, "and unawares shall destroy many." וּבְשַׁלְוָה does not exactly signify "in the midst of profound peace" (Job xv. 21), but more indefinitely, "with suddenness, by a malignant surprise," an illustration of the malice and dissimulation practised by this tyrant, which were already mentioned in v. 23. The circumstance that it is recorded of Antiochus Epiphanes, in 1 Macc. i. 30, *καὶ ἐπέπεσεν ἐπὶ τὴν πόλιν ἐξάπινα*, proves nothing in favor of a *vatic. ex eventu*, beyond the fact that malignant and sudden surprises are necessarily practised by every warlike foe of cruel disposition. ["In the רַבִּים (*many*) are comprehended 'the mighty (one) and the holy people' (ver. 24)."—*Keil.*]—**He shall also stand up against the Prince of princes,** etc. Cf. v. 11, and with regard to the being "broken without hand," cf. chap. ii. 34; also Job xxxiv. 20 and Lam. iv. 6. It is not necessary to seek a definite reference to the death of Epiphanes by sickness or extraordinary accident in this passage, instead of permitting him to fall on the battle-field, or by the hand of a murderer (against Bertholdt, Von Lengerke, Hävernick, etc.).†—Verse 26. **And the vision of the evening and the morning which was told,** namely, in v. 14. Since the observation in that place respecting the 2,300 evening-mornings was really a מִשְׁמָע, and not a מַרְאֶה, the words אֲשֶׁר נֶאֱמַר seem to refer back to the genitive הָעֶרֶב וגו׳, instead of to the *Stat. constr.* (thus Hitzig). *Words* and *things told*, however, form the subject of visions in other cases also (cf. Isa. ii. 1; Am. i. 1; Hab. ii. 1, etc.); and the remark concerning the 2,300 evening-mornings may consequently be termed a "vision" in this instance.—**Is true** (rather "truth"), *i.e.*, it is correct, deserves to be credited, inasmuch as 2,300 evening-mornings must elapse before the end of the period of affliction. That period is thus determined as an extended one, which shall not soon reach its close. On אֱמֶת, cf. chap. x. 1; xi. 2; also xii. 7; Jer. xxvi. 15; xxviii. 9; Rev. xix. 9; xxi. 5; xxii. 6.—**Wherefore shut thou up the vision;** rather, "and thou, conceal the vision," *i.e.*, do not publish it, do not be anxious to spread a report concerning it. סתם is not equivalent to חתם, "to seal up" (Theodotion, Hävernick, Von Lengerke); for "sealing" is added to the mere "concealing" in chap. xii. 4, as a strengthening term.—**For it shall be for many days,** *i.e.*, it (the vision) shall retain its prophetic value for a long period, it does not relate to a near, but to a distant future; cf. chap. xii. 4, 9. As the direction to conceal the vision is here based on the consideration that a long period must elapse before it shall be fulfilled, so, on the contrary, the prophet is directed, in Rev. xxii. 10, *not* to seal what has been revealed to him, because the time of its fulfilment is near. Notice the difference between the Old-Testament seer, who is far removed from the final future, and only sees it primarily in *types* (*e.g.*, instead of beholding the antichrist he only sees his forerunner Epiphanes), and the New-Testament prophet, who beholds the events of the last times in the history of the world much nearer at hand, and is therefore not obliged to conceal the prophecies relating to them, especially since he addresses a community composed exclusively of *θεοδιδακτοί* (Isa. liv. 3; John vi. 45; cf. 1 John ii. 20, 27).

Verse 27. *The effect of the vision upon the prophet.* **And I Daniel fainted, and was sick** (certain) **days.** Cf. vii. 28, and especially chap. ii. 1, in relation to נִהְיֵיתִי.—**Afterward I rose up,** namely, from the sick-bed. This formal statement by the prophet cannot be regarded as extraordinary, since not only the vision as such (*i.e.*, by reason of its startling character), but also the *fasting* which preceded it (cf. chap. ix. 3; x. 2 et seq.), comes under consideration as the cause of the complete exhaustion which followed.—**And did the king's business.** Concerning the extent to which Daniel might have transacted official business for the king in the reign of Belshazzar, without being personally known to him, see on chap. v. 7.—**And was astonished at** (rather, "dumb concerning")

* [" עֲצוּמִים does not here signify *many*, numerous, many individual Israelites (Von Leng., Maurer, Kliefoth [Stuart]), partly because in ver. 25 רַבִּים stands for that, partly because of the עַם קְדֹשִׁים, by which we are to understand *the people of Israel*."—*Keil.*]

† ["The language is adapted to the symbol, namely, the little horn. The meaning is, *totally destroyed.* Facts correspond. According to history, Antiochus, after marching into Persia, and robbing the temple at Elymaïs, was driven away by popular tumult; and on his return back towards Syria, he was met with the news of the total defeat of his army in Judæa, and of the restoration of the temple services there. Polybius (XXXI. 11) says of him, that '*he fell mad* (*δαιμονήσας*) and died;' 1 Macc. vi. 8 relates that he fell sick of grief for his losses; Appian (*De reb. Syr.*, LXVI.) says simply: *φθίνων ἐτελεύτησε*. Various shades are given to the picture by the different writers; *e.g.*, in 1 Macc. vi. 8 seq., which narrates his penitent confessions. But these have a strong tinge of *Jewish* coloring. So much is undoubtedly true, viz., that he perished suddenly by a violent sickness, during which he probably fell into a state of mania. He died, therefore, without violence by the hand of man, and so as to make a deep impression of perishing by a peculiar visitation of God."—*Stuart.*]

the vision, but ("and") **none understood** (rather, "became aware of") **it**; usually rendered, "none *understood* it," or, "and *to me* there was no understanding, *I* did not understand it" (thus Maurer, Hitzig, Kranichfeld, Kamphausen, etc., under comparison with chap. xii. 8). Since, however, the obvious design is to state what Daniel did "to conceal" the vision, the signification of "not noticing, not learning" seems to be the only logical and suitable one for לֹא הֵבִין in this passage; cf. on this interpretation, vs. 5, 17; Job xxviii. 23; Isa. xxviii. 19, etc.

ETHICO-FUNDAMENTAL PRINCIPLES RELATED TO THE HISTORY OF SALVATION, APOLOGETICAL REMARKS, AND HOMILETICAL SUGGESTIONS.

1. The principal difficulty to be met with in this section relates to the concrete number of 1150 days or 2300 evening-mornings, in v. 14, and in its failure to agree with the three and a half years of the preceding vision (chap. vii. 25). If simply the idea was to be expressed that the period of tribulation should expire in *something less* than three and a half years, why did the author not permit the angel to say, "even before three and a half years shall have passed," etc.? Or why did he not select really a round number, as 1200 days (to denote 1277, which amount exactly to three and a half years)? Or why did he not pursue the course adopted by the New-Test. apocalyptist, who substituted forty-two months for forty-two and a half, and hence 1260 days for 1277 (see Rev. xi. 2; xii. 6; xiii. 5)?—This strange feature admits of a correct explanation, only when it is remembered that prophecies relating to time are necessarily and unavoidably of a symbolic-concrete character, and that for this reason, no exact correspondence, or mechanically precise agreement of the prophetic numbers with the extent of the periods in which they are realized, can be expected. Neither the seventy years of being forgotten and of ruin which Isaiah predicted for the Tyrians (chap. xxv. 15–18), nor the seventy years of captivity in Babylon, which Jeremiah (chap. xxv. 11, et seq.; xxix. 10 et seq.) foretold to the Israelites of his time, were fulfilled with literal exactness* (cf. infra. on chap. ix.); and as the "two days" (יֹמַיִם) during which Israel's state of death or the period of its affliction was to continue, according to Hos. vi. 2, have primarily an ideal-symbolic value only, so the "three days and three nights," which were to be spent by the prophet in the belly of the great fish, according to Jon. ii. 1, were, in like manner, not an exact number, amounting to precisely seventy-two hours (cf. Kleinert on that passage)—and yet both these prophetic numbers were designed to foretell the resurrection of the Saviour on the third day, *i.e.*, after two whole nights and one entire day.* The prophets are accustomed to employ concrete conceptions of time, and to clothe them in definite form. This form might arise from any incident or event, most of which can no longer be discovered; but their relation to the duration of the events which fulfil the prophecy must as certainly be a merely approximate agreement, and not mathematically exact, as the manner in which God secures the fulfilment of the prophecies uttered by holy men through the Spirit, is in nowise a matter entrusted to man, but belongs only to the God who brings the predictions to pass (cf. 2 Pet. i. 20 et seq.)† The predictions of the prophets in the Church during the Middle Ages and in modern times (*e.g.*, St. Hildegard, Joachim, the Parisian professor Nicholas Oresmius, who, in 1364, foretold the great papal schism, which actually broke out in 1378; Huss and Savonarola, who predicted the Reformation; the Lutheran Michael Stiefel of Jena († 1567); the astrologer Nostradamus (†1566); and finally J. A. Benzel and Jung-Stilling) might be substantially treated in the same manner, so far as they assume a numerically exact, or definitely chronological form.‡ The partial non-agreement of their predictions with the points of time or periods of the future in which they were to be realized does not destroy their character as genuine prophets, or disprove that they were employed in a superior and heavenly calling; but the approximate agreement or partial coincidence of their vaticinations with the facts of fulfilment and their chronological relations, does not warrant a suspicion that they were forged subsequently to the beginning of their fulfilment, any more than the approximate agreement of either the 1150 days or the three and a half years, etc., in the prophecy before us, with the epochs of the Maccabæan history will justify the pseudo-Daniel tendency-hypothesis.

2. While the slight difference between the prophetic number and the events connected with its realization, discussed above, belongs undoubtedly to the category of those "slight discrepancies" which, according to M. v. Niebuhr,

* [With regard to the latter point at least the author concedes too much, for the Babylonian captivity was exactly seventy years in length, namely. from the fourth year of Jehoiakim, B. C. 606, to the edict of Cyrus, B.C. 536. See Browne's *Ordo Sædorum*, ch. iii. sec. i. §§ 161 et seq. Had we the data extant we might doubtless prove the truth of the other periods named in Scripture prophecy with equal precision.]

* [The "three days and three nights" in question are an exact expression according to Hebrew usage, which includes both extremes in all such periods.]

† Cf. Tholuck *Die Propheten und ihre Weissagungen; eine apologetisch-hermeneutische Studie* (Gotha, 1860), p. 113 et seq., where the remark is made concerning the seventy years of Jeremiah, considered as being a designation of time that agreed, generally at least, with the duration of the captivity. "Can any means of escaping this conclusion be discovered? Only that one, which, among others, Ewald has not despised, viz., to regard the number seventy as a round number, and therefore = 'a long time.' . . . . Is then, *round* number really = long time in the Oriental use of language? The master of Old-Test. language will certainly not attempt to deny that it rather denotes an 'approximate limitation of time!' . . . . Such numbers are clearly approximate, *e.g.*, in Am. ii. 4, where it is said, 'For three transgressions of Judah and for four, I will not turn away,' etc; Mic. v. 5, 'Then shall we raise against him seven shepherds and eight principal men;' cf. Hos. vi. 2. In like manner a desolation of forty years is predicted for Egypt, by Ezekiel, in chap. xxix. 11, 12, which is, indeed, a round number of probable reckoning, but is, at the same time, an approximate number, namely, 36 or 37," etc. [But these conventional numbers in a general statement are very different from those obviously given as chronological data.]

‡ In relation to the prophets of the Christian æra, above referred to, and also with regard to several others, cf. the interesting statements in Splittgerber, *Schlaf und Tod*, etc. (Halle. 1866), p. 235–253. [But sound theologians—indeed, accurate observers merely—would certainly place all these pseudo-predictions on a very different level from those of the prophets of Scripture.]

"must excite our awe, instead of begetting a doubt of the truth of the prophecy, or shaking our confidence in the chronology of ancient history" (*Geschichte Assurs und Babels*, p. 90), the relation between the character of the history of nations and kingdoms as described in the vision under consideration, and the condition of Israel during the æra of oppression and revolt in the Maccabæan age, which corresponds to it as a primary historical fulfilment, is such, that it unconditionally forbids the idea that the vision is a prophecy *ex eventu*, and was composed to favor a tendency. There is no complete and thorough correspondence between prophecy and fulfilment, that could favor the suspicion of its composition under such circumstances and for such a purpose; on the contrary, the discrepancies are so numerous, that to trace historical facts which shall correspond in every case to the particular features of the prophetic vision, involves the greatest uncertainty and difficulty. Bertholdt and v. Lengerke assume that the chapter was written shortly *after* the death of Antiochus Epiphanes; Hitzig, that it was composed shortly *before* that event; Bleek (*Jahrb. für deutsche Theologie*, 1860, No. 1, p. 57), that it was framed at least *about* that time. "According to this, the section was at any rate composed at a time when the Jews had already demonstrated their superiority in arms over the troops of the tyrant. At the same time, these bloody feats of arms, which formed the basis of all the hopes that animated the newly-awakened national consciousness of the Jews, are not mentioned with a single word. As in chap. vii. the heathen oppressor triumphs in battle over the holy people to the end of the three and a half times, so in this selection the host and sanctuary are represented as being trodden under foot until the close of the period mentioned in v. 14. Even the restoration of the sanctuary (v. 14), which might at least indirectly be interpreted as consequent on a warlike triumph of the Jews, is, in v. 25, referred only to a theocratic judgment imposed directly by God, and not to a national victory. The latter, indeed, is directly excluded. The great deeds of the oppressor only are spoken of, and his overthrow בְּאֶפֶס יָד is immediately connected with them. Every real foundation for the opinion that this section originated at that juncture which was marked by the triumphs over Apollonius and Seron, over Gorgias and Lysius, dearly bought as they were with the blood of the people, is thus taken away, since the situation described in the chapter, testifies only to defeat down to the time of restoring the temple, and denotes a disposition which looked for help only from a supernatural agency" (Kranichfeld, p. 286 et seq.).—Remarkable as is this total silence respecting the national revolt, which was so successfully introduced, when the author is regarded as a Maccabæan pseudo-Daniel, it is no less difficult to understand why, if the vision was recorded soon after the death of Antiochus, the Messianic hopes which must have been connected with that death, should not be mentioned with a single word. The only tolerable explanation of this fact is that the death of the oppressor (his "being broken without hand," v. 25) was future to the writer, as much so as everything else. Even the restoration of the temple-service, which had been abolished, is clearly placed in the future by the description in v. 14, and does not appear as an incident in the past experience of the prophet. The only comfort offered by him in the entire section has no relation to the sufferings of the present or the past, but to tribulations belonging to the far-distant future.

3. The only circumstance which seems seriously to favor the theory of a Maccabæan composition is the express mention of *Javan* in v. 21, as the world-power from which the impious oppressor of Israel should come forth (preceded, however, by a number of anti-theistic kingdoms [v. 22] and wicked sovereigns [v. 23]). But this circumstance also loses its apparent character, as disproving the origin of the chapter during the captivity, and becomes decidedly more intelligible, as soon as we remember the frequent contact of the orientals with Hellenic civilization and culture, as well as with Græcian military art and bravery, which began even before the time of Nebuchadnezzar (see Introd. § 7, Note 2). Let it also be remembered that the ancient prophecy by Balaam (Num. xxiv.), which threatened destruction to the Assyrians and Hebrews through "ships from Chittim," *i.e.*, through Greek *invasions* from the sea (cf. supra, on chap. ii.), must have been known to Daniel, even if it had originated as late as the age of Shalmaneser and Sennacherib, and afterward been incorporated with the early history in the Pentateuch. There is no lack of natural indications arising from the events of current history, which might suggest to a seer of the period of the exile, that precisely the distant nation of the Greeks would become a threatening rival, and eventually, a victorious opponent of the Persian power and greatness, and which might also awaken in him a presentiment of the internally divided and disunited, and therefore transient character of the future empire of the Greeks. The definite character of the predictions respecting the development of that Javanic empire is certainly marvellous and inexplicable, unless referred to the Divine Spirit of prophecy; but it is scarcely more wonderful than the equally definite character of Balaam's prophecy, which likewise related to the Greeks, or than the surprising clearness and confidence with which Amos foretold that the Israel of his day should "go into captivity beyond Damascus" (chap. v. 27), or Isaiah was able to predict that the successors of Hezekiah should be led into captivity at Babylon (chap. xxxix. 6 et seq.; 2 Kings xx. 17 et seq.), or Jeremiah could describe to his contemporaries the overthrow of Babylon by the Medo-Persians! Cf. also Kranichfeld, p. 128 et seq.

4. The real and fundamental Messianic feature of this section, and, at the same time, the thought which is pre-eminently adapted to practical homiletical treatment, is that already noticed in the exegesis of vs. 19 and 23, according to which the moral degradation and the wickedness of the world-power in its hostility to God becomes more excessive with each stage through which that power passes in its development, until it reaches its climax, when God interferes to judge and deliver—thus bringing it, in its character as an oppressive, pseudo-prophetic antichristianity, into the strongest contrast with the

transparent light and holiness of the Messiah and the community of His saints, who are born of God. This thought is also presented by the Saviour in the parable which describes the tares as growing together with the good seed in the field, and as ripening for the harvest at the judgment (Matt. xiii. 30 et seq.); it is the same Messianic truth and necessity to which he refers in the former half of his *oratio eschatologica* in thoroughly prophetic language (Matt. xxiv. 5 et seq.); it is the fundamental thought of all apocalyptic prophecy, of all prophecy relating to the future history of empires, as the analogous sections in 2 Thess. and the book of Revelation show with sufficient clearness. The *goats* triumph over the more harmless *rams* in the last times; the place of the weaker horns that arise against the Lord is supplied by others who succeed each other in constantly increasing strength. The "great power" of the enemy is reinforced by "great cunning," which increases with the lapse of time; and his insolence is joined to craft which steadily develops, and to malignant dissimulation (cf. vs. 23-25), until, through the instigation of the great arch-enemy, who is ever the same, nation rises against nation, and kingdom against kingdom. To increase the need and oppression of the righteous, many false prophets arise and practice their deceitful arts, and because iniquity abounds, the love of many waxes cold (Matt. xxiv. 7 et seq., 11 et seq.).—If all this, considered as the real fundamental idea of the visional representation, be duly regarded, the jejune character of this section, which at first sight seems to offer nothing that possesses practical value, or that is available for homiletical purposes, will speedily disappear; and as the danger of feeling that only unimportant features, such as the animal-symbols (vs. 3–7) or the doctrine of angels (vs. 13-18), are here presented, becomes less, the preacher will find the energetic warning and promise by the Saviour, "But he that endureth to the end shall be saved," available as an encouraging and hortatory theme that covers the ground of the whole chapter. This forms the pregnant and solemn expression of the New Testament, which marks the consoling and elevating Messianic back-ground in which the discouraging and stormy scene of the chapter is laid, but which here appears but for a brief moment in the concluding words of v. 19, like the cheering sun at evening against the border of the stormy cloud.

5. *Special homiletical suggestions relating to separate passages:*

On v. 3 et seq., Melancthon: "*Aliquoties dictum est, ad quid prosit tenere prædictiones de serie monarchiarum et omnium temporum usque ad extremum judicium? Est Ecclesiæ hac doctrina et consolatione opus, ne inter tot afflictiones et scandala desperet. Est etiam admonitione opus, ut causas cogitemus afflictionum. . . . . Hæ atroces comminationes exsuscitent nos, ut simus diligentiores in conservanda puritate doctrinæ et in vita, ne Deus sinat exoriri majores tenebras.*"—The *Tübing. Bib.*: "How uncertain is the glory and majesty of the kingdoms of earth! Even when they have attained the highest prosperity they must yet be humbled, fall, and pass away, like every other earthly good and honor. The kingdom of heaven alone is immutable, and forms the hope of every believer," Psa. cxlv. 13.

On v. 10 et seq., the *Tüb. Bib.*: "Nothing is more dangerous than pride, which leads man even to war against God, His Church, and the true worship. This must inevitably be followed by heavy judgments from God."—Starke: "An earthly ruler will not permit rebellion against his authority to pass unpunished. How shall he escape, who revolts against the Prince over the host of God (Isa. x. 13)?"

On v. 14, Cramer: "The persecution and rage of the godless is a storm that sweeps over us; God fixes its limits, results, and measure."—Starke: "God has indeed revealed something in relation to the hope of Christ's Church for better times on the earth, in order that no doubt may be entertained concerning the fact itself; but to seek to ascertain the particular time, would be fool-hardiness and useless trouble (Acts i. 7.)."

On v. 17 et seq., Jerome: "*Et Ezechiel et Daniel et Zacharias, quia sæpe inter angelos esse se cernunt, ne deventur in superbiam et angelicæ vel naturæ vel dignitatis se esse credant, admonentur fragilitatis suæ, et filii hominum appellantur, ut homines se esse noverint.*"—Geier: "If the presence of a holy angel was so insupportable to Daniel, how terrible will be the experience of the wicked when they shall behold the Lord of angels and Judge of the whole world, Jesus Christ Himself (Rev. vi. 15 et seq.)!"

On v. 24, Osiander: "God sometimes permits the plans of the wicked to succeed, in order that the saints may be tried."—Starke: "God requires no great preparation or mighty instruments to cast down a tyrant; He can adapt the most insignificant means to that end (Acts xii. 23)."

---

3. *The vision of the seventy weeks of years.*

CHAP. IX. 1–27.

1 In *the* first year of [to] Darius, *the* son of Ahasuerus, of *the* seed of *the* Medes
2 [Media], which [who] was made king over *the* realm of *the* Chaldæans; in *the*
first year of [to] his reign, I Daniel understood by [the] books *the* number of
the years, where*of* [which] *the* word of *the* Lord [Jehovah] came [was] to Jere-
miah the prophet, that *he would* accomplish [for fulfilling] seventy years in [for]
3 *the* desolations of Jerusalem. And I set [gave] my face unto *the* Lord God, to
seek [1] *by* prayer and supplications, with fasting, and sackcloth, and ashes.

4 And I prayed[2] unto *the* Lord [Jehovah] my God, and made my confession,
and said,[3] *O* Lord, the great and dreadful God, keeping the covenant and mercy[4]
5 to them that love him, and to them that keep his commandments; we have
sinned, and have committed iniquity, and have done wickedly, and have rebel-
led, even *by* [and *there has been* a] departing from thy precepts [commandments],
6 and from thy judgments; neither have we [and we have not] hearkened unto
thy servants the prophets, which [who] spake in thy name to our kings, our
7 princes, and our fathers, and to all *the* people of the land. *O* Lord, righteous-
ness *belongeth* unto thee; but [and] unto us confusion [shame] of faces,[4] as *at*
this day; to *the* men [man] of Judah, and to *the* inhabitants of Jerusalem, and
unto all Israel, *that are* near, and *that are* far *off*, through [in] all the countries
[lands] whither [where] thou hast driven them, because of [in] their trespass
[treachery] that they have trespassed [done treacherously] against [with] thee.
8 *O* Lord, to us *belongeth* confusion [shame] of face [faces], to our kings, to our
princes, and to our fathers, because we [*or*, we who] have sinned against [to]
9 thee. To *the* Lord our God *belong* mercies[4] and forgivenesses,[4] though [for] we
10 have rebelled against [with] him; neither have we [and we have not] obeyed
the voice of *the* Lord [Jehovah] our God, to walk in his laws, which he set
[gave] before us by [*the* hand of] his servants the prophets.
11 Yea, [And] all Israel have transgressed thy law, even by [and *there has been*
a] departing, that they might not [*so as* not *at all* to] obey thy voice; therefore
[and] the curse *is* [has] poured upon us, and the oath that *is* written in *the* law
12 of Moses *the* servant of God, because we have sinned against [to] him. And he
hath confirmed his words, which he spake against us, and against our judges
that judged us, by bringing [to bring] upon us *a*[5] great evil; for [, which]
under the whole heaven [heavens] hath not been done as [it] hath been done
13 upon [in] Jerusalem. As *it is* written in *the* law of Moses, [*as to*] all this evil
[, it] is [has] come upon us; yet [and] made we not our prayer before [we be-
sought not *the* face of] *the* Lord [Jehovah] our God, that we might [to] turn
14 from our iniquities, and understand [become wise in] thy truth. Therefore
[And] hath *the* Lord [Jehovah] watched upon the evil, and brought it upon us;
for *the* Lord [Jehovah] our God *is* righteous in [upon] all his works which he
doeth [has done]; for [and] we obeyed not his voice.
15 And now, *O* Lord our God, that hast brought thy people forth out of *the* land
of Egypt with a mighty hand, and hast gotten [made for] thee renown [a name],
16 as *at* this day; we have sinned, we have done wickedly. *O* Lord, according to
[in] all thy righteousness [righteousnesses], *I* beseech *thee*, let thine anger and
thy fury *be* turned *away* [return] from thy city Jerusalem, thy holy mountain
[*the* mountain of thy sanctuary]; because for [in] our sins, and for [in] *the* ini-
quities of our fathers, Jerusalem and thy people *are become* [*are* for] a reproach to
17 all *that are* about us. Now, therefore [And now], *O* our God, hear [hearken to] *the*
prayer of thy servant, and [to] his supplications, and cause thy face to shine upon
18 thy sanctuary *that is* desolate, for *the* Lord's sake. *O* my God, incline thine ear,
and hear; open thine eyes, and behold [see] our desolations, and the city which
is called by the name [upon which thy name has been called]: for we do not
present[6] our supplications before thee for [upon] our righteousness, but [for *it*
19 *is*] for [upon] thy great mercies. O Lord, hear; O Lord, forgive; O Lord,
hearken, and do; defer not: for thine *own* sake, *O* my God; for thy city and
thy people are called by thy name [thy name has been called upon thy city and
upon thy people].
20 And while I *was* [And I *was* yet] speaking, and praying, and confessing my
sin and *the* sin of my people Israel, and presenting my supplication before *the*
Lord [Jehovah] my God for *the* holy mountain [upon *the* mountain of *the* sanctuary]
21 of my God; yea, while I *was* [and I was yet] speaking in prayer,[4] even [and, *i.e.*,
then] the man Gabriel, whom I had seen in the vision at [in] the beginning,
being caused to fly swiftly, touched [reached] me about *the* time of *the* evening
22 oblation. And he informed *me*, and talked [spoke] with me, and said, *O*
23 Daniel, I am [have] now come forth to give thee skill *and* understanding. At
[In] *the* beginning of thy supplications *the* commandment [word] came [went]

forth, and I am [have] come to show *thee;* for thou *art* greatly beloved,[8] therefore [and] understand [in] the matter [word], and consider [have understanding in] the vision [appearance].
24 Seventy weeks [sevens] are determined[9] upon thy people and upon thy holy
city [*the* city of thy sanctuary], to finish the transgression, and to make an end
of [seal up] sins, and to make reconciliation for [cover] iniquity, and to bring
in everlasting righteousness, and to seal *up the* vision and prophecy, and to an-
25 oint *the* Most Holy [holy of holies]. Know, therefore [And thou shalt know],
and understand [be wise], *that* from *the* going forth of *the* commandment [word]
to restore [return] and to build Jerusalem, unto *the* Messiah *the* Prince, *shall be*
seven weeks [sevens], and threescore and two weeks [sevens]: *the* street shall
be built again, and *the* wall [trench], even [and, *i.e.*, but] in troublous [trouble
26 of the] times. And after [the] threescore and two weeks [sevens] shall Mes-
siah be cut off, but not for himself [and *there shall* be nothing to him]: and *the*
people of *the* prince that *shall* come shall destroy the city and the sanctuary;
and *the* end thereof [*or*, his end] *shall be* with a [the] flood, and unto [till] *the*
27 end of *the* war desolations *are* determined [*there is* a decision of desolations].
And he shall confirm *the* covenant with [to] many *for* one week [seven]: and *in the* midst [half] of the week [seven] he shall cause *the* sacrifice and *the* oblation to cease, and for [upon] *the* overspreading [wing] of abominations *he shall* make *it* desolate [*there shall be* a desolator], even [and] until *the* consummation, and *that* determined [decided], shall *be* poured [it shall pour] upon *the* desolate.

GRAMMATICAL NOTES.

[[1] בַּקֵּשׁ, used absolutely here, may be taken in the sense of *worshipping*, which it often bears, or we may supply "*information*" from the context.—[2] The form is very intensive. וָאֶתְפַּלְלָה, denoting extreme earnestness.—[3] Not only is this verb, like the others, emphatic, but the pronoun added gives it a reflexive reference, like the Hithp. of the other verbs, *i.q.*, *for myself*.—[4] The art. prefixed = *thy*, *our*, *his*, *my*, *etc.*—[5] The indef. art. here injures the sense by really making the noun definite.—[6] Literally, *let fall*, *i.e.*, *rest* or *base*.—[7] Literally, *to make thee wise* as to.—[8] Literally, *delights*.—[9] The verb being in the singular indicates the unity or singleness of this entire period.]

EXEGETICAL REMARKS.

Verses 1–3. *The time of the penitential prayer which led to the vision, and the occasion which inspired it.* **In the first year of Darius, the son of Ahasuerus.** Concerning both Darius the Mede and his father Ahasuerus (Theodot., Sept., Vulg., "Assuerus") or Astyages, see the Introd. § 8, note 4. The point of time referred to in the text belongs to a period later than that of the vision in the preceding chapter by more than twenty years, or about B.C. 537;* cf. on chap. v. 30 and vi. 1.—**Of the seed of the Medes.** The nationality of the new ruler is noticed, because the subject of the prayer which follows, and also of the prophecy respecting the seventy weeks of years vouchsafed in consequence, was conditioned by the circumstance that at the time when this incident transpired in the experience of Daniel, he was a *Medo-Persian subject*, and hence, *had seen the second world-power of his former vision replace the first.* The overthrow of Babylon by the Median king would naturally lead him to meditate on the question concerning the time of the restoration of Jerusalem and the realization of the further theocratic hopes connected with that event. In the nature of the case, such meditations would connect themselves at once with Jeremiah's prophecy relating to the seventy years which were to elapse, before Jerusalem, the desolate, should be restored; and such a reference was unavoidable in the case of a *vir desideriorum* (see v. 23, Vulg.), like Daniel, who searched the Scriptures.—**Which was made king.** The passive הָמְלַךְ denotes that he did not become king over the Chaldæan realm in the ordinary way and by right of inheritance, but that he reached the throne in an extraordinary and violent manner, through the agency of the victorious Persian army (led by his nephew, Cyrus).—Verse 2. **I Daniel, understood** (or "observed") **in books the number of years,** *i.e.*, I gave attention to that question, meditated upon it. With regard to בִּינֹתִי, a shortened Hiphil-form like בִּין, chap. x. 1, or like רִיבוֹתָ, for הֲרִיבוֹתָ, Job. xxxiii. 13, cf. Ewald, *Lehrb.* § 127 *a*, 1*—The construction with an accusative is similar to chap. x. 1; Prov. vii. 7; xxiii. 1. Von Lengerke renders it incorrectly, "I sought understanding in the books, in the number," etc., as if הֵבִין were here construed with בְּ, as in v. 23, and this בְּ were then dropped before the more definite מִסְפַּר.†—The "books" (or "writings," ספרים)

* [This anachronism results merely from the author's attempt to identify Belshazzar with Evil-Merodach. On the theory which we have adopted this chapter follows in immediate chronological order.]

* [It is simpler to make it at once an irregular Kal-form, with Gesenius.]

† ["מִסְפַּר (*number*) forms the object to בִּינֹתִי (*I understood*); cf. Prov. vii. 7. Neither the placing of בַּסְּפָרִים (*by books*) first, nor the Athnach under this word, controverts this view; for the object is placed after 'by books' because a further definition is annexed to it; and the sepa-

in which Daniel observed the number seventy, and thus made it the subject of his meditations, were, according to the context, those which would engage the attention of a captive, be familiar and adapted to him. They did not probably include the whole collection of O.-T. writings, the Torah, Nebiim, and Kethubim (as v. Lengerke, Hitzig, Ewald, and other defenders of the Maccabæan origin of the book suppose), nor were they limited to the letter of Jeremiah (Jer. xxix., although the plural הַסְּפָרִים might, without difficulty, designate a single letter; cf. Jer. xxix. 25; 2 Kings xix. 14) which contained the prophecy concerning the seventy years, but they were simply a collection of prophetic writings which Daniel had at command. It cannot be decided how great the extent of this collection was. Perhaps it was confined merely to prophecies by Jeremiah—possibly including only those which are now contained in chapters xxv. and xxix. (to which Wieseler, *Die* 70 *Wochen*, etc., p. 4, limits the סְפָרִים, as being the particular rolls of writing in which these oracles of Jeremiah were recorded), or extending to a larger number, or even comprehending all that are now found in the book of Jeremiah. Perhaps it comprehended a larger circle of prophetic and other writings, similar to the private collection which Jeremiah already must have owned (cf. Hengstenberg, *Beiträge*, etc., p. 33 et seq.). It is likely of itself that the Pentateuch was included among the sacred books belonging to Daniel, although no positive evidence of that fact can be derived from vs. 11 and 13 of this chapter; for the mention of the תּוֹרָה in those passages does not prove that the prophet classed them among the סְפָרִים which are here referred to.*—To what passage in Jeremiah's prophecies, then, does Daniel allude? Chiefly and primarily, no doubt, to chap. xxv., from which the term חֳרָבוֹת, "ruins," is evidently borrowed (see Jer. xxv. 9, 11); but likewise to chap. xxix., the 10th verse of which clearly refers back to chap. xxv. 11 et seq., and with which our prophet was doubtless as well acquainted as with the former. —**Whereof the word of the Lord came to Jeremiah the prophet.** אֲשֶׁר, "whereof, in regard to which" (namely, *years*); cf. the use of אֲשֶׁר in the same sense in chap. viii. 26. יִרְמְיָה, as found also in Ezra i. 1, and in chapters xxvii.–xxix. in the book of Jeremiah itself, is the later form of the name.—**That he would accomplish seventy years in the desolation of Jerusalem;** or, "that seventy years should be full in the ruins," etc. חֳרָבוֹת, "ruins, desolate condition;" cf. Lev. xxvi. 31; Ezek. xxxvi. 10, 33; xxxviii. 12, etc. Our prophet, as appears in v. 25 *a*, regards the destruction of Jerusalem by Nebuchadnezzar, in the year B.C. 587, as the *terminus a quo* of the seventy years of desolation, while, on the other hand, Jeremiah uttered his prophecy relating to the seventy years (Jer. xxvi. cf. xxix. 1 et seq.) as early as the "fourth year of Jehoiakim," *i.e.*, B.C. 605, or 19 years before that date, and accordingly seemed to favor the method which reckoned the seventy years from the first conquest of Judæa by Nebuchadnezzar, and ended them with Cyrus (606–536).* When and how the end of the seventy years should be realized, was therefore a question which would engage his special attention when the Chaldæan monarchy was supplanted by the Medo-Persian.†
—Verse 3. **And I set my face unto the Lord God,** *i.e.*, probably, heavenward (cf. Gen. xxi. 17; 1 Kings viii. 22; John xvii. 3); for the turning of his face toward Jerusalem or the site of the temple (cf. vi. 11), would certainly not be disregarded in *this* instance, when about to pray for the restoration of the city and temple. The name אֲדֹנָי is used here to designate God (instead of יְהוָֹה, which is found in several MSS.), as in chap. i. 2; Ezra x. 3; Neh. i. 11; iv. 8, and as in several places in the prayer itself, v. 4 et seq.—**To seek by prayer and supplications;** rather, "to seek prayer," etc. Prayer is conceived of as an operation of the Divine Spirit (cf. Zech. xii. 10; Rom. viii. 26), which must be sought after or elicited from within, by means of fasting, putting on mourning garments, etc.; cf. 2 Sam. vii. 27; xii. 16; Ezra ix. 3; Ecclus. xxxiv. 21; Luke ii. 37, etc. Upon this subject see my *Geschichte der Askese*, p. 136 et seq. תְּפִלָּה is "prayer" generally considered (Psa. lxv. 3), while תַּחֲנוּנִים, like תְּחִנָּה, v. 20, is "prayer for mercy, importunate, moving prayer."

Verses 4–19. *Daniel's prayer.* In order to justly appreciate the impressive beauty of this prayer, and to understand its plan and aim, cf. Ewald, p. 430 et seq.: "The motives that led him to pray are scarcely indicated in the introductory statements, vs. 1–3, and must be discovered in the nature of the circumstances. He had long been deeply afflicted because the sufferings of his people were protracted during so long a period, and thus found and meditated on those passages from Jeremiah in the Bible (?); but the difficulty of understanding the Divine meaning of the number, redoubled his grief. He comprehended, however, that if the period of Israel's punishment at the hand of God was so protracted, and the mystery relating to himself and the whole nation was so hard to solve, it must be charged solely to the consequences of

---

ration of the object from the verb by the Athnach is justified by this consideration, that the passage contains two statements, viz., that Daniel studied the Scriptures, and that his study was directed to the number of the years, etc."—*Keil*.]

*[" הַסְּפָרִים, τὰ βιβλία, is not synonymous with הַכְּתוּבִים, αἱ γραφαί, but denotes only writings in the plural, yet does not say that these writings already formed a recognized collection, so that from this expression nothing can be concluded regarding the formation of the O.-T. canon."—*Keil*.]

* [The discrepancy here surmised by the author is entirely imaginary. Daniel reckons the captivity precisely as Jeremiah, namely from the fourth of Jehoiakim, B.C. 606, when he was himself taken away by Nebuchadnezzar (Dan. i. 1, the *invasion* having taken place the preceding year). The present vision occurred B. C.538, when the captivity was near its close. "Jerusalem did not lie in ruins for seventy years [the *temple*, however, certainly did]; the expression is not thus to be interpreted, but is chosen partly with regard to the existing state of Jerusalem, and partly with reference to the words of Jerusalem."—*Keil*.]

† [Keil combats at length the notion of Bleek and Ewald that it was Daniel's *uncertainty* regarding the termination of the seventy years which moved him to prayer.]

the former grossly wayward course of the people as a whole, and in this concurrence of the most incongruous emotions he sought and found the proper plea to present before God. He does not plead for ability merely to solve this numerical riddle—the entire prayer contains no allusion to this; and what, indeed, is a mere number in the sight of God? The mystery of the number is oppressive to the heart of this individual supplicant who prays for light, and likewise to the whole nation, only because of other and entirely different errors, darknesses, and faults; and not until this supplicant has put forth all the powers of his soul in wrestling with God for the removal of those general sins, can he hope that the next uncertainty which bows him down and troubles him shall be dispelled by a gracious ray from the original source of all light. Thus the moving stream of this deeply agitated prayer gushes forth from a profound sense that only when the most earnest desire for renewed purification, forgiveness, and elevation at the hand of God shall take possession of the people as a whole, can Divine help be expected for the desolations of Jerusalem, for which after all Daniel also pleads. His words, resulting from the oppressive darkness of the present and from a further retrospect of all former history relating to this state, thus become at first the expression of a true confession, and then of genuine confidence and supplication. They become a sincere confession in view of the present, vs. 4–10, but still more so, vs. 11–14, in consequence of a retrospect of all former history, which is the more proper in this connection, because the blame for this exceeding great destruction and disintegration dates back, in the first instance, to the older times; but in vs. 15–19 the trustful prayer and supplication for mercy become gradually more fervent (at first in the name of the whole people, v. 15 et seq., but ultimately in the name of the individual supplicant himself, v. 17 et seq.), until they cease, so to speak, in disconnected sighs, and as if exhausted with the last glow of the fire (v. 19)."—However appropriate we may find this analysis to be in general,* we are nevertheless obliged to enter a decided protest against the presumption of a Maccabæan composition of the prayer, which forms its background. The proof of this presumption is found by Ewald, Hitzig, v. Lengerke, etc., in the similarity between this prayer and the penitential prayer found in Ezra ix. 6 et seq.; Neh. i. 5–11 and ix. 6 et seq., Bar. i. 14–ii. 19, which unquestionably exists, and which they believe indicates the imitation of those passages by an alleged pseudo-Daniel, who lived at a much later time. The points of contact referred to, however, are in part merely indirect and accidental, such as sprang naturally from the general type of thought produced by the period of the captivity and the age immediately subsequent to it. Other features belonging to them in common are more specific and direct; but in these cases the prayer before us must be regarded as the original, instead of the others (as, *e.g.*, בֹּשֶׁת הַפָּנִים, vs. 7, 8, cf. Ezra ix. 7; סְלִיחוֹת, v. 9, cf. Neh. ix. 17; also the combination "our kings, princes, fathers, and all the people of the land," v. 6, which is exactly repeated in Neh. ix. 32, and again in ix. 34, where [as here in v. 8] "all the people of the land" is omitted, etc.). The more verbose and diffuse style of these prayers, and especially of those found in Nehemiah and Baruch, is of itself sufficient to arouse the suspicion at a glance, that Daniel's prayer, with its comprehensive brevity and freshness, must be the original (cf. particularly Zündel, *Kritische Unterss.*, etc., p. 191, whose exposition has not been controverted in a single feature by anything adduced by Ewald, p. 485). The fact, moreover, that it represents the sufferings of Israel as deserved, but does not allude with a syllable to the damnable character of the human agent who executed the Divine punishment, nor yet to the raging of Israel's oppressors, which still continued, and to the Divine judgment which was certainly impending over them—all this is surely not conformable to the idea that this section is a compilation made in imitation of older models and dating as late as the Maccabæan age. "It is certainly conceivable that an author writing in the midst of the sufferings of the Maccabæan period, might occasionally avail himself of the opportunity to remind the people that their affliction was partly deserved, because of their general sinful conduct toward the God of their fathers, and thus attempt to remove their bitterness of heart in view of the fact that God had permitted such misery to come upon them. But it does not seem natural that he should fail to strengthen the courage of his nation by a direct reference, to say nothing of a passing allusion, to the excessive wickedness of the course of the persecuting despot, the μιαρός, at a juncture when they took their stand upon the ground of that very law of their fathers for which they suffered. Still more unnatural is it that here, where practical encouragement was needed in a time of decisive and terrible conflicts, he should neglect this for the mere purpose of keeping up a conformity to the prayers of Ezra and Nehemiah, which originated in circumstances of *a totally different character* and involved a reference to the *earlier* fact of the conquest and destruction of Jerusalem" (Kranichfeld). Cf. in addition the remarks in the Introd. § 6, respecting the relation of the book of Daniel to the writings of the period subsequent to the captivity, which refer to it; and also the exposition of the several passages.

Verses 4–10. *The introduction. A penitential confession of sin in the name of the people.* **And I prayed . . . . made my confession, and said.** הִתְוַדָּה, "to confess, acknowledge," as in v. 20; Ezra x. 1.—**O Lord, the great and dreadful God, keeping the covenant and mercy.** The same address to the mighty and terrible God, but who is good and merciful when His conditions are met, occurs also in Neh. i. 5; with this difference only, that the article is carelessly omitted before חֶסֶד, the second object of שֹׁמֵר, in the latter passage, while in the present instance and in Neh. ix. 32 and Deut. vii. 9, it is retained.—Verse 5. **We have sinned, and have committed iniquity, and have done**

* Cf. the similar, but more simple analysis by Melancthon which is adduced below, in connection with the homiletical suggestions. It divides the whole prayer into the two parts (1) of the *confessio* (vs. 4–14) and (2) of the *consolatio* (vs. 15–19).

wickedly, and have rebelled. Properly, "and sinned and rebelled," for the ו in וְהִרְשַׁעְנוּ is probably to be retained; its omission from several MSS. is explained from the desire to assimilate this passage to the parallels vs. 15 and 1 Kings viii. 47. The Hiphil הִרְשִׁיעַ, "to sin, do wickedly," is used instead of the more usual Kal רָשַׁע; cf. xi. 32; Neh. ix. 33; Psa. cvi. 6.—**By departing from thy precepts and from thy judgments.** The infinitive סוֹר is used as a continuation of the *v. finit.*, as in v. 11; cf. Neh. ix. 8, 13; Esth. iii. 13; ix. 1, 12, 16; vi. 9, etc.—Verse 6. **The prophets, which spake in thy name to our kings, our princes, and our fathers,** etc. The "fathers" in this place and in v. 8, as well as in Jer. xliv. 17, 21, denote the ancestors of the Israel of that day, including all but those who were of royal and princely blood; cf. the comprehensive "and to all the people of the land," which immediately follows. The same language occurs in Neh. ix. 32, where, however, the "prophets and priests" are also specially included, between the princes and the fathers—an extension which clearly reveals the thought of a later age, and which appears the more superfluous, inasmuch as both prophets and priests might unquestionably be comprehended in the term "fathers" (cf. Judg. xvii. 10; xviii. 19).—Verse 7. **O Lord, righteousness belongeth unto thee, but unto us confusion of faces,** *i.e.*, the confusion which depicts itself on the face (by blushing) because of our sin and the consequent disgrace and tribulation; cf. the familiar use of בּוֹשׁ, and the passage Ezra ix. 7, which paraphrases the thought here presented.—**As at this day** (so from time immemorial). In כַּיּוֹם הַזֶּה, כְּ does not indicate the indefinite temporal sense of "about, at" (as v. Lengerke, Hävernick, etc., think), but that of comparison, as always in this form of speech; cf. v. 15; Neh. ix. 10; Jer. xxv. 18, etc. Consequently the expression of God's righteousness and the contrasted being put to shame or disgrace of Israel are both described as having always been apparent and as being still evident.—**To the men of Judah, and to the inhabitants of Jerusalem.** Vs. 16–18, which represent Jerusalem as being in ruins, show clearly that this reference is not to inhabitants of Jerusalem who were contemporary with the prophet (Bertholdt, v. Lengerke, Stähelin, etc.).—Verse 8. **O Lord, to us belongeth confusion of face,** etc. cf. Jer. iii. 25; xiv. 20; Neh. ix. 34, etc.—Verse 9. **Though** (rather "for") **we have rebelled against him.** מָרַדְנוּ, as in v. 5. The clause with כִּי serves to explain why the mercy and forgiveness of God (סְלִיחוֹת; cf. Neh. ix. 17, and סְלִיחָה, Psa. cxxx. 4) are referred to, namely, because the children of Israel need mercy, etc., before all else, since they are guilty of rebellion against God. The thought is still farther developed in the following verse.—Verse 10. **Neither** (rather "and we") **have we obeyed the voice of the Lord our God, to walk in his laws;** cf. Jer. xliv. 23; 1 Kings viii. 61; Luke i. 6 etc. The תּוֹרֹת here mentioned differ from the תּוֹרָה of the next verse merely in the form of the word, the latter comprehending the commandments, *i.e.*, the several manifestations of God's will in a united whole. The prophets accordingly appear as the *guardians*, teachers, and enforcers of the law; cf. Isa. xxi. 11, where the term שֹׁמְרִים is applied to them; Jer. vi. 17; Ezek. xxxiii. 2; Mic. vii. 4, etc., which designate them by צֹפִים.

Verses 11–14. *Continuation.** *Reference to the past history of the nation.* **Therefore the curse is poured upon us, and the oath.** As in other places the anger of God (Jer. xlii. 18; xliv. 6; 2 Chron. xii. 7; xxxiv. 21, etc.), so here the curse which represents it, is characterized as, so to speak, a fiery hail (Gen. xix. 24; Ex. ix. 33; Nah. i. 6) which is poured out on the sinner. It is, moreover, not a simple curse, but stands connected with an oath, which supports and strengthens it; cf. Num. v. 21; Neh. x. 30; Psa. xcv. 11; Heb. iii. 11, 18; vi. 17.—**That is written in the law of Moses the servant of God.** Lev. xxvi. 14 et seq.; Deut. xxviii. 15 et seq.; xxix. 19. Concerning the designation as the servant of God, cf. Ex. iv. 10; xiv. 31; Num. xi. 11; xii. 7; Josh. i. 2; Heb. iii. 5. See also v. 5, where the same predicate is applied to the prophets.—Verse 12. **And he hath confirmed his words, which he spake.** הֵקִים, usually "to raise up," here signifies "to preserve intact, to maintain, to confirm in act;" cf. Num. xxx. 14, 15.—Instead of דְּבָרָיו the Keri has דְּבָרוֹ, referring back to the curse, v. 11; but all the ancient versions and also the parallels Neh. ix. 8; Bar. ii. 3 support the plural.—**Against us, and against our judges;** literally "*over* us," etc. שֹׁפְטֵינוּ, a comprehensive term denoting "our superiors" generally; cf. Psa. ii. 10; cxlviii. 11, and above, vs. 6 and 8, the separation of this idea into "kings and princes."—**By bringing upon us a great evil,** etc.; rather, "that he would bring upon us," etc.; cf. Lam. i. 12; ii. 17; Ezek. v. 9, etc.—Verse 13. **As it is written in the law of Moses, all this evil is come upon us;** rather, "as all this evil is written in the law of Moses, that is come," etc.† אֵת before כָּל־הָרָעָה serves to introduce the subject, as in 2 Kings x. 6; Jer. xlv. 4; Ezek. xliv. 3.‡ Concerning כַּאֲשֶׁר cf. Isa. xiv. 24 *b*.—**Yet made we not our prayer before the Lord our God;** rather, "yet conciliated we not the face of the Lord," etc.,—who prepares for our just punishment. It appears from the following verse that this neglect of propitiating his anger, hence an obstinate and hardened persistence in sin, was the immediate cause that brought misfortune to the nation. With regard to חִלָּה פְּנֵי, פ' which literally signifies "to stroke one's face, to smooth its stern furrows," cf. Ex. xxxii. 11; 1 Sam. xiii. 12; 1 Kings xiii. 6, etc.—**That we might** (or "should") **turn from our iniquities, and understand** (or "observe") **thy truth.**

* ["The confession of sin divides itself into two sections. Vers. 4–10 state the transgression and the guilt, while vers. 11–14 refer to the punishment from God for this guilt. Ver. 3 forms the introduction."—*Keil.*]

† [Against this construction, however, is the difference in gender of כָּתוּב and רָעָה.]

‡ [The subject, however, is here rather "stated *absolutely* as concerns all this evil, thus it has come upon us."—*Keil.*]

The truth of God which was not observed by the people is His immutability, by virtue of which He actually permits the punishment threatened against the sinner to be inflicted—hence His faithful adherence to His pledges from a negative point of view, which is identical with His punitive justice (cf. 1 John i. 9). Hitzig's adoption of a hendiadys, "that observing thy faithfulness, we should turn from our sins," is unnecessary.—Verse 14. **Therefore hath the Lord watched upon the evil,** *i.e.*, "He cared for it, was concerned about it;" cf. Jer. i. 12; xliv. 27.—**For the Lord our God is righteous in all his works which he doeth;** literally, "*on the ground* of all his works" (עַל־כָּל־מַעֲשָׂיו); cf. Neh. ix. 33. אֲשֶׁר עָשָׂה, "which he doeth," is aorist, like Jon. i. 14 (not pret., "which he has done").—**For** (rather "and") **we obeyed not his voice,** *i.e.*, despite that we obeyed not; cf. the similar expression, with וְלֹא וְגוֹ׳, in v. 13.

Verses 15–19. *Conclusion. The petition itself in its intensity and importunity, which increase from sentence to sentence.* **That hast brought thy people forth out of the land of Egypt with a mighty hand;** a glorious and striking proof of the grace and mercy which God formerly manifested towards his people; cf. Ex. xx. 2, etc.; Psa. cv.; cxiv. etc.—**And hast gotten thee renown, as at this day,** *i.e.*, by that wonderful act of deliverance hast acquired renown that continues to this day; cf. Jer. xxxii. 20; Neh. i. 10; ix. 10.—Verse 16. **O Lord, according to all thy righteousness . . . . let thine anger . . . be turned away,** *i.e.*, according to the displays of thy righteousness. צְדָקוֹת, whether it is to be regarded as the plural of צְדָקָה, as a majority hold, or as the plural of a singular צֶדֶק, which is Hitzig's view (cf. Isa. xli. 10; xlii. 6, 21), certainly denotes "proofs of *righteousness*," and not of mercy; but it is decidedly erroneous, and involves a gross weakening of the sense of the Scriptures, to assign the meaning "mercy" to the Old-Test term "righteousness," in a single instance.*—**From thy city Jerusalem, thy holy mountain.** The opposition is the more appropriate, as in Daniel's time nothing remained of Jerusalem but its site, its mountain.—**Jerusalem . . . .** (are become) **a reproach to all that are about us;** cf. Psa. lxxix. 4.—Verse 17. **Now therefore, O our God, hear.** וְעַתָּה is a conclusion from v. 16 *b*; and does not serve to resume v. 15.—**The prayer of thy servant, and his supplications.** Daniel applies the designation עַבְדְּךָ to himself in full consciousness of the mediatorial position occupied by him, as by Moses and the earlier prophets (cf. vs. 11, 5).—**Cause thy face to shine upon thy sanctuary that is desolate.** The ruined temple here takes the place of the city and the mountain which were mentioned before, indicating that the prayer constantly increases in fervor and importunity, and addresses God with motives whose effective character steadily grows stronger.—**For the Lord's sake,** *i.e.*, for thine own sake, for thy name's sake (v. 19). The noun is repeated, to the neglect of the pronoun, for the sake of emphasis, as in Gen. xix. 24, and as often in the usage of the New Test., *e.g.*, Rom. xv. 5, 6; Eph. ii. 21, etc.—Verse 18. **O my God, incline thine ear, and hear; open thine eyes,** etc. The Kethib פְּקָחָה is to be retained, in opposition to the Niphalizing Keri פְּקַח; cf. v. 19; Psa. xli. 5; Isa. vii. 11; xxxii. 11.—The thought of the phrase "incline thine ear" (cf. Psa. lxxxviii. 3; lxxxvi. 1; cii. 3; cxvi. 2, etc.), is also frequently expressed in the plural, "thine ears," *e.g.*, Psa. cxxx. 2; cf. Isa. lix. 1; Ezek. viii. 18; Psa. xxxiv. 16; 1 Pet. iii. 12; Jas. v. 4. Luther's translation generally disregards this distinction, and in almost every instance employs the plural, even where the original has the singular.—**And behold our desolations** (שֹׁמְמוֹת, as in v. 26, instead of the former חֳרָבוֹת, v. 2; cf. Isa. lxi. 4) **and the city which is called by thy name,** literally, "upon which thy name is called;" cf. Jer. vii. 10; xxv. 29; xxxiv. 15; Psa. xlviii. 3, 9, etc.—**For we do not present** (lit. "lay down") **our supplications before thee for our righteousness.** On the expression הִפִּיל תְּחִ׳, "to lay down or pour out supplications at one's feet," cf. v. 20; Jer. xxxviii. 26. ["The expression is derived from the custom of falling down before God in prayer."—*Keil.*] On the thought cf. Isa. lvii. 12; lviii. 2; Neh. ix. 19, 27, 31, etc.—Verse 19. **O Lord, hear; O Lord, forgive; O Lord, hearken,** etc. The two-fold repetition of the name Adonai, "Lord," denotes the highly importunate and almost uncontrollable character which the prayer assumes at the close; cf. Isa. vi. 3; Jer. vii. 4; xxii. 29.—**And do it, defer not.** It cannot be proved that Daniel intended to refer to the long delay attendant on the fulfilment of Jeremiah's prophecy of the seventy weeks by the expression "defer not" (cf. Psa. xl. 18; lxx. 6), as Ewald thinks. The expression is not sufficiently definite for this; and at any rate, nothing in favor of the Maccabæan origin of this passage can be deduced from it.—**For thine own sake, O my God; for thy city and thy people are called by thy name.** The explanatory clause "for . . . are called by thy name," implies that לְמַעַנְךָ is equivalent to לְמַעַן שְׁמֶךָ (Isa. xlviii. 9; Psa. xxiii. 3; xxv. 11), and therefore signifies, "for the sake of thy honor, of thy renown" (cf. on v. 18).

Verses 20–23. *Arrival of the angel Gabriel, who was sent from God to interpret Jeremiah's prophecy of the seventy weeks.* **And while I was speaking, and praying,** etc. This does not mean, "before I ceased praying"—for the prayer had evidently reached its conclusion with v. 19—but rather, "I was concluding my remarks, I was just speaking the last words," etc. Cf. Isa. xxviii. 4.—**My supplication . . . for the holy mountain of my God;** properly, "on the basis (or ground) of the holy mountain." The preposition עַל, by virtue of its fundamental meaning "over," may signify "against" (v. 12)

* ["צְדָקוֹת means the great deeds done by the Lord for his people, among which the signs and wonders accompanying their exodus from Egypt take the first place, so far as therein Jehovah gave proof of the righteousness of his covenant promise."—*Keil.*]

as well as "for." According to vs. 16 and 17 the "holy mountain" includes the "holy city" (Matt. iv. 5) and the temple.—Verse 21. **Yea** (lit., "and"), **while I was** (yet) **speaking in prayer;** rhetorical *epanalepsis* or brief repetition, designed to favor the connection.—**Even** (or "and") **the man Gabriel, whom I had seen in the vision at the beginning** (or "formerly"), a reference to chap. viii. 15 et seq., where the designation of the angel as a "man" was explained as being derived from his human form. Concerning בַּתְּחִלָּה see on chap. viii. 1.—**Being caused to fly swiftly;** rather, "come to me with flying speed." The expression מֻעָף בִּיעָף is difficult. The rendering, "wearied with an extended (or rapid) course," which is adopted by Ibn Ezra, Gesenius, etc. (substantially also by Kranichfeld, "very weary") appears to be supported by the circumstance that the same root יעף, which always signifies "to weary, become exhausted," lies at the bottom of both words. The sense of "being wearied," however, will not apply to angels generally, nor is it appropriate in the present instance, where the עַתָּה יָצָאתִי of the following verse clearly alludes to the rapidity of the angel's coming. This rapid approach does not indicate that he *ran* swiftly (Hävernick, v. Lengerke, etc.), but denotes hasty *flying*, with lightning speed, as may be seen (1) from the root יעף, which is unquestionably related to עוּף, "to fly," and therefore may involve that idea; (2) from the testimony of the ancient versions, which unanimously express the idea of flying rapidly (Sept. *τάχει φερόμενος*; Theodotion, *πετόμενος*; Vulg., *cito volans*, and also Syrus); (3) from the fact that the Scriptures frequently represent the angels as flying—a trait which is not confined to the New Test. (Rev. xiv. 6), but is found in the Old Test. also, as Isa. vi. 2 et seq.; Judg. xiii. 20; Psa. civ. 4, etc., demonstrate, despite the assertion to the contrary of Hitzig, Hävernick, and others (cf. also Matt. xxviii. 3 etc.).*—**About the time of the evening oblation,** or about sundown (Num. xxviii. 4). This theocratic and Levitical designation of time finds a simple explanation in the prophet's yearning recollection of the sacrifice that was offered at that hour in the temple-worship, and therefore does not in any way militate against the belief that this chapter originated during the captivity. It is no more remarkable, as uttered by the captive Daniel in the reign of Darius Medus, than it would be if a Christian youth of the Middle Ages who had fallen into the power of the Saracens, should, after being separated from scenes of Christian worship for many years, still have spoken of matins, or vespers, or the *completorium*. Cf. supra, on chap. vi. 11.—Verse 22. **And he informed me,** or "gave me to understand." Thus it is rendered, correctly, by most expositors; cf. הָבִין in chap. viii. 16. Hitzig's version, "and he became aware"—namely that the time of evening sacrifice was not yet past, and therefore that Daniel had just finished his evening prayer—is entirely too forced.—**I am now come forth,** namely from God, before whom Gabriel usually stands (Luke i. 19; cf. also Job i. 12). That he should *now* come forth (עַתָּה, like John xiv. 11) denotes that Daniel's importunate prayer had caused his being sent; cf. the next verse.—Verse 23. **At the beginning of thy supplications the commandment** (rather, "a word") **came forth,** *i.e.*, a *decree* (דָּבָר, as in Job iv. 12; Isa. ix. 7, etc.) intended to comfort and encourage thee (and consequently to answer thy prayer). It was not "*a commandment*," for this could only have been laid on the angel, and not on Daniel, who is nevertheless exhorted "to attend to the word" (בַּדָּבָר). Hitzig renders it correctly, "a decree, an oracle, which is recorded verbally in vs. 24-27."—**For thou art greatly beloved.** חֲמוּדוֹת, synonymous with אִישׁ־חֲמוּדוֹת, "man of costlinesses, of joys," *i.e.*, well-beloved, a favorite (Luther, "beloved man, beloved and precious;" Ewald, "a loved sweet one."). The "*vir desideriorum*" of Jerome is misleading; for חֲמוּדוֹת certainly does not relate to the prophet's anxiety to understand the mysteries of God ("*quod pro desiderio tuo Dei secreta audire mereuris, et esse conscius futurorum*"). With far greater correctness Jerome himself compares, in remarks immediately preceding, the predicate יְדִידְיָה, "the favorite of God," which was applied to Solomon (2 Sam. xii. 25); and several moderns have also adduced the cognomen of Titus, "*amor et deliciæ generis humani*," with equal justice.*—**Therefore understand thou** (or "observe") **the matter** ("word"), **and consider the vision.** "The transition from בין to הבין denotes a slight variation of meaning in the fundamental idea. The difference is not greater than exists between דָּבָר itself and מַרְאֶה, the latter of which = חָזוֹן, 'revelation,' the substance or soul of the spoken word" (Hitzig).†

* [Keil holds that these terms, מֻעָף בִּיעָף, "belong from their position to the relative clause, or specially to רָאִיתִי (*I had seen*), not to נֹגֵעַ, since no ground can be perceived for placing the adverbial idea before the verb." This is also countenanced by the Masoretic interpunction. Keil accordingly refers the phrase to Daniel himself, as being utterly exhausted; and compares ch. viii. 17 et seq., 27, "because Gabriel, at his former coming to him, not only helped to strengthen him, but also gave him understanding," etc. The epithet, however, as applied to Daniel, seems very inept and vague here, especially following the definite phrase "at first." Stuart maintains that יָעַף essentially means *to hasten*, and that it bears this signification here; but the usage of the word does not sustain this sense. Under these circumstances we can probably do no better than, with our author, to abide by the interpretation of the old translators, and regard both terms either as directly from עוּף or from יָעַף a cognate of that root.]

* ["The sentence, 'for thou art a man greatly beloved,' does not contain the reason for Gabriel's coming in haste, but for the principal thought of the verse, the going forth of the word of God immediately at the beginning of Daniel's prayer."—*Keil*].

† ["הַמַּרְאֶה stands not for revelation, but is the *vision*, the *appearance* of the angel by whom the word of God was communicated to the prophet. מַרְאֶה is accordingly not the contents of the word spoken, but the form of its communication to Daniel. To both—the word and the form of its revelation—Daniel must give heed. This revelation was, moreover, not communicated to him in a vision, but while in his natural consciousness."—*Keil.*]

Verses 24–27. *The interpretation of the seventy weeks of years.* **Seventy weeks are determined.** Literally, are "cut off;" for this is the proper meaning of נֶחְתַּךְ, in like manner as חָרַץ primarily signifies "to cut, to sharpen to a point," and then "to conclude, determine;" cf. Job xiv. 5; Isa. x. 22; 1 Kings xx. 40. The Vulgate, influenced by ἐκολοβώθησαν, Matt. xxiv. 22, has "*abbreviatæ sunt*," which conflicts with the context. Hitzig, on the contrary, is correct when he rejects the idea of "dividing" into two sections, which might seem to accord with v. 25 et seq., and instead applies the cutting off to the "sum of the time" as a whole, in consequence of which he paraphrases, "a *section of time* (consisting) of seventy years is *appointed*." –The construction is the familiar one of the impersonal passive with an accusative (cf. Gen. xxxv. 26; Ex. xiii. 7; Isa. xxi. 2; also supra, on v. 13). Entirely too artificial is the view which Wieseler adopts, that דָּבָר in v. 23 is the subject, while the seventy weeks form the predicate—"the word is cut off at seventy weeks." This view is opposed further, by the fact that נחתך cannot in this place denote the idea of "being abbreviated."—שָׁבֻעִים שִׁבְעִים, "seventy weeks." This cannot possibly denote seventy weeks in the ordinary sense, or 490 days; for the number has an obvious relation to the seventy years of Jeremiah, v. 2, and the brief limit of 490 days is not suited to serve as a mystical paraphrase of the period of three and a half years. Moreover, according to the descriptions in chapters vii. and viii., the three and a half years were throughout a period of suffering and oppression, while in v. 25 et seq. the latter and more extended subdivision (amounting to sixty-two weeks) of the seventy weeks is characterized as being comparatively free from sufferings. Finally, the three and a half years evidently reappear in v. 27, in the form of the "half-week" during which the sacrifices and oblations were to cease, etc.: and this undeniable identity of the small fraction at the end of the seventy weeks with the three and a half years of tribulation, heretofore described, removes it beyond the reach of doubt that the seventy weeks are to be regarded as *seventy weeks of years*, and therefore as an *amplification* of the seventy years of Jeremiah. Such a prophetic or mystical transformation of the seventy years into as many periods of seven years each is not unparalleled in the usage of the ancients; cf., *e.g.*, the remarks of Mark Varro, in Aul. Gellius, *N. A.* III., 10: "*Se jam undecimam annorum hebdomadem ingressum esse et ad eum diem septuaginta hedomadas librorum conscripsisse;*" also Aristotle, *Polit.*, VII. 16; Censorin., *de die natali*, C. 14. It was, however, peculiarly adapted to the prophet's purpose, and was especially intelligible to his readers, inasmuch as the Mosaic law (Lev. xxv. 2, 4 et seq.; xxvi. 34, 35, 43; cf. 2 Chron. xxxvi. 21) had designated every seventh year as a sabbath of the land, and had introduced the custom of dividing the years into hebdomads, which thus became familiar to every individual in the Jewish nation during all subsequent ages. The thought that instead of seventy years seven times seventy were to elapse before the theocracy should be restored in all its power and significance, and that, consequently, an extended period of delay should precede the advent of the Messianic æra, is "an integral feature in the mode of conception which prevails throughout the book" (Kranichfeld). It should also be observed that the idea *weeks*, as the principal idea, is placed before the numerical idea for emphasis: "*weeks* (of years, not simple years), seventy in number, are determined," etc. The masculine form of the noun occurs also in chap. x. 2, 3; cf. Gen. xxix. 27 et seq.; Lev. xii. 5.*—**Upon thy people and upon thy holy city.** "Thy" is used in the sense of "near thy heart, dear and precious unto thee;" cf. v. 20; chap. xii. 1. As the people of Jehovah (v. 19) is also Daniel's people (v. 20), so is Jerusalem *his* city, his favorite city. It may have been, in addition, his native place; but this circumstance cannot be determined from this passage; see the Introd. § 2, at the beginning. The predicate "holy" was deserved by Jerusalem, even when in ruins, and without regard to the length of the period during which it was desolate, since by virtue of all its history in the past, and in view of its importance for God's kingdom in the future, it was absolutely "the holy city," cf. vs. 16–20; Isa. lii. 1; Matt. iv. 5.—**To finish the transgression and to make an end of sins.** The infinitives with לְ which follow, to the end of the verse, "direct attention, with a view to comfort, to the blessed experiences connected with the close of the period in which the people and the city were then languishing," thus denoting from the outset that the vision is concerned with the realization of the *Messianic* hopes of Israel, in the time when "Zion's warfare" shall be accomplished (Isa. xl. 2 et seq.)—in short, that the prophetic remarks of the angel acquire a Messianic character from this point.—Theodot., Hengstenb., v. Leng., Wiesel., Kranichf., etc., punctuate the Kethib לְכַלֵּא הַפֶּשַׁע, and read "*to seal up* the transgression," which, according to v. Lengerke, signifies "*to forgive* the transgression," and according to Kranichfeld, means "to *hinder* or *restrain* the sin." The former rendering, however, would lead to an unsuitable tautology with לְכַפֵּר עָוֹן; and the idea of "*restraining* (*cohibere*) sin" would be more properly expressed by צרר; cf. Job xiv. 17; Hos. xiii. 2. The idea of "restraining," moreover, has not been presented by a single one of the more ancient translators, not even by Theodotion. It is better, therefore, to read לְכַלֵּא with a majority of moderns, and to regard this as standing for לְכַלֵּה, expressive of the idea of completing or filling up. This view is also supported by the parallel וּלְהָתֵם, as it should be read, with the Keri and all the ancient versions, excepting that of Theodotion; cf. chap. viii. 23; Isa. xvi. 4; xxxiii. 1, etc.

* [Keil maintains that neither the gender nor position of שָׁבֻעִים is here significant; but it is certain that the masc. plur. nowhere else occurs, except at chap. x. 2, 3, where it is defined by the addition of יָמִים, *days*. Even Stuart, who does not apply this prophecy to the Messianic age, candidly admits that *heptades* of years can only be designated by this expression.]

The "making full of sin," *i.e.*, of the measure of sin, is substantially identical with the finishing of the transgression, from which it differs only in expressing the idea more forcibly. The Kethib וְלַחְתֹּם (similarly Theodotion also: τοῦ σφραγίσαι ἁμαρτίας) is decisively rejected by the single fact that וְלַחְתֹּם, "and to seal up," is repeated in this passage, and in a sense that differs materially from what it would bear in the former half of the verse. It is certainly possible to refer (with Kranichfeld) to chap. vi. 18; xii. 4; Deut. xxxii. 34; Job ix. 7; xxxvii. 7, in support of this rendering, which would perhaps add to לְכַלֵּא, "to seal up, to hinder," the idea of a still more effective sealing up or of a more complete banishment. The sense of "filling up," however, which is secured by chap. viii. 23, and by which the language of the whole verse gains a harmonious variety and multiformity, is far more likely to prove correct; and, in addition, the substitution of ולחתם for ולהתם in the preceding line would, in and of itself, be an exceedingly probable error on the part of a copyist, which might be easily comprehended.—**To make reconciliation** (rather "expiation") **for iniquity, and to bring in everlasting righteousness.** These closely united members stand related to each other as antecedent and conclusion, or as a negative and a positive statement of the same fact. They form the central point of the acts of gracious blessing wrought by God, and both are introduced alike by the two infinitive clauses which precede, and appear to be conjoined and brought to a common conclusion by those which follow. According to this, three pairs of actions, or three double numbers, were designed in this verse, as Gesenius, Maurer, and Hitzig correctly observe; and for this reason the disjunctive accent ֑ seems less suitable after עָוֺן than it would have been after חַטָּאוֹת. The intimate collocation of כַּפֵּר עָוֺן with הָבִיא צֶדֶק ע׳ is warranted, further, by the fact that, without doubt, God is regarded as the efficient cause of both these results, and particularly of the "expiation" (literally "covering over") of sin; cf. Psa. xxxii. 2; lxv. 4, etc.—Righteousness, which is a characteristic of the Messianic period in other prophecies also (cf. Isa. liii. 11; Jer. xxxiii. 15 et seq.; Mal. iii. 20), is here described as "everlasting," in harmony with the eternal character of Messiah's kingdom (cf. chap. ii. 44; vii. 18. 27; Isa. li. 5-8). It is of course not to be limited to the sphere of a merely *external* (Levitical and theocratic) righteousness, as even Hitzig acknowledges, when he observes that external righteousness cannot be regarded as separate from internal in any case.—**And to seal up vision and prophet** (marg.), **and to anoint the most holy** (rather, "*a* holy of holies"). The relation between these final members of the whole series of Messianic results to be secured is that of the internal to the external, of the ethical to the ritual, or of religion to worship. Kranichfeld's remark is incorrect, when he observes that the third pair in the gracious series occupies an inverse relation to the first, in view of its form, inasmuch as the latter proceeds from the antecedent to the consequent, while that method is here reversed (namely, the sealing of prophecy precedes the anointing of the most Holy).* But Hitzig, Bleek, etc., are no less at fault, when they assume that the anointing of the most Holy is mentioned after the sealing of prophecy, and at the end of the entire series, because it *had not been foretold* by Jeremiah, while the other features had, directly or indirectly, formed the subject of the Messianic promises with that prophet. The opinion that the "sealing of vision and prophet" denotes specifically the confirmation of Jeremiah's prophecy respecting the seventy years (as v. Lengerke, Wieseler, Kamphausen, etc., also hold) in chap. xxv. and xxix. is wholly untenable, since the terms חָזוֹן and נָבִיא, without the article, evidently do not refer to any particular prophet or prophecy, but rather to the prophetic institution and its visions relating to the prospective salvation in general. The idea is, that everything in the form of prophetic visions and predictions which had been produced in the course of theocratic development from the time of Moses (נָבִיא and חָזוֹן are collective and general; cf. chap. xi. 14) should receive "sealing," *i.e.*, Divine confirmation and recognition, in the form of actual fulfilment (cf. 1 Kings xxi. 8; Esth. viii. 8).† Jeremiah's prophecy cannot be intended, either exclusively, or even by way of pre-eminence (as Ewald thinks), because it does not mention the expiation of sin and the establishing of everlasting Messianic righteousness, which nevertheless are here particularly emphasized. The sense is clearly general, similar to that found in New-Test. passages like Acts iii. 19; x. 43; 2 Cor. i. 20, etc.—The prospect of an "anointing of the most Holy," which is presented at the close, or

* ["The six statements (represented by the infinitives with לְ) are divided by Maurer, Hitzig, Kranichfeld, and others, into three passages of two members each, thus: After the expiration of seventy weeks there shall (1) be completed the measure of sin; (2) the sin shall be covered and righteousness brought in; (3) the prophecy shall be fulfilled, and the temple, which was desecrated by Antiochus, shall again be consecrated. The Masoretes, however, seem to have already conceived of this threefold division by placing the Athnach under צֶדֶק עֹלָמִים (the fourth clause); but it rests on a false construction of the individual members, especially of the first two passages. Rather we have two three-membered sentences before us. This appears evident from the arrangement of the six statements, *i.e.*, that the first three statements treat of the taking away of sin, and thus of the bringing in of everlasting righteousness, with its consequences, and thus of the positive deliverance, and in such a manner that in both classes the three members stand in reciprocal relation to each other; the fourth statement corresponds to the first, the fifth to the second, the sixth to the third—the second and the fifth present even the same verb חתם."—*Keil.* It is not necessary, however, to assume that these results were all to await the expiration of this entire period; they were only to be in the process of taking place during or after it; in a word, this was to be the final period of the Jewish economy, in or at the end of which all these consummations were to take place.]

† ["But for this figurative use of the word 'to seal' no proof-passages are adducted from the O. T. Add to this that the word cannot be used here in a different sense from that in which it is used in the second passage. The sealing of the prophecy corresponds to the sealing of the transgression, and must be similarly understood. The prophecy is sealed when it is laid under a seal, so that it can no longer actively show itself" (*Keil*); and correspondingly transgression is sealed, when its further demonstration is prevented In short, both are to be suppressed after that date; transgression by the Atoning Sacrifice, and prophecy by the close of the O.-T. canon.]

rather of *a* most Holy (קֹדֶשׁ ק׳, without the article) is evidently a solemn act of worship, which is substantially equivalent to the restoration of the theocratic worship as a whole. It is the anointing with oil or theocratic consecration of the *sacrificial altar* of the New Covenant, of the Messianic community of the redeemed, the pure sanctuary, which shall no more be profaned, that, according to chap. viii. 14 (cf. vii. 25; ix. 17), shall take the place of the desecrated and defiled altar of the Old Dispensation. From Lev. viii. 11, comp. with Ezek. xliii. 20, 26, where a consecration of the altar of burnt-offerings by means of an act of anointing is described (in Lev., l. c., with oil, in Ezek., l. c., with the blood of the sacrifice), and also from Ex. xxix. 37; xxx. 29; xl. 10, where the sacrificial altar is expressly designated as the קֹדֶשׁ קָדָשִׁים, it is evident that the altar of sacrifice is here intended, instead of the holy of holies in the temple at large, or even the Messiah himself (*sanctus sanctorum*), as Syrus, the Vulgate, and others suppose.—The prophecy under consideration has been twice fulfilled,—at first externally and in a literal sense, by the actual restoration of the Old-Test. services in the temple, with their bloody offerings of animals, which came to pass three years after they had been interrupted by Antiochus Epiphanes in the Maccabæan age (1 Macc. iv. 54–59),* and afterward in the antitype by the historical introduction of the more perfect sanctuary and worship of the New Covenant, which were likewise foretold by the prophet Zechariah (chap. iii. 9) and whose sacrificial altar is Christ, having become such through the *cross* which he anointed and consecrated by his own exalted priestly sacrifice and blood.†

Verse 25. **Know therefore and understand.** This exhortation is intended to introduce the more detailed explanation of the relation of the seventy year-weeks to the yet unexpired seventy years, and also to the subject of the earlier theocratic promises which follows. It directs the notice of both the hearer and the reader to the importance of the disclosures now to be made, and to the duty of subjecting them to serious and thoughtful consideration; cf. ὁ ἀναγινώσκων νοείτω, Matt. xxiv. 15.—**From the going forth of the commandment** (or "word") **to restore and to build Jerusalem, unto the Messiah the Prince shall be seven weeks**; rather, "unto *an* anointed one, *a* prince," etc. The expression מִצָּא דָבָר corresponds to יָצָא דָבָר at the beginning of the angel's remarks, and therefore probably denotes the promulgation of a Divine decree rather than of a royal edict (as Dereser, Hävernick, Weigl, etc., conceive with reference to the edict of Artaxerxes Longimanus, which commanded that the rebuilding of Jerusalem should be commenced). The latter idea would require that מֶלֶךְ should be connected with דבר, in order to its clear expression; and the observation of Hitzig is probably correct: "Gabriel could not speak so objectively, and with composure, of the decree of a heathen king that would imply his right to dispose of the holy city; such a decree would no more be a דָּבָר in the mind of a theocrat than the confederacy in Isa. viii. 12 would be a קֶשֶׁר."—Moreover, דבר cannot denote a decree at all, but rather a prophetic statement, an oracle, which in this instance promises the restoration of Jerusalem. This Divine prediction concerning the rebuilding of the holy city cannot differ materially from the repeated prophecy by Jeremiah (chap. xxv. and xxix.), which foretold the desolation of Jerusalem during seventy years, and the subsequent restoration of the exiles and punishment of their Chaldæan oppressors. Although the restoration of the theocracy, and especially the rebuilding of Jerusalem, are not expressly mentioned in the latter prophecies, these features are yet implicitly included in the prediction, chap. xxv. 12 et seq., concerning the judicial visitation of the Chaldæans and the re-adoption of Israel; and in chap. xxix. 10 the gracious visitation of the Jews is described directly as a restoration to their place, *i. e.*, their country. It is not necessary, therefore, to seek for a prophecy by Jeremiah that predicts the rebuilding of Jerusalem in more literal and explicit terms. If such a passage be found in Jer. xxx. 18, or xxxi. 38 (Hitzig, Ewald, Bleek, Kamphausen, etc.), it is nevertheless unnecessary to assume that Daniel here refers only to that prophecy (which was probably composed after the destruction of Jerusalem by Nebuchadnezzar, B.C. 588, according to chap. xxxi. 5 et seq.). It is more probable that our prophet made no chronological distinction between Jer. xxix. (a letter composed about B.C. 598) and the more extended prophecy in chap. xxx. and xxxi. They (and also chap. xxv.) were probably regarded by him as belonging, upon the whole, to the same period and the same circle of prophecies, namely, that of the overthrow of the kingdom of Judah which covered eighteen to twenty years, beginning with the first conquest of Jerusalem by Nebuchadnezzar in the fourth year of Jehoiakim, or B.C. 605, and ending with the destruction of the city in B.C. 588. His starting-point for the calculation of the seventy years thus naturally became uncertain and vacillating, and for that very reason became the inciting cause of the prophecy under consideration. See supra, on v. 2.*—It would conflict with the

* [Keil justly objects to this interpretation of the fulfilment that "it is opposed by the *actual fact*, that neither in the consecration of Zerubbabel's temple, nor at the reconsecration of the altar of burnt-offering desecrated by Antiochus, is mention made of any anointing. According to the definite, uniform tradition of the Jews, the holy anointing oil did not exist during the time of the second temple." The term "anoint," however, may here be taken in the metaphorical sense of *rededicating*.]

† [Keil likewise, after adducing several exegetical reasons against the interpretation of "most holy" here as referring to the temple, altar, or any of the sacred utensils, finally concludes that "the reference is to the anointing of a new sanctuary, temple, or most holy place." This, however, makes the whole expression metaphorical, while all the associated phrases are taken in a sense more or less literal. It seems to us that the rejection of the old reference of the language here to the Messiah, on the ground of the absence of the article, is rather hasty; for surely the words may justly be rendered "to anoint a most holy" (*one* as well as *thing*), and thus really refer to the inauguration of the Head of the New Dispensation. The expression is doubtless to be explained in conformity with the similar phraseology of the verses immediately following.]

* [Few will be disposed to adopt an interpretation that comes to so vague a conclusion, when the very object of these added verses is evidently to furnish a definite

general usage to take לְהָשִׁיב in an adverbial sense and to connect it with the following verb, so as to obtain the sense "to build Jerusalem again," since only שׁוּב in the Kal is used to designate our "again" (*rursus*, *iterum*) in other places (and also here, in the latter half of the verse). Wieseler's rendering, "to lead back," *i.e.*, the people, is opposed in part by the harshness of such an objective supplement, and partly by the impossibility of showing that this passage refers directly and exclusively back to Jer. xxix. 10, where לְהָשִׁיב certainly occurs in the sense of "to lead back." The second half of the verse, moreover, refers only to a rebuilding of the city (תָּשׁוּב וְנִבְנְתָה), and not to a *reductio populi exulis*, which is decisive in favor of a restoration, *i.e.*, of bringing back out of the state of desolation; cf. Ezek. xvi. 55.—Who is designated by מָשִׁיחַ נָגִיד, the "anointed one, the prince" (or, as it may be rendered with equal correctness, the "anointed prince;" cf. Ewald, *Lehrb.*, p. 741), in the sense of the prophet? Certainly not the *Messiah of Israel* in an immediate and primary sense, as the Jewish and orthodox exegesis has generally held, down to the latest time. He would scarcely have been referred to as "an anointed prince" without the article; nor would Daniel have introduced Him after the brief interval contained in the first seven of the seventy year-weeks, since he always places the advent of the Messiah in the distant future, when the fourth and last world-kingdom shall fall—which is especially apparent in chapters ii. and vii.* The reference is probably to a prince contemporary with Daniel and already well known, who was destined to exert a powerful influence in favor of the theocracy, and to fulfil the special Divine purpose relating to the Israel of that day (about forty-nine or fifty years after the destruction of Jerusalem)—hence, without doubt, to *Cyrus*, who is designated as Jehovah's Mashiach in Isa. xlviii. 1 also. Cf. Kranichfeld, p. 327: "Rather, the person referred to appears as a different prince, who has a theocratic dominion, and is endowed with the spirit of Jehovah for his calling; cf. 1 Sam. xvi. 13 et seq.; x. 1, 6 et seq. But since the special mention of the feature of anointing in the case of the ordinary, *i.e.*, non-Messianic national kings who came in contact with Israel would be strange, it is proper to search for a heathen prince, who became prominent as the promoter of the theocracy, and especially so, because of his relation to the Messianic hopes before referred to. As such a one, and unique in this respect, the theocratic literature conceives of *Koresh*, the victor from the east who effected the return of Israel from the exile. He is expressly designated in Isa. xlv. 1 as the Mashiach of Jehovah. He appears in the first year of the reign of Darius Medus over Babylon, therefore at the time of the vision, and was then at least the victorious leader of the armies of Darius. We are compelled to decide for him, in interpreting the משיח נגיד of Daniel's description. He was regarded as the executor of the will of Jehovah already referred to, agreeably to the description which immediately follows, and in harmony with the theoratic hopes which Israel based on him. Having realized other prophetic expectations, the author regarded him as the agent who should bring about the restoration and the rebuilding of Jerusalem; and consequently, the writer expressly confirms these expectations, since he merely separates from them the *direct Messianic idea*, which he finds himself obliged to refer to a more distant future, in view of the course of political events."*—The "Mashiach Nagid,"

chronological determination of the period spoken of. Keil, although no advocate of a strict literal fulfilment of this passage, justly remarks that "all such references (to Jeremiah) are excluded by the fact that the angel names the commandment for the restoration of Jerusalem as the *terminus a quo* for the seventy weeks, and could thus only mean a word of God whose going forth was somewhere determined, or could be determined, just as the appearance of the Anointed Prince is named as the termination of the seventy weeks. Accordingly, 'the going forth of the commandment to restore,' etc., must be a *factum* coming into visibility, the time of which could without difficulty be known—a word from God respecting the restoration of Jerusalem, which went forth by means of a man at a definite time, and received an observable historical execution." This last remark effectually disposes of the author's exegesis regarding דָּבָר here.]

* [This last argument is certainly out of place, for Daniel does not place the personage in question at an interval of only seven weeks, but of seven and sixty-two weeks, *i.e.*, all but at the close of the entire period of the prophecy. So likewise in the next verse. As to the objection against the reference to the Messiah, both here and in the following and preceding verses, on the ground of the absence of the article, this is greatly, if not wholly, made up by the *construction* of the noun with an adjunct, which in Hebrew often makes a word really definite, so that the article is readily dispensed with. Indeed, the simple term מָשִׁיחַ, *Messiah*, even anarthrous, is so emphatic that none but the Great Prophet of Deut. xviii. 18 (where נָבִיא is in like manner rendered definite only by the adjunct term) can well be thought of. Accordingly, those interpreters who have forsaken this old and widely-accepted reference, have signally failed to adduce any other historical personage to whom it can be fitly applied.]

* [Keil's remarks on this point seem to us so satisfactory that we transcribe them in full. "The words מָשִׁיחַ נָגִיד are not to be translated *an anointed one, a prince* (Bertholdt); for מָשִׁיחַ cannot be an adjective to נָגִיד, because in Hebr. the adjective is placed after the substantive, with few exceptions, which are inapplicable to this case; cf. in Ewald's *Lehrb.*, § 293 *b.* Nor can מָשִׁיחַ be a participle: *till a prince (is) anointed* (Steudel), but it is a noun, and נָגִיד is connected with it by apposition; *an anointed one (who is at the same time) a prince.* According to the O. T., kings and priests, and only these, were anointed. Since then, מָשִׁיחַ is brought forward as the principal designation, we may not by נָגִיד think of a priest-prince, but only of a prince of the people; nor by מָשִׁיחַ of a king, but only of a priest; and by מָשִׁיחַ נָגִיד we must understand a person who, first and specially, is a priest, and in addition is a prince of the people, a king. The separation of the two words in ver. 26, where נָגִיד is acknowledged as meaning a prince of the people, leads to the same conclusion. This priest-king can neither be Zerubbabel (according to many old interpreters), nor Ezra (Steudel), nor Onias III. (Wieseler); for Zerubbabel the prince was not anointed, and the priest Ezra and the high-priest Onias were not princes of the people. Nor can Cyrus be meant here, as Saadias, Gaon., Bertholdt, Von Lengerke, Maurer, Ewald, Hitzig, Kranichfeld, and others, think, by a reference to Isa. xlv. 1; for, supposing it to be the case that Daniel had reason from Isa. xlv. 1 to call Cyrus מָשִׁיחַ—which is doubted, since from his epithet מְשִׁיחוֹ, *His* (Jehovah's) *anointed*, which Isaiah uses of Cyrus, it does not follow, of course, that ne

accordingly, is in himself merely a type of the Messiah, corresponding to the person introduced in Isa. xlv., but is not Christ Himself (correctly rendered by Saad., Gaon., Bertholdt, Von Leng., Hitzig, Bleek, Kamph., etc., with the exception, however, that they generally reject the typical Messianic sense as well as the direct reference to Christ). This typical forerunner of Christ, the first restorer of the theocracy in the age of Daniel itself, is placed by the prophet at the close of the first cycle of seven Sabbatic years, and hence after the expiration of the first jubilee-period which had elapsed since the prophetic activity of Jeremiah, while he assigns sixty-two additional weeks of years (or nearly nine jubilee-periods) to the interval of tribulation that announced and prepared for the coming of the genuine antitypical Christ.* Several expositors attempt to substantiate the direct Messianic interpretation of מָשִׁיחַ נָגִיד, by placing the seven weeks referred to in this passage after the sixty-two weeks which follow (Von Hofmann, Wieseler in the *Göttinger Gelehrten-Anzeigen*, 1846, Delitzsch, etc.), and thus "reckon the contents of the seventy backward;" but if Daniel had preferred this order he would certainly have noticed the sixty-two weeks first and the seven weeks afterwards, and, moreover, the *one* week in v. 27 cannot be suitably provided for. Finally, all that has been heretofore observed against the direct Messianic interpretation of that expression, militates against their view. Upon the whole, cf. the "history of the exposition" in appendix to exeget. remarks.—**And three-score and two weeks; the street shall be built again**, etc.; rather, "and (during) three-score and two weeks (it) shall return (or 'be restored') and be built." * This period of sixty-two weeks, the "result of subtracting the significant seven at the beginning, and of one to be reserved for the end," covers the time during which the heathen world-kingdoms succeed each other, down to the fourth and most godless power, which is to attempt to entirely suppress the Divine kingdom of the Old Covenant that had meanwhile been perfectly restored, although with much labor, but which by that very effort secured its own destruction through the Messianic judgment (cf. viii. 11 et seq.; 23 et seq., and the preceding parallels). The subject of תָּשׁוּב וְנִבְנְתָה, which must be supplied, is doubtless Jerusalem, in analogy with the former half of the verse, where the same idea is presented in an active form. The specification of time, וְשָׁבֻעִים שִׁשִּׁים וש׳, which precedes in the accusative, "marks the limits of the period, within which, at different times, the building was prosecuted" (Hitzig).—The limitation of this period, beginning a new clause as it does, is properly preceded by an Athnach, which serves to divide the verse. The method adopted by the ancient translators, by Luther, and by a majority of subsequent expositors (including Hengstenb., Hävern., Auberl., Zündel, etc.—but not Kranichfeld, Kliefoth, and Füller), divides the verse so as to connect the "sixty-two weeks with the preceding clause, despite the Athnach, and thus obtains sixty-nine weeks as the time that should elapse before the coming of the anointed prince; but it is evidently based on the desire to give a direct Messianic bearing to the passage. It is opposed (1) by the fact that the sixty-two weeks are repeated in v. 26, where they are preceded by the article, which clearly marks them as an independent period; (2) that the clause תָּשׁוּב וגו׳ thus occupies a very abrupt and bare position, being without any designation of time, while the preceding clause has two; (3) that the sense of the writer clearly is that the rebuilding and restoration had not begun before the sixty-two weeks, while he evidently regards the seven weeks as a period of desolation and ruinous neglect of the city which afterward was to be built (cf. Hitzig, p. 160; also Kliefoth, p. 323 et seq.).†—**The**

should be named מָשִׁיחַ—the title ought at least to have been נָגִיד מָשִׁיחַ, the מָשִׁיחַ being an adjective following נָגִיד, because there is no evident reason for the express precedence of the adjective definition.

"The O. T. knows only one who shall be both priest and king in one person (Psa. cx. 4; Zech. vi. 13), Christ the Messias (John iv. 25), whom, with Hävernick, Hengstenberg, Hofmann, Auberlen, Delitzsch, and Kliefoth, we here understand by the מָשִׁיחַ נָגִיד, because in Him the two essential requisites of the theocratic king, the anointing and the appointment to be the נָגִיד of the people of God (cf. 1 Sam. x. 1; xiii. 14; xvi. 13; xxv. 30; 2 Sam. ii. 4; v. 2 seq.), are found in the most perfect manner. These requisites are here attributed to Him as predicates, and in such a manner that the being anointed goes before the being a prince, in order to make prominent the spiritual, priestly character of His royalty, and to designate Him, on the ground of the prophecies, Isa. lxi. 1–3 and lv. 4, as the person by whom 'the sure mercies of David' (Isa. lv. 3) shall be realized to the covenant people. The absence of the definite article is not to be explained by saying that מָשִׁיחַ, somewhat as צֶמַח, Zech. iii. 8; vi. 12, is used κατ' ἐξοχ. as a *nomen propr.* of the Messiah, the Anointed; for in that case נָגִיד ought to have the article, since in Hebrew we cannot say דָּוִד מֶלֶךְ, but only דָּוִד הַמֶּלֶךְ. Much rather the article is wanting, because it shall not be said: *till the Messiah, who is prince*, but only, *till one comes who is anointed and at the same time prince*, because He that is to come is not definitely designated as the expected Messiah, but must be made prominent by the predicates ascribed to Him as a personage altogether singular."]

* [How ill the chronological elements of the prophecy accord with the reference of this anointed one and prince to Cyrus, is evident from the fact that the author is obliged to sever Daniel's conjoined statement (7+62) in order to effect anything like an agreement. Yet even thus the historical fulfilment has to be vaguely *presumed*, and cannot be definitely verified.]

* [The only justification of this translation, which separates the two periods of seven weeks and sixty-two weeks, assigning the former as the *terminus ad quem* of the Anointed Prince, and the latter as the time of rebuilding, lies in the Masoretic interpunction, which places the Athnach between them. Some adduce also the fact that the ו connective is likewise at the point, and not at תָּשׁוּב. But these arguments, especially the latter, are not conclusive; and the rendering in question involves a harsh construction of the second member, being without a preposition. It is better, therefore, and simpler, to adhere to the Authorized Version, which follows all the older translations. Keil, indeed (although admitting that the Masoretic punctuation is neither authoritative nor decisive), departs from it, but endeavors to extricate himself from the chronological difficulties resulting by his interpretation of these "weeks" as not being heptades of years. Stuart, too, insists upon the Masoretic separation, but he is thereby led into a maze of interpretation from which he confesses he sees no satisfactory exit.]

† [These arguments, however, have little weight; for (1) the sixty two weeks are still "an independent period," namely, that following the seven weeks of rebuilding, *i.e.*, covering the whole period of the restored city down to the

street shall be built again, and the wall, even in troublous times; rather, (with) street and ditch, but in troublous times. רְחוֹב וְחָרוּץ, a combination that suggests חוֹמוֹת וָחֵל, Isa. xxvi. 1, is evidently an adverbial apposition to the subject יְרוּשָׁלַיִם; and there properly signifies "street-and-ditch-wise," *i.e.*, with streets and ditches. It was not to be a wretched, confused, and scattered, as well as a defenceless mass of houses, but was to be arranged in streets, and to be surrounded with a fortified (wall and) ditch. ["רְחוֹב means the street and the wide space before the gate" (*Keil*, who adds "before the temple," but this last is by no means certain.)] חָרוּץ is regarded by most moderns, and certainly with justice, as synonymous with the Chald. חֲרִיצָא, "ditch." This rendering is indirectly supported by the ancient versions also, which have "wall" (Sept., Theodot. : οἰκοδομηθήσεται πλατεῖα καὶ περίτειχος; Vulgate : "*rursum ædificabitur platea et muri*"). Hitzig arbitrarily asserts that the verb נִבְנְתָה will not admit of such an interpretation of חרוץ. On his view, the word is synonymous with גִּזְרָה, Ezek. xli. 12, and gives the meaning "according to street *and court.*" Hofmann adopts a similar rendering, "extension and bounded space," as do also Kliefoth and Füller, "opening and limitation." Grotius, on the other hand, conceives of an "aqueduct," Dathe, of the Divine "judgment," and several others take וְחָרוּץ as a parenthetic supplement, signifying "and it is determined" (decided), or, "as it is determined" (Hitzig, in *Stud. u. Krit.*, 1832, Hengstenb., Hävernick, Von Lengerke, Wieseler, Kranichfeld).*—וּבְצוֹק הָעִתִּים expresses the reason why so long a time is required to build and restore, and therefore stands in an adversative relation to the preceding (ו="but, however"). The historical commentary on this "but in troublous times" is found in the narratives of Ezra and Nehemiah, respecting the frequent disturbing and interruption of the rebuilding of the walls of Jerusalem in the time of the Persian kings; cf. especially Neh. ix. 36, 37. "The city was inhabited in the second year of Darius Hystaspis (Hag. i. 4), but had neither walls nor gates (cf. Zech. ii. 8, 9); up to that time the enemies of the Jews had prevented the building of the temple and of the walls either by cunning or by force (Ezra iv. 4, 5, 12, 23 et seq.). In the twentieth year of Artaxerxes Longimanus the walls and gates had again been destroyed (Neh. i. 3); and the renewed building succeeded only under manifold precautions: Neh. iii. 33; iv. 1, 2 et seq.; vi. 1 et seq." * (Hitzig). Any reference of the expression to disturbances encountered in the building up of the church, or the New-Test. kingdom of God, can only be admitted in a typical sense, since the primary reference of the passage is solely to Jerusalem in the period following the captivity. When Kranichfefd, p. 329, declares that וּבְצוֹק הָעִתִּים is "the modifying factor connected with oracles like Jer. xxxi. 38; Isa. liv. 11; lx. 10; Ezek. xlv. 6; xlviii. 8, 15 et seq.," he thereby substantially contradicts his ordinary interpretation of the passage, which is only typically Messianic, and he is guilty of an inconsequent vacillation in the direction of the strict Messianic theory.

Verse 26. **And after** (the †) **threescore and two weeks shall the Messiah be cut off;** rather, "an anointed one." Since the period covered by the sixty-two weeks (or 434 years) is preceded by the seven weeks (or forty-nine years) according to the above, the event here predicted must fall into the *last* of the seventy weeks in v. 24, as the next verse expressly states. Hence the מָשִׁיחַ who is to be cut off during that final year-week cannot possibly be identified with the מָשִׁיחַ נָגִיד whom the preceding verse introduced already on the expiration of the *seventh* of the seventy weeks of years.‡ Instead of an "anointed prince," we are here referred simply to an "anointed one," who is, moreover, placed in such an intimate relation to "the city and the sanctuary" in the second half of the verse—*i.e.*, to Jerusalem and the temple located there—that he is brought into sharp and clearly defined contrast with the "prince" and people who destroy that city and its sanctuary. A *high priest of Israel* is evidently intended, whom the people of the foreign and hostile prince "cuts off" (יִכָּרֵת), *i.e.*, "destroys, kills" (cf. Gen. ix. 11; Deut. xx. 20; Jer. xi. 19; Psa. xxxvii. 9; Prov. ii. 22;

appearance of the Anointed One and Prince; (2) the pause before the statement of the rebuilding of the "street and wall" is justified and even required by the fact that this is evidently a resumption of the former declaration of the "building of Jerusalem;" (3) so far from this period of rebuilding being delayed till some subsequent event, it is set forth as the very initial *terminus a quo* of the entire prophecy. We may add, that the subdivision of the sixty-nine weeks into two portions of seven and sixty-two weeks respectively perfectly corresponds with the assignment, in the same connection and order, of two distinct events, namely, the completed reconstruction for the former portion, and the Messianic advent for the latter. If, on the contrary view, we appropriate the sixty-two weeks to the reconstruction-period, we fall into several exegetical contradictions: (1) we confound it with the Messiah-period, which is described in very different terms, ver. 26; (2) we leave no special transaction for the preceding seven years; (3) we make the Messiah-period vastly too long for its definite limitation in ver. 27. Other difficulties of a historical character will be adduced presently.]

* [We suggest, as best suited to the etymological import of these two terms, as well as their proverbial antithesis and adverbial adjection to the sentence, the sense of "court and alley," *i.e.*, broad square, and close street; to denote the complete restoration of the city, with all its places of resort and thoroughfare.]

* [That the reconstruction of the city wall, however, was completed at this last date is certain from Neh. vi. 15. This was B. C. 446. The temple had been rebuilt a long time, Ezra vi. 15, B. C. 517. During Nehemiah's administration the whole process of restoration was evidently effected. It is impossible, therefore, to protract this period over the sixty-two year-weeks, as the author seeks to do. The historical interpretation here fails completely. From whatever point of time we reckon the first forty-nine years, they certainly included this work of reconstruction.]

† [The article here only shows that the period in question agrees in general with that similarly stated in the preceding verse. That they do not exactly coincide is clear from the fact that the *terminus ad quem* of the two is differently stated: in the one it is "till the Messiah," in the other, down to his "cutting off." The difference in time is accurately defined by the following verse.]

‡ [This objection to the identification of the *Mashiach* in both cases is entirely obviated by the above note of the variation in the limits of the two chronological terms.]

x. 31, etc.).* And since the hostile prince is unequivocally characterized in both vs. 26 *b* and 27 as the ruler of the antitheistic and anti-Christian world-power, and as the originator of the blasphemous and sacrilegious horrors which already appeared in chap. vii. 25; viii. 11 et seq., it will evidently be appropriate to regard a high priest who fell at the hands of heathen persecutors in the period of religious oppression under the Seleucidæ as the "anointed one," in whose death the prophecy before us was primarily, although but typically, fulfilled. Such a person is found in the high priest Onias III. who was murdered by Andronicus, the governor under Epiphanes, according to 2 Macc. iii. 31 et seq.; iv. 1 et seq., and to him the prophecy may be referred with the highest probability that the interpretation is correct. According to 2 Macc. iv. 34 et seq., the slaying of this anointed one took place before the second campaign undertaken by Epiphanes against Egypt, and shortly before the king arrived at Tyre on his return from Cilicia (cf. ibid., vs. 22, 30, 44; chap. v. 1). Hence, it certainly transpired before the abuse of the city and its sanctuary by the same king, a feature with which the description in this verse harmonizes well upon the whole [but with some fatal exceptions]. A discrepancy exists in a chronological aspect only between that event and the statements in the prophecy; for, while the sixty-two weeks of years extend, when reckoned from the end of the first seven year-weeks or B.C. 539, to B.C. 105 or into the reign of the Asmonæan Aristobulus I. or his successor Alexander Jannæus (after 105), the murder of Onias by Andronicus took place as early as 141 or 142 of the æra of the Seleucidæ, *i.e.*, B.C. 171 or 172, and therefore in the fifty-third week of years after B.C. 539. Consequently, if it be conceded that all the remaining assumptions are correct, it must be acknowledged that the prophecy is not consistent with itself in a chronological aspect, or that the prophet saw events belonging to different periods in a single comprehensive view—in other words, that he conceived of a catastrophe in the historical future, which was decidedly important to the nations concerned, as belonging to a period, later by a number of years (perhaps ten weeks of years, or seventy years) than it actually transpired. Cf. infra, eth.-fund. principles, etc. Nos. 1 and 2.†—The following diverging interpretations are to be rejected: (1) That adopted by Eichhorn, Corrodi, Wieseler, Hitzig, Kamphausen, etc., which comes especially near our own; they regard the anointed one as being Onias, but reckon the sixty-two year-weeks, which closed at the time of his death, from B.C. 604 instead of 539, so that the first seven weeks are not to be counted (?), or rather, are included in the sixty-two (?)—since 604-434 actually results in 170, the number of the year in which Onias died; (2) The similar view of Wieseler (*Gött. Gel.-Anz.* 1846) and of Delitzsch (upon the whole that of Hofmann also, *Weiss. und Erf.*, p. 303 et seq.), which holds that Onias is the anointed one, at whose cutting off the sixty-two weeks of years from B.C. 604 were to have expired; but that the seven weeks are to be placed after the year-week which began with the year of his death—hence are to be reckoned from B.C. 164 (cf. on the impossibility of this assumption, supra, on v. 25); (3) The opinion of Bleek, Maurer, v. Lengerke, Roesch, Ewald, etc., that the anointed one who was cut off was not the high priest Onias, but the king Seleucus IV. Philopater, of Syria, who was killed by the usurper Heliodorus in B.C. 176; this opinion involves still greater chronological difficulties than the former, inasmuch as the sixty-two weeks of years, when reckoned back from B.C. 176, would extend to B.C. 610; and it is opposed, moreover, by the inadmissible character of an attempt to explain מָשִׁיחַ by "king;" (4) That of Bertholdt, who believes that the passage refers to the death of Alexander the Great (!), who left no heir; (5) The assumption of Kranichfeld, that the anointed one is the Messiah of Israel, as in Psa, ii. 2; Isa. lxi. 1, and therefore not identical with the "anointed prince" of v. 25, but not less distinct also from Onias, the murdered high-priest of Maccabæan times; (6) The orthodox churchly view which identifies the "anointed one" with the "anointed prince" of the preceding verse, and believes that both denote Christ, whose sufferings and death are said to be predicted in a similar manner by יִכָּרֵת וְאֵין לֹא, as in Isa. liii. (held among moderns, *e.g.*, by Hävern., Hengstenb., Auberl., Pusey [Keil], etc.); (7) The assertion by Kliefoth (on Zech. xiii. 7 and also on this passage) that the anointed one is Christ, but only in the final stage of his work and government among the kingdoms of the earth; and further, that the passage, "like Luke xvii. 25; 2 Thess. ii. 7, describes the relation to the world and mankind which Christ shall occupy by reason of the great apostasy before the end of the world, as prophecy leads us to expect."—**But not for himself**; rather, "and he has no one," *i.e.*, "for his helper, his deliverer from death;" or "he has

* [Keil insists that יִכָּרֵת does not necessarily denote a violent death. But the passages adduced by the author are sufficient to establish this as the general meaning. The "orthodox" interpretation of this clause as referring to the crucifixion of the Messiah is certainly well sustained.]

† [This admission of failure to meet the chronological terms of the prophecy sufficiently points out the fallacy of the author's interpretation. The Anointed one of this verse can be no other than that of the preceding verse. "The circumstance that in ver. 26 מָשִׁיחַ has neither the article nor the addition נָגִיד following it appears to be in favor of this opinion. The absence of the one as well as of the other denotes that מָשִׁיחַ, after what is said of Him in consideration of the connection of the words, needs no more special description. If we observe that the destruction of the city and sanctuary is so connected with the *Mashiach* that we must consider this as the immediate or first consequence of the cutting off of the *Mashiach*, and that the destruction shall be brought about by a *Nagid*, then by *Mashiach* we can understand neither a secular prince or king, nor simply a high priest, but only an anointed one who stands in such a relation to the city and sanctuary, that with his being 'cut off' the city and the sanctuary lose not only their protection and their protector, but the sanctuary also loses at the same time, its character as the sanctuary which the Mashiach had given to it. This is suitable to no Jewish high-priest, but only to the Messias whom Jehovah anointed to be a Priest-King after the order of Melchizedek, and placed as Lord over Zion, his holy hill. We agree therefore with Hävernick, Hengstenberg, Auberlen, and Kliefoth, who regard the *Mashiach* of this verse as identical with the *Mashiach Nagid* of ver. 25 as Christ, who, in the fullest sense of the word, is the Anointed, and we hope to establish this view more fully in the following exposition of the historical reference of this word of the angel."—*Keil*].

nothing, there remains nothing to him" (אֵין לוֹ, namely מְאוּמָה, cf. Füller and Kranichfeld on this passage). This וְאֵין לוֹ meets with an extraordinary variety of interpretations, based respectively on the different explanations of מָשִׁיחַ. Theodotion: *καὶ κρίμα οὐκ ἔστιν ἐν αὐτῷ*; Jerome: "*et non erit ejus populus qui eum negaturus est*" (in like manner also Grotius, and a majority of Roman Catholic expositors); Bertholdt: "and he (Alex. the Gr.) shall have no successor;" v. Lengerke, Roesch, Bleek, Ewald, etc.: "and he (Seleucus Philopater) shall have no successor;" Wieseler: "and he (Onias) shall have no *son*;" Auberlen: "he, Christ, shall have no adherents;" Hofmann, Hengstenb., Kranichf., Kliefoth (and similarly also Calvin, Junius, Ebrard): "he, Christ, shall possess *nothing*, shall be without possessions, and be deprived of everything;" Hofmann (in *Weiss. und Erf.*): "and there shall not be to the people," *i.e.*, an anointed one, the people shall have no Messiah;* Hävernick: "and not for himself, *i.e.*, for his own sake,"—supply, "shall the Messiah die, but for the benefit of mankind, which is to be redeemed;" Michaelis, E. C. Schmidt (in Paulus' *Memorabil.* VII. 51), Wieseler (in *Gött. Gel.-Anz.*, 1846), Hitzig: "and he is not, *i.e.*, Onias" (— אֵין לוֹ consequently = אֵינֶנּוּ, cf. Gen v. 24). Upon the whole cf. Kliefoth, p. 357 et seq. Since the forcible cutting off of an anointed one is concerned, we are obliged to regard that explanation as being most consistent with the context, which supplies מַצִּיל, perhaps (cf. Psa. vii. 3; l. 22; Isa. v. 29) after וְאֵין לוֹ. It does not differ materially from that advocated by Hofmann, Hengstenberg, Kranichfeld, etc., which supplies מְאוּמָה; for whoever has no deliverer or helper is also without power, without possessions, without anything whatever. We differ from those expositors only in regarding the anointed one who is described as being without possessions and helpless, not directly as the Messiah, but more immediately as his type, the Jewish high priest who was killed in the course of the Antiochian persecution,—in short, in substituting the typical Messianic theory for the direct (in which we agree substantially with Füller).—**And the people of the prince that shall come shall destroy the city and the sanctuary, and the end thereof shall be with a flood**; rather, "and the people of *a* prince,† who shall come and end with overflowing,‡ shall destroy the city and the sanctuary." The words evidently refer to a catastrophe which follows immediately on the cutting off of the anointed one. The "coming prince" (נָגִיד הַבָּא) who approaches to cause destruction to the city and the sanctuary, or more exactly, who comes as the ruler of the people that brings ruin and destruction, is doubtless, therefore, the Old.-Test. antichrist, or the antitheistic horn of the earlier visions (chap. vii. 21, 25; viii. 11 et seq.; 24 et seq.), and consequently Antiochus Epiphanes, הַבָּא (=אֲשֶׁר יָבוֹא) describes this ruler as coming at the head of his army in a *hostile character* (cf. בּוֹא in i. 1; viii. 6; xi. 10, 13, 15, 16, 40, 41), and the definite article indicates that his coming was a familiar fact to the prophet, as having formed the subject of his earlier predictions.* The participle is therefore not employed without a purpose (Hofmann, *Weiss. und Erf.*, I. 304), nor does it refer to עָם, "people" (Schöll, Ebrard). It does not signify Epiphanes' "succession" to his predecessor Seleucus (Roesch, Maurer), nor denote the future "appearing" or mysterious presence of the New-Test. antichrist, in the sense of 2 Thess. ii. 9 (Kliefoth).—The ending of this prince "*with overflowing*" is probably not materially different from the "pouring out of annihilation and judicial punishment upon the desolator," at the close of the following verse. שֶׁטֶף, "a flood, an overflowing," accordingly denotes the *judgment inflicted by God in his anger* on the impious נָגִיד (Wieseler, Kliefoth), or, more probably, since in that case a genitive אַף (cf. Prov. xxvii. 4) would properly be required in order to define the sense more clearly, it is used *sensu bellico* to denote an overflowing with warlike hosts, which should lead to the end of his life, *i.e.*, his annihilation (chap. xi. 45; cf. vii. 26). Cf. the exactly similar use of שֶׁטֶף in chap. xi. 10, 22, 26, 40, and in Isa. viii. 8, together with שׁוֹטֵף צְדָקָה Isa. x. 22.—Here again we are obliged to reject a number of diverging explanations, and

* [Keil's interpretation is substantially like this, namely: "it is not to Him, viz., that which he must have, to be the *Mashiach*."]

† [On the contrary, נָגִיד is here rendered definite by the epithet or adjective following, and therefore may properly be translated "the prince." It simply "omits the article because it is different from that in ver. 25, and the article would give a wrong sense, or at least the insertion of it would make it dubious to the reader, inasmuch as it would naturally refer him to the נָגִיד in ver. 25. The נָגִיד here is merely a heathen prince acting in a civil (rather military) capacity, in distinction from a מָשִׁיחַ who belongs to the people of God."—*Stuart*].

‡ [This rendering of וְקִצּוֹ בַשֶּׁטֶף is quite unjustifiable. It is not a correlative clause appended to הַבָּא as a further definition of the נָגִיד, but an independent statement as to the result of that prince's coming. The suffix in קִצּוֹ doubtless refers to the נָגִיד, but in an *objective* not a subjective sense: it is *the end which he causes*, not any which he is to suffer. It is thus precisely parallel with the קֵץ of the clause immediately following. This view is confirmed by the article in בַּשֶּׁטֶף, which commentators have overlooked or misapplied, but which is here, as often, equivalent (like the Greek article) to a personal pronoun, *q.d.* "in his overflowing," evidently the military campaign or מִלְחָמָה immediately subjoined. The whole phrase thus indicates that the invasion should issue in the destruction of Jerusalem. This was certainly not done by Antiochus Epiphanes.]

* [The inconsistency of this explanation of the article after the above statement that הַבָּא = אֲשֶׁר יָבוֹא is obvious. It is not a Hebrew idiom to use the article with a *participle* or *adjective* in order to point out something well known; for that purpose the article should (also) be prefixed to the associated *noun*. It is evidently employed here simply in order to render definite the otherwise indefinite נָגִיד, *i.e.*, he is not a present or a past, but a *future* prince.]

especially that of Hitzig, v. Lengerke, etc., who refer the words to a warlike expedition undertaken by Antiochus Epiphanes, instead of one that should break in upon him like a flood and annihilate him; that of Ewald, who obtains the sense "who comes with his host overflowing" (or "in overflow") by a violent emendation, inasmuch as he substitutes וְחֵילוֹ, "and his host," or וְחֵצוֹ, "and his line of battle" (after Prov. xxx. 27), for וְקִצּוֹ; that of Gesenius, Rosenmüller, Roesch, etc., who take בַּשֶּׁטֶף in the sense of "suddenly, like a flood;" that of Auberlen, Hävernick, Delitzsch, etc., who refer the suffix in קִצּוֹ to the city and sanctuary, rather than to the "prince;" "their destruction shall come by overflowing," etc.*—**And unto the end of the war desolations are determined;** *i.e.*, the devastating of the city and sanctuary are to continue to the end of the warlike alarms excited by their impious oppressor, as a matter that is determined by God. מִלְחָמָה designates that state of war which begins with cutting off the anointed one, and eventually results in the destruction of the city and the sanctuary (so, correctly, Rosenmüller, Hofmann, Ewald, Füller, etc.). Others read, "and to the end shall be war, the determined desolations," in which method נֶחֱרֶצֶת שֹׁמֵמוֹת is either taken as an apposition (Hävern., v. Leng., Maur., Wieseler, Hitz., Auberlen), or as an explanatory clause to the foregoing, with the conjunctions omitted in the connection (Kranichfeld, Kliefoth), and in connection with which still further differences of opinion exist with regard to the meaning of קֵץ, some expositors referring it to the end of the prince (Wieseler), some to the end of the sanctuary (Häv., Aub.) or of the period of the seventy weeks—hence, to the last year-week of the seventy (v. Lengerke, Hitzig), and some even to the end of all things, the "absolute end" (Kliefoth). The reference of קֵץ to the exterminated prince is evidently the only one in harmony with the context, which thus identifies it with the קִצּוֹ of the preceding clause; but it is more appropriate to regard it in the sense of a *stat. constr.*, "to the end of the war," because of the more regular and connected character of the arrangement of the sentence.† נֶחֱרֶצֶת is also the construct state of נֶחֱרָצָה, which recurs at the close of the following verse, and here probably denotes the same idea as in chap. xi. 36, and Isa. x. 23; xxviii. 22, viz.: "determination, destiny, what is ordained." A "determination of the desolations" (שֹׁמֵמוֹת as in v. 18; cf. on that passage) is a decree that aims at desolations and has them for its object. Ewald: "the decision respecting the horrors," *i.e.*, the decision of God at the judgment of the world, which relates to the horrible actions and devastations of Antiochus, or which serves to punish them (?). Hofmann and Kliefoth are still more arbitrary: "a determined measure of desolations, which is thus limited and confined."—[This language was not fulfilled in any appropriate sense by Antiochus, who aimed merely at the suppression of Jehovah's worship, but left the city and sanctuary uninjured. It seems to us that the old interpretation, which refers it to the last war with the Romans when Titus seemed compelled by providence to persist in his attack till the temple itself was demolished, is the only adequate one. This was the retribution that eventually followed the rejection and murder of their Messiah by the Jews.]

Verse 27. **And he shall confirm the covenant with many for one week;** rather, "make a strong covenant,"* etc. This sentence (introduced by an explicative *vav*) is obviously an explanation and more particular illustration of the statements in the preceding verse. Its subject is neither the indefinite "it" (Füller), nor the "one week" (Theodot., Dereser, Hävern., Von Leng., Hengstenb., Hitz., Auberl.), but, beyond all question, נָגִיד, which governs the preceding sentence as a logical subject, is finally included in קִצּוֹ, and is the prominent subject of consideration, from v. 26 *b* (thus, correctly, Berth., Maur., Wiesel., Ewald, Kranichf., Klief., etc.).† It is observed, therefore, with regard to the anti-Christian prince of the final world-power, that "he shall confirm the covenant as to many," *i.e.*, "that he shall enter into a strong, firm covenant with many;" for the Hiphil הִגְבִּיר, which occurs elsewhere only in Psa. xii. 5, and there signifies "to be strong, to exhibit strength," in this place doubtless expresses the transitive idea of strengthening, and in connection with the idea "covenant," involves more particularly the notion of "confirming or establishing." The many (רַבִּים with the article) with whom the strong covenant is made by the prince are obviously the numerous apostate Jews, who were induced by the heathen tyrant to break their covenant with God and disobey His law, according to 1 Macc. i. 10 et seq., and thus to enter into an antitheocratic alliance that was hostile to God, *for one week*, *i.e.*, during a

* [These latter interpretations are refuted in detail by Keil, whose objections, however, do not apply to the explanations which are suggested above.]

† [Keil admits the grammatical propriety of this rendering, but objects that "in the preceding sentence no mention is expressly made of war; and if the war which consisted in the destruction of the city be meant, מִלְחָמָה ought to have the article." These arguments are of no force, as מִלְחָמָה is definite by reason of its construction with קֵץ, and the war itself was already distinctly alluded to in the שֶׁטֶף.]

* [The connection is unnecessary. The expression וְהִגְבִּיר בְּרִית properly and fairly signifies: "he shall confirm a covenant," which naturally implies one already made.]

† [On the contrary it seems to us that the subject of this clause is not the נָגִיד just spoken of, but the מָשִׁיחַ נָגִיד preceding, or, more definitely, the מָשִׁיחַ just before; for (1) this (as Hengstenberg rightly says) is the predominant or principal subject of the entire passage; and (2) each of the other portions of the seventy weeks is directly referred to that personage, so that this final week will not fill up the number appropriately if otherwise referred. The objections of Keil to this interpretation are unimportant. Moreover, the prophecy is not historically applicable to Antiochus, but does correspond to the term of the Messiah's ministry; as we shall endeavor to show.]

week of years (שָׁ׳ אֶחָד, accusative of time). Cf. the allusions to this fact in chap. xi. 22 (where בְּרִית is employed in the same antitheocratic sense as here), in xi. 32 (where the transgressors of [Jehovah's] covenant, the מַרְשִׁיעֵי בְרִית, are the same as the רַבִּים in this place), and also in chap. viii. 10 et seq., where the stars that were trodden under foot by the little horn may likewise represent the breakers of the covenant who are here mentioned (cf. also viii. 24 et seq.).*—A great diversity of opinion respecting the meaning of the "covenant" exists among the representatives of the theory which makes שָׁבוּעַ אֶחָד the subject of הִגְבִּיר. In illustration of this, cf. Hitzig, "the one week of years shall make the covenant—*i.e.*, the adherence to the faith in Jehovah, and to the theocratic law—*hard* for many;" Hofmann (*Schriftbeweis*, II. 2), "the one week of years shall confirm many in the covenant through tribulation and the trial of their faith" (similarly, Rosenmüller, before Hofmann); Von Lengerke, "A week shall confirm a covenant to many, through the seductive arts of Antiochus;" Hengstenberg, Hävernick, Auberlen, etc., "the one week, or rather the events belonging to it, especially the death of the Messiah referred to in v. 26, will lead to the conclusion of a new, strong, and firm covenant with many," etc.—**And in the midst of the week he shall cause the sacrifice and the oblation to cease**; *i.e.*, during one half of the week. חֲצִי הַשָּׁבוּעַ might of itself signify the middle of the week; but the following תַּחַת וגו׳ shows that something transpires during the חֲצִי הַשָּׁ׳, which naturally belongs to the close of the whole period of oppression here described, viz.: the punishment and annihilation of the impious persecutor. For this reason חֲצִי הַשָּׁ׳ must rather denote half of the week, and more particularly the *second* half, and it therefore corresponds to the three and a half years of persecution of chap. vii. 25; and יַשְׁבִּית—for which no other appropriate subject can be found than that of the preceding verb הִגְבִּיר—can therefore express no other sense than that of "causing to cease" during the period in question. The impious madman causes to cease during that period the זֶבַח וּמִנְחָה, the bloody and unbloody offerings, which are mentioned representatively for *all* the sacrifices required by the theocratic ritual, as being the two principal classes of offerings under the Mosaic economy, in a similar manner as that in which הַתָּמִיד, "the daily," was employed in chap. viii. 11 to express this concrete individualizing and comprehensive sense.* The expression here employed cannot be taken to refer to the superseding of the Old-Test. institution of sacrifices by the New-Test. worship in spirit and in truth, as being based on the perfect expiatory sacrifice of Christ (against Hävernick, Hengstenb., Auberl., etc.); for the verb השבית would not have been suited to express that idea, and, moreover, the *sin* offering (cf. v. 24) would hardly have been passed by without mention in that case. Kliefoth emphasizes correctly, "that in this place the נָגִיד of v. 26 must be considered the subject, and that the observation here relates not to the abrogation, but merely to the suspension of the sacrifices;" but he afterward arbitrarily applies the passage to a temporary suspension and suppression of the eucharist as the sacrifice of the New Covenant, to be caused by the antichrist in the last age of the church.—**And for the overspreading of abominations he shall make it desolate**; rather, "and abominations of desolation shall be on the wing." This וְעַל כְּנַף שִׁקּוּצִים מְשֹׁמֵם constitutes the actual climax of the many difficulties presented in this passage, the real *crux interpretum*, which has produced almost as many explanations as interpreters. Probably all those methods of explanation are to be at once rejected and avoided which contradict the most ancient quotation and translation of the words in the originally Hebrew Maccabæan book (chap. i. 54; cf. Matt. xxiv. 15; Mark xiii. 14), and the corresponding testimony of the most ancient translators, the Sept., Theodotion, and the Vulgate. All these render שִׁקּוּצִים מְשֹׁמֵם by "abominations of desolation" (1 Macc., l. c., τὸ βδέλυγμα τῆς ἐρημώσεως; Sept., Theodot., βδέλυγμα τῶν ἐρημώσεων; Vulg., *abominatio desolationis*), which probably resulted from the influence of primitive traditions that were certainly correct in the main. מְשֹׁמֵם was accordingly regarded as a genitive from the beginning, and probably by the author himself—not, however, as a genitive of possession, but as a genitive of *description;* or, what amounts to the same thing, it was considered an *apposition* to the preceding plural שִׁקּוּצִים, in support of which the analogy of חָזוּת אַרְבַּע in chap. viii. 8 may be adduced on the one hand (as also the similar connection of that plural with a singular in Jer. xlix. 11), and on the other, the appositional combination הַשִּׁקּוּץ מְשֹׁמֵם in chap. viii. 13 (cf. also הַכֹּהֵן

* [The passages adduced by the author, especially xi. 22, do not sustain the meaning he here assigns to בְּרִית, which, unless specially qualified, always refers to Jehovah's covenant as contained in the Law. Moreover, as Keil justly observes, "לָרַבִּים, with the article, signifies *the many*, *i.e.*, the great mass of the people in contrast with the few." But the mass of the Jews did not apostatize in the time of Antiochus. Still more inept is Keil's application: "That ungodly prince shall impose on the mass of the people a strong covenant that they should follow him and give themselves to him as their God." The language of the text can only have its appropriate fulfilment in the mission of the Redeemer, which was a completion of God's covenant with the race of man. How this took place during the last of the seventy weeks we will presently show.]

* [Or, on the usual Messianic interpretation, Christ shall forever do away with the Levitical sacrifices by the one perfect offering of himself (Heb. vii. 27; ix. 12–14, 26). On this view, it matters little whether we render חֲצִי "in the midst," or "during half," for our Lord's ministry was a process of supersedure of the legal sacrifices, which culminated in his death, and (should we even grant the author's position, that the *latter* half of the week is intended) was finally carried out by the release of Gentiles from the Levitical economy (Acts xi. 18). The author's objections, as to the sense of הִשְׁבִּית, etc., are inconclusive. Stuart thinks that "chap. vii. 11 settles the question" that Antiochus is referred to; but the language there employed is very different.]

ראשׁ, 1 Chron. xxvii. 5).* The plural שִׁקּוּצִים (for which, however, the writer of 1 Macc., l. c., substituted the sing. שִׁקּוּץ, *βδέλυγμα*, possibly with design, because the abomination of idolatry with which Epiphanes desecrated the temple was chief in his mind) at all events denotes "abominations, horrible things," and more particularly abominable things from a *religious* point of view, abominable idolatries, what is loathsome in the domain of Divine worship, "*res abominandæ ad cultum Deorum spectantes*;" cf. xi. 31; xii. 11. In like manner as this meaning of שִׁקּוּצִים is adequately secured by the *βδέλυγμα* or *abominatio* of the ancient translators, so that of מְשֹׁמֵם, by which it denotes "ravager or desolation," is evidently established by their *ἐρήμωσις*. This rendering may be substantiated by a comparison with שֹׁמֵמוֹת in the preceding verse, and also with שְׁמֹמוֹת in Ezek. xxxvi. 3 (cf. שָׁמֵם, "to be desolate, uninhabited," Lam. i. 4; 2 Sam. xiii. 20), and accords as well with the context as does the idea of an "object to be stared at, or of terror"—hence "what is terrible, dreadful,"—by which Hitzig, Ewald, *et al.*, prefer to render the term (by virtue of a one-sided application of the fund. meaning of שׁמם, "to stare, shudder"). If these considerations are accordingly sufficient to establish for שִׁקּוּץ מְשֹׁמֵם the sense of "abomination of desolation" = "desolating abomination of idolatry, hideously devastating nature of the idolatrous service," there remains only the difficult וְעַל כְּנַף to be interpreted. The ancient versions are agreed in rendering כנף by *ἱερόν*, *templum*, and also in not connecting it as a *stat. constr.* with the following term, but taking it separately as a *stat. absol.*, and reading it כָּנָף. It might be difficult to raise any material objection against this departure from the Masoret. punctuation, since it is only too easy to conceive of כנף as a *stat. constr.*, and thus reach the ordinary reading, in view of the temptation to obtain the sense of "wings of abomination, hideous wings," which is suggested by passages like Zech. v. 1, 9. Moreover, the interpretation of כנף by "sanctuary" has an almost irresistible though indirect support in the *πτερύγιον τοῦ ἱεροῦ* of Matt. iv. 5. כָּנָף, in itself equivalent to "screen, covering, roof" (from which fund. meaning all others, *e.g.*, wing, tassel, edge, border, etc., are readily derived), might without difficulty become the customary term to designate *the roof of the temple* or the "pinnacle of the temple" (Matt., l. c.), and afterward be applied, with equal adaptation, to the *entire edifice* of the temple (in view of its elevated site and its prominent buildings), by virtue of a synecdoche analogous to that which prevails in the Latin with reference to *tectum*, and in the Greek (cf. Matt. viii. 8) in the use of *στέγη*. If this view should not seem objectionable, it will not be necessary to limit the sense of כנף so as to apply to the roof-pinnacle, summit, or highest point of the temple (Gesenius, Hengstenberg, etc.), nor yet to violently amend וְעַל כְּנַף by supplying וּבְהֵיכָל, with J. D. Michaelis. It will then be possible to render it simply by, "and on the wing, *i. e.*, the temple," and to regard the "desolating idolatrous abominations found on it as any symbols or utensils of idolatrous worship whatever, whether idols, altars erected to their worship, or other similar fixtures. See especially Bleek, *Jahrb. f. d. Theol.*, 1860, p. 93 et seq.* — We adduce, by way of illustration merely, several of the more recent and noticeable of the many interpretations rejected in favor of the above (with reference to which Hitzig, p. 168, observes somewhat coarsely, but not without wit, and, were he to assign to his own a principal place among them, not incorrectly, that "the expositors themselves are here lying-in in the weeks, and being delivered of all manner of שִׁקּוּצִים"). Hitzig interprets, "and annihilation, even to its full consummation, is poured out on the extreme point of the horrible abomination" (by which expression is designated the idolatrous altar, which, according to 1 Macc. i. 59, was erected on the altar of burnt-offerings by Antiochus); Ewald, "and above shall be the horrible wing of abominations," *i. e.*, "the wing-shaped (! ?) point of the heathen altar shall appear over" the ruined altar of Jehovah; Wieseler, "and a desolator shall arise against the wing of abominations;" Von Lengerke, "the desolator comes upon the pinnacle of abomination" (also Hengstenberg, Maurer, Reinke); de Wette, "the abomination of the desolator shall stand on the pinnacle of the temple;" Hävernick, "on the head (or summit) of the abominations is a desolator;" Auberlen, "and because of the desolating wing of abominations . . . . the curse (?) shall drop down upon the desolate;" Delitzsch, "and indeed, because of the desolating wing of abominations (which spreads over the temple and the altar), the sacrifice shall be abolished;" Hofmann, "and upon the covering of the desolating idolatrous institutions (*i.e.*, on the new plate which Antiochus caused to be placed on the profaned altar with a view to the offering of heathen sacrifices) the sacrifice shall be interrupted for half a week;" Füller, "and over the covering of abominations stands a desolator;" Ebrard,

* [The author's construction of the words in question, although sanctioned by such early authority, is wholly ungrammatical. There is but one translation possible: *On a wing of abominations* shall be *a desolator*. The כּנף aptly designates the *eagles* of the Roman army, which were used as idolatrous images: and the "desolator," which was "over" them, of course, is the army itself or the commander. This is in pointed agreement with our Lord's warning, Matt. xxiv. 15; which, of course, must be regarded as a citation of this passage from the Sept., as *substantially* agreeing with its sense. The fact that the destruction of the city and temple by Titus did not immediately follow the Crucifixion is no objection to this interpretation of the clause, which is altogether parallel, both in import and phraseology, with the close of the preceding verse.]

* [Bleek, in the passage here cited, shows, as Keil well argues, that כנף is "used only of that which is extended horizontally (for end or extremity), but never of that which is extended perpendicularly (for peak)." Nor, as Keil continues, can the use of it in the latter sense be proved from the **πτερύγιον** of Matt. iv. 5; Luke iv. 9; for the genitive **τοῦ ἱεροῦ**, not **ναοῦ**, shows that not a pinnacle or summit of the temple edifice itself is meant, but a wing or adjoining building of the sanctuary. To the latter alone, indeed, could access have been had by our Lord on the occasion referred to.]

Kliefoth, "and a destroyer comes on the wings of idolatrous abominations" (so formerly Reichel, *Stud. u. Kritiken*, 1848, and also Kranichfeld [and substantially Keil]); Jahn, *Hermeneutic. Append.*, p. 161), Gesenius (*Thesaur.*), "desolation comes upon the horrible wing of the rebel's host;" [Stuart, "and a waster shall be over a winged fowl of abominations," *i.e.*, the winged statue of Jupiter Olympius placed by Antiochus in the temple], etc.—**Even until the consummation, and that determined shall be poured upon the desolate**; rather, "but (only) until extirpation and judicial punishment shall be poured out upon the desolator," *i.e.*, the abomination of desolation shall continue only until the Divinely determined judgment shall be poured out upon the desolator. The וְ in וְעַד may be rendered by "and indeed" (as וְ *epexegeticum*), or by "but yet;" in either case this closing sentence serves to *limit* the idea. It points out, in a comforting manner, how long the abomination of desolation should continue in the sanctuary, certifying that it could be maintained no longer than the providence of God should permit.* "The thought that the events of the entire period of severe tribulation in question are controlled by a Divine decree which predetermines their end and results was already expressed for the comfort of the pious in the נֶחֱרֶצֶת שֹׁמֵמוֹת of v. 26, and was also implied by יֶחְתַּךְ, v. 24" (Kranichfeld). The combination כָּלָה וְנֶחֱרָצָה is taken verbatim from Isa. x. 23; xxviii. 22, and signifies, as in those passages, "utter extinction (annihilation) and consummation,"—a hendiadys which denotes a "Divinely determined annihilation, extirpation imposed as a judicial punishment." This two-fold idea forms a unit in the intimate blending of its shades of meaning, and is the subject of the verb תִּתַּךְ; for עַד is not in this instance a preposition governing the two substantives, but a conjunction, signifying "until that," as elsewhere עַד־אֲשֶׁר; cf. Gen. xxxviii. 11; Hos. x. 12. The annihilation that was determined "drops down, is poured out" on the שֹׁמֵם, the impious desolator, as the curse and the oath were to descend upon the guilty Israelites, v. 11; cf. שֶׁטֶף, which does not materially differ from כָּלָה וְנֶחֱרָצָה; as has already been shown.—שֹׁמֵם, the Kal participle of שָׁמֵם, is probably equivalent in substance to מְשֹׁמֵם, the Piel partic. of the same verb (cf. chap. viii. 13; xii. 11 with chap. xi. 31).† Like that, it signifies "desolating, the desolating (agent), desolation," and probably does not primarily designate the person of the antichrist, but rather both antichrist and his host (cf. v. 26, "the people of a prince")—hence, the aggregate of the power that opposed God led Israel into apostasy and desecrated its sanctuary, and upon which the Divine judgment was for that reason poured out. Hitzig arbitrarily remarks (as did Ewald and Hofmann before him) that שֹׁמֵם does not designate the tyrant who resisted God, but rather the idol-altar erected by him or the heathen religion generally, against which destruction and judgment are here denounced, as being horrible to any Israelite in its nature.

APPENDIX

Relating to the history of the exposition of **vs.** 24–27.

1. *Jewish exposition* in pre-Christian times is united in referring this section to the Maccabæan æra of tribulation under Antiochus Epiphanes. This is established beyond controversy by the βδέλυγμα ἐρομώσεως of 1 Macc. i. 54, which corresponds to שִׁקּוּצִים מְשֹׁמֵם, v. 27, and in that place denotes the smaller idol-altar (βωμός, v. 59) erected by Antiochus Epiphanes on the altar of burnt-offerings. It is no less clearly indicated by the manner in which the Sept. renders this paragraph, and supplements it with various additions that obviously relate to the Maccabæan period. In this connection the mode of expressing the time indicated at the beginning of v. 26 is especially instructive. "And after threescore and two weeks," reads in that version, "μετὰ ἑπτὰ καὶ ἑβδομήκοντα καὶ ἑξήκοντα δύο," *i.e.*, after 139 (67 + 62) years. This was doubtless intended to designate the year 139 of the æra of the Seleucidæ (B.C. 174) as the time at which began the apostasy of the Jews who had been seduced by Antiochus; cf. 1 Macc. i. 11 et seq.; 2 Macc. iv. 9 et seq. See also Wieseler, *Die 70 Wochen*, etc., p. 201; Hävernick, *Komment.*, p. 387 et seq.—Several expressions in the New Test. appear to indicate that shortly before the advent of Christ the Jews again began to look for the fulfilment of the prophecy in question *in the future; e.g.*, Luke ii. 38 (cf. v. 24), προσδεχόμενοι λύτρωσιν Ἱερουσαλήμ; Matt. xi. 3, ὁ ἐρχόμενος, a designation of the Messiah that probably originated in a misunderstanding of הַבָּא in v. 26 (cf. Wieseler, p. 150); and also the allusions to the "abomination of desolation," v. 27, contained in the eschatological prophecies uttered by the Saviour (Matt. xxiv. 15; Mark xiii. 14) and by St. Paul (2 Thess. ii. 3 et seq.), which could only be understood by their contemporaries, in case a Messianic character were assigned to the paragraph before us, and consequently, in case its fulfilment were not exclusively looked for in the events of the Maccabæan period.*—Jose-

* [Rather, it shows that the abominable object should remain *even till* the complete desolation. Keil's objection to the use of וְעַד as a conjunction, that "though עַד is so used, וְעַד is not," has little force.]

† [Such a confusion of Kal and Piel is quite unauthorized. שׁוֹמֵם must here, as everywhere else, be treated as passive, *desolate*. It is certainly parallel with שׁוֹמְמוֹת of the preceding verse, as the connection with נחרצה in both instances shows.]

* Cf. the observation of Melancthon on the passage, which is certainly not incorrect upon the whole (p. 882): "*Ac Judæis quidem post Danielem facilis fuit observatio annorum, præsertim quum in eo populo sacerdotes tempora diligenter annotarent et multi essent longævi. Nehemias, qui Danielem senem viderat adolescens, Alexandrum senex vidit* (?) . . . . *Simeon qui Christum infantem gestavit in sinu, vidit adolescens senes, qui Maccabæum viderant. Tales viri tempore, quo Christus natus est, intellexerant, annos hic præfinitos exacte quadrare ad Christi adventum.*"

phus also bears witness that this Messianic-eschatological interpretation was current among the Jews of his day, in the repeated instances where he states, or at least implies, that the terrible incidents connected with the Jewish war and the destruction of Jerusalem by the Romans were predicted by the prophet Daniel; *e.g.*, *Ant.*, X. 11, 7: "Daniel also wrote concerning the Roman government, and that our country should be made desolate by them (ὅτι ὑπ' αὐτων ἐρημωθήσεται);" *De Bell. Jud.*, IV. 5, 2, where he applies the term "anointed one," v. 26, and again the expression "anointed one and prince," v. 25, to the high priest Ananus whom the Idumæans murdered; and *De Bell. Jud.*, VI. 5, 4, where the mysterious oracle "that then should their city be taken, when their temple should become four-square" seems to refer back to v. 27 (where they perhaps read רָבוּעַ instead of שָׁבוּעַ), etc. It is less certain whether any direct reference to this section is contained in the celebrated passage, *De Bell. Jud.*, VI., 5, 4, ὡς κατὰ τὸν καιρὸν ἐκεῖνον ἀπὸ τῆς χώρας τις αὐτῶν ἄρξει τῆς οἰκουμένης. In that case the parallel records in Tacitus, *Hist.*, V. 13 and Suet., *Vesp.*, 4, must, of course, be likewise rooted in the prophecy of Daniel that is before us. Concerning this question see Hävernick, p. 390; who, however, probably finds too much in the passage, since he refers the ἄρξει τῆς οἰκουμέν. directly to the נָגִיד of v. 25 and 26.*

2. The interpretation of Josephus, which applies the prophecy to the destruction of Jerusalem in A.D. 70 and to Titus as the נָגִיד הַבָּא, v. 26, seems to have been accepted, with scarcely an exception, by the *later Jews* of the Talmudic æra and the time immediately subsequent. The principal witness to this fact is Jerome (on v. 24 et seq.; *T. V.*, 2 ed. Vallars., p. 694). The "Hebræi" of his day calculated the 490 years or seventy weeks of years from the first year of Darius or B.C. 539 indeed, but none the less assigned their conclusion to the age of Jesus, even finding his death predicted therein (probably in the יִכָּרֵת מָשִׁיחַ, v. 26), since they held that "*non erit illius imperium, quod putabat se redemturum*" (as it should be read, instead of "*quod putabant se retenturos*," which is a later emendation). They also found a prediction of the approach of the Roman army under Vespasian and Titus, in the same place. Several added even the rising under Barcocheba or the three years' (three and a half years) war against Hadrian: "*Nec ignoramus, quosdam illorum dicere, quod una hebdomada, de qua scriptum est: confirmabit pactum multis hebdomada una, dividatur Vespasiano et Hadriano, quod juxta historiam Josephi Vespasianus et Titus tribus annis et sex mensibus pacem cum Judæis fecerint. Tres autem anni et sex menses sub Hadriano supputantur, quando Hierusalem omnino subversa est, et Judæorum gens catervatim cæsa, ita ut Judææ quoque finibus pellerentur.*"—The two Gemaras also refer this prophecy to the war against Vespasian; the Babylonian in *Nasir*, c. 5; *Sanhedr.*, c. 11, and the Jerusalem in *Kelim*, c. 9; and several Talmudic and Rabbinical traditions are likewise based on that interpretation, *e.g.*, that the Targumist had neglected to translate the Hagiographa, because it was taught in them that "the Messiah should be cut off" (v. 26. See Lightfoot, *Hor. Hebr.* ad Luc. xix. 11; Schöttgen, *Hor. Hebr.*, p. 211); and that the Messiah actually came at the time when Jerusalem was destroyed and the temple desolated, but as a sufferer and in disguise (Glæsener, *De gemin. Jud. Mess.*, p. 23 ss.; Corrodi, *Krit. Gesch. des Chilias mus*, I. 284 et seq.).—It was reserved for the later period of the middle ages to introduce several new and more independent explanations beside this variously modified Messianic interpretation of the prophecy; *e.g.*, by referring the מָשִׁיחַ נָגִיד to Cyrus (Saad. Gaon., Rashi, Jacchiad.), or to Nehemiah (Ibn-Ezra) or the high-priest Joshua (Levi b.-Gers.). Cf. Müller, *Judaism*, pp. 321, 342 et seq.; Carpzov, in his ed. of Raymond Martini's *Pugio fidei*, p. 233.—It was customary to follow the Seder Olam Rabba in reckoning the seventy weeks from the first destruction of the temple to the second; see Abendana, in the *Spicileg. ad Michl. Jophi*: "*Hebdomades hæ sept. sunt septimanæ annorum quadringentorum nonaginta, iidemque sine dubio a devastatione primi ad devastationem secundi templi, quia sept. anni fuere captivitatis Babylonicæ, et quadringenti viginti anni, quibus futura erit domus secunda in structura sua: atque sic majores nostri exposuere in Seder Olam.*" By this method of reckoning, the מֹצָא דָבָר, v. 25, is accordingly made to apply to the period of Jeremiah's prophecy respecting the seventy years' exile or to the year B.C. 588. Ibn-Ezra alone departs from this method, by referring that expression concerning the going forth of the oracle (v. 23) *to Daniel*, and consequently assigning the beginning of the 490 years to the year B.C. 539 and extending the first seven weeks of years belonging to that period, to Nehemiah, the restorer of the temple, or to the twentieth year of Artaxerxes. Concerning these Rabbinical methods of reckoning, and at the same time, concerning their fundamental incorrectness and untenable character in a chronological point of view, cf. Chr. B. Michaelis, *Annot. uberior*, III. 320 et seq. Individual Rabbins in modern times were convinced of the incorrectness of this usual anti-Messianic interpretation, as appears from the noteworthy expression of the Venetian chief-Rabbin Simon Luzzato, concerning this passage, as recorded by Wolf in the *Biblioth. Hebr.*, III. 1228. According to him, "the consequence of a too extended and profound investigation on the part of Jewish scholars would be that they would all become Christians; for it cannot be denied that according to Daniel's limitation of the time, the Messiah must have already appeared. But that Jesus was the true Messiah he felt himself unable to accept as certain."

3. *The Christian expositors of the older time* regarded the directly Messianic bearing of the passage as being generally incontrovertible, and especially the application of יִכָּרֵת מָשִׁיחַ to Christ the crucified, as also the reference of the "restoring and building" of the city and temple in v. 25 to the establishing of the church of the New Covenant; cf. Barnabas, *Ep.*, c. 16;

* [It is perhaps to these prophecies of Daniel in a general way that Josephus likewise alludes in the references to an ancient prediction that the city should be destroyed in a civil war, *De Bell. Jud.*, IV. 6, 3; VI., 2, 1.]

γέγραπται γὰρ καὶ ἔσται, ἑβδομάδης συντελουμένης, οἰκοδομηθήσεται ναὸς θεοῦ ἐνδόξως ἐπὶ τῷ ὀνόματι κυρίου, κτλ. The different exegetes varied exceedingly, however, in the mode of reckoning the years.* Jerome, on this passage, already mentions nine different methods of explaining them: (1) that of Jul. Africanus, who reckoned the 490 years from Nehemiah, or the 20th year of Artaxerxes, to the death of Christ, but in connection with this committed the error of reckoning by Jewish lunar years (resulting in only 465 solar years); (2) Three different theories of Eusebius, who (*a*) dates the first sixty-nine weeks from the return of the Jews in the reign of Cyrus to the death of Alexander Jannæus, the high priest and king, and Pompey's invasion (B.C. 536–B.C. 64; thus in *Dem. ev.*, VIII. 2, 55 et seq.); or (*b*) from the second year of Darius Hystaspis (B.C. 520 to the birth of Christ (ibid. and *Chronic.*, Ol. 184); or, (*c*) regards the last week as a period of seventy years, and attempts to calculate from the resurrection of Christ; (3) that of Hippolytus, who counted sixty-nine mystical weeks (comprising more than seven years each) from the first year of Cyrus to the incarnation of Christ, and declared that the *last* mystical week denotes the future period of the antichrist, which is connected with the end of the world; (4) that of Apollinaris of Laodicea, who reckoned the 490 years from the birth of Christ ("*ab exitu Verbi*," v. 25), and therefore expected the coming of the antichrist and the end of the world about a century after his day, in the "last week;" (5) that of Clemens Alex. who extended the seventy weeks of years, in the face of all chronology, from the first year of Cyrus to the second year of Vespasian (B.C. 560–A.D. 70); (6) that of Origen, who denies the possibility of any more exact chronological estimate, and therefore assumes 4900 years instead of 490, reaching from Adam to the destruction of Jerusalem by Titus (not indeed in vol. X. of his *Stromata*, which Jerome cites, but in his *Tract. XXIV.* on Matthew c, 24); (7) that of Tertullian (*adv. Judæos*, c. 8), who reckons the 437½ years from the first year of Darius Nothus (whom he strangely identifies with Darius Medus) to the birth of Christ, and fifty-two and a half from that event to the destruction of Jerusalem, thus obtaining 490.—Jerome himself expresses no opinion respecting the mode of reckoning to be observed, but seems to favor that of Africanus, which he preferred to all the others, and probably not without reason. That method is likewise adopted by Chrysostom, Theodoret, Isidore of Pelusium, Euthymius Zigabenus, and generally by a majority of expositors in the Oriental church, but few of whom assume an independent position. Among the latter are, *e.g.*, Cyril of Jerusalem (*Catech.* xii. 19), who attempts to extend the seventy weeks of years from the sixth year of Darius Medus to the birth of Christ, but violates historical accuracy by identifying Darius Medus with Darius Hystaspis; Ephraem Syrus who places the restoration of Jerusalem in the beginning of the seventieth week and the destruction by Titus at its close, without entering on a more careful calculation in other respects; Polychronius, a brother of Theodore of Mopsuestia, who reckons the first seven weeks from Darius Medus to the ninth year of Darius Hystaspis, when Zerubbabel's temple is said to have been completed, the sixty-two weeks from the twentieth year of Artaxerxes to the birth of Christ, and the final week from that date to Titus, while the death of Christ falls in its central point; Basil of Seleucia (*Orat.*, 38 in t. 85 of Migne's *Patrol.*), who calculates the first sixty-nine weeks from the completion of the walls of Jerusalem in the twenty-eighth year of Xerxes (!) to the resurrection of Christ, and identifies the seventieth week with the first seven years after the resurrection, while he declares the abomination of desolation erected in the middle of that week to have been the familiar attempt of Caligula to erect his image in the temple.—Among the later expositors of the Latin church, Augustine, following the example of Jerome, avoids every independent and detailed calculation of the seventy weeks. He contents himself with finding a fulfilment of the leading features of the prophecy Dan. ix. 24 et seq., in the earthly work of Christ and in the judgment of Jerusalem, and expressly rejects (especially in *Ep.* 199 "*de fine sæculii*") the opinion of those who looked for two periods of seventy weeks of years, the first of which should reach to Christ's advent in the flesh, and the second to the end of the world. This assumption of a double period of seventy weeks of years, or of an Old-Test. and typical realization of the prophecy, followed by a New-Test. antitypical fulfilment, was advocated as late as the sixth century by the unknown Arian author of the so-called *Opus imperfectum in Matthæum.* Sulpicius Severus (*Chron.*, II. 21) extends the sixty-nine weeks from the thirty-second year of Artaxerxes I. to Vespasian, or from the restoration of the temple to its second destruction. His contemporary, Julius Hilarianus, appears in his *Chronologia s. libellus de mundi duratione* (in Migne, t. 13, p. 1098) as the forerunner of the modern critical exposition, in consequence of his denial of the direct Messianic character of the prophecy, whose fulfilment he places in the age of Antiochus and the Maccabees; but he commits the gross chronological blunder of assigning 434 years (= 62 weeks) to the interval between the return of the Jews under Zerubbabel and the reign of Antiochus Epiphanes, while the period between B.C. 536 and B.C. 175 really amounts to but 361 years! Prosper Aquitan in his *Chronicon* adopts the view advocated by Eusebius in the *Demonstr. evangelica* and the *Chron.* (see supra, No. 2 *b*), and accordingly reckons the sixty-nine weeks from the building of the temple under Darius to Herod the Gr. and the birth of Christ. Finally, the venerable Bede adopts substantially the view of Julius Africanus (*Libell. de temporum ratione*, c. 7), as does also Thomas Aquinas (*Comm. in Dan.*, in *Opp.*, t. XIII. ed. Antverp).

* On this point, cf. Reusch, *Die patristischen Berechnungen der 70 Jahrwochen Daniels*, in the *Tübinger Theol. Quartalschrift*, 1868, No. iv., p. 535 et seq.: also Reinke, *Die Messianischen Weissagungen*, iv. 1, 389 et seq. The statements of the latter are, however, sadly in need of correction and supplementing by those of Reusch.

[In addition to Reusch's treatise, Keil refers to the following summaries: "for the period of the Middle Ages and of more modern times, Abr. Colovii Ἐξέτασις *theologica de septuaginta septimanis Danielis.* in the *Biblia illustr. ad* Dan. ix., and Hävernick's 'History of the Interpretation,' in his *Comment.*, p. 386 sq.; and for the most recent period, R. Baxmann, 'on the Book of Daniel,' in the *Theolog. Studien u. Kritiken*, 1863, III., p. 497 sq."]

4. *The expositors of modern times*, and more particularly of pre-rationalistic times, are agreed in recognizing the Messianic bearing of this prophecy, but differ exceedingly in their modes of reckoning the seventy weeks, or, what amounts to the same thing, in their interpretations of מֹצָא דָבָר, v. 25.* As the *terminus a quo* of the seventy weeks they accept one of the following dates:

a. The time of the *first* prophecy by Jeremiah (Jer. xxv. 11 et seq.), or the fourth year of Jehoiakim's reign; thus Harduin (*Chronol. Vet. Test.*, Amstel., 1709, p. 592 ss.); A. Calmet (*Dissert. sur les 70 semaines de Daniel*, *Dissertt.*, p. 1); A. Collins (*The scheme of liberal prophecy*, I. 109).

b. The time of Jeremiah's *second* prophecy (Jer. xxix. 10) or the fourth year of Zedekiah; so Seb. Münster, Vatablus (and also several expositors belonging to the last centuries in the Middle Ages, *e.g.*, Lyranus, in the *Postilla*, Raym. Martini, *Pugio fid.*, 2, 269, etc.).

c. The date of Daniel's prophecy itself (chap. ix. 1), and hence the first year of the reign of Darius Medus over Babylon, B. C. 539; so J. H. Jungmann (Cassel, 1681); J. Koch (*Entsiegelter Daniel*, II., § 206, and *Kurze Anfangsgründe der Chronologie*, II. 24), J. D. Michaelis (*Versuch über die 70 Wochen Daniels*, Gött. and Gotha, 1770; cf. his *Epistola de Septuag. hebdom. ad Jo. Pringle*, London, 1773); Matth. Hassenkamp (*Versuch einer neuen Erklärung der 70 Wochen Daniels*, Lemgo, 1772); Velthusen (*Muthmassungen über die siebenmal siebenzig Jahre beim Daniel* ix. 24–27, Hanover, 1774).

d. The first year of the reign of Cyrus, B.C. 560; Calvin, Œcolampadius, l'Empereur, Cocceius, Matth. Bervaldus (*Chronicon ss. auctoritate constitutum*, III. 7), B. Blayney (*A dissertation by way of Inquiry into Daniel's seventy Weeks*, Oxford, 1775), H. Uri (*Sept. hebdomadum, quas Gabriel ad Danielem detulerat, interpretatio, paraphrasis, computatio*, Oxford, 1788), also Dathe, Hegel, etc., in their commentaries.

e. The second year of the reign of Darius Hystaspis (B.C. 520), or the year of the prophecies of blessing by Haggai (i. 1 et seq.; ii. 1 et seq.) and Zechariah (i. 1 et seq.; iii. 8 et seq.; viii. 7 et seq.); so J. Driedo (*De scriptis et dogmatibus ecclesiasticis*, c. 5), Corn. Jansen (*Concord. evangel.*, c. 122), J. A. Bengel (*Ordo temporum*, etc., Stuttgart, 1741).

f. The *second* year of the reign of Darius Nothus (B.C. 423); so J. J. Scaliger (*De emendat. temporum*, l. 4), S. Calvisius (*Opus chronologicum*).

g. The second year of the reign of Artaxerxes Longimanus; so Luther (*D. Prophet Daniel deutsch*, etc., vol. 41, p. 247, ed. Erl.), Melancthon (*Comm.* p. 891), Sal. Glossius (*Philol. sacra*).

h. The *seventh* year of Artaxerxes Longimanus, or the date of the first decree by this king to rebuild Jerusalem (Ezra vii. 1; viii. 11 et seq.); so Abr. Calov (*De Septuag. septimanis mysterium*, Viteb., 1663; *Bibl. illustr.*, I., p. 119 ss.), M. Geier, in the *Comm.*, Isaac Newton (*Observations*, etc.), J. R. Rus (*Diss. de Sept. hebdom. Danielis*, Jenæ, 1740), H. Benzel (*Diss. de 70 hebdd. Danielis*, in the *Syntagma dissertatt.*, II., 21 ss.), H. Prideaux (*Connections*, etc.), Alex. Sostmann (*Comment. chronol. philol. et exeget. in orac. Dan.* ix. 24–27, Lugd. B. 1710), S. Deyling (*Progr. ad Dan.* ix. 24 ss., Lips., 1724), J. G. Franck (*Novum systema chronologiæ fundamentalis*, Gött., 1778), J. C. Döderlein (*Institutt. Theol. chr.*, II., p. 530 ss.).

i. The *twentieth* year of Artaxerxes Longimanus, or the date of the *second* edict by that king (Neh. ii. 1, 7 et seq.); so Luther (*Dass Jesus Christus ein geborner Jude sei*, vol. 29, p. 71 et seq., ed. Erl.),* H. J. Offerhaus (*Dissertat. de 70 septimanis Danielis*, Groning., 1756), J. G. Reinbeck (*Betrachtungen über die Augsb. Konfession*, III., 39), S. S. Weickhmann (*Carmen Danielis de 70 hebdd. Christo vindicat.*, Prog., Viteb., 1772), Starke (*Synops.*, p. 2614).

k. The *tenth* or *eleventh* year of Artaxerxes Longimanus, or the earlier date by about ten years assigned to his second edict, on the ground of his co-regency with his father Xerxes; so Dion. Petavius (*Doctrina tempp.*, L. 12, c. 29; *Rationarium tempp.*, II., 3, c. 9), Camp. Vitringa (*De Septuag. hebdom. Dan. advers. Marshamum, Observatt. sacr.*, II., p. 290 ss.), C. B. Michaelis (in *Annott. uberior.*, etc.).

l. The second year of the reign of Xerxes; so J. E. Faber (*Jesus ex natalium opportunitate Messias*, Jenæ, 1772, p. 125 ss.).

A great difference of opinion prevailed also with reference to the particular *terminus ad quem* of the prophecy referred to Christ, inasmuch as (*a*) some, following Eusebius, Cyril of Jerusalem, Jacob of Edessa, and other ancient churchly expositors, extended the seventy weeks merely to the death of Christ, others (*b*) continued them to the time of his presentation in the temple (Jungmann, Sostmann, etc.), others (*c*) to his baptism in the Jordan or to his anointing (Melancthon, Calvin, Vitringa; also W. Whiston, *Dissertation upon Daniel's weeks*, London, 1725), still others (*d*) to the year of our Lord's death (Luther, Calov, Prideaux, Buddeus, *H. Eccl. Vet. Ti.*, p. 854 ss.), and others finally (*e*) included the more general spread of the Gospel in the years immediately following the Saviour's death in the series of the seventy weeks (Petavius, Bengel, J. Brunsmann, etc.).—Various methods were adopted in order to obviate, by means of exact calculation, the discrepancy between the *termin. a quo* and *ad quem*, which was either too large or too small. According to Bertholdt, p. 574 et seq., they may be designated as follows:

(1). The method of *parallelism* by which the seven and the sixty-two weeks were reckoned from the same point of time, or by which these periods were not regarded as successive in their order, but as contemporaneous with each other (Harduin, Jungmann, Collins, Marsham, etc.).

(2). The method of *intercalation* which consisted in interpolating intervals of greater or less extent between the several periods of hebdomads, and especially between the sixty-ninth and seventieth weeks (l'Empereur, Newton, Koch, Beer, Uri, etc.).

(3). The method of *tranposition* by which the first two periods of hebdomads were enum-

* Cf. Bertholdt, *Daniel*, II. p., 567 et seq.

* Luther, however, confounds Artaxerxes I., who figures in the book of Nehemiah, with Cambyses, cf. also the work, *Von den Juden und ihren Lügen*, vol. 32, pp. 195 et seq., 212 et seq.

erated in inverted order, *i.e.*, the sixty-two first, and the seven afterward (thus, in imitation of Tertullian, Theodoret, etc., some of the most recent expositors, especially Hofmann, Delitzsch, Wieseler, etc.).

(4). The *analogical* method which estimates the hebdomads in the several sections by an unequal standard, *e.g.*, regarding the seventieth week as a "*septimana magna*" or Jubilee period of forty-nine years (Newton, Frank; similarly Calmet, A. Kluit [*Vaticinium de Messia duce primarium s. explic. Sept. hebdd. Dan.*, Mediol., 1774], and already many of the church fathers mentioned above, as Eusebius, Polychronius, etc.).

(5). The method of reckoning *by lunar years* of 354 days, without an intercalated month (Hassenkamp and J. D. Michaelis—after the precedent of Jul. Africanus and his patristic successors).

(6). The method of counting *by jubilee periods* of fifty years each, by which the seventy years appear to be exactly equal to 500 years (Sostmann and others).

(7). The method of reckoning by Chaldee years of 360 days, by which the seventy hebdomads are reduced to 483 years (Pet. Brinch, *Diss. chronol.-critica de 70 hebdomadd. Danielis*, Hafn., 1702).

(8). The *mystical* method of enumeration, which seeks either to limit or extend the seventy weeks of years by the use of a year of any abnormal and mystical length. Hippolytus and others led the way in the ancient church in this method; and following them we have J. J. Hainlinus (*Clavis sacror. temporum*, Tüb., 1692, and *Sol temporum s. Chronol. mystica*, Tüb., 1647); Bengel, Thube, Crusius (*Hypomnemata in theologiam propheticam*). Among them Hainlin assumed shorter years than the ordinary, giving them 343 days each, and thus obtained 460 Julian years for the seventy weeks. Bengel, Thube, etc., on the other hand, sought to amplify, and therefore fixed the length of a mystical year at $1\frac{5}{441}$ solar years, and thus obtained $555\frac{5}{9}$ years for the period of seventy weeks.

5. *The critico-rationalistic* or *anti-Messianic* expositors of recent times may be divided into two principal classes:

A. That of the *emendators who adopt a violent* course, and seek to remove the chronological difficulty by means of exegetical or critical assumptions of a more or less arbitrary character, *e.g.*, (1) by the assertion that the seventy weeks are ordinary weeks and therefore 490 days, and extended from the day of the vision to the time of Cyrus and of laying the foundations of the temple (thus the Eng.-work, *A free Inquiry into Daniel's vision or Prophecy of the Seventy Weeks*, London, 1776; cf. Bertholdt, p. 554 et seq.); (2) by the assertion that Daniel, who wrote after the time of Cyrus, predicted to the people an impending second destruction of the recently restored temple in this prophecy, which was therefore not fulfilled (Eckermann, *Theol. Beiträge*, I. 1, p. 132 et seq.); (3) by the assumption that vs. 25–27 are *the gloss of some rabbi* (Franz Löwenheim, *Inquisitio critica exegetica in diffi- cult. proph. Dan.*, c. ix., etc. Wirceb., 1787); (4) by several less important changes in the reading of v. 24 or 25, such as were proposed by Schmidt (in Paulus' *Memorabilia*, VII., 41 et seq.), Velthusen, J. D. Michaelis, Jahn, et al. The first (with whom Baumgarten-Crusius agrees, *Bibl. Theol.*, p. 370) reads v. 24, שִׁבְעִים שִׁבְעִים, "seventy, yea, seventy years" (which is intended to indicate the duration of the exile), and then translates v. 25, "from the present time to the Messiah are seventy, seven, sixty, and two weeks," which is interpreted to mean that "twice seventy years may elapse before his advent" (!). Velthusen (*Muthmassungen über die siebenmal 70 Jahre des Daniel*, Hanover, 1774) reads v. 25 שִׁבְעִים שְׁבָעָה שִׁבְעִים. J. D. Michaelis (*Versuch über die 70 Jahrwochen Daniels*, Gött., 1771) emends the same passage so as to read שִׁבְעִים שִׁבְעָה וְשִׁבְעִים. Jahn (*Herm. sacra*, Append., t. I.), on the other hand, reads v. 24, like Schmidt, שִׁבְעִים שִׁבְעִים (the seventy years of the captivity), and then renders v. 25 שִׁבְעִים שִׁבְעָה (70 × 7 or 490 years, which reach from Cyrus to B.C. 64), and adds in addition וְשִׁבְעִים שִׁשִּׁים וּשְׁנַיִם (*i.e.*, seventy years, to A.D. 7 or 8, and sixty-two years, to the destruction of Jerusalem by Titus).

B. The more considerate and scientific expositors of the critical school conceive of the passage as belonging to the times of Antiochus Epiphanes, and as a *Vaticinium ex eventu* relating to that age. In this view they were preceded by numerous Jewish and a few Christian representatives of the Maccabæan interpretation (*e.g.*, by Julius Hilarianus, about A.D. 400; by Marsham, an Englishman [*Canon chron.*, p. 610 ss.], the Jesuit Harduin [*Opp. selecta*, p. 592 ss.; cf. Köhler, *De Harduin nova sed inepta interpretatione vatic. apud Dan. de 70 hebd.*, Altorf, 1721], and the English free-thinker Ant. Collins [*Scheme of Literal Prophecy*, Lond., 1726]). So Corrodi (*Krit. Gesch. des Chiliasmus*, p. 247 et seq., and *Freimüthige Versuche über verschiedene in Theologie und biblische Kritik einschlagende Materien*, p. 42 et seq.), who, however, introduced much that is arbitrary in developing his scheme. He renewed, for instance, the questionable expedient of transposing the weeks [see No. 4 (3)], reckoning first sixty-two hebdomads from the beginning of the captivity to the first invasion of Judæa by Epiphanes, then seven hebdomads from the date of the composition of the book of pseudo-Daniel to the Maccabæan Messiah, who, it is alleged, was expected to appear about the year B.C. 115, and finally inserting a single hebdomad *between* the two former periods, to which last week he assigns the actual persecutions, which involved, *e.g.*, the murder of Onias III., the interruption of the sacrifices, etc.—Another representative of this tendency is Eichhorn (*Allgem. Bibliothek der biblischen Literatur*, III., 761 et seq.) who follows the method by parallelism [No. 4 (1)] rather than that of transposition, calculating the first seven hebdomads *backwards* from the edict of Cyrus in B.C. 536 to the destruction of Jerusalem by Nebuchadnezzar, but reckoning the sixty-two weeks *forward* from the fourth year of Jehoiakim (B.C. 605) to Ant. Epiphanes, and the final week from the death of Onias to the restoration of the temple services by Judas Maccabæus.—Eichhorn's hypothesis found an adherent in v. Ammon, who adopted it in his *Biblische Theologie* (II. 217 et seq.) with but few changes; but Bertholdt opposed it with keen criticism, and advanced instead the following explanation: "seventy weeks of years are determined upon the Jews until the expiation of their sin (*i.e.*, to the dedication of the temple by Judas Maccabæus), and, more particularly, from the destruction of Jerusalem by Nebuchadnezzar to the reign of Cyrus, forty-nine years or seven weeks of years; within a period of sixty-two further weeks of years Jerusalem is to be rebuilt (hence to the time of Epiphanes). At about the end of these sixty-two weeks (?!) Alexander the Gr. dies, without leaving a natural successor. Afterward Jerusalem is desolated by Antiochus Epiphanes, who forms an alliance with numerous apostate Jews, that continues during nearly a week of years. At the middle of that week he interrupts the temple services and erects the statue of Jupiter Olympus on a wing of the temple—until death overtakes him." So far as the chronological order of the seven and sixty-two weeks is concerned, this expositor is therefore not a parallelist, but a representative of the theory that they denote successive periods. To obviate the exorbitant interval of sixty-two weeks of years between B.C. 536 and B.C. 175, he assumes that, as a whole, the statements by the oracle respecting time "are not to be taken mathematically, but prophetically and indefinitely" (p. 613)!—Bertholdt's theory is accepted by Griesinger (*Neue Ansicht der Aufsätze im Buch Daniel*, 1815, p. 92) and substantially also by Bleek. The latter (*Theolog. Zeitschr.* of Schleiermacher, de Wette, and Lücke, 1822, and *Jahrbb. f. d. Theologie*, 1860) differs from Bertholdt in several particulars, *e.g.*, in not dating the commencement of the first seven weeks of years from the destruction of Jerusalem, but from the prophetic oracle of Jeremiah, chapters xxv. and xxix., and in extending the sixty-two weeks exactly to the death of Seleucus Philopater (the מָשִׁיחַ without a successor, v. 26). But they are entirely agreed in placing the seven, sixty-two, and one weeks in succession to each other, and in most positively rejecting every parallelism or transposition of these periods, as being contrary to the sense of the vision (*Jahrbb.*, etc., p. 83).—H. L. Reichel (*Die vier Weltreiche des Propheten Daniel*, in the *Theol. Stud. u. Krit.*, 1848) and Kamphausen in Bunsen's *Bibelwerk* advocate views similar to those of Bleek, excepting that the latter holds that the "anointed one" of v. 26 denotes the high priest Onias, instead of Seleucus Philopater. —Several others, however, again made use of parallelisms, *e.g.*, Rösch (*Die 70 Jahrwochen des Buches Daniel, genau chronologisch nachgewiesen*, *Stud. u. Krit.*, 1834), v. Lengerke, and Hitzig. The first takes the year B.C. 609 as the starting-point of the *two* parallel epochs as being the year which the alleged pseudo-Daniel assumed for the destruction of Jerusalem. The seven weeks of years, beginning at that date, were to continue until the commencement of the reign of Cyrus, B.C. 560, and the sixty-two weeks until the death of Seleucus Philopater, the "anointed one who should be cut off;" but this period is lengthened by the addition of eight farther weeks, which reach to B.C. 120 or to John Hyrcanus, the political Messiah of Judaism in the Maccabæan period. Von Lengerke likewise regards the seven and the sixty-two years as being parallel, but dates them from B.C. 588. The sixty- wo were to expire with the murder of Seleucus Philopater, the "anointed one," v. 26 (although this is said to involve an error of 21–22 years in the reckoning of pseudo-Daniel, since the 434 years, if calculated from 588, would, in fact, reach to B.C. 154), and the seventieth week was to reach from 170 to the death of Antiochus in B.C. 164. There is consequently a gap of about six years between the close of the sixty-second week and the beginning of the last! Hitzig subjects this hypothesis of v. Lengerke to a searching criticism, but on his part, likewise adopts an arbitrary explanation based on parallelisms. He (*a*) inserts the seven weeks of years between B.C. 588 and 539; (*b*) the sixty-two weeks or 434 years, on the other hand, are reckoned backward, from B.C. 172 to B.C. 606, the year in which Jeremiah uttered his prophecy respecting the seventy years; (*c*) the seventieth week extends from April, B.C. 170, to the end of March, 164, and the murder of Onias, the "anointed one," v. 26, falls in the beginning of this last week. This hypothesis comes nearest to that of Eichhorn, from which it differs merely in reckoning the seven weeks *forward* from 588, and the sixty-two backward from 172, while Eichhorn counts the seven weeks in a retrograde order, and the sixty-two progressively.—A peculiar mode of reckoning was adopted by Ewald, which may be characterized as the *abbreviating* method. It first reckons the seven weeks of years from B.C. 588 to 539, and the sixty-two weeks from thence to B.C. 105, but then assumes a shortening of the latter period of 434 years by seventy (which reduction, it is alleged, was formerly indicated in the text itself by a note after v. 25 or v. 27 that has now been lost), and by this method returns to the year B.C. 175, in which the "anointed one was cut off," *i.e.*, in which Seleucus Philopater died—and approximately at the same time, the year in which the momentous last week began, which extends from B.C. 174 to 167 (p. 424 et seq.).—Wieseler in substance (in his treatise, *Die 70 Wochen*, formerly followed the method of parallelism etc., Göttingen, 1839), but at a later period preferred a peculiar modification of the transposing method (in his review of the *Times of Daniel*, by the duke of Manchester, *Gött. Gel.-Anz.*, 1846). In the former instance he reckoned the sixty-two weeks from B.C. 606 to B.C. 172, and the last week from 172–165, and regarded the seven weeks as not admissible or to be counted beside the other sixty-three (pp. 102 et seq.; 123 et seq.); but in the latter, while he continues to reckon the sixty-three weeks from B.C. 606–165, he places the seven weeks after them, as representing the period which was to elapse between the week of severe tribulation and the advent of the Messiah (the מָשִׁיחַ נָגִיד, v. 25, who is to be carefully distinguished from the מָשִׁיחַ mentioned in v. 26, where Onias is intended). This period, which must not be calculated with mathematical exactness, but is to be interpreted spiritually, denotes a jubilee cycle, that has grown from a period of fifty years into one of more than 150 years, since Christ was born 160 years after the date of its beginning (p. 131 et seq.). Wieseler's modification of the transposing method may be denominated the *lengthening* hypothesis, in contradistinction from Ewald's abbreviating method. It obviously forms the point of transition to the Messianic conception of the text, and is intimately connected with the views of several representatives of the typical-Messianic interpretation in the latest times.

6. *The most recent Messianic expositors* are divided into two classes, who advocate respectively a direct-Messianic interpretation of the prophecy, or one that is merely typically Messianic.*

A. To the former class belong Less (*Beweis der Wahrheit der christlichen Religion*, p. 275 et seq.), Sack (*Apologetik*, p. 288 et seq.), Scholl (*Commentatio de Sept. hebdomadibus Danielis*, Francof., 1831), Dereser, Hävernick, Hengstenberg, Allioli, Reinke, Stawars, Sepp, Weigl, Auberlen, Duke George of Manchester, Pusey, Kliefoth, etc. [including the great body of English and American expositors, with the almost sole exception of Moses Stuart]. In general, they are agreed in referring both the מָשִׁיחַ נָגִיד, v. 25, and the מָשִׁיחַ, v. 26, to Jesus Christ, but they differ considerably as to the special *terminus a quo* of the prophecy, or its *terminus ad quem*. A majority regard the twentieth year of Artaxerxes Longimanus, or B.C. 455 (Neh. i. 1; ii. 1) as the starting point of the seventy weeks or the date of the מֹצָא דָבָר. They count sixty-nine weeks of years, or 483 years, from that date to the fifteenth year of the reign of Tiberius, twenty-eight ær. Dionysius, or 782 a. u. c. (Luke iii. 1), when the three and a half years of public activity on the part of our Lord began. They consequently place the Saviour's death and resurrection in the middle of the last week, and refer the יִכָּרֵת מָשִׁיחַ וְאֵין לוֹ, v. 26, to his crucifixion. The remaining three and a half years are regarded as a more or less variable terminus, admitting of no precise chronological determination, but rather transpiring indefinitely in the course of the founding of Christianity (so Less, Sack, Scholl, Dereser, Hävernick, Hengstenberg, Allioli, Reinke). Modifications of this theory are advocated (1) by Fr. Stawars (*Die Weissaguny Daniels ix. 24–27 in Bezug auf das Taufjahr Jesu*, in the *Tübinger Theol. Quartalschrift*, 1868, No. III., p. 416 et seq.), who translates מִן מֹצָא דָבָר, v. 25, "from the fulfilment of God's *promise* to rebuild Jerusalem," and contends that that promise was fulfilled in connection with the rebuilding of Jerusalem *as a city*, under Nehemiah, in the year 458; from that time to twenty-six ær. Dionysius 483 years or sixty-nine weeks elapsed, and immediately afterward, in Jan. 27, Jesus was baptized in the Jordan by John; (2) by Auberlen and Pusey, who begin the seventy weeks in B.C. 458, or the seventh year of Artaxerxes Longimanus (Ezra vii. 7), instead of the twentieth year of that reign, and thus obtain the twenty-sixth year of our æra as the close of the sixty-nine weeks, or the time of our Lord's baptism; (3) by Sepp (*Leben Jesu*, I., p. 248 et seq., second ed.), who regards Ezra as the *spiritual* rebuilder of Jerusalem, and therefore reckons from the year B.C. 460, locating the baptism of Jesus in the year 778 a. u. c., or A.D. 25; (4) by Weigl (*Ueber das wahre Geburts- und Sterbe-jahr Jesu Christi*, Part I., p. 103 et seq.), who renders the words at the commencement of v. 25 "from the *execution of the command* to rebuild Jerusalem," etc., and begins the seventy weeks with the year B.C. 453, thus obtaining the year 783 a. u. c., or A.D. 30, as the time of our Lord's baptism; (5) by Duke George of Manchester (in the work reviewed by Wieseler, *The times of Daniel, chronological and prophetical, examined with relation to the point of contact between sacred and profane chronology*, Lond. and Edinb., 1845), who takes the first year of Darius Medus as the *terminus a quo* of the seventy weeks—identifying that monarch with Darius Nothus, like Tertullian, Scaliger, Calvisius, etc.—and therefore calculates the 490 years from B.C. 424, which brings him to A.D. 66, the year in which the Christians fled from the besieged city of Jerusalem, and in which the Christian church was really founded. He assumes an entirely different *terminus a quo* for the sixty-nine weeks, namely B.C. 444, the alleged first year of Cyrus, whom he believes to have lived in the fifth instead of the sixth century before Christ (! !). The sixty-nine weeks, or 483 years, intervened tween that year and Christ's death on the cross in March, A.D. 38; (6) by Kliefoth, who goes back to the *mystical* theory of reckoning, and accordingly extends the *seven* weeks from the edict of Cyrus in B.C. 537 to the advent of Christ, regardless of the fact that that period does not consist of seven weeks of years, nor of seven centuries, nor of any cycle whatever, whose aggregate of years is divisible by seven—the sixty-two sevens from Christ to the time of the great apostacy, or of the antichrist at the end of earthly history (during which period of indefinite duration the church is to be "built" and "restored," or brought back to God), and finally, the last week from the great apostacy to the appearing of Christ, the last judgment, and the consummation of the world.

B. Hofmann, Delitzsch, Füller, Ebrard, and Kranichfeld [also substantially Keil] adopt the *typically Messianic* interpretation. The former three also favor the transposing theory followed by Wieseler (1846), inasmuch as they assign to the seven weeks of years a place after the 62 + 1 weeks. They reckon the latter from B.C. 606 or the fourth year of Jehoiakim to the time of the Maccabees (and more particularly, the sixty-two weeks from 606–172, and the one week from 172–165), regarding the events of the æra of the Antiochian persecution and the Maccabæan revolt as types and prefigurations of the history of the founding of Christianity; and they describe the seven weeks of years as a period of unmeasured length, whose beginning is coincident with the "going forth of the word to build Jerusalem," *i.e.*, with the first preaching of the Gospel in the time of Christ and the apostles, while their end is connected with the judgment of the world and the advent of Christ! There is therefore, on this theory, a "breaking of the thread," or a hiatus, between the sixty-three

* Cf. Kliefoth, *Daniel*, p. 329 et seq.

and the seven weeks amounting to about 160–190 years, and, in addition, an extension of the last seven weeks into periods of mysterious length; in other words, the aid of *intercalation* and of *mystical enumeration* is superadded to that of *transposition* [cf. supra, No. 4, (2), (3), and (8)]. These are employed at least by Hofmann and Delitzsch, who do not even shrink from the venturous experiment of amplifying the seventy weeks into quadratic Sabbatic periods,* while Füller, more sober and considerate, but assuredly not less arbitrary, interprets the six weeks as being wholly future, and as belonging to the distant end of the world. He endeavors to render this inordinate hiatus conceivable by the assumption that Daniel saw the post-Macedonian antichrist, Antiochus Epiphanes, and the post-Roman antichrist of the last times perspectively as one.—Ebrard avoids every method of transposition, but does not escape violently altering the text (in a review of Füller's *Daniel*, in the Güterslohe *Allgem. literar. Anzeiger*, Oct., 1868, p. 267, and earlier, in his *Offenbarung Johannis*, p. 67 et seq.), in his endeavor to demonstrate the typically Messianic sense of the passage. Supported by the amplifying version of the Sept. (see supra, No. 1), he reads שָׁבֻעִים in v. 25 *a* (scil. שִׁבְעִים), instead of שָׁבֻעִים, or he asserts that שִׁבְעִים was omitted after שָׁבֻעִים through the inadvertence of a copyist. He farther holds that v. 24 states, in general terms and round numbers, that seventy weeks of years were to elapse from the beginning of the captivity to Christ, and, by the method described above, obtains the more exact statement in v. 25, that 7 + 70 = 77 weeks of years should intervene between the edict of Cyrus (538) and Christ, and sixty-two weeks between the building of the city "with street and wall" by Nehemiah (B.C. 440) and Christ (six years earlier than the Christian æra). The time from Christ's birth to his death or the thirty-five years of his life on earth, in which he particularly includes the three and a half years of his official activity, are conceived by him as the former half of the last week, the whole of which is said to be a "larger mystical" week; and its latter half "reaches to the mystical three and a half years of the Apocalypse, which extend to the return of Christ."—Kranichfeld does less violence to the text than any of those referred to. Avoiding transposition, parallelisms, and emendations, he reckons the first seven weeks of years from the prophecy of Jeremiah, chap. xxix., and from the destruction of Jerusalem in B.C. 588 (cf. supra, on v. 25), the sixty-two weeks from the end of the former seven or the time of Daniel's vision in B.C. 539, and regards the מָשִׁיחַ נָגִיד, v. 25, who stands at the beginning of the sixty-two weeks, as representing Cyrus, while the מָשִׁיחַ, v. 26, who appears at their close, is supposed to denote Christ. This theory consequently postulates a gap of more than a century between the Maccabæan period, which bounds the sixty-two weeks (and to whose sufferings the prophetic descriptions of v. 26 *b* and 27 refer), and the time of Christ, the "anointed one who was to be cut off," v. 26 *a*, which interval was unnoticed by the prophet, in harmony with the law of perspective vision.*

The assumption of this interval between the close of the sixty-two weeks and the opening of the New-Test. æra of salvation does not constitute the feature which forms our only objection to Kranichfeld's theory; for, without some such interval the prophecy would lose its genuinely prophetic character, and instead of being an ideal description, possessing the future, it would present a calculation of arithmetical ex-

---

* Cf. Delitzsch, p. 284, "If the seventy weeks are not regarded as simple, but rather as quadrated Sabbatic periods, it follows that 70 × 49 or 3430 years are to intervene between the fourth year of Jehoiakim and Christ, whose parusia is considered as one such period. Consequently, if 3,595 years be added to that aggregate, as having passed from the creation to the fourth year of Jehoiakim, the suggestive amount will result in about 7000 years (diminished by only twenty-five years) as the duration of the world. For a criticism of this view cf. Kliefoth, p. 337 et seq.

* [Keil thus classifies the various interpretations: "1. Most of the church fathers and the older orthodox interpreters find prophesied here the appearance of Christ in the flesh, His death, and the destruction of Jerusalem by the Romans. This view is in our time fully and at length defended by Hävernick (*Comm.*), Hengstenberg (*Christol.*, III. 1, p. 19 sq., 2d ed.), and Auberlen (*Der Proph. Daniel*, etc., p. 103 sq., 3d ed.), and is adopted also by the Catholic theologian Laur. Reinke (*Die Messian. Weissag. bei den gr. u. kl. Proph. des A. T.*, IV. 1, p. 206 sq.), and by Dr. Pusey, of England. 2. The majority of modern (continental) interpreters, on the other hand, refer the whole passage to the time of Antiochus Epiphanes. This view presents itself in the Alexandrian translation of the prophecy, more distinctly in Julius Hilarianus (about A.D. 400) (*Chronologia s. libellus de mundi duratione*, in Migne's *Biblioth. cler. univ.*, t. 13, p. 1098), and in several rabbinical interpreters, but was first brought into special notice by the rationalistic interpreters Eichhorn, Bertholdt, v. Lengerke, Maurer, Ewald, Hitzig, [Rosenmüller], and the mediating theologians Bleek, Wieseler (*Die 70 Wochen u. die 63 Jahrwochen des Proph. Daniel*, Gött., 1839, with which compare the retractation in the *Göttinger. Gel. Anzeiger*, 1846, p. 113 sq.), who are followed by Lücke, Hilgenfeld, Kranichfeld [Stuart], and others. This verse has been defended by Hofmann (*Die 70 Jahre des Jer. u. die 70 Jahrwochen des Daniel*, Nürnb., 1836, and *Weissag. u. Erfüllung*, as also in the *Schriftbew.*), Delitzsch (art. *Daniel* in Herzog's *Real-encykl.* vol. III.), and Zündel (in the *Kritischen Unterss.*), but with this essential modification, that Hofmann and Delitzsch have united an eschatological reference to the primary historical reference of vers. 25–27 to Antiochus Epiphanes, in consequence of which the prophecy will be perfectly accomplished only in the appearance of antichrist and the final completion of the kingdom of God at the end of the days. 3. Finally, some of the church fathers and several modern theologians have interpreted the prophecy eschatologically, as an announcement of the development of the kingdom of God at the end of the exile on to the perfecting of the kingdom by the second coming of Christ at the end of the days. Of this view we have the first germs in Hippolytus and Apollinaris of Laodicea, who, having regard to the prophecy of Antichrist, ch. vii. 25, refer the statement of ver. 27 of this chap. regarding the last week to the end of the world, and the first half of this week they regard as the time of the return of Elias, the second half as the time of antichrist. This view is for the first time definitely stated in the *Berleburg Bible*. But Kliefoth, in his *Comm. on Daniel*, was the first who sought to investigate and establish this opinion exegetically, and Leyser (in Herzog's *Realenc.*, XVIII., p. 383) has thus briefly stated it: 'The seventy שְׁבֻעִים, *i.e.*, the καιροί of Daniel (ch. ix. 24 sq.), measured by sevens, within which the whole of God's plan of salvation in the world will be completed, are a symbolical period with reference to the seventy years of exile prophesied by Jeremiah, and with the accessory notion of œcumenicity. The seventy is again divided into three periods: into seven (till Christ), sixty-two (till the apostasy of antichrist), and *one*, שָׁבוּעַ, the last world, ἑπτά, divided into 2 × 3½ times, the rise and fall of antichrist.'" With the last view Keil's own interpretation essentially agrees. The great objection to it is that it *mixes* the literal with the mystical import of the prophecy, and fails to yield any exact fulfilment of the definite numbers of the text].

actness (cf. the following section, No. 1). Our difficulty consists in the circumstance that the "anointed one who should be cut off," v. 26 *a*, is held to be Jesus Christ, the Messiah, who was exalted through humiliation and sufferings to glory, while everything subsequently mentioned in the immediate context (the "prince" who should "destroy the city and the sanctuary," the "covenant with many" confirmed by him, the interruption of the sacrifice and oblation, the introduction of the abomination of desolation, and the judicial punishment of the destroyer) had its complete historical fulfilment in the events of the period of persecution and oppression under Antiochus, and serves merely as a typical illustration of the times of suffering and of the judgments under the New Covenant. The continuity of the prophetic description appears to be painfully broken by this application of v. 26 *a* to Christ, when the predictions of v. 26 *b* and v. 27 are simultaneously referred [by Kranichfeld, etc.] to the Maccabæan epoch. In addition to this contradiction of the context, this method of interpretation involves the logical inconsequence of a vacillation between the typical and the direct Messianic theory of exposition, or of an obscure intermixture of the prefigurative and the antitypical.

EXCURSUS.

(BY THE AMERICAN REVISOR.)

[*Identification of the Historical Periods comprised within the "Seventy Weeks" in Daniel* ix. 24–27.

Seventy heptades have been decreed [to transpire] upon thy nation, and upon thy holy city, for [entirely] closing the [punishment of] sin, and for sealing up [the retributive sentence against their] offences, and for expiating guilt, and for bringing in [the state of] perpetual righteousness, and for sealing up [the verification of] vision and prophet, and for anointing Holy of Holies. And thou shalt know and consider [that] from [the time of the] issuing of a command for restoring and building [*i.e.*, for rebuilding] Jerusalem till [the coming of] Messiah prince [shall intervene] seven heptades, and sixty and two heptades; [its] street shall return and be built [*i.e.*, shall be rebuilt], and [its] fosse, and [that] in distress of the times. And after the sixty and two heptades Messiah shall be cut off, and nothing [shall be left] to him; and people of the coming prince shall destroy the city and the holy [building], and his end [of fighting shall come] with [*or*, like] the flood, and until [the] end of warring [shall occur the] decreed [result] of desolations. And he shall establish a covenant for the many [during] one heptade, and [at the] middle of the heptade he shall cause to cease sacrifice and offering; and over a wing [*i.e.*, eagle as an ensign] of abominations [*i.e.*, idolatrous images], [shall preside the] desolator, and [this shall continue] till completion, and a decreed [one that] shall pour out upon [the] desolate.

I have been unable to satisfy myself of the entire consistency of any of the foregoing interpretations of this remarkable prophecy, and would therefore propose a partly new elucidation, in accordance with the preceding literal translation and the following diagram. In doing this I need not dwell upon the minor peculiarities of phraseology, which have been fully treated already.

	Last Reform begun [late in Summer] B. C. 410.		*Christ Baptized,* August, A. D. 25.	
Edict published at Jerusalem, July, B. C. 459.	7 w. = 49 y.	62 weeks = 434 years.	1 w. = 7 y.	*Jews rejected,* September, A. D. 32.
		70 heptades = 490 years.		
	52½ years.	62 weeks = 434 years.	Half w.	
	Reform Completed, [early in Spring] B. C. 405.		*Christ Sacrificed,* March 18, A. D. 29.	

Sequel.—Jerusalem razed by the Romans, A. D. 70.

In verse 24 we have a general view of the last great period of the Jewish Church (see the middle line in the *diagram*). It was to embrace four hundred and ninety years, from their permanent release from Babylonian bondage, till the time when God would finally cast them off for their incorrigible unbelief. Within this space Jehovah would fulfil what he had predicted, and accomplish all his designs respecting them under their special relation. The particulars noted in this cursory survey are, first, the conclusion of the then existing exile (expressed in three variations, of which the last phrase, "expiating guilt," explains the two former, "closing the sin" and "sealing up offences;") next, the fulfilment of ancient prophecy, by ushering in the religious prosperity of Gospel times; and, lastly, as the essential feature, the consecration of the Messiah to his redeeming office.

The only "command" answering to that of verse 25 is that of Artaxerxes Longimanus, issued in the seventh year of his reign, and recorded in the seventh chapter of Ezra, as Prideaux has abundantly shown, and as many cri tics agree. At this time, also, more Jews returned to their home than at any other, and the literal as well as spiritual "rebuilding of Jerusalem" was prosecuted with unsurpassed vigor. The period here referred to extends "*till* the Messiah" (see the upper line of the *diagram*); that is, as far as his public recognition as such by the Voice at his baptism, the "anointing" of the previous verse; and not to his *death*,—as is commonly supposed, but which is afterward referred to in very different language; nor to his *birth*—which would make the entire compass of the prophecy vary much from four hundred and ninety years. The period of this verse is divided into two portions of "seven heptades" and "sixty-two heptades," as if the "command" from which it dates were renewed at the end of the first portion; and this we find was the case. Ezra, under whom this reformation of the State and religion began, was succeeded in the work by Nehemiah, who, having occasion to return to Persia in the twenty-fifth year after the commencement of the work (Neh. xiii. 6), returned "after certain days," and found that it had so far retrograded that he was obliged to institute it anew. The length of his stay at court is not given, but it must have been considerable to allow so great a backsliding among the lately reformed Jews. Prideaux contends that his return to Judæa was after an absence of twenty-four years;* and I have supposed the new reform then set on foot by him to have occupied a little over three years, which is certainly none too much time for the task (see the lower line of the *diagram*). The "rebuilding of the streets and intrenchments in times of distress" seems to refer, in its literal sense, to the former part especially of the forty-nine years (compare Nehemiah iv.), very little having been previously done towards rebuilding the *city*, although former decrees had been issued for repairing the temple; † and, in its spiritual import, it applies to the whole time, and peculiarly to the three years of the last reform.

The "sixty-two weeks" of verse 26, be it observed, are not said to commence at the end of the "seven weeks" of verse 25, but, in more general terms, after the "distressing times" during which the reform was going on; hence, they properly date from the end of that reform, when things became permanently settled. It is in consequence of a failure to notice this variation in the limits of the two periods of sixty-two weeks referred to by the prophet (compare the middle portions of the upper and of the lower line in the *diagram*) that critics have thrown the whole scheme of this prophecy into disorder in applying to the same event such irreconcilable language as is used in describing some of its different elements. By the ravaging invasion of foreigners here foretold, is manifestly intended the destruction of Jerusalem by the Roman troops, whose emperor's son, Titus, is here styled a "prince" in command of them. The same allusion is also clear from the latter part of the following verse. But this event must not be included within the seventy weeks; because, in the first place, the accomplishment would not sustain such a view,—from the decree, B. C. 459, to the destruction of Jerusalem, A. D. 70, being five hundred and twenty-eight years; secondly, the language of verse 24 does not require it,—as it is not embraced in the purposes for which the seventy weeks are there stated to be appointed to Jerusalem and its inhabitants; and, lastly, the Jews then no longer formed a link in the chain of ecclesiastical history in the Divine sense,—Christian believers having become the true descendants of Abraham. At the close of the verse we have the judgments with which God would afflict the Jews for cutting off the Messiah: these would be so severe, that the prophet (or, rather, the angel instructing him) cannot refrain from introducing them here, in connection with that event, although he afterwards adverts to them in their proper order. What these sufferings were, Josephus narrates with a minuteness that chills the blood, affording a wonderful coincidence with the prediction of Moses in Deut. xxviii. 15–68; they are here called a "flood," the well-known Scripture emblem of terrible political calamities (as in Isa. viii. 7, 8; Dan. xi. 10, 22; Nah. i. 8).

Verse 27 has g ven the greatest trouble to critics of any in the whole passage; and, indeed, the common theory, by which the seventy weeks are made to end with the crucifixion, is flatly contradicted by the cessation of the daily sacrificial offerings at the temple, "in the middle of the week." All attempts to crowd aside this point are in vain; for such an abolition could not be said to occur in any pertinent sense before the offering of the Great Sacrifice, especially as Jesus himself, during his ministry, always countenanced their celebration. Besides, the advocates of this scheme are obliged to make this last "week" encroach upon the preceding "sixty-two weeks," so as to include John the Baptist's ministry, in order to make out seven years for "confirming the covenant;" and when they have done this they run counter to the previous explicit direction, which makes the first sixty-nine weeks come down "*to* the Messiah," and not end at John. By means of the double line of dates exhibited in the above *diagram*, all this is harmoniously adjusted; and at the same time the only satisfactory interpretation is retained, that after the true Atonement, these typical oblations ceased to have any meaning or efficacy, although before it they could not consistently be dispensed with, even by Christ and his Apostles.

The seventy weeks, therefore, were allotted to the Jews as their only season of favor or mercy as a Church, and we know that they were not immediately cast off upon their murder of Christ (see Luke xxiv. 27; Acts iii. 12–26). The gospel was specially directed to be first preached to them; and not only during our Saviour's personal ministry, but for several years afterward, the invitations of grace were confined to them. The first instance of a "turning to the Gentiles" proper was the baptism of the Roman centurion Cornelius, during the fourth year after the resurrection of Christ. In this interval the Jewish people had shown their de-

* [See the arguments in his *Connection*, sub anno 409. I place the whole prophecy a year earlier.]

† [Namely, by Cyrus, the Medo-Persian conqueror of the Babylonians, who thus put an end to the "seventy years' captivity," B. C. 536, as in Ezra i. 1; and by Darius Hystaspis, who renewed Cyrus's decree (Ezra iv. 24), B.C. 518, rescinding its prohibition by his immediate predecessors Cambyses and Smerdis.]

termined opposition to the New "Covenant" by imprisoning the Apostles, stoning Stephen to death, and officially proscribing Christianity through their Sanhedrim: soon after this martyrdom occurred the conversion of Saul, who "was a chosen vessel to bear God's name to the Gentiles": and about two years after this event the door was thrown wide open for their admission into the covenant relation of the church, instead of the Jews, by the vision of Peter and the conversion of Cornelius. Here we find a marked epoch, fixed by the finger of God in all the miraculous circumstances of the event, as well as by the formal apostolical decree, ratifying it, and obviously forming the great turning-point between the two dispensations. We find no evidence that "many" of the Jews embraced Christianity after this period, although they had been converted in great numbers on several occasions under the Apostles' preaching, not only in Judæa, but also in Galilee, and even among the semi-Jewish inhabitants of Samaria; the Jews had now rejected Christ as a nation with a tested and incorrigible hatred, and, having thus disowned their God, they were forsaken by him, and devoted to destruction, as the prophet intimates would be their retribution for that "decision," in which the four hundred and ninety years of this their second and last probation in the Promised Land would result. It is thus strictly true that Christ, personally and by his Apostles, "established the covenant," which had formerly been made, and was now renewed, with *many* of the chosen people, for precisely seven years after his public appearance as a Teacher; in the very *middle* of which space He superseded forever the sacrificial offerings of the Mosaic ritual by the one perfect and sufficient Offering of His own body on the cross.

In the latter part of this verse we have a graphic outline of the terrible catastrophe that should fall upon the Jews, in consequence of their rejection of the Messiah; a desolation that should not cease to cover them, but by the extinction of the oppressed nation; it forms an appendix to the main prophecy. Our Saviour's language leaves no doubt as to the application of this passage, in His memorable warning to His disciples, that when they should be about to "see the abomination of desolation spoken of by Daniel the prophet, stand in the holy place," they should then "flee into the mountains" (Matt. xxiv. 15, 16; comp. xxiii. 36, 38), in order to save themselves from that awful "*consummation*" of ruin, which he also pointed out as the "determined" fate of that impenitent city, after it should have endured the "desolating" ravages of a siege unparalleled in rigor and suffering, besides being "left desolate" by the abandonment of their God. The destined period of fulfilment arrived, and Josephus, who witnessed it, tells us that the standards of the Roman army, who held sacred the shrined silver eagles that surmounted their banners, were actually placed, during the capture, in the temple, opposite the eastern gate, and there sacrificed to (*De Bell. Jud.*, VI. 6, 1). Equally exact, if the view proposed above is correct, are all the specifications of this wonderful prophecy.

In the preceding investigation several chronological points have been partially assumed, which entire satisfaction with the results obtained would require to be fully proved. A minute investigation of the grounds on which all the dates involved rest would occupy too much space for the present discussion; I shall, therefore, content myself with determining the two boundary dates of the entire period, trusting the intermediate ones to such incidental evidences of their correctness as may have been afforded in the foregoing elucidation, or may arise in connection with the settlement proposed.* If these widely distant points can be fixed by definite data independently of each other, the correspondence of the *interval* will afford strong presumption that it is the true one, which will be heightened as the subdivisions fall naturally into their prescribed limits; and thus the above coincidence in the character of the *events* will receive all the confirmation that the nature of the case admits.

1. *The date of the Edict.* I have supposed this to be from the time of its taking effect at Jerusalem, rather than from that of its nominal issue at Babylon; the difference, however,—being only four months,—will not seriously affect the argument. Ezra states (chap. vii. 8), that "he arrived at Jerusalem in the fifth month (*Ab*, our July-August) of the seventh year of the king" Artaxerxes. Ctesias, who had every opportunity to know, makes Artaxerxes to have reigned forty-two years, and Thucydides states that an Athenian embassy, sent to Ephesus in the winter that closed the seventh year of the Peloponnesian war, was there met with the news of Artaxerxes' death, *πυθόμενοι . . . 'Αρταξέρξην . . . νεωστὶ τεθνηκότα (κατὰ γάρ τοῦτον τὸν χρόνον ἐτελεύτησεν)*, *Bell. Pelop.*, IV. 50. Now this war began in the spring of B.C. 431, as all allow (Thuc. ii. 2), and its seventh year expired with the spring of B.C. 424; consequently, Artaxerxes died in the winter introducing that year, and his reign began some time in B.C. 466. This latter historian also states that Themistocles, in his flight to Asia, having been driven by a storm into the Athenian fleet, at that time blockading Naxos, managed to get safely carried away to Ephesus, whence he dispatched a letter of solicitation to Artaxerxes, then lately invested with royalty, *νεωστὶ βασιλεύοντα* (*Bell. Pelop.*, I. 137). The date of the conquest of that island is B.C. 466, which is, therefore, also that of the Persian king's accession. It is now necessary to fix the *season* of the year in which he became king. If Ctesias means that his reign lasted forty-two *full* years, or a little over rather than under that length, the accession must be dated prior to the beginning of B.C. 466; but it is more in accordance with the usual computation of reigns to give the number of *current* years, if nearly full, and this will bring the date of accession down to about the beginning of summer, B.C. 466. This result is also more in accordance with the simultaneous capture of Naxos, which can hardly have occurred earlier in that year. I may add, that it likewise explains the length assigned to this reign (forty-one years) by Ptolemy, in his *Astronomical Canon*, although he has misled modern compilers of ancient history

* [On these chronological elements, see Browne's *Ordo Sæclorum*, pp. 202 and 96–107.]

by beginning it in B.C. 465, having apparently himself fallen into some confusion, from silently annexing the short intermediate periods of anarchy sometimes to the preceding and at others to the ensuing reign. The "seventh year" of Artaxerxes, therefore, began about the summer of B.C. 460, and the "first [Hebrew] month" (Nisan) occurring within that twelvemonth, gives the following March–April of B.C. 459 as the time when Ezra received his commission to proceed to Jerusalem for the purpose of executing the royal mandate.

2. *The date of the conversion of Cornelius.* The solution of this question will be the determination of the distance of this event from the time of our Saviour's Passion; the absolute date of this latter occurrence must, therefore, first be determined. This is ascertained to have taken place in A.D. 29, by a comparison of the duration of Christ's ministry with the historical data of Luke iii. 1–23; but the investigation is too long to be inserted here. (See Dr. Jarvis's *Introduction to the History of the Church.*) A ready mode of testing this conclusion is by observing that this is the only one of the adjacent series of years in which the calculated date of the equinoctial full moon coincides with that of the Friday of the crucifixion Passover, as any one may see—with sufficient accuracy for ordinary purposes—by computing the mean lunations and week-day back from the present time. This brings the date of Christ's baptism to A.D. 25; and the whole tenor of the Gospel narratives indicates that this took place in the latter part of summer. Other more definite criteria of the season cannot be specified here.

The chief chronological difficulties of the Acts occur in the arrangement of the events associated with Cornelius's conversion, and arise from the vague notes of time (or, rather, absence of any definite dates) by Luke, between the account of the Pentecostal effusion (chap. ii. 1) and the death of Herod Agrippa the elder (chap. xii. 23); indeed, but for the periods noted by Paul in Gal. i. and ii. it would be utterly impossible to adjust minutely the dates of this portion of the history. As it is, the subject is almost abandoned by most chronologers and commentators as hopelessly obscure and uncertain; but there is no occasion for such despair. The death of Herod is ascertained (by the help of Josephus, *Antiq.*, XIX. 8, 2) to have occurred in the early part of the year A.D. 44, between which time and the Pentecost of A.D. 29 is an interval of fifteen years, covered by the incidents contained in chapters ii.–xi. of the Acts. The visit of Paul, spoken of by him as his second to Jerusalem (Gal. ii. 1), appears at first sight to be the same with that narrated in Acts ii. 30, since there is no mention of any intervening visit; it was made in company with Barnabas, and the "revelation" (Gal. ii. 2) might answer to the prediction of the famine by Agabus (Acts xi. 28), which caused the journey. Now in that case it is certain that the date of this visit ("fourteen years after") is not reckoned from that of his former visit (Gal. i. 18), for then it would have occurred at least seventeen years (14+3) after his conversion, which would be two years more than the whole interval between this second visit and the Pentecost referred to; it is, therefore, reckoned from his *conversion*, which makes his journey to Damascus, on which he was converted occur one year (15—14) after this Pentecost. This is corroborated by two ancient ecclesiastical traditions, one of which states that Paul was converted in the year after the Ascension, and the other refers the martyrdom of Stephen (which was so connected with Paul's persecuting journey to Damascus, as not to have preceded it many months) to the close of the same year in which Christ suffered. If, on the other hand, as the best authorities mostly agree, the second visit spoken of in Gal. corresponds with that described in Acts xv., as the similarity of the subject debated at the time (the obligation of Mosaism) especially indicates, then we are at liberty to apply the natural interpretation to the intervals there given, and we shall thus have the visit in question occurring seventeen years after the conversion of Paul. Now, the date of the visit referred to in Acts xii. is known to be A.D. 44, and if we allow the reasonable space of three years for the first missionary journey, as recorded in the intervening chapters (Acts xiii., xiv.), and the considerable stay at Antioch upon its close (xiv. 28), we shall still have, as before, an interval of one year between the Crucifixion and Paul's conversion—a space, for all that we can see, sufficiently ample for the events related.

Paul's first visit (Gal. i. 8) must naturally be reckoned in like manner from his conversion, as it is mentioned to show the length of his stay in Damascus and its vicinity, and is put in contrast with his intentional avoidance of Jerusalem on his conversion (ver. 17); we have thus the date of this same visit in Acts ix. 26 fixed at A.D. 33, four years after the noted Pentecost. I need not here discuss the length nor precise time of the visit into Arabia (Gal. i. 17), nor the exact mode of adjusting this passage with Luke's account in the Acts; these points are capable of easy solution, and do not require the supposition of some intervening visit in either narrative. Neither need I stop to reconcile the mention of travels in Syria (Gal. i. 21) with the sea voyage direct from Cæsarea to Tarsus (Acts ix. 30); the visit to Jerusalem occupied only fifteen days (Gal. i. 18), and there is nothing here to disturb the above dates.

Most chronological schemes, blindly following the order of Acts ix. and x., without taking into special consideration this interval of three years spent by Paul at Damascus, have placed the conversion of Cornelius after that apostle's return to Tarsus, the arrangers being apparently actuated by a desire to fill up the period of fifteen years by sprinkling the events along as widely apart as possible for the sake of uniform intervals. But several considerations present themselves to my mind which cause me to think this arrangement erroneous. In the outset, the question arises on this supposition, What were the other apostles doing these three years? Was nothing going on at Jerusalem or in Judæa worth recording? But this interval is not thus left a blank by the sacred historian. Luke says (Acts ix. 31), "Then had the churches rest," etc.; that is, as I understand it, during these three years, the persecution stirred up by Saul after the martyrdom of Stephen being arrested by the conversion of that enemy, the Christian societies generally enjoyed great quiet and pros perity. I cannot discover any pertinent cause for this remark, unless we suppose it to refer to the period succeeding this event. The same idea is carried by the mention of the travels of Peter "through all parts" (verse 32), evidently during this season of outward peace, when his presence was no longer needed to sustain the Church at Jerusalem. It was during this tour that Peter was called to preach the Gospel to Cornelius; the year succeeding the conversion of Saul was probably spent by Peter in building up the society at the metropolis, his tour apparently occupied the summer of the year following; and in the third year Paul, on his visit to Jerusalem, finds Peter returned thither. This affords convenient time for all these occurrences, and connects them in their natural order. Lastly, under this view we can readily explain the plan of Luke's narrative in these chapters: after tracing the history of the Church (specially under the conduct of Peter) down to the persecution by Saul, he takes up the subject of this opponent's conversion, and does not quit him until he has left him in quiet at home—hence his omission of all reference to these three years as being unsuitable to his design of continuity; he then returns to Peter, and narrates his doings in the interim. This parallel method of narration is proved by the resumption of Paul's history in chapter xi. 19, where Luke evidently goes back to the time of Stephen, in order to show what the dispersed evangelists had been accomplishing during the four years succeeding that martyrdom, and thus connect the preaching to the Gentiles with the latter part of that period (ver. 20); and this again prepares the way for the visit to Antioch of Paul, who had lately returned to Tarsus.

It is true, in this scheme there is made an interval of ten years between the establishment of the Church at Antioch and the visit of Paul to Jerusalem, about the time of Herod's death; but it is much better to place such an interval, during which no incident of striking moment occurred, after the Gospel had become in a measure rooted in the community, than to intersperse considerable periods of uninteresting silence in its early planting, when matters which, had they transpired afterward, would be passed by as trivial, were of the greatest importance in the history. Intimations are given of the general prosperity of the cause, and there was no occasion to present the details of this period, until some remarkable event broke the even course of occurrences. Such an event was the visit of Paul, and especially the contemporaneous conduct and fate of Herod; and the latter account is accordingly introduced in the twelfth chapter by the phrase, *Κατ' ἐκεῖνον δὲ τὸν καιρόν*, always indicative of some fresh occurrence after a period of comparative monotony and silence. Nor is this interval left entirely devoid of incident; it is in fact filled up by the account of the preparation for the famine. It was "during those days" that the prophet Agabus visited Antioch from Jerusalem; some time after his arrival, he predicted the famine, and it is plainly intimated that the fulfilment did not take place immediately, but several years afterward, "in the days of Claudius Cæsar." That emperor, therefore, was not reigning at the time of its utterance, and as the famine took place in the *fourth* year of his reign (Josephus, *Ant.*, XX. 5, 2, compared with I. 2), there is here an interval of at least four years silently occurring between two closely related incidents of this period. The "whole year" during which Paul preached at Antioch (Acts xi. 26) is reckoned from his call thither by Barnabas, but does not extend to his visit to Jerusalem; it only covers his first labors confined to the city itself (after which he itinerated in the neighboring regions of Syria, Gal. i. 21), and extends merely to about the time of the arrival of Agabus. The above interval of ten years was occupied by Paul in such labors as are referred to in 2 Cor. xi. 23-27.

We thus arrive at the conclusion, based upon internal evidence, that the admission of the Gentiles by the conversion of Cornelius occurred near the close of Peter's summer tour, in A. D. 32; we cannot be far from certainty in fixing it as happening in the month of September of that year.]

ETHICO-FUNDAMENTAL PRINCIPLES RELATED TO THE HISTORY OF SALVATION, APOLOGETICAL REMARKS, AND HOMILETICAL SUGGESTIONS.

1. A truly unbiassed apprehension of the sense of the prophecy respecting the seventy weeks of years will succeed in demonstrating a typical reference to the Messiah only rather than any direct allusion.* The general character of the language in the introductory passage, v. 24, opens a prospect, indeed, of events such as are elsewhere foretold only in prophecies that are directly Messianic in their nature; but these events are here assigned to a time *immediately subsequent to the end of the seventy weeks of years*, which are made to begin with Jeremiah's דָּבָר concerning the seventy years, or at about the commencement of the captivity (B.C. 600 or 588). The prophet consequently saw the Messianic period of deliverance in a much closer proximity than its actual distance from his time would justify, and he connected it intimately with the æra of persecution under the Seleucidæ, which he saw in spirit as the closing period of the series of seventy sevens of years, as prophetically revealed to him. The theocratic seer, who could not calculate by centuries, but only by Sabbatic periods or cycles of jubilees, expected the advent of the Messianic deliverance after seventy Sabbatic years should have expired, instead of removing it to the distance of five or six centuries.† The limit assigned by the prophet certainly testifies to his wonderful range of vision, and exalts him far above his contemporaries in the captivity, none of whom would have been likely to remove the beginning of the Messianic æra to any considerable distance be-

* [On the contrary, there is good reason to believe that this remarkable prophecy sustained the faith of the pious Jews in their anticipations of the near approach of the Redeemer's coming (cf. Mark i. 15; Luke ii. 25, 38), as it has since been a powerful argument to prove his actual advent at the time predicted (cf. Gal. iv. 4; 1 Pet. i. 11).]

† [The learned and pious author does not seem to be aware how nugatory such a misconception on the part of the holy seer would render this prophecy, the marked peculiarity of which is that it designates the *time* of the events predicted.]

yond the close of the Babylonian captivity; but it still falls below the *historical* measure of the distance between Jeremiah's prophecy and the New-Test. fulfilment by 100–110 years,—or, in other words, instead of extending into the time of Christ, it merely reaches to the age of John Hyrcanus and his immediate successors. The principal stations in the course of pre-Christian development were doubtless sufficiently apparent to the prophet, and upon the whole, were seen as separated from each other by precisely the interval which actually resulted in the progress of events. In his younger contemporary Cyrus, the "anointed prince," v. 25, he recognized the introducer and founder of a period of *relative* salvation for the people of God (a period which should bring a restoration of Jerusalem, although for the time an imperfect, troubled, and oppressed restoration), and therefore saw in that prince a first typical forerunner of the Messiah. He saw a farther prefatory condition to the coming of the Messiah in the religious persecutions and antitheocratic abominations, with which the descendant of a royal Javanic house should afflict Israel in the distant future, slaying the anointed high priest (Onias III., B.C. 172), and even interrupting the theocratic worship for a time and desecrating its sanctuary; and he fixed the interval between the former positive and this later negative preparation for Messiah's coming, with approximate correctness, at sixty-two weeks (*i.e.*, the difference between the first seven, which had already expired at his time, and the momentous last week of the seventy—a number of years which certainly exceeds the actual historical interval between 539 and 175 or between Cyrus and Epiphanes by seventy years.* But the additional interval of more than one and a half centuries or twenty-three to twenty-four weeks of years, which, according to the Divine purpose, was to intervene between the typical ὠδῖνες τοῦ χριστοῦ of the Maccabæan age and the advent of Christ, escaped his vision while ranging in the distance. In the limitation of his earthly and human consciousness† he did not suspect that the Spirit of prophecy did not reveal to him any immediate, but only indirect preparations and types of the Messianic æra. He does not see the abysmal gap of renewed waiting during nearly two hundred years, which separated the bright exaltation of the victorious Maccabæan æra from the still more glorious and heavenly period in which the New Covenant should be established; and the prophets and observers of prophetic predictions immediately subsequent to him, probably noticed no more of that interval than did he (cf. the Eth.-fund. principles on chap. vii. No. 2). The pious theocratic searchers of the Scriptures in the Maccabæan period, and probably in the *later stages* of that period, who had themselves begun to experience a painful consciousness of the descent into the gap which Daniel had overlooked, were probably the first to arrive at an understanding of the merely typical nature of the contents of vs. 26 and 27, thus being taught to look for a more perfect and enduring realization of that oracle. Cf. Kranichfeld, p. 337: "This natural difference between the prophet's conception of events and their historical reality would ultimately lead to the inference that a farther realization of the prophecy was to be expected,* inasmuch as the Grecian empire, and more particularly that of Antiochus Epiphanes, did not appear as the last of the heathen monarchies, and the final supremacy of the Messianic kingdom of God was not yet introduced. Instead of charging the prophetic idea as such with being untrue in this respect, or of rejecting it without farther investigation as not having been fulfilled, the thoughtful circles among the people would probably treat that idea as Haggai, Zechariah, Malachi, and Daniel himself treated the Messianic hopes of Jeremiah or Isaiah, that were connected with the return from the captivity, since the prophetic description had been so remarkably fulfilled in other respects. The internal evidence demonstrated that the idea was in itself incontrovertibly *true*, and it was regarded as such, while its realization in the light of historical facts was referred to a more distant future. In like manner Christ unites the description of the Messianic future with its conflict, and its triumphs with his own time, and connects with the latter the thought of the erection of Messiah's kingdom; while the New-Test. Apocalypse, from *its* historical point of view, connects it with a still later time. Christ simply regards the destruction of Jerusalem and the end of all things, joined to the triumph of God's kingdom, as a comprehensive whole, on the authority of Daniel's description; and he consequently designates the present γενεά (Matt. xxiv. 31 and parallels) as the time in which the picture of the eschatological future should be realized.† The apostles imitate him in expecting the end of the world in the age in which they lived;‡ but the Revelator's field of vision lay beyond that γενεά, and beyond the destruction of Jerusalem. That such a transfer and reference from one period to another (which, as compared with its predecessor, is to bring a more complete, and ultimately, a full realization) is possible, without degrading the prophetic idea and destroying its value, is implied in the very character of the genuine prophetic oracle, as being *essentially comprehensive in its nature, even though the writer may primarily have intended it to refer only to some particular event in the progress of history.*—The reference of the prophecy respecting the future tribulation was doubtless accepted in the beginning of

* Cf. Bleek, in the *Jahrbücher f. deutsche Theologie*, 1860, p. 84; Reichel, in *Stud. u. Kritiken*, 1848, pp. 737, 748 et seq.

† [It should rather be borne in mind that this is not a question of Daniel's subjective intuition into the future; the dates in question were those explicitly given him by Gabriel commissioned direct from heaven for that very purpose.]

* [It is difficult to see how a discovery of Daniel's own error on the point in question should lead his readers either to entertain greater faith in his predictions or to seek for a more correct interpretation of them than he was able to attain himself.]

† [There is this essential difference, however, as to the point at issue between these eschatological sayings of our Lord and this of Daniel, that Christ expressly disclaimed any revelation or even knowledge of the "times and seasons" of the events predicted; whereas the prophecy before us is a pure series of such chronological notanda. Indeed our Lord in these very utterances explicitly refers to this identical passage of Daniel as affording the only clue that he gives to the date of their occurrence.]

‡ [This assertion is often made by expositors, but it is directly contradicted by Paul's emphatic language in 2 Thess. ii. 1 seq.]

the Maccabæan epoch, and among others, by the writer of the first book of Maccabees; but the Jewish Sibyl may serve to show that despite such reference, the circumstances of the times might make way for another interpretation in each instance, since, as early as about B.C. 140, and at the time of a newly founded hereditary Jewish-national dynasty, it makes the ten horns of Dan. vii. end beyond the Epiphanes with Demetrius I., finds the little horn in Alexander Balas, who seized the throne of the Seleucidæ, instead of referring it to Antiochus Epiphanes, and no longer regards the world-controlling power of the Jewish theocracy as bound to the ruin of the dead Hellenic influence, which is characterized in mild terms, but to the power of the hated Roman empire. The Romans, whom the Septuagint substitutes for the כִּתִּים in Dan. xi. 31, are here directly and practically installed in the place of the fourth world-kingdom of Daniel, in which position we afterward meet them in Josephus and the New Testament." Concerning the latter point cf. Hilgenfeld, *Die jüdische Apokalyptik*, pp. 69 et seq., 84 et seq., and also supra, § 6, note 3, of the Introd. to this work.

2. Despite the repeated specific references to facts and circumstances in the Maccabæan æra, the prophecy before us is no *vaticinium ex eventu*, that was invented in that age; for the want of agreement between its statements and the actual conditions of that time is far more general than their correspondence.* It is (1) a fundamental non-agreement between the prophecy and the fulfilment, that the sixty-two weeks of years, if reckoned from the end of the seven weeks, or from B.C. 538, in harmony with the context and the evident sense of the prophecy, extend down to B.C. 105, while the whole of the Antiochian-Maccabæan catastrophe, which forms the contents of the last week of years, was ended at least seventy years earlier; and (against Ewald) the text contains no indication whatever that the period of 434 years or sixty-two weeks is to be shortened by seventy years or ten weeks of years. Further (2), the murder of the high priest Onias, which we are compelled to regard as the Maccabæan or typical fulfilment of the יִכָּרֵת מָשִׁיחַ, v. 26, did not transpire exactly in the beginning of the sixty-ninth or last week, but somewhat earlier, in the year 141 æ. Sel., which was still included in the sixty-second week (cf. 2 Macc. iv. 7 et seq.; xxiii. 34). The prediction of v. 26, "and *after* the threescore and two weeks shall an anointed one be cut off," does not therefore harmonize exactly with the corresponding fact in the Maccabæan history (cf. supra, on that passage; also Kranichfeld, p. 309 et seq.); and if not Onias, but Seleucus Philopater is to be understood as denoted by the "anointed one who was cut off," as Bleek, Maurer, Roesch, v. Lengerke, Hitzig, etc., contend, the chronological discrepancy becomes still greater. To this must be added (3) that the temple and the altar did not remain in the profaned condition to which Antiochus Epiphanes had reduced them during "half a week or three and a half years, but only during three years and a few days (see Eth.-fund. principles, etc., on chap. vii. No. 3, *b*), and finally (4), that the detailed description of this desecrated state and of the "abomination of desolation," v. 27, which stood on the sanctuary while thus profaned, does not correspond more exactly to the statements in 1 Macc. i., than the allusions to the judicial punishment of the antitheistic madman, which are found in the close of the same and the preceding verse, accord precisely in any way with what history records concerning the end of Antiochus Epiphanes. In order to be understood by his contemporaries, a Maccabæan pseudo-Daniel would have clothed his allusions in a very different form, and would have made them everywhere less equivocal. The surroundings of the vision concerning the seventy weeks, and the preparations for it would likewise have received a different form at his hands; and the fervent penitential and intercessory prayer, by which the Spirit of prophecy was invoked and the Divine exposition of Jeremiah's oracle was secured, this especially would have been different in both contents and form, from what it is in vs. 4–19, had it been invented by a pseudo-Daniel. Instead of revealing a relationship to the similar prayers in the books of Ezra and Nehemiah, which were written immediately after the captivity, it would have displayed a character more nearly like that of the far more verbose and prolix apocryphal writings which originated during the last pre-Christian centuries, such as Baruch, Ecclus., Judith, and the additions to Esther and Daniel; cf., in addition to Bar. i. 14–ii. 19 (regarding which see above, on v. 4 et seq.), especially Ecclus. li.; Jud. ix.; Tob. iii. and xiii.; Ezek. iii. 1 et seq.; and also the Prayer of Azariah, Dan. iii. 26 et seq. Nor would the alleged pseudo-Daniel of the Maccabæan age have been likely to omit from a prayer written to favor a tendency, every allusion to the raging of the enemies of God's people, which still continued at his time, since that prayer would unquestionably be designed to contribute to the quickening of the religious and national zeal and courage (cf. *e.g.*, the prayer of Judith, chap. ix. which has already been referred to, and see again the remarks on v. 4 et seq.).

3. *The practical fundamental thought, and the central idea of this section* is to be looked for neither in Daniel's penitential prayer and fervent intercession for his nation only, nor yet merely in the equally serious and comforting disclosures of the vision of the weeks. It is rather contained in the relation of the two constituent elements to each other, *i.e.*, in the causal connection of the prayer, as the expression of a disposition of the heart, that showed it truly prepared to receive Divine revelations concerning the salvation connected with the future of God's kingdom, with the revelation itself that was thus obtained. Inasmuch as that preparation of the heart reaches its highest point in the disposition which constitutes the prophet a אִישׁ חֲמוּדוֹת (v. 23), a God-loving favorite of God, a needy, contrite, humble,

* [This effort of the author to turn to advantage in one direction an acknowledged failure in another, is ingenious, but unfortunately, if true, would prove too much; for if the prophecy does not tally with its alleged fulfilment, it is thereby shown not only to have been not written after the event, but to have been *no true prophecy at all.*]

and therefore worthy object of the yearning love of the Father of mercies, it may be said that this expression in v. 23, which states in a brief and striking manner the reason why the following prophetic disclosures are vouchsafed to the prophet, contains the central and fundamental thought of the whole chapter. Moreover, since by that very expression the prophet is characterized as an anxious searcher after the goal of the history of the Old-Test. empires, and as one of those humble and self-abasing servants of God, to whom He granted the most extended view of the future of His kingdom,* in reward of their humility and their faithful investigations in the documents containing His revelation of salvation, the *nature of genuine prophecy under the Old Dispensation, as being a longing and anxious preparation for the future manifestation of deliverance in Christ* may be found to have been characterized in this section, and to have been exemplified in one of the most prominent instances in the collective development of Old Testament. The theme for the homiletical treatment of the chapter as a whole might therefore read: "Daniel, the favorite of God; the leader and founder of that series of pious 'watchers' (*προσδεχόμενοι*, Luke ii. 25, 38) which reached to the time of Christ; the example and teacher of the only Divinely attested method of 'searching the Scriptures' (John v. 39); the model possessor of the Spirit in which the Scriptures are to be read and pondered; the ideal prophet in the sense indicated by Peter" (1 Pet. i. 10, 11: *περὶ ἧς σωτηρίας ἐξεζήτησαν καὶ ἐξηρεύνησαν προφῆται οἱ περὶ τῆς εἰς ὑμᾶς χάριτος προφητεύσαντες, ἐρευνῶντες εἰς τίνα ἢ ποῖον καιρὸν ἐδήλου τὸ ἐν αὐτοῖς πνεῦμα χριστοῦ προμαρτυρόμενον τὰ εἰς χριστὸν παθήματα καὶ τὰς μετὰ ταῦτα δόξας*). If a proper use were made of the key afforded by 1 Pet., l. c., to arrive at a correct understanding of the chapter and a correct estimate of the Messianic position of the prophet, thus securing the weapons with which to energetically refute the current rationalistic prejudice that Daniel no longer represented a normal and healthful stage of prophetic development, but rather one in which it had already begun to degenerate and to be "apocalyptically diseased," a sermon framed on some such plan would be able to achieve truly powerful results, both in a practical and an apologetic point of view. In view of the extraordinary wealth of matter, it might be well to divide it into two themes for sermons, in order to treat it thoroughly; for instance, let one sermon treat of the *spirit* in which the Scriptures should be read and the mysteries contained in them be approached (vs. 1–23), and another bear upon the principal feature disclosed by the Scriptures when thus perused, viz.: *the fundamental law of all the history of salvation—"through sufferings to glory"* (vs. 24–27).

* Cf. Füller, *Der Prophet Daniel*, p. 264, "We hear Daniel repeatedly characterized as a *jewel* of great value in the sight of God. Hence, for the reason that Daniel is precious with God, the latter meets his petitions and wishes kindly, and makes disclosures to him which would not otherwise have been imparted. If his nation may find comfort and encouragement in these disclosures at a later day, it is to know *to whom* it is indebted for them, and to learn that a man upon whom rests the favor of God may be a blessing to his people during subsequent centuries. For Daniel is not merely the instrument *through which*, but also the man *for whose sake* God imparts this revelation, which possesses incalculable value for Daniel's nation for centuries to come."

4. *Homiletical suggestions on particular passages.* On v. 2 et seq., Jerome: "*In cinere et sacco postulat impleri, quod promiserat Deus; non quo esset incredulus futurorum, sed ne securitas negligentiam et negligentia pareret offensam.*"—Melancthon: "*Etiamsi Deus promisit beneficia corporalia vel spiritualia, tamen precibus vult exerceri fidem, et vult crescere pœnitentiam sicut inquit Zacharias: Convertimini ad me, et ego convertar ad vos, etc. Et orat Daniel de restituenda Ecclesia; ita nos quoque officiamur vero dolore propter Ecclesiæ calamitates et oremus, ut Deus eam augeat, gubernet et servet.*" Spener: —(Penitential sermons on Daniel's penitential prayer): "All the Divine prophecies are obscure before their fulfilment, and can only be apprehended through special industry in the light of Divine truth; therefore, 'whoso readeth, let him understand' (Matt. xxiv. 14)."—Starke: "If Daniel read prophetic writings, although himself a prophet of the Most High, how silly is it to imagine that we can know everything of ourselves! Thence it results that dreams and false imaginings are taken for God's word (Ezek. xiii. 3 et seq.) . . . . It is certainly the duty of a Christian to exercise his faith continually in prayer; but when a special promise by God is before him, he should arouse himself to that exercise more fully (Acts iv. 24); for there are many promises which include the condition of true repentance and obedience to God, either expressed or implied," etc.—J. Lange: "Promise, prayer, and fulfilment always belong together (Psa. xxvii. 8)."

V. 4 et seq., Melancthon: "*Daniel fatetur peccata populi et tribuit Deo laudem justitiæ, quod juste puniverit populum. Deinde petit remissionem peccatorum et reductionem populi. Est ergo vera contritio, agnoscere iram Dei adversus nostra peccata, expavescere propter iram Dei, dolere quod Deum offenderimus, tribuere in laudem, quod juste nos puniat, et obedire in pœnis.—Nec tamen satis est peccata noscere, intueri pœnas, sed accedat quoque consolatio. Ergo Daniel non solum doctrinam contritionis proponit, sed addit partem alteram. Docet suo exemplo petere et expectare veniam propter misericordiam et promissiones.*" —Starke: "A conception of God's punitive justice is necessary, in order that man may more fully recognize the guilt of his sin, and may not lull himself into a mistaken security with the comforting thought of His mercy. . . . But despite this there is no other nor better comfort in the agony of sin, than God's goodness and mercy, through which alone we can obtain forgiveness by faith."—Hävernick: "At the same time, the prayer of the prophet was not merely one that proceeded from him as an individual, but one offered by him as a mediator of the whole nation, in whose name he now cried to the Merciful One. We may therefore ascribe a *liturgical* character to it with entire justice, and thus explain the frequent borrowing of former expressions in which it abounds."

Verses 11–14, Calvin: "*Daniel hic significat, non debere videri absurdum, quod Deus multo sit asperior in electum populum, quam in gentes profanas; quia scilicet major erat impietas illius populi quam gentium omnium, propter ingratitudinem, propter contumaciam, propter indomabilem illam pervicaciam. Quum ergo superarint Israelitæ gentes omnes et malitia et ingratitudin.*

et omni genere scelerum, Daniel hic prædicat, merito tum duriter ipsos affligi."—Geier: "The greater the favor shown by God toward a nation or country, the greater will afterward be the punishment which follows on its ingratitude (Deut. xxxii. 13, 22 et seq.)." —Spener: "Divine threatenings are recorded in order that man be deterred from sinning, and also that an evidence of God's righteousness and truthfulness may be drawn from their realization.—Without repentance, all other means to avert the wrath of God are useless. He that should endeavor to quench the fire with one hand, while pouring oil on it with the other, would increase the fire more than his attempt to quench it would diminish it (Jer. ii. 23)."

Verse 15 et seq., Starke: "Where genuine repentance exists it fills the heart, so that it cannot avoid breaking out in humble confession, and that repeatedly (Jer. vi. 11).—When man humbles himself under a sense of God's wrath, recognizes that the punishment was deserved, and flies to Divine mercy for refuge, God transforms His wrath and displeasure into grace (Psa. lxxxi. 14, 15).—If the church, and even every single member belonging to it, bears the name of Christ, it follows that this is the most powerful motive to hear our prayer for the church which we can present to God (cf. Acts iv. 27 et seq.)."—Hävernick: "As the strongest motive for a father to be careful for his child, is that it is called by his name—and that not in conformity with a custom having no significance, but as a sign that it belongs to him and must be considered as his property,—so the prophet here expresses his confidence in the grace of God most beautifully by the feature that he refers to the *city which is called by the name of God*, the city of Jehovah, the great King, which is founded in eternity (Psa. xlvi. 5; xlviii. 2, 9; lxxxvii. 3)."

Verses 20–23, Jerome: "*Non populi tantum peccata, sed et sua replicat, quia unus e populo est; sive humiliter, quum peccatum ipse non fecerit, se jungit populo peccatori, ut ex humilitate veniam consequatur.*"—Id. (on chap. x. 11): "*Congruenter 'vir desideriorum' vocatur, qui instantia precum et afflictione, corporisque jejuniorumque duritie cupit scire ventura et Dei secreta cognoscere.*"—Starke: "The prayer that is poured out before God for our personal wants and the common need is never unheard (Psa. xci. 15).—What will God not do for the sake of man! The princes of heaven are obliged to render Him service and reveal His will to the faithful, that they may be strengthened in faith and hope (Heb. i. 14).—True Christians imitate the angels, who seek to instruct each other more and more in the ways of God, till they all arrive at the unity of the faith and of the knowledge of the Son of God (Eph. iv. 13; 1 Pet. i. 12)." —Füller (see the note connected with No. 3).

Verses 24–27, Melancthon: "*Primum refutat hic locus errorem Judæorum de lege retinenda et de regno politico Christi. Si erit perpetua justitia, item: si Christus occidetur, sequitur legem Mosaicam non retinendam esse, nec fore mundanum regnum.—Secundo tradit testimonium de passione Christi.—Tertio cum politia jam desierit, ita ut nullos habeat duces, nullos prophetas, nulla tribuum discrimina* (cfr. Hos. iii. 4 s.), *constat impletum esse dictum Jacob: Non auferetur sceptrum de Juda, donec venerit Salvator* (Gen. xlix. 10). *Necesse est igitur, venisse Salvatorem.*" —Starke: "If everlasting righteousness shall be brought back, it follows that man has once possessed it, but has lost it.—While Christ is the true High-priest who atones for all men, and the great Prophet who has revealed the will of God concerning our salvation, He is also the true King, who has the power to place his atoning blood to our credit, and to protect His believing followers."—Hävernick: "The complete expiation of the great and numerous sins of Israel shall take place in the time of Messiah, the true High-priest; but His coming shall be delayed until after the expiration of the period that was indicated. But precisely because the sins of the people were as the sand of the sea, so that Daniel himself confessed their enormity (vs. 4–19), it was necessary to provide a perfect and wholly complete expiation, in contrast with that which had hitherto been made in the temple at Jerusalem, which was the mere foreshadowing of the future reality. The eyes of Daniel and of Israel were not to linger on the temple only, whose restoration the prophet so anxiously desired; they were to lift their eyes up farther, to Him who was to come, who is both the true temple, and the priest who ministers in it."—Füller: "Meanwhile the principal concern was that Israel should happily escape from the tribulation caused by the Old-Test. antichrist. When that was realized, it might be inquired why the seven weeks of years did not begin (?—rather, why Messiah did not come!)—At a later period, John, the New-Test. Daniel, appeared with his Revelation, which continued to build on the foundations laid by Daniel, and described the troubled times of the New-Test. antichrist, together with the deliverance from them, being designed to render the same service to the New-Test. people of God, which Daniel's prophecy formerly rendered to God's people under the Old Covenant."

---

4. *The prophet's last vision, containing the most thorough description of the future sufferings of Israel, and of its ultimate Messianic exaltation.*

CHAPTERS X.–XII.

a. *The appearance of the angel on the banks of the Tigris, as preparatory to the subsequent prophecies and introductory to them.*

CHAPS. X. 1–XI. 1.

1 In *the* third year of [to] Cyrus king of Persia, a thing [word] was revealed
unto Daniel, whose name was called Belteshazzar; and the thing [word] *was*

true [truth], but [and] *the* time *appointed* [warfare] *was* long [great]: and he
understood the thing [word], and had understanding of [in] the vision [appear-
ance.]
2 In those days I Daniel was[1] mourning three full weeks.[2] I ate no pleasant
3 bread, neither came flesh nor wine in [to] my mouth, neither did I anoint my-
self at all till three whole weeks were fulfilled.
4 And in *the* four and twentieth day of [to] the first month, as [and] I was by
5 [upon] *the* side of the great river, which [it] *is* Hiddekel, then [and] I lifted
up mine eyes, and looked [saw], and, behold, a certain [one] man clothed *in*
5 linen [linens], whose [and his] loins *were* girded with fine gold of Uphaz; his
body also [and his body] *was* like *the* beryl, and his face as *the* appearance of
lightning, and his eyes as lamps of fire, and his arms and his feet like in colour
to [*the* aspect of] polished brass, and *the* voice of his words like *the* voice of a
7 multitude. And I Daniel alone saw the vision [appearance]; for [and] the men
that were with me saw not the vision [appearance]; but a great quaking fell
upon them, so that [and] they fled to hide [in hiding] themselves.
8 Therefore [And] I was left alone, and saw this great vision [appearance], and
there remained no strength in me; for my comeliness was turned in [upon] me
9 *in*to corruption, and I retained no strength. Yet [And] heard I *the* voice of his
words: and when [as] I heard *the* voice of his words, then [and] was I in a deep
10 sleep [stupified] on my face, and my face toward *the* ground [earth]. And, be-
hold, a hand touched me, which [and] set me upon my knees and *upon the* palms
11 of my hands. And he said unto me, *O* Daniel, a man *greatly* beloved, under-
stand [have understanding in] the words that I speak unto thee, and stand up-
right; for unto thee am I now sent. And when he *had* spoken [at his speaking]
this word unto [with] me, I stood trembling.
12 Then [And] said he unto me, Fear not, Daniel; for from the first day that
thou didst set [give] thy heart to understand, and to chasten thyself before thy
13 God, thy words were heard, and I am [have] come for [at] thy words. But [And]
the prince of *the* kindom of Persia withstood [*was* standing in front of] me one
and twenty days: but [and], lo, Michael, one of the chief [first] princes, came
14 to help me; and I remained there with [beside] *the* kings of Persia. Now
[And] I am [have] come to make thee understand what shall befall thy people
in *the* latter [sequel of the] days: for yet *the* vision *is* for *many* days.
15 And when he had spoken [in his speaking] such like [like these] words unto
[with] me, I set [gave] my face toward *the* ground [earth], and I became dumb.
16 And, behold, *one* like *the* similitude of *the* sons of men [man] touched [touch-
ing upon] my lips: then [and] I opened my mouth and spake, and said unto
him that stood before me, *O* my lord, by the vision [appearance] my sorrows
17 are turned upon me, and I have retained no strength. For [And] how can *the*
servant of this my lord talk [speak] with this my lord? for [and] *as for* me
[I], straightway *there* remained [would stand] no strength in me, neither is
there breath left in me.
18 Then [And] *there* came again and touched me *one* like *the* appearance of a
19 man, and he strengthened me, and said, *O* man *greatly* beloved, fear not;
peace *be* unto thee; be strong, yea [and], be strong. And when he had spoken
unto [in his speaking with] me, I was strengthened, and said, Let my lord
speak; for thou hast strengthened me.
20 Then [And] said he, Knowest thou wherefore I [have] come unto thee? and
now will I return to fight with *the* prince of Persia: and *when* I *am* gone forth,
21 [then] lo, *the* prince of Græcia shall [has] come. But I will show [tell] thee
that *which is* noted [recorded] in *the* scripture of truth: and *there is* none that
1 holdeth with me in [upon] these things, but Michael your prince. Also [And]
I, in the first year of [to] Darius the Mede, *even* I, stood to confirm and to
strengthen him.

GRAMMATICAL NOTES.

[[1] הָיִיתִי here signifies *continued.*—[2] The phrase is peculiar, שָׁבֻעִים יָמִים, literally, *sevens days*, the latter being in epexegetical apposition. It is here used in contrast with chap. ix. 25 et seq., to show that literal weeks, and not hebdomades of years, are intended.]

PREFATORY REMARKS

Concerning the final vision of Daniel (chap. x.–xii.) *as a whole.*

The last section of the prophetically visional part of this book falls into three clearly defined subdivisions of unequal length, and was therefore not inappropriately treated by the person who divided the Holy Scriptures into chapters. It is not only the most comprehensive, but, because of its form and contents, also the most remarkable and difficult among the prophetic portions of the book. Having been composed later than the three preceding visions, namely subsequent to the captivity and when the return of the exiles had already begun (see on v. 1), it supplements their contents, and develops them still farther—especially those of the second vision (chap. viii.) and of the third (chap. ix.). The development of the fourth and last world-power to the stage of anti-Christianity, which was described with special interest in those two chapters, is now illustrated more fully than in any former instance, and at the same time, the ultimate triumph of the kingdom of God over that and all other opposing powers is brought into a clearer light and portrayed in more glowing colors than heretofore. The relation of the section to chap. vii. as serving to complement and still farther develop its subject, becomes especially prominent in this bright closing scene; while the prophecy is in so far complementary to chapters viii. and ix. as it describes the development of the anti-Christian world-power in predictions distinguished by a greater fulness of detail—to say nothing of the similarity between its preparatory scenery and that of chap. viii. and also of ix. 20–23. The section serves to complete the visions of chap. viii. by describing more exactly the hostile relations in which the various constituent sections of the fourth world-power stood to each other, as already symbolically indicated in chap. viii. 22 et seq.; and particularly by showing how the holy land, which lay between the contending sections of the divided empire, in some cases was drawn indirectly into suffering, and in others was made the object of direct attack. In like manner this vision becomes complementary to that in chap. ix. since it fills the outline of the sixty-two weeks and also of the one final week of tribulation [?], which were but briefly referred to in that chapter, with a wealth of contents, that displays a growing animation and interest as the description draws near to the close of the sixty-second and the beginning of the last week. In tracing the particular manner of the development of the anti-Christian power out of the fourth and last world-monarchy, there seems to have been *the occasional intervention of a later hand, which drew the prophecy with sharper lines and adapted it more fully to the subsequent facts connected with its historical fulfilment, than had been done in the general outline which was revealed to the prophet.** The statements in v. 5 et seq., concerning the geographical position of the two most powerful sections of the great divided Javanic world-empire, and also concerning the direction taken by the various expeditions for conquest which their rulers organized, the repeated attempts to unite the contending dynasties by means of matrimonial alliances, the insurrections and treasonable plots against individual sovereigns, etc., can hardly be regarded otherwise than as interpolations on the part of a pious Jewish apocalyptist of the Maccabæan age, although it may be impossible at this day to venture a definite estimate respecting the proportion of the whole section chap. xi. 5–45 that originated with Daniel, or as to how much is to be credited to the subsequent reviser (see the exeget. remarks on the several passages, particularly on vs. 5, 6, 8, 14, 17, 18, 25, 27, etc., and pre-eminently on v. 40 et seq.; and cf. supra, Introd. § 1, note 2, and § 4). While, for reasons that have been given (cf. Introd. § 4, note 1), we decidedly reject the hypothesis that the entire section chap. x. 1–xii. 13, excepting only the first four verses of chap. xii., is spurious, we regard the theory that chap. xi. has been interpolated as above suggested, as necessary, chiefly because details characterized by such unusual precision as is found in that chapter, seem to conflict with the nature of genuine and healthful prophecy, and with the analogy of all the remaining prophecies in the history of Old-Test. revelation.* We are entirely agreed with Kranichfeld (p. 340 et seq.) in holding that the nature or the "self-evident canon" of prophecy requires "*that the prediction should not usurp the place of historical development itself*, *i.e.*, that it should not adduce such future dates, as cannot be connected with the time of the prophetic originator, as the unfolding of a religious or moral idea animated by the operations of God—although in other respects a particularizing description may offer any amount of detailed representations in illustration, limited only by the confines established by that canon." We cannot, however, agree with him in believing that the entire vision before us, and especially that part contained in chap. xi., must be regarded "by that canon" *simply as a developing of the ideas contained elsewhere in the book.* The many surprising details of that chapter do not appear to an unbiassed mind as the mere development of former thoughts, but rather as concrete statements respecting the political and family history of the Seleucidæ and the Ptolemies, such as no other Old-Test. prophet would have attempted to furnish, even approximately, and such as conflict with the spirit of Old-Test. prophecy in general. We are certainly not compelled by any merely subjective reason to assume

* [We have repeatedly objected to this hypothesis of a later interpolation as purely subjective and gratuitous.]

* [That the prophecies in question are unique in this particular may readily be conceded without any impeachment of their genuineness. The whole book is remarkable for its vividness and personality of delineation. The details were so striking that Cyrus the Great and Alexander the Great are traditionally reported to have recognized their own portraits immediately. But the same is measurably true of other specifications in O.-T. prophecies, although not on so extended a scale. Even the *name* of Cyrus is mentioned by Isaiah nearly two centuries before his time; yet few, among evangelical interpreters at least, would on that account pronounce those passages a forgery. The author's reasoning for the rejection of the authenticity of these predictions of Daniel is entirely uncritical. Hengstenberg, in his work on the *Genuineness of the Book of Daniel* (Edinb. translation, sec. xii.), adduces other examples of equal definiteness in O.-T. prophecy, and meets this whole objection fully. The vague manner in which our author adduces the argument gives very little opportunity to do more than make this general demurral to his views on this point.]

an interpolation of the text of Daniel in this place, after having rejected that theory in every other instance. The only reason which prevents us from defending the genuineness of this closing section is based on the analogy of all the balance of O.-T. prophecy, which in no case affords a similar example of specific and detailed description of the future (cf. Tholuck, *Die Propheten und ihre Weissagungen*, p. 105 et seq.; *Die Grenzen einer Prädiktion*—an investigation, however, which seems to require a more strict apprehension).

The whole section divides itself, as has already been observed, into three parts, the first of which describes the general circumstances that conditioned the new vision, and also the introductory features of the vision itself (consisting in the appearance of a mighty angel, which at first excited the prophet's alarm and terror, but subsequently exercised a comforting and exalting influence over him); chap. x. 1–xi. 1. The special description of the future having been thus introduced is taken up by the second part and carried forward from the unfolding of the Persian world-empire, then upon the stage, to the highest point of conceited power developed by the antitheistic tyrant who ultimately sprang from the Javanic world-monarchy, and who became the antichrist of the Old Testament (chap. xi. 2–45).* Finally, the third part describes the triumph, the deliverance, and the exaltation of God's people in the Messianic period, and, if it does not certify the nearness of that æra of ultimate prosperity, it yet conveys the assurance that its approach is determined by immutable measurements and conditions fixed by God (chap. xii. 1–13).—The exorbitant length of the intermediate part, exceeding, as it does, the aggregate of the others nearly two-fold, might be adduced as an additional and highly probable evidence of its interpolation, as suggested above.*

* [Keil takes a different view of this whole prophecy, with a view to obviate any sudden transition, either from the Persian monarchy to the Antiochian tyranny, or from that to the final consummation of the kingdom of God. "The angel of the Lord will reveal to Daniel, not what shall happen from the third year of Cyrus to the time of Antiochus, and further to the resurrection of the dead, but, according to the express declaration of chap. x. 14, what shall happen to his people בְּאַחֲרִית הַיָּמִים, *i.e.*, in the Messianic future, because the prophecy relates to this time. In the אַחֲרִית יָמִים takes place the destruction of the world-power, and the setting up of the Messianic kingdom at the end of the present world-æon. All that the angel says regarding the Persian and the Javanic world-kingdoms, and the wars of the kings of the north and the south, has its aim to the end-time, and serves only to indicate briefly the chief elements of the development of the world-kingdoms till the time when the war that brings in the end shall burst forth, and to show how, after the overthrow of the Javanic world-kingdom, neither the kings of the north nor those of the south shall gain the possession of the dominion of the world." But this last would certainly seem to be a very inadequate reason for so great a detail of political delineation. Hence, after pursuing the exposition of the middle portion of this prophecy especially, Keil concludes thus: "From this comparison this much follows, that the prophecy does not furnish a prediction of the historical wars of the Seleucidæ and the Ptolemies, but an ideal description of the war of the kings of the north and the south in its general outlines, whereby, it is true, diverse special elements of the prophetical announcement have been historically fulfilled, but the historical reality does not correspond with the contents of the prophecy in anything like an exhaustive manner." Accordingly he everywhere exaggerates the minor discrepancies that occur between the prophecy and the history of Antiochus in particular, with a view to enhance this idealistic theory. The indefiniteness and inconsistency of thus carrying on at once a double line of interpretation renders his scheme on the whole very unsatisfactory. Yet it is in pursuance of his general theory concerning the absence of a design on the prophet's part to particularize the history or the Jews as such. To a certain point this theory is doubtless true; but he carries it so far as to render the predictions rather symbolical than real. The discrepancies upon which he chiefly relies for the support of his view we will examine in detail as they occur.]

* [On the contrary, the fact that in chap. xi. this detail is so minutely drawn out, is a strong proof of the genuineness of this portion, for it is precisely here that the same arch-enemy, the Antiochian antichrist, is most vividly depicted, who constitutes the prominent and culminating figure in all the preceding visions. The whole chapter evidently revolves around this, which is likewise the central point of the entire book. It is moreover in exact conformity with the spirit of O.-T. prophecy to dwell thus at length upon the *nearest* type of all the tableaux in the future of God's people, and to touch more lightly and dimly upon the more distant features.]

EXEGETICAL REMARKS.

Verse 1. *The time and significance of the vision.* **In the third year of Cyrus king of Persia**—therefore B.C. 536 or 535 [probably, 534], later than any other date in the book (cf. on chap. i. 21). It is significant and instructive, as bearing on the subject and design of the vision, which dwells with special interest on the aspect of affairs *subsequent to the Persian dominion*, that when it was imparted to Daniel, he had already lived under Medo-Persian rule during several years. Cf. Kranichfeld, p. 340: "After a series of prophetic announcements by Daniel had received a genuine prophetic fulfilment during the time of the exile itself, and, on the one hand the newly confirmed return of the exiles had been but lately realized, while on the other, the צוֹק הָעִתִּים, which had been predicted instead of the Messianic glory, was feelingly demonstrated, *e.g.*, by the disputes with the Samaritans, by the interruption of the building of the temple (cf. Ezra iii. 8 with iv. 8), and, above all, by the continued aversion of the supreme Persian powers (cf. Dan. x. 13, 20), it now became the interest of the seer to devote special attention to the last heathen empire of the earth, the only one remaining to be demonstrated, and to present theocratically this last characteristic picture of hostility, in colors that would constantly impress its nature, and in such detail as the confidence springing from the unvarying success of the past would justify. Thoroughly convinced as he was, on the ground of his own observation and of the teaching of earlier prophecy that the Javanic west would eventually displace the east in the dominion of the world, and that at the same time the ultimate form of heathen government would appear in connection with the former, he would naturally not regard the transient Persian empire, which had indeed been adequately characterized at its very beginning, as the אַחֲרִית הַיָּמִים (cf. x. 14; ii. 28; viii. 19) upon which prophecy elsewhere dwells by preference, but would rather consider the final form of heathen power over the theocracy in that light."—Hitzig inquires "Why Daniel was still at Babylon in the third year of Cyrus? Why so pious a theocrat, and so devoted a lover of Jerusalem and the holy land, had not returned thither? Why he should seem to place himself among the despisers of the holy mountain and among the apostates (Isa. lxv. 11; lxvi. 5), by disregarding the exhortations of Isa. ii. to return (Isa. xlviii. 20; lii. 11 et seq.)?"—to all of which the simple answer is, that while ranking as a highly esteemed and influential officer of the state, even under Persian rule (cf. chap. vi. 29), he must have been persuaded that he would be able to render his nation more important service with regard to the rebuilding of their city and temple, were he to remain behind to represent them at the court, than he possibly could were he to accompany them on their return to Judæa. As a secondary consideration his somewhat advanced age may have influenced his decision (despite Ezra iii. 12), cf. Hävernick on the passage.—**Unto Daniel, whose name was called Belteshazzar.** Cf. i. 7; ii. 26; iv. 5; v. 12. Both names are given in this place, for the reason, probably, that the two-fold relation which the prophet occupied (being connected with the Old-Test. people of God, and also filling an official station at the court of the world-kingdom) and which is thus indicated, constituted the feature by which he was enabled "to view the history of the conflict of Israel with the world-power, and to record for the benefit of his people what might be expected from the latter" (Füller).—**And the thing was true**; or, "and the word is truth," *i.e.*, the word of God which was revealed to the prophet, and which, unlike the words of so many false prophets of that time (Jer. xxix. 8 et seq., 15), is not a lying and deceptive word, but truth, that is worthy of credit and shall surely come to pass; cf. 2 Sam. vii. 28; 1 Kings viii. 26; also below, v. 21; xi. 2; xii. 7.—**But the time appointed was long**; rather, "and great tribulation," supply, "formed its subject" צָבָא גָדוֹל is an additional predicate of הַדָּבָר (cf. Gen. xi. 1; Isa. vii. 24; Jer. xxvi. 2). Maurer renders it correctly: "צ׳ ג׳ *oraculum vocatur ab argumento*," and also de Wette: "and refers to great wretchedness." צָבָא here denotes "warfare, oppression, trouble," exactly as in Isa. xl. 2; not "bravery, might" (Vulg., Syr.), nor "exertion," as if the great effort put forth by the prophet while receiving the revelation were alluded to (Hävern.), and least of all; "ministering," as Ewald strangely conceived, referring to the numerous angels whom he regarded as being engaged in this new revelation with industrious energy and care (!).—**And he understood the thing, and had understanding of the vision**; rather, "observed the word, and gave attention to the vision." בִּין is not an imperative (v. Lengerke, Ewald), but an infinitive with a perfect signification.* The construction with an accusative of the object is similar to that in chap. ix. 2; cf. xii. 8. The following בִּינָה, although *milel*, is not an imperative (as v. Lengerke supposes, but a noun, which has the accent here on the first syllable, because of the accented לוֹ that immediately follows; cf. Ezek. xix. 14. The probable design of the statement that Daniel gave careful heed to what was revealed was to emphasize the highly significant and profoundly important subject of the vision from the outset, and also to give assurance of the credibility of the prophet's narrative.

Verses 2, 3. *The frame of mind of Daniel and his outward deportment while receiving the revelation.* Verse 2. **In those days I Daniel was mourning three full weeks.** The tidings respecting the discouraging state of affairs among the Jews, who had returned to the holy land, which may have reached Daniel about this time, may be regarded as the probable cause of his sadness. An especial cause of grief to him probably lay in the fact, that as the intervention of the Samaritans had interrupted the building of the temple since the second year after the return of the exiles (Ezra iv. 4 et seq.; cf. iii. 8), the latter were prevented from observing the Passover in a lawful manner. His attention would be especially directed to that fact, since according to v. 4, the period of three weeks spent by him in mourning and fasting was included in the very month of the feast of the Passover, so as to precede the date fixed for the beginning of that feast (which continued from the 14th to the 21st Nisan, the "first month" of the Jewish year) by twelve days, and to extend three days beyond its close—to the 24th Nisan.—שָׁבֻעִים יָמִים. The addition of יָמִים, which is designed to indicate the full or enumerated measure of the weeks (cf. our "three full weeks"), is hardly intended to contrast with the weeks *of years* which are implied in chap. ix.; for the contrary cf. Gen. xxix. 14; xli 1; Num. xi. 20 et seq.; Jer. xxvi. 3, 11, etc.*—**I ate no pleasant bread.** לֶחֶם חֲמֻדוֹת, "bread of pleasures, of desires," is doubtless a contrast to the "bread of affliction," Deut. xvi. 3, *i.e.*, to the unleavened bread which was eaten during the Passover. Hence, the first expression of his grief mentioned by Daniel is that he abstained from the use of leavened bread, or from eating the לֶ׳ עֹנִי or מַצּוֹת.† Luther's rendering, "I ate no dainty food," is therefore mistaken and inexact; and also Bertholdt's, "I abstained even from the use of bread."—**Neither came flesh nor wine in my mouth.** A genuine fast, in which all dainty, attractive, or luxurious viands were avoided; cf. Gen. xxvii. 25; 2 Sam. xii. 20; Isa. xxii. 13, etc.—**Neither did I anoint myself**; another characteristic indication of a sorrowful disposition, cf. Ecc. ix. 8; Psa. xxiii. 5; Isa. lxi. 3, etc.—Hitzig's view is substantially correct: "The design of his mourning was not to support prayer and inter-

* [Keil, however, agrees with Gesenius and Fürst in regarding it as an anomalous third pers. masc. præter.]

* [In these phrases יָמִים is doubtless, as Gesenius explains, to be regarded as an *accusative* of limitation, the preceding noun being in the absolute, and not the construct state. Yet even this appositional relation seems to limit the שָׁבֻעִים, whether the latter be regarded as a noun = *weeks* or even simple = *seven*, to the usual hebdomadal sense. It thus stands really, though perhaps not intentionally, in contrast with the undefined שָׁבֻעִים of chap. ix. 24–27, and leaves the word in that passage to be interpreted by the exigencies of the context.]

† ["But this contrast is not well founded, for the מַצּוֹת (*unleavened cakes*) of the Passover was not (notwithstanding Deut. xvi. 3) bread of sorrow, but pure, holy bread, which Daniel did not eat, in opposition to the law, for three weeks. לֶחֶם is not to be limited to bread in its narrower sense, but denotes *food* generally."—*Keil.*]

cession as in chap. ix. (for which reason it does not assume its appropriate garb, cf. Psa. xxxv. 13, 14), but rather to prepare to receive a revelation. However, the writer by no means entertains the opinion that asceticism could secure or compel a revelation; for in that case the means employed would have been increased, particularly as the vision was delayed. Daniel rather confines himself to abstinence from worldly enjoyment, in order to maintain the serious frame of mind in which the desired revelation should be received, and which is the only one that may hope to be blessed with a revelation."

Verses 4–7. *Designation of the special time and place. Description of the appearance of the angel who conveys the revelation.* **And in the four and twentieth day of the first month.** Since, according to Esth. iii. 7, the "first month" was Nisan (cf. also 1 Macc. vii. 49; ix. 3), and since by vs. 12 and 13, the mourning and fasting of Daniel began precisely twenty-one days before the present date—therefore on the third Nisan,—the special reason why he commenced such exercises on that particular day may probably be found in the fact that the 1st and 2d Nisan were still observed, at the period of the captivity, as they were already in the time of Saul and David, as the festival of the New-year or of the first new moon in the year; and it was of course unsuitable for him to fast while that joyous festival continued (cf. 1 Sam. xx. 18, et seq.; xxvii. 34, with ii. 19, vi. 29).—**I was by the side of the great river, which is Hiddekel.** It cannot be easily determined whether he was there in vision merely, as in the similar case, chap viii. 2 (see on that passage), or likewise in body. The latter opinion (Hävern., v. Leng., Maurer, Hitzig, Kliefoth, Füller) appears to be preferable, in view of the subsequent mention of Daniel's companions on the bank of the river.—Concerning חִדֶּקֶל, *i.e.*, probably, the "swift, tearing" (from חדק), as the Scriptural designation of the Tigris, cf. Gesen.-Dietrich, s. v., and also the expositors of Gen. ii. 14. The latter passage, moreover, clearly asserts the distinction between the Hiddekel and the Euphrates, which is observed throughout the Old-Test. generally, and thereby demonstrates the mistake of Syrus, who regards the חד' in this place as denoting the Euphrates.—Verse 5. **Then I lifted up mine eyes and looked,** etc., exactly as in the vision on the banks of the Eulæus, chap. viii. 3.—**And behold a man clothed in linen.** The description begins with his clothing, hence proceeds from without inward (contrary to the method of, *e.g.*, Matt. xvii. 2; xxviii. 3). White linen (בַּדִּים, from בַּד, cf. Ezek. ix. 2) was the garb of priests, especially of the high-priests (cf. Lev. xvi. 4, 23; vi. 3 with Isa. xliii. 28), and therefore symbolizes *holiness;* the addition of golden ornaments denotes *princely rank.* The person here described was therefore at all events a שַׂר קֹדֶשׁ (cf. Isa. xliii. 28) or holy angelic prince, and more particularly, was identical with the "man's voice between the Ulai," chap. viii. 16, which directed Gabriel to interpret the vision for Daniel in that place, since according to chap. xii. 6, *he hovered over the river.* It was shown on the former passage, that the angel who uttered that command need not necessarily have been superior to Gabriel, but that he may have belonged, as well as the latter, to the class of archangels or שָׂרִים; and he may be regarded as the compeer of Michael as well, despite v. 13, where he refers to the aid he received from the latter against the prince of Persia. Hence, he was a *third* angel-prince besides Gabriel and Michael, whose name, however, is not given; and it is therefore vain to search for the specific name he bore. Hofmann, Auberlen and Füller conceive of this angelic prince as being the power of nature which operates for the kingdom of God in the entire heathen world, or as *the good principle in the world-power*, which is identical with the κατέχων, 2 Thess. ii. 6; but they fail to establish exegetically, and in an adequate manner this identity, as well as the character ascribed to the angel. Concerning the modicum of truth which may nevertheless underlie this opinion, see Eth.-fund. principles, etc., No. 1.—The identity of this angel with *Michael*, which Kranichfeld assumes, is opposed by the manner in which Michael is represented as *not being present*, in vs. 13 and 21. It is more probable that he was identical with *Gabriel* (Ewald et al.); but the appearance of the latter on his entrance in chap. viii. is described in different terms, and, moreover, the name of *Gabriel* is not expressly mentioned; cf. infra, on v. 13.—**Whose loins were girded with fine gold of Uphaz;** *i.e.*, with the finest and most valuable gold; cf. Psa. xlv. 8, "gold of Ophir." The identity of אוּפָז and אוֹפִיר, which is assumed by, *e.g.*, the Vulg., Chald., and Syr. (but not by Theodot.), is opposed by the different form of the name, and by the impossibility of transforming ר into ז.* The country here referred to (and in Jer. xii. 8) was probably a region in the south or east, and perhaps adjoining to Ophir, which abounded in gold, and like the latter, constituted a principal source from whence the people of hither Asia derived their precious metals in ancient times. The theory which seems best recommended is that of Hitzig, who combines the Sancr. name *vipâçâ = Hyphasis*, with the supposition based on that etymology, that the country derived its name from a colony which came to Arabia Felix from the river Hyphasis in India. Cf. Nägelsbach on Jer., l. c., concerning this question.—Verse 6. **His body also was like the beryl,** or "crysolite," hence having the golden lustre of topaz or amber, which shone through his garb of white linen. With regard to תַּרְשִׁישׁ—whose primary signification was doubtless "the sea" (=Sanscr. *tarisha*), and which afterward became the name of the celebrated colony of Phœnician merchants located in Spain near the Mediterranean sea, and still later was employed to designate the precious stone brought from thence, which the Sept and Josephus term the χρυσόλιθος with probable correctness—see Hitzig on Ezek. i. 16; Gesen.-Dietrich in the *Handwörterbuch;* and also my observation on Cant. v. 14.—**And his face as the appearance of lightning**; cf. Ezek. i. 13; Matt. xxviii. 3. On the comparison

* [The predominant opinion, nevertheless, among scholars identifies Ophir with Uphaz.]

of his eyes with lamps of fire cf. Rev. i. 14, which passage is wholly imitated from the one before us.—**And his arms and feet like in colour to polished brass**; rather, "arms and feet like the gleam of glowing brass." מַרְגְּלֹת, which primarily denotes the "place of the feet," is here synonymous with רַגְלַיִם, "feet," as appears from the mention of זְרֹעֹת, "arms," in the same connection; for why, if the arms glowed like brass, should the *place* only of the feet present the same appearance and not rather the feet themselves? (against Kranichfeld, etc.).*—קָלָל, the attribute of נְחשֶׁת, together with כְּעֵין (cf. Num. xi. 7), is taken from Ezek. i. 7. It denotes brass in a glowing and liquid or molten state (קָלָל, a fuller form of the more usual קַל, light, swiftly moving, *volubilis*), not merely "shining or gleaming" brass (Ewald, etc.), nor yet "brass of the smelting furnace," as Hitzig assumes, putting entirely too artificial a sense on the idea. Cf., however, the parallel Rev. i. 15, οἱ πόδες αὐτοῦ ὅμοιοι χαλχολιβάνῳ ὡς ἐν καμίνῳ πεπυρομένῳ.—**And the voice of his words like the voice of a multitude,** or "of a roaring." קוֹל הָמוֹן primarily signifies the "voice (sound) of a roaring," and may denote the roaring of the sea, of the stormy waves of the ocean, or of a great multitude of people (Theod., Vulg., Syr., and also moderns, *e.g.*, Kranichfeld, Füller, etc.). The parallels, Ezek. i. 24 (כְּקוֹל מַיִם רַבִּים); xliii. 2; Isa. xvii. 12; Rev. i. 15, determine in favor of the former interpretation. The terrified prophet does not at first recognize what the speaker says in so dreadful a voice, either here or in v. 9. Cf. the analogous circumstance in chap. viii. 13 *a*.—Verse 7. **The men that were with me saw not the vision**; a feature similar to that connected with the conversion of St. Paul, Acts ix. 7; xxii. 11. It is impossible to determine who the prophet's companions were; they may as well have been the *servants* of the highly esteemed "prince" Daniel (chap. vi. 21), as associates of a different rank.—**But a great quaking fell upon them**; evidently because they *heard* the dreadful sound of the roaring, although they saw nothing; cf. Gen iii. 8; Am. iii. 6; Acts ix. 7.†—**They fled to hide themselves**; rather, "they fled hiding themselves." בְּהֵחָבֵא, properly, "while hiding themselves," a periphrase of the gerund; cf. Gesenius, *Thesaur.*, p. 175 *a*. The infinitive with לְ would have expressed the somewhat different idea, "they fled to hide themselves;" cf. 1 Kings xxii. 25; 2 Kings xix. 11.

Verses 8–11. *The impression made on Daniel by the appearance of the angel. His temporary stupor, and subsequent and gradual restoration.* **I . . . . saw this great vision.** The same language is used with reference to the appearance of the Lord in the burning bush to Moses, Ex. iii. 3.—**My comeliness was turned in me into corruption**; rather, "the color of my face was changed into disfigurement for me." Literally, "and my brightness," etc. (thus Ewald et al). הוֹד, "brightness, freshness of color," here corresponds to the Chald. זִיו, chap. v. 6, 9; vii. 28. עָלַי, "on me," seems to be a Chaldaism employed as a periphrase for the dative, and therefore to be equivalent to אֵלַי (unlike v. 16). It is hardly to be separated from the verb and to be immediately connected with הוֹדִי, thus periphrasing the genitive (against Hitzig).—לְמַשְׁחִית, properly, "to destruction;" cf. 2 Chron. xx. 23. The following context indicates the nature of this destruction or disfigurement, by stating that the loss of color was joined to faintness and a total loss of strength.—Verse 9. **Then was I in a deep sleep on my face**, *i.e.*, in a stupefied state, during which a total loss of his senses and of consciousness was depicted on his countenance.—**And my face** (sank) **toward the ground**; *i.e.*, the loss of consciousness was not momentary, but was protracted during some time, and brought him to the ground on his face. With a strange arbitrariness Hitzig finds "an attention to trivial details that border closely on the comical" in the statement that the *face* was toward the ground; as if the frequent expression אַפַּיִם אַרְצָה (Gen. xix. 1; xlii. 6) or וַיִּשְׁתַּחוּ אַרְצָה (Gen. xxxiii. 3, etc.) did not likewise indicate the apparently general use of אַרְצָה in this sense! On the subject cf. chap. viii. 17.—Verse 10. **And behold, a hand touched me.** The stunned prophet is not able to say whose hand it was; but the tenor of the entire representation shows, beyond the reach of doubt, that it was the hand of the same person who had hitherto been in his presence (cf. viii. 18; Ezek. ii. 9). Kranichfeld (see above, on v. 5) is therefore in error when, after having assumed that the angel described above was Michael, he regards the one who now appears and henceforth addresses Daniel as being *Gabriel* (as do Hävernick, Hengstenberg, etc.). Such a multiplication of persons is unnecessary, and is opposed by the total silence of the author with regard to the names of the appearance here introduced. Maurer, Hitzig, v. Hofmann, Füller, Kliefoth, etc., correctly hold to the identity of the angel who touches Daniel with the one introduced in v. 5.—**Set me** (rather "shook me") **upon my knees and upon the palms of my hands**; a *constr. prægnans*, for "shook me and helped me," etc. The couching position which he accordingly assumed at first is the natural posture of one who is stunned and overwhelmed with awe in the presence of a superior being.—Verse 11. **O Daniel, a man greatly beloved.** See on chap. ix. 23.—**For unto thee am I now sent**; namely, sent at this precise moment, as the servant of God and the bearer of a message of blessing and comfort. The angel designs by this encouraging address not merely to induce Daniel to arise to an erect position, but also to

* [Keil, however contends that מַרְגְּלֹת, *place of feet*, does not stand for *feet*, but denotes that part of the human frame where the feet are; and the word indicates that not the feet alone, but the under parts of the body shone like burnished brass.]

† [Keil thinks that "the voice was not heard till after Daniel's companions had fled;" but this is by no means certain from the text.]

fix his attention on the words about to be spoken.—**I stood trembling**—in fearful expectation of the things to which he should listen; cf. Ezra x. 9.

Verses 12–14. *The angel's statement respecting the design of his coming and the reason of his delay to that time.* Cf. chap. ix. 23.—**For from the first day** (therefore from the third Nisan, according to v. 4) **that thou didst set thine heart**; properly "gavest thy heart;" cf. Eccles. i. 13, 17.—**To understand, and to chasten** (or "humble") **thyself before God.** V. 14 *a* states what Daniel desired to understand, viz.: the future experiences of his people. He sought to obtain the knowledge of this *by humbling himself* before God in fasting, etc. Consequently לְהָבִין וּלְהִתְעַנּוֹת וגו׳ may be considered a hendiadys, to the extent to which the implied verbal idea *is co-ordinated.*—**And I am come for thy words**, *i.e.*, in consequence of the words of thy prayer to which reference has just been made. On כִּדְבָרֶיךָ, "according to thy words," cf. for instance, Esth. i. 12; iii. 15; viii. 14; 1 Kings xiii. 1, etc. The perfect בָּאתִי, "I have come," denotes that the coming of the angel, which had already been determined on at the beginning of the prophet's prayer, had only then become an accomplished fact. The delay in his coming, which was caused by the interference of a hostile angelic power, is accounted for in the following verse.—Verse 13. **But the prince of the kingdom of Persia withstood me one and twenty days.** שַׂר מַלְכוּת פָּרַס. Jerome observes correctly, although upon a possibly inadequate exegetical foundation: "*Videtur mihi hic esse angelus, cui Persis credita est, juxta illud quod in Deuteronomio* (xxxii. 8, lxx.) *legimus: 'Quando dividebat Altissimus gentes et disseminabat filios Adam, statuit terminos gentium juxta numerum angelorum Dei.' Isti sunt principes, de quibus Paulus apostolus loquitur: 'Sapientiam loquimur inter perfectos, quam nullus principum sæculi hujus cognovit; si enim cognovissent, nunquam Dominum gloriæ crucifixissent.' Restitit autem princeps, i.e., angelus Persarum, faciens pro credita sibi provincia, ne captivorum omnis populus dimitteretur.*" This interpretation is supported, and that of Calvin, Hävernick, Kranichfeld, et al., which takes שַׂר in the sense of "king, earthly and human sovereign," is opposed by the following considerations: (1) in chap. xi. 5, where שַׂר is unquestionably employed in the latter sense, the connection is entirely different from the character of the present passage, where the הַשָּׂרִים which immediately follows obviously denotes *angelic princes;* (2) the Persian kings, on the other hand, are termed מַלְכֵי פָרַס at the end of the verse; (3) the idea of an angel's conflict with a *human* king seems very inappropriate; (4) the angel Michael was Israel's "prince," *i.e.*, guardian angel, according to v. 21; chap. xii. 1; and corresponding to this, the prince of Persia who is here noticed, and the prince of Græcia mentioned in v. 20, were, without doubt, the *angels* of Persia and Javan respectively; (5) the idea of guardian angels over entire realms, whether friendly or hostile in their disposition toward the theocracy, is attested by various Old-Test. parallels, particularly by Isa. xxiv. 21 (see Knobel on that passage); Isa. xlvi. 2; Jer. xlvi. 25; xlix. 3 (where the gods of heathen nations take the place of the guardian angels); Deut. xxxii 8; and Psa. xcvi. 4, lxx.; also Bar. iv. 7 and Ecclus. xvii. 17 (where ἡγούμενος seems to designate an angel prince, exactly like שַׂר in this passage),—to say nothing of New-Test. passages, such as 1 Cor. viii. 5; x. 20 et seq.—The withstanding or resisting during twenty-one days is obviously to be understood *sensu hostili* (לְנֶגֶד, as in Prov. xxi. 30; cf. 2 Sam. xviii. 13), without, however, involving the idea that the *Persian court*, or any earthly locality whatever, was the scene of such opposition or warfare (as, *e.g.*, Füller assumes). That *adversari* may more probably have taken place in super-mundane regions; and that this was the case seems to have been attested by parallels like 1 Kings xxii. 19 et seq.; Job i. 6; ii. 1 et seq.; Luke x. 18; xxii. 31. Hofmann (*Schriftbew.*, I. 286 et seq.) and Füller hold that "the prince of the kingdom of Persia" does not denote an actual guardian angel of that realm, but any evil spirit whatever, who may have sought to exert an influence on the decisions of the Persian king, while on the contrary the angel who appeared to Daniel sought to counteract that influence by his own, as being more beneficial to Israel; * but this opinion is altogether too artificial, because it supposes two spiritual powers—the one good and the other evil—in every case (a "court-angel" and a "royal court-devil," in the language of Starke), as exerting influence over the ruler of a kingdom. Moreover, the idea of the spirit ruling at a court, as being either good or bad, either peaceful or warlike, has too modern an aspect, and is foreign to the modes of conception that were current among the ancient Orientals. The strongest argument against this opinion, however, consists in the consideration that the title שַׂר מַלְכוּת פָּרַס, and farther on, the appellations שַׂר יָוָן and שַׂרְכֶם (Michael, the prince of *Israel;* v. 21, cf. v. 20), imply a more intimate connection, a much closer and more constant relation between the angel and the corresponding nation than is involved in a merely temporary influence over the governmental policy of any particular ruler. A spirit who may have exercised a temporary control over the decisions of one or more Persian kings could not on that account simply be designated the שַׂר פָּרַס. The angel who is thus entitled must be considered the *constant* patron of the Persian

* Cf. especially Füller on this passage, p. 274: "The question is, which of the two spirits shall succeed in exercising the greater influence over the Persian court and king. It becomes an object to gain the consent of the Persian king and the holders of power under him, that he may decide thus or otherwise . . . . It is conceivable that in such a case the good spirit, who operated on the world-ruler, would occupy a more difficult position, and be engaged in a harder task than the evil spirit, to whom the heart of the natural man, to say nothing of the heart of a heathen, is more accessible than it is to the former. It was then that Michael came to his support by causing, as Hofmann remarks (as above, p. 288), the relations which Cyrus had assumed toward the Jewish people to operate on that king, and to gain increased influence over his inclinations and views," etc.

nation and state, as much so as Michael was the constant patron of Israel, having been known as such in the age of Joshua (Josh. v. 13) as well as in that of Daniel, and still later, in that of the New-Test. apocalyptist (Rev. xii. 7; Jude v. 9). For additional thoughts on the subject see on vs. 20, 21, and the Eth.-fund. principles.

And lo, Michael, one of the chief princes; properly, "one of the first" (הָרִאשֹׁנִים), *i.e.*, of the most eminent; cf. 1 Chron. xviii. 17, and also הַשַּׂר הַגָּדוֹל, chap. xii. 1. The name Michael, "*quis sicut Deus*" (cf., *e.g.*, Ex. xv. 11; Psa. lxxxix. 7), and also the name of Isaiah's prophetic contemporary מִיכָה (= מִיכָיָהוּ) is, according to Haneberg's correct observation (in Reusch's *Theol. Literaturbl.*, 1867, No. 3, p. 72), "a name that sounds like a decided monotheistic protest against every undue exaltation of the angelic dignity." It expresses still more strongly than the similar name of Gabriel (cf. on viii. 16), the idea of God's incomparable and assisting power, as whose instrument the angelic being who bears this name must be regarded (Kranichfeld). His "coming to help" is probably to be conceived of as an armed intervention, and supported by celestial hosts, as is suggested by the preceding warlike phrase עֹמֵד לְנֶגְדִּי, and as the term לְהִלָּחֵם in v. 20 indicates still more clearly. Michael must be conceived of in this place as battling at the head of an angelic host, as in Josh. v. 14 and Rev. xii. 7; cf. also Gen. xxxii. 2; 2 Kings vi. 17, and other references to hosts of celestial angels. How little this belligerent attitude of Michael comports with the view of Hofmann and Füller, that the speaker was a special "good spirit of the heathen world-power," whose battle with the prince of Persia was fought in the circles of the Persian court, will be apparent at once. Concerning the theory of the older exegetes and also of Hävernick, which directly identifies Michael with Christ, see Eth. fund. principles, No. 1, and also on chap. xii. 1.—**And I remained there with the kings of Persia**; rather, "and I became superfluous there," etc., namely, because another who was still more powerful than I had relieved me, and now represented me in the resistance to be made to the prince of Persia. The angel says that his presence became superfluous "with the kings of Persia" because he refers to all the powers who operate at the head of the Persian empire, including both the earthly and the super-earthly, the guardian spirit and the king beside his chief officers (cf. Isa. xxiv. 21 et seq.; lvii. 9; Psa. lxxxii. 6; also the more extended signification of "kings" [= great ones, mighty ones], which occurs, *e.g.*, in Psa. ii. 2; Job xxix. 25; Ezek. xxvi. 7; 1 Kings xi. 24). The difficult וַאֲנִי נוֹתַרְתִּי שָׁם אֵצֶל מַלְכֵי פָרָס must probably be explained in this way (with Ewald and partly also with Hitzig). The explanation offered by others, "and thus it happened that I *remained or tarried* during an extended period with the kings of Persia" (Vulg.: "*et ego remansi ibi*," etc.; Syr., Dereser, Rosenm., Kranichf., etc.), is opposed by the fact that נוֹתַר does not properly signify "to remain behind," but "to remain over, to be superfluous" (at the most, it might be possible to adduce Gen. xxxii. 25 in support of the former meaning); and also that the construction of the sentence does not justify its being regarded as a supplement or complementary explanation of the remainder of the verse. The translation of Luther, Geier, Winer, Gesenius, Hävernick, etc.: "and I gained the *ascendancy*, or the *victory*, with the kings of Persia," is likewise at variance with the general usage of נוֹתַר. The explanation of Füller (and Hofmann [also Keil]), "and I then maintained my place beside the kings of Persia," certainly accords better with the usage; but it is opposed by the consideration adduced above, concerning the assumption of two angelic powers who contend for the greatest influence over the Persian king. Nor can it be understood on that theory why the plural מַלְכֵי פ׳ was used instead of the singular; for, although the opinion that the writer intended Cyrus together with his successors, hence the entire Persian dynasty, by his "kings of Persia," has recently become an especial favorite (being accepted likewise by Füller and Hofmann), it seems to us so improbable in itself, that even the adoption of the theory which asserts the Maccabæan origin of the book, could scarcely serve to establish it (cf. especially Hitzig, who contends for the more extended signification of מַלְכֵי upon substantial grounds). The Sept. (and Theodot.) renders the passage correctly with regard to its meaning: καὶ αὐτὸν (sc. τὸν Μιχαὴλ) κατέλιπον ἐκεῖ μετὰ τοῦ ἄρχοντος βασιλείας Περῶν.—Verse 14. **I am come to make thee understand what shall befall thy people in the latter days.** Cf. the introductory words of Jacob's blessing, Gen. xlix. 1; also Num. xxiv. 14. Concerning אַחֲרִית הַיָּמִים as a designation of the Messianic future (the "issue of the ages," Füller), cf. on chap. ii. 28. The "end of the indignation," mentioned in chap. viii. 19, is not materially different from this end of (pre-Messianic) days.—**For yet the vision is for many days**; rather, "for yet a vision for those days," supply "I now bring, am about to reveal." הַיָּמִים, *the* days, *those* days, viz.: the latter days just mentioned. עוֹד is probably to be taken (with Füller and C. B. Michaelis) as referring indirectly back to the two preceding visions which treated of the latter days, hence to chapters viii. and ix. (cf. especially chap. viii. 19 *b* and chap. ix. 23 et seq.). Consequently the angel now brings *yet* an eschatological prophecy, *yet* a vision of the last times which forms the final and most specific revelation. None of the other interpretations yield a clear sense that agrees with the context, *e.g.*, that by Hitzig: "but it is yet continually a prophecy for ages;" by Hävernick, "for the prophecy to be imparted to thee shall extend to this time" (similarly Kranichfeld: "עוֹד, exceeding the present and the immediate future in its range"); the highly artificial one by Coccejus: "*expectatio promissionis adhuc protelabitur, nempe per ista tempora, quæ partim c. 8, partim c. 9 descripta sunt*," etc.

Verses 15–17. *The prophet's renewed consternation, in consequence of the reverential awe felt by him in the presence of his super-human visitor, who therefore now assumes an increasingly human bearing* (see v. 16 *a;* cf. v. 18 *a*). . . . . **I set my face toward the ground and became dumb**; the same attitude of reverential awe as in Luke xviii. 13; xxiv. 5.—The prophet's dumbness was twice removed by the comforting interference of the angel (v. 16 et seq. and v. 19); but he afterward remained speechless, excepting that he asked the brief question in chap. xii. 8. —**And behold one like the similitude of the sons of men touched my lips**, or, "like the sons of men he touched my lips;" the subject is not indicated here (and in v. 18), which does not, however, permit a doubt to arise that the one "after the similitude . . . of men" is identical with the angel who was hitherto present. כִּדְמוּת בְּנֵי אָדָם serves to recall the כְּבַר אֱנָשׁ, chap. vii. 13, as כְּמַרְאֵה אָדָם in v. 18 recalls the similar expression in chap. viii. 15. An identity with *Gabriel*, however, cannot be established on this repeated assurance of the angel's manlike appearance (against Kranichf.).—The touching of the lips (for the purpose of unsealing and opening them) is similar to the incident in Isa. vi. 7; Jer. i. 9.—**O my lord, by the vision my sorrows are turned upon me.** There is nothing strange in the form of the prophet's address to the angel, which terms him "my lord," particularly since the angel belonged to the class of "chief princes;" cf. Josh. v. 14; Judg. vi. 13. With regard to צִירִים, "sorrows," properly, "pains," cf. Isa. xiii. 8; xxi. 3; 1 Sam. iv. 19. צִירַי, "my sorrows" (cf. Psa. xviii. 24), characterizes the acuteness of the terrified sensation alluded to more impressively than could have been done by צִירִים merely; and since the term is obviously employed in a tropical sense only, it does not sound strange from the lips of a man (against Hitzig), and does not require to be obviated by means of putting an unusual sense on צִירַי, *e.g.*, by "my *joints* trembled in me" (Vulg., Luther, Berth., Hävernick, Füller), or by "my features were changed" (Ewald, following Psa. xlix. 15).—Verse 17. **And how can the servant of my lord talk**, etc. הֵיךְ, as in 1 Chron. xiii. 2, a Chaldaism for אֵיךְ.—**As for me** (properly "and I") **straightway there remained no strength in me, neither is there breath left in me**; *i.e.*, the power to stand and breathe regularly (1 Kings x. 5; Josh. ii. 11) departed from me afresh. The renewed consternation described in these words was not as great as the former, in v. 9; the "ceasing of the breath" was not in a literal sense as in 1 Kings xvii. 17, but only figurative, as in the similar form of speech, Cant. v. 6.—A majority of recent expositors correctly regard this second member of the verse as no longer belonging to Daniel's address to the angel; for if it were still included, the words "there is no strength in me" would have been employed twice in close proximity (v. 16 *b* and here) and in nearly the same form. Moreover, the incident of the two following verses requires a suitable preparation.—Füller, however, is entirely too artificial when he includes the words "and I—" in Daniel's explanation to the angel, but excludes everything else, to the close of his remarks.

Verses 18, 19. *The prophet is touched and strengthened* for the *third* time, and more effectually than before (cf. vs. 5 and 16). The being touched and strengthened *three times* by the angel (in which old-churchly exegetes, *e.g.*, Ephraem, etc., sought to find an allusion to the Trinity) was certainly not accidental; cf. the conflict of Christ in Gethsemane, Matt. xxvi. 38 et seq.; his being tempted thrice in the desert, Matt. iv. 1 et seq.; also such passages as John xxi. 15 et seq.; Acts x. 16; 2 Cor. xii. 8 et seq., etc. Hitzig, however, being utterly unaware of the profound mystical meaning of the description, thinks that "the broad representation that he was gradually invigorated, at first to speak himself, and afterward to listen to speech (v. 16 *b*, 19 *b*), has a manufactured appearance, and does not impress."—**Like the appearance of a man**; cf. on v. 16.—Verse 19. **Peace be unto thee; be strong, yea, be strong.** חֲזַק וַחֲזָק; cf. חֲזַק וֶאֱמָץ, Josh. i. 6, 7, 9; and with regard to the repetition of the verb, as strengthening the idea, cf. Jer. x. 25; li. 34, etc.—**For thou hast strengthened me,** viz. sufficiently to enable me to listen with courageous composure to all that is to be revealed, not excepting even what is calamitous and terrible.

Verse 20—chap. xi. 1. *Solemn and circumstantial introduction of the subsequent detailed description of the future*, connected with an encouraging reference to the constant readiness of God to assist Israel, despite the serious character of the situation of the time (and particularly, despite the dangers which threatened from the direction of Persia and Javan).—**Knowest thou wherefore I come unto thee?** *i. e.*, art thou aware of the serious and highly important character of the message which I am to deliver unto thee? Dost thou sufficiently estimate the tremendous earnestness of the situation, in consequence of which my mission became necessary?—**And now will I return to fight with the prince of Persia.** That is, the peaceful service of disclosing the future unto thee, in which I am now engaged, forms but a brief interruption to the great war which I must continue steadily to wage against the guardian spirit of the Persian power. With regard to הִלָּחֵם, considered as denoting an actual warfare rather than a mere altercation or dispute in the council of the angels of God (as Bertholdt and others think), see on v. 13.—**And when** (as soon as) **I am gone forth, lo, the prince of Græcia shall come.** The "going forth" in this passage, as often in descriptions of warlike incidents (*e.g.*, Josh. xiv. 11; 1 Kings ii. 7; 1 Sam. viii. 20; Isa. xlii. 12; Zech. xiv. 10), certainly denotes a going forth to battle rather than the mere departing from a locality (Hofmann, Füller, etc.). The observation does not, however, refer to his going forth to meet the prince of Persia, but a going forth to other conflicts after the war with the latter shall have been brought to a close; or, in other words, it denotes a going forth *out of* the war against the prince of Persia (so Jacchiad., Bertholdt, Hitzig, Kranichfeld, etc.—correctly). The sense is therefore: "Scarcely shall the Persian war be ended, when the Greek arises against me; the conflict with the Græcian world-power shall be immediately consequent on the war with that of

Persia." * Cf. the similar contrasting of יָצָא and בּוֹא in 2 Kings xi. 5, 7. Hofmann's exposition of the passage is altogether too labored: "The prince of the Græcians enters into the quarrel against the prince of the Persians, from which the angel retires; but, after the Persian empire has fallen, the angel renews the conflict with the new adversary, and, as in the former instance, is supported by Michael, the prince of Israel" (*Schriftbew.*, I. 290; cf. *Weissag. und Erfüllung*, I. 312 et seq.). Hofmann, however, properly rejects V. Lengerke's view, on which the coming of the prince of Græcia must be regarded as *victorious*, and leading to the defeat of the angel. Hitzig, on the other hand, comes especially near to the latter theory, in his venturesome assertion that the angelic prince who converses with Daniel, and who is to battle against Persia and afterward against Greece, represents the *guardian spirit of Egypt*, as of a power that had been friendly to the Jews in former ages and that especially made common cause with them against Syria (= Javan) in the period of the Seleucidæ!—a bold hypothesis, that has no support in the context, and that is absolutely incompatible with the expressions of sacred awe and reverence which Daniel made use of toward this celestial שַׂר, according to v. 5 et seq. Daniel would have been an idolater of the coarsest kind had he rendered such homage as is described in this chapter, and particularly in vs. 16–19, to the angelic patron and representative of Egypt (whom he assuredly regarded as a *dæmonic* power inimical to God, no less than those of Persia and Javan). And a possible Maccabæan pseudo-Daniel would have been still less likely than the Daniel of the æra of the captivity, to involve himself in the guilt of so gross a violation of the monotheistic principle and of disobedience to the first commandment in the decalogue.—Verse 21. **But I will show thee that which is noted in the Scripture** (or book) **of truth.** אֲבָל, "but still," a strong adversative particle, serves here to introduce the antidote to the fears for the theocracy excited by v. 20—in the shape of a comforting allusion to the ultimate welfare and blessing which are awaiting God's people according to the book of Divine providence, despite all the conflicts and sufferings that must precede them. Properly, "in a book of truth," *i.e.*, in a Divine document upon which "the yet unrevealed (Deut. xxxii. 34) fortunes of nations (Rev. v. 1) as well as of individuals (Psa. cxxxix. 16) in the future are entered" (Hitzig). Cf. the books of judgment in chap. vii. 10, and also the term אֱמֶת in chap. xi. 2, which briefly comprehends the contents of the book of truth.—**And there is none that holds with me in these things;** rather, "and yet there is none that exerts himself with me against these," *i.e.*, against the guardian angels of Persia and Javan, the dæmonic patrons of the heathen world-powers. On מִתְחַזֵּק עִם, exerting oneself with another, battling beside one, supporting one, cf 1 Sam. iv. 9; 2 Sam. x. 12. The participle characterizes the action, although future, as nevertheless being constant.—**But** (only) **Michael your prince,**—namely, in the sense of Josh. v. 13 et seq.; cf. supra, on v. 13. The sentence "and there is none . . . . your prince," taken as a whole, is not intended to justify the greatness of the sufferings through which Israel must pass (Hofmann), or the long duration of the prospective conflict with the world-powers (Füller); it simply aims to place in a clearer light the help afforded by the grace of God, which requires no foreign support in order to protect, and eventually to fully deliver Israel" (Kranichf.). The sentence would still express the idea of the self-sufficiency of the good spiritual powers in the kingdom of God, which require no aid from the world, and also of their ability to effect all things, even if it were made (as Füller proposes) dependent on אַגִּיד לְךָ, and consequently if (in disregard of the accentuation) it were translated, "But I will show thee that which is noted," etc., ". . . . . and the absence of one to help me," etc. In that case, however, it would present two very dissimilar objects of the angel's remarks as co-ordinate with each other, the former of which is very general in its character, and the latter equally specific; and this rendering would not obviate the incongruous relation between the contents of the former half of the verse and those of the latter, which exists in any case.—Chap. xi. 1. **Also I in the first year of Darius the Mede, even I, stood to confirm and to strengthen him,** or, "As I also . . . . . stood by him as a supporter and helper;" properly, "and I also." וַאֲנִי begins a new sentence (cf. Psa. xxx. 7; Job xix. 25) which does not stand in an adversative relation to the preceding verse (Hitzig), nor serve to explain it (Luther, etc.), but which is *comparative*. It describes the relation by which the angel who now speaks and Michael, the prince of Israel, assisted each other, as being reciprocal. עָמְדִי serves to repeat the אֲנִי, without regard to sequence, "and I . . . . . my *standing* was as his support," etc. Cf. Job ix. 27; Zeph. iii. 20; and respecting the use of עָמַד *sensu bellico s. militari* cf. supra, v. 13 and chap. viii. 25.—לוֹ "to him." Hävernick and Hitzig propose to refer this particle to דָּרְיָוֶשׁ rather than to Michael, because the strong terms מָעוֹז and מַחֲזִיק are supposed to warrant the conclusion that the one to whose support he came was a being inferior to the assisting angel, which would not apply to the relation of the latter to Michael. But in view of all the teaching of this section, a martial angelic prince may well be in occasional need of the aid and support of another, without being inferior to the latter on that account; and in support of the view that Michael, the guardian angel of Israel, was obliged to put forth special efforts in behalf of his wards, and therefore required the assistance of other good angelic powers to an unusual degree, precisely "in the first year of Darius the Mede," or at the period when the world-power passed from the Chaldæans to the Medo-Persians, it will be sufficien

* [Yet "we must not, with Kranichfeld, supply the clause, 'to another more extensive conflict,' because this supplement is arbitrary; but rather, with Kliefoth, interpret the word generally, as it stands, of the going out of the angel to fight for the people of God, without excluding the war with the prince of Persia, or limiting it to this war" (Keil).]

refer to chap. vi. and to chap. ix. 1 et seq. (cf. Zech. i. 12). Cf. Hofmann, *Schriftbew.*, I. 289, and also Füller, p. 279: "The first verse of chap. xi. is thus intimately connected with the last verse of chap. x.; and it was unwise to separate them, and thereby to confuse the train of thought (by referring לִי to Darius the Mede). If it be asked, what interests were at stake in the first year of Darius, the answer will be, *the position which the new dynasty should occupy toward the people of Israel.* And it may be seen from the narrative in chap. vi. that efforts were made in that particular year to place it in a hostile attitude toward that people. It was in that juncture that the good angel of the world-power stood by Michael, the prince of Israel, until he prevailed; in the coming conflict Michael shall support *him.*"

ETHICO-FUNDAMENTAL PRINCIPLES RELATED TO THE HISTORY OF SALVATION, APOLOGETICAL REMARKS, AND HOMILETICAL SUGGESTIONS.

1. The characteristic and leading feature of the contents of this section is *angelological* in its nature. An angelic being is introduced and described in an unusually minute and life-like manner, whom we (see on vs. 5 and 13) cannot regard as being identical with the Gabriel of chapters viii. and ix., nor yet with Michael, to whom he repeatedly refers in the communications addressed by him to Daniel; but the important disclosures made by this being respecting the nature and functions of several leading representatives of the angelic world, and the exalted rank and powerful influence within that world claimed by him, no less than his tremendous influence on the fortunes of earthly empires, justify the careful description of which he is the object (vs. 5–7), as well as the expressions of profound reverence addressed to him by Daniel (according to vs. 8–11; 15–19). These expressions, together with the counteracting efforts of the angel called forth by them, by which he designed to strengthen and encourage the terrified and overwhelmed prophet, are analogous to the incidents connected with the appearance of Gabriel to Daniel in chap. viii. 15 et seq.; but while the prophet's fainting and his restoration by Gabriel occurred but once in that instance (see on v. 18), the same features appear *thrice* in this connection, leading to the conclusion that this nameless angelic prince is of extraordinary importance, and at least equals, if he does not outrank Michael, the "captain of the Lord's host" (Josh. v. 13). As the latter comes to his assistance (vs. 13, 21), so he affords aid to that prince in return (chap. xi. 1) in the conflict with the "princes" of Persia and Javan, the angels who fight against God at the head of the heathen world-power. The latter likewise appear to be possessed of exalted power, and therefore as terrible spiritual beings who are dangerous to the kingdom of God and its representatives. They are powerful dæmons who bear the name שָׂרִים "princes, archangels," by virtue of their influential rank in the kingdom of darkness, with as much propriety as do Gabriel, Michael, etc., by virtue of their position in the kingdom of light. The power of the evil angels, however, is only transient and perishable, like that of the empires over which they rule, while the angelic princes of light, Michael and the nameless one, who stand in the service of God, triumph over them all in succession, although the victory may only be achieved by effort and determined conflict.

But who is this nameless one, this mysterious being, to whom not even the predicate שַׂר is applied, although doubtless belonging to him, to say nothing of a definite *nomen proprium* being assigned to him?—Are we, in connection with many older expositors (*e.g.*, Vitringa, C. B. Michaelis, Rambach, Starke, etc.), to identify him with Christ, the "uncreated angel of the Lord," whom Daniel repeatedly addressed as אֲדֹנִי, and whose description is said to be strikingly similar to that of the "Son of man" in chap. vii. 13 et seq. (with which compare especially vs. 16, 18), and also to that of Christ in the Apocalypse (Rev. i. 13–18; x. 1–6)? This opinion is at all events more probable than that of the interpreters who identify Michael instead with Christ (Melancthon, Geier, Jo. Lange, Neubauer, *Disput. de Michaele archangelo*, Hävernick, etc.); but it is opposed, and the created nature of the angel is implied, by the following considerations: (1) he describes himself in v. 11 as a *messenger* sent from God to bear a Divine message to Daniel (similar to Gabriel in chap. viii. 16 et seq.; ix. 20 et seq.); (2) his difficulty in combating the protecting angels of the world-powers, even necessitating his being supported by other angelic princes, contrasts strongly with the manner in which the former visions describe the triumph of Christ over the world-empires opposed to him; see especially chap. ii. 44 et seq. and chap. vii. 13, 22, 26; (3) the circumstance already noticed in v. 16, that the address "my lord," together with the other features of the description which aim at the exaltation and glorifying of this angel, are elsewhere applied to angels who were certainly created; *e.g.*, in Josh. v. 14, to the captain of the Lord's host; Judg. vi. 13, to the angel who appeared to Gideon; Judg. xiii. 8, to the angel whom Manoah saw; cf. also Rev. xix. 10; xxii. 8 et seq. We shall consequently be compelled to assume that the messenger sent from God to Daniel, as here introduced, was an angel proper, and distinct from the Son of God (see Jerome, Theodoret, and a majority of church fathers, on this passage). But what position of rank and power is to be attributed to him, or—in case he is at once coordinated with Michael and Gabriel in these respects (as we have done on v. 5), and is therefore regarded as an archangel—what particular office and functions are to be assigned to him, is after all a difficult question, and can hardly be answered with full exegetical certainty. The range of the angel's activity would become *too limited* if he were identified with the third of the archangels mentioned by name in the Old Test., beside Gabriel and Michael, viz.: with the Raphael of the apocryphal book Tobit, or if he were degraded to the rank of a mere guardian angel over *Egypt* (Hitzig; see on v. 20). On the other hand, his authority would become too *extensive*, and his position too exalted, if he were conceived of as the mighty governor of all earthly nature, the Divinely appointed ruler and spiritual guide of the whole terrestrial world, thus assigning to him a sphere similar to that occupied by the demiurge of the Gnostics, or the "earth-spirit" of Goethe in his prologue to *Faust*, or to that given by the ingenious natural philosopher, Max Perty (in his work *über die mystischen Erscheinungen der menschlichen Natur*, 1862), to the *geodæmon*, the regent of our planet, who is regarded as the spiritual principle that presides over the earth, the human race, and the development of both. To assume such an earth-spirit, which is neither Scriptural nor natural, and which has no support even in the magical and mystical phenomena of human life (cf. the thorough criticism of this hypothesis in L. Giesebrecht's lecture on *Das Wunder in der deutschen Geschichtbeschreibung neuerer Zeit*, Stettin, 1868, p. 10 et seq.), would be to disregard the tenor of this section, as certainly as it characterizes the angel as being decidedly supernatural, and at the same time (in v. 5 et seq.) endows him with external attributes of his rank such as would be but poorly adapted to the position and functions of a telluric planetary spirit. —Accordingly, if any particular explanation whatever of the nature and office of this angel is to be attempted, the opinion of Hofmann which was noticed above, on v. 5, is to be decidedly preferred to all others (*Weissagung und Erfüllung*, I. 312 et seq.; *Schriftbeweis*, I. 287 et seq.). That opinion has also been adopted by Auberlen (*Daniel*, etc., p. 67), Füller, Baumgarten, Luthardt, Riggenbach (on 2 Thess. ii. 6), and others. It assumes that the angel in question represents "*the good spirit of the heathen world-power*," while the "princes" of Persia and Javan opposed by him and Michael, represent the evil principle which is hostile to God, and which manifests itself in the development of the heathen world-power. The former is that "power in nature which operates in favor of God's kingdom throughout the heathen world," the "good spirit, which is to promote in the heathen world the realization of God's purpose of salvation;" the latter are powers opposed to God, who seek to cross and neutralize the plans of God and of the good angel, which aim at the salvation of the world. The former is the restraining principle (τὸ κατέχον, 2 Thess., l. c.) which restrains and prevents the ascendancy and prevalence of the height of Satanic wickedness in human history; the latter, on the contrary, endeavor to hinder and retard the progress of the kingdom of God. We regard this view as harmonizing well with the contents of the chapter before us, and can permit a partial departure from it only in so far as (1) we must consider it doubtful whether St. Paul intended to definitely and consciously allude precisely to the angel here described by the word κατέχων or κατέχον; (2) so far as we regard the conflict of the angel with those foes as an *actual warfare* in the invisible regions of the spirit-world, and not as a mere supplanting in the favor of the king and his court, because of the *termini bellici* employed in vs. 13 and 20 et seq.; (3) so far as we are compelled to regard the foes against whom the angel contended, as being the actual spiritual protectors of the world-kingdoms in question, and as dæmonic powers or Satanic angels, who have entered on a permanent connection with the kingdoms over which they rule, in consequence of which they stand or fall with them (cf. on v. 13). The idea of guardian angels, or, more exactly, the idea of certain dæmonic spiritual beings (ἄγγελοι Σατάν, 2 Cor. xii. 7) as being at the head of the antitheistic world-monarchies and as fundamentally opposed to Michael, the prince of the theocracy, is not only countenanced by the leading authorities of the older exegetical tradition (Luther, Melanc., Calov, Geier, C. B. Michaelis, Starke, and in substance also Jerome, Theodoret, and the older Roman Catholic expositors, excepting that they mistake the Satanic evil character of the "princes" of Persia, etc., to a greater or less extent), but it is likewise based on all the passages in both the Old and New-Test. Scriptures, which represent the gods of the heathen world as dæmons, and consequently, the heathen lands or states over which they rule and exercise spiritual authority as being provinces of the kingdom of darkness (cf. the expositors of 1 Cor. viii. 6; x. 20 et seq., especially Kling, vol. 7 of the New-Test. part of the *Bible-work*).*

2. This estimate of the contents of the chapter does not affect its credibility, nor does it oblige us to conclude that the section originated at the hands of a pseudo-Daniel in the Maccabæan age. Füller's remarks on these points, p. 272 et seq., are especially pertinent. We transfer to this place an epitome of this author's apology for the doctrine of angels, as contained in this section, although it is connected with views that diverge somewhat from ours, and that especially contain no correct estimate of the idea of guardian angels: "This is the meaning of our text. Shall we consider it a rabbinical idea and a Jewish fable? I cannot even find that it is entirely foreign to our modern conceptions. Do we not frequently speak of the spirit that reigns in the influential circles of a court? Is it not well understood that propositions which conflict with that spirit have no prospect of being approved, unless the prevailing spirit should be superseded by a different one? That is exactly what the text affirms—although certainly with a difference; for our age speaks of spirit without understanding a personal spiritual being by that term. 'Spirit' is a current word in its mouth, but it becomes embarrassed when asked how it conceives of spirit. As *God*, in the consciousness of modern times, has taken

* [The vagueness and indecision of this interpretation of the "prince" in question is no less an objection to it than its evidently heathenish character. The author's arguments adduced above against the common view which identifies this angelic prince with Christ himself are entirely inconclusive: for (1) Jesus likewise calls himself a *messenger* of God (John iii. 17, 34); (2) the Son of God himself did not disdain angelic aid (Matt. iv. 11; Luke xxii. 43); (3) the other O.-T. instances cited (especially Josh. v. 14) are clearly allusions to the Messianic theophany. "This heavenly form has thus, it is true, the shining white *talar* common to the angel, Ezek. ix. 9, but all the other features, as prescribed—the shining of the body, the brightness of his countenance, his eyes like a lamp of fire, arms and feet like glittering brass, the sound of his speaking—all these point to the revelation of the כְּבוֹד יְהוָה, the glorious appearance of the Lord, Ezek. i., and teach us that the אִישׁ seen by Daniel was no common angel-prince, but a manifestation of Jehovah, *i.e.*, the Logos. This is placed beyond a doubt by a comparison with Rev. i. 13–15, where the form of the Son of man, whom John saw walking in the midst of the golden candlesticks, is described like the glorious appearance seen by Ezekiel and Daniel" (Keil).]

refuge in the guise of a universal spirit, of which it may be affirmed that it is, and that it is not, with equal propriety, so the spirits are involved in a similar predicament; they have dissolved into vapor. The Scriptures, however, teach a different doctrine. They have and know a *personal* God and *personal* spirits, and teach that the latter include some who do the will of God, while others resist it. If we assume accordingly that such spirits *exist*, it will not surprise any mind that they should be active and influential (cf. Gen. xxxii. 1 et seq.; 2 Kings vi. 17, etc.). . . . . According to the Scriptures as a whole, the angels are the agents through whom God governs the world, and they are concerned in many things where we do not suspect their presence. The only new feature in the passage is that they are employed in influencing the decisions of the rulers of the world; but this is not surprising, since they are concerned to realize or prevent the Divine purposes. The world-power interferes in the fortunes of Israel; should God quietly look on while His will is counteracted? In such a case he opposes the evil spirit by *His* spirit, so that spirit combats against spirit," etc. —Auberlen expresses ideas exactly similar, p. 67: "The Holy Scriptures only ask of us that we should take in a real sense the language we are accustomed to employ in a figurative sense, respecting a conflict of the good and the evil spirit in man. Similar ideas prevail in 1 Sam. xvi. 13.15; 1 Kings xxii. 22; the Satanic influences with which we become better acquainted through the words of Jesus and the apostles are nothing different in their nature. This does not argue that the freedom of human action is thereby destroyed; for the influence of spirits over the inner nature of man is not irresistible, and their principal attention may perhaps be given to the shaping of external circumstances. The question concerning the relation of the Divine government to the freedom of man does not become more difficult by the additional feature of the service of angels, but, on the contrary, becomes more intelligible."—Cf. also Blumhardt, *Ueber die Lehre von den Engeln*, in Vilmar's *Pastoral-Theol. Blättern*, 1865, I. p. 32: "If Christ is presented to us as he who shall reign until all his foes are made the footstool for his feet, his reigning is always realized through the means of angels who are sent forth, and over whom is placed a special angel, Michael being prominent among them; and the fact that so little is said respecting the persons of the warring angels, who must be regarded as constantly reappearing, produces in us the more positive and elevating impression, as it is always the same battle from the beginning and down to the consummation of God's kingdom, when he shall have put down all opposing rule, and all authority and power (1 Cor. xv. 24). In this light we learn to lose sight of the strangeness of a name also, *e.g.*, that of Michael ('who is like God?'), and see that the names found in the Scriptures have not the slightest connection with the follies of the Jewish doctrine concerning angels, which includes extended registers of angels' names. But we also learn how easy it is, when the Word is carefully and thoroughly studied, to set aside the sneering objections of opponents, who judge everything superficially by its appearance, and are ready to throw it into the lumber-room of superstitions, if we only guard against being moved from our simplicity by the power of a worldly wisdom that overlooks the kernel of everything."

3. Nor does the chapter contain anything aside from the doctrine of angels that is not well adapted to the time of Daniel, and to the captive prophet Daniel as its author. This has already been shown with reference to several particulars. It only remains to call attention to the alleged "historical improbability" contained in v. 1, that Daniel did not return to the holy land with Zerubbabel and Joshua, as being a circumstance that on the contrary lends very little support to the Maccabæan-tendency hypothesis. For while it is a sufficient explanation of that fact that the aged and esteemed prophet remained at Babylon for the special purpose of promoting the welfare of his compatriots and of the theocracy (see on that passage), it is certainly improbable that a writer of the Maccabæan period, who should have invented this narrative in the interest of a tendency, would have left his hero in a strange land, among the many indifferent and apostate ones (cf. 1 Macc. i. 13 et seq.; xliv. 55), when a suitable opportunity was presented for his return, and while his own heart was animated with a glowing love for the "pleasant land" (אֶרֶץ־צְבִי, chap. viii. 9; xi. 16).—The zealous *fasting* of Daniel (v. 2 et seq.) serves as little as the circumstance above referred to, to render probable the composition of the chapter in the Maccabæan age; for the prophet's fasting does not bear an ascetic and work-righteous character, such as was adapted to the spirit of the later Judaism, and especially to the Alexandrian Judaism, inasmuch as the cause of the gracious acceptance of the supplicant while yearning for deliverance, is shown by v. 12 to have been, not his fasting, but the fervent and persistent prayer which accompanied it. In this character of a mere accompaniment and outward sign of sorrow because of national and religious misfortunes, fasting (together with related usages connected with mourning, *e.g.*, abstaining from anointing, the wearing of sackcloth, sitting in ashes, etc.) was practised, long prior to the captivity, by the earliest representatives of the prophetic order, such as Elijah, Joel, Isaiah, etc. (cf. 1 Kings xvii. 6; xix. 4 et seq.; Joel i. 14; ii. 12; Isa. xx. 2 et seq.); so that the similar conduct of Daniel, which becomes additionally appropriate in view of its being connected with the occurrence of the feast of the Passover, does not seem remarkable or untimely in the least.—In opposition to Hitzig's assertion that the remarks of the angel in chap. x. 21; xi. 1, contain an allusion to the political relations of Egypt with Syria and Palestine in the Maccabæan period, see supra, on these passages.

4. The *homiletical* treatment of the chapter will have regard primarily and principally to its angelological features. In this respect attention will naturally be directed less to the nature and employment of the angels brought to our notice than to their relation to the designs and modes of operation of the *Divine providence* which employs them as instruments in its service. *The influence of God on the fortunes of the world-empires and the decisions of their rulers, as being*

exerted through the agency of angels, and as employing the power of the mighty princes of the spirit-world for the welfare of man—such will probably be the theme of a meditation on the contents of the section as a whole. In connection with this it will be proper to refer to passages like Psa. xxxiv. 3; ciii. 20 et seq.; Heb. i. 14, etc., and to illustrate and enforce them in their profound truth and comforting power, by the subject of this chapter.

Homiletical suggestions on particular passages: On v. 1, Melancthon: "*Nova visio exhibetur jam Daniel, non solum ut ipse et cæteri pii in hoc præsenti periculo confirmentur, sed etiam et posteritas præmoneatur de præcipuis mutationibus imperiorum et de iis calamitatibus, quæ Judææ impendebant. . . . . Habes Ecclesiæ imaginem, quam Deus vult et exerceri afflictionibus et fide expectare liberationem. Et cum liberat, tamen eventus non respondent nostris conjecturis. Cum Cyri beneficium impeditum esset, postea magis conspici potuit, a Deo gubernari hanc liberationem, cum tot impedimenta incidissent, quæ humanis consiliis tolli non poterant.*"

On v. 2, Jerome: "*Secundum anagogen vero hoc dicendum est, quod qui in luctu est et sponsi luget absentiam, non comedit panem desiderabilem, qui de cœlo descendit, neque solidum capit cibum, qui intelligitur in carne, nec bibit vinum, quod lætificat cor hominis, nec exhilarat faciem in oleo* (Ps. civ. 15). *Hoc autem jejunio sponsa impetrabiles facit lacrimas, quondo sponsus fuerit ablatus ab ea,*" etc.—Cramer: "To fast and prepare the body is indeed a proper external discipline, not to deserve something thereby, as the Papists do, but in order to a still better preparation: Matt. vi. 17 et seq."

On v. 4, Geier: "*Juxta hunc fluvium se fuisse ilicit propheta, jejunio hactenus maceratus precibusque vacans devotis, sine dubio, ut animum nonnihil recrearet hac loci jucundioris contemplatione, si quidem ad hujusmodi fluviorum ripas amœni nonnunquam dantur colles, valles aut luci arboribus consiti, ubi undarum suaviter audiuntur susurri adeoque non exigua simul suppeditatur ansa recolendi beneficia tam creationis, quam conservationis redemtionis,*" etc. Cf. Psa. cxxxvii. 1 et seq.; Ezek. i. 1 etc.

On v. 8 et seq., Calvin: "*Deus non ideo terret suos, quoniam ipsum oblectet nostra perturbatio, sed quoniam id nobis utile est, quia scilicet nunquam erimus idonei ad discendum, nisi carne nostra prorsus subacta. Hoc autem necesse fieri violento modo propter pervicaciam nobis ingenitam.*"—Starke: "Behold in this the goodness and friendliness of God, who not only knows how to terrify, but also causes the terrified ones to be comforted and strengthened!"

On v. 11, Theodoret: Καλεῖ αὐτὸν οὐ Βαλτασάρ, ἀλλὰ Δανιήλ· τὸ μὲν γὰρ ἦν Χαλδαίων, τὸ δὲ Ἑβραίων ὄνομα· καὶ τὸ μὲν ὑπὸ εὐσεβῶν ἐτέθη, τὸ δὲ ὑπὸ δυσσεβῶν προσετέθη.—Starke: "It is difficult for a timid and sorrowful heart to appropriate to itself the Divine comfort; wherefore God sometimes calls them by name; cf. Acts x. 31."

On v. 13, Jerome (see supra, on that passage). —Melancthon: "*Angelus pius narrat Danieli, se dimicasse cum principe Persarum, i.e., cum diabolo moliente dissipationes regni Persici. Etsi enim ignoramus, quomodo inter se pugnent boni et mali spiritus, tamen certamina esse non dubium est, sive disputatione fiant, sive aliis modis. Ait ergo bonus Angelus repressum a se esse malum spiritum, qui Cambysen juvenem et aulicos impios incitabat, vel ad delendam gentem Judaicam, vel ad interficiendum Danielem, vel ad alias malas actiones tentandas, quæ novos motus in regno allaturæ erant.*"—Auberlen, Blumhardt, Füller (see supra, No. 2).

On v. 15 et seq., Starke: "If needless terror and alarm can deprive a *pious* soul of his speech, is it a wonder that wicked persons shall be dumb when Christ addresses them with the words, Friend, how camest thou in hither, etc.? (Matt. xxii. 12).—If God does not first open our lips, either directly or indirectly, we shall be unable to speak what pleases Him (Rom. viii. 26; x. 15)."

On v. 20 et seq., Melancthon: "*Hæc exempla ostendunt satis inquietam fuisse provinciam. Fuerunt igitur et angelorum certamina, qui malos spiritus, seditionum et discordiarum inflammatores depellebant.*"—Starke: "When one kingdom of the world has been destroyed, Satan will reign through another; and thus the church is compelled to contend constantly against the prince of this world, until all kingdoms shall belong to God and Christ.—The fact that the power of angels is limited appears from their requiring the assistance of others."

D. *Detailed prophetic description of the Persian and Græcian world-kingdoms, and also of the kingdoms which should arise from the latter, together with their conflicts.*

CHAP. XI. 2-45.

2 And now will I shew thee *the* truth. Behold, *there shall* stand *up* yet three
kings in [to] Persia; and the fourth shall be far richer than *they* all: and by
[according to] his strength through [by] his riches he shall stir *up* all [the
whole] against [with] *the* realm of Græcia [kingdom of Javan].
3 And a mighty king [a king, a hero] shall stand *up*, that shall rule *with* great
4 dominion [rule], and do according to his will. And when he shall stand *up*,
his kingdom shall be broken, and shall be divided [partitioned] *toward the* four
winds of heaven [the heavens]; and not to his posterity, nor according to his
dominion [rule] which he ruled: for his kingdom shall be plucked *up*, even for
[and *given* to] others besides those [these].

5 And *the* king of the south shall be strong, and [*become*] *one* of his princes;
and he shall be strong above him, and have dominion [rule]; his dominion
6 [rule] *shall be* a great dominion [rule]. And in [to] the end of years they shall
join [associate] themselves *together*; for [and] *the* king's daughter [daughter of
the king] of the south shall come to the king of the north to make an agreement;
but [and] she shall not retain *the* power of the arm; neither shall he stand, nor
[and] his arm; but [and] she shall be given *up*, and *they* that brought her, and
he that begat her, and *he* that strengthened her in *these* [the] times.
7 But [And] out of a branch [shoot] of her roots shall *one* stand *up in* his
estate [basis, *i.e.*, stead], which [and he] shall come with an army [to the force],
and shall enter into [come in] *the* fortress of *the* king of the north, and shall deal
8 against [do with] them, and shall prevail [strengthen *himself*]; and shall also
carry captives [cause to go in the captivity] *into* Egypt their gods, with their
princes [anointed *ones*], *and* with their precious [prized] vessels of silver and of
9 gold; and he [2] shall continue [stand] *more* years than *the* king of the north. So
the king of the south shall come in*to his* kingdom [And he shall come in*to* the
kingdom of *the* king of the south], and shall return *in*to his *own* land [ground].
10 But his sons shall be stirred up [strengthen themselves], and shall assemble
a multitude of great forces: and *one* shall certainly come, and overflow, and
pass through; then [and] shall he return, and be stirred up [*or*, they shall
11 strengthen themselves], *even* to his [*or*, their] fortress. And *the* king of the
south shall be moved with choler [become very bitter], and shall come forth
and fight with him, *even* with *the* king of the north: and he shall set forth [cause
to stand] a great multitude; but the multitude shall be given in*to* his hand.
12 And *when* he hath taken *away* the multitude [*or*, the multitude shall be taken
away], his heart shall be lifted *up* [*or*, raised *up*]; and he shall cast down [cause
to fall] *many* ten thousands: but [and] he shall not be strengthened *by it.*
13 For [And] *the* king of the north shall return and shall set forth [cause to
stand] a multitude greater than the former, and shall certainly come after cer-
tain [at *the* end of the times *the*] years with a great army [force] and with much
14 riches. And in those times *there* shall many stand *up* against *the* king of the
south: also [and] *the* robbers [sons of tyrants] of thy people shall exalt them-
selves [be lifted *up*] to establish [cause to stand] *the* vision; but [and] they
shall fall [be stumbled].
15 So [And] *the* king of the north shall come, and cast up [pour *out*] a mount
[mound], and take [catch] *the* most fenced cities [city of defences]; and *the*
arms of the south shall not *with*stand, neither [and, *i.e.*, or] his chosen people
16 [*the* people of his choice], neither *shall there be any* strength to *with*stand. But
[And] he that cometh against [to] him shall do according to his *own* will, and
none *shall* stand before him; and he shall stand in *the* glorious land [land of
17 comeliness], which [and] by his hand [he] shall be consumed. He shall also
[And he shall] set his face to enter [come] with *the* strength of his whole king-
dom, and upright *ones* [3] with him; thus [and] shall he do: and he shall give
him *the* daughter of [the] women, corrupting [to corrupt, *or*, destroy] her; but
18 [and] she shall not stand *on his side*, neither [nor] be for him. After this [And]
shall he turn his face unto *the* isles, and shall take [catch] many; but a prince
[general] for his *own behalf* [his reproach] shall cause *the* reproach *offered* by
him [for him] to cease; without his *own* reproach he shall cause *it* to turn upon
19 [to] him. Then [And] he shall turn his face toward *the* fort [fortresses] of his
own land; but [and] he shall stumble [be stumbled] and fall, and not be
found.
20 Then [And] shall stand *up* in his estate [on his basis, *i.e.*, stead] a raiser of
taxes *in* [*one* causing *the* exactor to pass *through*] *the* glory of *the* kingdom: but
within few days [and in single days] he shall be destroyed [broken], neither
[and not] in anger nor in battle.
21 And in his estate [on his basis, *i.e.*, stead] shall stand *up* a vile [despised]
person, to whom [and on him] they shall not give *the* honour of *the* kingdom:
but [and] he shall come *in* peaceably [with tranquillity], and obtain [*or*
22 strengthen] *the* kingdom by flatteries. And *with* the arms of a [the] flood shall

they be overflown from before him, and shall be broken; yea [and], also *the*
23 prince of *the* covenant. And after the league *made* with [from the covenanting
to] him he shall work deceit*fully:* for [and] he shall come up, and shall become
24 strong with a small people. He shall enter [come] peaceably [with tranquillity]
even upon [and with] the fattest *places* of *the* province; and he shall do *that*
which his fathers have not done, nor [and] his fathers' fathers; he shall scatter
among [to] them *the* prey, and spoil, and riches; *yea*, and he shall forecast
[devise] his devices against *the* strong holds, even [and *that*] for [till] a
time.

25 And he shall stir *up* his power and his courage [heart] against *the* king of the
south with a great army [force]; and *the* king of the south shall be stirred *up* to
[the] battle with a very great and mighty army [force]; but [and] he shall not
26 stand: for they shall forecast [devise] devices against him. Yea [And], *they*
that feed [eat] of *the* portion of his meat [*dainty* food] shall destroy [break]
27 him, and his army [force] shall overflow; and many shall fall *down* slain. And
both these kings' hearts [the kings, their heart] *shall be* to do mischief [wrong],
and they shall speak lies [falsehood] at [over] one table; but *it* shall not pros-
per: for yet *the* end *shall be* at [to] the time *appointed.*

28 Then [And] shall he return *into* his land with great riches; and his heart
shall be against *the* holy covenant; and he shall do *exploits* and return to his
29 *own* land. At [To] the time *appointed* he shall return, and come toward [in]
30 the south: but [and] it shall not be as the former, or [and] as the latter. For
[And] *the* ships of Chittim shall come against [in] him; therefore [and] he shall
be grieved [dejected], and return, and have indignation against *the* holy cove-
nant; so [and] shall he do; he shall even [and he shall] return, and have intelli-
gence with *them* that forsake *the* holy covenant.

31 And arms shall stand on his part [from him], and they shall pollute the sanc-
tuary *of* trength [the stronghold], and shall take [cause to turn] *away* the
daily [continual] *sacrifice*, and they shall place [give] the abomination that
32 maketh desolate. And *such as* do wickedly *against* [*the* wicked doers of] *the*
covenant shall he corrupt [pollute] by flatteries: but [and] *the* people that *do*
33 know their [its] God shall be strong, and do *exploits.* And *they* that under-
stand *among* [the prudent of] *the* people shall instruct [understand for the]
many; yet [and] they shall fall [be stumbled] by *the* sword, and by flame,
34 by captivity, and by spoil, *many* days. Now [And] when they *shall* fall [be
stumbled], they shall be holpen [helped] *with* a little help: but [and] many
35 shall cleave [be joined] to them with flatteries. And *some* of them of under-
standing [the prudent] shall fall [be stumbled], to try [*lit.*, smelt in] them, and
to purge [purify], and to make *them* white, *even* to [till] *the* time of *the* end:
36 because *it is* yet for a [to the] time *appointed.* And the king shall do accord-
ing to his will; and he shall exalt himself, and magnify himself above every
god, and shall speak marvellous [distinguished] *things* against *the* God of gods,
and shall prosper till *the* indignation be accomplished [fail]: for *that that is*
determined shall be done.

37 Neither shall he regard [And he will not have understanding upon] *the* God of
his fathers, nor [and upon] *the* desire of women, nor regard [and he will not have
38 understanding upon] any god: for he shall magnify himself above all. But in His
estate [And on his base, *i.e.*, stead] shall he honour [give glory to] *the* god of forces
[strongholds]; and [to] a god whom his fathers knew not shall he honour [give
glory] with gold, and [with] silver, and with precious stones [stone], and plea-
39 sant *things.* Thus [And] shall he do in *the* most [fortresses of] strongholds
with a strange god, whom he shall acknowledge *and* increase [increase to ac-
knowledge] *with* glory: and he shall cause them to rule over [the] many, and
shall divide *the* land for gain [distribute ground with a price].

40 And at [in] *the* time of *the* end shall the king of the south push at [wage *war*
with] him: and *the* king of the north shall come against him like a whirlwind
[will storm upon him], with chariots [chariot], and with horsemen [horses], and
with many ships [boats]; and he shall enter [come] in*to the* countries [lands],
41 and shall overflow and pass *over.* He shall enter also [And he will come] in*to*

the glorious land [land of comeliness], and many *countries* shall be overthrown
[stumbled]: but [and] these shall escape out of his hand, *even* Edom, and Moab,
42 and *the* chief [first] of *the* children of Ammon. He shall stretch forth his hand
also [And he shall send his hand] upon [in] *the* countries [lands]; and *the* land
43 of Egypt shall not escape [be for an escaped *one*, *i.e.*, exempt]. But [And] he
shall have power [rule] over *the* treasures of gold and of silver, and over all the
precious [pleasant] *things* of Egypt: and *the* Libyans and *the* Ethiopians *shall*
44 *be* at [in] his steps. But [And] tidings out of *the* east and out of *the* north
shall trouble him: therefore [and] he shall go forth with great fury to destroy,
45 and utterly to make away [devote to extermination] many. And he shall
plant *the* tabernacles [tents] of his palace [pavilion] between *the* seas in [at]
the glorious holy mountain [holy mountain of comeliness]; yet [and] he shall
come to his end, and none *shall* help him.

8

LEXICAL AND GRAMMATICAL NOTES.

[[1] מֵישָׁרִים, literally *equities*, hence a *compact* as to what is agreed upon as right between the parties. It here seems to refer especially to the terms or provisos of the alliance, the marriage being one of the main conditions or *considerations*.—[2] The pronoun is emphatic.—[3] יְשָׁרִים probably, like מֵישָׁרִים above, contains an allusion to the *rights* of a contract, and may therefore signify *allies*.]

EXEGETICAL REMARKS.

Verse 2. *Touching upon the last kings of Persia in a hasty and summary review.* **And now will I show thee the truth.** אֱמֶת, see chap. x. 21.—**Behold, there shall stand up yet three kings in Persia;** *i.e.*, doubtless, after the present king, hence after Cyrus (see chap. x. 1), there shall be three more kings of Persia,—the Persian state shall have three more kings. The author therefore assigns altogether four kings to Persia, from which, however, it by no means follows that he "knew" only that number; nor can it be shown from Ezra iv. 5, 7 that the writer of that book knew of four Persian kings (Hitzig, Ewald).* The number four is rather to be regarded as a *symbolic* number, exactly like that of the wings and heads of the leopard in chap. vii. 6 (see on that passage), which indicates that the development of the kingdom in question is completed, and is, to that extent, parallel with the number of the world-monarchies and with other significant quadruples; cf. Eth.-fund principles, etc., on chap. ii. No. 3.†—**And the fourth shall be far richer than they all;** rather, "shall acquire greater riches," etc. This fourth one does not denote the last of all the Persian kings, Darius Codomannus, but the fourth from the beginning (or, in other words, the *third* of the three just mentioned),* and therefore *Xerxes*, as pseudo-Smerdis, is probably not included, and Cyrus, Cambyses, and Darius Hystaspis are considered the first three. The characteristic noticed in this place applies well to Xerxes, as he became especially famous because of his immense riches (Herodotus, III. 96; IV. 27–29), and as his expedition into Greece obscured those of his father by the excessive greatness of his armament. The significance of this fourth member of the old Persian dynasty (whose identity with Xerxes was naturally not yet apprehended by the prophet [?], especially as the angel did not see fit to state his name) is that he represents, on the one hand, the acme of the development in power of the kingdom in question, and, on the other, the beginning of its dissolution.—**And by his strength through his riches,** or, "when he has become strong through his riches. וּכְחֶזְקָתוֹ, an infinitive (cf. 2 Chron. xii. 1; also infra, v. 4, and chap. viii. 8, 23), is not co-ordinated with the following בְּעָשְׁרוֹ, but is placed above it.—**He shall stir up all against the realm of Græcia,** *i.e.*, "stake all." הַכֹּל, properly, "*the* all," *i.e.*, all that has been mentioned, all the immense treasures and forces referred to. יָעִיר, properly, "shall excite, stir up," does not allude so much to inanimate treasures as to the subjects of this king as being the objects of his exciting activity; cf. v. 25; Job xli. 2; Jer. l. 9.—אֵת מַלְכוּת יָוָן is not properly "*against* the realm of Javan," but "*to* the realm," etc.; אֵת serves to introduce the accusative denoting the direction of the movement.—It accords fully with the position of the seer *prior* to Xerxes, that Greece (with regard to Javan, cf. on chap. viii. 21) should be represented as a *kingdom*. A Maccabæan writer, who might aim to sketch the history of that king, and of his expedition against the Greeks, would

* ["Moreover, this assertion (that the O. T. only knows of four Persian kings) is not at all correct; for in Neh. xii. 22, besides those four, there is mention made also of a Darius, and to the Jews, in the age of the Maccabbees there was well known, according to 1 Macc. i. 1, also the name of the last Persian king, Darius, who was put to death (defeated) by Alexander."—*Keil.*]

† [This interpretation is altogether vague and unnecessary. The meaning obviously is not that there should thereafter be only four more Persian kings in all, but merely that the next three should bring down the history as far as the prophetic vision extended in this regard, *i.e.*, down to the breaking out of the conflict between Persia and Greece. Thus "the three kings who shall yet (עֹמְדִים) arise are the three successors of Cyrus, viz., Cambyses, the pseudo-Smerdis, and Darius Hystaspis: the fourth is then Xerxes, with whom all that is said regarding the fourth perfectly agrees. Thus Hävernick, Ebrard, Delitzsch, Auberlen, and Kliefoth interpret."—*Keil.*]

* [This computation is manifestly inconsistent, for it confounds the "fourth" with the one just said to be the third.]

assuredly have known, and indicated, that at that time Javan was not yet a מַלְכוּת.

Verses 3, 4. *Alexander the Great and his immediate successors.** **And a mighty king shall stand up.** מֶלֶךְ גִּבּוֹר, a herioc, warlike king; cf. אֵל גִּבּוֹר, Isa. ix. 5, and also the symbolic description of Alexander's martial greatness in chap. viii. 5 et seq., 21. עָמַד, "he stands up," *i.e.*, comes up and presents a warlike and threatening appearance; cf. vs. 4, 14, and also v. 1. – **And do according to his will.** Cf. chap. viii. 4 and infra, v. 16. The sovereign arbitrariness with which Alexander ruled all the persons of his time is likewise attested by Curtius, X. 5, 35: "*Fortunam solus omnium mortalium in potestate habuit.*"—Verse 4. **And when he shall stand up** (rather, "when he has stood up"), **his kingdom shall be broken, and shall be divided toward the four winds of heaven.** וּכְעָמְדוֹ is probably to be closely connected with the idea presented by עָמַד in the preceding verse: "*and when*," or, "and *as soon as* he shall have stood up" (Von Lengerke, Füller, etc.); so that the brief duration of Alexander's reign is here indicated. Others, *e.g.*, Hävernick, Kranichfeld, Ewald, etc., render it, "and when he shall stand in his power, when his power has reached its highest point" (Luther); but this view is questionable, because of the entirely too pregnant meaning which is thus attributed to עמד. Hitzig's assertion that עמד in this place is synonymous with the Syr. עֲנַד, "to depart in death, to die," and that the following תִּשָּׁבֵר (with which cf. chap. viii. 8) is not passive in its signification, and therefore does not denote "to be broken," but "to break apart," must certainly be rejected.—On the phrase, "be divided toward the four winds of heaven," cf. the analogous symbolic description in chap. viii. 8.—**And not to his posterity,** namely, "shall it be divided;" they shall not be benefited by the division, but shall be entirely deprived of their patrimony, thus realizing a feature that was common in the early experience of the theocracy, 1 Sam. xv. 28; 2 Sam. iii. 10; 1 Kings xi. 11; xiv. 7-10; xv. 29; xvi. 3 et seq.; xxi. 21. It is well known that this actually was the case with Alexander's sons, Hercules (whose mother was Barsina, and who was murdered by Polysperchon) and Alexander (a *filius posthumus*, born of Roxana, and likewise murdered). Cf. Diodorus, XIX. 105; XX. 28; Pausan., IX. 7; Justin., XV. 2; Appian, *Syr.*, C. 51.—**Nor according to his dominion which he ruled,** "shall the divided kingdom be;" on the contrary, it shall present a painful picture of impotence; cf. וְלֹא בְכֹחוֹ in the parallel, chap. viii. 22.—**For his kingdom shall be plucked up, even for others besides those.** מִלְּבַד אֵלֶּה, to the exclusion of those, *i.e.*, of the natural heirs and rightful successors of this ruler. Concerning the phrase, "to be torn out, uprooted," cf. on chap. iv. 12, 12; also Job xiv. 7 et seq.; Isa. vi. 10, etc.

Verses 5, 6. *The first Seleucidæ and Lagidæ.* While the prophetic description, upon the whole, has hitherto confined itself to general outlines, and has not materially deviated from the ordinary methods of prophecy, it begins at this point to assume a suspiciously specific character, which arouses the thought that later hands may have improved on the prophecy by interpolating various features of detail. The fact that only the two states, emanating from the great Græcian world-empire, which bordered immediately on the "pleasant land," are more carefully followed in their further development, is not, indeed, enough to arouse this suspicion; for the other kingdoms of the Diadochi might have been passed over as too unimportant in their relations with the theocracy. It was, moreover, to be expected that Israel should be alternately oppressed by a southern and a northern neighbor, in view of the similar parts taken in earlier prophecies by the Assyrio-Babylonian north on the one hand, and by Egypt in the south, on the other (cf., *e.g.*, Isa. xxx. 6; xliii. 6; Jer. iii. 12, 18; vi. 22; xlvi. 20, 24; Zeph. ii. 13; Zech. x. 10, 11). But the manner in which the transactions between the two kingdoms, whether peaceful or hostile in their character, are described with regard to their changeful course, is too exact, and covers too extended a succession of reigns and events, to find even a remote parallel in any other part of the prophetic literature of the Old-Test. canon.* The unique character of the section in this respect was recognized at an early period, and has been made use of by the opponents of the authenticity and genuine prophetic dignity of the book (*e.g.*, early by Porphyry), in order to attack its character, and has also been employed for apologetic purposes, in order to demonstrate the inspired character of the prophecy, and the astonishing exactness with which its predictions corresponded with the actual development of the dominion of the Seleucidæ and the Lagidæ. With this view it is employed by Luther in his preface to Daniel and in his exposition of chap. xii. (which begins, according to his opinion, with chap. xi. 36;—see vol. 41, pp. 252 et seq., 294 et seq.); by Venema, *Commentarius ad Danielis* cap. XI. 5-XII. 3 (Leovard., 1752); by Hengstenberg, *Beitr.*, p. 173 et seq.; and, generally, by a majority of orthodox expositors in ancient and modern times. Cf. especially Ebrard, *Die Offenb. Joh.*, p. 81 et seq., where a thorough

* ["From the conflict of Persia with Greece, the angel (ver. 3) passes immediately over to the founder of the Græcian (Macedonian) world-kingdom; for the prophecy proceeds not to the prediction of historical details, but mentions only the elements or factors which constitute the historical development. The expedition of Xerxes against Greece brings to the foreground the world-historical conflict between Persia and Greece, which led to the destruction of the Persian kingdom by Alexander the Great."—*Keil.*]

* [As we have already remarked, this peculiarity of detail does not argue a want of genuineness here. It is impossible to sever this portion from the preceding and following predictions, which present no such "suspicious" features, without making an irreparable hiatus in the prophecy as a whole. Indeed this very part constitutes the gist of the entire disclosure, for it is this alone that immediately and intimately concerns the theocracy. The unprecedented and unparalleled character of the Antiochian persecution, as a chapter in Jewish history, justifies the minuteness and earnestness of the portraiture. The rest of this prophecy is but introduction and sequel to this central delineation. The careful reader will note that Daniel does not give a syllabus of *secular* history, but only sketches the course of those collisions which should affect the *religious* status and relations of Israel. The character and conduct of the Antiochian antichrist could not be fully appreciated without a setting forth of these connections.]

illustration of the harmony between the contents of this section and the facts of history precedes the remark: "For that very reason—this is the internal design of the specializing prophecy, chap. xi.—the coming of the Macedonian tyrant is connected with the age of Daniel by an unbroken chain of the most particular events, that it might be thoroughly apparent *that no interval for the coming of the Messiah and his rejection should intervene between the time of Daniel and that tyrant.*" But Ebrard himself does not seem to have remained permanently satisfied with this mode of justifying the remarkably specific character of the prophecy on the supposition of a higher plane of revelation; for, in his review of Füller's commentary, he confesses that he "has not yet found any exposition of chap. xi. that was entirely satisfactory" (p. 267).—We shall attend specially to Kranichfeld's view in the following exposition of the several passages. He likewise contends for the genuine character of the section throughout, but on the frequently forced assumption that the modern exegesis applies what was indefinite and merely ideal in the mind of the prophet to the facts of history in the corresponding period in far too pointed a manner.—**And the king of the south shall be** (or "become") **strong**, *i.e.*, the ruler to whom the south, or Egypt, has fallen; cf. v. 8, where the south is expressly designated as מִצְרַיִם; also the Sept. on this passage, and Zech. vi. 6.—**And one of his princes; and he shall be strong above him**; rather, "but one of his princes—*he* shall be strong above him." With regard to the partitive מִן in וּמִן שָׂרָיו, cf. Gen. xxviii. 11; Ex. vi. 26; Neh. xiii. 28. The subject, "one of his princes," occupies a detached position at the beginning (cf. Ezek. xxxiv. 19); the copula, however, restores the connection: "(so far as he is concerned) he shall still be stronger."—Others (Luther, etc., Bertholdt, Rosenm., Kranichfeld, Füller, etc.) regard the ו in וּמִן שָׂרָיו as the definite "*and indeed*, namely," and refer the suffix to the subject of the preceding verse: "and the king of the south, namely one of his (Alexander's) princes, shall become strong." This, however, is opposed by the lack of a definite subject of וַיֶּחֱזַק in that case, and by the unanimous authority of the ancient versions, which regard this second ויחזק as the predicate of ומן שריו, despite the *Athnach*. Consequently, the event to which the passage alludes is the founding of the dynasty of the Seleucidæ in the year B.C. 312, by Seleucus Nicator, the general of Ptolemy Lagus (Diodorus, XIX. 55, 58; Appian, *Syr.*, C. 52),* who extended his dominion from Phrygia to the Indus, and thus greatly exceeded his former lord in power, approaching to the position of power and greatness occupied by Alexander himself more nearly than any other of the Diadochi (Appian, *Syr.*, 55; Arrian, *Anab.*, VII. 22. 9).—**And** (shall) **have dominion; his dominion shall be a great dominion.** מִמְשָׁל רַב is the predicate, followed by the subject in regular order. The whole clause, however, is logically subordinated to וּמָשַׁל; cf. Gen. xii. 8.—Verse 6. **And in the end of years they shall join themselves together.** וּלְקֵץ שָׁנִים, "and after the lapse of several years," cf. 2 Chron. xviii. 2; also infra, vs. 8 and 13. The subjects of the sentence are the kings of the northern and of the southern kingdoms, and the alliance referred to is the marriage of Antiochus II. Theos (the son and successor of Antiochus I. Soter, who had followed Seleucus Nicator upon the throne of the Seleucidæ as its second possessor, B.C. 281–261, but who is wholly unnoticed in this prophecy) with Berenice, the daughter of Ptolemy Philadelphus (280–247), the second of the line of Ptolemies. Antiochus was obliged, on that occasion, to banish Loadice, his former wife and half-sister, and to disinherit the children she had borne to him (Appian, *Syr.*, C. 55; cf. Jerome on this passage). It is impossible to doubt that this event is referred to in this place, in view of what follows, and Kranichfeld therefore wastes his labor when he observes, with reference to מֶלֶךְ הַצָּפוֹן, and with an apologetic aim, that "it is an interpolation to assume that Daniel here intended precisely a king of *Syria*."—**To make an agreement**; properly, "to make a straightening, to establish a just and peaceful condition." Cf. יְשָׁרִים, v. 17, and the corresponding δίκαια, 1 Macc. vii. 12.—**But she shall not retain the power of the arm; neither shall he stand, nor his arm**; *i.e.*, probably, neither her arm nor his, which had strengthened themselves by that union, shall be able to retain the power thus acquired;* their union shall again be dissolved, and the political alliance, with its strengthening influence upon both kingdoms, shall thus be set aside. It seems unnecessary, upon this view, to adopt Hitzig's emendation, וְלֹא יַעַמְדוּ זְרֹעָו ("his [*i.e.*, the arm of Berenice] arms shall not stand," which is held to be equivalent to "her father as well as her consort, who were hitherto her protectors, shall forsake her), and also Kranichfeld's rendering of זְרֹעוֹ in the sense of *host*, in support of which vs. 15, 22, and 31 may indeed be adduced, but this is decidedly opposed by the context, which treats solely of an intermarriage and its immediate consequences, and not at all of warlike events. It is likewise arbitrary to take זְרֹעַ in the sense of "support, protector," with Hävernick, Von Lengerke, etc., and accordingly to find the assistance to be derived by Berenice from Egypt referred to in the former half of the sentence, and in the latter half the

* [Keil lays great stress upon the objection that Seleucus was *not* one of Ptolemy's generals, as the text requires; but his own account of the history makes him out to have been so at least for a time.]

* [This substantially agrees with the rendering of Keil, who, however, is rather refined in his view of the construction: "The subject to לֹא יַעֲמֹד is the מֶלֶךְ נֶגֶד; and his, *i.e.*, this king's, help is his own daughter, who should establish מֵישָׁרִים by her marriage with the king of the north. וּזְרֹעוֹ is a second subject subordinated or co-ordinated to the subject lying in the verb: *he together with his help*. We may not explain the passage: *neither he nor his help*, because in this case הוּא could not be wanting, particularly in comparison with the following הִיא."]

aid rendered to her husband by Berenice herself. "Arm" is intended in each case to simply denote the *physical* or *political* power of the respective royal personages, and consequently, in the first instance, that of the Egyptian princess, and in the next that of her consort.—**But she shall be given up and they that brought her, and he that begat her, and he that strengthened her in these times**; or, "he that begat her and he that led her away in the times." מְבִיאֶיהָ, "they that brought her," denotes either the "begetter" who is mentioned immediately afterward, and the one that "led her home," hence her father and her husband (Hävernick, Füller, etc.), or the company of her followers, her train when she left Egypt (Ewald), [or "who brought her into the marriage" (Keil)]. The word is hardly to be taken, with Hitzig, as a categorical plural, and thus to be limited to the husband. מַחֲזִקָהּ properly signifies "he that holds her, that obtains possession of her," *i.e.*, her consort (thus correctly Von Lengerke and Hävernick, while Hitzig, Kranichfeld, [Keil], etc., contend for the rendering of הֶחֱזִיק by "maintaining or supporting," which is too artificial).—בָּעִתִּים, "in the times," is an idiom signifying "at that time," *i.e.*, when his critical situation obliged him to marry her. תִּנָּתֵן, "she shall be given up, be given over to ruin, overthrown (*in perniciem traditur*)," is a very general expression that does not necessarily imply death by violence; cf. Isa. v. 12; also infra, v. 11.—The historical commentary on the latter half of this verse is as follows: As soon as Ptolemy Philadelphus had died in B.C. 247, Antiochus Theos expelled Berenice, and recalled the formerly rejected Laodice. The latter, however, aimed at farther revenge, and to achieve it she poisoned the king, had her son by him, Seleucus II. Callinicus, declared his successor, and sent assassins against Berenice, who had fled to the sanctuary of Daphne. The latter queen was slain, together with her little son, and the hope of the Ptolemies to behold one of their lineage on the throne of the Seleucidæ was thus wholly destroyed. Cf. Polyæn., VIII. 50; Justin., XXVII. 1; Appian, l. c.—Kranichfeld vainly attempts to shake the evident correspondence of this series of facts with the language of the passage by regarding תִּנָּתֵן as denoting a violent death, and consequently as not harmonizing with the natural death of Ptolemy Philadelphus.* He farther translates זְרוֹעַ in the sense of "host," and attributes to מְבִיאֶיהָ the questionable meaning, "the *promoters* of her marrriage" (the "furtherers of the whole Delilah-like match"), by all of which he obviously becomes liable to the charge of arbitrary "interpolation," to a far greater degree than the opponents whom he accuses of that crime because they frankly recognize the reference to those events.

Verses 7-9. *Ptolemy Evergetes and Seleucus Callinicus.* **But out of a branch of her roots shall one stand up in his place** (marg.). The partitive מִן, as in v. 5. נֵצֶר שׁ׳, "the sprouting of her roots" (cf. Isa. xi. 1) signifies the lineage, the immediate ancestry of Berenice; the person referred to was consequently the son of her parents and her own brother, viz.: Ptolemy III. Evergetes, the successor of Ptolemy Philadelphus, B.C. 247-221. כַּנּוֹ, an accusative of the direction (cf. v. 2, at the end); in vs. 20, 21, it is replaced by a definite עַל כַּנּוֹ.—**Which** (or "and he") **shall come with an** (rather, "against the") **army, and shall enter into the fortress of the king of the north** אֶל־הַחַיִל וְיָבֹא signifies neither, "he shall come to his host" (Hitzig), nor "he shall come to power" (Hävernick); the former rendering is as forced as the latter is contrary to the language (owing to the missing article). עַל is rather equivalent to *against*, and the "host" is that of the northern king. The "coming into his fortress" which follows, designates the result of the expedition as a whole, the taking of the northern king's fortress by the king of the south. It must, however, remain undecided whether this "fortress" denotes specially the strongly fortified maritime city of Seleucia (as Hitzig thinks). It is more probable that מָעוֹז is used collectively (cf. v. 19), and that therefore בּוֹא בְּ does not denote the entering into the fortresses, but only the arrival before them.—**And shall deal** (or "execute it") **against them and prevail.** "Against them" refers to the subjects of the northern kingdom, not to the fortresses. With regard to עָשָׂה בְּ, "to do to, or against one," namely, according to pleasure, cf. Jer. xviii. 23; also the more definite עָשָׂה כִּרְצוֹנוֹ, vs. 3, 36; chap. viii. 4. Concerning the magnificent success achieved by Ptolemy Evergetes during his expedition against Syria (the conquest of almost the entire Syrian realm from Cilicia to beyond the Tigris, the taking of numerous fortresses, and the slaying of Laodice, the rival and murderess of his sister Berenice) cf. Appian, *Syr.*, C. 65; Justin., XXVII. 1; Jerome on the passage.—Verse 8. **And shall also carry captive into Egypt their gods, with their princes** (rather "molten images"), etc. The suffix in אֱלֹהֵיהֶם and also in נְסִכֵיהֶם refers to the inhabitants of Syria, the same to whom בָּהֶם in the preceding verse referred. נְסִכִים does not signify "princes" in this passage (as it does, *e.g.*, in Josh. xiii. 21; Ezek. xxxii. 30), but "molten images, cast images, brazen statues;" and consequently נָסִיךְ is employed in the sense which is more generally denoted by נֶסֶךְ (Isa. xli. 29; xlviii. 5) or מַסֵּכָה (Ex. xxxii. 4, 8; xxxiv. 17, etc.). The express mention of the molten images besides the gods arises from the fact that the existence of the latter is made wholly dependent on the former. The transportation of

* [Keil somewhat extends this objection: "The prophecy differs from the historical facts, not merely in regard to the consequences of the events, but also in regard to the matter itself; for it speaks not only of the daughter but also of her father, being given up to death, while the natural death of her father is in no way connected with that marriage, and not till after his death did the consequences fatal to his daughter and her child develop themselves." Such niceties of verification in a prophecy so concise and incidental we may safely leave to the candor of the reader.]

the idols in itself is the significant evidence of the total subjugation of an opposing kingdom (cf. Isa. xlvi. 1, 2: Jer. xlviii. 7; xlix. 3; Hos. x. 5 et seq.); and likewise the removal of the "precious vessels of silver and gold" which is afterward noticed (כְּסֶף וְזָהָב, *genit. materiæ*, depending on the immediately preceding *gen. qualitatis*, כְּלֵי חֶמְדָּתָם), cf. Nah. ii. 10; Jer. xxvii. 18 et seq.; Ezek. vii. 19 et seq.; Zeph. i. 18; Dan. i. 2.—The historical event which corresponds to this was the return of Ptolemy Evergetes to Egypt, occasioned by a revolt, when he carried away from Syria a booty of 4,000 talents of gold, numerous jewels, and 2,500 idol-statues, the latter including among their number those which Cambyses had formerly transported to Persia. It was the restoration of these that secured to this third Ptolemy the name of Εὐεργέτης. Cf. Jerome on the passage, and the *Marmor Adulitanum*, the monument erected by the victor in commemoration of his deeds, which boasts that he had united Mesopotamia, Babylonia, Persia, Susiana, Media, and all the countries as far as Bactria, under his sceptre. In view of this exact correspondence of our passage to the facts of history, which, it is alleged, occurred subsequently to the composition of the prophecy, the suspicion that the oracle was conformed to the history appears to be only too well founded, especially as *Egypt* (מִצְרַיִם) is expressly mentioned as the goal of the magnificent triumphal march.* The predictions by other prophets relating to expeditions that secured great booty and that captured immense numbers of idol-images, *e.g.*, those of Isaiah, Jeremiah, Nahum, Ezekiel, etc., in the passages cited above, are always associated with very different surroundings, and present fewer circumstances of detail to be particularly fulfilled.† For this reason it cannot be admitted that the neglect to mention the death of Laodice forms a proof of the undimmed originality of the prophecy (against Kranichfeld).—**And he shall continue more years than the king of the north**; rather, "and shall abstain from the king of the north (several) years," *i.e.*, shall refrain from waging war against him, shall leave him in peace. Thus Hävernick, Von Lengerke, Maurer, Hitzig, etc., correctly render the sense. On the other hand, Syr., Vulg., Luther, Kranichfeld, Füller, etc., render: "and for years he shall maintain himself before the king of the north," *i.e.*, preserve his superiority over him, *prævalebit adversus regem Aquilonis* (Vulg.). This interpretation is opposed by the usage of עָמַד מִן in the sense of "to cease, abstain from something," which occurs elsewhere also; cf. Gen. xxix. 35; xxx. 9; 2 Kings iv. 6; xiii. 18.‡—

Verse 9. **So the king of the south shall come into his kingdom**; rather, "and he shall (now) come into the kingdom of the king of the south." The subject obviously is the northern king, who was mentioned at the close of the preceding verse, for מֶלֶךְ הַנֶּגֶב is clearly a genitive depending on מַלְכוּת (against Kranichfeld).—**And shall return unto his own land**, *i.e.*, to the northern kingdom, to Syria. The reference to the expedition against Egypt by sea (with a fleet that was soon destroyed in a storm) and also by land, which Seleucus Callinicus undertook about B.C. 240, or two years after the departure of Ptolemy Evergetes from Syria, but which resulted in his total defeat and hasty flight, is sufficiently obvious; cf. Euseb., *Chron.*, I. 346; Justin., XXVII. 2.

Verses 10–12. *Seleucus Ceraunus and Antiochus the Great against Ptolemy IV. Philopater.* **But his sons shall be stirred up** (or "prepare for war") **and shall assemble a multitude of great forces.** If the Keri וּבָנָיו is to be followed, it is unquestionable that the suffix of this plural refers back to the last named Syrian king Seleucus II. Callinicus, and that his two sons, Seleucus III. Ceraunus (B.C. 227–224) and Antiochus III. the Great (224–187), are intended. It is reported concerning the latter, although only by the somewhat credulous and hasty Jerome (on the passage), that, in connection with his younger brother, Antiochus, he made war on Egypt; but it is hardly possible that he should have attempted a war against Ptolemy Evergetes, who lived and reigned until B.C. 221, three years beyond the reign of Ceraunus. But the writer does not probably intend to assert by יִתְגָּרוּ that the warlike expedition undertaken by the brothers was primarily and directly aimed against Egypt. The verb is rather used in a comprehensive sense, so as to cover the campaign of Seleucus Ceraunus (in which he met his death, B.C. 224) against Attalus of Pergamus, and also that commenced several years afterward by Antiochus Magnus, which was directed against the indolent Ptolemy IV. Philopater of Egypt; cf. Polyb., IV. 48; Appian, *Syr.*, C. 66 (Hävernick, Von Lengerke, Maurer, Hitzig, Füller, etc., are substantially correct). This counteracts the attempt of Venema, Bertholdt, and Kranichfeld to read וּבְנוֹ with the Kethib, and to understand Ptolemy Philopater, the son of Evergetes, by this "son," by proving it to be superfluous, and, moreover, to be conflicting with the plural יִתְגָּרוּ וְאָסְפוּ.*—**And** (one) **shall certainly come, overflow, and pass**

* [Surely the exact agreement of prophecy with history ought not to be an objection with any except those who deny the possibility of prediction at all. At other times the *lack* of this agreement is made by the author the ground of the same objection.]

† [This argument resolves itself simply into the conceded fact that the prophecy in question is unusually specific. But what of that? Was not the Spirit of revelation competent to impart particulars, if need be? The author's reasoning is purely of a piece with the *presumptions* of rationalism.]

‡ [Keil likewise, though he admits that וְעָמַד מִן might well bear the sense of *abstaining from*, yet adduces plausible reasons from the context in favor of the sense *to stand before*. It is difficult, however, to see how this signification can be legitimately extracted from the words.]

* [The author's remarks sufficiently meet the objection of Keil that "the announcement of the war of his (Callinicus') sons with many hosts overflowing the land is not confirmed by history;" but to make all clear we add the following from Stuart: "The sons of Seleucus Callinicus were Seleucus Ceraunus and Antiochus Magnus. The former of these two began the war against Egypt, in Asia Minor, where Egypt had tributary or allied provinces. He perished in the contest there. Antiochus Magnus then led on his army toward Egypt; and hence וּבָא בוֹא in the singular. The infin. being after the definite verb denotes the *continued* advance of the army under Antiochus."]

through (or "inundate"). וּבָא בוֹא, a strong description of the protracted but irresistible advance, followed by a portrayal of the overflowing masses of warriors that recalls the similar description in Isa. viii. 8. Beginning with this point, the subject is singular, denoting Antiochus the Great alone, who became king of Syria after the death of his brother Seleucus III., and after that of Ptolemy Evergetes became the terrible and victorious foe of Egypt, whose luxurious and cowardly king, Ptolemy Philopater, quietly permitted him to take the fortress of Seleucia on the Orontes, to capture Tyre and Ptolemais through the treachery of Theodotus, and finally to besiege the fortress of Dora during a protracted period, while entering into a four months' truce with him in connection with that siege (Polyb., V. 45–66).—**Then shall he return, and be stirred up** (or, "and they wage war"), **even to his fortress.** וְיָשֹׁב can in no case designate the return of Antiochus to Seleucia on the Orontes, after concluding the truce above referred to, in order to go into winter quarters at that place (Polyb., V. 66), but rather, as appears from the *verb. bellicum* וְיִתְגָּרוּ (as it must be read with the Kethib, instead of יִתְגָּרֶה, as the Keri prefers) which immediately follows, it denotes a renewal of his operations against the Egyptians in the spring of 218, in the course of which he surrounded the Egyptians in the strong city of Sidon, to which they had advanced, conquered all Phœnicia and Palestine, and finally established himself in Gaza (Polyb., V. 68–80). מָעֻזֹּה (as it should be read, or even מָעֻזּוֹ, with the Keri, but not מְעֻזָּה, as Kranichfeld desires), "his fortress," doubtless refers to the great and exceedingly strong city of Gaza, so that its suffix points back to the king of the north, the subject of יָשֹׁב. It is arbitrary, however, to assume a designed assimilation in sound between מעזה and עַזָּה, as do Venema and Hitzig. —Verse 11. **And the king of the south shall be moved with choler,** etc. On וְיִתְמַרְמַר cf. chap. viii. 7. The king of the south who is "moved with choler" is Ptolemy Philopater, and his "coming forth," as here described, denotes his moving to attack Antiochus the Great in the year 217, with 70,000 foot, 5,000 horse, and 73 elephants (Polyb., V. 79).—**And he shall set forth a great multitude; but** (rather, "and") **the multitude shall be given into his hand.** The southern king is the subject here likewise, whose success, as based on the support of a great army, is described in this and the following verse (not the king of the north, as Kranichfeld supposes). הָמוֹן רָב designates the great host before described, at whose head the aroused Egyptian king goes forth, and הֶהָמוֹן the host, of nearly equal strength (62,000 foot, 6,000 horse, and 102 elephants) with which the Syrian opposed him. Hitzig arbitrarily assumes that instead of וְנִתַּן we should read וְנָתַן; so that the sense would be, "and he (Ptolemy Philopater) gave the great multitude into his own hand."—Verse 12. **And when he hath taken away the multitude, his heart shall be lifted up**; rather, "and the multitude shall rise up (or "lift itself up"), and his courage (or "heart") increase." The "multitude" denotes the powerful host of the Egyptians (= הָמוֹן רָב, v. 11) which is now advancing;* "his courage" (לְבָבוֹ) is the courage of the hitherto cowardly, dissipated, and lustful Ptolemy Philopater (cf. 2 Kings xiv. 10). The Kethib יָרוּם is probably to be retained, instead of replacing it by the Keri וְרָם, which is simply an easier reading. וְנִשָּׂא is spoken of a warlike "rising up" to battle, as in Isa. xxxiii. 10.—**And he shall cast down ten thousands** ("myriads"). This occurred near Raphia (southwest of Gaza), where Ptolemy Philopater inflicted a heavy defeat on Antiochus the Great, in which the Syrians lost in killed 10,000 foot, 300 horse, and five elephants, and more than 4,000 prisoners (Polyb., V. 86).—**But he shall not be strengthened by it**; or, "but yet he shall not become strong," *i.e.*, inasmuch as he followed up his victory very negligently (see Justin., XXX. 1: "*Spoliasset regem Antiochum, si fortunam virtute juvisset;*" cf. Polyb., V. 87), and immediately returned to Egypt after garrisoning the cities that had formerly been lost, in order to resume his former dissipated life. The Vulgate, "*sed non prævalebit,*" is incorrect.

Verses 13, 14. *Farther description of the warlike deeds of Antiochus Magnus.* **For the king of the north shall return, and set forth** (rather "shall again set forth") **a multitude, greater than the former.** This new adventure falls fully thirteen years after the defeat of Antiochus near Raphia. Not until he had carried on fortunate wars during an extended period against the Parthians, the Bactrians, and even to the borders of India, and until he had likewise conquered Asia Minor and the Thracian Chersonnesus, did he turn his arms against Egypt in B.C. 203, where Ptolemy Philopater had recently died and left the throne to his son Epiphanes, a child of five years, who was placed under the guardianship of the voluptuous and cruel Agathocles. In league with Philip of Macedon, who concluded a formal treaty for the division of the Egyptian empire with him, he advanced toward Egypt at the head of the immense army which he had formed while engaged in his protracted eastern wars, and which he had especially strengthened by the addition of a great number of Indian elephants, and succeeded in depriving it again of Phœnicia and southern Syria; see Justin., XXX. 2; XXXI. 1; Polyb., XV. 20; Jerome, on this passage.—**And shall certainly come after certain years**; rather, "and toward the end of times he shall come (repeatedly) during a period of years." The "times" at whose end his annually repeated coming shall begin (שָׁנִים, during several years, as in v. 8 *b*) are the thirteen years be-

* [Keil, however, somewhat arbitrarily declares that "הֶהָמוֹן, with the article, can only be the host of the king of the north." He contends that "the meaning is this: 'As the multitude rises up, so his heart is lifted up.'"]

tween the battle near Raphia and the death of Ptolemy Philopater (B.C. 217–204). — **With a great army and with much riches** (rather, "equipment"). In connection with this equipment we are probably to conceive of the rich treasures secured in past wars, in addition to the Indian elephants.—**And in those times there shall many stand up against the king of the south.** Insurrections occurred in upper Egypt as early as the first year of the reign of Ptolemy Epiphanes, occasioned by the bad administration and the cruelty of his guardian Agathocles; and these were followed in subsequent years by renewed insurrections, the revolt of subjugated countries, etc. Before his eighth year had expired, the king was obliged to conquer Lycopolis, a stronghold of the rebels (see *Corp. inscr.*, III. 339: *Inscr. of Rosetta*, 20, 26, 28; Jerome, on the passage).—**Also the robbers of thy people shall exalt themselves**; rather, "and criminal sons of thy people shall revolt." The literal reading is, "and sons of the ravenous ones, of the oppressors of thy people." פָּרִיצִים denotes persons who overturn the law and justice (cf. Psa. xvii. 4; Ezek. vii. 22; xviii. 10; Isa. xxxv. 9), hence violent persons, robbers. With regard to the occurrence of two *stat. constr.* in immediate succession (בְּנֵי פָּרִיצֵי), which must not be strained so as to denote robbers' *sons*, robbers *by birth* (Füller), cf. the examples collected by Ewald (*Lehrb.*, § 289 *c.*). The oracle refers to the league against Egypt, into which a large number of Jews entered with Antiochus the Great, and to their participation in his warlike operations against that country, *e.g.*, in his attacks on the garrison which the Egyptian general Scopas had left in the citadel of Jerusalem (Josephus, *Ant.*, XII. 3, 3). The theocratic writer sternly condemns this partial revolt to the Syrians as a criminal course or as common robbery, because of the many benefits conferred on the Jewish nation by the earlier Ptolemies.—**To establish the vision** (rather, "visions"), namely, the visions respecting the afflictions of the Jews under Ant. Epiphanes already recorded in chap. viii. and ix., which could appropriately be regarded as a consequence or punishment of the revolt from the Egyptians as here described. חָזוֹן is used collectively in this passage, in the sense of "what there is of prophecy, such visions as exist."—**But they shall fall.** נִכְשָׁלוּ does not probably denote stumbling or falling in a *moral* point of view (Hävernick, etc.), but to be unfortunate in war, to be oppressed politically and religiously, etc. The special event referred to, whether a punishment imposed by Scopas, in the shape of taking away various nobles as hostages (cf. Polyb., XVI. 39; Josephus, *Ant.*, XII. 3, 4), or otherwise, must remain undetermined. It is not to be denied that at any rate this particular passage presents a somewhat considerable discrepancy between the prophetic text of the section and the corresponding historical events; cf. Kranichfeld on the passage, p. 368.*

Verses 15–19. *Last wars and death of Antiochus Magnus.* **So** (rather, "and") **the king of the north shall come, and cast up a mount, and take the most fenced cities**; rather, "a strongly fortified city." The reference is probably to the siege and ultimate capture of Sidon, into which "city of fortifications" (עִיר מִבְצָרוֹת, cf. Ewald, § 177 *c*) the Egyptian leader Scopas had thrown himself after suffering a severe defeat at the hands of Antiochus at Paneas, near the sources of the Jordan, which reduced his army to 10,000 men (B.C. 198). While Antiochus was carrying on a war in Asia Minor against Attalus in the preceding year, Scopas had again brought Cœle-Syria under the dominion of Egypt; but in consequence of that terrible defeat he was deprived not only of that province, but also of the whole of Palestine as far as Gaza by the Syrian king. After enduring a protracted siege in Sidon, in the course of which an Egyptian army under Eropus, Menocles, and Damoxenus had vainly attempted to extricate him, he was compelled by hunger to surrender himself into the victor's hands (Polyb., XXVIII. 1; Livy, XXXIII. 19; Josephus and Jerome, l. c.). The text, consequently, does not expressly notice the repeated advance of the Egyptians and the great battle near Paneas, but contents itself with referring to the final results of this new war, viz.: the capitulation of the remaining Egyptian troops in Sidon. The idea that עִיר מִבְצָ׳ is used collectively (Theodot., Syr., Vulg., Kranichfeld) must be rejected, because this event is so obviously referred to as appears especially from the second half of the verse.—**And the arms of the south shall not withstand,** etc.; an allusion to the unsuccessful nature of the attempt made by the three Egyptian leaders to come to the assistance of the besieged Scopas. זְרֹעוֹת is evidently used in the sense of military forces (arms = army), hence not as in v. 6; on the other hand, cf. vs. 22 and 31.—Verse 16. **But he that cometh against him shall do according to his own will**; *i.e.*, Antiochus, the victor of Paneas and conqueror of Sidon, who now subjugated the whole of Palestine (the "pleasant land" or "land of beauty,"—cf. on chap. viii. 9).—**Which by his hand shall be consumed**; rather, "and destruction is in his hand." כָּלָה בְיָדוֹ, as in Isa. x. 32; cf. xliv. 20; Job xi. 14. If there were no other reason, these parallels would be sufficient to show that כָּלָה cannot here denote "to consummate" (Luther), nor yet "completeness or totality," which would result in the meaning, "and it is *wholly* in his hand," *i.e.*, the glorious land (Hävern., Von Leng., van Ess, Füller, etc.; also Bertholdt and Dereser, who

* [It certainly may with justice "be denied that there is here such a *discrepancy*." There is, indeed, some indistinctness, owing chiefly to our inability to determine the exact application of the term "fall" here. It is clear, however, that it indicates a failure of their expectations; and of this, in the case of the apostate Jews referred to, history affords sufficient confirmation. "The apostasy of one party among the Jews from the law of their fathers, and their adoption of heathen customs contributed to bring about that oppression with which the theocracy was visited by Antiochus Epiphanes" (Keil). On the author's view, that these specifications were interpolated into the prophecy by a later hand, it is impossible to account for any such vagueness, much less "discrepancy;" for the forger would certainly have taken pains to conform his language to the well-known facts.]

prefer, however, to read כִּלָּה).*—Verse 17. **He shall also set his face to enter with the strength of his whole kingdom.** "To set his face" is equivalent to "fixing his aim" upon something; cf. 2 Kings xii. 18, and for the rest of the sentence, cf. Psa. lxxi. 16; Isa. xl. 10. Livy, XXXIII. 19, plainly asserts that Antiochus was temporarily inclined to follow up his victories in Cœle-Syria and Phœnicia by a powerful attack on Egypt: "*Omnibus regni viribus connixus, cum ingentes copias terrestres maritimasque comparasset*," etc. The same author records also an attack on the cities on the coast of Cilicia and Caria belonging to Ptolemy, as being an introductory step toward the execution of that plan. The reference of the text to this fact is so unequivocal, that all explanations which do not accord with it must be rejected, *e.g.*, that of Hävernick, Von Lengerke, etc.: "to come *against the strength* of his (the Egyptian monarch's) whole kingdom;" and of Füller, "to come *in the power* of his (Antiochus') whole kingdom," which is interpreted to mean, that he should secure the complete possession of the royal power throughout Syria, and re-establish its former limits.—**And upright ones with him;** rather, "and an agreement shall he make with him." This rendering of וִישָׁרִים עִמּוֹ וְעָשָׂה was adopted by the Sept. (*καὶ συνήκας μετ' αὐτοῦ ποιήσεται*), Vulg., Luther, Berth., Dereser, Von Leng., and Hitzig, although the two last-named writers attempt emendations of the text (Von Leng., וּמֵישָׁרִים instead of וִישָׁרִים; Hitzig, יַעֲשֶׂה instead of וְעָשָׂה) which are entirely uncalled for. It is certainly obvious that the words refer to the treaty concluded in the year 198 between Antiochus and the defeated Ptolemy Epiphanes, by which Cœle-Syria was left in the hands of the victor, and in connection with which the marriage of Cleopatra, the daughter of Antiochus, with Ptol. Epiphanes was agreed upon, although not consummated until five years afterward (Polyb., XXVIII. 17; Josephus, *Ant.*, XII. 4, 1); see what follows. Such explanations as the following must therefore be rejected, "and upright ones shall be with him,"—*i.e.*, the Jews (!)—"and he shall succeed in it" (Gesenius, Winer, etc.); "and *strong ones* come with him, and he conducts it successfully" (Füller); or, "and uprightness with him, and he shall accomplish it" (Hävernick, Kranichf.), etc.—**And he shall give him the daughter of women,** *i.e.*, his daughter Cleopatra, who is here designated as "a daughter of the women" (*i.e.*, of her mother, grandmother, etc., who were still employed with her education), probably *on account of her youth;* cf. Zech. ix. 9, where בֶּן־אֲתֹנוֹת in like manner denotes a *young* ass-colt.* As Ptolemy himself was but seven years old when this treaty was made, the agreement primarily involves a *betrothal* only, the marriage being postponed during five years to B.C. 193.—**Corrupting her;** rather, "to destroy it," *i.e.*, his league with Egypt; his purpose was to ruin his former opponent and present ally. לְהַשְׁחִיתָהּ is probably to be taken in this sense, without substituting לְהַשְׁחִית for it with Hitzig, or, with others, referring the suffix to the daughter. If the latter interpretation ("to destroy *her*") were adopted, the לְ would certainly lose its telic signification, and become consecutive: "so that he destroys her, so that he ruins her in this way" (Kranichf.), but the following clause does not accord with this view.—**But she shall not stand on his side, neither be for him;** rather, "but it shall not succeed, nor result to his advantage," *i.e.*, Antiochus shall not realize the expected benefits from the agreement. Others, less appropriately, conceive of Cleopatra as the subject, "*she* shall not stand on his side (?), neither be for him (?), but rather take sides with her husband, the king of Egypt" (cf. Jerome on the passage). The rendering preferred by us is supported by the exactly similar expressions in Isa. vii. 7; xiv. 24.†—Verse 18. **And he shall turn his face unto the isles** (or coast-lands), **and shall take many** (of them). The Kethib וְיָשֵׁב is to be retained in opposition to the Keri וְיָשֵׂם, which is transferred to this place from v. 17 for the sake of analogy. אִיִּים, *i.e.*, "the isles and coast-lands" probably denotes the coasts of Asia Minor, which Antiochus

---

* [Keil again objects: "Here also the historical events fall far behind the contents of the prophecy, which points to the complete subjugation of the king of the south, whereas this war was carried on solely for the possession of the Asiatic provinces of the Egyptian kingdom. Also the rising up of many (רַבִּים, ver. 14) against the king of the south is not historically verified; and even the relation spoken of by Josephus (*Ant.*, XII. 3, 3) in which the Jews stood to Antiochus the Great was not of such a kind as to be capable of being regarded as a fulfilling of the 'exalting themselves' of the בְּנֵי פָּרִיצִים, ver. 14. Still less does the statement of ver. 16, that the king of the north would stand in the glorious land, agree with the כָּלָה interpreted of the conduct of Antiochus the Great against the Jews; for, according to Josephus (*Ant.*, l. c.), he treated the Jews about Jerusalem favorably, because of their own accord they had submitted to him, and had supported his army; and he granted to them not only indulgence in regard to the observance of their religious ordinances, but also afforded them protection." These minute points of apparent variation are sufficiently met by the explanations given above. We cannot refrain, however, from observing here how completely these seeming discrepancies with the facts of history disprove our author's theory of an interpolation of this part of the prophecy by a later writer; for such a person would surely have been careful to conform his writing scrupulously to the known historical data.]

* ["הַנָּשִׁים, *of women*, the plural of the class, as in Judg. xiv. 5" (Keil). The plur. gives a kind of superlative force, indicating her choiceness, beauty, etc.]

† [Still the construction proposed is harsh, for the subject of the verb is naturally בַּת הַנָּשִׁים. Her destruction, "it is true, was not the object of the marriage, but only its consequence; but the consequence is set forth as had in view, so as forcibly to express the thought that the marriage could lead, according to a higher direction, only to the destruction of the daughter. The last clauses of the verse express the failure of the measure adopted. The verbs are fem., not neut.; thus the meaning is: . . . 'she (the daughter) shall not stand,' not be able to carry out the plan contemplated by her father. The words וְלֹא־לוֹ תִהְיֶה do not stand for וְלֹא תִהְיֶה לוֹ, 'she shall not be to him,' or 'for him.' In that case, לֹא must be connected with the verb. According to the text, לֹא־לוֹ forms one idea, as לֹא כֹחַ, *impotent* (cf. Ewald, § 270); 'she shall be a *not for him*, *i.e.*, he shall have nothing at all from her."—*Keil.*]

subjected to his power through the aid of his fleet and army in the summer of 197, and also Macedon and Hellas, which were attacked and conquered by him in the following year, after having spent the intervening winter at Ephesus and crossed the Hellespont in the spring (Livy, XXXIII. 19, 38, 40; Polyb., XVIII. 34).*—**But a prince . . . . shall cause the reproach offered by him to cease;** or, "but a general (military leader) shall stifle his scorn," *i.e.*, his scornful and contemptuous declaration to the Roman ambassadors at a meeting in Lysimachia, that "Asia did not concern them, the Romans, and he was not subject to their orders" (Polyb. and Livy, l. c.). The leader (קָצִין, as in Josh. x. 24; Judg. xi. 6, 11) who stifled the scornfulness of the Syrian king (הִשְׁבִּית, literally, "to cause to cease" [to *teach* it to cease, Luther]), was Lucius Scipio Asiaticus, whose brilliant victory near Magnesia on the Sipylus in Lydia, B.C. 190, enabled him to force Antiochus to conclude an immediate peace on very severe and humiliating terms (Polyb., XXI. 14; Livy, XXXVIII. 38; Appian, *Syr.*, 38, 39, etc.).—**Without his own reproach he shall cause it to turn upon him;** rather, "he shall assuredly give him back his reproach;" he shall retaliate by inflicting a more bitter reproach on his part. בִּלְתִּי in this place is synonymous with אַךְ or כִּי־אִם, and does not signify "except that" (Hävernick).†—Kranichfeld attempts in vain to obviate and obscure the manifest reference of this representation to the defeat of Antiochus near Magnesia, as being an artful "fabrication of history" on the part of the "positivists in prophetic interpretation."—Verse 19. **And he shall turn his face toward the fort ("forts") of his own land.** These words are probably ironical; instead of advancing against the fortresses of foreign lands, he is thenceforward to be employed only with those of his own realm, perhaps in the direction of placing them in good condition for defence. Füller's remark, that here and in vs. 24, 31, and 39, מָעוּזִּים denotes temples, which Antiochus was eventually obliged to plunder, because of the distracting state of his finances, is entirely too artificial and without adequate support from the customary usage of the term. History is acquainted with but a single instance in which Antiochus pillaged the temples, viz.: that of the temple of the Elymaic Zeus, or Bel, in connection with which he was slain, together with his warriors, in a rising of the people; and it is arbitrary to argue a number of similar acts from this single fact.‡—**But he shall stumble and fall, and not (or, "no more") be found.** Cf. what has just been remarked, and see Strabo, XVI. 1, 18; Justin., XXXII. 2; Diodorus, *Fragm.*, 26, 39, 40.*

Verse 20. *Seleucus Philopater, the son and successor of Antiochus Magnus,* B.C. 187–176. **Then shall stand up in his estate a raiser of taxes (in) the glory of the kingdom;** rather, "one that causeth an exacter of taxes to pass over" (marg.), or "one that sendeth out a driver," to the ornament of the kingdom. The driver was obviously a collector of money, or of tribute, and the person intended was the treasurer *Heliodorus*, who was sent out by Seleucus Philopater (according to 2 Macc. iii. 7 et seq.) to Jerusalem to confiscate the treasure in the Jewish temple. הֲדַר מַלְכוּת, "the splendor or ornament of the kingdom," doubtless designates Jerusalem (as does also the צְבִי of Judæa, chap. viii. 9); cf. the similar laudatory terms applied to that city in Psa. xlviii. 3; l. 2; Lam. ii. 15.† The accusative הֲדַר מ׳ accordingly indicates the direction rather than the measure ("who causes to pass through the extent (?) of the land," Füller et al.), and cannot in any case be regarded as a nominative in apposition with the subject מַעֲבִיר נוֹגֵשׂ, as Kranichfeld proposes, who consequently translates: "(one) who shall lead drivers thither, the ornament of dominion."—**But in few days he shall be destroyed, neither in anger, nor in battle.** Soon after Heliodorus was despatched to plunder the temple of Jehovah, B.C. 176 or 175, Seleucus Philopater was suddenly and mysteriously removed, possibly by poison which had been administered to him by the same Heliodorus (Appian, *Syr.*, C. 45). The words "after some (or 'a few') days" doubtless refer to the brief interval between the departure of that officer and the king's death, rather than to the brief duration of his reign of only twelve years, as they are generally applied.‡ On the statement

---

* [Yet Keil insists that "this prophecy of the undertaking of the king of the north against the islands has not its historical fulfilment in the expedition of Antiochus the Great against the coasts and islands of Asia Minor and the Hellespont."]

† [Keil objects to the signification *moreover*, assigned to בִּלְתִּי, that "in all places where it is so rendered a negative sentence goes before it, cf. Gen. xliii. 3; xlvii. 18; Judg. vii. 14, or a sentence asking a question with a negative sense, as Amos iii. 3, 4. Hence בִּלְתִּי here has the idea of *exception*, and can only be rendered after an affirmative statement by *however*, for the passage introduced by it limits the statement going before."]

‡ [Nevertheless, the plur. here is not to be strained to exactness, and the temple referred to may very well be taken as a representative of the native fortifications, especially as it was so vigorously defended as to cause the death of the assailant.]

* [Keil still insists that "what is said regarding his return to the fortresses of his own land and his own throne, does not so correspond with the historical issue of the reign of this king, that one would be able to recognize therein a prediction of it." Yet such a prediction has actually been recognized by interpreters of all ages.]

† [Keil, however, objects to "this interpretation of the words as too limited. נָגַשׂ denotes, no doubt (2 Kings xxiii. 35), to collect gold and silver; but it does not thence follow that נוֹגֵשׂ, when silver and gold are not spoken of, means to collect tribute. The word in general designates the *taskmaster* who urges on the people to severe labor, afflicts and oppresses them as cattle. הֶדֶר מַלְכוּת is not synonymous with אֶרֶץ הַצְּבִי, ver. 16, but stands much nearer to הוֹד מַלְכוּת, ver. 21, and designates *the glory of the kingdom.* The glory of the kingdom was brought down by נוֹגֵשׂ, and הֶזֱבִיר refers to the whole kingdom of the king spoken of, not merely to the Holy Land, which formed but a part of his kingdom. By these oppressions of his kingdom he prepared himself in a short time for destruction."]

‡ [Keil's objection: "The reference of these words, '*in days few*,' to the time *after* the pillage of the temple of Jerusalem by Heliodorus is not only an arbitrary proceed-

that he was to be destroyed "neither in anger, nor in battle," the remarks of Appian respecting the mode of Philopater's death (ἐξ ἐπιβουλῆς) should be compared.*

Verses 21–24. *The rise of Antiochus Epiphanes; his first Egyptian campaign.* **And in his estate shall stand up a vile person.** נִבְזֶה does not probably denote "a despised one, whose birth deprived him of every right to the throne" (Kranichfeld), but rather one who is deservedly despised, who is despicable, morally contemptible, thus corresponding to נִמְאָס, Jer. vi. 30, and contrasting with מֵיטָב, 1 Sam. xv. 9 (cf. Hitzig on the passage). The symbolic description of the person here introduced, as a "little horn," chap. vii. 8; viii. 9, is in any case appropriate. A contrast with the cognomen Ἐπιφανής was probably not intended, since the term appears to be one of the original constituents of the section, rather than an interpolation; for a Maccabæan interpolator would hardly have avoided the temptation to avail himself of the suggestion afforded by the familiar perversion of Ἐπιφανής into Ἐπιμανής to make use of a term like מְשֻׁגָּע, for instance (cf. 1 Sam. xxi. 16; Jer. xxix. 26; Hos. ix. 7).—**To whom they shall not give the honour of the kingdom;** rather, "to whom was not given," etc.—who has seized the royal dignity instead, in opposition to the will of his nation. Cf. the Eth.-fund. principles, etc., on chap. vii., No. 3; and with reference to the expression הוֹד מַלְכוּת, cf. 1 Chron. xxix. 25; Psa. xxi. 6.—**He shall come in peaceably** (or "unexpectedly"—בְּשַׁלְוָה, as in v. 24 and chap. viii. 25) **and obtain the kingdom by flatteries;** rather, by "dissimulations." חֲלַקְלַקּוֹת does not denote smooth speeches or flattering words merely, but dissimulating words and actions, a hypocritical and deceitful bearing in both word and deed. It occurs in the same sense in v. 34. The historical tradition, indeed, speaks only of the application of military force by Antiochus, when seeking to obtain the Syrian throne for himself, and of the assistance which Eumenes and Attalus rendered him to that end, by expelling the usurper Heliodorus. But this assuredly did not exclude the employment of all manner of cunning arts and secret manœuverings, which probably were the only means by which he could secure the countenance of those kings of Pergamos. The difference between the language of the passage and the historical fact is at any rate inconsiderable; and it is not necessary to assume that to obviate *that difficulty* the Sept. substituted the more appropriate בַּחֲלָקוֹת or בְּחֶלְקָה for בחלקלקות, and translated it by κατισχύσει βασιλεὺς ἐν κληροδοσίᾳ αὐτοῦ, on the ground that they "could find no historical equivalent for the former term" (against Kranichfeld).—Verse 22. **And with the arms of a flood shall they be overflown from before him;** rather, "and the overflowing power of the host shall be swept away and broken before him;" literally, "and the arms of the overflowing—before his face they shall be swept away," etc. On זְרֹעוֹת, cf. vs. 15, 31; on שֶׁטֶף, cf. chap. ix. 26. The tropical expression זרעוֹת הַשֶּׁטֶף, when taken as a whole, involves a metaphor that is not entirely unmixed, similar to שׁוֹט שׁוֹטֵף, "the overflowing scourge," in Isa. xxviii. 15. The "overflowing hosts" probably represent in part the troops of Heliodorus, whom Antiochus routed with the assistance of his Pergamenian allies, and in part the Egyptian forces which sought to deprive him of Cœle-Syria soon after his accession to the throne. "For after the death of Cleopatra (v. 17), Eulaus and Lenæus, the guardians of her son, Ptolemy Philometor, demanded the cession of Cœle-Syria, the dowry which had hitherto been refused (Polyb., XXVIII. 1; Diodor., *Leg.* 18, p. 624 Wess.; Livy, XLII. 49). Antiochus, on the other hand, would not acknowledge that his father had promised such a dowry (Polyb., XXVIII. 17), and therefore refused to grant it. Finding that the Egyptians were preparing for war, he took the initiative, and succeeded in defeating the generals of Ptolemy between the Casian mountains and Pelusium. On every calculation, that event transpired in B.C. 171" (Hitzig).—**Yea, also the** (rather, "a") **prince of the covenant;** supply יִשָּׁבֵר, "shall be broken." The person referred to was probably the high priest Onias III., who was put to death by command of Antiochus Epiphanes in the year 172, and hence about the time of the war between that king and Ptol. Philometor. He was denominated a מָשִׁיחַ in chap. ix. 26 (see on that passage),* and here bears the title of נְגִיד בְּרִית, "prince of the covenant," because he was the actual head of the theocracy at that time; cf. the repeated designation of the theocracy by the term בְּרִית in the following verses, *e.g.*, vs. 28 and 32 (thus correctly Theodoret, Rosenm., Hitzig, Hofm., Füller). A majority of recent writers refer this expression to Ptol. Philometor; but this is opposed (1) by the fact that at the time which is here indicated, that prince was by no means in league with Antiochus; (2) that if it were really intended to represent him as having entered into such an alliance, it would have been necessary to employ the words נְגִיד־בְּרִיתוֹ, or rather בַּעַל

ing, but is also contrary to the import of the words, since בְּ in בְּיָמִים does not mean *past*," has little force, even if we accept his interpretation of נוֹגֵשׂ preceding; for that term evidently constitutes a fresh date or starting-point.]

* [Keil once more urges that "of Seleucus Philopater, to whom ver. 20 must refer, if the foregoing verses treat of Antiochus the Great, nothing further is communicated than that he, '*quum paternis cladibus fractas admodum Syriæ opes accepisset, post otiosum nullisque admodum rebus gestis nobilitatum annorum duodecim regnum*,' was put to death through the treachery of Heliodorus, *unius ex purpuratis* (Livy, XLI. 19: cf. App., *Syr.*, C. 45), and the mission of Heliodorus to Jerusalem to seize the treasures of the temple, which is fabulously described in 2 Macc. iii. 4 ff. The יִשָּׁבֵר (*shall be destroyed*) of this king בְּיָמִים אֲחָדִים (*within a few days*) does not harmonize with the fact of his twelve years' reign."]

* [The fact that he is not here styled מָשִׁיחַ serves to distinguish him from the personage so designated there.]

בְּרִיתוֹ. (cf. Gen. xiv. 13); (3) that the Egyptian is always designated as מֶלֶךְ הַנֶּגֶב in this chapter, while, on the other hand, בְּרִית always refers to the theocracy.*—Verse 23. **And after the league made with him he shall work deceitfully,** *i.e.*, as soon as he shall have established friendly relations, and allied himself with his defeated opponent, which his victory near Pelusium enabled him to accomplish. Even while the battle was raging, Antiochus displayed great kindness toward the Egyptians, everywhere interfering to check the slaughter by his soldiers, and thus won the hearts of his foes (see Diodorus, Exc. in Wess., p. 579). This conduct seems to have subsequently been of material value to him in the capture of Pelusium, Memphis, and generally of all lower and central Egypt (cf. Diodor., l. c.; Polyb., XXVIII. 16 et seq.; Jerome, on this passage).—**And shall come up, and shall become strong** (or "prevail") **with a small people, unexpectedly.** Cf. Jerome: "*Ascendit Memphin et ibi ex more Ægypti regnum accipiens puerique* (*i.e.*, *Ptolemæi Philometoris*) *rebus se providere dicens, cum modico populo omnem Ægyptum subjugavit sibi, et abundantes atque uberrimas ingressus est civitates.*" Several expositors propose to refer וְעָלָה to the king's invasion of Cœle-Syria and Palestine only, instead of understanding his victorious march up the Nile as far as Memphis (*e.g.*, Kranichfeld, Hofmann, Ewald, and especially Füller, who had already interpreted the preceding וּמִן־הִתְחַבְּרוּת as referring to the league of Antiochus with the Pergamenian kings Eumenes and Attalus); but this interrupts the regular progress of the narrative by transposing an event from the beginning of the war to the history of its close. בְּשַׁלְוָה, "unexpedly," is probably to be included in this verse, as Von Lengerke, Hitzig, etc., propose. It states that the victor had penetrated into the heart of their country before the Egyptians were fully aware of the fact, or had made arrangements to resist his progress. Hitzig's explanation, "with confidence (= בּוֹטֵחַ) as if he were not in an enemy's country," is unnecessary; and also that offered by others, "with a peaceful object" ("in the midst of peace," Füller). — Verse 24. Concerning בְּשַׁלְוָה, see what immediately precedes.—**And he shall enter even upon the fattest places of the province.** The extraordinary fertility of lower Egypt is well known; cf. Plin., *H. N.*, XXI. 15: "*Ægyptus frugum fertilissima*," etc. With regard to the genitive combination מִשְׁמַנֵּי מְדִינָה, cf., *e.g.*, אֶבְיוֹנֵי אדם, Isa. xxix. 19. Concerning מְדִינָה, a "territorial jurisdiction or province," see on chap. ii. 48; iii. 2.—**He shall scatter among them the prey** (rather "prey"—without the article), **and spoil, and riches.** This defines "that which his fathers had not done, nor his fathers' fathers." It consisted of an immoderate squandering, by which he not only divided among his soldiers the money provided for carrying on the war, but also the spoil of Pelusium and all other booty that had been acquired. Even the Egyptians (to whom לָהֶם is perhaps to be specially referred) were not excluded from his liberality. Thus he bestowed on each Greek a piece of gold at that time, while at Naucratis, according to Polyb., XXVIII. 17. His unusual liberality during this campaign in Egypt is also attested by 1 Macc. iii. 30.*—**He shall forecast his devices against the strong holds, even for a time.** מִבְצָרִים unquestionably denotes fortresses in the proper sense, or strong cities, rather than *temples*, as Füller supposes (cf. on v. 19).—It refers, *e.g.*, to the taking of Pelusium, and to the siege of the fortified cities of Naucratis and Alexandria, etc. (Polyb., XXVIII. 17-19).—וְעַד־עֵת, "and that until a time," *i.e.*, until a time that has been determined by a higher power—for a time. Cf. שָׁנִים in v. 8, and the similar terms in vs. 6 and 13.

Verses 25-27. *The second Egyptian campaign of Antiochus Epiphanes.* **And he shall stir up his power and his courage.** Concerning וְיָעֵר, cf. יָעִיר הַכֹּל in v. 2; also Psa. lxxviii. 38; 1 Macc. ii. 24.—**Against the king of the south.** This was not probably Ptolemy Philometor, but his younger brother Ptolemy Physcon, who had thrown himself, together with his sister Cleopatra, into the strong city of Alexandria, at the time when Antiochus was conquering Egypt, and had there been declared king in the stead of his brother, who had fallen into the hands of the Syrians. After the departure of Antiochus

* [Keil objects that the interpretation of this cutting off of the "prince of the covenant," as referring to the murder of Onias III., "is not warranted by the facts of history. That murder does not at all relate to the matter before us, not only because the Jewish high-priest at Antioch did not sustain the relation of a 'prince of the covenant,' but also because the murder was perpetrated without the previous knowledge of Antiochus, and when the matter was reported to him, the murderer was put to death by his command (2 Macc. iv. 36-38)." Still the fact remains that Onias was slain by his agents, however much he disavowed or even regretted the occurrence. To deny the propriety of the epithet "prince of the covenant" as a title of the high-priest is arbitrary, as also the interpretation: "We must, therefore, with Kranichfeld, understand נְגִיד בְּרִית, in undefined generality, of covenant princes in general." There is little force in Stuart's comment that the latter phrase is "not the high-priest Onias, the prince of the Jewish covenant, as Rosenmüller maintains, for then הַבְּרִית would of course be employed. בְּרִית is designed for a mere adjective of quality or condition here, and the article is omitted, as it is more generally in such cases. . . . . If Rosenmüller be in the right, the order of time would be inverted, and a ὕστερον πρότερον must consequently be admitted in the course of the narrative, which is improbable." "The absence of the article in בְּרִית is no proof against the reference of the word to the holy covenant. The article is wanting where otherwise the determination is found from the connection, *e.g.*, ch. viii. 13" (Keil).]

* ["But to distribute money and spoil is nothing unheard of, and in no way does it agree with the 'fattest provinces.' The context decidedly refers to conduct which injured the fat provinces. This can only consist in squandering and dissipating the wealth of this province which he had plundered to its injury (לָהֶם [*to them*], *dativ. incommodi*). A historical confirmation is found in 1 Macc. iii. 29-31. To bring the provinces wholly under his power he devised plans against the fortresses that he might subdue them."—*Keil.*]

(occasioned by a revolt of the Tarsians and the Mallotes in Cilicia), this usurper had probably brought the entire kingdom into his power, as seems to be implied in Livy, XLIV. 19: "*Antiochus, Syriæ rex—per honestam speciem majoris Ptolemæi reducendi in regnum, bellum cum minore fratre ejus, qui tum Alexandream tenebat, gerens*," etc.—**But he shall not stand; for they shall forecast devices against him**; *i.e.*, despite the magnitude of his army, this Ptolemy shall offer no resistance to the Syrian king (לֹא יַעֲמֹד, cf. viii. 4, 7; 2 Kings x. 4), because treason in his own camp (cf. what immediately follows), of which his opponent is able to make skilful use, shall cause his defeat.—Verse 26. **Yea, they that feed of the portion of his meat shall destroy him.** With regard to פַּתְבַּג, cf. on i. 8. The אֹכְלֵי פַתְבָּגוֹ were of course members of the royal household and servants of the king, therefore serpents whom he had cherished in his own bosom, like the traitorous אֹכֵל לַחְמִי in Psa. xli. 10 (John xiii. 18); cf. v. 27 and 2 Sam. ix. 11 et seq.; xix. 29; 1 Kings ii. 7; xviii. 19, etc.—**And his army shall overflow** (or "flow away, dissolve"); **and many shall fall down slain.** Concerning the "flowing away," which is here equivalent to "dissolving, turning away to flee," cf. v. 22; also 1 Sam. xiv. 16, where נָמוֹג expresses about the same idea. On the second member of the sentence, cf. Judg. ix. 40; 1 Chron. v. 22; 1 Macc. i. 18.—The decisive victory of this *second* Egyptian war (the δευτέρα ἔφοδος, 2 Macc. v. 1), which Antiochus achieved over Physcon and Cleopatra, was not gained on land, so far as we know, but in a great and fortunate naval action near Pelusium; and וְחֵילוֹ יִשְׁטוֹף seems to be applicable only to a battle of the former kind, not to the scattering or destruction of a fleet. Nor is there any definite record of treason committed against Ptol. Physcon by the Egyptians.* But, after making due allowance for this discrepancy [?], the whole description seems more appropriate when applied to the *second* Egyptian campaign of Epiphanes than when it is altogether referred to the events of the former war, as Ewald, Füller, etc., attempt to do.—Verse 27. **And both those kings' hearts shall be to do mischief.** This does not allude, probably, to their evil designs against their enemy Physcon, but to those entertained *against each other;* cf. Prov. xxvii. 19; and on the term לְמֵרַע (*i.e.*, literally, "belonging to do evil"), cf. Isa. i. 5; Judges v. 9. The two kings themselves are certainly not Physcon and his victorious opponent Epiphanes, nor yet the two brothers Philometor and Physcon, but Antiochus and Philometor, who were leagued against Physcon, and concerning whom Livy (XLV. 11) and Polyb. (XXIX. 8) expressly state, that at that time they had taken the field in company against the latter king.—**And they shall speak lies at one table.** Probably an allusion to a particular incident which is no longer known.* Their "speaking of lies" was naturally a hypocritical profession of disinterestedness on the part of Antiochus, as if his only concern were to reconquer the kingdom for his nephew Philometor (*cui regnum quæri suis viribus simulabat*, Livy, l. c.), while the latter pretended reverence and gratitude toward his uncle, but in his heart was anxious to have him removed from his path.—**But it shall not prosper,** *i.e.*, their joint endeavor to overthrow Physcon; the latter, on the contrary, retained possession of Alexandria and of his usurped crown.—**For yet the end shall be at the time appointed;** rather, "for yet the end is (reserved) to the appointed time." "The end," namely of the Syrio-Egyptian wars, and consequently of the sufferings of Judæa, which was intermediate between the contending kingdoms. The time indicated by לַמּוֹעֵד in v. 29 is not identical with this קֵץ, or "end of the appointed time," but rather that denoted by וּבְעֵת קֵץ in v. 40, and by עֵת קֵץ in v. 35.

Verses 28–30. *The third Egyptian campaign of Antiochus.* **Then shall he return into his land with great riches,** *i.e.*, with much booty, which he partly secured in Egypt, and partly on his homeward march through Judæa, which was now in a state of insurrection. Cf. 1 Macc. i. 19, 20; 2 Macc. v. 11 with Livy, l. c.—**His heart** (shall be) **against the holy covenant.** Cf. the detailed descriptions of the rapine and other atrocities committed by Antiochus while marching through Judæa; 1 Macc. i. 20–29; 2 Macc. v. 11–17. בְּרִית קֹדֶשׁ denotes the theocracy with reference to its territory and its adherents.—**And he shall do exploits;** rather, "accomplish it," *i.e.*, his malicious intention, the design of his לֵבָב.—Verse 29. **At the time appointed he shall return, and come toward the south.** לַמּוֹעֵד, "at the appointed time," *i.e.*, the time appointed by *God*. The reference is to the spring of the year B.C. 168, in which Antiochus began his third campaign against Egypt, this time against the two Ptolemies, Philometor and Physcon. The brothers had become reconciled to each other in the preceding year, through the influence of their sister Cleopatra, and had made common cause against the Syrian, whose conduct in leaving behind him a strong garrison in Pelusium had indicated his purpose to secure a permanent influence over Egypt. Incensed by the course of the Ptolemies, Antiochus led a large army through Cœle-Syria and Palestine to Egypt in the spring of 168 (*primo vere*, Livy, XLV. 11), and would have inflicted heavy penalties on the brothers had not the

* [The expression, "*those who eat of his choice food* probably means Lennæus and Eulæus, the guardians and state ministers of the young Ptolemy," the same persons alluded to in the preceding verse as the members of his own court corrupted by the bribes of the Syrians.—*Stuart.*]

* [The phrase is sufficiently justified by the hypocritical alliance. "*At one table* designates the dissembled amity and intimacy of the parties, who said and did all they could to mislead each other" (Stuart). Keil, after interpreting: "The *evil doing* consists in this, that the one seeks to overthrow and destroy the other under the cloak of feigned friendship; for they eat as friends at one table, and 'speak lies'—the one tells lies to the other, professing friendship. But their design shall not succeed;" yet captiously adds "All interpretations of these words which are determined by historical *facta* are arbitrary. The history of Antiochus Epiphanes furnishes no illustrations for this." The above league affords abundant presumption of these facts, even if strictly understood.]

Romans interfered (cf. Livy, l. c.; Polyb., XXIX. 8; Justin., XXXIV. 2).—**But it shall not be as the former, or as the latter,** *i.e.*, a success similar to the triumphs of the first and second expeditions shall not be realized; cf. for instance, v. 12.—כְּ־וּכְ, "as—so also;" cf. Ezek. xviii. 4; Josh. xiv. 11 (Ewald, *Lehrb.*, p. 851). The two substantives are in the *cas. adverbialis.* —Verse 30. **For ships of Chittim** (צִיִּים כִּתִּים) **shall come against him.** The expression is derived from Num. xxiv. 24, where Balaam predicted the humiliation of Assyria through the agency of ships of Chittim. In that place Græcian ships were probably intended, but the reference here is certainly to ships belonging to the Romans, namely, the fleet of C. Popilius Lænas, which sailed to Egypt after the victory over Perseus near Pydna (June 22d, B.C. 168), in order to prevent the Syrian king from subjugating that country, as he designed to do (Livy, XLV. 10; Polyb., XXIX. 1). It is not necessary to assume, with Bertholdt and Dereser, that the "ships of Chittim" denote the Macedonian fleet which fell into the hands of the Romans at the victory of Pydna, and was afterward employed by Lænas for his voyage to Egypt. Aside from the fact that Polybius and Livy do not mention this fact, to designate ships that had been taken by the Romans as *Macedonian* vessels would obviously be inappropriate; and, moreover, the customary usage throughout this book would lead us to expect יְוָנִים instead. The term כִּתִּים is very broad and indefinite in its application, as appears already from Gen. x. 4. It denotes all the islands and coast-lands along the northern shores of the Mediterranean sea, beginning with Cyprus (which is referred to under that name in Isa. xxiii. 1, 12; Ezek. xxvii. 6), and extending as far as Spain, and therefore might appropriately be employed to designate Rome or Italy in particular (cf. Knobel, *Völkertafel*, p. 95 et seq.). The Sept. is correct (Ῥωμαῖοι), and also Jerome; but the latter overlooked the adjective nature of כִּתִּים (plur. of כִּתִּי), and therefore inserted a copula between the two nouns: "*venient super eum trieres* et *Romani.*" —**Therefore shall he be grieved** (rather, "discouraged") **and return.** It is known that Popilius Lænas, on meeting with Antiochus four miles from Alexandria, did not grasp the hand extended by the latter in greeting, but at once presented the message entrusted by the senate to his care, and that when the king requested time to consider its contents, the Roman drew a circle about him, and did not permit him to pass beyond it before he had given the desired answer (Livy, XLV. 12; Polyb., XXIX. 11; Appian, *Syr.*, 66; Justin., XXXIV. 3).—**And have indignation against the holy covenant: so shall he do;** or, "and shall accomplish it." Füller says well, "The rage which he was unable to vent on Egypt is now turned against the holy covenant; in his displeasure he turns against Israel, without being hindered" (וְעָשָׂה, as in v. 28). Several writers, among whom are Rosenm. and Kranichfeld (the latter being guided by his desire to render the prophecy as dissimilar to the history as possible), take the preceding וְשָׁב adverbially, and regard it as qualifying וְזָעַם: "and *again* he shall have indignation," etc. שׁוּב, however, is not used as a mere auxiliary in any other part of this section; and the return of the northern king from Egypt could not be passed over without notice in this place, since not to have mentioned it would have made Egypt the scene of the subsequent warlike operations in v. 31 *a*, which would thus conflict with v. 31 *b* (cf. Hitzig on the passage).—**He shall even return and have intelligence with them that forsake the holy covenant**; rather, "and he shall return, and fix his attention on them," etc. The second "and he returns" denotes his journey to Antioch from Palestine, where he had halted by the way. His "fixing attention" (הֵבִין עַל, as in v. 37; Job. xxxi. 1; Jer. xxxix. 12) on the apostates from the covenant (עֹזְבֵי בְרִית = פָּרִיצִים, v. 14) is to be understood in the sense of affiliating with them, who became his favorites and protegés, and for whom he endeavored to erect a new and idolatrous system of worship; cf. 1 Macc. ii. 18; 2 Macc. vi. 1. Also infra, on v. 39.

Verses 31–36. *Attacks on the sacred institutions of the theocracy, and the persecution of its faithful adherents by Antiochus.* **And arms shall stand on his part**; rather, "and armed hosts of his shall remain," namely, in the holy land. Consequently זְרֹעִים יַעֲמֹדוּ is used substantially as in v. 15, to denote the standing still of an armed host (cf. the leaving of a Syrian garrison in the citadel of Zion, which is mentioned in 1 Macc. i. 34). The usual rendering is, "and armed bands *shall arise* from him"—which, however, seems more appropriate and conformable to the context than Kranichfeld's strange interpretation, "and accomplices (*i.e.*, traitorous Israelites) shall stand up through his influence" (!). מִמֶּנּוּ probably does not signify "at his bidding" (cf. 2 Sam. iii. 37), but is a partitive, or rather expresses dependence on the possessor.—**And pollute the sanctuary of strength**; rather, "the sanctuary, the stronghold." The sanctuary is probably termed the stronghold (הַמָּעוֹז, an apposition) in a *spiritual sense*, as being the refuge and support of Israel; cf. Psa. xviii. 3; xxxi. 3–5; Isa. xxv. 4, etc., where Jehovah himself is termed Israel's strong tower (Von Leng., Kranichfeld, Füller). The reference of the expression to the fortifications with which the second temple was certainly provided (1 Macc. vi. 7; v. 60) is less probable. However, cf. 1 Macc. i. 37; 2 Macc. vi. 4.—**And shall take away the daily sacrifice.** Cf. the parallels, chap. viii. 11–13; ix. 27; xii. 11; and with regard to the historical fulfilment, cf. 1 Macc. i. 45, 54.—Verse 32. **And such as do wickedly against** (or "by") **the covenant shall he corrupt by flatteries**; Hitzig: "the *condemners* of the covenant, its accusers." The מַרְשִׁיעֵי בְרִית, however, are evidently the same as the עֹזְבֵי בְרִית in v. 30; בְּרִית is simply an accusative of specification; cf. Ewald, *Lehrb.*, § 288, 2 et seq.—הַחֲנִיף, pro perly, "to desecrate," here signifies "to cause to revolt," utterly to sever their union with the theocracy, against which they had already sinned. Consequently, the expression does not involve a tautology, as if a successful effort to lead such as had already cast off their allegiance to apostatize were asserted. Kranichfeld interprets very harshly and arbitrarily, "and so far as the sinner against the covenant is concerned, he shall pollute it (the covenant) by his insinuating deportment." בַּחֲלַקּוֹת, "with smoothnesses," *i.e.*, with smooth words and dissimulating arts (doubtless including deceitful *promises*, cf. 1 Macc. ii. 17 et seq.) probably differs merely in form from בַּחֲלַקְלַקּוֹת in v. 21; cf. v. 34.—**But people that do know their God shall be** (or "prove themselves") **strong** (*i.e.*, to resist his seductive efforts), **and do exploits**; rather, "do it." Cf. vs. 17, 28, 30, and for the historical fulfilment, see 1 Macc. i. 62 et seq.; ii. 3 et seq.—Verse 33. **And they that understand among the people shall instruct** (the) **many.** מַשְׂכִּילֵי עָם does not denote "*teachers* of the people" (Dereser, Hitzig), and the analogy of לְהַשְׂכִּילְךָ in chap. ix. 22 is not sufficient to establish that rendering. מַשְׂכִּיל is rather to be taken as equivalent to *intelligens* (cf. Sept., Theodot.: οἱ συνετοὶ λαοῦ; Vulg., *docti*), in harmony with the usual intransitive sense השׂכּיל (see chap. i. 4, 17; ix. 13, 25). This rendering finds a special support in the contrasting of the מַשְׂכִּילִים and the רְשָׁעִים in chap. xii. 10. These understanding ones, *i.e.*, these genuine theocrats, *e.g.*, a Mattathias (1 Macc. ii. 1 et seq.), an Eleazar (2 Macc. vi. 18), etc., shall "impart understanding (יָבִינוּ; cf. Job vi. 24) to *the many*, *i.e.*, the not inconsiderable number of the "people that do know their God," v. 32, who were faithful to the covenant and capable of being saved, and of whom 1 Macc. i. 65 et seq. testifies that they were somewhat numerous.—**Yet they shall fall by the sword, and by flame,** etc. "They," viz.: the many who hearken to the voice of the understanding ones, not the latter in person; see v. 35. For the narrative of the fulfilment, see 1 Macc. i. 57; ii. 38; iii. 41; v. 13; 2 Macc. vi. 11.—Verse 34. **Now when they fall they shall be holpen with a little help**, or, "they shall obtain but little help" (עֵזֶר מְעָט), referring to the efforts of Judas Maccabæus (1 Macc. iii. 11 et seq.; iv. 14 et seq.), which were not sufficient to put an end to all the suffering and persecution at a single stroke; cf., *e.g.*, 1 Macc. v. 60 et seq.—**But many shall cleave to them with flatteries,** or "hypocrisies;" *i.e.*, in addition to the limited aid received by them, the party of faithful adherents shall absorb many impure elements, which associate themselves hypocritically (בחלקלקות, cf. on v. 32) with the "many." It appears from passages like 1 Macc. vi. 21 et seq.; ix. 23, that this was actually the case in the Maccabæan age, principally as a consequence of the bloody severity with which Judas Maccabæus treated all apostates (1 Macc. ii. 44; iii. 5, 8).—Verse 35. **And some of them of understanding** (see v. 33) **shall fall**, *e.g.*, certain priests, 1 Macc. v. 67; Eleazar, 2 Macc. vi. 18, etc., and Judas Maccabæus himself, etc. נכשׁל can have no other meaning in this place than that in which it occurs in vs. 33 and 34.—**To try** ("smelt") **them, and to purge and to make them white** (or, "cleanse them"), **even to the time of the end**; literally, "among them." This is a statement of the Divine purpose in imposing the specified sufferings. "Among them" (בָּהֶם), *i.e.*, not merely among the "understanding ones," but also among their followers, among the theocratic party as a whole, which, according to v. 34, stood in some need of being sifted and purified. לְבָרֵר alludes to the separation or removal of the dross that was expelled by the צרוף, and לְלַבֵּן to the polishing and brightening of the metal that was thus freed from its impure elements. "The three-fold description is also probably designed to indicate that the purifying should be effected by various processes. Not only are the pretended adherents to Jehovah's party to separate themselves from His sincere followers, but the latter themselves, incited thereto by the example of steadfastness and self-denial furnished by their martyrs, shall cast out from themselves everything that is impure; and they shall succeed in gaining over all those who share their convictions in their hearts, but have been hindered by fear and timidity from avowing an open connection with them. In like manner a Nicodemus and a Joseph of Arimathæa were induced by the very death of Christ on the cross to confess their allegiance to him. —Thus Antiochus attempts to annihilate the party among the Jews that is devoted to its God, but succeeds only in contributing to its purifying" (Füller).—The "time of the end" (עֵת־קֵץ) down to which the painful process of purifying is to be continued, denotes, in the sense of the prophecy, the end of the pre-Messianic period as a whole, as appears from chap. viii. 17; ix. 27; but it coincides essentially with the end of Antiochus himself.—**Because it is yet for a time appointed**; *i.e.*, the period of tribulation shall be protracted until then; cf. v. 27.—Verse 36. **And the king shall do according to his will.** The מֶלֶךְ can be no other than the one hitherto represented, the antitheistic persecutor of Israel, the king of the north, Antiochus Epiphanes. It is therefore not Constantine the Great (Ibn-Ezra, Jacchiad., Abarbanel, etc.), or the Roman state as a whole (Rashi, Calvin, etc.), or the New-Test. antichrist (Jerome, Theodor., Luther, Œcolamp., Geier, Calov, Kliefoth)—all of which interpretations contradict the context, and arbitrarily interpose a hiatus of centuries between v. 35 and the closing verses of the chapter.*—**And**

* [Keil contends for the last of the above views, in accordance with his adopted theory of the final Antichristian "little horn;" but his arguments have little weight, in the face of the admitted identity of the persecuting "king" throughout this passage. His chief point is this: "If the contents of vers. 36-45 lie beyond the end of the enemy who has hitherto been spoken of, then ought his destruction to have been mentioned, especially since with the words, 'to the time of the end, because yet for a time appointed,' ver. 35, the words of ver. 27, 'for yet the end of the time appointed,' are resumed. All attempts to give to the former of these expressions, ver. 35, a different meaning from that

magnify himself above every god, *i.e.*, subjectively, in his proud imagination; cf. 2 Macc. ix. 12; 2 Thess. ii. 4; also chap. viii. 25. Jerome, Luther, Füller, etc., render the words, "*against* every god;" but this interpretation of עַל is antagonized by its use in v. 37 *b*, where it is likewise connected with יִתְגַּדֵּל, but notedly in the sense of "above."—**And shall speak marvellous things against the God of gods.** Cf. chap. vii. 8, 25; and concerning אֵל אֵלִים, see chap. ii. 47.—**And shall prosper,** *i.e.*, in his undertakings generally; cf. viii. 12, 24 et seq. — **Till the indignation be accomplished;** namely, God's anger against His people, in whose execution He employed Antiochus as a scourge or "saw" (Isa. x. 15). Cf. viii. 19; ix. 27; and on the whole expression, see Isa. x. 23, 25.

Verses 37–39. *Description of the general godlessness of Antiochus Epiphanes, without confining it to its relations to the theocracy.* **Neither** (or, "and not") **shall he regard the god** ("gods") **of his fathers,** hence, shall manifest his impiety even with reference to the requirements of the religious sense of the heathen. This will include his robbery of temples (Polyb., XXXI. 4), and his efforts to destroy national bounds by tearing down their several religious systems (Diodor., XXXI. 1; 1 Macc. i. 43).*—**Nor the desire of women, nor regard any god;** rather, "nor the desire of women nor any god shall he regard." In view of the connection חֶמְדַּת נָשִׁים cannot possibly signify anything else than a god, and does not, therefore, denote chaste conjugal love (Luther, J. Gerhard, etc., who support their view by a reference to κωλύειν γαμεῖν, 1 Tim. iv. 3), or a love for women, susceptibility to amorous emotions generally (Grotius), nor yet "the *supplications* of women" (Dathe, Stäudlin), or "*the favorites* of women," *i.e.*, children (cf. Hos. ix. 16; Mic. i 16, etc.—thus Bertholdt). We are to conceive, rather, of the goddess of nature among the Asiatics, the Baaltis, Astarte, or Mylitta of the Babylonians, the Persian Artemis. and the Nanæa of the Syrians. This is the more certain, as it is expressly reported of Antiochus that he had inflicted a gross indignity on the worship of this goddess (who is identical with the "queen of heaven," Jer. vii. 18; xliv. 17 et seq.), by attempting to plunder a temple of Artemis or Aphrodite in Elymais (Polyb., XXXI. 11; Appian, *Syr.*, c. 66; 1 Macc. vi. 1–4; 2 Macc. ix. 2). For this reason modern expositors since J. D. Michaelis, Gesenius, Derreser, and Hävernick are, with few exceptions, agreed in applying the words to this divinity. Concerning the designation as "the desire of women," cf. Isa. xliv. 9, where the heathen gods in general are characterized as חֲמוּדִים, "favorites."* — **He shall magnify himself above all;** above everything, whether Divine or human (the addition of אֱלוֹהַּ merely to כֹּל would be one-sided). Cf. 2 Thess. ii. 4: ἐπὶ πάντα λεγόμενον θεὸν ἢ σέβασμα.—Verse 38. **But in his estate shall he honour the god of forces;** rather, "but he shall honor the god of fortresses in his place." אֱלֹהַּ מָעֻזִּים is not properly a *nom. propr.*: the god "Mauzzim" or "Mæusim" (Luther, following the Sept., Theodot., and the Vulg., which have Μαωξείμ, *Maozim*), but rather, as appears from the repeated mention in this chapter of מָעֻזִּים (vs. 7, 10, 19, 31) or מִבְצָרוֹת (v. 15) or מִבְצָרִים, it denotes a martial god to whom the Syrian king paid special reverence—a "god of fortresses or castles," who must be regarded as being Jupiter Capitolinus, because he is subsequently described as formerly unknown to the Asiatics. There is no question respecting the character of this divinity, as being pre-eminently warlike, nor yet respecting the special reverence which Epiphanes entertained for him. "To him, the Capitoline Jupiter, were devoted the *spolia opima;* he was called Jupiter Stator, because he brought the Romans to a stand in answer to the prayer of Romulus, when they fled before the Sabines. But the surname Capitolinus accords fully with

contained in the latter, ver. 27 (Calovius, Geier, Kliefoth), amount to verbally impossible interpretations." But surely this phrase might be understood to refer to different points of time, if the change in the connection required it. Even this, however, is not necessary. It is sufficient to apply it to the general issue of these troubles of the theocracy, and thus room is still left to introduce the sequel of Antiochus's career, which in fact did not take place till the controversy about the Jewish worship was pretty well decided at Jerusalem by the first successes of the Maccabees.]

* [Keil objects. "This does not agree with Antiochus. The ἰσόθεα φρονεῖν ὑπερηφανῶς which is said of him, 2 Macc. ix. 12, is not an exalting of himself above every god. 'Antiochus was not an ἄθεος; he even wished to render the worship of Zeus universal; and that he once spoiled the temple does not imply his raising himself above every god' (Kliefoth). Of Antiochus much rather, as is said by Livy (XLI. 20), '*in duobus tamen honestisque rebus fere regius erat animus, in urbium donis et deorum cultu.*'" But this misses the main point of the portraiture of this persecuting tyrant throughout the entire series of these prophecies, which is not so much his utter godlessness and violence as the direction of these traits against the hitherto established usages of his own subjects: intolerance now first made religion a crime, and *foreign* deities were now for the first time forcibly imposed upon them. "The next verse shows that he had no regard for his country's gods; and his whole course of life, his plundering the temple at Jerusalem, and finally in Elymais, shows the reckless and impious character of the tyrant. . . . The intimation here given, *of disregarding the gods of his fathers*, shows that the previous Græcian kings of Syria had adopted the gods of the Syrian nation; while Antiochus, who had lived some years at Rome, had learned to despise the Syrian gods, and to prefer the Jupiter Olympius and Xenias of the Greeks and Romans. The establishment of the worship of the former at Jerusalem, and of the latter at Samaria, shows that Antiochus was ambitious at times of imitating the Greeks and Romans" (Stuart). For this he was naturally applauded by Pagan historians, but the sacred seer penetrates the motives of policy that led to these occasional freaks of so-called piety, and paints his secret contempt for all religion. That the person here described, however, was not wholly or externally irreligious is proved by vers. 38, 39, which bring out the precise point of his impiety, namely, its foreign character.]

* [Keil's defence of the abstract interpretation is signally weak: "A verbal proof that חֶמְדַּת נָשִׁים denotes Anaïtis or Adonis as the favorite deity of women has not been adduced. For these words, *desiderium mulierum*, denote not that which women desire, but that which women possess which is desirable; cf. under 1 Sam. ix. 20. But it is impossible that this can be Anaïtis or Adonis, but it is a possession or precious treasure of women. This desirable possession of women is without doubt *love*; so that, as C. B. Michaelis has remarked, the expression is not materially different from אַהֲבַת נָשִׁים, *the love of women*, 2 Sam. i. 26." On the contrary, all the associated terms compel us to understand a concrete object of regard. As Keil himself admits, "The connection requires us to think of a deity, because these words are placed between two expressions which refer to the gods."]

the god of fortresses; for the capitol was, so to speak, the seat of the Roman empire, the *arx omnium nationum* (Cicero, *Verr.*, VII. 72), as being the citadel of Rome, beside which stood its temple. There the generals sacrificed and paid their vows; and when they returned from their victories, they were taken thither in triumph.—It is readily conceivable that Antiochus should honor this foreign god; he had learned to know him and his worship while at Rome." Antiochus did not, probably, regard the principal god of the Romans as distinct from the Olympic Zeus of the Greeks, whom he adored with a special zeal, according to Livy, XLI. 20; Polyb. XXVI. 10; 2 Macc. vi. 2, and for whom he caused a splendid temple to be erected at Athens; as a genuine Oriental syncretist he rather identified the two. Probably the magnificent temple which, according to Livy, XLI. 20, he began to build at his capital, Antiochia, but which did not arrive at its completion, was dedicated indifferently to both the Capitoline and the Olympic Zeus, the principal god of the Romans and the Greeks. The interpretations which deviate from this are accordingly to be rejected, *e.g.*, that of several rabbins, Grotius, Bertholdt, Stäudlin, etc., who think of *Mars* (who was evidently not a god of fortresses, but rather a god of *battles*), and that of Hitzig, who proposes to read אֱלוֹהַּ מָעֹז יָם, not to render "god of the sea fortress," and that it should be referred to Melcarth or the Tyrian Heracles, making only the latter sentence of the verse to apply to Jupiter Capitolinus. The correct view is advocated by Gesenius, Dereser, Von Lengerke, Hävernick, Maurer, Ewald, and, generally, by a majority of recent writers, among them Vaihinger, Art. *Meussim* in Herzog's *Real-Encyklop.**—עַל־כַּנּוֹ, "upon his basis," probably indicates that Antiochus should honor the specified divinity "on its pedestal," hence in the form of a statue or an idol-image (Bertholdt, Hävernick, Von Lengerke, Maurer, Hitzig, etc.). A less probable opinion is that the words refer to the temple of Jupiter at Rome, as being the headquarters or seat of that god, to which Antiochus forwarded gifts (Kamphausen); and finally, the rendering "in his stead," which was formerly current (Luther, Gesenius, de Wette, and more recently Kranichfeld and Füller), conflicts with the general usage and with the context, because the preceding verse did not confine its statements to a single Oriental deity, in the stead of which this new god was to arise, while the sing. suffix in כַּנּוֹ can hardly be held to possess a "distributive and illustrative" force (cf. vs. 20, 21).*—**And** (the) **god whom his fathers knew not shall he honor with gold and silver,** etc. This god with whom the ancestors of Antiochus were not acquainted was the god of fortresses just mentioned, not a different god (Hitzig), and still less *qualiscunque Deus alius* (Venema). Livy, XLII. 6, expressly mentions an embassy which Antiochus sent to Rome with a votive offering of golden vessels valued at 500 pounds (a portion of which would naturally be placed in the temple of the principal god).—חֲמֻדוֹת, "jewels, precious articles of small size," is here equivalent to כְּלֵי חֶמְדּוֹת, 2 Chron. xx. 25.-Verse 39. **Thus shall he do in the most strong holds with a strange god;** rather, "and he shall pursue the same course with the fortifications of the fortresses as with the strange god;" *i.e.*, he shall recognize and honor *them only*, shall fix his attention on nothing else, *the fortresses are his idols.* The words are significant merely as an introduction to what is to follow; עִם in this place is merely a stronger form of כְּ, cf. Job xl. 15; ix. 26; Psa. cxx. 4; cxliii. 7; Ecc. ii. 16. By approving of this explanation, which originated with Ewald, and which we are compelled to consider the only one that accords with the context, and that is adequately supported by the general usage of the language, we reject the numerous renderings which deviate from it, that have been imposed on the passage from of old, *e.g.*, Vulg., "*Et faciet, ut muniat Maozim cum Deo alieno, quem cognovit;*" Luther, "And shall greatly honor those who aid him to strengthen Maeusim, with the strange god whom he has selected;" Bertholdt and Dereser, "And shall store them (the jewels) in the temples of the god of war; all who hold with the strange god," etc.; Rosenmüller, Von Lengerke, Hävernick, "And in the manner which has been described he

* [Keil still objects; (1) "But according to the following passage, this god (worshipped by the person in question) was not known to his fathers. That could not be said either of Mars, Jupiter, or Melkart." Keil has overlooked the description of this deity, which is not his ancestral god (although even then it would doubtless mean, as in ver. 37, the deity commonly worshipped in the country, *i.e.*, Asiatic or Syrian), but "a *strange* god" (אֱלוֹהַּ נֵכָר, ver. 39). (2) "Add to this, 'that if the statement here refers to the honoring of Hercules, or Mars, or Zeus, or Jupiter, then therewith all would be denied that was previously said of the king's being destitute of all religion' (Kliefoth)." We cannot see that this last discrepancy would be at all improved by the identification with any other deity whatever. It simply shows that the latter passage must not be so strictly interpreted. (3) "The words thus in no respect (?) agree with Antiochus, and do not permit us to think of any definite heathen deity." Strange then that the descriptive epithet מָעֻזִּים should have been added by the sacred writer if he had so indefinite a worship in view, and stranger still that he should go on to characterize that reverence by the particulars given in this and the following verse.]

* [On this Keil's criticism seems in the main to be just: "עַל כַּנּוֹ does not signify *on his foundation, pedestal,* because the remark that he honored the god on his pedestal would be quite inappropriate, unless it had also been said that he had erected a statue to him. עַל כַּנּוֹ has here the same meaning as in vers. 20, 21, and 7, 'in his place or stead.' But the suffix is not, with Kliefoth, to be referred to עַל כֹּל, 'in the place of all that which he did not regard,' but it refers to כָּל אֱלוֹהַּ, 'in the peace of every god;' which is not overthrown by the objection that in that case the suffix should have been in the plur., because the suffix is connected with the sing. אלוה. The 'god of fortresses' is the personification of war, and the thought is this: He will regard no other god, but only war; the taking of fortresses he will make his god; and he will worship this god above all as the means of his gaining the world-power. Of this war god as the object of deification, it might be said that his fathers knew nothing, because no other king had made war his religion, his god, to whom he offered up in sacrifice all, gold, silver, precious stones, jewels." We must take exception, however, to the incongruous idea of this last sentence respecting the deification of an abstract passion; nor can we see that in any reasonable or conceivable sense this could be said to characterize the king in question—be he who he may—above all his forefathers.]

shall proceed with regard to the true feasts together with the strange gods," etc.; Maurer, "*Et sic ille versabitur in obtrudendo urbibus munitis Jove Capitolino, qui agnoverit illum,*" etc.; Kranichfeld (and similarly de Wette), "And he shall do it to the defensive fortresses with the aid of the strange god;" Füller, "And he is active for the fortifying of the strong holds with the strange god; whoso shall acknowledge," etc.; Kliefoth, "And he shall act with the defensive fortress according to the mind of the strange god; whoso shall acknowledge," etc.; Hitzig and Kamphausen, "And he shall provide for the defensive fortresses the *people* of a strange god, *i.e.*, heathen colonists" (the two latter consequently transform עִם into עַם); [Keil, "With the help of this god, who was unknown to his fathers, he will so proceed against the strong fortresses that he will reward with honor, might, and wealth those who acknowledge him."]—**Whom he shall acknowledge and increase with glory**; rather, "To him who shall acknowledge (them), he shall make the honor great;" *i.e.*, he shall confer great honor on those who, like himself, adore the god of fortresses, and consequently make an idol of fortifications and war in general. The persons in view are probably not the heathen subjects and military officers of the king, who naturally were already devoted to this martial god and the worship of fortresses, but primarily the Jews who apostatized to that religion, such as, *e.g.*, a Jason, Menelaus, and others (2 Macc. iv. 10, 25; v. 15).—**And shall cause them to rule** (or "be lords") **among** (the) **many**; *i.e.*, among the great mass of their nation. Füller, who identifies the הָרַבִּים with those noticed in v. 33, *i.e.*, with the theocratic Jews, probably goes too far in this; but he is doubtless correct in distinguishing the phrase "set them to be lords *among many*" from "to make them lords *over many*."—**And shall divide the land for gain**, or "in reward," *i.e.*, in recompense for their apostasy. Nothing definite is stated with reference to a division of lands among the apostates by Antiochus in the passages that report his briberies and promises, 1 Macc. ii. 18; iii. 30 et seq.; but it can scarcely be doubted that he employed this means also, and that especially such property as had been confiscated from obstinate Jews was conferred on the apostates.

Verses 40–45. *Recapitulation of the warlike career of Antiochus Epiphanes*, not distinguishing between his several campaigns against Egypt, as was the case in v. 22 et seq., but merely noticing the general character of his attacks on that country, and their unfortunate results upon Judæa. The rather general character of this paragraph, which is analogous in this respect to the descriptions of the future drawn by earlier prophets, raises the expectation that these verses will prove to be especially original and free from interpolating additions—an expectation that will be verified by the exegesis of the several verses. Influenced by the words וּבְעֵת קֵץ, "and at the time of the end," which appeared to relate to the final stages of the reign of Epiphanes, although the prophet probably employed it in the same general sense as in chap. viii. 17 (with reference to the closing period of the pre-Messianic history in general); and led astray to a no less extent by the example of Porphyry, who, according to Jerome on this place, discovered the description of a fourth and last Egyptian campaign in this paragraph, which he supposed to belong to the year before that in which the reign of Antiochus closed (B.C. 165),* a majority of modern expositors have also regarded these verses as a continuation of the historical narrative, whose special object was to describe the last warlike operations of Epiphanes against Egypt, Phœnicia, and Armenia. The Maccabæan books make no mention of these final wars of Antiochus, but report that he marched toward the east only, namely, to Babylonia, Elymaïs, and Persia, and that he died in the latter country (see 1 Macc. iii. 37; vi. 1 et seq.); but this circumstance is explained, either by assuming that the writer of those books *designedly ignored* the wars in question, especially the fourth Egyptian and the Armenian campaigns (Hofmann, *De bellis ab Antiocho gestis*), or by declaring that his representations as a whole are *not worthy of credit*, and for that reason giving the preference to Porphyry's statements as reported by Jerome (so especially Füller on this passage, p. 328 et seq.). The report of Porphyry, however, appears rather to have originated in a misapprehension of the paragraph under consideration; for the remaining historians of the time, and particularly Livy, Polybius, and Appian, are entirely ignorant of a fourth Egyptian campaign of Epiphanes, and the credibility of the Maccabæan books, especially of the first, cannot be assailed upon the ground of their statements respecting the final actions and the death of Epiphanes, nor in any other respect; see Wernsdorf, *De fide Maccab.*, p. 58 ss., and Wieseler, Art. *Antiochus Epiphanes* in Herzog's *Real-Encyklop.*, I., 386 et seq. We therefore agree with Dereser, Von Lengerke, Maurer, Hitzig, Ewald, and Kamphausen, in regarding vs. 40–45 as being in fact a kind of abbreviating and generalizing résumé of the contents of vs. 22–39; but we explain this peculiar feature by regarding that detailed narrative of the military career of Epiphanes, as the product of the interpolating activity of a pious Jew in the Maccabæan period, while we consider vs. 40–45 as being a portion of Daniel's original prophecies uttered during the æra of the Captivity, which was left untouched upon the whole by the interpolator.†—**And at the time of the end**

* Jerome, *T. V.*, p. 2, p. 720: "*Et hæc Porphyrius ad Antiochum refert, quod undecimo anno regni sui rursus contra sororis filium, Ptolemæum Philometorem dimicaverit. Qui audiens venire Antiochum congregaverit multa populorum millia: sed Antiochus quasi tempestas valida in curribus et in equitibus et in classe magna ingressus sit terras plurimas et transeundo universa vestaverit; veneritque ad terram inclytam, i.e., Judæam . . . . et arcem munierit de ruinis murorum civitatis et sic perrexerit in Ægyptum.*"—Cf. farther the statements respecting the result of this expedition to Egypt, and respecting the connected expeditions toward the north and east, p. 721: ". . . . *Pugnans contra Ægyptios et Libyas Æthiopiasque pertransiens audiet sibi ab Aquilone et Oriente prœlia concitari, unde et regrediens capit Aradios resistentes et omnem in litore Phœnicis vastavit provinciam; confestimque pergit ad Artaxiam regem Armeniæ, qui de Orientis partibus movebitur; et interfectis plurimis de ejus exercitu, ponet tabernaculum suum in loco Apedno, qui inter duo latissima situs est flumina, Tigrim et Euphratem* (v. 45)."

† [The author's views here have evidently been biassed by his favorite theory of an interpolation of part of this pro-

the king of the south shall push at him. On וּבְעֵת קֵץ, see immediately above. יִתְנַגַּח, "shall push at," accords fully with the genuine prophetic description of chap. viii. 4. The Egyptian king clearly appears as the beginner of this conflict, for he is mentioned before the northern king. Consequently, on the assumption that a *fourth* Egyptian war is here spoken of, it will be necessary to hold that Ptol. Physcon and Philometor, *encouraged by their alliance with the Romans*, had ventured to attack the Syrian. It is hardly to be credited that the Roman historians, and especially Livy, should have been uninformed with regard to such a war, waged by one ally against another.*—**And he shall enter into the countries**, *i.e.*, into the countries adjoining to Egypt through which his march against the latter kingdom would lead him, hence, into Cœle-Syria, Phœnicia, and Palestine. — **And shall overflow** (or "flow along") **and pass** (or "surge") **over.** The phrase employed in v. 10, with reference to the war of Antiochus Epiphanes against Ptolemy Philopater, is entirely similar.—Verse 41. **He shall enter also**—rather, "and he shall enter"—**into the glorious land, and many countries shall be overthrown**; rather, "and many shall be caused to fall." The description is scarcely as concrete as the parallel in chap. viii. 9–11, and may therefore be an original prophecy with equal probability. The case differs in vs. 28, 31 et seq. The "many" who shall be caused to fall by the northern king are probably *countries or nations*, as appears clearly from *b*, and as the fem. רַבּוֹת likewise indicates (namely, אֲרָצוֹת). That plural is consequently not to be pointed רִבּוֹת, "ten thousands" (Psa. xci. 7), nor to be translated, with Ewald, by "rabbins, teachers of high grade," and that interpretation to be taken as an evidence of the later composition of the book. —**But these shall escape out of his hand,** (even) **Edom and Moab and the chief** (or "kernel") **of the children of Ammon.** רֵאשִׁית בְּנֵי עַמּוֹן, properly, the principal power, the "*firstlings* of the power" of the children of Ammon (cf. Num. xxiv. 20; Jer. xlix. 35; Am. vi. 1), which probably relates to Rabbah, their chief city, and the principal seat of their power. The entire prophecy before us relative to the neighbors of Israel does not bear the look of a *vatic. ex eventu*; for although the Maccabæan book (1 Macc. iv. 61; v. 3–8) notices the assistance rendered to Epiphanes by the Edomites and Ammonites against the Jews, the mention of the Moabites in this place is so much the more remarkable, as that nation is never mentioned after the captivity as maintaining an independent existence (Ezra ix. 1 and Neh. xiii. 1 afford no proof to contradict this statement, since the Moabites are not referred to in those passages from a historical point of view, but dogmatically, with reference to the passage in the law, Deut. xxiii. 3), and since the name of the Moabites had already been lost in the more comprehensive one of Arabians in the Maccabæan age. It is not strange, on the other hand, that a prophet of the time immediately subsequent to the Captivity should adduce the nations of Edom, Moab, and Ammon as leading representatives of tribal hostility to the theocracy,—not remarkable in the least; cf. the older prophetic parallels, Psa. x. 10; Isa. xi. 14; xxv. 10, 15, 16; Zeph. ii. 8; Jer. xliii.; xlix. 1–6; Ezek. xxv. 1–14; xxi. 20, 28, etc. Kranichfeld remarks correctly: "The Edomites, like the Moabites and Ammonites, showed themselves the most persistent allies of the oppressors of Israel among

phecy. But the whole prediction is consecutive and naturally connected, without any repetition or redundancy. Keil, admitting a primary reference of this passage to Antiochus, argues against this supposition of a recapitulation or summary here. "If thus, according to ver. 35, the tribulation with which the people of God shall be visited by the hostile king for their purification shall last till the time of the end, then the time of the end to which the prophecies of vers. 40–45 fall cannot designate the whole duration of the conduct of this enemy, but only the end of his reign and of his persecutions, in which he perished (ver. 40). On the contrary, the reference to chap. viii. 17 avails nothing, because there also עֵת קֵץ has the same meaning as here, *i.e.*, it denotes the termination of the epoch referred to, and is there only made a more general expression by means of לְעֵת than here, where by בְּעֵת and the connection with ver. 35 the end is more sharply defined. To this is to be added that the contents of vers. 40–45 are irreconcilable with the supposition that in them is repeated in a comprehensive form what has already been said of Antiochus, for here something new is announced, something of which nothing has been said before. This even Maurer and Hitzig have not been able to deny, but have sought to conceal as much as possible,—Maurer by the remark: '*Res a scriptore iterum ac sævius pertractatas esse, extremam vero manum operi defuisse;*' and Hitzig by various turnings—'as it seems,' 'but is not precisely acknowledged,' 'the fact is nowhere else communicated'—which are obviously mere makeshifts." Stuart thus defends the belief in another and final campaign of Antiochus: "Lengerke asserts the entire improbability of another and fourth invasion of Egypt and Palestine, on the ground that Antiochus was too weak and too poor to collect forces enough to carry on such a war with success. But 1 Macc. i. 27 seq. shows us that after Antiochus had heard of the notable defeat by Judas of his general Seron, 'he was enraged, and gathered together all the forces of his kingdom, παρεβολὴν ἰσχυρὰν σφόδρα, *an exceedingly great encampment.*' These he paid profusely, while in an attitude of preparation for active service, and thus exhausted his treasury, 1 Macc. i. 28, 29. To Lysias, his general, he left one-half of his troops (1 Macc. i. 34), which amounted to 47,000 (v. 39), with orders to subdue and partition out Palestine (vs. 35, 36). *Weak*, then, Antiochus was not, at that time. It is indeed true that neither Appian, nor Polybius, nor Justin, nor Livy, nor Josephus have given us any particulars about this latest war of Antiochus; but who that has read their Syrian histories does not know that mere summaries, scraps, and fragments are all that remain of these writers in respect to Antiochus? Josephus depends on 1 Macc.; and this is mainly confined to the exploits of Judas and his brethren. Rosenmüller very appositely remarks: '*Caremus omnino integra aliqua et continua de rebus Antiochi narratione, quæ a suæ ætatis scriptore aliquo fide digno literis sit mandat.*' The *argumentum a silentio*, specially in respect to ancient history, is far from being cogent and satisfactory. On the other hand, the accuracy of the statements in the book of Daniel, respecting the domain of Alexander's successors, is on all hands admitted in other cases. Here it has narrated the events of an expedition, in vs. 40–43, with its usual minuteness, and apparently in good order. Why should this testimony be rejected? Nor does it stand alone. Jerome refers to Porphyry, who wrote against the book of Daniel, as saying with respect to vs. 40–43, that they relate to the last war of Antiochus, near the close of his life. . . . Let it be remembered that Jerome does not say a word to contradict this statement, although it made for his favorite object to do so if he could, inasmuch as he might then refer the passage to his favorite *Antichrist*. I do not see why the testimony of the book before us, the full confirmation of it by Porphyry, and the apparent consenting attitude of Jerome, do not place the matter before us fairly out of the reach of *destructive* criticism."]

* [The inconclusiveness of this reasoning is evident, for as the Romans themselves were not directly involved in this last campaign, a Roman historian may well have been ignorant or indifferent respecting it.]

all its neighboring relatives; and when the Chaldæan catastrophe broke in upon Judah, they proved themselves her most bitter enemies. From that period, the complaint against this treacherous nation, so regardless of fraternal ties, is poured out more persistently, and the cry for revenge upon it is repeated more urgently, than against Babylon itself; cf. Obadiah; Jer. xlix. 7–22; Lam. iv. 21, 22; Ezek. xxv. 12–14; xxxv.; xxxvi. 5; Psa. cxxxvii. 7 et seq.; Mal. i. 1–3. Although Edom, Moab, and Ammon, of all others, were connected with Israel by ties of relationship, and therefore were bound to maintain cordial relations with it in the very nature of their connection, it is precisely these nations, the unnatural oppressors of Israel, that enter into the conception of every theocrat, and especially of the prophets, as the historical representatives of all hostility against the theocracy; and as their subjugation revives the Messianic hopes (Psa. xl. 10; Isa. xi. 14; xxv. 10), so the picture of the bloody humiliation of Edom is occasionally introduced to represent the Messianic universal triumph in Isa. lxiii. 1–6," etc.—Verse 42. **He shall stretch forth his hand also upon the countries**, *i.e.*, upon the aggregate of the southern countries generally; cf. v. 41 *a*, to which the words before us are related as a generalizing repetition. [?]—**And the land of Egypt shall not escape.*** לֹא תִהְיֶה לִפְלֵיטָה, properly, "shall not be among the escaped ones;" cf. Joel ii. 3; Jer. l. 29; 2 Chron. xx. 24; Ezra ix. 14.—Verse 43. **And he shall have power over the treasures of gold and of silver, and over all the precious things of Egypt.** Cf. supra, v. 28, where the great booty was mentioned which Antiochus carried away on his return from the second Egyptian campaign, while the statement here is very general in its character, and notices the confiscation of treasures in Egypt once for all.—**And the Libyans and the Ethiopians shall be at his steps**, as enforced auxiliaries, who were compelled to follow the victorious king of the north, as was Egypt in former times (cf. Ezek. xxx. 5; Jer. xlvi. 9). The fact that this feature is recorded in no other authorities is an additional evidence for the genuine character of this prophecy (against Hitzig).† Concerning בְּמִצְעָדָיו, "in his following or train," cf. the analogous בְּרַגְלָיו, in Judg. iv. 10; v. 15; also Ex. xi. 8.—Verse 44. **But tidings** ("rumors") **out of the east and out of the north shall trouble** (or "alarm") **him; therefore he shall go forth with great fury, to destroy and utterly to make away many.** The masculine plural יְבַהֲלֻוהוּ is employed here, "in view of the omission from the general idea of the statement, of the subject which originates the rumors." Cf. the analogous case in chap. ii. 33. The "alarming rumors out of the east and north" may, in fact, be referred to the expedition which Antiochus undertook shortly before he died (B.C. 166, or 147 ær. Sel.—see 1 Macc. iii. 37), against the Parthians under Arsaces and against the Armenians under Artaxias, and which resulted in at least the subjugation and capture of the Armenian king (see Tacitus, *Hist.*, v. 8; Appian, *Syr.* 45, 46). This thought is at any rate less forced than that which refers the words to the brutal treatment accorded to Jerusalem, which was mentioned in v. 30 et seq., and also to the alleged rebellion of the Aradians in Phœnicia, which is mentioned only by Porphyry in the passage cited by Jerome (see note above; against Hitzig). It is, however, by no means necessary to regard this passage as a *vatic. ex eventu*; on the contrary, it is exceedingly possible that the remarkable correspondence between its statements and the historical fact that Antiochus Epiphanes was recalled from his warlike operations in the south by those insurrections in the north and east, became the very occasion which led the Maccabæan interpolator to introduce into the preceding verses (22–39) allusions, still more specific in character, to the history of the wars of the antitheistic tyrant, with a view to represent his entire career as having been foretold by Daniel in all its successive stages.*—Verse 45. **And he shall plant the tabernacles of his palace † between the seas in the glorious holy mountain**; rather, "between seas and the mountain of the holy ornament." הַר צְבִי־קֹדֶשׁ, the "mount of the holy ornament," certainly denotes Mount Zion, the mount on which the temple at Jerusalem was erected (cf. צבי, chap. viii. 9, and ארץ הצבי, vs. 16, 41, as designations of the holy land); and the plural יַמִּים must be regarded, with Hitzig, Kranichfeld, etc., and with equal certainty, either as a poetical designation of the Mediterranean Sea (cf. Job vi. 3; Ecclus. i. 2), or, with Venema, Füller, and others, as denoting the two seas between which mount Zion is situated—the Dead Sea and the Mediterranean. The latter view, on which the plural is employed for the dual, is the best recommended, on account of the absence of the article from יַמִּים. There is certainly no reference to any locality outside of the holy land, as Porphyry, l. c., held, referring the two "seas" to the rivers Euphrates and Tigris, and misunderstanding the choice poetical expression אָהֳלֵי אַפַּדְנוֹ, "tents of his palace" (cf. the corresponding Syr. word for אַפֶּדֶן, "palace," and also Jer. xliii. 10, Targ.), to the extent of assuming a place between those rivers, and bearing the name of Apedno, as the resting-place of Antiochus while contending against the Armenians and Parthians; or, as Dereser and Hävernick have interpreted it in modern times, ren-

* [No one can fail to see how inept and trivial this statement would be if a mere recapitulation of what had been before declared so much more fully and explicitly.]

† [But a later interpolator would not have failed to seize upon so remarkable a point, and would surely have incorporated it into his part, and even enlarged upon it from the history at his command.]

* [On the contrary, had these clauses been introduced by such an interpolator, he would surely have been more definite in his allusions.]

† ["נָטַע of planting a tent, only here used instead of the usual נָטָה, to spread out, to set up, probably with reference to the great palace-like tent of the Oriental ruler, whose poles must be struck very deep into the earth. Cf. the description of the tent of Alexander the Great, which was erected after the Oriental type, in Polyæn., *Strateg.*, IV. 3, 24, and of the tent of Nadir-Shah, in Rosenmüller, *A. u. N. Morgenl.*, IV., p. 364 *f*. These tents were surrounded by a multitude of smaller tents for the guards and servants, a circumstance which explains the use of the plural."—*Keil.*]

dering אַפַּדְנוֹ correctly, but making the "mount of the holy ornament" to designate the "mount of the sanctuary of Nanæa," which lies between the Persian Gulf and the Caspian Sea, and near which they believe Antiochus to have died,—a view which Hitzig justly characterizes as "a monstrosity," and which is equally unfortunate in interpreting either הַר צְבִי־קֹדֶשׁ or יַמִּים.—**But he shall come to his end, and none shall help him.** The death of Antiochus did not take place in Judæa itself, nor did it occur immediately after his final sojourn in that country, when his camp was in the vicinity of Jerusalem (having returned from the third Egyptian war in B.C. 168.—On the location of his camp, cf. 2 Macc. v. 24 with 1 Macc. i. 29 et seq.), but rather from two to three years later, in connection with the campaign against the Parthians and Armenians, and in the Persian town of Tabæ (Τάβαι), which Polyb., XXXI. 11, and Porphyry, in Jerome on this passage, agree in representing as the place of his decease; cf. in addition 1 Macc. vi. 4, 8.* So sudden a transition from the scene of the over-confident oppressor's sojourn in the holy land to that of his irretrievable destruction, which did not take place until after a considerable interval, is a decided proof of the genuine prophetic character of this passage.† A testimony of no less weight is found in the analogy of the peculiar expression קִצּוֹ וּבָא עַד to the former descriptions in chap. viii. 25; ix. 26, and in the *poetic* coloring of the entire representation. As a characteristic feature in the latter regard, we notice the words וְאֵין עוֹזֵר לוֹ (cf. the shorter וְאֵין לוֹ, chap. ix. 26), which serve as a transition to chap. xii. 1-3, and form an expression that refers in very general terms to the irretrievable and irrevocable character of his destruction. It would be useless to look for an indication of insanity (Polyb., l. c.) or of painful disease (2 Macc. ix. 5, 9, 28), as having preceded the death of Epiphanes, in these words.

ETHICO-FUNDAMENTAL PRINCIPLES RELATED TO THE HISTORY OF SALVATION, APOLOGETICAL REMARKS, AND HOMILETICAL SUGGESTIONS.

1. Our exegetical examination has resulted in leading us to regard the *opening and closing verses* of the section as having originated with Daniel, or more particularly, those portions of the prophecy which relate to the development of the Persian empire and to the first beginnings of the Javanic world-power (vs. 2-4), together with those that refer to the Old-Test. antichrist as the last representative of the Græcian world-kingdom (vs. 40-45); while we saw cause to regard the portion intervening between the two just indicated (vs. 5-39) as being composed of both genuine and interpolated elements. It is impossible to assert that the intermediate section is spurious throughout, because it affords many traces of original prophecy, which may be recognized by the comparative discrepancy of their statements with the corresponding facts in the history of the Seleucidæ and the Lagidæ (see, *e.g.*, vs. 14, 19, 26, 34, 39). By far the larger portion, however, seems to have been inserted by a later hand, since the parallels found in former descriptions of the future, viz.: chap. vii. 24, and viii. 9,—passages which likewise refer to the period intervening between Alexander the Great and Antiochus Epiphanes,—are exceeded by it to an almost incredible degree in regard to the specific character of its predicted details.* It follows the succession of the Seleucid monarchs and their conflicts with the Ptolemies with such conscientious accuracy, that it may almost be considered an attempt to demonstrate the ideal tenfold number of the horns of the fourth beast in chap. vii. 24, in the particulars of history. This, however, becomes improbable from the circumstance that the number of the Syrian kings who are mentioned is by no means exactly ten, but that, on the contrary, their succession is followed in a decidedly imperfect manner, as appears from the overlooking of Antiochus Soter (see on v. 6), and from the confused interchange of the earliest kings in general (see on vs. 5-9). We observed in a former paragraph (Eth.-fund. principles on chap. vii. No. 3, *a*) that it could not be proven that the writer of this book assigns exactly ten kings to the period from Alexander the Great to Antiochus Epiphanes, or that he was acquainted with precisely *four* kings of Persia, and no more (see on chap. xi. 2). The arrangement of the series of Seleucid kings according to a numerically symbolic plan, can in nowise be asserted, whether the chapter before us be regarded as the genuine production of Daniel throughout, or as enriched [?] by later additions of the Maccabæan age. On the other hand, there can be no question that it was the design of the originator of this exact description of the history of the Seleucidæ and the Lagidæ, whether Daniel himself or an inspired [?] reader of his book in the Maccabæan period were that writer, to demonstrate that the Maccabæan period, and it alone, formed the point in which the entire series of prophecies in the book are centred, and consequently that it constituted the immediate preparation for the Messianic period of salvation. It became necessary, "on the beginning of the predicted unexampled

* [Stuart thus explains this seeming discrepancy: "But why is the mention of Antiochus's encampment between the Mediterranean and Jerusalem here brought again to view, after the speaker had already followed him to the East? For the purpose of *impression*, I should say, rather than from any necessity of the case. 'Look at the contrast' (the speaker would seem to say); '*now* Antiochus encamps in his lofty tent like a palace, meditating the overthrow of the holy city and temple; *next* we see him in disgrace, and even in the agonies of death, stricken by an invisible and irresistible hand.' The interest with which a Hebrew would survey this picture may be imagined, but cannot well be described."]

† [This remark of the author is doubtless by way of contrast with the more definite and historically correct utterances of the presumed interpolation preceding; as if an inexact—not to say untrue—prediction were a sure mark of authenticity in a prophet!]

* [We dismiss this theory of the author by once more calling attention to the fact that these so-called interpolations are so intimately blended as component parts with the rest of the prophecy in which they are imbedded, that our author does not attempt to eliminate them, or even distinctly designate them. To do so would result in enervating and dislocating the whole. The authenticity of the entire passage must stand or fall together.]

trial, to enable the Jewish nation to trace, step by step, that it was by the counsel of God that it should begin under precisely those circumstances, and in precisely that juncture of the progress of history" (Delitzsch). It was necessary "to connect the advent of the post-Macedonian tyrant with the time of Daniel by so continuous a chain of the most particular events, that it would be evident that no hiatus could intervene between the time of Daniel and that tyrant, in which the Messiah might appear" (Ebrard; see supra on v. 5). Cf. also Füller, pp. 362, et. seq., 368.

2. *The fundamental ethical and Messianic principle* of the section coincides substantially with its aim, as it was pointed out in the preceding paragraph, and as we are compelled to formulate it in common with nearly all the orthodox expositors of recent times, despite our doubts concerning its unimpaired genuineness. God will not desert his people in the changing fortunes of the world, or amid the tempestuous thronging of the nations and the tumults of the wars incited by the monarchs of the earth. Even though they be pressed during centuries between mighty contending empires as between two millstones, and be unable in their own power to prevent the raging of such foes, God will not permit them to be either ground or crushed. He does not permit the chosen people of His heritage to be overwhelmed, even though the oppressor's power should reach its highest stage, and though to his violent attempts to suppress that people by force should be added the most flattering arts of dissimulation and the most dangerous spiritual trials (cf. v. 31 et seq.). Indeed, it is precisely when the need is highest, that He comes nighest with His aid and deliverance; precisely when to human wisdom every prospect of rescue has been lost, does the judgment of God break in on the oppressor and snatch him away to irretrievable ruin—"and there is none to help him" (v. 45). The particularizing description of the tedious conflicts between the kingdoms of the north and south is evidently designed to illustrate these truths, which are closely connected with the fundamental thought of chap. viii. These truths would still constitute the ethical kernel of this section, even if the portion that is probably interpolated, vs. 5–39 (where the prophecy becomes transformed into actual history), were conceived of as being *wholly* expunged; but they form its leading thought in a more obvious sense, when it is remembered that that portion is at least *largely* composed of genuine prophecies relating to the time between Alexander and Antiochus Epiphanes. It must accordingly be admitted, even on the assumption of the partially interpolated character of the section which we have adopted, that the prophecy enters upon the course of history from the Persian æra to the Asmonæan period with an unusual fulness of detail, and does this because it accorded with the Divine purpose to afford the suffering confessors of the latter epoch a strong certainty that their afflictions constituted the woes, the immediate precursors of the Messianic æra of deliverance. To the extraordinary trials of the Maccabæan age, the wise providence of God designed to oppose a means of comfort and strength possessing extraordinary power, in this unusually specific portion of Daniel's prophecies. "If that affliction was unique in its kind, is it wonderful that the people was armed against it, and strengthened to endure it, by means that are likewise unique in their kind? . . . The war which Antiochus waged against Israel was not like other wars. He aimed to destroy its religion; and therefore this war is represented as a contest against God and His service. In such a war Israel stood alone and without allies, in the resistance it opposed to the powerful king and his armies. In proportion as it was deprived of ordinary means of power and resistance, and was confined to the exercise of confidence in the aid of its God, in that proportion it was necessary to strengthen its trust; and this was accomplished by means of this unique detailed prophetic description of the tribulation and the history which should precede it" (Füller, p. 363; cf. Hofmann, *Weissag. u. Erf.*, I. 313).—We have assumed that a pious [!] theocratic investigator of the Scriptures in that period of trial, affected and surprised by the marvellously exact correspondence between the prophecy and the history of his time, sought to give a still more direct form to that correspondence, and to remove the last remains of apparent discrepancy between the prediction and the recent historical past, by inserting into the prophetic text a series of *vaticinia ex eventu;* but this can no more destroy the incomparable value and the inspired character of the prophecy before us, than, for instance, the interpolations perpetrated on the somewhat analogous predictions of the abbot Joachim of Floris († 1202) by later mystical observers of the history of the Middle Ages, for the purpose of adapting them as accurately as possible to the facts in which they were realized, can throw doubt upon the high prophetic endowment of that personage [?], or can bring into question the occurrence of really genuine prophecies in his writings (cf. Neander, *Kirchengesch.*, vol. II., p. 451 et seq.; Gieseler, II. 2, p. 354, No. 8; 356, No. 9). The interpolating activity of his later admirers did not destroy the fame as a genuine prophet of that celebrated apocalyptist of the twelfth century, who, as is well known, foretold the rise of two new orders, a preaching order and a contemplative order, during the period immediately subsequent to his own, and by that very means gave occasion to the more strict (or spiritual) party among the Franciscans in the thirteenth century to construct as perfect a concordance as was possible between his predictions and the history of the origin of their own order and that of the Dominicans; nor was his contemporary, S. Hildegard († 1197), who predicted the Reformation and the order of the Jesuits (*Epist.*, p. 160; cf. Neander, *ibid.*, p. 448 et seq.) deprived of her fame as a richly endowed prophetess [?], by the interpolated additions which were doubtless made to her prophecies at a later period.* With equal, and still greater truthfulness, it may be asserted that the prophetic and inspired character of this book is not materially injured, in any

* The *Revelationes* of S. Bridget († 1373) might also be adduced as an example in point; likewise the *Quatrains* of Nostradamus († 1566), etc. [The Rationalistic tone of these comparisons of a book of Holy Writ with pseudo-apocryphal pretenders of modern times, is palpable.]

way whatever, by the opinion that the present section has received certain adaptations and particularizing additions from a later hand, and that by this opinion, *e.g.*, its accurate references to the expedition of Ptol. Evergetes for conquest (vs. 7, 8), to the warlike operations of Antiochus Magnus (vs. 11–19), and to the three Egyptian campaigns of Epiphanes (vs. 22–30) are most readily explained.*

3. This chapter apparently presents but few points, or none at all, for *practical or homiletical* treatment, as it is composed almost exclusively of prophetic descriptions of special historical events. Even the thought just presented, that the wonderful adaptation of the prediction to particular events, was conditioned upon the extraordinary severity of the Maccabæan sufferings and oppressions, seems to afford but little opportunity for practical and edifying application. Instead of emphasizing that idea in a one-sided manner, it will be better to seize on the ethical centre of the entire prophetic historical picture, or, in other words, on the truth that *God will not desert His people and His holy covenant in any of the storms and changing events of the history of the nations, but that He will send deliverance in the precise moment when their need has reached its highest point*—and to make this the starting-point and principal object of study. The practical fundamental thought of the section is consequently the same in substance as that contained in Psa. xlvi. 2–6: "God is our refuge and strength, a very present help in trouble. Therefore will we not fear though the earth be removed, and though the mountains be carried into the midst of the sea; though the waters thereof roar and be troubled, though the mountains shake with the swelling thereof. Still the city of God shall be glad with its fountain [so Luther], where are the holy tabernacles of the Most High. God is in the midst of her; she shall not be moved; God shall help her, and that right early."—The fundamental thought, reduced to a briefer form, may also be expressed as follows: The Lord causes the mighty millstones (the northern and southern kingdoms) between which the people of his heritage is placed like an insignificant and impotent grain of corn, to crush each other rather than that object of their bitter oppression; or, Where the need is highest, there is God's aid nighest; or, "For a small moment have I forsaken thee; but with great mercies will I gather thee" (Isa. liv. 7; cf. Lam. v. 20; Psa. xxxvii. 25; Heb. xiii. 5, etc.).

Homiletic suggestions on particular passages. On v. 2, Melancthon, "*Est hæc prædictio testimonium illustre, quod a Deo traditam esse Prophetarum doctrinam ostendit. Et quia pollicetur liberationem, significat Deo curæ esse hunc populum, qui doctrinam propheticam amplectitur. Confirmantur ergo pii, ne a Deo deficiant, ne abjiciant hujus doctrinæ professionem. Pertinet autem postrema pars hujus longæ concionis etiam ad hanc ultimam mundi ætatem et ad Ecclesiæ ærumnas, quas tulit jam multis sæculis; dum alibi Mahometica rabies conatur prorsus delere nomen Filii Dei, alibi regnant Episcopi ethnico more et studia ecclesiastica negligunt, sinunt extingui lucem Evangelii, proponunt idola et libidines, injuste occidunt homines innocentes propter veræ doctrinæ professionem* (therefore the supplanting of Christianity by the Pope and the Turks—a New-Test. counterpart to the advance of the northern and southern kingdoms against Israel). *Hæc mala pii considerent, ut primum a Deo petant, ut ipse Ecclesiam suam servet, regat, foveat et augeat; deinde si qui possunt aliquibus vulneribus mederi, annitantur pro sua vocatione*," etc.

On v. 33, Calvin: "*Hæc circumstantia magnum pondus in se continet, quia videmus multos ad tempus satis virili esse et intrepido animo, postea languescere et tandem evanescere, ut fiant prorsus sui dissimiles. Angelus autem hic promittit fore insuperabilem constantiam eorum, qui sustinebuntur Dei spiritu, ita ut non uno tantum die vel mense vel anno certent, sed subinde colligant animos et nova certamina, neque unquam deficiant.*"—Cramer: "God supports his own even in the most violent persecutions, and preserves them from apostasy."—Starke: "A real Christian must venture his body, life, and all that he has, for the glory of God."

On v. 35, Calvin: "*Sequitur, nullos pollere tanta sanctimonia et puritate, quin adhuc resideant in ipsis aliquæ sordes, quæ purgationem exigunt, ita ut ipsis necesse sit transire per fornacem, et mundari instar auri et argenti. Hoc ad omnes Dei martyres extenditur. Unde etiam videmus, quam insulse Papistæ imaginentur merita Sanctorum ad nos redundare, quoniam plus quam necesse erat præstiterint.*"—Osiander: "God has set a limit to every persecution, beyond which it cannot pass."—Starke: "The trial is succeeded by the time of refreshing, and the suffering by the time of rejoicing; Tob. iii. 31."

On v. 39 et seq.: "Upon the surface the worshippers of the beast seem to prosper, but they are eventually compelled to realize that their honors and possessions are not eternal in their duration, while the followers of the Lamb shall enjoy everlasting glory . . . . (On v. 44 et seq.): Although God permits many an evil purpose to be executed, His forbearance toward the godless is always merely for a time; Psa. l. 21."

* [This apology of the author for the wrecks of this passage after the expurgation from spurious additions—to an ill-defined extent—is a vain plea. Once admit the fact of such interpolations, in any considerable degree at least, and the credit of the prophecy is irretrievably destroyed. Every one will be at liberty to expunge *ad libitum* what he fancies to be a *vaticinium ex eventu.*]

c. *Conclusion of the vision. The Messianic deliverance and glorifying of God's people, together with a reference to the definite determination by God of the time at which the Messiah's coming to deliver should transpire.*

CHAP. XII.

1 And at [in] that time shall Michael stand *up*, the great prince which [who]
standeth for [*over* against] *the* children of thy people; and *there* shall be a time
of trouble, such as [which] never was[1] since *there* was a nation *even* to [till]
that *same* time: and at [in] that time thy people shall be delivered, every one
2 that *shall be* found written in the book. And many of *them* that sleep *in the*
dust [ground] of *the* earth [dust] shall awake, some [these] to everlasting life,
3 and some [these] to shame [reproaches] *and* [to] everlasting contempt. And
they that *be* wise shall shine as *the* brightness of the firmament; and *they* that
turn [the] many to righteousness, as the stars for ever and ever.
4 But [And] thou, O Daniel, shut *up* the words, and seal the book, *even* to
[till] *the* time of *the* end: many shall run to and fro [run through *the book*],
and [the] knowledge [*of it*] shall *be* increased.
5 Then [And] I Daniel looked, and, behold, *there* stood other two, *the* one on
this side of the bank [hither at *the* lip] of the river,[2] and *the* other [one] on that
6 side of the bank [hither at *the* lip] of the river.[2] And *one* said to the man
clothed *in* linen, which [who] *was* upon *the* waters[3] of the river,[2] How long
7 [Till when] *shall it be to the* end of these [the] wonders? And I heard the man
clothed *in* linen, which [who] *was* upon *the* waters[3] of the river, when [and]
he held up his right hand and his left hand unto heaven [toward the heavens],
and sware by him *that* liveth *for* ever, that *it shall be* for a time, times, and a
half; and when *he shall have* accomplished to scatter [as (at) *the* finishing of
scattering] *the* power [hand] of *the* holy people, all these *things* shall be fin-
ished.
8 And I[4] heard, but I understood not [could not understand]: then [and] said
9 I, *O* my Lord, what *shall be the* end [sequel] of these *things?* And he said, Go
thy way, Daniel; for the words *are* closed *up* and sealed till *the* time of *the*
end.
10 Many shall be purified [purify themselves], and made white [whiten them-
selves], and tried [be smelted]; but *the* wicked shall do wickedly: and none
of the wicked shall understand; but [and] *the* wise [prudent] shall understand.
11 And from *the* time *that* the daily [continual] *sacrifice shall be* taken away, and
the abomination *that maketh* desolate set *up* [to *the* giving of *the* desolate
12 abomination], *there shall be* a thousand two hundred and ninety days. Blessed
is he that waiteth, and cometh to *the* thousand three hundred and five and
thirty days.
13 But [And] go thou[4] *thy way* till [to] the end *be:* for [and] thou shalt rest,
and stand in [to (at)] thy lot at *the* end of the days.

LEXICAL AND GRAMMATICAL NOTES.

[[1] נִהְיְתָה, *was made to exist*, or *was gone through*, contains the idea of exhaustion.—[2] הַיְאֹר, strictly, *the canal*, properly applied to the *Nile*, but here used of any alluvial stream.—[3] The reduplicated forms מִמַּעַל לְמֵימֵי seem to call special attention to the position of this being, which was not precisely defined before, ch. x. 5.—[4] The pronoun is emphatic.]

EXEGETICAL REMARKS.

Verses 1-3. *The Messianic deliverance and the judgment for eternal retribution.* **And at that time;** *i.e.*, at the time just indicated (xi. 45), when judgment shall overtake the impious oppressor, Antiochus Epiphanes, and when he shall come to his end "without a helper." * In

* [Keil (as we have seen) makes the transition from the Antiochian to the Messianic æra occur at an earlier point in the prophecy, and he urges the connective force of the introductory clause of the verse, especially the ו of consecution, as a proof that no break or interval can be admitted here. This is an unnecessary straining of the phraseology. In fact, phrases of date, like בָּעֵת הַהִיא here, usually

opposition to Hävernick's attempt to interpret וּבָעֵת הַהִיא in the indefinite sense of "once, at a certain time," nearly all recent expositors have justly contended: (1) that the copula ו connects this new designation of time most intimately with the preceding; (2) that it is impossible to regard the words בַּיּוֹם הַהוּא, which Hävernick adduces in comparison, otherwise than as a reference to the time indicated in the context immediately preceding; (3) that the time referred to is immediately afterward characterized as a time of trouble, which shows with sufficient clearness, that, like the mention of the מַשְׂכִּלִים in v. 3 (cf. xi. 35), the allusion is to the period of persecution under Antiochus as heretofore described.*—**Shall Michael stand up, the great prince, which standeth for the children of thy people.** This introduction of Michael as the heavenly ally and protector of Israel (not as the Son of God or the Messiah himself,—as Hävernick, in accord with the older exegesis, still supposes), refers back to chap. xi. 1, and also to the preliminaries to the vision as a whole in chap. x., and especially to x., 13, 21, in the same way as וּבָעֵת הַהִיא refers to the close of the preceding chapter. In both places עמד is employed *sensu bellico*, and denotes an armed and martial appearance (cf. xi. 14, 16, etc.). עַל, following הָעֹמֵד, serves to express the idea of protecting oversight over, etc., as in Esth. viii. 11; ix. 16. He "stands up" or "stands there" for the children of thy people, *i.e.*, he represents their interests in the way of actively supporting them and of protecting them; cf. chap. x. 13.—**And there shall be a time of trouble, such as never was since there was a nation even to that same time**; *i.e.*, the trouble of the faithful shall then reach its highest intensity, shall have reached its climax when deliverance finally arrives; cf. chap. xi. 45; ix. 26, 27. * On the relative clause אֲשֶׁר לֹא נִהְיְתָה וגו׳, which describes this as a time of unheard of, unprecedented trouble, cf. Ex. ix. 18, 24; Joel ii. 2, and particularly Jer. xxx. 7, which latter passage seems to have served generally as a prototype of the text.—**And at that time thy people shall be delivered.** Kranichfeld remarks properly, that "the deliverance of Israel (יִמָּלֵט) which is here conceived of as accomplished under the direction of מִיכָאֵל, is coincident in fact with the descriptions of chap. vii. 18, 26 et seq., 14; ix. 24; and the entrance to the Ancient of days (vii. 13) of him who was like the son of man, and who was the spiritually endowed leader of Israel, *i.e.*, the Mashiach, sprung from Israel itself, receives notice as being the final result and attestation of the victorious conflict maintained, under the invisible direction of the angel מִיכָאֵל, against the adversary of the theocracy, who appears in the history of the nations. The absolute identity of the Mashiach with מִיכָאֵל, whose spiritual endowments and official relations were similar to his, does not, however, become manifest from this observation—as Hävernick and others assert—despite the appropriate and well-founded *application* of the description to the glorified Son of man in person, in the New-Test. Apocalypse,—any more than the direct identity of Satan, the adversary of God in the angelic world, with the New-Test. antichrist, who stands under his ægis, can be demonstrated."—**Every one that shall be found written in the book**; or, "whosoever shall find himself recorded in the book." The A. V. is literal. On כֹּל in the sense of "whosoever, *quicunque*," cf. Isa. xliii. 7; 2 Sam. ii. 23. The book is the same as that mentioned in the similar passage, Isa. iv. 3, and hence, the book of life; cf. on chap. vii. 10. It is, of course, not to be regarded as a "list of *living* Israelites" (cf. Psa. lxix. 29; Ex. xxxii. 32); nor, probably, as a "record of those who shall be delivered in the decisive hour and be permitted to live." It is rather a record of those who shall inherit *eternal* life, a "list of the subjects of Messiah's kingdom" (cf. Hitzig on the passage), of those *who shall stand approved in the judgment*, whether they live until it transpires, or are raised from the dead to meet it, according to v. 2. Hofmann (*Schriftbew.*, I. 209) is in substantial accord with this view—the "Divine register of Israel, upon which are entered all who *truly* belong to Israel,"—while Füller arbitrarily applies the expression in this place to the "book of truth," chap. x. 21.—Verse 2. **And many of them that sleep in the dust of the earth**; rather, "and many of them that sleep under the earth;" literally, "many of the sleepers of the *dust-land*." אַדְמַת־עָפָר, "land, earth of dust" (*i.e.*, the dust *of the grave*, cf. Psa. xxii. 16, 30; Isa. xxvi. 19, etc), is substantially equivalent to "earth-dust, soil;" the יְשֵׁנֵי א׳־ע׳ are those who sleep the sleep of *death* in that dust of the earth; cf. Psa. xiii. 4; Job iii. 13; Jer. li. 39, 57; and also the New-Test. κοιμώμενοι, κεκοιμημένοι.—**Shall awake, some to everlasting life,** etc. While all the ancient Christian expositors regard this as referring to the *general* resurrection of the dead, and, among moderns, Hävernick, Hofmann, Auberlen, Zündel, Kliefoth, etc., still agree with that view, which makes

---

indicate a transition rather than a close sequence. Cf. Stuart, who instances especially Isa. xix. 23; xxvi. 1; and even Dan. ii. 44.]

* [Keil, on the other hand, thinks that "וּבָעֵת הַהִיא points back to בְּעֵת קֵץ (ch. xi. 40)," which he interprets as "the time of the end, when the hostile persecutor rises up to subdue the whole world," *i.e.*, the final Antichrist. The transition appears to us precisely analogous to that found in our Lord's eschatological discourse, Matt. xxiv. 29; Mark xiii. 24; and it seems to stand here, as there, for a connecting link between the near and the remote application of the prediction. The distress of the Antiochian persecution, like that of the final siege of Jerusalem, is made the symbol of the ecclesiastico-political throes of the final catastrophe, the downfall of Judaism being there the precursor of that of the world itself. The phrase, "In that time," thus becomes parallel with the formula, "In that day," or, "In those days," "In the last day," etc., as a stereotyped designation of the Messianic æra. It is the constant practice of the prophets to view these series of future events on the same plane and in the same perspective, the interval, as well that between the close of the Old Dispensation and the introduction of the New, as that between the establishment of the latter and its ultimate triumph, being left out of view. There is thus always a measure of indefiniteness in the prophetical utterances on these points, especially in the phraseology relating to these "times and seasons."]

"many" to be equivalent to "all" (or translates, with Hofmann, *Schriftbew.*, II. 2, 549, "and *in multitudes* shall they arise from the world of the dead"), a majority of writers since Bertholdt (also Kranichfeld, Füller, Köstlin, in *Stud. und Krit.*, 1869, No. 2, p. 252) hold that the many who awake from their sleep *belong solely to the nation of Israel;* as Füller expresses it, p. 339: the resurrection of the dead foretold in this place is "not the last and general resurrection, but a partial one which precedes that, and is confined to Daniel's nation." It is manifest, however, that the final and general resurrection is here intended, (1) because the expression, the "sleepers of the dust of the earth" is far too general in its character, to admit of its being limited to the deceased Israelites; (2) because the mention of the eternal punishment of the wicked in the closing words of the verse would be incomprehensible, and serve no purpose, if they refer only to Israelites who are to be punished eternally (see the context immediately below); (3) further, רַבִּים, which primarily implies the immeasurable extent of the multitude of the resurrected dead (cf. Hofmann's rendering: "in multitudes"), may as well designate the entire world of dead arising from their graves as a large fraction of it—in the same way as πολλοί or οἱ πολλοί is frequently employed in the New Test. as synonymous with πάντες; cf., *e.g.*, Matt. xx. 28; xxvi. 28, with 1 John ii. 2; 1 Cor. xv. 22; Rom. v. 15, 16, with v. 12; * (4) if the earlier prophetic parallels, Isa. xxvi. 19; lxvi. 24; Ezek. xxxvii. 1–15, actually do foretell a partial resurrection which is confined to Israel (which can by no means be positively established, since they rest, without exception, on the pre-supposition of an ultimate resurrection of *all* men, cf. Hofmann, *Schriftbew.*, II. 2, 461 et seq.), this will not involve that the passage before us has a similar bearing; (5) on the contrary, the expectation of a *general* resurrection of the dead, whose existence is abundantly evidenced in the Jewish apocalyptic literature (2 Macc. vii. 14) and in the New Test. (see especially John v. 28 et seq.; Acts xxiv. 15), would require *that there should not be wanting basal testimonies to that fact in the canonical Old Test. as well*, which would obviously be the case if this passage referred exclusively to a particular resurrection of the Israelites; (6) nor does the intimate connection of the passage with the preceding context, or, in other words, the concatenation of the eschatological prophecies in vs. 1–3 with the æra of the Antiochian-Maccabæan troubles, as described in the preceding chapter, militate against the universal character of the resurrection in question. It is evident that in the mind of the prophet that period of trial was the immediate precursor of the end of the world.* As he viewed it, the end of the persecution by Antiochus and the advent of the Messiah to introduce a new and eternal period of blessing were substantially coincident. He saw nothing at all of the long series of years that were to intervene between those Old-Test. "*woes* of the Messiah" and his actual birth and incarnation, nor did he observe the many centuries between His first and second advent, between the *beginning* of the end and the ultimate end of all things, because it was inconsistent with the nature of prophetic vision (cf. supra, Eth.-fund. principles, etc., on chap. ix. No. 1). The antitypical general judgment of all flesh was identical with the typical judgment that came upon the Old-Test. oppressor of God's people, to his understanding; and it is therefore equally one-sided to deprive the judgment here referred to of its universal character, and to reduce it to a special judgment over the good and the wicked Israelites, as Bertholdt, Hitzig, and the remaining rationalistic expositors contend, —or to arbitrarily refer v. 1 to the deliverance of Israel from the oppression of Antiochus, and therefore interpret it typically and distinctively, but vs. 2 and 3 to the general resurrection and judgment, making them antitypical and eschatological, so that an immense chasm between the time of vs. 1 and 2 is postulated, of whose existence there is no indication in the text. Against this arbitrary disruption of a description that obviously forms a unit, see Hilgenfeld, *Die Propheten Ezra und Daniel*, p. 84, and also Kranichfeld, p. 402. A hiatus of centuries certainly exists; but it belongs between chap. xi. 45 and chap. xii. 1, and is of such a character that the prophet could have been in no way conscious of its presence.†—**And some to shame, and everlasting contempt.** As the awaking "to everlasting life" recalls Isa. xxvi. 19, so the arising "to shame, to everlasting contempt" (דִּרְאוֹן, *stat. constr.* of דֵּרָאוֹן, similar to זִכְרוֹן, constr. of זִכָּרוֹן) suggests Isa. lxvi. 24. Cf. the New-Test. expressions ἀνάστασις κρίσεως, John v. 29, and θάνατος δεύτερος, Rev. xx. 14.—Füller supposes, very arbitrarily, that "the resurrection to shame" is "merely a passing observation," which might be omitted from the passage without damaging its meaning. On the contrary, the mention of the eternal shame and torment which await the wicked at the judgment is a *leading thought*, which was not only suggested, but positively demanded, by the recent mention of the helpless and irretrievable ruin of the antichristian madman (xi. 45), and which deserves consideration as a leading proof that the judgment here foretold is not to be distinctively Jewish, but universal in its character, precisely because of this undeniable reference to chap. xi. 45 *b*; see supra, No. 2.—Verse 3. **And they**

* Cf. Calvin on that passage: "MULTOS *hic ponit pro* OMNIBUS, *ut certum est. Neque hæc locutio debet nobis videri absurda. Non enim* RABBINO *opponit angelus omnibus vel paucis, sed opponit* UNI; cfr. Rom. v. 15, 19." [Keil observes that "the angel has it not in view to give a general statement regarding the resurrection of the dead, but only discloses on this point that the final salvation of the people shall not be limited to those still living at the end of the great tribulation, but shall include also those who have lost their lives during the period of the tribulation." This, however, seems an unnecessary limitation of the "many," which Keil himself admits "can only be rightly interpreted from the context." Stuart clearly argues that the connection gives it here the universal sense.]

* [This view is unnecessary, and places the prophet in a false light. Daniel does not explicitly say that these events are simultaneous, if we have rightly apprehended and expounded his language. He did not indeed clearly apprehend the length of the interval, but we are not warranted in saying that he was not aware there was any. Much less does he assert it.]

† [Keil of course disputes this interval at the place assigned to it by our author. Stuart also is unable to discover it there. Both lay undue stress upon the connecting link, "In that time."]

that be wise shall shine as the brightness of the firmament. There is no more reason here than in chap. xi. 33, 35, to translate הַמַּשְׂכִּלִים otherwise than "the wise, prudent, or understanding" ones. It does not characterize the pious generally (who were designated as the "many," רַבִּים, in chap. xi. 33, and who are again mentioned by the same term in *b* of this verse), but "those who were prominent among the people by their piety, fidelity, and steadfastness, who accomplished more than others by word and deed, and suffered more than others for the holy covenant" (Füller). It is self-evident that the activity of such theocratically wise or prudent persons would include the work of *teaching*, but this does not involve the necessity of rendering משכילים directly by "*teachers.*" This over-precise adaptation of the idea is not established by the parallel מַצְדִּיקֵי הָרַבִּים, nor by the designation of Jehovah's servant by מַשְׂכִּיל, in Isa. lii. 13 (against Hitzig). On the other hand, the too general and diluted rendering, "pious, well-disposed ones" (de Wette), has no sufficient support, *e.g.*, in Matt. xiii. 44; for Christ's statement respecting the "righteous" in general, that "they shall shine as the sun in the kingdom of their Father," is a free application, but not a translation or an explanation of this passage.—On the comparison of the shining of the "wise (הַזְהִר, properly, "to radiate brightness, to shine brightly") with that of the bright arch of heaven (רָקִיעַ, "the firmament," cf. the expositors on Gen. i. 6), see especially Ex. xxiv. 10; also Ezek. i. 22, 26, etc.—**And they that turn** (the) **many to righteousness, as the stars for ever and ever.** The words מַצְדִּיקֵי הָרַבִּים seem to have been borrowed from Isa. liii. 11, but do not on that account justify the assertion of Kranichfeld, that only originators of the righteousness *mediated by the priestly function*,—hence *priests*, "who take away the sins of the people through the *sacrificial* ceremonial"—are to be understood thereby;—a view concerning הַצַּדִּיק that is entirely too contracted, and, at the same time, interpolating in character, which finds no support either in the former mention of theocratic sacrifices (vii. 25; viii. 11, 13; ix. 26), or in the passage, chap. ix. 24.—The stars are mentioned as symbols of the heavenly condition of the righteous who have been glorified after the image of God in 1 Cor. xv. 40 et seq.; Rev. ii. 28; cf. also supra, on chap. viii. 10.

Verse 4. *Concluding exhortation of the prophesying angel.* **But thou, O Daniel shut up** (or "conceal") **the words, and seal the book.** The "words" and the "book" can hardly designate the entire book of Daniel's prophecies, but refer merely to the final vision, chap. xi. 2–xii. 3 (Hävern., Von Leng., Kranichf., Füller, etc., are correct). On סֵפֶר as denoting a limited section of connected writing, which occupies *a single* roll, cf. Neh. i. 1; Jer. li. 63; also supra, on chap. ix. 2.* On סתם, "to conceal," —*i.e.*, to preserve in secret, or not publish it—and חתם, "to seal," which is added to strengthen the idea, see on chap. viii. 6. Neither of the words was to be taken literally, of course (against Hitzig). What the angel required of the prophet, and to which the latter doubtless consented, was merely that he should avoid any intentional or inconsiderate publishing of the prophecy, hence, that he should transmit it into chaste, approved, and trustworthy hands, that would be prepared to treat it in accordance with its mysterious and awe-compelling subject.—**To the time of the end;** *i.e.*, until the juncture indicated in v. 1, to which the entire prophecy, beginning with chap. xi. 2, is directed.—**Many shall run to and fro, and knowledge shall be increased;** rather, "many shall search it through, and the understanding shall become great." יְשֹׁטְטוּ, properly, "they shall run about," namely, for the purpose of searching or investigating; cf. Jer. v. 1; Am. viii. 12; Zech. iv. 10; 2 Chron. xvi. 9. The interpretation by "wandering about, roving about without a guide" (as contrasted with the assured guidance afforded by God's word), which was advocated by J. D. Michaelis and Von Lengerke, cannot be established; nor can the sense of "careful reading," which was adopted by Maurer, Hitzig, Ewald, etc., be demonstrated, despite the citation of the rabbinical שִׁטָּה, שִׁטִּים, "a line (of reading), a straight line," which is alleged as underlying the words in the text.—The whole observation was evidently intended to assign a reason for the exhortation to conceal the imparted prophecy, and treat it sacredly, and to prevent its falling into profane hands; for that prophecy was not unimportant and ordinary in its character, but a means to secure to many, who should zealously examine it in the future, a deeper insight into the ways of God, the controller of all earthly fortunes. For that reason it would be sinful to profane it. ["If Daniel, therefore, must only place the prophecy securely, that it may continue to the time of the end, the sealing then does not exclude the use of it in transcriptions, and there exists no reason for thinking that the searching into it will take place only for the first time in the end" (Keil).]

Verses 5–7. *Solemn averment, by oath, of the assured realizing of the prophecy until a determined point in the future*—namely, until the expiration of the mystical three and a half years, to whose close the prophet had already been referred, chap. vii. 25 (cf. viii. 14; ix. 27). The recurrence of this comforting designation of time indicates that the contents of these verses to the end of the chapter are designed to form an *epilogue*, not merely to the last prophetic vision (chap. x.–xii. 3), but to the entire prophetic

* [Keil, on the other hand, inclines (with Bertholdt, Hitzig, Auberlen, Kliefoth) to "understand by הַסֵּפֶר the whole book. For, as Kliefoth remarks, the angel will close, ver. 4, the last revelation, and along with it the whole prophetical work of Daniel, and dismiss him from his prophetical office, as he afterwards, ver. 13, does, after he has given him, vers. 5-12, disclosures regarding the periods of these wonderful things that were announced. He must seal the book, *i.e.*, guard it securely from disfigurement, 'till the time of the end,' because its contents stretch out to the end. Cf. ch. viii. 26, where the reason for the sealing is stated in the words, 'for yet it shall be for many days.' Instead of such a statement as that, the time of the end is here briefly named as the *terminus*, down to which the revelation reaches, in harmony with the contents of ch. xi. 40–xii. 3, which comprehends the events of the time of the end."]

part of the book, and even to the whole book itself. The new scene, however, which begins with this verse, and serves to introduce the epilogue, obviously occupies a more intimate relation to the scene, chap. x. 4 et seq., which introduces the last great vision, than to the others, and may even be regarded as a resumption of that scene, with but little modification. Compare, on the one hand, the words indicating a new beginning, "Then I, Daniel, looked," etc., which recall chap. x. 5, and, on the other hand, the circumstance that the principal person in the former scene, the mighty angelic prince, "clothed in linen," still continues to be the principal person in word and action (v. 6 et seq.), although two other angels, who had not been present hitherto, now appeared (as *witnesses* of the oath to be taken by him; see immediately below), so that the number present was now double its former size, when only Daniel and the angelic prince in linen clothing were on the scene.—**And behold, there stood other two;** *i.e.*, other than the one who had hitherto spoken and who again resumes in v. 7,—other than the priestly angelic prince in linen garments. אֲחֵרִים is certainly not used with reference to the speaker introduced in v. 6 (Hengstenb.), but refers, as it always does, to what has been previously mentioned, so that it distinguishes two other persons besides the angel who was thus far the speaker; and these enter into the prophet's range of vision at this point. There can be no doubt that these persons were likewise angels; and the following verses leave no room to question that their number was precisely two, that they might be recognized as *witnesses* to the oath in v. 7; cf. Deut. xix. 15; xxxi. 28; 2 Cor. xiii. 1, etc. (thus correctly, Hitzig, Kranichfeld, and in substance Kliefoth also). It would be useless, however, to venture any supposition as to who the two angels were, for the simple reason that the writer did not see fit to furnish their names. It is scarcely probable that they were Gabriel and Michael, for Daniel would certainly have noticed *their* presence, since he had already mentioned these two chief princes among the angels in several instances. Probably angels of *inferior* rank are to be conceived of, since they were capable of being witnesses in the present case. Whether they were identical with the two saints whom the prophet heard conversing together in chap. viii. 13, or not, must remain undecided. In any case, the following theories, which conflict with the context, must be rejected: (1) that one of the two אֲחֵרִים was Gabriel, whose disappearance was nowhere mentioned (Von Lengerke); (2) that one of them was Gabriel, but the other was a different angel, who was already introduced in the former scene, chap. x. 5 et seq., but had not yet been designated by name (thus Hävernick, who consequently finds the three angels of this scene present in chap. x., without exception, but without being clearly distinguished from each other); (3) that the אֲחֵרִים were the guardian angels or princes of Persia and Græcia, mentioned in chap. x. 20 (Jerome, Luther, Grotius, Sanctius, etc.); (4) that they were Judas and Simon Maccabæus (!—so J. D. Michaelis); (5) that they were the representatives of all who in the future should wait for the kingdom of God and inquire after the time of its coming (Cocceius); (6) that they were a mystical personification either of the law and prophecy (thus a gloss in the margin of the *cod. Chisian.*) or of reason and imagination (rabbins, *e.g.*, Jos. Jacchiades). M. Geier already remarks respecting these and other theories of a similar character: "*Hæc figmenta sunt hominum; textus auctoritate destituta.*"—**The one on this side of the bank of the river, and the other on that side of the bank of the river;** rather, "the one here on the bank of the river, the other yonder on the bank," etc. הַיְאֹר, usually the Heb. name for the Nile (which in the Egypt. itself is called *ior* [Sahid. *jero*, Memphit. *jaro*]; cf. Gesen.-Dietr., s. v., יְאֹר), is here used to designate the "great river" Tigris, chap. x. 4. The reason is probably to be found in the fact that at an early period יְאֹר had acquired a purely appellative signification = הַנָּהָר הַגָּדוֹל, as may appear from the poetic use of יְאֹרִים in the sense of "channels" (cf. Job xxviii. 10; Isa. xxxiii. 21). It is useless for Hitzig and Kranichfeld to deny the purely appellative use of יְאֹר in this place, and to contend instead that the Tigris is here termed the Nile by way of *metonymy*—from which position they deduce consequences of a more or less arbitrary character (the former, that this designation reveals that the angel who had hitherto spoken, and who now, v. 6 et seq., hovered over the water, was the *guardian spirit of Egypt* [cf. on chap. x. 5] and also that the author of the entire book was of Egyptian descent [!]; the latter, that "the metonymical co-ordination in fact of the Nile, representing Egypt, and the Hiddekel, the representative of the coming time of trouble [?], was designed to indicate *a second Egyptian deliverance*" *).—Verse 6. **And one said to the man clothed in linen,** etc. The subject of וַיֹּאמֶר is certainly not "each of the two, the one on this side and one on the other" (Theod., Syr., Kranichf., Kliefoth), but rather only *one of them* (הָאֶחָד מֵהֶם, Ibn-Ezra), as the analogy of chap. viii. 13 clearly suggests, and probably the one nearest to the prophet, on the same side of the stream as the latter, and the only one whom he could hear. This angel represents the prophet himself in his inquiry, similar to chap. viii. 13 (cf. v. 14); Jerome is therefore not in the wrong to that extent, when he substitutes "*et dixi*" for "*et dixit* (*alter eorum*)," without further question.—**Which upon** (or "above") **the waters of the river;** supply "stood," or "hovered." This hovering over the waters of the Tigris denotes a new position, which was not mentioned in connection with the former introduction and description of the "man clothed in linen," chap. x., and with which chap. viii. 16 is probably not to

* [Keil (after Kliefoth) thus moderates the latter position: "The river Hiddekel (Tigris) was a figure of the Persian world-power, through whose territory it flowed (cf. for the prophetic type, Isa. viii. 6, 7: Psa. cxxiv. 3, 4), and the designation of the river as יְאֹר, *Nile*, contains an allusion to the deliverance of Israel from the power of Egypt, which in its essence was to be repeated in the future."]

be compared (see on that passage). The fact that the revealing angel hovered over the stream was hardly for the mere purpose of placing him between the two inquiring angels on its banks, nor was it merely designed to recall the brooding of God's Spirit over the waters, Gen. i. 2 (Hitzig), but rather serves to designate the mighty and swiftly flowing stream of the Tigris —as formerly the sea (chap. vii. 2)—as a symbol of the surging world of nations over which "the good spirit of the world-power" exercises sway as a beneficent and guiding principle of order (so Füller, probably with correctness; but he combines with it the extremely forced hypothesis that the angels on the banks of the river were intended to denote the two-fold end of the world-period, hence the two manifestations of Christ, the first in lowliness and the second in glory!)—**How long to the end of the wonders?** *i.e.*, "when (עַד־מָתַי, here equivalent to מָתַי) shall the end, the consummation, come of the wondrous things foretold by thee?" The קֵץ is evidently that referred to in v. 1 (cf. chap. xi. 45), and therefore different from the אַחֲרִית, "the *last* end," concerning which Daniel makes inquiry in v. 8. The "wondrous things" (פְּלָאוֹת) themselves are the *extraordinary* sufferings and judicial punishments, whose instrument Antiochus, the Old-Test. Antichrist, was to become, and which are described at the end, beginning with chap. xi. 30; cf. the similar use of נִפְלָאוֹת in chap. viii. 24; xi. 36; and particularly Isa. xxix. 14.—Verse 7. **And he held up his right hand and his left hand.** The raising of *both* hands was designed to impart a solemn emphasis to the act of taking the oath; cf. Deut. xxxii. 40; Ezek. xx. 5.—**And sware by him that liveth for ever.** בְּחֵי־עוֹלָם, cf. iv. 31; Deut., l. c., and Rev. x. 6. חַי is an adjective, not a substantive, in this place. Cf. the similar predicates connected with the names of *heathen* gods also, *e.g.*, ἀείζωος θεός in the inscrip. at Shakka (Burkhardt, *Reisen*, etc., pp. 147, 503); Πτολεμαῖος αἰωνόβιος on the Rosetta stone, lines 4, 9, 54. In connection with the true God Jehovah, the predicate *vivens in æternum* has the profounder significance, that He not only lives for ever, but also fixes the limit of evil for ever (Ewald, on this passage).—**That for a time, times, and a half**; *i.e.*, after a time, and two times, and a half time, or, briefly, after three and a half (mystical [rather, literal]) years; cf. on chap. vii. 25. To this limitation of time, which has become familiar from its former occurrence (cf. also chap. viii. 14; ix. 27), is now added a further one, which, however, substantially coincides with it:—**and when he shall have accomplished to scatter the power of the holy people**; rather, "and when the scattering of a part of the holy people shall have ceased." No material objection can be brought to bear against this exposition of the words וּכְכַלּוֹת נַפֵּץ יַד־עַם־קֹדֶשׁ, since נַפֵּץ almost invariably has the meaning "to scatter, disperse," in the *prophetic* usage (cf. Isa. xi. 12; Jer. xiii. 14; li. 20, 23), while that of "break, shatter," seems to be confined more particularly to poetry (cf. Psa. ii. 9; cxxxvii. 9), and further, since the rendering of יָד by "part, division," seems to be adequately supported by parallels like Gen. xlvii. 24; 2 Kings xi. 7; Neh. xi. 1. It is not necessary, in order to obtain this meaning, to change the pointing so as to read וּכְכַלּוֹת נֹפֵץ 'וגו, as Hitzig proposes. The correct view is represented by Bertholdt, Dereser, Gesenius, Hävernick, Von Lengerke, Zündel, and substantially by Theodot., Vulg., Luther, etc., excepting only that the latter neglect to render יַד by "part," and either interpret it by "might, warlike power," or leave it altogether untranslated. On the other hand, Hengstenberg, Hofmann, Maurer, Auberlen, Kranichfeld, Füller, Kliefoth, Ewald, etc., render: "When the shattering of the hand of the holy people shall have ceased" (*i.e.*, when its power shall have been entirely broken). In support of this view it is usually contended (with Hofmann, *Weiss. und Erf.*, I. 314 et seq.) that the idea of reuniting the scattered Israel, which occurs nowhere else in Daniel, would be presented in this place without any preparation whatever. This is as if the chapter under consideration did not present a number of other ideas, which are wholly new and have never occurred previously, *e.g.*, the prophecy of the resurrection in v. 2; the shining of the wise like the brightness of the firmament, in v. 3; and also the contents of v. 10; or as if the mention in this book of the expectation that the dispersed people of God should be reunited, which was so familiar to the earlier prophets, could be in any way remarkable, when taken in connection with the correspondence, usually so thorough, of the range of this prophet's ideas with that of his predecessors (cf. Joel iii. 5 et seq.; Am. ix. 11 et seq.; Isa. xi. 12; Jer. li. 20 et seq., etc., etc.).* It is entirely unnecessary to adopt the historical reference to 1 Macc. v. 23, 45, 53 et seq.; 2 Macc. xii. 32, which Hitzig discovers in this passage, and regards as a proof that in this instance there is another *vatic. ex eventu.* There is not the slightest difficulty, however, connected with the opinion that the facts recorded in those passages of the Maccabæan books (relating to the bringing back to Judæa of the scattered Jews who lived in Galilee and Gilead among the heathen, by Judas and Simon Maccabæus), constituted a first typical fulfilment and historical exemplification of the present prophecy.†—**All this shall be finished.** כָּל־אֵלֶּה, not the foregoing words, but the things spoken of, the sum of the prophecy beginning with chap. xi. 2 (inclusive of the contents of chap. xii. 1–3). ‡

---

* [Keil defends the rendering of נַפֵּץ by *shatter*, rather than "scatter," and of כַּלּוֹת by *completion*, rather than "ceasing;" but the sense is not materially different in either case, if the prophecy refer to the persecution by Antiochus, for the hour of striking for independence was coincident with that of the deepest oppression. The metaphorical signification of *power* for יָד, however, seems preferable as being more usual and natural than that of *part*; and the latter savors too much of a diplomatic rendering.]

† [It may reasonably be objected to this reference that it is too petty, and requires too special a rendering of the words to be of any great value.]

‡ [The "fulfilment of all these things" obviously is

Verses 8, 9. *The prophet's question concerning the* FINAL *end, and the angel's encouraging reply.* **And I heard, but I understood not,** namely, the information just imparted by the angel, involving a two-fold designation of the time, and also including the statement, which was especially incomprehensible to the prophet, that at the expiration of the three and a half times the dispersion of a part of Israel should have reached its end.—**What shall be the end of these things?** *i.e.*, "which event is to be the last of these 'wondrous things?'" (v. 6); by the occurrence of what event shall it be possible to know that the last end of the entire series of the predicted troubles and judgments has been reached?—Hence the אַחֲרִית, concerning which Daniel now inquires, does not directly coincide with the קֵץ to which the question of the angel in v. 6 referred, but stands related to it as the final *point* in a course of development is related to a final *period* of extended duration.* —Verse 9. **And he said, Go thy way, Daniel,** etc. לֵךְ, as in v. 13, an encouraging remark addressed to the prophet, who had approached with anxious questioning; cf. Ecc. ix. 7. This parallel demonstrates, if there were no other reason, that it is impossible to take הֵלֵךְ in the sense of "to die, to die peacefully, to lie down to sleep," in this place, as Bertholdt, Hävernick, etc., propose.—**For the words are closed up** (or "concealed") **and sealed till the time of the end.** Cf. v. 4, where הַדְּבָרִים, "the words," is evidently employed in the same sense as here, namely, as designating the words of the prophecy, chap. xi. 2–xii. 3. The statement that these words are "concealed and sealed" till the time of the end, has, of course, a different meaning from the exhortation in that passage, "to conceal and seal" them. While that exhortation was intended to *warn* him earnestly against an inconsiderate desire to publish and prostitute to common uses the statements of the prophecy, the present reference to their hidden condition (*i.e.*, to the mysterious nature of the revealed facts), is designed to *encourage and to lead to humble submission to the Divine guidance, whose purposes cannot at first be understood.* עֵת קֵץ, however, has no other signification in this place than in v. 4, or than קֵץ in v. 6.†

Verses 10–12. *Approximate* determination of the final point* (the אַחֲרִית) *of the predicted development,* for the purpose of affording additional comfort and encouragement to the prophet, in his anxiety to receive information. **Many shall be purified and made white, and tried,** rather, "shall purify and cleanse themselves, and shall be thoroughly tried." The terms recur from chap. xi. 35, excepting that they are differently arranged, and that the two leading verbs, ברר "to purify," and לבן "to cleanse," are to be taken in a reflexive sense, corresponding to the Hithpael, while the third צרף (Niph.) expresses the passive sense of being thoroughly tried, or of being thoroughly purified (cf. Psa. xii. 7; Prov. xxx. 5). With each of the verbs the idea of *suffering and persecution* on account of the faith is of course again involved, as forming the media of purifying.—**But the wicked shall do wickedly.** The ו in וְהִרְשִׁיעוּ is adversative, and serves to contrast the conduct of the wicked in the last time with the contemporaneous course pursued by the faithful. Cf. the free rendering of the passage in Rev. xxii. 11.—**And none of the wicked shall understand; but the wise shall understand,** namely, what is the meaning and ultimate aim of the predictions relating to the last time; consequently they shall then understand the prophecy, and by its light shall be able to correctly interpret the signs of the time (cf. Matt. xxiv. 32 et seq.; Luke xxi. 28 et seq.), and accordingly, to act and regulate their conduct with reference to the salvation of their souls.† —Hitzig himself realizes that it would be exceedingly inappropriate to render מַשְׂכִּלִים by "teachers" in this passage; but why should he arbitrarily refuse to assign to it the meaning of "understanding ones," which is the only one

explained by the more definite statement in vers. 11 and 12, for the prophet's inquiry was expressly in order to elicit such an explanation. This is precisely analogous to our Lord's eschatological data, Matt. xxv. 34, etc.; where the *nearer* event alone is chronologically determined, and the final one left vague (Matt. xxv. 36).]

* [Keil likewise distinguishes between קֵץ and אַחֲרִית, but neither his nor the author's distinction seems to be very clear or well founded. In the present instance אחרית seems to denote the nearer *sequel* of the pressing emergencies in immediate view, and קֵץ the more distant *consummation* of the entire prophecy. If so, the angel does not fully answer the inquiry of ver. 6, but does Daniel's, by designating only the terminus of the Antiochian history. "Hitzig is altogether correct in thus stating the (latter) question: 'What, *i.e.*, which event is the uttermost, the last of the פְּלָאוֹת, that stands before the end?'" (Keil).]

† [In like manner the "closing and sealing" (סתם and חתם in both cases) can be no other here than in ver. 4. "But since, according to ver. 4, Daniel himself must shut up and seal the book, the participles in this clause, assigning the reason for לֵךְ, cannot have the meaning of the perfect, but only state what is or shall be done; shut up—they shall be (remain) till the time of the end; thus they only denote the shutting up and sealing, which must be accomplished by Daniel. . . . . The shutting up and sealing . . . . can only consist in this, that the book should be preserved in security against any defacement of its contents, so that it might be capable of being read at all times down to the time of the end, and might be used by God's people for the strengthening of their faith; cf. ch. viii. 26."—*Keil.*]

* [It is strange that a commentator will persist in calling this an "approximate estimate," when its sole object was to clear up uncertainty as to the duration of the events in prospect, and when, accordingly, precise periods of time are assigned in explicit and varied terms. Surely the whole subject is designedly left in doubt if this language does not definitely determine it.]

† [It is thus true that history in a measure interprets prophecy, or rather enables the interpreter to give vividness and detail to predictions in themselves general and obscure. So also *seeing* is better than reading a description, however clear. But it is not necessary to wait for the accomplishment of prophecy in order to gain an intelligent comprehension of its essential import. To maintain this would be equivalent to denying any intelligible use of language. Nor is it true, as many expositors assert, that Daniel himself did not understand these prophecies. Ver. 8 only means that he did not clearly see the application of the announcement in ver. 7 to the previous prophetic declarations, especially the mode of computing the note of time there given. This point is cleared up by the particular specifications of the present communication, and Daniel is therefore dismissed with a peaceful sense of full intelligence.]

that can be admitted here, in the former passages (xi. 35; xii. 1), where it is no less appropriate?—Verse 11. **And from the time that the daily sacrifice shall be taken away, and an abomination that maketh desolate set up, there shall be a thousand two hundred and ninety days.** On the construction of the words וּמֵעֵת הוּסַר וגו׳, which denote the beginning of the 1290 days, cf., *e.g.*, chap. ii. 16; v. 15; Ecc. ix. 1; Jer. xvii. 10, etc. הוּסַר, as appears from the following לָתֵת, which does not depend on עֵת after the manner of the genitive, is not an infinitive, but a "relative asyndetic connection of the *præt. propheticum* with עֵת." The לְ in לָתֵת may be regarded as "expressing the fateful purpose of God," and therefore as taking the place of the jussive imperfect, which ordinarily serves that purpose (cf. xi. 18).—The expression שִׁקּוּץ שֹׁמֵם is distinguished from the synonymous הַשִּׁקּוּץ מְשׁוֹמֵם, chap. xi. 31, and also from שִׁקּוּצִים מְשֹׁמֵם, solely by its greater brevity, which may be indicated by the combination "desolating abomination" (cf. also the substantially identical הַפֶּשַׁע שֹׁמֵם, chap. viii. 13).* It seems to be inadmissible because of the substantial identity of the expression with those former parallels, to translate this passage, with Wieseler (*Die siebzig Wochen* etc., p. 109): "From the time that the daily sacrifice shall be taken away, *till the desolating of the abomination, i.e.*, till the destruction of the idol-altar and the rededication of the temple by Judas Maccabæus."—It has already been shown, on chap. viii. 14, that the 1290 days are substantially identical with the half year-week (ix. 27), or with the three and a half times (vii. 25; xii. 7), and that they involve *an extension of that period by about half a month only* (twelve to thirteen days); and it was also shown on that passage, that on the other hand the 2300 evening-mornings or 1,150 days *shorten* the same period by about four months. According to all the passages relating to the period of three and a half years as thus determined (in the one case exceeding those years by a few days, in the other falling below them by a few months), and especially according to the present passage, the *terminus a quo* for that period was the juncture when the daily sacrifice was taken away, and when the abomination of desolation was placed in the sanctuary. Our passage is *silent* with regard to the special *terminus ad quem*, which had in former passages been described as coincident, on the one hand with the *judgment* of the wicked author of such profanation (chap. vii. 26; ix. 27), and on the other with the rededication of the profaned sanctuary (chap. viii. 14); in other words, the revealing angel *does not precisely determine the final point of the last time of trouble* (the אַחֲרִית, concerning which Daniel inquired, v. 8).* He affords an indication, indeed, that a period of blessing should ensue on the expiration of the mystical three and a half years, by employing the beatitude of the following verse: "Blessed is he that waiteth," etc.; but he refrains from determining the exact point of time in which it should begin. Upon this point his language is even undecided and equivocal, inasmuch as he fixes the limits of the intervening time, at first at 1290, but afterwards at 1335 days—thus in the one case exceeding the measure of exactly 1277 days by thirteen, and in the other by fifty-eight days. The troubled events of the Maccabæan period, which might deserve notice as the points of the beginning and the end of the historical equivalent of the three and a half years, do not present a satisfactory reason for such vacillating predictions; for the exact period required cannot be found in that epoch, however its limits may be fixed. *E.g.*, if, with Bertholdt, Hävernick, Von Lengerke, et al., its conclusion is assigned to the day of rededicating the temple by Judas Maccabæus, or the 25th Chisleu (Dec. 15th) of the year B.C. 164 (1 Macc. iv. 52), and the 1290 days are reckoned backward from that date, their beginning will fall on June 10th, B.C. 167, or more than five and a half months *earlier* than the event which is generally regarded as marking the commencement of the three and a half years (*i.e.*, earlier than the abrogation of the daily sacrifice on the 15th Chisleu, 167; cf. 1 Macc. i. 54); nor will that reckoning consist with the arrival in Jerusalem of Apollonius, the commissioner of taxes, which might possibly be regarded as the introductory event of the period in question; for according to 1 Macc. i. 29, his arrival took place only about three months prior to the 15th Chisleu, 167, instead of 5th (cf. supra, on chap. vii.). Further, the attempt to regard the Maccabæan dedication of the temple as the characteristic fact that marked the conclusion of the 1290 days, is antagonized by the circumstance that the troubles of the Jews had by no means reached their end at that time, since the dreadful tyrant Antiochus yet lived, the citadel of Zion was still garrisoned by enemies, their leader, Lysias, who had gone to Antioch, was employed in making preparation for farther extensive operations, in order to wipe out the shame of his former defeat by Judas, and, in addition, the Ammonites, Edomites, and other heathen neighbors threatened the little band of Jews led by the Maccabees with dangerous attacks (cf. 1 Macc. iv. 35, 41; v. 1 et seq.).† If we assume, with Hitzig, Bleek, Hofmann, Delitzsch,

* [The neut. שֹׁמֵם, however, is not in itself synonymous with the act. מְשֹׁמֵם; it here becomes equivalent to it only by reason of the connection with שִׁקּוּץ. "In ch. xi. 31, where the subject spoken of is the proceedings of the enemy causing desolation, the abomination is viewed as מְשֹׁמֵם, *bringing desolation;* here, with reference to the end of those proceedings" (rather, with reference to the persecuted sufferers as being profaned by it), "as שֹׁמֵם, *brought to desolation;* cf. on ch. ix. 27" (Keil).]

* [After the precise designation of the *terminus ad quem* in the passage which our author last refers to, there seemed to the prophet, or rather to his angelic instructor, no need of its repetition here. Every reader would spontaneously understand the period in question, dating from an idolatrous installation, to continue till the removal of the offensive and impious object. It is evidently the term of the sacrilege.]

† [It ought to be observed, on the contrary, that the 1,290 days are not assigned as the limit of the *troubles*, but only of the *profanation*.]

Füller, etc., that the *death of Epiphanes*, which took place somewhat later than the dedication of the temple, ended the 1290 days, we are met by the difficulty of ascertaining the *date* of his death, which has not been preserved by any historical authorities that have descended to our times, and for that reason cannot be definitely settled. That Epiphanes died precisely 140 days *after* the dedication of the temple, is a mere assumption of Hitzig, Bleek, etc., based on a comparison of the 1150 days of chap. viii. 14,—which, it is asserted, extend exactly to the dedication—with the 1290 days of the present passage. This assumption appears the more uncertain, in proportion as, on the one hand, it becomes impossible to exactly accommodate those 1150 days between the desecration of the temple and the ascertained date of its rededication (cf. on chap. viii. 14), and as, on the other hand, it becomes difficult to reconcile the date of the death of Antiochus, as thus assumed, with historical statements respecting his end which have been preserved to us.* We are accordingly compelled to abandon every attempt to demonstrate an exact correspondence between the time indicated in the text and the periods of the Maccabæan æra of persecution, and to remain content with the hypothesis that the 1290 days have a merely mystical and symbolical significance.† The merely approximate character of the correspondence between the prophetic measurement of time and the chronological relations of the history of its typical realization, with which we were obliged to content ourselves in a former instance, in connection with the 1150 days, returns here in a somewhat different manner. In that instance we found a considerable *minus* in comparison with the number 1277, and here a smaller *plus*.‡ It will scarcely become possible to ever assign a more definite reason for this two-fold discrepancy than that the seer's attention was to be emphatically called to the *approximation* of the designation of time. Cf. Kranichfeld also, p. 413, who justly observes in opposition to the artificial attempts to ascertain the exact historical grounds for the difference between the 1150 and 1290 days, which he adduces, that "it is, moreover, an assertion which can never be exegetically established, that the deliverance of the nation, the destruction of the foe, and the restoration of the order of worship are everywhere in this book regarded as separate in time. On the contrary, they designate the same juncture of time at the end, as seen in the prophet's perspective, which appears from their indiscriminate application, or in other words, from the substitution of one for another; cf. vii. 25 with 26; viii. 14 with 25 et seq.; ix. 24 with 26, 27; xi. 45 with xii. 1. . . . . For the rest, the profanation of the temple which an Antiochus Epiphanes imposed on Israel during three years, continues to be a historical exemplification of the facts revealed to Daniel's prophetic vision, in the face of the 1290 days, and despite the fact that in the nature of the case *it accords but relatively with them in a formal aspect.*" *—Verse 12. **Blessed is he that waiteth** (or "is steadfast to the end") **and cometh to the thousand three hundred and five and thirty days.** In view of its connection with the foregoing, the meaning of this exclamation can only be as follows: "After 1290 days have expired, the tribulation shall end; it shall not be *completely* ended, however, until forty-five additional days (one and a half months) have elapsed, hence, until a total of 1335 days has been reached." Here again we believe ourselves obliged to rest satisfied with finding a symbolic and approximate value in the relation of the several numbers to each other; cf. the remarks on this point in a former connection, Eth.-fund. principles, etc., on chap. viii. No. 1. Among the various attempts that have been made to explain with historical accuracy the difference of forty-five days between the time fixed by v. 11 and that given in v. 12, none have succeeded in realizing an entirely satisfactory result: *e.g.*, (1) that of Hitzig, based on the assumption that the 1335 days extend to the reception from Tabæ of the tidings respecting the death of Antiochus, forty-five (?) days subsequent to his demise; (2) the

---

* The precarious character of all combinations bearing on this question may appear from the following calculation by Hitzig (p. 225 et seq.): ". . . . Antiochus (1 Macc. i. 10) ascended the throne in the year 137 æ. Sel., and he died (1 Macc. vi. 16) in the year 149; consequently his reign falls between April, B.C. 176 and March, 163. But we possess a coin of Seleucus bearing the number of the year ΡΛΖ (see Eckhel, *Doctr. num.*, III. 222), which shows that Seleucus still reigned at least at the beginning of the last quarter of B.C. 176. Antiochus became king during the month of October, 176, at the earliest; and if he reigned not quite twelve years, according to Appian, *Syr.*, c. 66, we may perhaps regard the eleven years 175–165 as being full; and obtain, in addition, the fraction of the twelfth year by including a remnant of 176 possibly, and certainly by adding the first months of 164 (at least as far as April). Accordingly if, as we believe, the author referred in v. 11 to the death of Antiochus as the end of the period, it follows that the latter died 140 days after the dedication of the temple (see on viii. 14), on the fifteenth to eighteenth day of the second month 149 (Jewish), *i.e.*, on the thirteenth of the eighth month (Artemisius) 148 Sel. This result harmonizes excellently with that coin, and also with Appian (?). On the other hand, when Eusebius (Chron. i. 348) assigns eleven years to the reign of Antiochus, from Olymp. 151, 3, to Olymp. 154, 1, or from B.C. 174 to 164, there is an error, not only with respect to the point of departure, but also with regard to the end, since the death of the king transpired during the second half of the Olympiad; Antiochus died in Olymp. 153, 4." Bleek ventures a similar calculation (*Theolög. Zeitschr.*, p. 293 et seq.), in which the words "perhaps, probably, I believe," occur suspiciously often.

† [But this convenient refuge of the puzzled expositor is cut off by the repeated and varied form of the numbers so absolutely given. If all was symbolical, why these changes, and why these particular numbers?]

‡ [This excess or deficiency is occasioned by the erroneous interpretation of the "2300 evening-mornings" as being 1150 days (cf. on ch. viii. 14), and by taking the three and a half years too strictly.]

* [It seems to us that the following explanations of Stuart fairly and sufficiently meet the difficulties or "discrepancies" raised by the author: "The 1290 days are more specific than the phrase, 'time, times and a half,' in ver. 7, and also in vii. 25. The latter ('time,' etc.) is, as it were, a round number, three and a half first equalling the one half of the sacred number seven, and the fractional part equalling the half of one year. In such a case minute exactness of course is not to be expected. But the thirty additional days here (over 1260 days = forty-two months = three and a half years) are doubtless designed as an *exact* account of time during which the detestable (desolating) abomination continued in the temple. The *terminus a quo* is the time when Antiochus first removed the daily sacrifice, which probably was near the end of May or at the beginning of June in B.C. 168. Judas Maccabæus removed this שִׁקּוּץ, and purified the temple, Dec. 25th of B.C. 165, making the time in question, *i.e.*, three and a half years, as nearly as history will enable us to compute it. There can hardly be room for doubt that the statement in our text is minutely correct. The work of Judas there is the *terminus ad quem* of the period in question."]

assumption of Füller, that the 15th Xanthicus (April) of the year B.C. 164 (?), when a letter from Antiochus V. Eupator to the Jews reached Jerusalem, according to 2 Macc. xi., which contained the welcome proffer of peace, marks the end of the 1335 days; and (3) the theory of Bertholdt, Hävernick, Von Lengerke, Wieseler, etc., that while the 1290 days extended to the dedication of the temple, the 1335 days reached down to the death of Antiochus, forty-five days afterward. Against the latter opinion it may be objected that the interval between the dedication of the temple and the death of Antiochus was unquestionably longer than forty-five days; or, in other words, that Epiphanes did not die as early as the month of Shebat in the year 148 æ. Sel., as those scholars (including Wieseler in Herzog's *Real-Encyklop.*, I. 387, Art. *Antiochus*) assume, in contradiction of 1 Macc. vi. 16 (cf. also Hitzig, p. 226, and Füller, p. 357 et seq.).* The two former theories, on the other hand, are open to the objection that the reception of the news from Tabæ of the king's death, and also of the offers of peace from Antioch, were events of far too little importance to lead the writer (whether prophesying *ex eventu*, or by virtue of a disclosure of the future from God) to assign to either of them the dignity of marking the final conclusion of all troubles. The letter from Eupator was merely an offer of peace, and not the peace itself; and at the time both of its arrival and of the tidings from Tabæ, the horizon of Judæa was far too dark to enable a pseudo-Daniel, writing at that day, to announce the end of all the sufferings of his nation as having already arrived, or as being immediately at hand (cf. 1 Macc. iv. 35; vi. 17 et seq.), on the ground merely that such messages had been received. The mode of escape from the difficulty that is adopted by Kirmss, Bleek, Delitzsch, et al., is however still more questionable than the reference of the 1335 days to any of the events that were adduced in support of the foregoing theories. It assumes that some other fact of an encouraging nature, which is no longer found in our historical documents, formed the *terminus ad quem* of the 1335 days of the prophet; and is clearly nothing more than an expedient prompted by embarrassment and helpless discouragement, which feelings our theory of the merely symbolic value of the designation of time serves to justify better than any other hypothesis. Cf. Kliefoth, p. 514: "In extending this period of 1290 days by forty-five, the design probably was merely to indicate that whoever should live in patience and religious faith beyond the 1290 days, *i.e.*, beyond the death of the wicked oppressor Antiochus, should be accounted blessed. The forty-five days are mentioned for the purpose merely of expressing that idea of surviving, and the form of the expression was governed solely by a desire to retain the analogy of v. 11." Also Kranichfeld, p. 416: "The period of final conflict which leads to the victory is here described as being very brief, comparatively, for the purpose of comforting and encouraging the pious ones; it is not measured by years, but merely by fractions of months. The half of a cycle of three months, here takes the place of the limited period in the mind of the writer, according to ix. 26; viii. 25, etc.; and by the arithmetical measurement of time by days which is current in this book, it obtains the forty-five days which lie outside of the period of 1290 days or three and a half times," etc. Cf. also the Eth.-fund. principles, No. 2.

Verse 13. *Concluding exhortation and promise.* **But go thou thy way** (rather, "on") **till the end.** וְאַתָּה, properly, "and thou," with conclusive וְ, but which may also be taken in an adversative sense, because it leads over from the foregoing to the close in an encouraging manner. לֵךְ לַקֵּץ is of course to be understood according to the analogy of v. 9: "go on, toward the final point of the predicted events;" not "go thy way" (Hitzig), nor yet "go toward *thy* end" (Hävernick, Füller, Kliefoth, etc.), for קֵץ is clearly shown by the article to refer to the same end as that mentioned in v. 9.—**For thou shalt rest and stand in thy lot at the end of the days;** *i.e.*, thou shalt rest in the grave, in the quiet sleep of death (cf. Isa. lvii. 2, and supra, v. 2). The meaning is, "that thou mayest rest, and enter on thy lot," etc., *i.e.*, that thou mayest receive thy portion of the inheritance at the judgment of eternal recompense; cf. chap. vii. 18, 27; Rev. xx. 6. The thought refers back undeniably to vs. 2, 3, hence to the Messianic recompense, of which Daniel also should par-

* [The author is far too positive concerning the irreconcilability of this period with the death of Antiochus, as the following computation by Stuart will suffice to show: "It appears from chap. xi. 40–44 above, that Antiochus made another and final invasion of Egypt, near the close of his life, after which he marched against Palestine. Mattathias and his sons, in the mean time, had been organizing the party of the pious, and Antiochus was exceedingly indignant at the efforts which they made and the success with which they were attended. In 1 Macc. ii. 26–37, we have an account of the situation of Antiochus while in the 'glorious land.' His treasury was empty. He had already robbed the temple of all which it contained that was of any value, and he was necessitated to look to another quarter. He left half of his army, therefore, with Lysias, one of his favorite officers, and passed over the Euphrates in order to rifle the countries of the East. First he went through and subdued Armenia (τὰς ἐπάνω χώρας, v. 37), and then turned off to rob the temple at Elymais, where he met with disgrace, and finally with death. Not long after the departure of Antiochus, Lysias began the contest in Palestine in serious earnest; but Judas uniformly triumphed in all his encounters; and so decisive was one of them over Lysias, that Judas proceeded to purify the temple and to restore its worship, 1 Macc. iv. 36 seq. All this must have occupied some months; and the consecration of the temple took place the 25th of Dec. 165 B.C. Of course Antiochus had had sufficient time for his conquest in Armenia and for his advance to Elymais before the winter had far advanced. It was in early spring that he undertook the robbery of the temple in Elymais; after which, on his retreat, the news met him of total defeat in Palestine, and helped to increase the malady under which he was then laboring. In 1 Macc. vi. 1 seq., is an account of the close of the life of Antiochus, and of his failure at Elymais. If we now count onward, from the consecration of the temple by Judas to the time when Antiochus deceased, we shall perceive at once that the period of 1335 days is in all probability the period of Antiochus' death. From the time that the daily burnt-offering was removed by Apollonius, at the command of Antiochus, to the time of the reconsecration, were 1290. From the same *terminus a quo* to the death of Antiochus were 1335 days, *i.e.*, forty-five days more than is included in the preceding period. History has not anywhere recorded the precise day of Antiochus' death; so that we cannot compare the passage before us with that. But we are certain as to the order of events, and as to the season of the year, as well as the year itself, in which the death of this king took place. Of the *general* accuracy there can be no doubt; and such are the chronological designations of this book that we may safely rely, in this case, on its minute accuracy."]

take, and a majority of interpreters recognize that fact; but they generally pervert the meaning of וְתַעֲמֹד, so as to make it apply to the resurrection (standing up) for the purpose of being thus recompensed. The correct view in this respect is advocated, *e.g.*, by Ewald, Kamphausen, Kranichfeld, etc.—Hitzig's interpretation is very flat and exceedingly forced (in partial imitation of Grotius and Dathe): "And thou, go on to the goal, and thou mayest be content (!), and attend to thy office (!) for the end of days."—[" גּוֹרָל, *lot*, of the inheritance divided to the Israelites by lot, referred to the inheritance of the saints in light (Col. i. 12), which shall be possessed by the righteous after the resurrection from the dead in the heavenly Jerusalem. לְקֵץ הַיָּמִים, *to = at the end of the days*, *i.e.*, not = אַחֲרִית הַיָּמִים, in the Messianic (rather Antiochian) time, but in the last days, when, after the judgment of the world, the kingdom of glory shall appear.—Well shall it be for us if in the end of our days we too are able to depart hence with such consolation of hope!"—*Keil.*]

ETHICO-FUNDAMENTAL PRINCIPLES RELATED TO THE HISTORY OF SALVATION, APOLOGETICAL REMARKS, AND HOMILETICAL SUGGESTIONS.

1. The fundamental dogmatic thought that is especially prominent in this closing section is *the future resurrection of the dead and their eternal destiny*, as predicted in vs. 1–3, and as again repeated and confirmed in the closing words of v. 13. That in the meaning of the book this resurrection is not to be regarded as confined to Israel only, but rather as universal in its scope, has been shown in the remarks on v. 2. It remains only to briefly answer the important question respecting the relation of that prediction to the Maccabæan age, which primarily afforded a typical and preliminary realization only of the prophecies of Daniel in general. Is it necessary, for instance, to take the entire prophecy in a *figurative* sense, as Dereser does, and to apply it merely to a spiritual or national resurrection of the nation from its former condition of apparent helplessness and death?* Or are we, with Bertholdt, Hitzig, and the remaining rationalistic exegetes, to charge the prophet with having committed a gross error, in conceiving of the end of the world, the resurrection, and the judgment as immediately consequent on the death of Ant. Epiphanes?—Neither of the two would be correct; on the contrary, we are again reminded of the perspective character of prophetic vision in this connection, according to which the interval between the preliminary and the ultimate end was overlooked, from the point of view occupied by the prophesying seer long before either came to pass. By virtue of this perspective vision, the Old-Test. and the New-Test. Antichrists become one, which is true also of all the circumstances and results connected with their appearance. "As Antiochus became a type of Antichrist, so the oppression of the Old-Test. community of God's people by him became a type of the oppression of the New-Test. congregation of the people of God by the latter. And as little as it surprises us that Joel iii. 1 et seq. should make the preliminary signs of the end follow immediately upon the pouring out of God's Spirit, with which the last world-period begins, without remarking the period intervening between them; or as easily as we can explain the fact that Amos ix. should predict the restoration of the fallen tabernacle of David and the final return of Israel to its native land, immediately after the judgment which he denounces upon the nation, thus overlooking the whole of the immense period in the course of which Israel indeed returned to its country, but was a second time expelled by the Romans; or as little as we charge untruthfulness upon the prophet Ezekiel, when, in chap. xxxvi., he announces to the mountains of Israel the future return of the nation, and adds that God would show greater kindness to them than ever before, because this was not fulfilled on their first return; or as natural as we find it that in chap. xi. Isaiah should connect a description of the glory and peace of Christ's kingdom, which shall only be realized at His second coming, with the words, "there shall come forth a rod out of the stem of Jesse," which are regarded as bearing on the appearance of Christ in lowliness, thus viewing Christ's first and second advents together; so little should it surprise us or seem incompatible with the nature of prophecy, that the present prediction should represent the Seleucid persecution as being immediately followed by *the full and final deliverance of the nation*, without observing that a long series of years intervenes between the two. . . . Call it prophetic limitation, or whatever else we will, it is nevertheless the manner of the prophets; and the fact that we find it exemplified in the present instance is to us an evidence that the prophecy is genuine. Why do its opponents neglect to show how the prophecy respecting the resurrection of the dead immediately after the decease of Antiochus can be reconciled with their view concerning the composition of the book? If it was written immediately *before* the death of Antiochus, what was there to excite the hope that the time of blessing and the resurrection of the dead should follow immediately afterward? And if it was felt that such a hope was warranted, and it was *not realized*, were men not deceived? Who would have attached further value to such a mistaken prophecy?—But if it was composed *after* the death of Antiochus, *it becomes wholly inconceivable that the false prophet should have compromised his pretended prophecy by* THIS *conclusion*. But the features that are inconceivable on the presumption that the prophecy is spurious, are readily explained on the view that it was the actual Daniel who prophesied thus, centuries before Antiochus. The truth of his prophecy was in that case so incontestably assured in the time of Antiochus, that

* Cf. Dereser on the passage: "Many Israelites who lived during the persecution . . . . . in rocky caverns, where the dead were bestowed, or who seemed to lie in the dust like a lifeless corpse, shall, so to speak, awake to renewed life through the goodness and power of God, and shall perform actions by which they shall live forever in history. On the other hand, the apostate Jews — — shall be branded with everlasting shame."

the apparent failure of its prediction concerning the resurrection of the dead (or, more properly, the delay of its fulfilment) was no longer sufficient to cast a doubt upon it. In one word, this passage of our book, usually considered so difficult, is so little worthy to be regarded as the heel of Achilles in the case, that it rather constitutes its strength, before which its assailants are put to shame" (Füller, p. 343 et seq.).—It should, however, be observed in this connection that the leading idea in the prophecy in vs. 1-3 is not the prediction of the resurrection, but rather the universal and eternal *recompense* to be meted out to them. The rising of the many "sleepers in the dust of the earth," as predicted in v. 2, is at bottom a mere auxiliary thought, or a preparation for the principal feature of the prophecy, consisting in the promise of everlasting life to the pious, and the denouncing of everlasting shame and torment upon the wicked. Inasmuch as the judgment upon the Old-Test. Antichrist, as foretold in a former passage (chap. xi. 45), forms, in a measure, the opening act and point of commencement of this great recompensing judgment, all subsequent instances of such judgment must appear as a continued series of displays of the Divine righteousness, whose final conclusion at the last judgment will constitute the highest and most perfect, but not the only fulfilment of this prophetic passage. Among such displays of God's justice may be reckoned the end of the tyrant Herod and the destruction of Jerusalem by the Romans, the subjugation of the Eastern churches by Islamism and the overthrow of the Middle-age Papal church by the Reformation.—As the eternal recompense, so the awaking of the dead, which forms its substratum and preliminary condition, reaches far into the history of time and earth, extending itself close to the historical position of our prophet, even though Jesus Christ, as the first fruits of them that sleep, began the blessed series of those who shall have a part in the "resurrection of the just" (Luke xiv. 14; xx. 36; 1 Cor. xv. 20 et seq.), and though, consequently, He was the first who could say with entire truth, "The hour is coming, *and now* is, when the dead shall hear the voice of the Son of God; and they that hear him shall live" (John v. 25; cf. vs. 28, 29). Both the preliminary judgment of the world, which is transpiring in the events of history, and the ethical resurrection in Christ Jesus of the spiritually dead, which is the basis and pre-condition of the future resurrection of all flesh,—both these have their beginning at the very point where the prophet's scope of vision ends, and by that fact attest the truth and the Divine origin of his predictions, to which the Lord would assuredly not have repeatedly appealed and referred, had He not considered this book equal, in its inspired character, to any of the remaining prophets of the Old Covenant (cf. the Introd. § 6).

2. The prophecy, which forms the second leading thought of this section, relates to *the point of time of the end*. It repeats in substance the mystical [?] measure of time noticed in a former section, by which the last severe trouble of God's people should continue during three and a half times, and adds a further period of one and a half months, during which the last remnants of suffering and trouble shall be removed. It was shown above that the historical conditions of the Maccabæan period afford but little countenance to the assumption that these periods of 1290 and 1335 days were invented to accord with the course of events in the experience of the past. It was also shown in a former instance (on chap. vii. 25) that the underlying idea, which is common to all the parallel mystical limitations of time (the half-week, the three and a half times, the 1150, 1290, 1335 days), is that *the time of suffering should be shortened*,—that the time of tribulation should indeed begin, but should be broken through at the middle, and by the grace of God should quickly be brought to its close. It is consequently a time to which the words of the Saviour respecting the shortening of the days of tribulation (κολοβωθῆναι, Matt. xxiv. 22; Mark xiii. 20) will apply. It will be sufficient to notice, in this connection, that this mysterious period, which received a first approximate [!] fulfilment in the great religious persecution of the Jews by Antiochus Epiphanes, appeared a second time in the Jewish war, which ended in the destruction of Jerusalem by Titus (A.D. 66-70), and that a third and final fulfilment of the same period is in anticipation, in the last days before the return of Christ, according to Rev. xii. 14; xiii. 5, when the church shall be overtaken by a time of severe trial and purification. Cf. Auberlen (*Daniel*, p. 287), who, somewhat vaguely and generally characterizes the three and a half times as "the period of the world-power, during which the supremacy over the kingdom of heaven is given to the earthly kingdoms," and then proceeds: "So, then, this number is resumed in the Apocalypse, in order to characterize the times of the heathen, during which Jerusalem is trodden under foot, and in which, consequently, the kingdom of God has wholly lost its outward and visible existence in the earth—hence the times from the Roman destruction of Jerusalem to the return of Christ (more correctly, without doubt, the last and most momentous epoch of that time, or the epoch of the New-Test. Antichrist). Cf. Luke xxi. 24, and Rev. xi. 2, both of which speak of the treading under foot of the holy city by the heathen, to continue, according to the former passage, until the times of the Gentiles are fulfilled, and, according to the latter, until forty-two months(= $3\frac{1}{2}$ years = 1260 days) are past. To this negative designation Rev. xiii. 5 adds a positive, according to which the forty-two months denote the duration of the power of the beast, *i.e.*, of the world-power. The only remaining passage in the Apocalypse which mentions the 1260 days, chap. xi. 3, might likewise be explained by this opinion. . . . The congregation therefore finds room in the heathen world, but it is also given over to the dominion of the world-power; it rests under the protection of that power, but also under its pressure; it is a suffering and militant church to this day. Precisely this correlation of protection and oppression forms the specific feature of the relation of the congregation to the world-power throughout the history of the church." Delitzsch (p. 285) is more cautious, that is, he avoids the excessive extension of the three and a half times until they cover a period of many centuries, and contents himself with observing that "in the antitypical history of the last times, these measures

of time, the three and a half years, 1290 and 1335 days, shall yet become important;" and Kliefoth (p. 503) contends for that interpretation of the three and a half times which holds that they denote "the highest development of the power of Antichrist, and his end," immediately before the manifestation of Christ.

Probably the opinion of those is likewise not to be at once rejected, who hold that there was also a typical relation between the three and a half times of Daniel and the public life of Jesus, which covered three to four years, whether they regard the latter period as a period of continued trial and suffering, which became more intense toward its close (cf. Luke xiii. 6–9: the three years of laborious and vain attempts on the part of the Lord to convert the barren fig-tree, Israel), or whether they find in it the *first* half of the mystical week mentioned in chap. ix. 27, and let the *second*, which corresponds directly to the three and a half years, follow immediately afterward (cf. supra, the history of the exposition of chap. ix. 24–27). Ebrard has recently put forth a particularly noteworthy effort to carry out the latter of these views, with special regard to the chronology of the leading events in the life of Christ, although his attempt involves much that is artificial and arbitrary (*Christliche Dogmatik*, 2d ed., II. 747; cf. his *Kritik der evang. Geschichte*, 3d ed., pp. 165, 196 et seq.;—and for a criticism of his views, cf. Bähring, in Schenkel's *Allg. kirchl. Zeitschrift*, 1867, p. 579).

3. *Homiletical suggestions.*—As in the *Oratio eschatologica* by Christ (Matt. xxiv. par.) and especially in its intermediate parts (vs. 29–36), so in the present section there are two principal questions whose investigation devolves on the homiletical student; and they succeed each other in the same order as in that section of the gospels: (1) the question concerning *the preconditions and the course of the end of the world and the final judgment* (see vs. 1–3); and (2) the question relating to the preceding development, or to *the time of the end of* the world (see v. 5 et seq.). In answer to the *first* question, vs. 1–3 indicate that the sufferings and sorrows of God's people shall attain to an unprecedented height, as a necessary preparation for their deliverance by the Messiah; and further, that the general resurrection of all the dead, whether pious or godless, forms a prerequisite and preparation to pave the way for the judgment of the world, which is to dispense eternal rewards and punishments. The revealing angel answers the *second* question in vs. 7, 11, and 12, so far as to state that the last times shall constitute a period of suffering, through which the faithful ones must urge their way, but which shall be shortened and broken through at the middle by the grace of God,—in which is contained, at the same time, a reference to the sudden and unexpected introduction of the final time of the end, or to the coming of the judge of the world like a thief in the night (Matt. xxiv. 36, 42, 44; Luke xxi. 34 et seq.; 1 Thess. v. 2 et seq.). The solution of both questions leads to an exhortation to patient, contented, and watchful waiting for the fulfilment of the prophecy respecting the last end (vs. 4, 9, 13—cf. Matt. xxiv. 32 et seq., 42 et seq.; xxv. 1 et seq.). Thus all the leading features of the Scriptural doctrine of the last things (*Mors tua, judicium postremum, gloria cœli, et dolor inferni*, etc.) are comprehended within the narrow limits of this chapter, and are there properly arranged for practical and edifying discussion, either in a single study or in several.

Single passages.

On v. 1, Luther: "This does not signify physical sufferings, which were far greater at the destruction of Jerusalem, in Rome, and in many other cities and countries; but the suffering of souls, or the *spiritual* affliction of the church, as prefigured by the sufferings of Christ. For physical sufferings are temporary, and cease with the body. But the question here is whether the church shall fall or stand, which the devil had attacked in two directions through the agency of Antichrist: on the one hand, by an Epicurean contempt for the sacraments and the Word of God, on the other, by the terrors and despair of conscience, in which no proper comfort of the graces (was found), but only wretched tortures, which vexed men with the sufficiency of their own doings and with their works (of which, however, the Epicureans and heathen know nothing); hence, that it was time that Michael should arouse himself, and not suffer Christendom to be destroyed at its last gasp, but to comfort and collect it again by his beneficent word of grace."—Melancthon: "*Semper oportet nobis notam esse et infixam animis hanc doctrinam, quod Ecclesia sit subjecta cruci, et cur sit subjecta, videlicit, quia vult Deus intelligi ab Ecclesia iram adversus peccatum, quam mundus contemnit. . . . Agnoscant igitur pii Ecclesiæ ærumnas, et propter Dei gloriam ac propriam salutem et publicam necessitatem acrius incumbant in Evangelii studium, et toto pectore Deum invocent, ut Ecclesiam conservet, defendat, et augeat.—Quatuor autem consolationes h. l. traduntur, quæ piis omnibus semper in conspectu esse debent:* 1. *Prima est, quod Ecclesia non sit penitus interitura, sed tunc quoque in illis periculis duratura.* 2. *Secunda consolatio, quod ibi sunt futura Ecclesiæ membra, ubicumque erunt amplectentes puram Evangelii doctrinam; erit enim, ut inquit, dispersio populi* (cfr. v. 7). 3. *Tertia consolatio, quod in his tantis periculis habitura sit Ecclesia defensorem Filium Dei* (*Michaelem*). 4. *Quarta consolatio est, quam hic quoque proponit Angelus: Quum ærumnæ non sint futuræ perpetuæ, hac spe facilius eas feramus, quod piis promittitur gloriosa liberatio et æterna lætitia; impiis vero denuntiantur æterni cruciatus.*"—Starke: "God permits the persecution of His church to reach its highest point that His help may be so much the more glorious."

On vs. 2, 3, Jerome: "*Oppresso Antichristo et spiritu Salvatoris extincto salvabitur populus, qui scriptus fuerit in libro Dei, et pro diversitate meritorum alii resurgent in vitam æternam, et alii in opprobrium sempiternum. Magistri autem habebunt similitudinem cœli, et qui alios erudierunt, stellarum fulgori comparabuntur.* NON ENIM SUFFICIT SCIRE SAPIENTIAM, NISI ET ALIOS ERUDIAS; TACITUSQUE SERMO DOCTRINÆ, ALIUM NON ÆDIFICANS (cfr. 1 Cor. xiv. 3 ss.), MERCEDEM OPERIS RECIPERE NON POTEST."—Melancthon: "*Facilius ferimus hujus vitæ miserias, cum quasi metam prospicimus, et scimus aliquando Ecclesiam ex tantis malis eluctaturam esse. . . . Videmus nunc quidem misere dissipatum esse populum Dei: quare non procul abest resuscitatio mortuorum.*"—Starke: "Since the faithful martyrs, who loved not their lives unto the death, are to have the preference over others in the resurrection (1 Cor. xv. 23 et seq.), should it contradict the righteousness of God that the greatest persecutors of the church, as the first-born sons of hell, should be raised before the general resurrection of the dead, and be the first to be cast into hell with soul and body (comp. Rev. xix. 20 with Rom. ii. 9)?—Forward, then, ye teachers of the Gospel! do not become wearied in your office! Rather devote tongue, pen, and life to point men to Christ as the true righteousness! Suffer in patience everything that the wicked world can do to you on that account! The magnitude of your gracious reward is well worth such industry and patience!" On v. 4, Jerome: "*Etiam in Apocalypsi Joannis liber videtur signatus septem sigillis intus et foris. . . . . Librum autem illum potest solvere, qui Scripturarum sacramenta cognovit, et intelligit ænigmata et verba tenebrosa propter mysteriorum magnitudinem, et interpretatur parabolas, et occiddentem literam transfert in spiritum vivificantem.*" — Osiander: "The Divine prophecies are only then correctly understood when they are in course of fulfilment (cf. 2 Pet. i. 20)."

On vs. 7, 11, 12, Melancthon: "*Metæ sunt temporum mirabili consilio Dei constitutæ. Et quanquam Christus diem illum soli patri notum esse inquit nec vult nos curiose quærere certum diem aut annum, sed semper velut in statione paratos expectare illum lætissimum diem, quo se ostendet universo humano generi et cum sua Ecclesia triumphabit; tamen brevitas hujus mundi varie significata est.*"—Calvin: "*Quamvis Daniel non stulta curiositate inductus quæsierit ex Angelo de fine mirabilium, tamen non obtinet, quod petebat, quià scilicet voluit Deus ad modum aliquem intelligi, quæ prædixerat, sed tamen aliquid manere occultum, usquedum veniret maturum plenæ revalationis tempus. Hœc igitur ratio est, cur Angelus non exaudiat Danielem. Pium quidem erat ejus votum (neque enim optat quicquam scire plus quam jus esset), verum Deus scit quid opus sit, ideo non concessit, quod optabat.*"—Geier (in Starke): "The last times will be terrible and dangerous; but they have their definite limits."

On v. 10, Theodoret: *Οὐδὲ γὰρ δεῖ πᾶσιν ἁπλῶς προσκεῖσθαι τὰ θεῖα, ἀλλ' οἱ μὲν νοήμονες διὰ τῆς ἄνωθεν αὐτοῖς χορηγουμένης γνώσεως συνήσουσιν, οἱ δὲ ἀνομίᾳ καὶ δυσσεβείᾳ συζῶντες οὐδὲν τῶν ἐγκειμένων νοῆσαι δυνήσονται, ὅταν δὲ ἔλθῃ τὰ πράγματα, σαφῶς τὰς περὶ τούτων μαθήσονται προφητείας.*—Luther: "For however brightly and powerfully the Gospel moves, and however strong the church may be, there must still be heretics and false teachers to prove her, in order that the approved ones may be manifest; and these same heretics are fond of taking sides with kings and great lords. Consequently the heretics will continue to the end. . . . . But to the godless he (the prophet, or, rather, his prophecy) is of no service, as he himself remarks: the wicked shall remain wicked, and not regard it. For this prophecy and similar ones were not written that we might (beforehand exactly) know history and the troubles of the future, so as to feed our curiosity as with an item of news; but that the pious might comfort themselves and rejoice over them, and that they should strengthen their faith and hope in patience, as those that see and hear that their wretchedness shall have an end, and that they, delivered from sin, death, the devil, and every evil, shall come to Christ in heaven, in his blessed eternal kingdom."

On v. 13, *Tübing. Bibel:* "How blessed will it seem to rest in the bosom of the Lord, after the work of this life is done, until the day of restitution shall come, when we shall arise, every one to the gracious lot that shall fall to him."—Starke: "At length the sufferings of the faithful reach a joyous end; then follow rest and sweet refreshing, and finally a glorious resurrection, when with their glorified bodies they shall enter into the joy of their Lord." Blessed is he who with Daniel shall receive a similar lot. Amen.